Moral Psychology

Moral Psychology
Historical and Contemporary Readings

Edited by
Thomas Nadelhoffer, Eddy Nahmias,
and Shaun Nichols

A John Wiley & Sons, Ltd., Publication

Blackwell Publishing was acquired by John Wiley & Sons in February 2007. Blackwell's publishing program has been merged with Wiley's global Scientific, Technical, and Medical business to form Wiley-Blackwell.

Registered Office
John Wiley & Sons Ltd, The Atrium, Southern Gate, Chichester, West Sussex, PO19 8SQ, United Kingdom

Editorial Offices
350 Main Street, Malden, MA 02148–5020, USA
9600 Garsington Road, Oxford, OX4 2DQ, UK
The Atrium, Southern Gate, Chichester, West Sussex, PO19 8SQ, UK

For details of our global editorial offices, for customer services, and for information about how to apply for permission to reuse the copyright material in this book please see our website at www.wiley.com/wiley-blackwell.

Library of Congress Cataloging-in-Publication Data
Moral psychology : historical and contemporary readings / edited by Thomas Nadelhoffer, Eddy Nahmias, Shaun Nichols.
    p. cm.
  Includes bibliographical references and index.
    ISBN 978-1-4051-9020-6 (hbk. : alk. paper) – ISBN 978-1-4051-9019-0 (pbk. : alk. paper)   1. Ethics.
2. Moral development.   3. Psychology–Moral and ethical aspects.   4. Psychology and philosophy.
I. Nadelhoffer, Thomas.   II. Nahmias, Eddy A., 1969–   III. Nichols, Shaun.
  BJ45.M665 2010
  170.1′9–dc22

                                                                                    2010025064

A catalogue record for this book is available from the British Library.

Set in 9.5/11.5pt Minion by Graphicraft Limited, Hong Kong
Printed and bound in Malaysia by Vivar Printing Sdn Bhd

01   2010

Contents

Acknowledgements   viii

Introduction   1
Thomas Nadelhoffer, Eddy Nahmias, and Shaun Nichols

Part I: Reason & Passion   **5**

Introduction
Shaun Nichols   7

1   Selections from *A Discourse of Natural Religion*
Samuel Clarke   11

2   Selections from *An Inquiry into the Original of Our Ideas of Beauty and Virtue*
Francis Hutcheson   21

3   Selections from *An Essay on the Nature and Conduct of the Passions and Affections, with Illustrations on the Moral Sense*
Francis Hutcheson   24

4   Selections from *Enquiries Concerning the Principles of Morals*
David Hume   32

5   Introduction to *Groundwork for the Metaphysics of Morals*
Immanuel Kant   37

6   The Claim to Moral Adequacy of a Highest Stage of Moral Judgment
Lawrence Kohlberg   40

7   A Cognitive Developmental Approach to Morality: Investigating the Psychopath
Robert James Blair   48

8   Selections from *The Moral Problem*
Michael Smith   64

9   How Psychopaths Threaten Moral Rationalism: Is it Irrational to be Amoral?
    Shaun Nichols   73

Part II: Altruism & Egoism   85

Introduction
Thomas Nadelhoffer and Shaun Nichols   87

10 Selections from *Republic*
    Plato   93

11 Selections from *Leviathan* and *The Elements of Law Natural and Politic*
    Thomas Hobbes   97

12 Selections from *Human Nature and Other Sermons*
    Joseph Butler   103

13 Selections from *An Inquiry into the Original of our Ideas of Beauty and Virtue*
    Francis Hutcheson   111

14 How Social an Animal: the Human Capacity for Caring
    C. Daniel Batson   117

15 The Evolution of Reciprocal Altruism
    Robert L. Trivers   124

16 Summary of *Unto Others: The Evolution and Psychology of Unselfish Behavior*
    Elliott Sober and David Sloan Wilson   135

17 Why Altruism Is Impossible … and Ubiquitous
    Barry Schwartz   148

Part III: Virtue & Character   161

Introduction
Eddy Nahmias   163

18 Selections from *Protagoras*
    Plato   167

19 Selections from *Nicomachean Ethics*
    Aristotle   172

20 Behavioral Study of Obedience
    Stanley Milgram   179

21 Selections from *The Person and the Situation*
    Lee Ross and Richard Nisbett   187

22 Persons, Situations, and Virtue Ethics
    John M. Doris   197

23 Situationism and Virtue Ethics on the Content of Our Character
    Rachana Kamtekar   210

24 Virtue Ethics and Situationist Personality Psychology
    Maria Merritt   224

Part IV: Agency & Responsibility   231

Introduction
Eddy Nahmias   233

25   Selections from *Nicomachean Ethics*
     Aristotle   239

26   Selections from *Essays on the Active Powers of Man*
     Thomas Reid   246

27   Selections from *Beyond Good and Evil* and *Twilight of the Idols*
     Friedrich Nietzsche   251

28   Selections from *Beyond Freedom and Dignity*
     B.F. Skinner   256

29   Apparent Mental Causation: Sources of the Experience of Will
     Daniel M. Wegner and Thalia Wheatley   264

30   Agency, Authorship, and Illusion
     Eddy Nahmias   276

31   Free Will in Scientific Psychology
     Roy F. Baumeister   288

32   Scientific Skepticism About Free Will
     Alfred R. Mele   295

Part V: Moral Intuitions   307

Introduction
Thomas Nadelhoffer   309

33   Selections from *The Methods of Ethics*
     Henry Sidgwick   315

34   Selections from *The Right and the Good*
     W.D. Ross   321

35   The Trolley Problem
     Judith Jarvis Thomson   327

36   Selections from *Living High and Letting Die: Our Illusion of Innocence*
     Peter Unger   335

37   The Emotional Dog and Its Rational Tail: A Social Intuitionist Approach to
     Moral Judgment
     Jonathan Haidt   343

38   The Secret Joke of Kant's Soul
     Joshua Greene   359

39   Moral Intuitionism Meets Empirical Psychology
     Walter Sinnott-Armstrong   373

Sources   388

Acknowledgments

Thomas Nadelhoffer worked on this volume while doing a post-doctoral fellowship with The MacArthur Law and Neuroscience Project. He would like to thank The John D. and Catherine T. MacArthur Foundation, the Law and Neuroscience Project, and The Regents of the University of California for their support. Thomas Nadelhoffer would also like to thank Dickinson College for giving him a leave of absence to be a post-doctoral fellow.

Eddy Nahmias would like to thank Manual Vargas, Al Mele, John Doris, Rachana Kamtekar, and students in his seminars on moral psychology for their helpful suggestions on this volume. Eddy Nahmias completed work on this volume in part with support from a grant from the John Templeton Foundation administered by the University of Chicago's Arete Initiative.

Shaun Nichols would like to thank Michael Gill, Mark Timmons, and Walter Sinnott-Armstrong for their helpful suggestions on this volume.

The editors would also like to thank the anonymous reviewers for helpful advice and Jeff Dean and all of the other people at Wiley-Blackwell who have helped bring this volume to fruition.

Introduction

Thomas Nadelhoffer, Eddy Nahmias, and Shaun Nichols

What is Moral Psychology?

Philosophers have long been captivated by the distinctively human capacity for making moral judgments and engaging in moral behavior. Not only do we sometimes help strangers we'll never meet and donate time and money to saving species we'll never see, but we also engage in heated debates about moral issues and write treatises of moral philosophy. What is it about human beings that enables (or compels) us to engage in such complicated moral thought and behavior? What biological and psychological capacities underlie our moral judgments? What drives us to help those in need? What enables us to follow moral norms and to be responsible for transgressing them? Philosophers ranging from Plato and Aristotle to Hume and Kant have weighed in on these issues. More recently, psychologists and researchers in other cognate fields have joined the conversation and taken a similar interest in the origin, nature, and limitations of human morality.

Moral psychology is the field that addresses these and related issues – it is the study of the way humans think about morality, make moral judgments, and behave in moral situations. While the immediate goal of the field is to understand moral cognition and behavior, the inquiry also has possible implications for how we should make moral judgments and how we should behave. Even though we cannot move directly from

data concerning how we actually do think and behave to theories about how we ought to think and behave, by exploring morality in an inter-disciplinary way, moral psychologists are, at a minimum, able to place empirical constraints on normative theorizing. Moral psychology thus involves the intersection of philosophy and empir-ical sciences ranging from evolutionary biology and game theory to neuroscience and social psychology. Given both the breath of the issues to be explored and the multitude of research methodologies currently at our disposal, it is an exciting time to be studying moral psychology. This anthology focuses on five issues that have their roots in traditional philosophy but have also been explored in contemporary scientific research.

- *Part I (Reason & Passion)*: How do humans arrive at moral judgments and how should they? Is moral judgment a kind of rational judgment? What role do emotions play in moral judgment?
- *Part II (Altruism & Egoism)*: Are humans ultimately selfish or can they be genuinely altruistic? If they can be altruistic, how is that possible? What evolutionary and psycho-logical processes might explain empathy and altruism?
- *Part III (Virtue & Character)*: Is virtue an attainable goal for humans? What are character traits and what role do they play in explaining

virtuous action? To what extent do humans have robust character traits, including virtues, and how might we inculcate virtuous traits and behaviors?

• *Part IV (Agency & Responsibility)*: Are humans autonomous and responsible agents? If so, what features of human decision-making and action allow us to be morally responsible agents? If not, what scientific discoveries threaten free and responsible agency?

• *Part V (Moral Intuitions)*: What are people's immediate intuitions about right and wrong? What accounts for those moral intuitions? Are they reliable? How should our moral concepts and intuitions inform moral theory?

Of course, the five key topics we selected do not exhaust all of the important questions in moral psychology. There are several other fascinating topics that we regrettably do not have the space to investigate – for instance, the puzzling nature of self-deception and weakness of will, the innateness of moral judgment, moral disagreement between and within cultures, the development of morality in children, and the relevance of moral luck, to name but a few. However, we selected the readings for this volume not only because they raise a number of intriguing questions about the nature of morality, but also because they can be collectively used to illustrate the recent trend in moral psychology towards a more thoroughly interdisciplinary approach. In each section, we first offer classic selections from the history of philosophy that raise the central questions and frame the ensuing debates. The philosophical pieces are followed by selections from twentieth-century scientists whose work informs these debates. Finally, we offer contemporary selections by both philosophers and scientists whose work exemplifies the struggle to understand the nature of human morality in a thoroughly interdisciplinary way.

Each section of this volume is designed to explore the various ways that moral philosophers commonly make claims that rely, in one way or another, on facts about human psychology. These empirical commitments may be more or less explicit. And often it is very difficult both to discern what they are and to determine how exactly the theoretical conclusions depend on

them. When it comes to doing interdisciplinary moral psychology, one of the first steps is to examine ethical theories and try to elucidate their empirical commitments. Then, one should review the existing work in the relevant sciences – for example, social psychology, neuroscience, cognitive science, evolutionary theory, anthropology, linguistics – to see whether the data support those empirical commitments. Where the evidence conflicts or does not exist, the moral psychologist can then either offer suggestions about how best to gather the data needed to resolve the conflict or she can take active steps to fill the gaps. The primary goal of *Moral Psychology: Historical and Contemporary Readings* is to show that by moving back and forth between philosophy and the sciences of the mind in this way, researchers can shed interesting and important new light on some of the most difficult and interesting problems in moral psychology.

Questions for Further Study

As you work your way through the various Parts and selections of this volume, here are a few of the questions to keep in mind:

• What are the various philosophical debates about moral reasoning and behavior and the various positions that are possible for one to take in those debates?

• What empirical commitments do each of those positions make about how humans actually think about morality and about what leads humans to behave as they do? Are there reasons to think that any of these positions are immune to empirical considerations?

• To the extent that theories *prescribe* a proper way of thinking and acting, do they suggest ways to achieve these goals and are those suggestions empirically viable?

• What empirical research would be most relevant to exploring these questions?

• Is the existing research relevant in the ways that the scientists and philosophers suggest? What does such research show?

• What methods and experiments would be useful to test the empirical commitments of moral theories?

Suggested Readings

Anscombe, G.E.M. (1958). Modern moral philosophy. *Philosophy*, 33, 1–19.

Appiah, A. (2008). *Experiments in Ethics*. Cambridge: Harvard University Press.

Broad, C.D. (1930). *Five Types of Ethical Theory*. New York: Harcourt, Brace.

Cooper, J. (1999). *Reason and Emotion: Essays on Ancient Moral Psychology and Ethical Theory*. Princeton University Press.

Doris, J.M. and Stich, S.P. (2005). As a matter of fact: Empirical perspectives on ethics. In F. Jackson and M. Smith (eds.), *The Oxford Handbook of Contemporary Philosophy*. Oxford: Oxford University Press.

Flanagan, O. (1991). *Varieties of Moral Personality: Ethics and Psychological Realism*. Cambridge: Harvard University Press.

Flanagan, O. and Rorty, A., eds. 1993. *Identity, Character, and Morality: Essays in Moral Psychology*. MIT Press.

Frankena, W. (1939). The naturalistic fallacy. *Mind*, 48, 464–77.

Knobe, J. and Nichols, S. (eds.) (2008). *Experimental Philosophy*. Oxford: Oxford University Press.

Schoeman, F. ed. 1987. *Responsibility, Character, and the Emotions: New Essays in Moral Psychology*. Cambridge University Press.

Sinnott-Armstrong, W. (ed.). (2008). *Moral Psychology: Volumes 1–3*. Cambridge: The MIT Press.

Smith, M. (2004). *Ethics and the A Priori: Selected Essays in Moral Psychology and Meta-ethics*. Cambridge: Cambridge University Press.

Stocker, M. (1979). Desiring the Bad: An Essay in Moral Psychology. *Journal of Philosophy* 76, 738–53.

Part I
Reason & Passion

Introduction

Shaun Nichols

Metaethics concerns questions about the nature of morality. For instance, in metaethics we ask whether some moral claims are objectively true or only true relative to some cultural group? Perhaps moral claims are never true. One historically prominent entry to such issues concerns the psychological foundations of moral judgment itself. Some philosophers, moral rationalists, maintain that morality flows from *reason*. If that's right, morality has a special authority and all creatures with sufficient rationality should arrive at roughly the same moral conclusions, if they are presented with the same nonmoral facts. This would suggest that morality isn't merely relative to culture, and it would lend credence to the idea that there are objectively true moral claims. The central opposing camp of philosophers – sentimentalists – maintains that morality originates in the emotions. If that's right, this suggests that morality does not have the kind of authority that is suggested by rationalism. Rather, the morality we have is a function of the emotions we happen to have, and rational creatures with different emotions could have different moral views, or perhaps no moral views at all. This sentimentalist picture of morality would provide reason to doubt that moral claims are objectively true.

With such weighty issues hanging in the balance, it is not surprising that the debate between rationalism and sentimentalism has been central to metaethics since the issue first rose to prominence in the early eighteenth century. British philosopher **Samuel Clarke** (1675–1729) provides one of the first explicit presentations of a rationalist picture. According to Clarke, it is an objective fact that it's wrong to injure someone without any provocation. We come to appreciate that this is objectively wrong by exercising our basic rational capacities. When presented with a claim like "it is wrong to injure the innocent," so long as we understand the terms, we are compelled by rationality to recognize the truth of the claim. Who is thus endowed to appreciate such moral truths? Almost everyone, it would seem. Clarke claims that apart from perversion, only the "extremest stupidity" could lead any person to doubt such things.

Mathematics provides a captivating model for how to think about moral rationalism; for we tend to think that we reach objective mathematical truths by reason alone. And Clarke maintains that there is a clear parallel between mathematics and morality. Once you understand the claim that $4 + 5 = 9$, you can't help but appreciate that it is true. Its truth is self-evident and overwhelming. Similarly, the idea that you shouldn't injure an innocent person is self-evident. As soon as you think about it, you will find it obvious.

According to Clarke, rationalism is further supported by the fact that unprejudiced minds converge on the same views about morality. Again we can exploit the analogy with mathematics. We expect all unprejudiced minds to appreciate that $4 + 5 = 9$. And it's plausible that anyone who

Moral Psychology: Historical and Contemporary Readings, edited by Thomas Nadelhoffer, Eddy Nahmias, and Shaun Nichols.
© 2010 Blackwell Publishing Ltd except for editorial material and organization © 2010 Thomas Nadelhoffer, Eddy Nahmias, and Shaun Nichols.

understands the terms also appreciates the truth of the claim. Similarly, Clarke says that we find widespread agreement on moral claims. As Clarke notes, even people who commit morally wrong acts will typically acknowledge that the action they performed was wrong, at least if they consider the action as done by someone else. According to Clarke, everyone agrees that 4 + 5 = 9 because everyone has sufficient rationality to appreciate this mathematical truth. Similarly then, the best explanation for why everyone agrees that it's wrong to injure the innocent is that everyone has sufficient rationality to appreciate this moral truth.

Francis Hutcheson (1694–1746) would not begrudge Clarke the claim that every rational human being would agree that it is wrong to injure the innocent. But these common judgments are not, according to Hutcheson, issued by purely rational capacities. Rather, moral verdicts are based in a kind of emotional response. When something bad happens to me, say a tree limb falls on my head, this generates an unpleasant sensation. But, Hutcheson says, this is much different from what happens if someone *hits* me over the head. In that case, in addition to the pain on my head, I also form a distinctive moral reaction – a sentiment of disapproval towards the person who performed the action. And this isn't restricted to things that happen to *me*. This sentiment of disapproval is also triggered when I see a person hit someone else over the head without provocation. The sentiment of disapproval flows from the *moral sense*, which is analogous in important ways to other senses or emotions. Hutcheson thinks that our moral reactions "arise in us as necessarily as any other Sensations; nor can we alter, or stop them, while our *previous Opinion* or *Apprehension* of the *Affection, Temper*, or *Intention* of the Agent continues the same; any more than we can make the Taste of Wormwood sweet, or that of Honey bitter."[1] The moral sense generates approval or disapproval automatically, just as other senses and primitive emotions their outputs automatically.

One of Hutcheson's central arguments against rationalism is that reasons have to come to an end somewhere. Hutcheson distinguishes between *exciting* reasons, which motivate us to action, and *justifying* reasons, which provide warrant or justification for our judgments. Justifications bottom out in both cases, according to Hutcheson. We might give some justification for why drunk

driving, for example, is wrong – it's wrong because it poses a risk to others. But then we need to give a justification for why it's wrong to pose a risk to others. And eventually (pretty quickly, in fact), we are going to run out of reasons. Otherwise there would have to be an endless chain of justifications, which doesn't seem possible. Hutcheson maintains that at the bottom of the pile we find sentiments rather than reasons.

Hutcheson was a central figure in the *Scottish Enlightenment*, which also boasted Adam Smith and **David Hume** (1711–76). Hume followed Hutcheson in maintaining that morality originates in the emotions rather than reason. Hume allows that reason is crucial in one sense – we need reasoning to identify the facts of the case before us, and until that has been accomplished, we should not submit a case to moral evaluation. But once we know all the relevant facts, reason has done what it can, and moral judgment now depends on our emotional reaction to the facts.

In defending sentimentalism, Hume confronts the mathematical analogy directly. Hume would agree with Clarke that it's transparent that 4 + 5 = 9, but this is because the relations between 4 + 5 and 9 are simple and transparent – I can see how adding 4 to 5 *has* to yield 9. But Hume maintains that there is no such simple and transparent set of relations revealing that ingratitude *has* to be immoral. For instance, Hume would maintain that there is nothing logically contradictory about denying that ingratitude is immoral. It is left obscure how rational relations alone make ingratitude immoral. In contrast to this obscure view of morality, Hume says, the sentimentalist theory is plain and simple. Rather than think of morality on analogy with mathematics, Hume suggests that a more apt analogy is aesthetics. Our appreciation of natural beauty is partly a matter of relations like proportion and balance, but it would be absurd to conclude that the appreciation of beauty depends entirely on reason. Rather, our evaluation of natural beauty depends on our sentiments. As such, Hume suggests that our aesthetic sense provides the most apt analogy for how to think about *moral* beauty.

Writing in the wake of Hume, **Immanuel Kant** (1724–1804) reaffirms a rationalist approach to morality. Kant maintains that the wrongness of actions is grounded in a fundamental moral law (the "categorical imperative"), according to which, roughly, *I should never perform an action unless I could rationally intend that everyone else in a similar situation do the same thing*. This moral law rules out actions like stealing, for while stealing might benefit me, it would be irrational for me to intend that everyone steal.

What is of interest for the debate between rationalists and sentimentalists is that Kant thinks that the moral law is delivered by reason – "common human reason." The moral law isn't supposed to be some recondite principle that you only learn in college. Kant says that while people might not think of the moral law in the abstract formulation he offers, they are nonetheless guided by it when they make judgments about what is right and wrong. Thus, Kant maintains, the role for philosophy in this domain is not to provide a novel basis for morality – *common* reason already gives us the right basis. Rather, the role of philosophy is to give a fuller defense of the moral law that we all know.

On natural interpretations of these historical philosophers, some of their claims were *empirical* claims about the psychological basis of everyday moral judgment. Empirical exploration of these claims waited until the tentieth century. The first systematic empirical investigation of moral judgment was initiated by the developmental psychologist **Lawrence Kohlberg** (1927–87). Taking Kant as philosophical inspiration, Kohlberg offers a rationalist account of moral development according to which there are six stages in moral development. The first stage is driven simply by the desire to avoid punishment. The final stage is driven by abstract moral principles, like Kant's moral law.

Kohlberg's six stage model generated an enormous research program. In typical Kolbergian studies, people are presented with morally complex scenarios (e.g., a person stealing a drug for his sick wife) and then asked to explain why the agent's action was right or wrong. The explanations are then coded as corresponding to one of the six stages. One significant finding is that not everyone achieves the highest stage of morality. Nonetheless, Kohlberg suggests that the process that normal people go through as they advance through the stages is akin to the process that moral philosophers go through in justifying higher stages of moral reasoning. According to Kohlberg, each stage is morally superior to the earlier one. Specifically, Kohlberg takes certain conditions, like the universalizability of Kant's moral law, to be demanded by a rational morality, and he maintains that each stage of moral development meets these conditions better than the earlier stages.

The tasks inspired by Kohlberg's stage theory are rather demanding – the subjects have to give detailed reasons for their evaluations about situations involving competing moral considerations. The psychologist Elliott Turiel developed a much simpler method – the "moral/conventional" task – to explore moral understanding in children. Children are asked a series of questions about simple violations, which are antecedently regarded as moral violations (e.g., one child hitting another) or conventional violations (e.g., talking during story time). Research indicates that even 3-year old children will distinguish moral from conventional violations on several dimensions.

R. James Blair builds on this tradition of work by giving the moral/conventional task to psychopaths. He compared prisoners who were diagnosed as psychopathic with prisoners who did not meet the diagnostic criteria for psychopathy. Blair found that non-psychopathic prisoners drew a clear moral/conventional distinction, but this was not the case for psychopathic prisoners. In addition, Blair compared how psychopaths and non-psychopaths react to images of suffering, for example, a picture of a crying child. He found that while non-psychopaths showed very significant bodily reactions to such images, psychopaths responses were much more muted. This leads Blair to suggest that the abnormal responses psychopaths give to the moral/conventional task are a result of their diminished emotional responsiveness to the suffering of others. Thus Blair's proposal is that the basic capacity for moral understanding is founded on an emotional response. Having a deficit in that basic emotional response leads to a deficit in moral understanding. This seems to provide empirical evidence for the importance of emotions in moral judgments. It is accordingly natural to view Blair as an heir to the sentimentalist tradition in philosophy.

In the contemporary philosophical literature, **Michael Smith** is heir to the rationalist tradition. He offers one of the clearest and most sophisticated defenses of moral rationalism. Smith distinguishes between *conceptual* and *substantive* rationalism. According to conceptual rationalism, to say that John is morally required to help the injured child entails that it is *rational* for John to want to help the injured child. Still, as Smith notes, our concept of morality might not correspond to anything in the world. Substantive rationalism goes further and claims that there really are such rational moral facts. To support the substantive claim that there really are moral facts, Smith, like Clarke before him, adverts to the widespread agreement that we find about basic moral claims. However, Smith is more cautious about whether or not we would in fact find widespread convergence in moral views. If there are rational moral facts, he says, then we should find such convergence. Perhaps we will not find such convergence, but Smith maintains that at this point we have little reason to be pessimistic.

Shaun Nichols draws on the psychological research on psychopaths to argue against moral rationalism, focusing especially on Smith's rationalist theory. Blair's evidence suggests that psychopaths have a deficiency in basic moral understanding. But psychopaths also have relatively intact rational capacities, says Nichols. At any rate, the rational capacities of psychopaths are equal to the rational capacities of many people (e.g. young children) who do exhibit a normal basic moral understanding. What explains the moral deficiencies of psychopaths is an *emotional* deficit. According to Nichols, this suggests that rationalism fails to provide an adequate account of basic moral judgment.

Questions for Further Study

- Can a rationalist allow that emotions play some role in moral judgment?
- What are the different ways in which emotions might be implicated in the processes leading to moral judgment?
- Can a person make normal moral judgments if they have lost their emotional sensitivity, for example, through brain damage?
- If morality does depend on the emotions, does this undermine the idea that morality is objective?
- If morality depends on the emotions, does this give reason to think that moral claims are all false?

- What are important disanalogies between morality and aesthetics?
- What are important disanalogies between morality and mathematics?

Notes

Thanks to Michael Gill and Mark Timmons for discussion and comments on an early draft of this introduction.
[1] *An Essay on the Nature and Conduct of the Passions and Affections, with Illustrations on the Moral Sense,* ed. Aaron Garrett (Indianapolis: Liberty Fund, 2002), Treatise 1, Section 1.

Suggested Readings

Blasi, A. (1983). Moral cognition and moral action: A theoretical perspective. *Developmental Review*, 3, 178–210.

Gill, M. (2006). Moral rationalism vs. moral sentimentalism: Is morality more like math or beauty? *Philosophy Compass*, 2, 16–30.

Huebner, B., Dwyer, S., and Hauser, M. (2009). The role of emotion in moral psychology, *Trends in Cognitive Sciences*, 13, 1–6

Joyce, R. (2008). What neuroscience can (and cannot) contribute to metaethics. In W. Sinnott-Armstrong (ed.), *Moral Psychology, vol 3: The Neuroscience of Morality: Emotion, Brain Disorders, and Development.* Cambridge, MA: MIT Press, pp. 371–94

Koenigs, M., Young, L., Adolphs, R., Tranel, D., Cushman, F.A., Hauser, M.D., et al. (2007). Damage to the prefrontal cortex increases utilitarian moral judgments. *Nature*, 446, 908–11.

Maibom, H. (2005). Moral unreason: The case of psychopathy. *Mind & Language*, 20, 237–57.

Pizarro, D. and Bloom, P. (2003). The intelligence of the moral intuitions. *Psychological Review*, 110, 193–6.

Prinz, J. (2006). The emotional basis of moral judgment. *Philosophical Explorations*, 9, 1, 29–43.

Roskies, A. (2003). Are ethical judgments intrinsically motivational? Lessons from "acquired sociopathy." *Philosophical Psychology*, 16, 51–66.

Rozin, P., Lowery, L., Imada, S., & Haidt, J. (1999). The CAD triad hypothesis: A mapping between three moral emotions (contempt, anger, disgust) and three moral codes (community, autonomy, divinity). *Journal of Personality and Social Psychology*, 76, 574–86.

Smetana, J. (1993). Understanding of social rules. In M. Bennett (ed.), *The Development of Social Cognition: The Child as Psychologist.* New York: Guilford Press, pp. 111–41.

1

A Discourse of Natural Religion

Samuel Clarke

1. That there are differences of things; and different relations, respects or proportions, of some things towards others; is as evident and undeniable, as that one magnitude or number, is greater, equal to, or smaller than another. That from these different relations of different things, there necessarily arises an agreement or disagreement of some things with others, or a fitness or unfitness of the application of different things or different relations one to another; is likewise as plain, as that there is any such thing as proportion or disproportion in geometry and arithmetic, or uniformity or difformity in comparing together the respective figures of bodies. Further, that there is a fitness or suitableness of certain circumstances to certain persons, and an unsuitableness of others; founded in the nature of things and the qualifications of persons, antecedent to all positive appointment whatsoever; also that from the different relations of different persons one to another, there necessarily arises a fitness or unfitness of certain manners of behaviour of some persons towards others: is as manifest, as that the properties which flow from the essences of different mathematical figures, have different congruities or incongruities between themselves; or that, in mechanics, certain weights or powers have very different forces, and different effects one upon another, according to their different distances, or different positions and situations in

respect of each other. For instance: that God is infinitely superior to men; is as clear, as that infinity is larger than a point, or eternity longer than a moment. And it is as certainly fit, that men should honour and worship, obey and imitate God, rather than on the contrary in all their actions endeavour to dishonor and disobey him; as it is certainly true, that they have an entire dependence on him, and he on the contrary can in no respect receive any advantage from them; and not only so, but also that his will is as certainly and unalterably just and equitable in giving his commands, as his power is irresistible in requiring submission to it. Again; it is a thing absolutely and necessarily fitter in itself, that the supreme author and creator of the universe, should govern, order, and direct all things to certain constant and regular ends; than that every thing should be permitted to go on at adventures, and produce uncertain effects merely by chance and in the utmost confusion, without any determinate view or design at all. It is a thing manifestly fitter in itself, that the all-powerful governor of the world, should do always what is best in the whole, and what tends most to the universal good of the whole creation; than that he should make the whole continually miserable; or that, to satisfy the unreasonable desires of any particular depraved natures, he should at any time suffer the order of the whole to be altered and perverted. Lastly, it is a

From *A Discourse concerning the Unchangeable Obligations of Natural Religion, and the Truth and certainty of the Christian Revelation.* First printed, 1709. This text taken from corrected 7th edition (1728).

Moral Psychology: Historical and Contemporary Readings, edited by Thomas Nadelhoffer, Eddy Nahmias, and Shaun Nichols. © 2010 Blackwell Publishing Ltd except for editorial material and organization © 2010 Thomas Nadelhoffer, Eddy Nahmias, and Shaun Nichols.

thing evidently and infinitely more fit, that any one particular innocent and good being, should by the supreme ruler and disposer of all things, be placed and preserved in an easy and happy estate; than that, without any fault or demerit of its own, it should be made extremely, remedilessly, and endlessly miserable. In like manner; in men's dealing and conversing one with another; it is undeniably more fit, absolutely and in the nature of the thing itself, that all men should endeavour to promote the universal good and welfare of all; than that all men should be continually contriving the ruin and destruction of all. It is evidently more fit, even before all positive bargains and compacts, that men should deal one with another according to the known rules of justice and equity; than that every man for his own present advantage, should without scruple disappoint the most reasonable and equitable expectations of his neighbours, and cheat and defraud, or spoil by violence, all others without restraint. Lastly, it is without dispute more fit and reasonable in itself, that I should preserve the life of an innocent man, that happens at any time to be in my power; or deliver him from any imminent danger, though I have never made any promise so to do; than that I should suffer him to perish, or take away his life, without any reason or provocation at all.

These things are so notoriously plain and self-evident, that nothing but the extremest stupidity of mind, corruption of manners, or perverseness of spirit, can possibly make any man entertain the least doubt concerning them. For a man endued with reason, to deny the truth of these things; is the very same thing, as if a man that has the use of his sight, should at the same time that he beholds the sun, deny that there is any such thing as light in the world; or as if a man that understands geometry or arithmetic, should deny the most obvious and known proportions of lines or numbers, and perversely contend that the whole is not equal to all its parts, or that a square is not double to a triangle of equal base and height. Any man of ordinary capacity, and unbiassed judgment, plainness and simplicity; who had never read, and had never been told, that there were men and philosophers, who had in earnest asserted and attempted to prove, that there is no natural and unalterable difference between good and evil; would at the first hearing be as hardly persuaded to believe, that it could ever really enter into the heart of any intelligent man, to deny all natural

difference between right and wrong; as he would be to believe, that ever there could be any geometer who would seriously and in good earnest lay it down as a first principle, that a crooked line is as straight as a right one. So that indeed it might justly seem altogether a needless undertaking, to attempt to prove and establish the eternal difference of good and evil; had there not appeared certain men, as Mr. Hobbes and some few others, who have presumed, contrary to the plainest and most obvious reason of mankind, to assert, and not without some subtlety endeavoured to prove, that there is no such real difference originally, necessarily, and absolutely in the nature of things; but that all obligation of duty to God, arises merely from his absolute irresistible power; and all duty towards men, merely from positive compact: and have founded their whole scheme of politics upon that opinion. Wherein as they have contradicted the judgment of all the wisest and soberest part of mankind, so they have not been able to avoid contradicting themselves also. For (not to mention now, that they have no way to show how compacts themselves come to be obligatory, but by inconsistently owning an eternal original fitness in the thing itself, which I shall have occasion to observe hereafter: besides this, I say,) if there be naturally and absolutely in things themselves, no difference between good and evil, just and unjust; then in the state of nature, before any compact be made, it is equally as good, just and reasonable, for one man to destroy the life of another, not only when it is necessary for his own preservation, but also arbitrarily and without any provocation at all, or any appearance of advantage to himself; as to preserve or save another man's life, when he may do it without any hazard of his own. The consequence of which, is; that not only the first and most obvious way for every particular man to secure himself effectually, would be (as Mr. Hobbes teaches) to endeavour to prevent and cut off all others; but also that men might destroy one another upon every foolish and peevish or arbitrary humour, even when they did not think any such thing necessary for their own preservation. And the effect of this practice must needs be, that it would terminate in the destruction of all mankind. Which being undeniably a great and insufferable evil; Mr. Hobbes himself confesses it reasonable, that, to prevent this evil, men should enter into certain compacts to preserve one another. Now if the destruction of mankind by each other's hands, be such an evil, that, to prevent it, it was fit and reasonable that men should enter into compacts to preserve each other; then, before any such compacts, it was manifestly a thing unfit and unreasonable in itself, that mankind should all destroy one another. And if so, then for the same reason it was also unfit and unreasonable, antecedent to all compacts, that any one man should destroy another arbitrarily and without any provocation, or at any time when it was not absolutely and immediately necessary for the preservation of himself. Which is directly contradictory to Mr. Hobbes's first supposition, of there being no natural and absolute difference between good and evil, just and unjust, antecedent to positive compact. And in like manner all others, who upon any pretence whatsoever, teach that good and evil depend originally on the constitution of positive laws, whether divine or human; must unavoidably run into the same absurdity. For if there be no such thing as good and evil in the nature of things, antecedent to all laws; then neither can any one law be better than another; nor any one thing whatever, be more justly established, and enforced by laws, than the contrary; nor can any reason be given, why any laws should ever be made at all: but all laws equally, will be either arbitrary and tyrannical, or frivolous and needless; because the contrary might with equal reason have been established, if, before the making of the laws, all things had been alike indifferent in their own nature. There is no possible way to avoid this absurdity, but by saying, that out of things in their own nature absolutely indifferent, those are chosen by wise governors to be made obligatory by law, the practice of which they judge will tend to the public benefit of the community. But this is an express contradiction in the very terms. For if the practice of certain things tends to the public benefit of the world, and the contrary would tend to the public disadvantage; then those things are not in their own nature indifferent, but were good and reasonable to be practised before any law was made, and can only for that very reason be wisely enforced by the authority of laws. Only here it is to be observed, that by the public benefit must not be understood the interest of any one particular nation, to the plain injury or prejudice of the rest of mankind; any more than the interest of one city or family, in opposition to their neighbours of the same country: but those things only are truly good in their own nature, which either tend to the universal benefit and welfare of all men, or at least are not destructive of it. The true state therefore of this case, is plainly this. Some things are in their own nature good and reasonable and fit to be done; such as keeping faith, and performing equitable compacts, and the like; and these receive not their obligatory power, from any law or authority; but are only declared, confirmed and enforced by penalties, upon such as would not perhaps be governed by right reason only. Other things are in their own nature absolutely evil; such as breaking faith, refusing to perform equitable compacts, cruelly destroying those who have neither directly nor indirectly given any occasion for any such treatment, and the like; and these cannot by any law or authority whatsoever, be made fit and reasonable, or excusable to be practised. Lastly, other things are in their own nature indifferent; that is, (not absolutely and strictly so; as such trivial actions, which have no way any tendency at all either to the public welfare or damage; for concerning such things, it would be childish and trifling to suppose any laws to be made at all; but they are) such things, whose tendency to the public benefit or disadvantage, is either so small or so remote, or so obscure and involved, that the generality of people are not able of themselves to discern on which side they ought to act: and these things are made obligatory by the authority of laws; though perhaps every one cannot distinctly perceive the reason and fitness of their being enjoined: of which sort are many particular penal laws, in several countries and nations. But to proceed.

The principal thing that can, with any colour of reason, seem to countenance the opinion of those who deny the natural and eternal difference of good and evil; (for Mr. Hobbes's false reasonings I shall hereafter consider by themselves;) is the difficulty there may sometimes be, to define exactly the bounds of right and wrong: the variety of opinions, that have obtained even among understanding and learned men concerning certain questions of just and unjust, especially in political matters: and the many contrary laws that have been made in divers ages and in different countries, concerning these matters. But as, in painting, two very different colours, by diluting each other very slowly and gradually, may from the highest intenseness in either extreme, terminate in the midst insensibly, and so run one into the other, that it shall not be possible even for a skilful eye to determine exactly where the one ends, and the other begins; and yet the colours may really differ as much as can be, not in degree only but entirely in kind, as red and blue, or white and black: So, though it may perhaps be very difficult in some nice and perplexed cases (which yet are very far from occurring frequently,) to define exactly the bounds of right and wrong, just and unjust; and there may be some latitude in the judgment of different men, and the laws of divers nations; yet right and wrong are nevertheless in themselves totally and essentially different; even altogether as much, as white and black, light and darkness. The Spartan law perhaps, which permitted their youth to steal; may, as absurd as it was, bear much dispute whether it was absolutely unjust or no; because every man having an absolute right in his own goods, it may seem that the members of any society may agree to transfer or alter their own properties upon what conditions they shall think fit. But if it could be supposed that a law had been made at Sparta; or at Rome, or in India, or in any other part of the world; whereby it had been commanded or allowed, that every man might rob by violence, and murder whomsoever he met with; or that no faith should be kept with any man, nor any equitable compacts performed; no man, with any tolerable use of his reason, whatever diversity of judgment might be among them in other matters, would have thought that such a law could have authorized or excused, much less have justified such actions, and have made them become good: because it is plainly not in men's power to make falsehood be truth, though they may alter the property of their goods as they please. Now if in flagrant cases, the natural and essential difference between good and evil, right and wrong, cannot but be confessed to be plainly and undeniably evident; the difference between them must be also essential and unalterable in all even the smallest and nicest and most intricate cases, though it be not so easy to be discerned and accurately distinguished. For if from the difficulty of determining exactly the bounds of right and wrong in many perplexed cases, it could truly be concluded that just and unjust were not essentially different by nature, but only by positive constitution and custom; it would follow equally, that they were not really, essentially, and unalterably different, even in the most flagrant

cases that can be supposed. Which is an assertion so very absurd, that Mr. Hobbes himself could hardly vent it without blushing, and discovering plainly, by his shifting expressions, his secret self-condemnation. There are therefore certain necessary and eternal differences of things; and certain consequent fitnesses or unfitnesses of the application of different things or different relations one to another; not depending on any positive constitutions, but founded unchangeably in the nature and reason of things, and unavoidably arising from the differences of the things themselves. Which is the first branch of the general proposition I proposed to prove.

2. Now what these eternal and unalterable relations, respects, or proportions of things, with their consequent agreements or disagreements, fitnesses or unfitnesses, absolutely and necessarily are in themselves; that also they appear to be, to the understandings of all intelligent beings; except those only, who understand things to be what they are not, that is, whose understandings are either very imperfect, or very much depraved. And by this understanding or knowledge of the natural and necessary relations, fitnesses, and proportions of things, the wills likewise of all intelligent beings are constantly directed, and must needs be determined to act accordingly; excepting those only, who will things to be what they are not and cannot be; that is, whose wills are corrupted by particular interest or affection, or swayed by some unreasonable and prevailing passion. Wherefore since the natural attributes of God, his infinite knowledge, wisdom and power, set him infinitely above all possibility of being deceived by any error, or of being influenced by any wrong affection; it is manifest his divine will cannot but always and necessarily determine itself to choose to do what in the whole is absolutely best and fittest to be done; that is, to act constantly according to the eternal rules of infinite goodness, justice and truth. As I have endeavoured to show distinctly in my former discourse, in deducing severally the moral attributes of God.

3. And now, that the same reason of things, with regard to which the will of God always and necessarily does determine itself to act in constant conformity to the eternal rules of justice, equity, goodness and truth; ought also constantly to

determine the wills of all subordinate rational beings, to govern all their actions by the same rules; is very evident. For, as it is absolutely impossible in nature, that God should be deceived by any error, or influenced by any wrong affection: so it is very unreasonable and blame-worthy in practice, that any intelligent creatures, whom God has made so far like unto himself, as to endue them with those excellent faculties of reason and will, whereby they are enabled to distinguish good from evil, and to choose the one and refuse the other; should either negligently suffer themselves to be imposed upon and deceived in matters of good and evil, right and wrong; or wilfully and perversely allow themselves to be over-ruled by absurd passions, and corrupt or partial affections, to act contrary to what they know is fit to be done. Which two things, viz. negligent misunderstanding and wilful passions or lusts, are, as I said, the only causes which can make a reasonable creature act contrary to reason, that is, contrary to the eternal rules of justice, equity, righteousness and truth. For, was it not for these inexcusable corruptions and depravations; it is impossible but the same proportions and fitnesses of things, which have so much weight and so much excellency and beauty in them, that the all-powerful creator and governor of the universe, (who has the absolute and uncontrollable dominion of all things in his own hands, and is accountable to none for what he does, yet) thinks it no diminution of his power to make this reason of things the unalterable rule and law of his own actions in the government of the world, and does nothing by mere will and arbitrariness; it is impossible (I say,) if it was not for inexcusable corruption and depravation, but the same eternal reason of things must much more have weight enough to determine constantly the wills and actions of all subordinate, finite, dependent and accountable beings. For originally and in reality, it is as natural and (morally speaking) necessary, that the will should be determined in every action by the reason of the thing, and the right of the case; as it is natural and (absolutely speaking) necessary, that the understanding should submit to a demonstrated truth. And it is as absurd and blame-worthy, to mistake negligently plain right and wrong, that is, to understand the proportions of things in morality to be what they are not; or wilfully to act contrary to known justice and equity, that is, to will things

to be what they are not and cannot be; as it would be absurd and ridiculous for a man in arithmetical matters, ignorantly to believe that twice two is not equal to four; or wilfully and obstinately to contend, against his own clear knowledge, that the whole is not equal to all its parts. The only difference is, that assent to a plain speculative truth, is not in a man's power to withhold; but to act according to the plain right and reason of things, this he may, by the natural liberty of his will, forbear. But the one he ought to do; and it is as much his plain and indispensable duty; as the other he cannot but do, and it is the necessity of his nature to do it. He that wilfully refuses to honour and obey God, from whom he received his being, and to whom he continually owes his preservation; is really guilty of an equal absurdity and inconsistency in practice; as he that in speculation denies the effect to owe anything to its cause, or the whole to be bigger than its part. He that refuses to deal with all men equitably, and with every man as he desires they should deal with him: is guilty of the very same unreasonableness and contradiction in one case; as he that in another case should affirm one number or quantity to be equal to another, and yet that other at the same time not to be equal to the first. Lastly, he that acknowledges himself obliged to the practice of certain duties both towards God and towards men, and yet takes no care either to preserve his own being, or at least not to preserve himself in such a state and temper of mind and body, as may best enable him to perform those duties; is altogether as inexcusable and ridiculous, as he that in any other matter should affirm one thing at the same time that he denies another, without which the former could not possibly be true; or undertake one thing, at the same time that he obstinately omits another, without which the former is by no means practicable. Wherefore all rational creatures, whose wills are not constantly and regularly determined, and their actions governed, by right reason and the necessary differences of good and evil, according to the eternal and invariable rules of justice, equity, goodness and truth; but suffer themselves to be swayed by unaccountable arbitrary humours, and rash passions, by lusts, vanity and pride; by private interest, or present sensual pleasures: these, setting up their own unreasonable self-will in opposition to the nature and reason of things, endeavour (as much as in them lies) to make things be what they are not, and cannot be. Which is the highest presumption and greatest insolence, as well as the greatest absurdity, imaginable. It is acting contrary to that understanding, reason and judgment, which God has implanted in their natures on purpose to enable them to discern the difference between good and evil. It is attempting to destroy that order, by which the universe subsists. It is offering the highest affront imaginable to the creator of all things, who made things to be what they are, and governs everything himself according to the laws of their several natures. In a word; all wilful wickedness and perversion of right, is the very same insolence and absurdity in moral matters; as it would be in natural things, for a man to pretend to alter the certain proportions of numbers, to take away the demonstrable relations and properties of mathematical figures; to make light darkness, and darkness light; or to call sweet bitter, and bitter sweet.

Further: as it appears thus from the abstract and absolute reason and nature of things, that all rational creatures ought, that is, are obliged to take care that their wills and actions be constantly determined and governed by the eternal rule of right and equity: so the certainty and universality of that obligation is plainly confirmed, and the force of it particularly discovered and applied to every man, by this; that in like manner as no one, who is instructed in mathematics, can forbear giving his assent to every geometrical demonstration, of which he understands the terms, either by his own study, or by having had them explained to him by others; so no man, who either has patience and opportunities to examine and consider things himself, or has the means of being taught and instructed in any tolerable manner by others, concerning the necessary relations and dependencies of things; can avoid giving his assent to the fitness and reasonableness of his governing all his actions by the law or rule before mentioned, even though his practice, through the prevalence of brutish lusts, be most absurdly contradictory to that assent. That is to say: by the reason of his mind, he cannot but be compelled to own and acknowledge, that there is really such an obligation indispensably incumbent upon him; even at the same time that in the actions of his life he is endeavouring to throw it off and despise it. For the judgment and conscience of a man's own mind, concerning the reasonableness and fitness

of the thing, that his actions should be conformed to such or such a rule or law; is the truest and formallest obligation; even more properly and strictly so, than any opinion whatsoever of the authority of the giver of a law, or any regard he may have to its sanction by rewards and punishments. For whoever acts contrary to this sense and conscience of his own mind, is necessarily self-condemned; and the greatest and strongest of all obligations is that, which a man cannot break through without condemning himself. The dread of superior power and authority, and the sanction of rewards and punishments; however indeed absolutely necessary to the government of frail and fallible creatures, and truly the most effectual means of keeping them in their duty; is yet really in itself, only a secondary and additional obligation, or enforcement of the first. The original obligation of all, (the ambiguous use of which word as a term of art, has caused some perplexity and confusion in this matter,) is the eternal reason of things; that reason, which God himself, who has no superior to direct him, and to whose happiness nothing can be added nor anything diminished from it, yet constantly obliges himself to govern the world by: and the more excellent and perfect any creatures are, the more cheerfully and steadily are their wills always determined by this supreme obligation, in conformity to the nature, and in imitation of the most perfect will of God. So far therefore as men are conscious of what is right and wrong, so far they are under an obligation to act accordingly; and consequently that eternal rule of right, which I have been hitherto describing, it is evident ought as indispensably to govern men's actions, as it cannot but necessarily determine their assent.

Now that the case is truly thus; that the eternal differences of good and evil, the unalterable rule of right and equity, do necessarily and unavoidably determine the judgment, and force the assent of all men that use any consideration; is undeniably manifest from the universal experience of mankind. For no man willingly and deliberately transgresses this rule, in any great and considerable instance; but he acts contrary to the judgment and reason of his own mind, and secretly reproaches himself for so doing. And no man observes and obeys it steadily, especially in cases of difficulty and temptation, when it interferes with any present interest, pleasure or passion; but his own mind commends and applauds him for his resolution, in executing what his conscience could not forbear giving its assent to, as just and right. And this is what St. Paul means, when he says, (Rom. ii; 14, 15.) that "when the Gentiles which have not the law, do by nature the things contained in the law, these having not the law, are a law unto themselves; which show the work of the law written in their hearts, their conscience also bearing witness, and their thoughts the mean while accusing, or else excusing one another".

It was a very wise observation of Plato, which he received from Socrates; that if you take a young man, impartial and unprejudiced, one that never had any learning, nor any experience in the world; and examine him about the natural relations and proportions of things, [or the moral differences of good and evil;] you may, only by asking him questions, without teaching him any thing at all directly, cause him to express in his answers just and adequate notions of geometrical truths, [and true and exact determinations concerning matters of right and wrong.] From whence he thought it was to be concluded, that all knowledge and learning is nothing but memory, or only a recollecting upon every new occasion, what had been before known in a state of pre-existence. And some others both ancient and moderns, have concluded that the ideas of all first and simple truths, either natural or moral, are innate and originally impressed or stamped upon the mind. In their inference from the observation, the authors of both these opinions seem to be mistaken. But thus much it proves unavoidably; that the differences, relations, and proportions of things both natural and moral, in which all unprejudiced minds thus naturally agree, are certain, unalterable, and real in the things themselves; and do not at all depend on the variable opinions, fancies, or imaginations of men prejudiced by education, laws, customs, or evil practices: and also that the mind of man naturally and unavoidably gives its assent, as to natural and geometrical truth, so also to the moral differences of things, and to the fitness and reasonableness of the obligation of the everlasting law of righteousness, whenever fairly and plainly proposed.

Some men indeed, who, by means of a very evil and vicious education, or through a long habit of wickedness and debauchery, have extremely corrupted the principles of their nature, and have long accustomed themselves to bear down their own reason, by the force of prejudice, lust and passion; that they may not be forced to confess themselves self-condemned, will confidently and absolutely contend that they do not really see any natural and necessary difference between what we call *right* and *wrong*, *just* and *unjust*; that the reason and judgment of their own mind, does not tell them they are under any such indispensable obligations, as we would endeavour to persuade them; and that they are not sensible they ought to be governed by any other rule, than their own will and pleasure. But even these men, the most abandoned of all mankind; however industriously they endeavour to conceal and deny their self-condemnation; yet they cannot avoid making a discovery of it sometimes when they are not aware of it. For example: there is no man so vile and desperate, who commits at any time a murder and robbery, with the most unrelenting mind; but would choose, if such a thing could be proposed to him, to obtain all the same profit or advantage, whatsoever it be that he aims at, without committing the crime, rather than with it; even though he was sure to go unpunished for committing the crime. Nay, I believe, there is no man, even in Mr. Hobbes's state of nature, and of Mr. Hobbes's own principles; but if he was equally assured of securing his main end, his self-preservation, by either way; would choose to preserve himself rather without destroying all his fellow-creatures, than with it; even supposing all impunity, and all other future conveniencies of life, equal in either case. Mr. Hobbes's own scheme, of men's agreeing by compact to preserve one another, can hardly be supposed without this. And this plainly evinces, that the mind of man unavoidably acknowledges a natural and necessary difference between good and evil, antecedent to all arbitrary and positive constitution whatsoever.

But the truth of this, that the mind of man naturally and necessarily assents to the eternal law of righteousness; may still better and more clearly and more universally appear, from the judgment that men pass upon each other's actions, than from what we can discern concerning their consciousness of their own. For men may dissemble and conceal from the world, the judgment of their own conscience; nay, by a strange partiality, they may even impose upon and deceive themselves; (for who is there, that does not sometimes allow himself, nay, and even justify himself in that, wherein he condemns another?) But men's judgments concerning the actions of others, especially where they have no relation to themselves, or repugnance to their interest, are commonly impartial; and from this we may judge, what sense men naturally have of the unalterable difference of right and wrong. Now the observation which everyone cannot but make in this matter, is this; that virtue and true goodness, righteousness and equity, are things so truly noble and excellent, so lovely and venerable in themselves, and do so necessarily approve themselves to the reason and consciences of men; that even those very persons, who, by the prevailing power of some interest or lust, are themselves drawn aside out of the paths of virtue, can yet hardly ever forbear to give it its true character and commendation in others. And this observation holds true, not only in the generality of vicious men, but very frequently even in the worst sort of them, viz. those who persecute others for being better than themselves. [. . .] Plato judiciously observes that even the worst of men seldom or never make so wrong judgment concerning persons, as they do concerning things; there being in virtue an unaccountable and as it were divine force, which, whatever confusion men endeavour to introduce in things by their vicious discourses and debauched practices, yet almost always compels them to distinguish right concerning persons, and makes them admire and praise just and equitable and honest men. On the contrary, vice and injustice, profaneness and debauchery, are things so absolutely odious in their own nature, that, however they insinuate themselves into the practice, yet they can never gain over to themselves the judgment of mankind. They who do evil, yet see and approve what is good; and condemn in others, what they blindly allow in themselves; nay and very frequently condemn even themselves also, not without great disorder and uneasiness of mind, in those very things wherein they allow themselves. At least, there is hardly any wicked man, but when his own case is represented to him under the person of another, will freely enough pass sentence against the wickedness he himself is guilty of; and, with sufficient severity, exclaim against all iniquity. This shows abundantly, that all variation from the eternal rule of right, is absolutely and in the nature of the thing itself to be abhorred and detested; and that the unprejudiced mind of man, as naturally disapproves injustice in moral matters, as in natural things it cannot but dissent from falsehood, or dislike incongruities. Even in reading the histories of past and far distant ages, where it is plain we can have no concern for the events of things, nor prejudices concerning the characters of persons; who is there, that does not praise and admire, nay highly esteem and in his imagination love (as it were) the equity, justice, truth and fidelity of some persons; and with the greatest indignation and hatred, detest the barbarity, injustice, and treachery of others? Nay further; when the prejudices of corrupt minds lie all on the side of injustice; as when we have obtained some very great profit or advantage through another man's treachery or breach of faith; yet who is there, that upon that very occasion does not (even to a proverb) dislike the person and the action, how much soever he may rejoice at the event? But when we come ourselves to suffer by iniquity, then where are all the arguments and sophistries, by which unjust men, while they are oppressing others, would persuade themselves that they are not sensible of any natural difference between good and evil? When it comes to be these men's own case, to be oppressed by violence, or over-reached by fraud; where then are all their pleas against the eternal distinction of right and wrong? How, on the contrary, do they then cry out for equity, and exclaim against injustice! How do they then challenge and object against Providence, and think neither God nor man severe enough, in punishing the violators of right and truth! Whereas, if there was no natural and eternal difference between just and unjust; no man could have any reason to complain of injury, any other than what laws and compacts made so; which in innumerable cases will be always to be evaded.

There is but one thing, that I am sensible of, which can here with any colour be objected against what has been hitherto said concerning the necessity of the mind's giving its assent to the eternal law of righteousness; and that is, the total ignorance, which some whole nations are reported to lie under, of the nature and force of these moral obligations. The matter of fact, is not very true: but if it was, it is certain there are more nations and people totally ignorant of the plainest mathematical truths; as, of the proportion, for example, of a square to a triangle of the same base and height: and yet these truths are such, to which the mind cannot but give its assent necessarily and unavoidably, as soon as they are distinctly proposed to it. All that this objection proves therefore, supposing the matter of it to be true, is only this; not, that the mind of man can ever dissent from the rule of right; much less, that there is no necessary difference in nature, between moral good and evil; any more than it proves, that there are no certain and necessary proportions of numbers, lines, or figures: but this it proves only, that men have great need to be taught and instructed in some very plain and easy, as well as certain truths; and, if they be important truths, that then men have need also to have them frequently inculcated, and strongly enforced upon them. Which is very true: and is (as shall hereafter be particularly made to appear) one good argument for the reasonableness of expecting a revelation.

4. Thus it appears in general, that the mind of man cannot avoid giving its assent to the eternal law of righteousness; that is, cannot but acknowledge the reasonableness and fitness of men's governing all their actions by the rule of right or equity: and also that this assent is a formal obligation upon every man, actually and constantly to conform himself to that rule. I might now from hence deduce in particular, all the several duties of morality or natural religion. But because this would take up too large a portion of my intended discourse, and may easily be supplied abundantly out of several late excellent writers; I shall only mention the three great and principal branches, from which all the other and smaller instances of duty do naturally flow, or may without difficulty be derived.

[. . .]

In respect of our fellow-creatures, the rule of righteousness is; that in particular we so deal with every man, as in like circumstances we could reasonably expect he should deal with us; and that in general we endeavour, by an universal benevolence, to promote the welfare and happiness of all men. The former branch of this rule, is equity; the latter, is love.

As to the former, viz. equity: the reason which obliges every man in practice, so to deal always with another, as he would reasonably expect that others should in like circumstances deal with him; is the very same, as that which forces him in speculation to affirm, that if one line or number be equal to another, that other is reciprocally equal to it. Iniquity is the very same in action, as falsity or contradiction in theory; and the same cause which makes the one absurd, makes the other unreasonable. Whatever relation or proportion one man in any case bears to another; the same that other, when put in like circumstances, bears to him. Whatever I judge reasonable or unreasonable for another to do for me; that, by the same judgment, I declare reasonable or unreasonable, that I in the like case should do for him. And to deny this either in word or action, is as if a man should contend, that, though two and three are equal to five, yet five are not equal to two and three. Wherefore, were not men strangely and most unnaturally corrupted, by perverse and unaccountably false opinions, and monstrous evil customs and habits, prevailing against the clearest and plainest reason in the world: it would be impossible, that universal equity should not be practised by all mankind; and especially among equals, where the proportion of equity is simple and obvious, and every man's own case is already the same with all others, without any nice comparing or transposing of circumstances. It would be as impossible, that a man, contrary to the eternal reason of things, should desire to gain some small profit to himself, by doing violence and damage to his neighbour; as that he should be willing to be deprived of necessaries himself, to satisfy the unreasonable covetousness or ambition of another. In a word; it would be impossible for men not to be as much ashamed of doing iniquity, as they are of believing contradictions. In considering indeed the duties of superiors and inferiors in various relations, the proportion of equity is somewhat more complex; but still it may always be deduced from the same rule of doing as we would be done by, if careful regard be had at the same time to the difference of relation: that is, if in considering what is fit for you to do to another, you always take into the account, not only every circumstance of the action, but also every circumstance wherein the person differs from you; and in judging what you would desire that another, if your circumstances were transposed, should do to you; you always consider, not what any unreasonable passion or private interest would prompt you, but what impartial reason would dictate to you to desire. For example: a magistrate, in order to deal equitably with a criminal, is not to consider what fear or self-love would cause him, in the criminal's case, to desire; but what reason and the public good would oblige him to acknowledge was fit and just for him to expect. And the same proportion is to be observed, in deducing the duties of parents and children, of masters and servants, of governors and subjects, of citizens and foreigners; in what manner every person is obliged by the rule of equity, to behave himself in each of these and all other relations. In the regular and uniform practice of all which duties among all mankind, in their several and respective relations, through the whole earth; consists that universal justice, which is the top and perfection of all virtues.

Notes

This text taken from the corrected seventh edition (1728). Spelling has been adjusted. In addition italics and initial capital letters have been minimized.

2

An Inquiry into the Original of Our Ideas of Beauty and Virtue

Francis Hutcheson

Introduction

The word *moral goodness*, in this treatise, denotes our idea of some quality apprehended in actions, which procures approbation, attended with desire of the agent's happiness. *Moral evil* denotes our idea of a contrary quality, which excites condemnation or dislike. Approbation and condemnation are probably simple ideas, which cannot be farther explained. We must be contented with these imperfect descriptions, until we discover whether we really have such ideas, and what general foundation there is in nature for this difference of actions, as morally good or evil.

[. . .]

Section II: Of the Moral Sense by which We Perceive Virtue and Vice, and Approve or Disapprove them in Others

I. That the perceptions of moral good and evil, are perfectly different from those of natural good or advantage, every one must convince himself, by reflecting upon the different manner in which he finds himself affected when these objects occur to him. Had we no sense of good distinct from the advantage or interest arising from the external senses, and the perceptions of beauty and harmony; the sensations and affections toward a fruitful field, or commodious habitation, would be much the same with what we have toward a generous friend, or any noble character; for both are or may be advantageous to us: and we should no more admire any action, or love any person in a distant country, or age, whose influence could not extend to us, than we love the mountains of Peru, while we are unconcerned in the Spanish trade. We should have the same sentiments and affections toward inanimate beings, which we have toward rational agents, which yet every one knows to be false. Upon comparison, we say, "Why should we approve or love inanimate beings? They have no intention of good to us, or to any other person; their nature makes them fit for our uses, which they neither know nor study to serve. But it is not so with rational agents: they study the interest, and desire the happiness of other beings with whom they converse."

We are all then conscious of the difference between that approbation or perception of moral excellence, which benevolence excites toward the person in whom we observe it, and that opinion of natural goodness, which only raises desire of possession toward the good object. Now "what should make this difference, if all approbation, or sense of good be from prospect of advantage? Do not inanimate objects promote our advantage as well as benevolent persons, who do us offices of kindness and friendship? should we not then have

From *An Inquiry into the Original of our Ideas of Beauty and Virtue*. First printed 1725. This text taken from revised 4th edition (1738).

Moral Psychology: Historical and Contemporary Readings, edited by Thomas Nadelhoffer, Eddy Nahmias, and Shaun Nichols.
© 2010 Blackwell Publishing Ltd except for editorial material and organization © 2010 Thomas Nadelhoffer, Eddy Nahmias, and Shaun Nichols.

the same endearing approbation of both? or only the same cold opinion of advantage in both?" The reason why it is not so, must be this, "that we have a distinct perception of *beauty* or *excellence* in the kind affections of rational agents; whence we are determined to admire and love such characters and persons."

Suppose we reap the same advantage from two men, one of whom serves us from an ultimate desire of our happiness, or good-will toward us; the other from views of self-interest, or by constraint: both are in this case equally beneficial or advantageous to us, and yet we shall have quite different sentiments of them. We must then certainly have other perceptions of moral actions, than those of advantage: and that power of receiving these perceptions may be called a *moral sense*, since the definition agrees to it, viz. a determination of the mind, to receive any idea from the presence of an object which occurs to us, independent on our will.

This perhaps will be equally evident from our ideas of evil, done to us designedly by a rational agent. Our senses of natural good and evil would make us receive, with equal serenity and composure, an assault, a buffet, an affront from a neighbour, a cheat from a partner, or trustee, as we would an equal damage from the fall of a beam, a tile, or a tempest; and we should have the same affections and sentiments on both occasions. Villainy, treachery, cruelty, would be as meekly resented as a blast, or mildew, or an overflowing stream. But I fancy every one is very differently affected on these occasions, though there may be equal natural evil in both. Nay, actions no way detrimental may occasion the strongest anger and indignation, if they evidence only impotent hatred or contempt. And, on the other hand, the intervention of moral ideas may prevent our condemnation of the agent, or bad moral apprehension of that action, which causes to us the greatest natural evil. Thus the opinion of justice in any sentence, will prevent all ideas of moral evil in the execution, or hatred toward the magistrate, who is the immediate cause of our greatest sufferings.

II. In our sentiments of actions which affect ourselves, there is indeed a mixture of the ideas of natural and moral good, which require some attention to separate them. But when we reflect upon the actions which affect other persons only,

we may observe the moral ideas unmixed with those of natural good or evil. For let it be here observed, that those senses by which we perceive pleasure in natural objects, whence they are constituted advantageous, could never raise in us any desire of public good, but only of what was good to ourselves in particular. Nor could they ever make us approve an action merely because of its promoting the happiness of others. And yet, as soon as any action is represented to us as flowing from love, humanity, gratitude, compassion, a study of the good of others, and an ultimate desire of their happiness, although it were in the most distant part of the world, or in some past age, we feel joy within us, admire the lovely action, and praise its author. And on the contrary, every action represented as flowing from ill-will, desire of the misery of others without view to any prevalent good to the public, or ingratitude, raises abhorrence and aversion.

[. . .]

It remains then, "that as the Author of nature has determined us to receive, by our external senses, pleasant or disagreeable ideas of objects, according as they are useful or hurtful to our bodies; and to receive from uniform objects the pleasures of beauty and harmony, to excite us to the pursuit of knowledge, and to reward us for it; or to be an argument to us of his goodness, as the uniformity itself proves his existence, whether we had a sense of beauty in uniformity or not; in the same manner he has given us a *moral sense*, to direct our actions, and to give us still nobler pleasures: so that while we are only intending the good of others, we undesignedly promote our own greatest private good."

We are not to imagine, that this moral sense, more than the other senses, supposes any innate ideas, knowledge, or practical proposition: we mean by it only a determination of our minds to receive the simple ideas of approbation or condemnation, from actions observed, antecedent to any opinions of advantage or loss to redound to ourselves from them; even as we are pleased with a regular form, or an harmonious composition, without having any knowledge of mathematics, or seeing any advantage in that form or composition, different from the immediate pleasure.

That we may discern more distinctly the difference between moral perceptions and others, let us consider, when we taste a pleasant fruit, we are conscious of pleasure; when another tastes it, we only conclude or form an opinion that he enjoys pleasure; and, abstracting from some previous good-will or anger, his enjoying this pleasure is to us a matter wholly indifferent, raising no new sentiment or affection. But when we are under the influence of a virtuous temper, and thereby engaged in virtuous actions, we are not always conscious of any pleasure, nor are we only pursuing private pleasures, as will appear hereafter: it is only by *reflex acts* upon our temper and conduct that we enjoy the delights of virtue. When also we judge the temper of another to be virtuous, we do not necessarily imagine him *then* to enjoy pleasure, though we know *reflection* will give it to him: and farther, our apprehension of his virtuous temper raises sentiments of approbation, esteem or admiration, and the affection of good-will toward him. The quality approved by our moral sense is conceived to reside in the person approved, and to be a perfection and dignity in him: approbation of another's virtue is not conceived as making the approver happy, or virtuous, or worthy, though it is attended with some small pleasure. Virtue is then called *amiable* or *lovely*, from its raising good-will or love in spectators toward the agent; and not from the agent's perceiving the virtuous temper to be advantageous to him, or desiring to obtain it under that view. A virtuous temper is called *good* or *beatific*, not that it is always attended with pleasure in the agent; much less that some small pleasure attends the contemplation of it in the approver: but from this, that every spectator is persuaded that the reflex acts of the virtuous agent upon his own temper will give him the highest pleasures. The admired quality is conceived as the perfection of the agent, and such a one as is distinct from the pleasure either in the agent or the approver; though it is a sure source of pleasure to the agent. The perception of the approver, though attended with pleasure, plainly represents something quite distinct from this pleasure; even as the perception of external forms is attended with pleasure, and yet represents something distinct from this pleasure. This may prevent many cavils upon this subject.

Note

This text from the revised fourth edition (1738). Spelling has been adjusted and footnotes eliminated. Italics and initial capital letters have been minimized.

3

An Essay on the Nature and Conduct of the Passions and Affections, with Illustrations on the Moral Sense

Treatise II: Illustrations Upon the Moral Sense

Francis Hutcheson

Section I: Concerning the Character of Virtue, Agreeable to Truth or Reason

Since reason is understood to denote our power of finding out true propositions, reasonableness must denote the same thing, with conformity to true propositions, or to truth.

Reasonableness in an action is a very common expression, but yet upon inquiry, it will appear very confused, whether we suppose it the motive to election, or the quality determining approbation.

[. . .]

If reasonableness, the character of virtue, denote some other sort of conformity to truth, it were to be wished that these gentlemen, who make it the original idea of moral good, antecedent to any sense or affections, would explain it, and show how it determines us antecedently to a sense, either to election or approbation.

They tell us, "we must have some standard antecedently to all sense or affections, since we judge even of our senses and affections themselves, and approve or disapprove them: this standard must be our reason, conformity to which must be the original idea of moral good."

But what is this conformity of actions to reason? When we ask the reason of an action, we sometimes mean, "What truth shows a quality in the action, exciting the agent to do it?" Thus, why does a luxurious man pursue wealth? The reason is given by this truth, "Wealth is useful to purchase pleasures." Sometimes for a reason of actions we show the truth expressing a quality, engaging our approbation. Thus the reason of hazarding life in just war, is, that "it tends to preserve our honest countrymen, or evidences public spirit:" The reason for temperance, and against luxury is given thus, "Luxury evidences a selfish base temper." The former sort of reasons we will call *exciting*, and the latter *justifying*. Now we shall find that all exciting reasons presuppose instincts and affections; and the justifying presuppose a moral sense.

As to exciting reasons, in every calm rational action some end is desired or intended; no end can be intended or desired previously to some one of these classes of affections, self-love, self-hatred, or desire of private misery, (if this be possible) benevolence toward others, or malice: All affections are included under these; no end can be previous to them all; there can therefore be no exciting reason previous to affection.

We have indeed many confused harangues on this subject, telling us, "We have two principles of action, reason, and affection or passion: the former in common with angels, the latter with brutes: no action is wise, or good, or reasonable, to which we are not excited by reason, as distinct

From *Treatise II: Illustrations Upon the Moral Sense*, 3rd edition, London 1742.

Moral Psychology: Historical and Contemporary Readings, edited by Thomas Nadelhoffer, Eddy Nahmias, and Shaun Nichols.

from all affections; or, if any such actions as flow from affections be good, it is only by chance, or materially and not formally." As if indeed reason, or the knowledge of the relations of things, could excite to action when we proposed no end, or as if ends could be intended without desire or affection.

But are there not also exciting reasons, even previous to any end, moving us to propose one end rather than another? To this Aristotle long ago answered, "that there are ultimate ends desired without a view to any thing else, and subordinate ends or objects desired with a view to something else." To subordinate ends those reasons or truths excite, which show them to be conducive to the ultimate end, and show one object to be more effectual than another: thus subordinate ends may be called *reasonable*. But as to the ultimate ends, to suppose exciting reasons for them, would infer, that there is no ultimate end, but that we desire one thing for another in an infinite series.

Thus ask a being who desires private happiness, or has self-love, "what reason excites him to desire wealth?" He will give this reason, that "wealth tends to procure pleasure and ease." Ask his reason for desiring pleasure or happiness: one cannot imagine what proposition he could assign as his exciting reason. This proposition is indeed true, "There is an instinct or desire fixed in his nature, determining him to pursue his happiness;" but it is not this reflection on his own nature, or this proposition which excites or determines him, but the instinct itself. This is a truth, "rhubarb strengthens the stomach." But it is not a proposition which strengthens the stomach, but the quality in that medicine. The effect is not produced by propositions showing the cause, but by the cause itself.

In like manner, what reason can a benevolent being give, as exciting him to hazard his life in just war? This perhaps, "such conduct tends to the happiness of his country." Ask him, "why he serves his country?" he will say, "his country is a very valuable part of mankind." Why does he study the happiness of mankind? If his affections be really disinterested, he can give no exciting reasons for it: the happiness of mankind in general, or of any valuable part of it, is an ultimate end to that series of desires.

[. . .]

Let us examine the truths assigned as *exciting* to the pursuit of public good, even by those, who, though they allow disinterested affections, and a moral sense, yet suppose something reasonable in it antecedently. They assign such as these, "public good is the end proposed by the deity." Then what reason excites men to concur with the deity? Is it this, "concurring with the deity will make the agent happy?" This is an exciting reason indeed, but plainly supposes self-love: And let any one assign the exciting reason to the desire of happiness. Is the reason exciting to concur with the deity this, "The deity is our benefactor?" Then what reason excites to concur with benefactors? Here we must recur to an instinct. Is it this truth, "The divine ends are reasonable ends?" Then what means the word *reasonable*? Does it mean, that "the deity has reasons exciting him to promote the public good?" What are these reasons? Why, perhaps "we do not know them particularly, but in general are sure that the deity has reasons for them." Then the question recurs, "What reason excites us to implicit concurrence with the ends of the deity?" The reasons which excite one nature may not excite another: The tendency of an action to the happiness of one agent may excite him, but will not excite another agent to concur, unless there appears a like tendency to the happiness of that other. They may say, "they are sure the divine ends are good." What means *goodness*? Is it moral or natural? If the divine ends be natural good, i.e. pleasant, or the cause of pleasure, to whom is this pleasure? If to the deity, then why do we study the happiness or the pleasing of the deity? What reason excites us? All the possible reasons must either presuppose some affection, if they are exciting; or some moral sense, if they are justifying. – Is the divine end naturally good to us? This is an exciting Reason, but supposes self-love. If we say the divine ends are morally good, we are just where we began. What is moral goodness? Conformity to reason. What are the reasons exciting or justifying?

If any allege as the reason exciting us to pursue public good, this truth, that "the happiness of a system, a thousand, or a million, is a greater quantity of happiness than that of one person: and consequently, if men desire happiness, they must have stronger desires toward the greater sum, than toward the less." This reason still supposes an instinct toward happiness as previous to it: And again, to whom is the happiness of a system a greater happiness? To one individual, or to the system? If to the individual, then his reason exciting his desire of a happy system supposes self-love: If to the system, then what reason can excite to desire the greater happiness of a system, or any happiness to be in the possession of others? None surely which does not presuppose public affections. Without such affections this truth, "that an hundred felicities is a greater sum than one felicity," will no more excite to study the happiness of the hundred, than this truth, "an hundred stones are greater than one," will excite a man, who has no desire of heaps, to cast them together.

The same may be observed concerning that proposition, assigned by some as the ultimate reason both exciting to, and justifying the pursuit of public good, viz. "It is best that all should be happy." Best is most good: Good to whom? To the whole, or to each individual? If to the former, when this truth excites to action, it must presuppose kind affections; if it is good to each individual, it must suppose self-love.

Let us once suppose affections, instincts or desires previously implanted in our nature: and we shall easily understand the exciting reasons for actions, viz. "These truths which show them to be conducive toward some ultimate end, or toward the greatest end of that kind in our power." He acts reasonably, who considers the various actions in his power, and forms true opinions of their tendencies; and then chooses to do that which will obtain the highest degree of that, to which the instincts of his nature incline him, with the smallest degree of those things from which the affections in his nature make him averse.

More particularly, the exciting reasons to a nature which had only selfish affections, are those truths which showed "what object or event would occasion to it the greatest quantity of pleasure:" these would excite to the prosecution of it. The exciting truths about means, would be only those which pointed out some means as more certainly effectual than any other, or with less pain or trouble to the agent. Public usefulness of ends or means, or public hurtfulness would neither excite nor dissuade, farther than the public state might affect that of the agent.

If there is any nature with public affections: The truths exciting to any end in this order, are such as show, "that any event would promote the happiness of others." That end is called most *reasonable*, which our reason discovers to contain a greater quantity of public good, than any other in our power.

When any event may affect both the agent and others, if the agent have both self-love and public affections, he acts according to that affection which is strongest, when there is any opposition of interests; if there be no opposition, he follows both. If he discovers this truth, that "his constant pursuit of public good is the most probable way of promoting his own happiness," then his pursuit is truly reasonable and constant; thus both affections are at once gratified, and he is consistent with himself. Without knowledge of that truth he does not act reasonably for his own happiness, but follows it by means not tending effectually to this end: and must frequently, from the power of self-love, neglect or counteract his other end, the public good. If there be also a moral sense in such an agent, while yet he is inadvertent to the connection of private happiness with the study of the public; he must be perpetually yet more uneasy, either through the apprehended neglect of private interest when he serves the public; or when he pursues only private interest, he will have perpetual remorse and dissatisfaction with his own temper, through his moral sense. So that the knowledge of this connection of private interest, with the study of public good, seems absolutely necessary to preserve a constant satisfaction of mind, and to prevent an alternate prevalence of seemingly contrary desires.

Should any one ask even concerning these two ultimate ends, private good and public, is not the latter more reasonable than the former? – What means the word *reasonable* in this question? If we are allowed to presuppose instincts and affections, then the truth just now supposed to be discoverable concerning our state, is an exciting reason to serve the public interest, since this conduct is the most effectual means to obtain both ends. But I doubt if any truth can be assigned which excites in us either the desire of private happiness or public. For the former none ever alleged any exciting reason: and a benevolent temper finds as little reason exciting him to the latter; which he desires without any view to private good. If the meaning of the question be this, "does not every spectator approve the pursuit of public good more than private?" The answer is obvious that he does: but not for any reason or truth, but from a moral sense in the constitution of the soul.

This leads to consider approbation of actions, whether it be for conformity to any truth, or reasonableness, that actions are ultimately approved, independently of any moral sense? Or if all justifying reasons do not presuppose it?

If conformity to truth, or reasonable, denote nothing else but that "an action is the object of a true proposition," it is plain, that all actions should be approved equally, since as many truths may be made about the worst, as can be made about the best. See what was said above about exciting reasons.

But let the truths commonly assigned as *justifying* be examined. Here it is plain, "A truth showing an action to be fit to attain an end," does not justify it; nor do we approve a subordinate end for any truth, which only shows it to be fit to promote the ultimate end; for the worst actions may be conducive to their ends, and reasonable in that sense. The justifying reasons then must be about the ends themselves, especially the ultimate ends. The question then is, "Does a conformity to any truth make us approve an ultimate end, previously to any moral sense?" For example, we approve pursuing the public good. For what reason? Or what is the truth for conformity to which we call it a *reasonable end*? I fancy we can find none in these cases, more than we could give for our liking any pleasant fruit.

The reasons assigned are such as these; "it is the end proposed by the deity." But why do we approve concurring with the divine ends? This reason is given, "He is our benefactor." But then, for what reason do we approve concurrence with a benefactor? Here we must recur to a sense. Is this the reason moving to approbation, "Study of public good tends to the advantage of the approver?" Then the quality moving us to approve an action, is its being advantageous to us, and not conformity to a truth. This scheme is intelligible, but not true in fact. Men approve without perception of private advantage; and often do not condemn or disapprove what is plainly pernicious; as in the execution of a just sentence, which even the sufferer may approve.

If any allege, that this is the justifying reason of the pursuit of public good, "that it is best all be happy," then we approve actions for their tendency to that state which is best, and not for conformity to reason. But here again, what means *best*? morally best, or naturally best? If the former,

they explain the same word by itself in a circle: If they mean the latter, that "it is the most happy state where all are happy;" then, most happy, for whom? the system, or the individual? If for the former, what reason makes us approve the happiness of a system? Here we must recur to a sense or kind affections. Is it most happy for the individual? Then the quality moving approbation is again tendency to private happiness, not reasonableness.

[...]

Before we quit this character *reasonableness*, let us consider the arguments brought to prove that there must be some standard of moral good antecedent to any sense. Say they, "Perceptions of sense are deceitful, we must have some perception or idea of virtue more stable and certain; this must be conformity to reason: Truth discovered by our reason is certain and invariable: That then alone is the original idea of virtue, agreement with reason." But in like manner our sight and sense of beauty is deceitful, and does not always represent the true forms of objects. We must not call that *beautiful* or *regular*, which pleases the sight, or an internal sense; but beauty in external forms too, consists in conformity to reason. So our taste may be vitiated: we must not say that savour is perceived by taste, but must place the original idea of grateful savours in conformity to reason, and of ungrateful in contrariety to reason. We may mistake the real extent of bodies, or their proportions, by making a conclusion upon the first sensible appearance: Therefore ideas of extension are not originally acquired by a sense, but consist in conformity to reason.

If what is intended in this conformity to reason be this, "That we should call no action *virtuous*, unless we have some reason to conclude it to be virtuous, or some truth showing it to be so." This is very true; but then in like manner we should count no action vicious, unless we have some reason for counting it so, or when it is truth "that it is vicious." If this be intended by conformity to truth, then at the same rate we may make conformity to truth the original idea of vice as well as virtue; nay, of every attribute whatsoever. That taste alone is sweet, which there is reason to count sweet; that taste alone is bitter, concerning which it is true that it is bitter; that form alone is beautiful, concerning which it is true that it is beautiful; and that alone deformed, which is truly deformed. Thus virtue, vice, sweet, bitter, beautiful, or deformed, originally denote conformity to reason, antecedently to perceptions of any sense. The idea of virtue is particularly that concerning which it is truth, that it is virtue; or virtue is virtue; a wonderful discovery!

So when some tell us, "that truth is naturally pleasant, and more so than any sensible perception; this must therefore engage men more than any other motive, if they attend to it." Let them observe, that as much truth is known about vice as virtue. We may demonstrate the public miseries which would ensue upon perjury, murder, and robbery. These demonstrations would be attended with that pleasure which is peculiar to truth; as well as the demonstrations of the public happiness to ensue from faith, humanity and justice. There is equal truth on both sides.

We may transiently observe what has occasioned the use of the word *reasonable*, as an epithet of only virtuous actions. Though we have instincts determining us to desire ends, without supposing any previous reasoning; yet it is by use of our reason that we find out the means of obtaining our ends. When we do not use our reason, we often are disappointed of our end. We therefore call those actions which are effectual to their ends, *reasonable* in one sense of that word.

Again, in all men there is probably a moral sense, making publicly useful actions and kind affections grateful to the agent, and to every observer: Most men who have thought of human actions, agree, that the publicly useful are in the whole also privately useful to the agent, either in this life or the next: We conclude, that all men have the same affections and senses: We are convinced by our reason, that it is by publicly useful actions alone that we can promote all our ends. Whoever then acts in a contrary manner, we presume is mistaken, ignorant of, or inadvertent to, these truths which he might know; and say he acts unreasonably. Hence some have been led to imagine, some reasons either exciting or justifying previously to all affections or a moral sense.

Two arguments are brought in defense of this epithet, as antecedent to any sense, viz. "That we judge even of our affections and senses themselves, whether they are morally good or evil."

The second argument is, that "if all moral ideas depend upon the constitution of our sense, then all constitutions would have been alike reasonable and good to the deity, which is absurd."

As to the first argument, it is plain we judge of our own affections, or those of others by our moral sense, by which we approve kind affections, and disapprove the contrary. But none can apply moral attributes to the very faculty of perceiving moral qualities; or call his moral sense morally good or evil, any more than he calls the power of tasting, sweet or bitter; or of seeing, straight or crooked, white or black.

Every one judges the affections of others by his own sense; so that it seems not impossible that in these senses men might differ as they do in taste. A sense approving benevolence would disapprove that temper, which a sense approving malice would delight in. The former would judge of the latter by his own sense, so would the latter of the former. Each one would at first view think the sense of the other perverted. But then, is there no difference? Are both senses equally good? No certainly, any man who observed them would think the sense of the former more desirable than of the latter; but this is, because the moral sense of every man is constituted in the former manner. But were there any nature with no moral sense at all observing these two persons, would he not think the state of the former preferable to that of the latter? Yes, he might: but not from any perception of moral goodness in the one sense more than in the other. Any rational nature observing two men thus constituted, with opposite senses, might by reasoning see, not moral goodness in one sense more than in the contrary, but a tendency to the happiness of the person himself, who had the former sense in the one constitution, and a contrary tendency in the opposite constitution: nay, the persons themselves might observe this; since the former sense would make these actions grateful to the agent which were useful to others; who, if they had a like sense, would love him, and return good offices; whereas the latter sense would make all such Actions as are useful to others, and apt to engage their good offices, ungrateful to the agent; and would lead him into publicly hurtful actions, which would not only procure the hatred of others, if they had a contrary sense, but engage them out of their self-love to study his destruction, though their senses agreed. Thus any observer, or the agent himself with this latter sense, might perceive that the pains to be feared, as the consequence of malicious actions, did over-balance the pleasures of this sense; so that it would be to the agent's interest to counteract it. Thus one constitution of the moral sense might appear to be more advantageous to those who had it, than the contrary; as we may call that sense of tasting healthful, which made wholesome meat pleasant; and we would call a contrary taste pernicious. And yet we should no more call the moral sense morally good or evil, than we call the sense of tasting savoury or unsavoury, sweet or bitter.

But must we not own, that we judge of all our senses by our reason, and often correct their reports of the magnitude, figure, colour, taste of objects, and pronounce them right or wrong, as they agree or disagree with reason? This is true. But does it then follow, that *extension, figure, colour, taste,* are not sensible ideas, but only denote *reasonableness,* or agreement with reason? Or that these qualities are perceivable antecedently to any sense, by our power of finding out truth? Just so a compassionate temper may rashly imagine the correction of a child, or the execution of a criminal, to be cruel and inhuman: but by reasoning may discover the superior good arising from them in the whole; and then the same moral sense may determine the observer to approve them. But we must not hence conclude, that it is any reasoning antecedent to a moral sense, which determines us to approve the study of public good, any more than we can in the former case conclude, that we perceive extension, figure, colour, taste, antecedently to a sense. All these sensations are often corrected by reasoning, as well as our approbations of actions as good or evil: and yet no body ever placed the original idea of *extension, figure, colour,* or *taste,* in conformity to reason.

Thus though no man can immediately either approve or disapprove as morally good or evil his own moral sense, by which he approves only affections and actions consequent upon them; yet he may see whether it be advantageous to him in other respects, to have it constituted one way rather than another. One constitution may make these actions grateful to this sense which tend to procure other pleasures also. A contrary constitution may be known to the very person himself to be disadvantageous, as making these actions immediately grateful, which shall occasion all other sorts of misery. His self-love may excite him, though with dissatisfaction, to counteract this sense, in order to avoid a greater evil. Mr. Hobbes seems to have had no better notions of the natural state of mankind. An observer, who was benevolent, would desire that all had the former sort of sense; a malicious observer, if he feared no evil to himself, from the actions of the persons observed, would desire the latter constitution. If this observer had a moral sense, he would think that constitution which was contrary to his own, strange and surprizing, or unnatural. If the observer had no affections toward others, and were disjoined from mankind, so as to have neither hopes nor fears from their actions, he would be indifferent about their constitutions, and have no desire or preference of one above another; though he might see which were advantageous to them, and which pernicious.

[. . .]

We have got some strange phrases, "that some things are antecedently reasonable in the nature of the thing," which some insist upon: "That otherwise, say they, if before man was created, any nature without a moral sense had existed, this nature would not have approved as morally good in the deity, his constituting our sense as it is at present." Very true; and what next? If there had been no moral sense in that nature, there would have been no perception of morality. But "could not such natures have seen something reasonable in one constitution more than in another?" They might no doubt have reasoned about the various constitutions, and foreseen that the present one would tend to the happiness of mankind, and would evidence benevolence in the deity; So also they might have reasoned about the contrary constitution, that it would make men miserable, and evidence malice in the deity. They would have reasoned about both, and found out truths: are both constitutions alike reasonable to these observers? No, say they, "the benevolent one is reasonable, and the malicious unreasonable:" And yet these observers reasoned and discovered truths about both: An action then is called by us *reasonable* when it is benevolent, and unreasonable when malicious. This is plainly making the word *reasonable* denote whatever is approved by our moral sense, without relation to true propositions. We often use that word in such a confused manner; But these antecedent natures, supposed without a moral sense, would not have approved one constitution of the deity as morally better than another.

Had it been left to the choice of these antecedent minds, what manner of sense they would have desired for mankind; would they have seen no difference? Yes they would, according to their affections which are presupposed in all election. If they were benevolent, as we suppose the deity, the tendency of the present sense to the happiness of men would have excited their choice. Had they been malicious, as we suppose the devil, the contrary tendency of the contrary sense would have excited their election of it. But is there nothing preferable, or eligible antecedently to all affections too? No certainly, unless there can be desire without affections, or superior desire, i.e. election antecedently to all desire.

Some farther perplex this subject, by asserting, that "the same reasons determining approbation, ought also to excite to election." Here, 1. We often see justifying reasons where we can have no election; viz. when we observe the actions of others, which were even prior to our existence. 2. The quality moving us to election very often cannot excite approbation; viz. private usefulness, not publicly pernicious. This both does and ought to move election, and yet I believe few will say, "they approve as virtuous the eating a bunch of grapes, taking a glass of wine, or sitting down when one is tired." Approbation is not what we can voluntarily bring upon ourselves. When we are contemplating actions, we do not choose to approve, because approbation is pleasant; otherwise we would always approve, and never condemn any action; because this is some way uneasy. Approbation is plainly a perception arising without previous volition, or choice of it, because of any concomitant pleasure. The occasion of it is the perception of benevolent affections in ourselves, or the discovering the like in others, even when we are incapable of any action or election. The reasons determining approbation are such as show that an action evidenced kind affections, and that in others, as often as in ourselves. Whereas, the reasons moving to election are such as show the tendency of an action to gratify some affection in the agent.

The prospect of the pleasure of self-approbation, is indeed often a motive to choose one action rather than another; but this supposes the moral sense, or determination to approve, prior to the election. Were approbation voluntarily chosen, from the prospect of its concomitant pleasure, then there could be no condemnation of our own actions, for that is unpleasant. . . .

Section II: Concerning that Character of Virtue and Vice, The Fitness or Unfitness of Actions

We come next to examine some other explications of morality, which have been much insisted on of late. We are told, "that there are eternal and immutable differences of things, absolutely and antecedently: that there are also eternal and unalterable relations in the natures of the things themselves, from which arise agreements and disagreements, congruities and incongruities, fitness and unfitness of the application of circumstances, to the qualifications of persons; that actions agreeable to these relations are morally good, and that the contrary actions are morally evil." These expressions are sometimes made of the same import with those more common ones: "acting agreeably to the eternal reason and truth of things." It is asserted, that "God who knows all these relations, etc. does guide his actions by them, since he has no wrong affection" (the word 'wrong' should have been first explained): "And that in like manner these relations, etc. ought" (another unlucky word in morals) "to determine the choice of all rationals, abstractly from any views of interest. If they do not, these creatures are insolently counteracting their creator, and as far as they can, making things to be what they are not, which is the greatest impiety."

That things are now different is certain. That ideas, to which there is no object yet existing conformable, are also different, is certain. That upon comparing two ideas there arises a relative idea, generally when the two ideas compared have in them any modes of the same simple idea, is also obvious. Thus every extended being may be compared to any other of the same kinds of dimensions; and relative ideas be formed of greater, less, equal, double, triple, subduple, etc. with infinite variety. This may let us see that relations are not real qualities inherent in external natures, but only ideas necessarily accompanying our perception of two objects at once, and comparing them. Relative ideas continue, when the external objects do not exist, provided we retain the two ideas. But what the eternal relations in the natures of things do mean, is not so easy perhaps to be conceived. [. . .]

Now let us examine what fitnesses or unfitnesses arise from any of these sorts of relations, in which the morality of actions may consist; and whether we can place morality in them, without presupposing a moral sense. It is plain, that ingenious Author[1] says nothing against the supposition of a moral sense: But many imagine, that his account of moral ideas is independent upon a moral sense, and therefore are less willing to allow that we have such an immediate perception, or sense of virtue and vice. What follows is not intended to oppose his scheme, but rather to suggest what seems a necessary explication of it; by showing that it is no otherwise intelligible, but upon supposition of a moral sense.

[. . .]

There is certainly, independently of fancy or custom, a natural tendency in some actions to give pleasure, either to the agent or to others; and a contrary tendency in other actions to give pain, either to the agent or others. This sort of relation of actions to the agents or objects is indisputable. If we call these relations *fitnesses*, then the most contrary actions have equal fitnesses for contrary ends; and each one is unfit for the end of the other. Thus Compassion is fit to make others happy, and unfit to make others miserable. Violation of property is fit to make men miserable, and unfit to make them happy. Each of these is both fit and unfit, with respect to different ends. The bare fitness then to an end, is not the idea of moral goodness.

Perhaps the virtuous fitness is that of ends. The fitness of a subordinate end to the ultimate, can-

not constitute the action good, unless the ultimate end be good. To keep a conspiracy secret is not a good end, though it be fit for obtaining a farther end, the success of the conspiracy. The moral fitness must be that of the ultimate end itself: The public good alone is a fit end, therefore the means fit for this end alone are good.

What means the *fitness of an ultimate end*? For what is it fit? Why, it is an ultimate end, not fit for any thing farther, but absolutely fit. What means that word *fit*? If it notes a simple idea it must be the perception of some sense: thus we must recur, upon this scheme too, to a moral Sense.

If fitness be not a simple idea, let it be defined. Some tell us, that it is "an agreement of an affection, desire, action, or end, to the relations of agents." But what means *agreement*? [. . .]

There is one meaning perhaps intended, however it be obscurely expressed, "That certain affections or actions of an agent, standing in a certain relation to other agents, is approved by every observer, or raises in him a grateful perception, or moves the observer to love the agent." This meaning is the same with the notion of pleasing a moral sense.

Whoever explains virtue or vice by justice or injustice, right or wrong, uses only more ambiguous words, which will equally lead to acknowledge a moral sense.

Note

Third edition. London, 1742. Spelling has been adjusted and footnotes eliminated. Italics and initial capital letters have been minimized.
[1]   Hutcheson is referring to John Locke.

4

Enquiries Concerning the Principles of Morals
Appendix I: *Concerning Moral Sentiment*

David Hume

[...]

The chief foundation of moral praise being supposed to lie in the usefulness of any quality or action; 'tis evident, that *Reason* must enter for a considerable share in all determinations of this kind; since nothing but that faculty can instruct us in the tendency of qualities and actions, and point out their beneficial consequences to society and to their possessors. In many cases, this is an affair liable to great controversy: Doubts may arise; opposite interests occur; and a preference must be given to one side, from very nice views and a small overballance of utility. This is particularly remarkable in questions with regard to justice; as is, indeed, natural to suppose from that species of utility, which attends this virtue. Were every single instance of justice, like that of benevolence, beneficial and useful to society; this would be a more simple state of the case, and seldom liable to great controversy. But as single instances of justice are often pernicious, in their first and immediate tendency, and as the advantage to society results only from the observance of the general rule, and from the concurrence and combination of several persons in the same equitable conduct; the case here becomes more intricate and involved. The various circumstances of society; the various consequences of any practice; the various interests, which may be proposed: These on many occasions are doubtful,

and subject to great discussion and enquiry. The object of municipal laws is to fix all questions with regard to justice: the debates of civilians; the reflections of politicians; the precedents of Histories and public records, are all directed to the same Purpose. And a very accurate *reason* or *judgment* is often requisite, to give the true determination, amidst such intricate doubts arising from obscure or opposite utilities.

But tho' reason, when fully assisted and improved, be sufficient to instruct us in the pernicious or useful tendencies of qualities and actions; it is not alone sufficient to produce any moral blame or approbation. Utility is only a tendency to a certain end; and were the end totally indifferent to us, we should feel the same indifference towards the means. 'Tis requisite a *sentiment* should here display itself, in order to give a Preference to the useful above the pernicious tendencies. This sentiment can be no other than a feeling for the happiness of mankind, and a resentment of their misery; since these are the different ends, which virtue and vice have a tendency to promote. Here therefore, *reason* instructs us in the several tendencies of actions, and *humanity* makes a distinction in favour of those, which are useful and beneficial.

This partition betwixt the faculties of understanding and sentiment, in all moral decisions, seems clear from the preceding hypothesis. But I

From An Enquiry concernnging the *Principles of Morals* by David Hume, Efq; London Printed for A. Millar, over_againft Catberine_Street in the Strand. 1751 pages 197–212.

Moral Psychology: Historical and Contemporary Readings, edited by Thomas Nadelhoffer, Eddy Nahmias, and Shaun Nichols.

shall suppose that hypothesis false: 'Twill then be requisite to look out for some other theory, that may be satisfactory; and I dare venture to affirm, that none such will ever be found, as long as we suppose reason to be the sole source of morals. To prove this, it will be proper to weigh the five following considerations.

I. 'Tis easy for a false hypothesis to maintain some appearance of truth, while it keeps altogether in generals, makes use of undefined terms, and employs comparisons, instead of instances. This is particularly remarkable in that philosophy, which ascribes the discernment of all moral distinctions to reason alone without the concurrence of sentiment. 'Tis impossible, in any particular instance, that this hypothesis can so much as be rendered intelligible; whatever specious figure it may make in general declamations and discourses. Examine the crime of *ingratitude*, for instance; which has place, wherever we observe good-will, exprest and known, along with good-offices performed, on the one side, and a return of ill-will or indifference, with ill-offices or neglect, on the other: Anatomize all these circumstances and examine, by your reason alone, wherein consists the demerit or blame: You never will come to any issue or conclusion.

Reason judges either of *matter of fact* or of *relations*. Enquire then, *first,* where is that matter of fact, which we here call *crime*; point it out; determine the time of its existence; describe its essence or nature; explain the sense or faculty, to which it discovers itself. It resides in the mind of the person, who is ungrateful. He must, therefore, feel it and be conscious of it. But nothing is there, except the passion of ill will or absolute indifference. You cannot say, that these, of themselves, always, and in all circumstances, are crimes. No: They are only crimes, when directed towards persons, who have before expressed and displayed good will towards us. Consequently, we may infer, that the crime of ingratitude is not any particular individual *fact*; but arises from a complication of circumstances, which, being presented to the spectator, excites the *sentiment* of blame, by the particular structure and fabric of his mind.

This representation, you say, is false. Crime, indeed, consists not in a particular *fact*, of whose reality we are assured by *reason*: But it consists in certain *moral relations*, discovered by reason, in the same manner as we discover, by reason, the truths of geometry or algebra. But what are the relations, I ask, of which you here talk? In the case stated above, I see first good-will and good-offices, in one person; then Ill-will and Ill-offices in the other: Betwixt these, there is the relation of *contrariety*. Does the crime consist in that relation? But suppose a person bore me Ill-will or did me Ill-offices; and I, in return, were indifferent towards him, or did him good-offices: Here is the same relation of *contrariety*; and yet my conduct is often highly laudable. Twist and turn this matter, as much as you will, you can never rest the morality on relation; but must have recourse to the decisions of sentiment.

When 'tis affirmed, that two and three are equal to the half of ten; this relation of equality, I understand perfectly. I conceive, that if ten be divided into two parts, of which one has as many units as the other; and if any of these parts be compared to two added to three, it will contain as many units as that compound number. But when you draw thence a comparison to moral relations, I own, I am altogether at a loss to understand you. A moral action, a crime, such as ingratitude, is a complicated object. Does the morality consist in the relation of its parts to each other? How? After what Manner? Specify the relation: Be more particular and explicit in your propositions; and you will easily see their falsehood.

No, say you, the morality consists in the relation of actions to the rule of right; and they are denominated good or ill, according as they agree or disagree with it. What then is this rule of right? Wherein does it consist? How is it determined? By reason, you'll say, which examines the moral relations of actions. So that moral relations are determined by the comparison of actions to a rule. And that rule is determined by considering the moral relations of objects. Is not this fine reasoning?

All this is metaphysics, you cry. That is enough: There needs nothing more to give a strong Presumption of falsehood. Yes, reply I: Here are metaphysics surely: But they are all on your side, who advance an abstruse hypothesis, which can never be made intelligible, nor quadrate to any particular instance or illustration. The hypothesis we embrace is plain. It maintains, that morality is determined by sentiment. It defines virtue to be, *whatever mental action or quality gives to a spectator the pleasing sentiment of approbation*; and vice the contrary. We then proceed to examine a plain matter of fact, *viz.* what actions have this influence: We consider all the circumstances, in which these actions agree: And from thence endeavour to extract some general observations with regard to these sentiments. If you call this metaphysics, and find any thing abstruse here, you need only conclude, that your turn of mind is not suited to the moral sciences.

II. When a man, at any time, deliberates concerning his own conduct, (as, whether he had better, in a particular emergence, assist a Brother or a benefactor) he must consider these separate relations, with the whole Circumstances and situation of the persons, in order to determine his superior duty and obligation: And in order to determine the proportion of lines in any triangle, 'tis necessary to examine the nature of that figure, and the relations, which its several parts bear to each other. But notwithstanding this apparent similarity in the two cases, there is, at the bottom, an extreme difference betwixt them. A speculative reasoner concerning triangles or circles considers the several known and given relations of the parts of these figures; and from thence infers some unknown relation, which is dependent on the former. But in moral deliberations, we must be acquainted, before-hand, with all the objects, and all their relations to each other; and from a comparison of the whole, fix our choice or approbation. No new fact to be ascertained: No new relation to be discovered. The whole circumstances of the case are supposed to be laid before us, 'ere we can fix any sentence of blame or approbation. If any material circumstance be yet unknown or doubtful, we must first employ our enquiry or intellectual faculties to assure us of it; and suspend for a time all moral decision or sentiment. While we are ignorant, whether a man was aggressor or not, how can we determine, whether the person, who killed him, be criminal or innocent? But after every circumstance, every relation is known, the understanding has no further room to operate, nor any object, on which it could employ itself. The approbation or blame, which then ensues, cannot be the work of the judgment, but of the heart, and is not a speculative proposition or affirmation, but an active feeling or sentiment: In the disquisitions of the understanding, from known circumstances and relations, we infer some new and unknown. In moral decisions, the whole circumstances and relations must be antecedently known; and the mind, from the contemplation of the whole, feels some new impression of affection or disgust, esteem or contempt, approbation or blame.

Hence the great difference betwixt a mistake of *fact* and one of *right;* and hence the reason, why the one is commonly criminal, and not the other. When *Oedipus* killed *Laius*, he was ignorant of the relation, and from circumstances, innocent and involuntary, formed erroneous opinions concerning the action he committed. But when *Nero* killed *Agrippina*, all the relations betwixt himself and the person, and all the circumstances of the fact were antecedently known to him: But the motive of revenge, or fear or interest, in his savage heart, prevailed over the sentiments of duty and humanity. And when we express a detestation against him, to which he, himself, in a little time, became insensible; 'tis not, that we see any relations, of which he was ignorant, but that, from the rectitude of our disposition, we feel sentiments, against which he was hardened, from flattery and a long perseverance in the most enormous crimes. In these sentiments, then, not in a discovery of relations of any kind, do all moral determinations consist. Before we can pretend to form any decision of this kind, every thing must be known and ascertained on the side of the object or action. Nothing remains but to feel, on our part, some sentiment of blame or approbation, whence we pronounce the action criminal or virtuous.

III. This doctrine will become still more evident, if we compare moral beauty with natural, to which, in many particulars, it bears so near a resemblance. 'Tis on the proportion, relation, and position of parts, that all natural beauty depends; but 'twould be absurd thence to infer, that the perception of beauty, like that of truth in geometrical problems, consists altogether in the perception of relations, and was performed entirely by the understanding or intellectual faculties. In all the sciences, our mind, from the known relations, investigates the unknown: But in all decisions of taste or external beauty, the whole relations are before-hand obvious to the eye, and we thence proceed to feel a sentiment of complacency or disgust, according to the nature of the object, and disposition of our organs.

Euclid has fully explained all the qualities of the circle; but has not, in any proposition, said a word of its beauty. The reason is evident. The beauty is not a quality of the circle. It lies not in any part of the line, whose parts are all equally distant from a common centre. It is only the effect, which that figure operates upon the mind, whose peculiar fabric or structure renders it susceptible of such sentiments. In vain, would you look for it in the circle, or seek it, either by your Senses or by mathematical reasonings, in all the properties of that figure.

Attend to *Palladio* and *Perrault*, while they explain all the parts and proportions of a pillar: They talk of the cornice and freeze and base and entablature and shaft and architrave; and give the Description and position of each of these members. But should you ask the description and position of its beauty, they would readily reply, that the beauty is not any of the parts or members of a pillar, but results from the whole, when that complicated figure is presented to an intelligent mind, susceptible of those finer sensations 'Till such a spectator appear, there is nothing but a figure of such particular dimensions and proportions: From his sentiments alone arises its elegance and beauty.

Again; attend to *Cicero*, while he paints the crimes of a *Verres* or a *Catiline*; you must acknowledge, that the moral turpitude results, in the same manner, from the contemplation of the whole, when presented to a being, whose organs have such a particular structure and formation. The orator may paint rage, insolence barbarity on the one side: Meekness, sufferance, sorrow, innocence on the other. But if you feel no indignation or compassion arise in you from this complication of circumstances, you would in vain ask him, wherein consists the crime or villainy, which he so vehemently exclaims against? At what time, or on what subject it first began to exist? And what has a few months afterwards become of it, when every disposition and thought of all the actors is totally altered or annihilated? No satisfactory answer can be given to any of these questions, upon the abstract hypothesis of morals; and we must at last acknowledge, that the crime or immorality is no particular fact or relation, which can be the object of the understanding: But arises altogether from the sentiment of disapprobation, which, by the structure of human nature, we unavoidably feel on the apprehension of barbarity or treachery.

IV. Inanimate objects may bear to each other all the same relations, which we observe in moral agents; tho' the former can never be the object of love or hatred, nor are consequently susceptible of merit or iniquity. A young tree, that over-tops or destroys its parent, from whose seed it sprung, stands in all the same relations with *Nero*, when he murdered *Agrippina*; and if morality consisted in any abstract relations, would, no doubt, be equally criminal.

V. It appears evident, that the ultimate ends of human actions can never, in any case, be accounted for by *reason*, but recommend themselves entirely to the sentiments and affections of mankind, without any dependance on the intellectual faculties. Ask a man, *why he uses Exercise*; he will answer, *because he desires to keep his health*. If you then enquire, *why he desires health*, he will readily reply, *because Sickness is painful*. If you push your enquiries farther, and desire a reason, *why he hates pain*, 'tis impossible he can ever give any. This is an ultimate end, and is never refered to any other object.

Perhaps, to your second question, *why he desires health*, he may also reply, that *'tis requisite for the exercise of his calling*. If you ask, *why he is anxious on that head*, he will answer, *because he desires to get money*. If you demand, *Why? It is the Instrument of pleasure*, says he. And beyond this, 'tis an absurdity to ask for a reason. 'Tis impossible there can be a Progress *in infinitum*; and that one thing can always be the reason, why another is desired. Something must be desirable on its own account, and because of its immediate accord or agreement with human sentiment and affection.

Now as virtue is an end, and is desirable on its own account, without fee or reward, merely for the immediate satisfaction it conveys; 'tis requisite there should be some sentiment, which it touches; some internal taste or feeling, or whatever you please to call it, which distinguishes moral good and evil, and which embraces the one and rejects the other.

Thus the distinct boundaries and offices of *reason* and *taste* are easily ascertained. The former conveys the knowledge of truth and falsehood: The latter gives the sentiment of beauty and deformity, vice and virtue. The one discovers objects, as they really stand in nature, without addition or diminution: The other has a productive faculty, and guilding or staining all natural objects with the colours, borrowed from internal sentiment, raises in a manner, a new creation. Reason, being cool and disengaged, is no motive to action, and

directs only the impulse, received from appetite or inclination, by showing us the means of
obtaining happiness or avoiding misery: Taste,
as it gives pleasure or pain, and thereby constitutes happiness or misery, becomes a motive to
action, and is the first spring or impulse to desire
and volition. From circumstances and relations,
known or supposed, the former leads us to the
discovery of the concealed and unknown: After
all circumstances and relations are laid before us,
the latter makes us feel from the whole a new
sentiment of blame or approbation. The standard
of the one, being founded on the nature of
things, is eternal and inflexible, even by the will
of the Supreme Being: The standard of the other,
arising from the internal frame and constitution
of animals, is ultimately derived from that
supreme will, who bestowed on each being its
peculiar nature, and arranged the several classes
and orders of existence.

5

Introduction to *Groundwork for the Metaphysics of Morals*

Immanuel Kant

First Section: Transition from Common Rational Moral Cognition to Philosophical Moral Cognition

[. . .]

What kind of law can it be, whose representation, without even taking account of the effect expected from it, must determine the will, so that it can be called good absolutely and without limitation? Since I have robbed the will of every impulse that could have arisen from the obedience to any law, there is nothing left over except the universal lawfulness of the action in general which alone is to serve the will as its principle, i.e., I ought never to conduct myself except so *that I could also will that my maxim become a universal law*. Here it is mere lawfulness in general (without grounding it on any law determining certain actions) that serves the will as its principle, and also must so serve it, if duty is not to be everywhere an empty delusion and a chimerical concept; common human reason,[1] indeed, agrees perfectly with this in its practical judgment, and has the principle just cited always before its eyes.

Let the question be, e.g.: When I am in a tight spot, may I not make a promise with the intention of not keeping it? Here I easily make a distinction in the signification the question can have, whether it is prudent, or whether it is in conformity with duty, to make a false promise. The first can

without doubt often occur. I do see very well that it is not sufficient to get myself out of a present embarrassment by means of this subterfuge, but rather it must be reflected upon whether from this lie there could later arise much greater inconvenience than that from which I am now freeing myself, and, since the consequences of my supposed *cunning* are not so easy to foresee, and a trust once lost to me might become much more disadvantageous than any ill I think I am avoiding, whether it might not be more *prudent* to conduct myself in accordance with a universal maxim and make it into a habit not to promise anything except with the intention of keeping it. Yet it soon occurs to me here that such a maxim has as its ground only the worrisome consequences. Now to be truthful from duty is something entirely different from being truthful out of worry over disadvantageous consequences; in the first case, the concept of the action in itself already contains a law for me, whereas in the second I must look around elsewhere to see which effects might be bound up with it for me. For if I deviate from the principle of duty, then this is quite certainly evil; but if I desert my maxim of prudence, then that can sometimes be very advantageous to me, even though it is safer to remain with it. Meanwhile, to inform myself in the shortest and least deceptive way in regard to my answer to this problem, whether a lying promise is in conformity with

From Immanual Kant, *Groundwork for the Metaphysics of Morals* (translated by Allen Wood). (Yale University Press 2002). Pp. 18–21.

Moral Psychology: Historical and Contemporary Readings, edited by Thomas Nadelhoffer, Eddy Nahmias, and Shaun Nichols.

duty, I ask myself: Would I be content with it if my maxim (of getting myself out of embarrassment through an untruthful promise) should be valid as a universal law (for myself as well as for others), and would I be able to say to myself that anyone may make an untruthful promise when he finds himself in embarrassment which he cannot get out of in any other way? Then I soon become aware that I can will the lie but not at all a universal law to lie; for in accordance with such a law there would properly be no promises, because it would be pointless to avow my will in regard to my future actions to those who would not believe this avowal, or, if they rashly did so, who would pay me back in the same coin; hence my maxim, as soon as it were made into a universal law, would destroy itself.

Thus I need no well-informed shrewdness to know what I have to do in order to make my volition morally good. Inexperienced in regard to the course of the world, incapable of being prepared for all the occurrences that might eventuate in it, I ask myself only: Can you will also that your maxim should become a universal law? If not, then it is reprehensible, and this not for the sake of any disadvantage impending for you or someone else, but because it cannot fit as a principle into a possible universal legislation; but for this legislation reason extorts immediate respect from me, from which, to be sure, I still do not have *insight* into that on which it is grounded (which the philosopher may investigate), but I at least understand this much, that it is an estimation of a worth which far outweighs everything whose worth is commended by inclination, and that the necessity of my actions from *pure* respect for the practical law is what constitutes duty, before which every other motive must give way because it is the condition of a will that is good *in itself*, whose worth surpasses everything.

Thus in the moral cognition of common human reason we have attained to its principle, which it obviously does not think abstractly in such a universal form, but actually has always before its eyes and uses as its standard of judgment. It would be easy here to show how, with this compass in its hand, it knows its way around very well in all the cases that come before it, how to distinguish what is good, what is evil, what conforms to duty or is contrary to duty, if, without teaching it the least new thing, one only makes it

aware of its own principle, as Socrates did;[2] and thus that it needs no science and philosophy to know what one has to do in order to be honest and good, or indeed, even wise and virtuous. It might even have been conjectured in advance that the acquaintance with what every human being is obliged to do, hence to know, would also be the affair of everyone, even of the most common human being. Here[3] one cannot regard without admiration the way the practical faculty of judgment is so far ahead of the theoretical in the common human understanding. In the latter, if common reason ventures to depart from the laws of experience and perceptions of sense, then it falls into sheer inconceivabilities and self-contradictions, or at least into a chaos of uncertainty, obscurity, and inconstancy. But in the practical, the power of judgment first begins to show itself to advantage when the common understanding excludes from practical laws all sensuous incentives. It then even becomes subtle, caviling with its conscience, or with other claims in reference to what is to be called right, or even in wanting sincerely to determine the worth of actions for its own instruction,[4] and, what is most striking, it can in the latter case do so with just as good a hope of getting things right as any philosopher might promise to do; indeed, it is almost more secure in this even than the latter, because the philosopher has[5] no other principle than the common understanding, but the philosopher's judgment is easily confused by a multiplicity of considerations that are alien and do not belong to the matter and can make it deviate from the straight direction. Would it not accordingly be more advisable in moral things to stay with the judgment of common reason, and bring in philosophy at most only in order to exhibit the system of morals all the more completely and comprehensibly, and its rules in a way that is more convenient for their use (still more for disputation), but not in order to remove the common human understanding in a practical respect out of its happy simplicity, and through philosophy to set it on a new route of investigation and instruction?

There is something splendid about innocence, but it is in turn very bad that it cannot be protected very well and is easily seduced. On this account even wisdom – which consists more in deeds and omissions than in knowledge – also needs science, not in order to learn from it but in order to provide entry and durability for its precepts. The human being feels in himself a powerful counterweight against all commands of duty, which reason represents to him as so worthy of esteem, in his needs and inclinations, whose satisfaction he summarizes under the name of 'happiness'. Now reason commands its precepts unremittingly, without promising anything to inclinations, thus snubbing and disrespecting, as it were, those impetuous claims, which at the same time seem so reasonable (and will not be done away with by any command). From this, however, arises a *natural dialectic*, that is, a propensity to ratiocinate against those strict laws of duty and to bring into doubt their validity, or at least their purity and strictness, and,[6] where possible, to make them better suited to our wishes and inclinations, i.e., at ground to corrupt them and deprive them of their entire dignity, which not even common practical reason can in the end call good.

Thus *common human reason* is impelled, not through any need of speculation (which never assaults it as long as it is satisfied with being mere healthy reason), but rather from practical grounds themselves, to go outside its sphere and to take a step into the field of *practical philosophy*,

in order to receive information and distinct directions about the source of its principle and its correct determination in opposition to the maxims based on need and inclination, so that it may escape from its embarrassment concerning the claims of both sides and not run the risk of being deprived, through the ambiguity into which it easily falls, of all genuine ethical principles. Thus even in common practical reason, when it is cultivated, there ensues unnoticed a *dialectic*, which necessitates it to seek help in philosophy, just as befalls it in its theoretical use; and therefore the first will find no more tranquillity than the other anywhere except in a complete critique of our reason.

Notes

1   1785: "but common human reason".
2   This would appeal to be Kant's interpretation of Socrates' "human wisdom" (Plato, *Apology* 20c–24b). Compare *Metaphysics of Morals*, Ak 6:411.
3   1785: "Nevertheless".
4   1785: *Belohnung* ("reward"); 1786: *Belehrung* ("instruction").
5   1785: "can have".
6   1875: "at least".

6

The Claim to Moral Adequacy of a Highest Stage of Moral Judgment

Lawrence Kohlberg

In previous publications I have outlined: (a) the extensive research facts concerning culturally universal stages of moral judgment,[1] (b) the psychological theory of development which best fits those facts,[2] and (c) a metaethical view which attempts to bridge the gap between naturalistic and nonnaturalistic theories of moral judgment and their grounds of adequacy.[3] The present paper elaborates a claim made in the previous paper[3]: the claim that a higher or later stage of moral judgment is "objectively" preferable to or more adequate than an earlier stage of judgment according to certain *moral* criteria. Since these criteria of adequacy are those central to judgment at our most advanced stage, "stage 6," the problem becomes one of justifying the structure of moral judgment at stage 6. First, however, we shall briefly review the position taken in our earlier paper, and introduce the claims of the present one.

I. Review of Psychological Theory

Over a period of almost 20 years of empirical research, my colleagues and I have rather firmly established a culturally universal invariant sequence of stages of moral judgment; these stages are grossly summarized in Box 6.1:

Box 6.1.   Definition of moral stages

I. Preconventional level
At this level the child is responsive to cultural rules and labels of good and bad, right or wrong, but interprets these labels either in terms of the physical or the hedonistic consequences of action (punishment, reward, exchange of favors) or in terms of the physical power of those who enunciate the rules and labels. The level is divided into the following two stages:

Stage 1: *The punishment-and-obedience orientation*. The physical consequences of action determine its goodness or badness regardless of the human meaning or value of these consequences. Avoidance of punishment and unquestioning deference to power are valued in their own right, not in terms of respect for an underlying moral order supported by punishment and authority (the latter being stage 4).

Stage 2: *The instrumental-relativist orientation*. Right action consists of that which instrumentally satisfies one's own needs and occasionally the needs of others. Human relations are viewed in terms like those of the market place. Elements of fairness, of reciprocity,

The Claim to Moral Adequacy of a Highest Stage of Moral Judgment, abridged from Lawrence Kohlberg, (1973). The claim to moral adequacy of a highest stage of moral judgment. *The Journal of Philosophy*, 70, pp. 630–5, 641–6. Reprinted with permission.

Moral Psychology: Historical and Contemporary Readings, edited by Thomas Nadelhoffer, Eddy Nahmias, and Shaun Nichols.
© 2010 Blackwell Publishing Ltd except for editorial material and organization © 2010 Thomas Nadelhoffer, Eddy Nahmias, and Shaun Nichols.

and of equal sharing are present, but they are always interpreted in a physical pragmatic way. Reciprocity is a matter of "you scratch my back and I'll scratch yours," not of loyalty, gratitude, or justice.

II. Conventional level

At this level, maintaining the expectations of the individual's family, group, or nation is perceived as valuable in its own right, regardless of immediate and obvious consequences. The attitude is not only one of *conformity* to personal expectations and social order, but of loyalty to it, of actively *maintaining*, supporting, and justifying the order, and of identifying with the persons or group involved in it. At this level, there are the following two stages:

Stage 3: *The interpersonal concordance or "good boy – nice girl" orientation.* Good behavior is that which pleases or helps others and is approved by them. There is much conformity to stereotypical images of what is majority or "natural" behavior. Behavior is frequently judged by intention – "he means well" becomes important for the first time. One earns approval by being "nice."

Stage 4: *The "law and order" orientation.* There is orientation toward authority, fixed rules, and the maintenance of the social order. Right behavior consists of doing one's duty, showing respect for authority, and maintaining the given social order for its own sake.

III. Postconventional, autonomous, or principled level

At this level, there is a clear effort to define moral values and principles that have validity and application apart from the authority of the groups or persons holding these principles and apart from the individual's own identification with these groups. This level again has two stages:

Stage 5: *The social-contract legalistic orientation,* generally with utilitarian overtones. Right action tends to be defined in terms of general individual rights, and standards which have been critically examined and agreed upon by the whole society. There is a clear awareness of the relativism of personal values and opinions and a corresponding emphasis upon procedural rules for reaching consensus. Aside from what is constitutionally and democratically agreed upon, the right is a matter of personal "values" and "opinion." The result is an emphasis upon the "legal point of view," but with an emphasis upon the possibility of changing law in terms of rational considerations of social utility (rather than freezing it in terms of stage 4 "law and order"). Outside the legal realm, free agreement and contract is the binding element of obligation. This is the "official" morality of the American government and constitution.

Stage 6: *The universal-ethical-principle orientation.* Right is defined by the decision of conscience in accord with self-chosen *ethical principles* appealing to logical comprehensiveness, universality, and consistency. These principles are abstract and ethical (the Golden Rule, the categorical imperative); they are not concrete moral rules like the Ten Commandments. At heart, these are universal principles of *justice*, of the *reciprocity* and *equality* of human *rights*, and of respect for the dignity of human beings as *individual persons* ("From Is to Ought," pp. 164–5).

As Box 6.1 indicates, the last stage, stage 6, has a distinctively Kantian ring, centering moral judgment on concepts of obligation as these are defined by principles of respect for persons and of justice. In part, this corresponds to an initial "formalist" or "structuralist" bias of both our moral and our psychological theory. Our psychological theory of morality derives largely from Piaget,[4] who claims that both logic and morality develop through stages and that each stage is a structure which, formally considered, is in better equilibrium than its predecessor. It assumes, that is, that each new (logical or moral) stage is a new structure which includes elements of earlier structures but transforms them in such a way as to represent a more stable and extensive equilibrium. Our theory assumes that new moral structures presuppose new logical structures, i.e., that a new logical stage (or substage) is a necessary but not sufficient condition for a new moral stage. It assumes, however, that moral judgments (or moral equilibrium) involves two related processes or conditions absent in the logical domain. First, moral judgments involve role-taking, taking the point of view of others conceived as *subjects* and coordinating those points of view, whereas logic involves only coordinating points of view upon objects. Second, equilibrated moral judgments involve principles of justice or fairness. A moral situation in disequilibrium is one in which there are unresolved conflicting claims. A resolution of the situation is one in which each is "given his due" according to some principle of justice that can be recognized as fair by all the conflicting parties involved. These "equilibration" assumptions of our psychological theory are naturally allied to the formalistic tradition in philosophic ethics from Kant to Rawls. This isomorphism of psychological and normative theory generates the claim that a psychologically more advanced stage of moral judgment is more morally adequate, by moral-philosophic criteria. The isomorphism assumption is a two-way street. While moral philosophical criteria of adequacy of moral judgment help define a standard of psychological adequacy or advance, the study of psychological advance feeds back and clarifies these criteria. Our psychological theory as to why individuals move from one stage to the next is grounded on a moral-philosophical theory which specifies that the later stage is morally better or more adequate than the earlier stage. Our psychological theory claims that individuals prefer the highest stage of reasoning they comprehend, a claim supported by research.[5] This claim of our psychological theory derives from a philosophical claim that a later stage is "objectively" preferable or more adequate by certain *moral* criteria. This philosophic claim, however, would for us be thrown into question if the facts of moral advance were inconsistent with its psychological implications.

Our assumption of isomorphism implies first the assumption of continuity between the context of discovery of moral viewpoints (studied by the psychology of moral development) and the context of justification of moral viewpoints (studied by formal moral philosophy). This implies that the philosopher's *justification* of a higher stage of moral reasoning maps into the psychologist's *explanation* of movement to that stage, and vice versa. The isomorphism assumption is plausible if one believes that the developing human being and the moral philosopher are engaged in fundamentally the same moral task.

II.   Moral Theories and Natural Structures

Our notions of moral philosophic adequacy derive, then, from the notion that moral theories are derivative from the natural structures we term "stages." The structures are "natural," not in the sense of being innate, but in the sense of being the sequential results of processing moral experience, not derivative from particular teachings or particular moral ideologies or theories. In this sense notions of natural rights, social contract, and utility are "natural structures" emerging in non-philosophers from reflection upon the limits of customary morality in very varied cultural and educational circumstances. To clarify the relation of philosophic moral theories to this, we have interviewed moral philosophers concerning our moral dilemmas and tried to relate their published theory to their reasoning on the dilemmas. We feel that our results justify the notion that a philosopher's formal moral theory is an elaboration of certain portions of his "natural" moral-stage structure. Not only do philosophers use their published moral theories to reason about interview dilemmas, but we see that their theories interlock with "natural" or unformalized elements of their moral reasoning unstated in their published theories but required for actually making moral decisions. Further, hardly to our surprise, all philosophers interviewed reason at the two highest stages, being stage 5, stage 6, or some mixture of the two. We believe our data on philosophers are consistent with our assumptions, that: (1) stages are natural structures generating families of moral theories, and (2) the two major families of formal normative moral theory tend to be generated by two natural structures which we term "stage 5" and "stage 6."

Our own approach to moral theory is to view it as a constructive systematization of these natural structures. Without formal moral theory men naturally attain to a "stage 5" in which they judge laws by the light of a social contract, by rule-utilitarianism, and by some notion of universal or natural rights. Much moral philosophy may be understood as a systematization of this mode of thought, and most moral philosophers have, in some sense, assumed this to be their task. Other philosophers, however, have attempted to generalize, or raise to a higher level, these "stage 5" postulates, to define a basis for individually principled moral decision. As George Herbert Mead[6] put it:

Kant generalized the position involved in the theory of natural rights and social contract, which was that one could claim for himself only that which he recognized equally for others. He made a generalization of this the basis for his moral doctrine, the categorical imperative that every act should be of such a character that it could be made universal for everyone under the same conditions.

As John Rawls[7] states it:

My aim is to present a conception of justice which generalizes and carries to a higher level of abstraction the familiar theory of the social contract as found, say, in Locke, Rousseau and Kant.

In our view, there is a family of theories that have the purpose just stated of Kant and Rawls. This family of theories may be looked at as derivatives of a natural structure I term "stage 6." Rawls's theory, when traced back to its natural structural roots, is not merely a "generalization" and "abstraction" of the theory of social contract, but derives from a new way of thought, a new system of assumptions, a new decision making process. This is true in the same sense that "the familiar theory of social contract" is not merely a "generalization" and "abstraction" of the stage 4 conception of an overriding need for social order, but is an expression of a natural structure we term "stage 5."

[. . .]

The sense in which each stage is *better integrated* is seen in the fact that only at stage 6 are rights and duties completely correlative. The meaning of correlativity of rights and duties is suggested in the following passage by Raphael.[8]

We have accepted the deontological view that the moral use of "ought" is a basic concept that cannot be derived from the idea of goodness. – We turn next to the notion of "rights." There are two senses of the word, the first meaning, "I have no duty to refrain from so acting," the second in which I describe the same fact as I describe by saying, "Someone else has a duty to me." The second kind of a right might be called "a right of

recipience." Whenever I have a right of action, I also have a right of recipience. In virtue of the second definition of rights, the two forms of expression: "A has a duty to B" and "B has a right (of recipience) against A" are correlative in the sense of analytically implying each other. They may not be connotatively tautologous in ordinary speech, though they are in the more precise language we are recommending (pp. 47–49).

Let us accept, for the moment, Raphael's view that using rights and duties on correlative terms is either more "precise" or more "integrated." We have found that such usage, consistently maintained, is found only at stage 6. At stage 5, "rights" categories are completely reciprocal; i.e., the concept and limits of rights are completely reciprocal with the rights of others, but individual rights and individual duties are not completely correlative.

An example is case 2, age 24, who said:

Morality to me means recognizing the rights of others first to life and then to do as they please as long as it doesn't interfere with somebody else's rights.

Although case 2 is able to define rights clearly, he is unable to specify clearly the conditions under which awareness of rights generates correlative duties. At stage 5, for every right, society has some duty to protect that right. Duties to other individuals, however, are not clearly specified in the absence of either individual contract or social contract. At stage 5 there are obligations to the law and there are obligations to the welfare of others, of a rule- or act-utilitarian sort. But recognition of individual rights does not directly generate individual duties; i.e., rights and duties are not directly correlative. Even moral philosophers, like our "natural" stage 5 subjects, need not accept that rights directly imply duties. This is indicated in philosophers' responses to the following dilemma:

In Europe, a woman was near death from a very bad disease, a special kind of cancer. There was one drug that the doctors thought might save her. It was a form of radium for which a druggist was charging ten times what the drug cost him to make. The sick woman's husband, Heinz, went to everyone he knew to borrow the money, but he could only get together about half of what it cost.

He told the druggist that his wife was dying, and asked him to sell it cheaper or let him pay later. But the druggist said, "No, I discovered the drug and I'm going to make money from it." So Heinz got desperate and broke into the man's store to steal the drug for his wife.

In general, subjects whom we classify on other grounds as stage 5 recognize the woman's right to live, but do not believe that it directly generates an obligation to steal to save her. Or they may recognize a duty to steal for the wife, based on contract, but recognize no duty to steal for the friend or stranger who equally has a right to life. This, too, is the position taken by a number of moral philosophers, two of whom are quoted elsewhere ("From Is to Ought," pp. 206–7).

Examples are as follows:

Philosopher 1:

What Heinz did was not wrong. The distribution of scarce drugs should be regulated by principles of fairness. In the absence of such regulations, the druggist was within his legal rights, but in the circumstances he has no moral complaint. He still was within his moral rights, however, unless it was within his society a strongly disapproved thing to do. While what Heinz did was not wrong, it was not his duty to do it. In this case it is not wrong for Heinz to steal the drug, but it goes beyond the call of duty; it is a deed of supererogation.

Philosopher 2:

It is a husband's duty to steal the drug. The principle that husbands should look after their wives to the best of their ability is one whose general observance does more good than harm. He should also steal it for a friend, if he were a very close friend (close enough for it to be understood that they would do this sort of thing for each other). The reasons are similar to those in the case of wives. If the person with cancer were a less close friend, or even a stranger, Heinz would be doing a good act if he stole the drug, but he has no duty to.

These philosophers agree that stealing to save a life in the situation is right, but disagree on when it is a duty. Using rule-utilitarian criteria of duty,

it is difficult to make duties and rights correlative. In contrast, here is the response of philosopher 3, who responds quite differently to duty questions about this dilemma:

IF THE HUSBAND DOES NOT FEEL VERY CLOSE OF AFFECTIONATE TO HIS WIFE, SHOULD HE STEAL THE DRUG?
Yes. The value of her life is independent of any personal ties. The value of human life is based on the fact that it offers the only possible source of a categorical moral "ought" to a rational being acting in the role of a moral agent.
SUPPOSE IT WERE A FRIEND OR AN ACQUAINTANCE?
Yes, the value of a human life remains the same.

In general, philosopher 3's conceptions of rights and duties were correlative. In this sense his thinking appears more differentiated and integrated than that of the other two philosophers. We must note, however, that the greater integration of a structure making rights and duties correlative is not a mere matter of increased logical or analytical tidiness, as Raphael suggests, but that it imposes a severe price. The price in question is, baldly, that philosopher 3 has to be prepared to go to jail to steal for a friend or acquaintance, and philosophers 1 and 2 do not. According to Raphael (*op. cit.*):

From an objective point of view, the so-called duties of supererogation are not duties. For the agent, they are duties but from the objective standpoint, i.e., from the standpoint of what we take to be the average moral agent, they are thought to go beyond duty. Correspondingly, in the eyes of the agent, the beneficiary has a right while from the objective standpoint (of the average impartial spectator) the person benefited does not have a right (51).

We would question whether duties and rights could be made correlative, as Raphael wishes, if the moral point of view adopted is that recommended by Raphael, i.e., "the average moral agent" or "the average impartial spectator." To make duties and rights correlative, we must take not the standpoint of the "average moral agent," but philosopher 3's standpoint of the "rational moral agent." The rational moral agent is not a self-sacrificial saint, since the saint's duties do not imply that he has corresponding rights. The rational moral agent is fair, not saintly, he does as a duty only what his is rationally prepared to demand that others do as a duty, or that to which he has a right. The fact that a dying acquaintance in need of the medicine has the right to life does not define a duty for the average moral agent, but it may for the rational or just moral agent.

[. . .]

IV. Universalizability and Reversibility at Stage 6

Since Kant, formalists have argued that rational moral judgments must be reversible, consistent, and universalizable, and that this implies the prescriptivity of such judgments. We claim that only the substantive moral judgments made at stage 6 fully meet these conditions, and that each higher stage meets these conditions better than each lower stage. In fully meeting these conditions, stage 6 moral structures are ultimately equilibrated.

For developmental theory, meeting these conditions of moral judgment is parallel with the equilibration of fully logical thought in the realm of physical or logical facts. According to Piaget and others, the keystone of logic is reversibility. A logical train of thought is one in which one can move back and forth between premises and conclusions without distortion. Mathematical thinking is an example; $A + B$ is the same as $B + A$. Or again, the operation $A + B = C$ is reversible by the operation $C - B = A$. In one sense, the elements of reversible moral thought are the moral categories as these apply to the universe of moral actors. To say that rights and duties are correlative is to say that one can move from rights to duties and back without change or distortion. Universalizability and consistency are fully attained by the reversibility of prescriptions of actions. Reversibility of moral judgment is what is ultimately meant by the criterion of the fairness of a moral decision. Procedurally, fairness as impartiality means reversibility in the sense of a decision on which all interested parties could agree insofar as they can consider their own claims impartially, as the just decider would. If we have a reversible solution, we have one that could be reached as right starting from anyone's perspective in the situation, given each

person's intent to put himself in the shoes of the other.

Reversibility meets a second criterion of formalism: universalizability. As reversibility starts with the slogan, "Put yourself in the other guy's shoes when you decide," universalizability starts with the slogan, "What if everyone did it; what if everyone used this principle of choice?" It is clear that universalizability is implied by reversibility. If something is fair or right to do from the conflicting points of view of all those involved in the situation, it is something we can wish all men to do in all similar situations. Reversibility tells us more than universalizability, then, in resolving dilemmas, but it implies universalizability.

The concept of reversibility explains the intuitive plausibility of Rawls's conception of justice (*op. cit.*) as a rational choice in an original position in which one is under a veil of ignorance as to one's role or identity. Rawls argues that this conception leads to the choice of a justice principle of equality, with inequalities accepted only when it is to the benefit of the least advantaged. This conception of choice in the veil of ignorance is a formalization of the conception of fairness involved in having one person cut the cake and a second person distribute it. This conception leads to a mini-maximization solution in the sense that the division must be such that the least advantaged person is better off, i.e., that the cake is so cut that the person cutting the cake is willing to live with getting the smallest piece.

Our conception of stage 6 helps to clarify the intuitive plausibility of Rawls's notion of the original position. This is because the concept of fairness as reversibility is the ultimate elaboration of the concept that fairness is reciprocity, a conception held at every stage. At stage 1, the conception of reciprocity is mechanical equivalence, an eye for an eye and a tooth for a tooth. At stage 2, reciprocity is mediated by awareness that self and others are subjectively evaluating actors with different interests and aware of one another's interests. The result is a notion of fairness as positive (or negative) exchange of gratifications: if you contribute to my needs and interests, it's fair for me to contribute to yours. At stage 3, reversibility becomes the Golden Rule, i.e., putting yourself in the other guy's shoes regardless of exchange of interests or values. The difficult attainment of this Golden Rule conception is illustrated by the following interpretation of the Golden Rule by a ten-year-old:

> Well, it's like your brain has to leave your head and go into the other guy's head and then come back into your head but you still see it like it was in the other guy's head and then you decide that way.

Stage 3 interpretations of Golden Rule reversibility, however, do not yield fair decisions nor are they completely reversible. As a result, they lead to no determinate moral resolution of a situation. In the "Heinz steals the drug" dilemma, the husband reaches one solution if he puts himself in his wife's shoes, another in the druggist's. Or again, in the Talmudic dilemma of a man with a water bottle encountering another man equally in danger of dying of thirst, a stage 3 interpretation of the Golden Rule logically leads to their passing the water bottle back and forth like Alphonse and Gaston.

At higher stages, e.g., stage 5, these problems are handled by the conceptions of prior rights and contractual agreements. Reversibility at stage 5 means reciprocity of rights. In the stage 5 subject's words:

> Morality means recognizing the rights of other individuals to do as they please as long as it doesn't interfere with somebody else's rights.

At stage 6, reversibility is attained by a second-order conception of Golden Rule role-taking. In the Heinz dilemma, Heinz must imagine whether the druggist could put himself in the wife's position and still maintain his claim and whether the wife could put herself in the druggist's position and still maintain her claim. Intuitively we feel the wife could, the druggist could not. As a result, it is fair for the husband to act on the basis of the wife's claim. We call the process by which a reversible moral decision is reached, "ideal role-taking." Stage 6 moral judgment is based on role-taking the claim of each actor under the assumption that all other actors' claims are also governed by the Golden Rule and accommodated accordingly. This is what is meant by calling stage 6 reversibility the second-order application of the Golden Rule. The steps for an actor involved in making such a decision based on ideal role-taking are:

1. To imagine onself in each person's position in that situation (including the self) and to consider all the claims he could make (or which the self could make in his position).
2. Then to imagine that the individual does not know which person he is in the situation and to ask whether he would still uphold that claim.
3. Then to act in accordance with these reversible claims in the situation.

This is clearly similar to Rawls's notion of choice under a veil of ignorance as to who in a moral situation one is to be. Differences involved spring from the facts that: (1) we are trying to arrive at concrete decisions in addition to a choice of principles governing a society, and (2) An ideal moral agent decides with knowledge of all the facts of interest and claims, and is under the veil of ignorance only as to who he is in the situation. Also eliminated is the opposition between a mini-maximization and a maximization basis of making a decision.

For the purpose of solving individual moral dilemmas, we do not want to assume that the individual is ignorant of the probabilities of outcome of a given decision to each person involved, only that he is ignorant of the probability of being any particular person in the situation, i.e., that he is likely to be any particular person in that situation.

Returning to the stealing-the-drug situation, let us imagine someone making the decision under the veil of ignorance, i.e., not knowing whether he is to be assigned the role of husband, wife, or druggist. Clearly, the rational solution is to steal the drug; i.e., this leads to the least loss (or the most gain) to an individual who could be in any role. This corresponds to our intuition of the primacy of the woman's right to life over the druggist's right to property and makes it a duty to act in terms of those rights. If the situation is that the dying person is a friend or acquaintaince, the same holds true. Here a solution achieved under the veil of ignorance is equivalent to one obtained by ideal role-taking, or "moral musical chairs" as described earlier.

The notion of stage 6 as a natural structure implies the following:

1. A decision reached by playing moral musical chairs corresponds to a decision as to what is

ultimately "just" or "fair." Ideal role-taking is the decision procedure ultimately required by the attitudes of respect for persons and of justice as equity recognized at higher stages. This is suggested by Rawls's derivation of principles of justice as equity from the original position.

2. Accordingly, the decision reached by ideal role-taking defines duties correlative to rights rather than acts of supererogation.

3. If we engage in ideal role-taking in most situations, we reach a determinate decision. Our stage 6 moral judges do agree on a choice alternative in our dilemmas where facts and probabilities are specified.

4. A decision reached in that way is in "equilibrium" in the sense that it is "right" from the point of view of all involved insofar as they are concerned to be governed by a moral attitude or a conception of justice, i.e., insofar as they are willing to take the roles of others.

5. The procedure integrates "absolute rights" or equality notions and utilitarian conceptions in conflict at stage 5.

To support these claims convincingly involves elaborating a "stage 6" analysis and choice in various moral dilemmas, a procedure not possible in a limited space. An example of the integration of utility and deontological justice more difficult than that of stealing the drug is that of an individual drowning in the river. A passerby can save him, but at a 25% risk of death (and a 75% chance that both will be saved). Stated in terms of ideal role-taking, from the point of view of the drowning person, he should. If the drowning person put himself in the bystander's shoes and returned to his own position, he still could make the claim. If the passerby took the drowning person's position, he could not maintain his claim to inaction. Stated in terms of the "veil of ignorance," if an individual did not know whether he was the bystander or the drowning person, he would judge the right decision that of jumping in as long as the risk of death for jumping was definitely less than 50%. Utility maximization (or minimaximization) leads to the choice of jumping in if the actor does not know the probabilities of which party he will end up being, but does know the probabilities of the outcome of each alternative (jumping/not-jumping) for both parties. In other words, in these situations "stage 5" utilitarian considerations are perceived from the point of view of stage 6 notions of correlative rights and duties based upon the fundamental equality of persons.

The notion that these claims correspond to a greater psychological equilibration of moral judgment becomes truly plausible in empirical study. A. Erdynast[9] gave subjects instructions to assume the original position. This could not be done or was meaningless to highly intelligent subjects below stage 5. Stage 5 subjects, however, would often change their choices after assuming the original position and would feel that the new solution was more adequate. A number of Harvard undergraduates engaged in small-group discussions in which original-position solutions were elaborated by the group leader and were discussed in relation to alternative ultimates of decision. A number of those who were initially stage 5 retained and elaborated this mode of moral thought, a change we called a movement from stage 5 to stage 6. The fact that only students previously at stage 5 adopted this mode of thinking suggests that it is a stepwise progression of an intuitive natural structure rather than one more moral theory.

Notes

1 *Moralization: The Cognitive-Developmental Approach* (New York: Holt, Rinehart & Winston, 1974).

2 "Stage and Sequence: The Cognitive-Developmental Approach to Socialization," in D. Goslin, ed., *Handbook of Socialization Theory and Research* (New York: Rand McNally, 1969).

3 "From Is to Ought: How to Commit the Naturalistic Fallacy and Get Away with It in the Study of Moral Development," in T. Mischel, ed., *Cognitive Development and Epistemology* (New York: Academic Press, 1971).

4 Jean Piaget, *The Moral Judgment of the Child* (Glencoe, Ill.: Free Press, 1948; first edn, 1932).

5 See my *Moralization, op. cit.*

6 *Movements of Thought in the Nineteenth Century* (Chicago: University Press, 1936).

7 *A Theory of Justice* (Cambridge, Mass.: Harvard, 1971).

8 D. Daiches Raphael, *Moral Judgement* (London: Allen & Unwin, 1955).

9 "Relationships between Moral Stage and Reversibility of Moral Judgment in an Original Position." Unpublished PhD thesis, Harvard University, 1973.

7

A Cognitive Developmental Approach to Morality
Investigating the Psychopath

R.J.R. Blair

[...]

1.1. A violence inhibition mechanism

Several ethologists (Eibl-Eibesfeldt, 1970; Lorenz, 1966) have proposed the existence of mechanisms which control aggression in some social animal species. These ethologists noted that the display of submission cues to a conspecific aggressor resulted in the termination of the attack. For example, dogs when attacked by a stronger opponent bare their throats. This results in the cessation of the fight. Blair (1993) proposed a model of the development of morality which implies a specific cause for psychopathy. He suggested that humans might possess a functionally analogous mechanism: a violence inhibition mechanism (VIM). He considered VIM to be a cognitive mechanism which, when activated by non-verbal communications of distress (i.e., sad facial expression, the sight and sound of tears), initiates a withdrawal response; a schema will be activated predisposing the individual to withdraw from the attack. In line with this suggestion, Camras (1977) has observed that the display of distress cues (a sad facial expression) does result in the termination of aggression in 4- to 7-year-olds. She studied the use and the effect of facial expressions in children defending possessions. When a child displayed a sad facial expression

when resisting another child's attempt to take a possession, the aggressor child usually terminated his/her demands and allowed the original possessor to continue playing "for a relatively long time".

Distress cues are assumed to activate predispositions to withdraw in any observer who processes them, regardless of whether that observer is the aggressor or a bystander. However, this does not imply that the final behavioural responses of all observers who process a victim's distress cues are the same. The activation of VIM in any observer will predispose him/her to withdraw from the situation. However, VIM is not the only cognitive device controlling behaviour; for example, there are the executive functions (e.g., the Supervisory Attentional System; see Norman & Shallice, 1986). These other cognitive devices may determine the final response. Thus, in a given aggressive situation, an attacker may continue to attack and an observer initiate an intervention; in both cases, the VIM-mediated predisposition to withdraw will have been overruled by executive functioning. Finally, the strength of the withdrawal response is assumed to be a function of the degree of activation of VIM. An isolated sad facial expression may excite limited withdrawal. A screaming, sobbing individual may excite much greater withdrawal.[1]

[...]

A Cognitive Developmental Approach to Morality: Investigating the Psychopath, from Robert James Blair (1995). A cognitive developmental approach to morality: Investigating the psychopath. *Cognition*, 57, 2–3, 5–18, 20–5. Reprinted with permission of Elsevier.

(2) *The inhibition of violent action.* As stated above, the postulated operation of VIM initiates a withdrawal response resulting in the on-line interruption of violent action. However, and in addition, it is suggested that *developmentally* VIM results in the inhibition of violent action. The normally developing child will be negatively reinforced by the distress cues every time he engages in any aggressive activity. Through classical conditioning this should result in even the thought of aggression being aversively reinforced; the thought of the aggression will come to trigger VIM. Hence, over time, the child will be less likely, *ceteris paribus*, to engage in violent actions.[2]

(3) *The moral/conventional distinction.* The moral/conventional distinction is the distinction between moral and conventional transgressions found in the judgements of children and adults. Within the literature on this distinction (e.g., Arsenio & Ford, 1985; Nucci & Turiel, 1978; Siegal & Storey, 1985; Smetana, 1981, 1985; Smetana & Braeges, 1990; Tisak & Turiel, 1988; see, for a review, Turiel, Killen, & Helwig, 1987), moral transgressions have been defined by their consequences for the rights and welfare of others, and social conventional transgressions have been defined as violations of the behavioural uniformities that structure social interactions within social systems.

The judgements, "criterion judgements" as Turiel (1983) termed them, that children have been asked to make about moral and conventional transgressions can be divided into two broad categories: seriousness and modifiability. Usually, children and adults judge moral transgressions as more serious than conventional transgressions. For example, while all of the transgression situations, whether moral or conventional, are generally judged not *permissible*, conventional transgressions are more likely to be judged *permissible* than moral transgressions (Smetana, 1985, 1986; Smetana & Braeges, 1990; Tisak & Turiel, 1988; Weston & Turiel, 1980). In addition, subjects generally state that moral transgressions are more *serious* than conventional transgressions or rank them as more *serious* than conventional transgressions (Nucci, 1981; Smetana, 1981, 1985; Smetana & Braeges, 1990; Smetana, Bridgeman, & Turiel, 1983; Stoddart & Turiel, 1985). As regards the modifiability category of criterion judgements, the research

indicates that moral transgressions are judged *differently* from conventional transgressions. For example, moral transgressions are judged less *rule contingent* than conventional transgressions (Arsenio & Ford, 1985; Nucci, 1981; Nucci & Nucci, 1982; Nucci & Turiel, 1978; Smetana, 1981, 1985; Smetana et al., 1983; Smetana, Kelly, & Twentyman, 1984; Weston & Turiel, 1980); individuals state that moral transgressions are not permissible even in the absence of prohibiting rules while conventional transgressions are judged permissible if there is no rule prohibiting them. In addition, moral transgressions are less under *authority jurisdiction* (the act would not be permissible even if the teacher says that you can do the act) than conventional transgressions (Laupa & Turiel, 1986; Tisak & Turiel, 1984, 1988; Turiel, 1983). The moral/conventional distinction has been found in the judgements of children from the age of 39 months (Smetana, 1981) and across cultures (e.g., Hollos, Leis, & Turiel, 1986; Nucci, Turiel, & Encarnacion-Gawrych, 1983; Song, Smetana, & Kim, 1987).

1.3. Theories of the moral/conventional distinction

The existing framework of models of the moral/conventional distinction (e.g., Smetana, 1983; Turiel, 1977, 1983; Turiel et al., 1987; Turiel & Smetana, 1984) involves the suggestion that the distinction is a result of the formation of two, independent conceptual domains (see Turiel & Davidson, 1986). These authors have proposed that the child *constructs* these domains from the qualitatively different social interactional consequences of moral and conventional transgressions. This *construction* process has not been well specified by most authors. However, Turiel (1983) has described two forms of manipulation of gathered data which result in the *construction* of what he terms "judgements of moral necessity". These two forms are: manipulations of past experiences and counter-factual reasoning. Turiel (1983) states that "the child will connect his or her experience of pain (an undesirable experience) to the observed experience of the victim" (p. 43). According to Turiel, by forming this connection the child will generate a proscription against the event which resulted in the victim. In addition, Turiel (1983) states that the child will arrive at "judgements of moral necessity" through comparison of the performance of the act itself with its opposite. If the constructed consequences of its non-occurrence (there is no victim) are judged to be more "desirable" than the consequences of its occurrence (the victim is harmed), then inferences will be made regarding how people should act in these circumstances. As stated above, the child will judge the presence of a victim as undesirable if he has connected his own experience of pain with that of the victim.

According to Turiel, these same manipulations, when applied to conventional transgressions, will not result in automatic proscriptions. First, Turiel does not consider that there are any past experiences that might result in the generation of proscriptions. Second, Turiel argues that comparison of a conventional act with its opposite will not result in one situation being judged as obviously superior to the other. Taking, for example, the conventional transgression of talking in class, Turiel considers that there is no intrinsic basis for a requirement that children do not talk in class. According to Turiel (1983), it is social organizational factors, such as consensus, rules and authority, that provide meaning to conventional proscriptions.

In summary, therefore, the origin of the moral/conventional distinction, according to Turiel, is the child's *construed* connection between his personal experience of pain and the observed experience of the victim. It is a consequence of this connection that the child judges any act that results in a victim as wrong whatever the context. It is the child's experience of his own pain that makes the observed experience of the victim aversive. It would thus be predicted from this that an individual who has never experienced pain would not make the moral/conventional distinction.

Blair (1993), in contrast, suggested that VIM is a prerequisite for the development of the moral/conventional distinction. He claimed that the activation of VIM mediates the performance on the moral/conventional distinction task but that this only occurs after representations of moral transgressions have become stimuli for the activation of VIM. He suggested that repeated pairing of representations of the transgression with the distress cues that are being caused by the act results in these representations of the transgression becoming, through classical conditioning, conditioned stimuli for the activation of VIM. Since conventional transgressions, by definition,

do not result in victims, they are therefore never paired with distress cues and will not therefore become stimuli for the activation of VIM. Blair (1993) claimed that it was the on-line operation of VIM which determines the moral/conventional distinction. He suggested that the withdrawal response following the activation of VIM is experienced, through meaning analysis, as aversive (following Mandler's, 1984, position on value). He suggested that it was this sense of aversion to the moral transgression that resulted in the act being judged as bad. Manipulations of the transgression's context (i.e., stating that there is no rule against the transgression) would not alter the activation of VIM by the details of the transgression. Thus, according to this position, the transgression would still be judged bad. Conventional transgressions would not generate this sense of aversion. They are defined as transgressions only by the presence of rules. Removal of the rule, by modifying the transgression context, and the transgression should no longer be judged as bad to do.[3]

1.4.   A developmental account of morality

In Figure 7.1, the developmental consequences of VIM are represented as a causal model. Causal models are divided into three levels: physiological, cognitive and behavioural (see Morton & Frith, 1993). The relationship of connected elements within a causal model is one of causality. Normally, causal models are applied to abnormal development where the absence of a particular neural structure has cognitive and behavioural consequences; e.g., in autism. In this case, "cause" has a straightforward meaning. In the case of normal development, it has the implication of critical necessity. Thus, the model in Figure 7.1 represents the claim that VIM causes the development of the moral emotions; i.e., VIM is critically necessary if the moral emotions are to develop normally. Figure 7.1 also represents two alternative accounts of the development of VIM: either as the maturation of a physiological structure or as the result of the experience of certain early socialization events. It is possible that VIM is an innately specified physiological structure. Alternatively, VIM may be a consequence of the very early experience of socialization to withdraw from certain distress cue contexts; e.g., when another's distress cues have been caused by the self. Figure 7.1

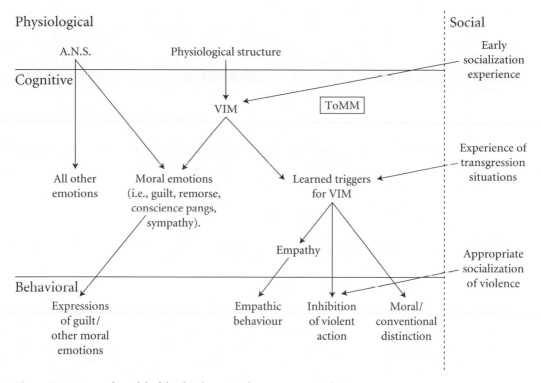

Figure 7.1 A causal model of the developmental consequences of VIM.

represents the claim that the autonomic nervous system (ANS) is necessary for the development of all emotions; the ANS provides the arousal which is interpreted as an emotion through meaning analysis (Mandler, 1984). VIM, specifically, allows the development of the moral emotions. VIM, when activated, generates arousal which will be interpreted as one of the moral emotions (see above). In addition, pairing of the activation of VIM with representations of the transgression situation or representations formed through role taking of the victim's experience will, through classical conditioning, result in the expansion of the VIM trigger database.[4] This expansion allows the experience of empathy,[5] the development of additional inhibitions on violence and the expression of the moral/conventional distinction (see above).

1.5. A developmental account of psychopathic disorder

Figure 7.2 represents the hypothesized consequences of an absence of VIM as a causal model.

Elements within a causal model that are unaffected by the absence of another element are shown "protected" within boxes. Thus, in Figure 7.2, the Theory of Mind Mechanism (Leslie, 1987, 1988) and "All other emotions" are shown as independent of the development of VIM. In line with this, Blair et al. (1996) found that psychopaths, relative to non-psychopaths, are not impoverished on "Theory of Mind" tasks while Patrick, Bradley, and Lang (1993) observed that psychopaths showed arousal to fear stimuli.

In Figure 7.2, the absence of VIM is conceptualized as either a consequence of a physiological deficit or the absence of early socialization experiences. The lack of VIM will result in the absence of the moral emotions. An absence of the moral emotions is reported in the clinical description of psychopathy (Karpman, 1941; Hare, 1985). The lack of VIM will obviously prevent the addition of learned triggers for the activation of VIM. Normally, representations held during the display of distress cues will come to activate VIM through classical conditioning. For example, representations of the victim's internal state, formed

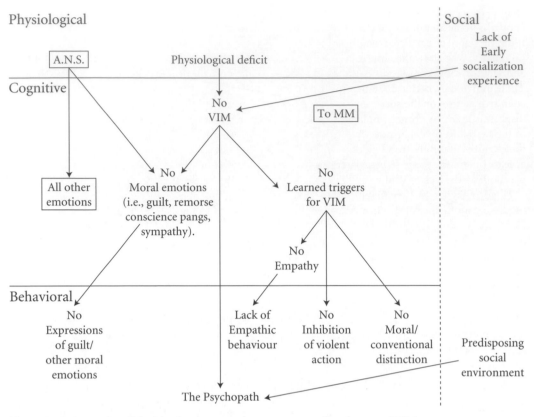

Figure 7.2   A causal model of the developmental consequences of an absence of VIM.

through role taking, will come to activate VIM. Obviously, without VIM, this will not occur; there will be no pairings of representations of the victim's internal state with the activation of VIM because there will be no activation of VIM. Psychopathy is associated with the inability to feel empathy with the victim (Hare, 1985). As stated above, not only does VIM interrupt violent action on line (in the context of distress cues) but it also developmentally inhibits violent action. The child with VIM will be, *ceterus paribus*, negatively reinforced following any action that results in the display of distress cues by a victim. The child without VIM would not be negatively reinforced; he would, therefore, be much more likely to show violent tendencies from a very early age. Psychopaths are associated with considerable violent tendencies from a very early age (American Psychological Association, 1987; Hare, 1985). Thus, the core features of the behavioural description of the psychopath – the early onset of extremely aggressive behaviour that is not

tempered by any sense of guilt or empathy with the victim – are all direct causal predictions of a lack of VIM.

Now it is the case that, in general, a cognitive deficit is not determinate at the behavioural level. Thus, a lack of VIM need not result in the individual becoming a psychopath. Psychopaths are defined, for clinical purposes, by the frequency of their criminal and other antisocial acts. A lack of VIM does not of itself motivate an individual to commit aggressive acts. A lack of VIM just means that one source of the interruption of violent action is lost. Thus, in Figure 7.2, the development of the psychopath is represented as a consequence of the lack of VIM together with either unspecified cognitive or environmental factors. It is perhaps possible that the development of the psychopath may require deficits within executive functioning as well as within VIM; that both sources of behavioural inhibition must be impaired in order for the child to develop as a psychopath. Certainly, there have been reports of impairments in executive functioning in psychopaths in the literature (e.g., Gorenstein, 1982). It can therefore be predicted that there may exist a population who show the same callous behaviour and lack of moral emotions as the psychopath. These individuals, because of either the lack of the cognitive factors or the social environment predisposing them to crime, would not be known to the legal and psychiatric services. However, at the cognitive level, these individuals would show at least one of the same structural deficits as the psychopath: the lack of VIM.

Finally, Figure 7.2 represents two unique predictions of the VIM position: individuals lacking VIM should fail the moral/conventional distinction and fail to internally generate moral justifications. Blair (1993) has suggested that the operation of VIM mediates the moral/conventional distinction (see above). If psychopaths lack VIM they should fail to demonstrate this distinction. VIM may also be a prerequisite for the internal generation of moral meta-knowledge; i.e., the individual's consciously accessible theories about why moral transgressions are bad to do. Children have been consistently found to justify their opinions about moral transgressions by references to the *victim's welfare* and by *appeals to fairness* (e.g., Arsenio & Ford, 1985; Nucci, 1981; Smetana, 1985; Song et al., 1987). Blair (1993) suggested that when the individual is asked why a moral transgression is bad, he should be able to do some sort of causal analysis which will determine that the distress to the other is the object which activated the withdrawal response; i.e., it is the object that is bad. Blair suggested that without VIM the individual will judge acts as bad only because he has been told that they are bad (by parents/peers). Without VIM, if the subject is asked about why the act is bad, he will make reference to what he has been told.

Previous investigations of the moral reasoning of the psychopath have been exclusively conducted within the paradigmatic framework of Kohlberg (1969; Colby & Kohlberg, 1987). While it appears clear that the moral reasoning of delinquents is at a lower level than that of normal controls[6] (see Blasi, 1980; Trevathan & Walker, 1989) it is more debatable whether the moral reasoning of psychopaths is at a lower level than that of criminal controls. Fodor (1973) found that the moral reasoning of psychopathic youths was at a

lower level than the moral reasoning of other delinquents. Campagna and Harter (1975) found the moral reasoning of sociopaths to be lower than that of non-incarcerated normals, even when controlling for mental age. Jurkovic and Prentice (1977) found that psychopaths give evidence of less mature moral reasoning than other groups of delinquent and normal youths. However, Lee, and Prentice (1988) only found that delinquents responded at a lower level than non-delinquents; the psychopaths did not reason at a lower level than the other delinquent groups.

Also, the above studies used scales of psychopathy (e.g., Quay's Behaviour Problem Checklist) that are of doubtful validity (see Hare & Cox, 1978). This methodological deficit was remedied by Trevathan and Walker (1989), who utilized Hare's Psychopathy Checklist. Trevathan and Walker (1989) observed a tendency for the psychopaths to reason at a lower level than non-psychopathic controls but this was not significant. However, both groups of delinquents scored at a significantly lower level than non-incarcerated controls. Thus, while it is clear that criminal groups may reason at a lower level than non-criminal controls, it is uncertain whether the moral reasoning of psychopaths is lower than that of other criminal groups.

No previous work has investigated whether the psychopath makes a distinction between moral and conventional rules. No previous work has looked at moral meta-knowledge. This is despite the fact that both of these are fundamental aspects of the normal development of morality. The VIM position would predict that the psychopath should fail to make a distinction in his judgements between moral and conventional transgressions and that he will not make victim-based justifications of why moral transgressions are bad to do. In summary, it was predicted that:

1 psychopaths will not make a distinction between moral and conventional rules;

2 psychopaths will treat moral rules as if they were conventional; that is, under permission conditions, the psychopaths will say that moral as well as conventional transgressions are OK to do;

3 psychopaths will be less likely to make references to the pain or discomfort of victims than the non-psychopath controls.

2.   Method

2.1.   Design

The experiment involved a 2 × 2 repeated measures factorial design. The independent variables were the two different subject groups (psychopaths and non-psychopathic controls) and the two different domains of story (moral and conventional). The dependent variable was the responses of the subjects to the questions about the transgression situation.

2.2.   Subjects

Ten psychopaths and 10 non-psychopaths controls took part in this study. All were obtained through contacts in Broadmoor and Ashworth Special Hospitals and had been admitted to the hospitals under the *legal* category of Psychopathic Disorder. The files of all the subjects were examined to obtain a Psychopathy Checklist (PCL) score in accordance with the guidelines of Hare (1985). Wong (1988) has shown that PCL scores derived entirely from file data can be valid and reliable. Four items on the PCL were not scored: items 1 ("Glibness/superficial charm"), 2 ("Grandiose sense of self worth"), 4 ("Pathological lying") and 13 ("Lack of realistic, long term goals"). These items were neglected because of the difficulty of obtaining such information from the files. However, Hare states that "as many as 5 items can be omitted without any appreciable reduction in reliability" (Hare, 1985, p. 10). The subjects were then divided into two groups according to their score on the PCL: one high for psychopathy (the psychopaths), one low for psychopathy (the nonpsychopaths). All of the subjects were male and white. All of the subjects had committed crimes of violence. Indeed, all of the subjects apart from one of the high PCL scorers (i.e., one of the psychopaths) had killed. Full subject characteristics are shown in Table 7.1.

Two-way ANOVAs (comparing the two subject groups) were undertaken for each of the subject criteria. These revealed no significant differences in age between the two groups ($F(1, 18) = 1.10$; n.s.). The two tests of intelligence revealed no significant differences between the groups either when using the WAIS[7] ($F(1, 12) = 0.08$; n.s.) or Raven's Advanced matrices ($F(1, 18) = 0.01$; n.s.).

2.3.   Materials

The stories used to measure the moral/conventional distinction were all taken from the literature. The four moral stories involved a child hitting another child, a child pulling the hair of another child and the victim cries, a child smashing a piano and a child breaking the swing in the playground. The four conventional stories involved a boy child wearing a skirt, two children talking in class, a child walking out of the classroom without permission and a child who stops paying attention to the lesson and turns his back on the teacher. Subject's responses to questions were recorded on standard scoring sheets.

2.4.   Procedure

Subjects were tested in one of the interview rooms attached to the ward on which the subject was housed. Before the study commenced the subjects were introduced to the experimenter and

Table 7.1   Means for each of the subject criteria (standard deviations in parentheses)

Group	N	Age	IQ (WAIS)	Raven's matrices score	Hare's psychopathy score[a]
Psychopaths	10	33.3 (7.7)	91.6 (17.2)	6.4 (2.1)	31.6 (2.1)
Non-psychopaths	10	37.5 (9.43)	92.7 (16.0)	6.3 (3.3)	16.1 (4.6)

[a] To gain a score out of 40 when only 16 items were being measured the score from the 16 items (out of 32) was multiplied by 40/32.

informed about what they were to do. Subject consent forms were taken.

Before any of the transgressions scenes were read out to the subjects, they were informed that all of the scenes would occur within a school environment. It was decided to place the transgressions scenes within a school environment, as opposed to a ward or other adult environment, because piloting had shown that teachers were regarded by the subjects as legitimate authority figures for children. Some subjects did not regard nurses as legitimate authority figures for other adults.

Each of the transgression scenes was read out to the subject one at a time. The order of presentation of the transgression scenes was randomized across subjects. After the transgression scene had been presented, the subject was asked four questions:

1   "Was it OK for X to do Y?" (Examining the subject's judgement of the *permissibility* of the act.)
2   "Was it bad for X to do [the transgression?]" and then "On a scale of one to ten, how bad was it for X to do [the transgression]?" (Examining the subject's judgement of the *seriousness* of the act.)
3   "Why was it bad for X to do [the transgression]?" (Examining the subject's *justification categories* for the act.)

The subject was then told:

"Now what if the teacher said before the lesson, before X did [the transgression], that "At this school anybody can Y if they want to. Anybody can Y."

The subject was then asked a final question:

4   "Would it be OK for X to Y if the teacher says X can?" (Examining the rule's *authority jurisdiction*.)

All responses were recorded by hand on a standard scoring sheet.

2.5. Scoring procedure

The scoring procedure followed that commonly used in the literature (e.g., Smetana, 1981; Smetana & Braeges, 1990). The answers to all questions, except three, were scored categorically. *Yes* responses were assigned a score of 0, and *no* (*not OK*) responses a score of 1. Subjects could thus achieve a cumulative score of between 0 and 4 for each of the domains for each of the questions. Question 3 was scored according to the value (between 1 and 10) the subject had given that transgression. The justifications of the subjects were scored according to categories similar to those used in previous research (e.g., Smetana, 1985). The justification categories are shown in Table 7.2. Two coders scored all justifications, and inter-rater reliability was high (91%).

3. Results

3.1. Criterion judgements

Table 7.3 presents the means and standard deviations of moral and conventional judgements for each of the criterion judgements for both subject groups. Three 2 (Domain) × 2 (Group) ANOVAs were performed on the subject's responses for

Table 7.2   A description of the justification categories

	Description
Other's welfare	Any reference to the welfare of the victim (e.g., "it will hurt him")
Normative references	Any reference, even implicit (e.g., "It's not acceptable to do that"), to rules
Disorder statements	Any reference to the disruption caused by the transgression (e.g., "It will distract the class").
Lack of change	Any reference to the long-term implications of the transgression (e.g., "If he gets away with it now he'll always do it)
Rudeness	Any reference to the rudeness of the transgression (e.g., "It's bad manners")
Other	Any other response

Table 7.3   The means and standard deviations of moral (M) and conventional (C) judgements for each of the criterion judgements for each of the subject groups

	Criterion judgements Permissibility		Seriousness		Modifiability	
	M	C	M	C	M	C
Psychopaths	0.98	0.93	8.28	6.42	0.95	0.80
	(0.08)	(0.17)	(1.66)	(3.04)	(0.16)	(0.33)
Non-psychopaths	1.00	0.75	8.04	4.72	1.00	0.38
	(0.00)	(0.26)	(2.11)	(3.29)	(0.00)	(0.34)

each of the three criterion judgements. These three ANOVAs revealed main effects of domain for all three judgements: *permissibility*, $F(1, 38) = 9.51$, $p = .05$; *seriousness*, $F(1, 38) = 8.83$, $p < .01$, and; *authority jurisdiction* (modifiability), $F(1, 38) = 30.07$, $p < .001$). Moral transgressions were judged significantly less *permissible*, more *serious* and less *authority dependent* than conventional transgressions.

Significant group differences were only shown in the results of the ANOVA on the *authority jurisdiction* (modifiability) criterion judgement. This ANOVA showed a main effect of group $F(1, 38) = 5.53$, $p < .05$ and a significant Domain × Group interaction $F(1, 38) = 9.97$, $p < .01$. However, a simple effects analysis using two-way ANOVAs to examine the moral/conventional distinction of the two groups independently revealed different patterns of responding for the two groups. The non-psychopaths made a significant moral/conventional distinction on all three criterion judgements (*permissibility*, $F(1, 18) = 11.76$, $p < .05$; *seriousness*, $F(1, 18) = 6.49$, $p < .05$; *authority jurisdiction*, $F(1, 18) = 53.47$, $p < .001$). However, the psychopaths did not make a significant moral/conventional distinction on any of the criterion judgements (*permissibility*, $F(1, 18) = 0.56$, n.s.; *seriousness*, $F(1, 18) = 2.58$, n.s.; *authority jurisdiction*, $F(1, 18) = 2.08$, n.s.).

It seems therefore that while the responding of the psychopaths and non-psychopaths was only significantly different for the *authority jurisdiction* (modifiability) criterion judgement, the two groups can be differentiated. As predicted (prediction 1; see the simple effects analysis), the psychopaths did not show a moral/conventional distinction on any of the criterion judgements. However, in contrast to prediction 2, the psy-

chopaths did not judge moral transgressions as conventional on the *authority jurisdiction* criterion judgement; i.e., *authority dependent*. Indeed, psychopaths did the opposite, judging conventional transgressions as moral on this criterion judgement; i.e., not *authority independent*.

Analysis of individual subject data reveals the difference in the pattern of responding of the two subject groups even more clearly. Table 7.4 reveals the differences between individuals in the two groups in their pattern of responding on the *authority jurisdiction* question. Table 7.4 reveals how many of the subjects in each of the two groups judged how many of the conventional transgressions to be *authority independent*. All of the subjects (other than one psychopath) judged that all of the moral transgressions were *authority independent*.

Table 7.4 clearly shows the difference between the two groups. Six psychopaths (as opposed to 1 non-psychopath) subjects did not distinguish between moral and conventional transgressions on the *authority jurisdiction* question at all; all of these subjects thought that the transgression was not OK even if the teacher said that it was. In addition, a two (group)-way ANOVA, performed on the "quality of the moral/conventional distinction" score, revealed that the psychopaths were judging significantly more of the conventional transgressions as moral ($F(1, 18) = 8.10$; $p < .05$).

Only two psychopaths as opposed to eight controls made a clear moral/conventional transgression (i.e., considered that more than two of the conventional transgressions were OK to do under the permission conditions). Even then, one of these two psychopaths actually viewed all transgressions, apart from the two physical violence transgressions, as permissible under permission

Table 7.4 The number of psychopaths and non-psychopaths in each of the "quality of the moral/conventional distinction" categories

	Quality of the moral/conventional distinction		
Group	No distinction	Mild distinction	Clear distinction
Psychopaths	6	2	2
Non-psychopaths	1	1	8

No distinction = no transgressions were judged *authority dependent*; mild distinction = 1 transgression was judged *authority independent*; clear distinction = 2 or more transgressions were judged *authority dependent*.

conditions; this subject, unlike all the other 19 studied, considered that property damage, under permission conditions, was permissible.

3.2. Justification categories

Table 7.5 and Figure 7.4 depict subjects' proportionate use of justifications for (combined) moral and conventional items. It seems that, regardless of group, *victim's welfare* reasoning was more commonly used to justify moral items while *disorder* statements and *rudeness* were more commonly used to justify conventional items. Indeed, a 2 (Group) × 2 (Domain) ANOVA, performed on the *victim's welfare* justification category, revealed a main effect for domain. This ANOVA also revealed a main effect of group ($F(1, 38) = 6.76; p < .05$). As predicted (prediction 3), psychopaths are significantly less likely to justify items by references to the victim's welfare. There was also a significant Group × Domain interaction ($F(1,36) = 6.76; p < .05$). This was a product of the fact that this difference between the groups

was only present for the moral items; no conventional items were justified through references to *victim's welfare*.

Examination of *victim's welfare* justification by the individual subject revealed that 5 of the psychopaths and 9 of the non-psychopaths used this form of justification at least once. Of the 5 psychopaths who used this justification, 2 were the 2 subjects who showed a clear moral/conventional distinction (see Table 7.4) and 1 was 1 of the subjects who made a mild moral/conventional distinction. The 1 non-psychopath who did not use *other's welfare* justifications did, however, make a clear moral/conventional distinction.

[...]

4. Discussion

The present study examined the form of the moral/conventional distinction made by psychopaths and non-psychopaths and the categories used by these subjects when they justify their

Table 7.5 The proportionate use by the psychopath and non-psychopath subjects of the justification categories

	Group			
	Psychopath		Non-psychopath	
	M	C	M	C
Other's welfare	17.5	0.00	52.50	0.00
Normative references	52.50	42.50	35.00	25.00
Disorder statements	0.05	22.50	2.50	32.50
Lack of change	12.50	7.50	2.50	12.50
Rudeness	0.00	17.50	2.50	17.50
Other	12.5	10.00	5.00	12.5

M, moral; C, conventional.

judgements. This study revealed: first, and in line with predictions, that while the non-psychopaths made the moral/conventional distinction, the psychopaths did not; secondly, and in contrast with predictions, that psychopaths treated conventional transgressions like moral transgressions rather than treating moral transgressions like conventional transgressions; and thirdly, and in line with predictions, that psychopaths were much less likely to justify their items with reference to *victim's welfare*.

It should be noted that while these results were broadly in line with predictions, they would not be expected from an analysis of the literature. As reported above, the observation in individuals of a moral/conventional distinction is a particularly robust phenomenon; it is found across ages (e.g., Nucci, 1981) and across cultures (e.g., Song et al., 1987). Indeed, Blair (1996) found that children with autism made the distinction. In fact, all other populations examined have been found to make this distinction.

It should also be noted that these findings cannot be explained as a result of poor parenting strategies (this includes neglect or child abuse). While clinicians have reported that many psychopaths have been abused as children, not all have, nor have the non-psychopath population used here been free of this abuse. More importantly, Smetana et al. (1984), examining the moral/conventional distinction in abused children, found that these children did make the distinction.

Indeed, these findings cannot easily be accommodated within the existing framework of accounts of the moral/conventional distinction (e.g., Smetana, 1983; Turiel, 1977, 1983; Turiel et al., 1987; Turiel & Smetana, 1984). These authors have suggested that the moral/conventional distinction is a result of the formation of two, independent conceptual domains (see Turiel & Davidson, 1986). These authors have proposed that the child *constructs* these domains from the qualitatively different social interactional consequences of moral and conventional transgressions. Such a framework would have to account for the present findings as indicating that the psychopath has not *constructed* the moral domain either because of a failure in the construction process or because of a lack of experience of the social interactional consequences of moral and conventional transgressions. Taking the second possibility first: given the activities of the psychopath it is highly unlikely that they have not been exposed to the social interactional consequences of moral and conventional transgressions. It would therefore probably be easier to explain the present findings in terms of a deficit within the *construction* process in psychopaths. The only detailed description of the *construction* process is that provided by Turiel (1983). He states that two forms of the manipulation of gathered data result in the *construction* of "judgements of moral necessity": manipulations of past experience and counter-factual reasoning. In summary, both of these manipulations result in judgements of moral necessity if the child has *constructed* a connection between his own personal experience of pain and the observed experience of the victim. It would thus be predicted that an individual who has never experienced pain would not make the moral/conventional distinction. However, there is no reason to believe the psychopaths do not experience pain. Nor is there any empirical reason to believe that psychopaths are any less likely to form *connections* between concepts than the normal population.

Two potential alternative ways of generating "judgements of moral necessity" might be by either role taking or empathizing with the victim. Representations of another's plight, formed through role taking, have previously been suggested to motivate the observer to alleviate that plight (Gough, 1948). In addition, emphatic responses are assumed to motivate prosocial behaviour (Hoffman, 1987) and inhibit violent action (Feshbach, 1983; Gibbs, 1987; Perry & Perry, 1974; Samenov, 1984). As stated above, role taking is defined as the "imaginative transposing of oneself into the thinking and acting of another" (Feshbach, 1978). As Batson states: "Perspective taking is the psychological variable most often assumed to be the antecedent of specifically empathic reactions to another's distress" (Batson et al., 1987, p.172). Thus, empathizing involves role taking. To role take an individual must be able to "mentalize" (see Leslie, 1987, 1988) where "mentalizing" involves the representation of mental states of others. If, when the individual is role taking, he is forming a representation of the mental state of the other he is, by definition, "mentalizing". Children with autism

Table 7.6 Intercorrelations of total PCL score, tendency to judge conventional transgressions as moral and tendency to make *victim's welfare* justifications

	Tendency to judge conventional transgressions as moral	Tendency to make victim's welfare justifications
Total PCL score	0.45[a]	−0.47
Tendency to make *victim's* welfare justifications	−0.54	

[a] This correlation is not significant.

have been demonstrated to be incapable of "mentalizing" (e.g., Baron-Cohen, Leslie & Frith, 1985; Leslie & Frith, 1988). Therefore, according to the above definitions, these children cannot either role take or empathize. However, children with autism do make the moral/conventional distinction (Blair, 1996). Therefore, neither role taking nor empathy can be prerequisites for successful performance on the moral/conventional distinction task.

Turning to the position detailed in the Introduction, there is no reason to believe that children with autism lack VIM and, therefore, their demonstration of the moral/conventional distinction is not surprising. While children with autism may not be able to represent a mental state of another's distress, this distress, as a visual or aural cue, will activate their VIM. Developmentally, representations of transgressions which commonly cause distress in victims (moral transgressions) will become triggers for VIM due to their pairing with VIM activation as a consequence of the observation of distress cues (see above). Thus, in children with autism, as in normally developing children, representations of moral transgressions will activate VIM.

As regards the three predictions made in the Introduction for psychopaths, it can be seen that two out of the three were confirmed. If psychopaths lack VIM they should fail to distinguish in their judgments between moral and conventional transgressions. Most of the psychopaths in the present study did not distinguish between these two transgression situations in their judgements. If psychopaths lack VIM they should show impoverished victim-based moral meta-knowledge. The psychopaths in the present study demonstrated significantly less reference to victim-based moral meta-knowledge than the non-psychopaths.

In addition, as regards the VIM position, the findings displayed in Table 7.6 . . . should be considered. Total PCL score correlated with both tendency to judge conventional transgressions as moral and tendency to make *victim's welfare* justifications. There is an association between degree of psychopathy and both failure to make the moral/conventional distinction and failure to make *victim's welfare justifications*. More important, however, are the significant correlations between individual PCL items and both moral/conventional scores. All the individual PCL items which correlate significantly with either of the measures of failure on the moral/conventional distinction task would be predicted primary consequences of a lack of VIM. In particular, in this respect, is the very significant correlation between lack of remorse or guilt and tendency to judge conventional items as moral. The causal model presented in Figure 7.2 specifically predicts the absence of moral emotions in the psychopath.

The third prediction, that the psychopaths should treat moral transgressions as conventional, was disconfirmed. The psychopaths treated conventional transgressions as if they were moral. In the Introduction, it was suggested that when an individual learns of a moral transgression, VIM is activated by the presence of a victim. It was suggested that VIM activation results in a withdrawal response resulting in arousal. This arousal, associated with the withdrawal response, is experienced as aversive. The act which elicited this arousal is associated with the aversiveness; it is considered undesirable. Even if the transgression situation is changed, i.e., there is no rule prohibiting the moral transgression, VIM will still be activated by the presence of the victim, and so the act will still be considered not OK to do. In contrast, when an individual processes a conventional transgression

VIM will not be activated and there will be no aversive arousal. The individual will therefore consider that any conventional transgression that is not prohibited by a rule is OK to do.

This account implies: first, that the psychopath should judge moral and conventional transgressions similarly; and, secondly, that the psychopath should process all transgressions as conventional (*authority dependent*) because, given the lack of VIM, no aversive arousal should be generated. As stated above, the first prediction was confirmed; psychopaths did judge moral and conventional transgressions similarly. However, psychopaths judged all transgressions as moral, not conventional. However, this second finding is not incompatible with the VIM position. Indeed, perhaps this finding is not surprising. These subjects were all incarcerated and presumably motivated to be released. All wished to demonstrate that the treatments they were receiving were effective. They therefore would be motivated to show how they had learned the rules of society (notice the predominance of normative statement justifications from both groups; 45% of the psychopaths and 34% of the non-psychopaths justifications were of this form). The psychopaths manifest this desire on the *authority jurisdiction* criterion judgement, by suggesting that all transgressions are *authority independent*. I suggest that this is because the psychopaths lack VIM and thus are unable to identify the distinguishing features differentiating moral and conventional transgressions. This inability, coupled with a desire to demonstrate adherence to societal rules, results in their judgement of all the transgressions as *authority independent*. The non-psychopaths, in contrast, though presumably equally motivated to be released, are incapable of ignoring the distinguishing features of moral and conventional transgressions because of the operation of VIM, and thus answer the *authority jurisdiction* question appropriately.

Examining the justifications produced by subjects when they were explaining why they thought the transgressions were not OK to do (see Table 7.5), it can be seen that psychopaths and non-psychopaths used similar justifications if the transgression was conventional but not if the transgression was moral. If the transgression was moral, nonpsychopaths used predominantly *other's welfare* justifications ("it hurts") while psychopaths used predominantly *normative* justifications (i.e., "its wrong" or "its not socially acceptable"). This result was as predicted. Without VIM, the individual may not associate the pain of the other with the transgression and thus will not justify the act's wrongness by referring to the welfare of others.

It could be suggested, from Table 7.5, that the psychopaths, though they failed to make a moral/conventional distinction in their criterion judgements, are making a moral/conventional distinction in their justifications. They certainly do show a tendency to give different justifications for moral and conventional transgressions. However, this cannot be taken as evidence against the position proposed here. In the Introduction, the moral/conventional transgressions was defined as the distinction in an individual's *judgements* between moral and conventional transgressions. It was suggested that the activation of VIM by representations of moral, but not conventional, transgressions was responsible for this distinction. It was also suggested that VIM was a prerequisite for the internal generation of justifications centred on the plight of the victim. However, it was not suggested that VIM had a role in the generation of any other form of justification category. Indeed, there is no reason to believe that it should have. What justification category an individual gives for a specific transgression will be a function of the salient aspects of that transgression. There is no reason to believe that the salient features of a moral transgression should be identical to those of a conventional transgression (outside of the fact that moral transgressions necessarily result in victims). Indeed, there is reason to believe that they should not be. Moral transgressions (e.g., one individual hitting another) need not result in classroom disorder. The conventional transgressions used in the present study (e.g., talking in class) necessitate classroom disorder. Thus, the fact that the psychopaths give different, non-victim based justifications for moral and conventional transgression cannot be used against the position being advocated here.

In conclusion, this study confirmed two predictions of the causal model presented as Figure 7.1. Psychopaths are significantly more likely to fail to make the moral/conventional distinction and they are significantly less likely to make reference to the welfare of others. While this study has not proven that psychopaths lack VIM, it has provided evidence that is in line with the position.

Notes

[1] Again, it should be noted that the activation of VIM does not inevitably result in the withdrawal of the individual from the situation. The operation of executive functions may overrule the activation of VIM; the individual may help the distressed person. Frequent instances of helping a distressed individual may result in the development of an approach schema. In this case helping behaviour could become the prepotent response to certain distress cue situations.

[2] Of course, if the child is rewarded for his attacks, particularly during the attack, either by material gain or by peer/parental praise, the child is likely to overrule VIM and continue the attack. Such a child, by continuing to fight, will obviously not experience a withdrawal response. Consequently, such a child will not experience the aggression as aversive (assuming they do not have to withdraw from the fight because they lost the conflict). Indeed, they may even enjoy the violence (if the aggressor continues to approach the victim child). Such a child will not be less likely to engage in future violent action. Indeed, they may be more likely to aggress.

[3] It should be noted that a distinction between morality and convention is also made for positive acts. For example, Smetana et al. (1983) found that moral positive actions (e.g., comforting a young child) were ranked by subjects as better to do than conventional positive actions (e.g., wearing the school's uniform). The VIM position makes no direct predictions about the moral/conventional distinction in positive actions nor does it make specific claims as to why we should approve of moral positive actions. It could be argued that moral positive actions are evaluated as good if they result in the termination of a situation evaluated as bad because of the activation of VIM (i.e., a distressed other). In this case, VIM would be conceptualized as a prerequisite for the development of the moral/conventional distinction in positive acts. Alternatively, it could be argued that VIM has no role in the development of approval for moral positive acts, that VIM is only involved in the development of disapproval for moral transgressions. In this case, VIM would have no role in the development of the moral/conventional distinction for positive acts. At present, these two positions have not been empirically resolved.

[4] For this expansion of the trigger database to occur, VIM must actually control behaviour: the individual must withdraw from the transgression situation. If the individual continues to approach the victim (perhaps because of peer pressure to inflict greater damage), the individual will associate any representations of the victim's plight or the transgression situation with the approach response. Such an individual is more likely to be aggressive in future.

[5] Empathy, defined as above, is an emotional reaction to a representation of the distressed internal state of another; i.e., an emotional response to a representation of the form "she's suffering"; "what a poor little boy"; "he must be cold and hungry".

[6] Though the reasons for this are not (see Blasi, 1980).

[7] WAIS scores were obtained from the patients' files and not by the present experimenter. WAIS scores were not available for three of the psychopaths and three of the non-psychopaths. Because of the incompleteness of these data, all of the subjects were submitted Raven's Advanced matrices.

References

American Psychological Association (1987). *Diagnostic and Statistical Manual of Mental Disorders, 3rd revised edn. (DSM-III-R)*. Washington, DC: American Psychological Association.

Arsenio, W.F., & Ford, M.E. (1985). The role of affective information in social-cognitive development: children's differentiation of moral and conventional events. *Merrill-Palmer Quarterly, 31*, 1–17.

Baron-Cohen, S., Leslie, A.M. & Frith, U. (1985). Does the autistic have a "Theory of Mind"? *Cognition, 21*, 37–46.

Batson, C.D., Fultz, J., & Schoenrade, P.A. (1987). Adults' emotional reactions to the distress of others. In N. Eisenberg & J. Strayer (eds.), *Empathy and its development* (pp. 163–85). Cambridge, UK: Cambridge University Press.

Blair, R. (1993). *The development of morality*. Unpublished PhD thesis, University of London.

Blair, R.J.R. (1996). Brief report: Morality in the autistic child. *Journal of Autism and Developmental Disorders, 26*, 571–9.

Blair, R.J.R., Sellars, C., Strickland, I., Clark, F., Williams, A.O., Smith, M., & Jones, J. (1996). Theory of mind in the psychopath. *Journal of Forensic Psychology, 7*, 15–25.

Blasi, A. (1980). Bridging moral cognition and moral action: a critical review of the literature. *Psychological Bulletin, 88*, 1–45.

Campagna, A.F., & Harter, S. (1975). Moral judgements in sociopathic and normal children. *Journal of Personality and Social Psychology, 31*, 199–205.

Camras, L.A. (1977). Facial expressions used by children in a conflict situation. *Child Development, 48*, 1431–5.

Colby, A., & Kohlberg, L. (1987). *The measurement of moral judgement*. New York: Cambridge University Press.

Eibl-Eibesfeldt, I. (1970). *Ethology: The biology of behaviour*. New York: Holt, Rinehart & Winston.

Feshbach, N.D. (1978). Studies of empathic behaviour in children: In B.A. Maher (ed.), *Progress in experimental personality research*, New York: Academic Press.

Feshbach, N.D. (1983). Learning to care: a positive approach to child training and discipline. *Journal of Clinical Child Psychology, 12*, 266–71.

Fodor, E.M. (1973). Moral development and parent behaviour antecedents in adolescent psychopaths. *Journal of Genetic Psychology, 122*, 37–43.

Gibbs, J.C. (1987). Social processes in delinquency: the need to facilitate empathy as well as sociomoral reasoning. In W.M. Kurtines & J.L. Gewirtz (eds.), *Moral development through social interaction* (pp. 301–21). New York: Wiley.

Gorenstein, E.E. (1982). Frontal lobe functions in psychopaths. *Journal of Abnormal Psychology, 91*, 368–79.

Gough, H.G. (1948). A sociological theory of psychopathy. *American Journal of Sociology, 53*, 359–66.

Hare, R.D. (1980). A research scale for the assessment of psychopathy in criminal populations. *Personality and Individual Differences, 1*, 111–19.

Hare, R.D. (1985). *Scoring manual for the psychopathy checklist*. Unpublished manuscript. University of British Columbia, Vancouver, Canada.

Hare, R.D., & Cox, D.N. (1978). Clinical and empirical conceptions of psychopathy, and the selection of subjects for research. In R.D. Hare & D. Schalling (eds.), *Psychopathic behaviour: Approaches to research*. Chichester: Wiley.

Hoffman, M.L. (1987). The contribution of empathy to justice and moral judgment. In N. Eisenberg & J. Strayer (eds.), *Empathy and its development* (pp. 47–80). Cambridge, UK: Cambridge University Press.

Hollos, M., Leis, P., & Turiel, E. (1986). Social reasoning children and adolescents. *Journal of Cross Cultural Psychology, 17*, 352–74.

Jurkovic, G.J., & Prentice, N.M. (1977). Relation of moral and cognitive development to dimensions of juvenile delinquency. *Journal of Abnormal Psychology, 86*, 414–20.

Karpman, B. (1941). On the need for separating psychopathy into two distinct types: the symptomatic and the idiopathic. *Journal of Criminal Psychopathy, 3*, 112–37.

Kohlberg, L. (1969). Stage and sequence: the cognitive-developmental approach to socialization. In D.A. Goslin (ed.), *Handbook of socialisation theory and research*. Chicago: Rand McNally.

Laupa, M., & Turiel, E. (1986). Children's conceptions of adult and peer authority. *Child Development, 57*, 405–12.

Lee, M., & Prentice, N.M. (1988). Interrelations of empathy, cognition, and moral reasoning with dimensions of juvenile delinquency. *Journal of Abnormal Child Psychology, 16*, 127–39.

Leslie, A.M. (1987). Pretence and representation: the origins of "Theory of Mind". *Psychological Review, 94*, 412–26.

Leslie, A.M. (1988). Some implications of pretence for mechanisms underlying the child's theory of mind. In P.L. Astington, P.L. Harris, & D.R. Olson (eds.), *Developing theories of the mind*. Cambridge: Cambridge University Press.

Leslie, A.M., & Frith, U. (1988). Autistic children's understanding of seeing, knowing and believing. *British Journal of Developmental Psychology, 6*, 315–24.

Lorenz, K. (1966). *On aggression*. New York: Harcourt Brace Jovanovich.

Mandler, G. (1984). *Mind and body*. New York: Norton.

Morton, J., & Frith, U. (1993). Causal modelling: a structural approach to developmental psychopathology. In D. Cicchetti & D.H. Cohen (eds.), *Manual of developmental Psychopathology*. New York: Wiley.

Norman, D., & Shallice, T. (1986). Attention to action: willed and automatic control of behaviour. In R.J. Davidson, G.E. Schwartz, & D. Shapiro (eds.), *Consciousness and self-regulation*. New York: Plenum Press.

Nucci, L. (1981). Conceptions of personal issues: a domain distinct from moral or societal concepts. *Child Development, 52*, 114–21.

Nucci, L., & Nucci, M. (1982). Children's responses to moral and conventional transgressions in free-play settings. *Child Development, 52*, 1337–42.

Nucci, L., & Turiel, E. (1978) Social interactions and the development of social concepts in preschool children. *Child Development, 49*, 400–7.

Nucci, L., Turiel, E., & Encarnacion-Gawrych, G.E. (1983). Social interactions and social concepts: analysis of morality and convention in the Virgin Islands. *Journal of Cross Cultural Psychology, 14*, 469–87.

Patrick, C.J., Bradley, M.M., & Lang, P.J. (1993). Emotion in the criminal psychopath: startle reflex modulation. *Journal of Abnormal Psychology, 102*, 82–92.

Perry, D.G., & Perry, L.C. (1974). Denial of suffering in the victim as a stimulus to violence in aggressive boys. *Child Development, 45*, 55–62.

Samenov, S.E. (1984). *Inside the criminal mind*. New York: Random House.

Siegal, M., & Storey, R.M. (1985). Day care and children's conceptions of moral and social rules. *Child Development, 56*, 1001–8.

Smetana, J. (1981). Preschool children's conceptions of moral and social rules. *Child Development, 52,* 1333–6.

Smetana, J. (1983). Social-cognitive development: domain distinctions and coordinations. *Developmental Review, 3,* 131–47.

Smetana, J. (1985). Preschool children's conceptions of transgressions: effects of varying moral and conventional domain-related attributes. *Developmental Psychology, 21,* 18–29.

Smetana, J. (1986). Preschool children's conceptions of sex-role transgressions. *Child Development, 57,* 862–71.

Smetana, J., & Braeges, J.L. (1990). The development of toddlers moral and conventional judgements. *Merrill-Palmer Quarterly, 36,* 329–46.

Smetana, J., Bridgeman, D.L., & Turiel, E. (1983). Differentiation of domains and prosocial behaviour. In D.L. Bridgeman (ed.), *The nature of prosocial development: Interdisciplinary theories and strategies.* New York: Academic Press.

Smetana, J., Kelly, M., & Twentyman, C.T. (1984). Abused, neglected and nonmaltreated children's conceptions of moral and social-conventional transgressions. *Child Development, 55,* 277–87.

Song, M., Smetana, J.G., & Kim, S.Y. (1987). Korean children's conceptions of moral and conventional transgressions. *Developmental Psychology, 23,* 577–82.

Stoddart, T., & Turiel, E. (1985) Children's concepts of cross-gender activities. *Child Development, 56,* 1241–52.

Tisak, M.S., & Turiel, E. (1984). Children's conception of moral and prudential rules. *Child Development, 55,* 1030–9.

Tisak, M.S., & Turiel, E. (1988). Variation in seriousness of transgressions and children's moral and conventional concepts. *Developmental Psychology, 24,* 352–7.

Trevathan, S., & Walker, L.J. (1989). Hypothetical versus real-life moral reasoning among psychopatic and delinquent youth. *Development and Psychopathology, 1,* 91–103.

Turiel, E. (1977). Distinct conceptual and developmental domains: social convention and morality. In H.E. Howe & C.B. Keasey (eds.), *Nebraska symposium on motivation.* Lincoln: University of Nebraska Press.

Turiel E. (1983). *The development of social knowledge: Morality and convention.* Cambridge: UK. Cambridge University Press.

Turiel, E., & Davidson, P. (1986). Heterogeneity, inconsistency, and asynchrony in the development of cognitive structures. In I. Levin (ed.), *Stage and structure: Reopening the debate.* Norwood, NJ: Ablex Press.

Turiel, E., Killen, M., & Helwig, C.C. (1987). Morality: its structure, functions, and vagaries. In J. Kagan & S. Lamb (eds.), *The emergence of morality in young children* (pp. 155–245). Chicago: University of Chicago Press.

Turiel, E., & Smetana, J. (1984). Social knowledge and action: the coordination of domains. In W.M. Kurtines & J.L. Gewirtz (eds.), *Morality, moral behaviour and moral development: Basic issues in theories and research.* New York: Wiley.

Weston, D., & Turiel, E. (1980). Act–Rule relations: children's concepts of social rules. *Development Psychology, 236,* 417–24.

Wong, S. (1988). Is Hare's Psychopathy Checklist reliable with the interview? *Psychological Reports, 62,* 931–4.

8

The Moral Problem

Michael Smith

Suppose we debate the pros and cons of giving to famine relief and you convince me that I should give. However when the occasion arises for me to hand over my money I say 'But wait! I know I *should* give to famine relief. But you haven't convinced me that I have any *reason* to do so!' And so I don't.

I suggested earlier that such an outburst would occasion serious puzzlement. Having convinced me that I should give to famine relief you seem to have done everything you need to do to convince me that I have a reason to do so. And having convinced me that I have a reason to give to famine relief – absent weakness of will or some other such psychological failure – you seem to have done everything you need to do to motivate me to do so. Puzzlement would thus naturally arise because, having convinced me that I should donate, you would quite rightly expect me to hand over my money. *Believing I should* seems to bring with it *my being motivated to* – at least absent weakness of will and the like.

This idea, that moral judgement has a practical upshot, is generally referred to as 'internalism' (Falk, 1948; Frankena, 1958; Davidson, 1970; Williams, 1980; Railton, 1986; Korsgaard, 1986; Brink, 1986; Wallace, 1990; Darwall, Gibbard and Railton, 1992). Unfortunately, however, 'internalism' is a vague label in the philosophical litera-

ture, used to refer to several quite different claims about the connection between moral facts or judgements on the one hand, and having reasons or being motivated on the other (as noted by both Brink and Wallace). Let me begin by spelling out some of these rather different claims.

Sometimes the idea behind internalism is that there is the following conceptual connection between moral judgement and the will (Nagel, 1970; McDowell, 1978, 1979, 1985; Platts, 1979, 1981).

If an agent judges that it is right for her to φ in circumstances C, then she is motivated to φ in C.

In other words, moral judgement brings motivation with it *simpliciter*. This is a very strong claim. It commits us to denying that, for example, weakness of the will and the like may defeat an agent's moral motivations while leaving her appreciation of her moral reasons intact. And for this very reason it is, I think, a manifestly implausible claim as well. However I will not have anything more to say about it here; . . .

More plausibly, then, the idea behind internalism is sometimes that though there is a conceptual connection between moral judgement and the will, the connection involved is the following *defeasible* one (Blackburn, 1984: 187–9, 1998; Johnston, 1989; Pettit and Smith, 1993).

From Michael Smith (1994). *The Moral Problem* (Blackwell) (pp. 60–71 & pp. 185–9).

If an agent judges that it is right for her to φ in circumstances C, then either she is motivated to φ in C or she is practically irrational.

In other words, agents who judge it right to act in various ways are so motivated, and necessarily so, absent the distorting influences of weakness of the will and other similar forms of practical unreason on their motivations. I will have more to say about this idea in what follows.

And sometimes the idea behind the internalism requirement is not, or at least is not primarily, that there is a conceptual connection of some sort between moral judgement and motivation, but that there is the following conceptual connection between the content of a moral judgement – the moral facts – and our reasons for action (Nagel, 1970; Korsgaard, 1986).

If it is right for agents to φ in circumstances C, then there is a reason for those agents to φ in C.

In other words, moral facts are facts about our reasons for action; they are themselves simply requirements of rationality or reason.

This last internalist claim might be offered as an explanation of the previous one, for it plausibly entails the previous claim. The proof of this will be spelled out in some detail later (chapter 5 [of the original book]), but in general terms the idea can be put like this. It is a platitude that an agent has a reason to act in a certain way just in case she would be motivated to act in that way if she were rational (Korsgaard, 1986). And it is a consequence of this platitude that an agent who judges herself to have a reason to act in a certain way – who judges that she would be so motivated if she were rational – is practically irrational if she is not motivated to act accordingly. For if she is not motivated accordingly then she fails to be rational by her own lights (Smith, 1992). But if this is right then it is clear that the third form of internalism entails the second. For, according to the third form, the judgement that it is right to act in a certain way is simply equivalent to the judgement that there is a reason to act in that way.

The reverse does not hold, however. The second internalist claim does not entail the third. Expressivists, for example, agree that someone who judges it right to act in a certain way is either motivated accordingly or practically irrational in

some way, but deny that moral requirements are requirements of rationality or reason. They thus accept the second internalist claim because they think that a moral judgement is the expression of a preference, or perhaps the expression of a disposition to have a preference; but they reject the third because they think that fully rational creatures may yet differ in the preferences that they have, or are disposed to have.

Let me give the second and third internalist claims names. I will call the second, the one that may be accepted even by those who deny the third internalist claim, 'the practicality requirement on moral judgement'. And, for obvious reasons, I will call the third internalist claim 'rationalism'. These two forms of internalism allow us to distinguish corresponding forms of externalism.

One form of externalism amounts to a denial of rationalism. This kind of externalism is consistent with the practicality requirement. Expressivists are typically both externalists and internalists in this sense (Ayer, 1936; Hare, 1952; Blackburn, 1984). They are externalists in so far as they are anti-rationalists, and yet they are also internalists in so far as they accept the practicality requirement on moral judgement. But the other kind of externalism, the stronger form, amounts to a denial of the practicality requirement. Since rationalism entails the practicality requirement, this form of externalism therefore excludes rationalism as well. Many of those who think, against the expressivists, that moral judgements purport to be descriptive are externalists in this stronger sense (Foot, 1972; Sturgeon, 1985; Railton, 1986; Brink, 1986, 1989).

My task in the present chapter is to defend both these forms of internalism – both rationalism and the practicality requirement – against two recent externalist challenges. The first comes from David Brink (1986). Brink's challenge is directed primarily against the weaker internalist claim: that is, against the practicality requirement. The second comes from Philippa Foot (1972). Her challenge is directed primarily against the stronger internalist claim: that is, against rationalism.

In what follows I will begin by clarifying the kind of rationalism to which we are committed by the stronger internalist claim. I then consider Brink's and Foot's challenges in turn. As a matter of fact both Brink and Foot accept the stronger form of externalism, the form that excludes both rationalism and the practicality requirement. However, as we will see, being an externalist of either kind involves far more controversial and counter-intuitive commitments than either Brink or Foot seem to realize.

Rationalism as a Conceptual Claim vs. Rationalism as a Substantive Claim

John Mackie draws a distinction between two quite different claims a rationalist might make (Mackie, 1977: 27–30). As I see it, it is Mackie's appreciation of this distinction that allows him to argue for his 'error theory': the view that all moral thought and talk is infected with an error of pre-supposition; the presupposition that the world contains objectively prescriptive features (Smith, 1993).

We can best introduce this distinction by way of an analogy. Suppose we are interested in whether or not there are any witches. How are we to go about answering our question? First we must ask a *conceptual question*. What is our concept of a witch? Let's suppose we answer this conceptual question as follows. Our concept of a witch is the concept of a person who exploits his or her relationship with a supernatural agency in order to cause events to happen in the natural world. Then, second, we must ask a *substantive question*. That is, having now fixed on what our concept of a witch is, we must ask whether there is anything in the world instantiating our concept of a witch. If we do not think that there are any supernatural agencies for anyone to have a relationship with, then we will answer this substantive question in the negative. We will say that there are no witches.

Mackie's idea is that, when we ask whether there are any moral facts, we have to follow exactly the same procedure. We must first of all ask a conceptual question. What is our concept of a moral fact? Mackie answers that our concept of a moral fact is the concept of an 'objectively prescriptive' feature of the world. And then, according to Mackie, we must go on to ask a substantive question. Is there anything in the world answering to our concept of a moral fact? Mackie's answer to this question is, famously, that once we are clear about what it is that we are looking for, we see that there are no moral facts.

For we see that our concept of an objectively prescriptive feature is not instantiated anywhere in the world.

I said that Mackie draws our attention to two different claims a rationalist might make. This is because, in light of his distinction between conceptual claims and substantive claims, rationalism might now be taken to be a conceptual claim: the claim that our concept of a moral requirement is the concept of a reason for action; a requirement of rationality or reason. Or alternatively, rationalism might be taken to be a substantive claim. That is, rationalists might be telling us that there are requirements of rationality or reason corresponding to the various moral requirements. Taken in the first way, rationalism is a claim about the best analysis of moral terms. Taken in the second way, rationalism is a claim about the deliverances of the theory of rational action.

As I see it, when Mackie tells us that our concept of a moral fact is the concept of an objectively prescriptive feature of the world, he is telling us that the rationalists' conceptual claim is true. And when he tells us that there are no objectively prescriptive features in the world, he is telling us that the rationalists' substantive claim is false. That is, as I see it, Mackie's argument for the error theory may be reconstructed as follows.

Conceptual truth:	If agents are morally required to ϕ in circumstances C then there is a requirement of rationality or reason for all agents to ϕ in circumstances C
Substantive claim:	There is no requirement of rationality or reason for all agents who find themselves in circumstances C to ϕ
Conclusion:	Agents are not morally required to ϕ in circumstances C

That we are able to reconstruct Mackie's argument in this way is important, for it shows that in defending the rationalists' conceptual claim we do not thereby beg any questions. Even if we accept the rationalists' conceptual claim, we must still go on to defend the rationalists' substantive claim. And conversely, even if we deny the rationalists' substantive claim, we must still engage with the rationalists' conceptual claim.

This distinction between rationalism as a conceptual claim and rationalism as a substantive claim is to be central in what follows. For note that the stronger internalist claim – what I have called 'rationalism' – is simply a claim about our concept of rightness: it is a claim about the content of an agent's judgement that her action is right, not a claim to effect that judgements with such contents are *true*. Moreover, note that it is this conceptual claim that entails the practicality requirement. The *truth* of the substantive claim is simply not required for that entailment to hold.

It is thus rationalism as a conceptual claim that is to be at issue in the present chapter, not rationalism as a substantive claim. Rationalism as a substantive claim will come up for discussion in later chapters, but for now the focus is to be purely conceptual.

Brink's "Amoralist" Challenge

In 'Externalist Moral Realism' David Brink argues that we must reject the practicality requirement. Since the rationalists' conceptual claim entails the practicality requirement, his argument thus threatens to refute rationalism as well. Here is Brink.

> Much moral skepticism is skepticism about the objectivity of morality, that is, skepticism about the existence of moral facts. But another traditional kind of skepticism accepts the existence of moral facts and asks why we should care about these facts. Amoralists are the traditional way of representing this second kind of skepticism; the amoralist is someone who recognizes the existence of moral considerations and remains unmoved.
>
> The ... [defender of the practicality requirement] ... must dismiss the amoralist challenge as incoherent ... We may think that the amoralist challenge is coherent, but this can only be because we confuse moral senses of terms and 'inverted commas' senses of those same terms ... Thus ... apparent amoralists ... remain unmoved, not by what they regard as moral considerations, but only by what others regard as moral considerations.

> The problem ... is that ... [this] ... does not take the amoralist's challenge seriously enough ... We can imagine someone who regards certain demands as moral demands – and not simply as conventional moral demands – and yet remains unmoved ... [If] ... we are to take the amoralist challenge seriously, we must attempt to explain why the amoralist should care about morality. (1986: 30)

Brink's argument is simple enough.

According to defenders of the practicality requirement, it is supposed to be a conceptual truth that agents who make moral judgements are motivated accordingly, at least absent weakness of will and the like. But far from this being a conceptual truth, it isn't any sort of truth at all. For amoralists use moral terms to pick out the very same properties we pick out when we use moral terms. Their use of moral terms may therefore be reliably guided by the moral facts in the same way as our uses of those terms. But amoralists differ from us in that they see no reason at all to do what they thus take to be morally required. In other words, amoralists make moral judgements without being motivated accordingly, and without suffering from any sort of practical irrationality either. The practicality requirement is thus false.

As Brink notes, defenders of the requirement have generally not responded to this challenge by boldly denying that amoralists exist. And nor could they with any credibility, for amoralists are among the more popular heroes of both philosophical fantasy and non-philosophical fiction. Brink mentions Plato's Thrasymachus and Dickens's Uriah Heep. But nor are amoralists confined to the world of make-believe. There are, after all, real-life sociopaths like Robert Harris, the thrill-killer whose story is faithfully retold and analysed by Gary Watson (1987). Harris claims that he knew that what he was doing was wrong and that he simply chose to do it anyway; that he felt no conflict. It therefore seems quite wrong to suppose that he suffered from weakness of will, or, perhaps, from any other kind of practical irrationality either.

What defenders of the requirement have tended to deny is therefore rather that, properly described, the existence of amoralists is not inconsistent with the practicality requirement. For, they claim, amoralists do not *really* make moral judgements at all. Even if they do use moral words to pick out the same properties that we pick out when we use moral words, they do not really judge acts to be right and wrong; rather they judge acts to be 'right' and 'wrong'. That is to say they use moral words in a different sense; in the inverted commas sense Brink mentions.

According to Hare, for example, the sentence 'φ-ing is right' as used by an amoralist does not mean 'φ-ing is right'; but rather means 'φ-ing is in accordance with what other people judge to be right' (Hare, 1952: 124–6, 163–5). And, as such, the fact that an amoralist may judge it 'right' to φ without being either motivated to φ or suffering from weakness of will is no counter-example to the requirement. For the requirement tells us that those who judge it right to φ are motivated accordingly, absent weakness of will, not that those who judge it 'right' to φ are motivated accordingly, absent weakness of will.

Now Brink thinks that this inverted commas response doesn't take the amoralist challenge 'seriously' enough. And I must confess that I share his misgivings, at least as regards the details of Hare's version of the response. For, as Brink points out, there seems to be nothing incoherent about the idea of an amoralist who claims to have special insight into what is *really* right and wrong; an amoralist whose judgements about what it is right and wrong to do are therefore, even by her own lights, out of line with the judgements of others. But if this is right, then the judgements of amoralists can hardly be thought of as judgements about what other people judge to be right and wrong.

Despite these misgivings, however, I think that the inverted commas response to the amoralist challenge is along exactly the right lines. In what follows I want therefore to give a two part reply to Brink. First I will say what the inverted commas response really amounts to; how it differs from what Hare says. And second I will say why defenders of the requirement are right to think that the requirement is a conceptual truth.

Reply to Brink's Claim that Amoralists Really Make Moral Judgements

As I see it, defenders of the practicality requirement are right to say that amoralists do not really make moral judgements, they simply go wrong in trying to say more than this. The point is not that amoralists really make judgements of some other kind: about what other people judge to be right and wrong, for example. The point is rather that the *very best we* can say about amoralists is that they try to make moral judgements but fail. In order to see why this is not *ad hoc*, consider an analogy.

There is a familiar problem about the conditions under which we should say of someone that she really makes colour judgements (Peacocke, 1985: chapter 2; Tawil, 1987). The problem can be brought out by reflecting on the case of someone, blind from birth, who has a reliable method of using colour terms. We might imagine that she has been hooked up to a machine from birth that allows her to feel, through her skin, when an object has the appropriate surface reflectance properties.

Now such a person certainly has a facility with colour terms, a facility that allows her to engage in many aspects of the ordinary practice of colour ascription. For she uses terms with the same extension as our colour terms, and the properties of objects that explain her uses of those terms are the very same properties as those that explain our uses of colour terms. (This is similar to what we said earlier about the amoralist's use of moral language.) And we can even imagine, if we like, that her colour judgements are far more accurate and reliable than those made by sighted folk. When she makes colour judgements, she is therefore not appropriately thought of as making judgements about what other people judge to be red, green and the like. (This is again similar to what we have said about the amoralist.)

However, despite the facility such a blind person has with colour language, many theorists have thought that we should still deny that she possesses colour concepts or mastery of colour terms. For, they say, the ability to have the appropriate visual experiences under suitable conditions is partially constitutive of possession of colour concepts and mastery of colour terms (Peacocke, 1985: 29–30, 37–8). And what such theorists thereby commit themselves to saying is that, despite her facility with colour terms, such a blind person does not *really* make colour judgements at all. They do not have to say that she is really making judgements of some other kind, of course. Rather they can insist that though she is trying to make colour judgements, because she doesn't count as a possessor of colour concepts, she fails. When she says 'Fire-engines are red', 'Grass is green' and the like, she is therefore best interpreted as using colour terms in an inverted commas sense: she is saying that fire-engines are 'red', grass is 'green' and so on.

It is, I hope, clear that the structure of this debate over the conditions for mastery of colour terms is in crucial respects identical to the structure of the debate we are engaged in with Brink. One side says that a subject has mastery of colour terms (moral terms), and thus really makes colour judgements (moral judgements), only if, under certain conditions, being in the psychological state that we express when we make colour judgements (moral judgements) entails having an appropriate visual experience (motivation). The other side denies this holding instead that the ability to use a term whose use is reliably explained by the relevant properties of objects is enough to credit her with mastery of colour terms (moral terms) and the ability really to make colour judgements (moral judgements). Having the appropriate visual experience (motivation) under appropriate conditions is an entirely contingent, and optional, extra. The debate is a real one, so how are we to decide who wins?

Imagine someone objecting that those who say that the capacity to have certain visual experiences is partially constitutive of mastery of colour terms do not take 'seriously' enough the challenge posed by people who can reliably say 'Grass is green', 'Fire-engines are red', and so on, while yet being completely blind. Suppose the objector insists that since blind people can reliably use colour terms in this way, it just follows that they have full mastery of colour terms. Would the objection be a good one? I do not think so. For the objection simply assumes the conclusion it is supposed to be arguing for. It assumes that blind people have mastery of colour terms, something that those who think that mastery requires the capacity to have the appropriate visual experiences under the appropriate conditions deny.

It seems to me that Brink's amoralist challenge is flawed in just this way. He puts a prejudicial interpretation on the amoralist's reliable use of moral terms. He assumes that the amoralist's reliable use is evidence of her mastery of those

terms; assumes that being suitably motivated under the appropriate conditions is not a condition of mastery of moral terms. But those who accept the practicality requirement do not accept the account of what it is to have mastery of moral terms that makes this prejudicial interpretation of the amoralist's use of moral terms appropriate.

What this suggests is that, in order to adjudicate the debate with Brink, what we really need is an independent reason for accepting one or the other account of mastery. In what follows I want therefore to provide such an independent reason. The argument is to be that the account of mastery offered by those who defend the practicality requirement is to be preferred because it alone is able to provide a plausible explanation of the reliable connection between moral judgement and motivation in the good and strong-willed person.

[. . .]

The Solution to the Moral Problem

We now have a solution to the moral problem at hand. That is, we can now explain why the following three propositions:

1   Moral judgements of the form 'It is right that I φ' express a subject's beliefs about an objective matter of fact, a fact about what it is right for her to do.
2   If someone judges that it is right that she φs then, *ceteris paribus*, she is motivated to φ.
3   An agent is motivated to act in a certain way just in case she has an appropriate desire and a means-end belief, where belief and desire are, in Hume's terms, distinct existences.

are both consistent and true. Let me briefly explain why.

If our concept of rightness is the concept of what we would desire ourselves to do if we were fully rational, where this is a desire for something of the appropriate substantive kind, then it does indeed follow that our moral judgements are expressions of our beliefs about an objective matter of fact. For our moral judgements are expressions of our beliefs about what we have normative reason to do, where such reasons are in turn categorical requirements of rationality. (1) is thus true. Moreover, as we have seen, such beliefs do indeed connect with motivation in the manner of (2). And, again as we have seen, their doing so does not in any way compomise the claim that motivation is to be explained in Humean terms: that is, in terms of belief and desire, where belief and desire are distinct existences. (3) too is thus true. So far so good. But does the analysis allow us not only to solve the moral problem, but to do so in a way that allows us to square morality with a broader naturalism? It seems to me that it does.

The analysis tells us that the rightness of acts in certain circumstances C – using our earlier terminology, let's call this the 'evaluated possible world' – is the feature that we would want acts to have in C if we were fully rational, where these wants have the appropriate content – and, again, using our earlier terminology, let's call this world, the world in which we are fully rational, the 'evaluating possible world'. Now though, for reasons already given, this does not itself constitute a naturalistic definition of rightness – though it is merely a non-reductive, summary style analysis [. . .] – it does provide us with the materials to construct a two-stage argument of the following kind.

Conceptual claim:	Rightness in circumstances C is the feature we would want acts to have in C if we were fully rational, where these wants have the appropriate content
Substantive claim:	Fness is the feature we would want acts to have in C if we were fully rational, and Fness is a feature of the appropriate kind
Conclusion:	Rightness in C is Fness

And this argument is, in turn, broadly naturalistic in two respects. First, it is naturalistic in so far as the features that we would want our acts to have under conditions of full rationality, the features that we would want acts to instantiate in the evaluated possible world, are themselves all natural features whenever the evaluated world is itself naturalistic. Our non-reductive, summary style definition of rightness, in conjunction with a substantive claim of the kind described, thus allows us to identify rightness with a natural feature of acts in naturalistic worlds like the actual world: for example, in this case, with Fness.

And second, even though the analysis is not itself naturalistic – even though it defines rightness in terms of full rationality where this may not itself be definable in naturalistic terms – fully rational creatures in the evaluating possible world are themselves naturalistically realized. For a fully rational creature is simply someone with a certain psychology and, as you will recall, a natural feature is simply a feature that figures in one of the natural or social sciences, *including psychology* [. . .]. Of course, the psychology of a fully rational creature is an idealized psychology, but such an idealization requires nothing non-natural for its realization. Thus, if we wanted to, we could construct non-reductive analyses of the key normative concepts we use to characterize the normative features of such an idealized creature's psychology – the unity, the coherence, and the like, of its desires – and then use these analyses to construct two-stage arguments, much like that just given, in order to identify these normative features of a fully rational creature's psychology with natural features of its psychology [. . .]. Coherence and unity, though not naturalistically definable are therefore themselves just natural features of a psychology. The evaluating possible world is therefore naturalistic in the relevant respect as well.

The analysis of rightness provided thus makes the legitimacy of moral talk depend ultimately upon the possibility of identifying moral features, like rightness, with natural features of acts. Absent such identifications, we would have to conclude that moral features are simply not instantiated at all; that moral talk is, much as Mackie thought, based on an error of presupposition. But can we say more? Can we say whether moral talk is or is not legitimate?

Are there any Moral Facts?

The substantive claim in the two-stage argument described above tells us that moral talk is legitimate just in case a certain condition is met. My handing back a wallet I found in the street in such and such circumstances is right, for example, only if, under conditions of full rationality, we would all want that if we find a wallet in the street in such and such circumstances, then we hand it back. Of course, if this is indeed true, then it is an *a priori* truth. The fact that we would have such a desire under conditions of full rationality will be a consequence of the theory that systematically justifies our desires, and this task of theory construction is itself a relatively *a priori* enterprise; it is a task that requires reflection and conversation, not empirical investigation. However that does not mean that it is an *obvious* truth. For it might not only take a good deal of reflection and conversation for any individual to discover this to be true, it might also take time and effort to convince anyone else. And of course, even after all of that time and effort, it might turn out that we are wrong. What we thought was an *a priori* truth might have been no truth at all. In deciding whether or not moral talk is legitimate, then, it seems to me that we have no alternative but to admit that we are venturing an opinion on something about which we can have no cast-iron guarantee.

However, for all that, it seems to me that we should none the less have some confidence in the legitimacy of moral talk. For, in short, the empirical fact that moral argument tends to elicit the agreement of our fellows gives us reason to believe that there will be a convergence in our desires under conditions of full rationality. For the best explanation of that tendency is our convergence upon a set of extremely unobvious *a priori* moral truths. And the truth of these unobvious *a priori* moral truths requires, in turn, a convergence in the desires that fully rational creatures would have.

Now this argument is likely to meet with some resistance. After all, isn't there currently much entrenched moral disagreement? And don't such disagreements constitute profound obstacles to a convergence in our desires in fact emerging? This is true, but it does not count against the force of the argument. Indeed, once we remember the following three points, such disagreements can be seen to add to the force of the argument.

First, we must remember that alongside such entrenched disagreements as we in fact find we also find massive areas of entrenched agreement. As I see it, this is the real significance of the fact that we have and use the so-called 'thick' moral concepts, concepts that at once both describe some naturalistic state of affairs and positively or negatively evaluate it: concepts like courage, brutality, honesty, duplicity, loyalty, meanness, kindness, treachery, and the like (Williams, 1985:

129). For what the prevalence of such concepts suggests is that there is in fact considerable agreement about what is right and wrong: acts of brutality, duplicity, meanness and treachery are wrong, at least other things being equal, whereas acts of courage, honesty, loyalty, and kindness are right, again, other things being equal. What the prevalence of such concepts suggests is therefore that moral agreement is in fact *so* extensive that our language has developed in such a way as to build an evaluative component into certain naturalistically descriptive concepts.

Second, when we look at current areas of entrenched disagreement, we must remember that in the past similarly entrenched disagreements were removed *inter alia* via a process of moral argument. I am thinking in particular of the historical, and in some places still current, debates over slavery, worker's rights, women's rights, democracy and the like. We must not forget that there has been considerable moral progress, and that what moral progress consists in is the removal of entrenched disagreements of just the kind that we currently face.

And third and finally, we must remember that where entrenched disagreements currently seem utterly intractable we can often explain why this is the case in ways that make them seem less threatening to the idea of a convergence in the opinions of fully rational creatures. For example, one or the other parties to the disagreement all too often forms their moral beliefs in response to the directives of a religious authority rather than as the result of the exercise of their own free thought in concert with their fellows. But beliefs formed exclusively in this way have dubious rational credentials. They require that we privilege one group's opinions about what is to be done – those of the religious authority – over another's – those of the followers – for no good reason. The fact that disagreement persists for this sort of reason thus casts no doubt on the possibility of an agreement if we were to engage in free and rational debate.

In light of these points it seems to me that, notwithstanding such disagreements as there are and will perhaps remain, we should therefore in fact be quite optimistic about the possibility of an agreement about what is right and wrong being reached under more idealized conditions of reflection and discussion. We might eventually come to be pessimistic, of course. Our epistemic situation might deteriorate, widespread disagreements might emerge, disagreements that seem both unresolvable and inexplicable. And if that were to happen, then we might well quite justifiably come to think that Mackie was right after all, that there are no moral facts, though there would still be room for doubt. The point is simply that this *is not* our current epistemic situation.

References

Ayer, A.J. 1936: *Language, Truth and Logic*. Gollancz. Second edn. 1946.

Blackburn, S. 1984: *Spreading the Word*. Oxford University Press.

Blackburn, S. 1998: 'The Flight to Reality' in Rosalind Hursthouse, Gavin Lawrence and Warren Quinn, eds., *Virtues and Reasons, a Festschrift for Philippa Foot*. Oxford University Press, pp. 35–56.

Brink, D. 1986: 'Externalist Moral Realism', *Southern Journal of Philosophy* Supplement. 23–42.

Brink, D. 1989: *Moral Realism and the Foundations of Ethics*. Cambridge University Press.

Darwall, S., Gibbard, A. and Railton, P. 1992: 'Toward *Fin de siecle* Ethics: Some Trends', *Philosophical Review*. 115–89.

Davidson, D. 1970: 'How is Weakness of the Will Possible?' reprinted in Davidson 1980, *Essays on Actions and Events*. Oxford University Press, pp. 21–42.

Falk, W.D. 1948: ' "Ought" and Motivation', *Proceedings of the Aristotelian Society*. 111–38.

Foot, P., 1972: 'Morality as a System of Hypothetical Imperatives,' reprinted in Foot 1978. *Virtues and Vices*. University of California Press, pp. 157–73.

Frankena, W. 1958: 'Obligation and Motivation in Recent Moral Philosophy' in A.I. Melden, ed., *Essays on Moral Philosophy*. University of Washington Press.

Hare, R.M. 1952: *The Language of Morals*. Oxford University Press.

Johnston, M. 1989: 'Dispositional Theories of Value', *Proceedings of the Aristotelian Society* Supplementary Volume. 139–74.

Korsgaard, C. 1986: 'Skepticism about Practical Reason', *Journal of Philosophy*. 5–25.

Mackie, J.L. 1977: Ethics: *Inventing Right and Wrong*. Penguin.

McDowell, J. 1978: 'Are Moral Requirements Hypothetical Imperatives?', *Proceedings of the Aristotelian Society* Supplementary Volume. 13–29.

McDowell, J. 1979: 'Virtue and Reason', *The Monist*, 331–50.

McDowell, J. 1985: 'Values and Secondary Qualities' in Honderich 1985. 110–29.

Nagel, T. 1970: *The Possibility of Altruism*. Princeton University Press.

Peacocke, C. 1985: *Sense and Content*. Oxford University Press.

Pettit, P. and Smith, M. 1993: 'Practical Unreason', *Mind*. 53–79.

Platts, M. 1979: *Ways of Meaning*. Routledge and Kegan Paul.

Platts, M. 1981: 'Moral Reality and the End of Desire' in Mark Platts, ed., *Reference, Truth and Reality*. Routledge and Kegan Paul, pp. 69–82.

Railton, P. 1986: 'Moral Realism', *Philosophical Review*. 163–207.

Smith, M. 1992: 'Valuing: Desiring or Believing?' in D. Charles and K. Lennon, eds., *Reduction, Explanation, and Realism*. Oxford University Press, pp. 323–60.

Smith, M. 1993: 'Objectivity and Moral Realism: On the Significance of the Phenomenology of Moral Experience' in J. Haldane and C. Wright, eds., *Reality, Representation and Projection*. Oxford University Press, pp. 235–6.

Sturgeon, N. 1985: 'Moral Explanations' in D. Copp and D. Zimmerman, eds., *Morality, Reason and Truth*. Rowman and Allanheld, pp. 49–78.

Tawil, N. 1987: *Reference and Intentionality*. PhD Dissertation, Princeton University.

Wallace, J. 1990: *Motivation and Moral Reality*. Bachelor of Philosophy thesis. Oxford University.

Watson, G. 1987: 'Responsibility and the Limits of Evil' in Ferdinand Schoeman, ed., *Responsibility, Character and the Emotions: New Essays in Moral Psychology*. Cambridge University Press, pp. 256–86.

Williams, B. 1980: 'Internal and External Reasons' reprinted in Williams 1981, *Moral Luck*. Cambridge University Press.

Williams, B. 1985: *Ethics and the Limits of Philosophy*. Harvard University Press.

9

How Psychopaths Threaten Moral Rationalism

Is it Irrational to be Amoral?

Shaun Nichols

Over the last twenty years, a number of central figures in moral philosophy have defended some version of moral rationalism, the idea that morality is based on reason or rationality (e.g., Gewirth 1978, Darwall 1983, Nagel 1970, 1986, Korsgaard 1986, Singer 1995, Smith 1994, 1997). According to rationalism, morality is based on reason or rationality rather than the emotions or cultural idiosyncrasies, and this has seemed to many to be the best way of securing a kind of objectivism about moral claims. Consider the following representative statements:

> Just as there are rational requirements on thought, there are rational requirements on action, and altruism is one of them. . . . If the requirements of ethics are rational requirements, it follows that the motive for submitting to them must be one which it would be contrary to reason to ignore (Nagel 1970, p. 3).

The Kantian approach to moral philosophy is to try to show that ethics is based on practical reason: that is, that our ethical judgments can be explained in terms of rational standards that apply directly to conduct or to deliberation. Part of the appeal of this approach lies in the way that it avoids certain sources of skepticism that some other approaches meet with inevitably. If ethically good action is simply rational action, we do not need to postulate special ethical properties in the world or

faculties in the mind in order to provide ethics with a foundation (Korsgaard 1986, p. 311).

> If our concept of lightness is the concept of what we would desire ourselves to do if we were fully rational, where this is a desire for something of the appropriate substantive kind, then it does indeed follow that our moral judgements are expressions of our beliefs about an objective matter of fact (Smith 1994, p. 185).

Despite the appealing consequences promised by rationalism, I'll argue that the view is implausible. There are, I maintain, two quite different kinds of claims available to the rationalist, a conceptual claim and an empirical claim. I'll argue that each of these claims is threatened by considerations about psychopaths, but in radically different ways. Conceptual Rationalism claims that it is part of our concept of morality that moral requirements are requirements of reason. The problem with this proposal is that common views about psychopaths suggest that Conceptual Rationalism does not capture our *concept* of moral requirements. Empirical Rationalism is immune to these criticisms, for it claims only that it is an empirical fact about human psychology that moral judgment derives from our rational capacities. However, Empirical Rationalism is seriously threatened by empirical evidence on the *psychology* of psychopathy. For recent evidence

From Shaun Nichols (2002). *How Psychopaths Threaten Moral Rationalism*. Monist 85 (pp. 285–303).

Moral Psychology: Historical and Contemporary Readings, edited by Thomas Nadelhoffer, Eddy Nahmias, and Shaun Nichols.

indicates that the capacity for moral judgment is in fact seriously disrupted in psychopaths, but this seems to be the result of an emotional deficit rather than any rational shortcomings.

I.   Conceptual Rationalism

The basic idea of Conceptual Rationalism is that it is a conceptual truth that a moral requirement is a reason for action (Nagel 1970, Korsgaard 1986, Smith 1994). For instance, Michael Smith writes that the rationalist's conceptual claim is that "our concept of a moral requirement is the concept of a reason for action; a requirement of rationality or reason" (1994, p. 64). He goes on to say, "according to the rationalist, it is a conceptual truth that claims about what we are morally required to do are claims about our reasons" (1994, p. 84). I will focus on Smith's version of this position, since it is largely insulated from empirical problems raised against classical conceptual analysis (e.g., Stich 1992). Smith adopts David Lewis's view that the terms of common-sense theories are defined by the set of platitudes in which they occur (Lewis 1970, 1972). So, as Smith envisions the project of conceptual analysis, "an analysis of a concept is successful just in case it gives us knowledge of all and only the platitudes which are such that, by coming to treat those platitudes as platitudinous, we come to have mastery of that concept" (1994, p. 31). This approach elegantly sidesteps empirical problems about the way that concepts are mentally represented. It is clearly the case that lay people know a number of platitudes about morality (e.g., "It's wrong to hit a person without a good reason"). The project of charting those platitudes is both practicable and interesting.

For current purposes (viz., exploring the importance of psychopaths for moral rationalism), the crucial feature of Conceptual Rationalism is its account of the link between moral judgment and motivation. Smith maintains that Conceptual Rationalism entails the Practicality Requirement, according to which "It is supposed to be a conceptual truth that agents who make moral judgments are motivated accordingly, at least absent weakness of the will and the like" (Smith 1994, p. 66). Thus, Conceptual Rationalism is committed to the claim that it's a conceptual truth that people who make moral judgments are motivated by them.[1] It is at this point that considerations about psychopaths start to raise trouble.

II.   Conceptual Rationalism and Platitudes about Psychopathy

It was almost as if he [I] said it was wrong for all these things to happen. 'It is wrong for me to jaywalk. It is wrong to rob a bank. It is wrong to break into other people's houses. It is wrong for me to drive without a driver's license. It is wrong not to pay your parking tickets. It is wrong not to vote in elections. It is wrong to intentionally embarrass people.'

Presumed psychopath Ted Bundy
(Michaud & Aynesworth 1989, p. 116).[2]

Psychopaths pose a familiar problem for Conceptual Rationalism because, contrary to the Practicality Requirement, it seems possible that a psychopath can be fully rational and judge that some action is morally required without being motivated to do it. This sort of worry is typically traced back to Hume's "sensible knave" thought experiment. Hume sets up the case as follows:

according to the imperfect way in which human affairs are conducted, a sensible knave, in particular incidents, may think that an act of iniquity or infidelity will make a considerable addition to his fortune, without causing any considerable breach in the social union and confederacy. That *honesty is the best policy*, may be a good general rule, but is liable to many exceptions; and he, it may perhaps be thought, conducts himself with most wisdom, who observes the general rule, and takes advantage of all the exceptions.

I must confess that, if a man think that this reasoning much requires an answer, it will be a little difficult to find any which will to him appear satisfactory and convincing. If his heart rebel not against such pernicious maxims, if he feel no reluctance to the thoughts of villainy or baseness, he has indeed lost a considerable motive to virtue; and we may expect that his practice will be answerable to his speculation (Hume 1777/1966, pp. 282–3).

In the contemporary literature, David Brink develops Hume's example and argues that these sorts of cases show that it is conceptually possible for a rational amoralist to make moral judgments without being appropriately motivated by them (e.g., Brink 1989). Although he ultimately tries to defend Conceptual Rationalism against Brink, Smith himself suggests that such apparent cases of rational amoralists aren't "confined to the world of make-believe. There are, after all, real-life sociopaths" (1994, p. 67).

The standard Conceptual Rationalist response to this problem is to maintain that sociopaths or psychopaths do not "*really* make moral judgments at all" (Smith 1994, p. 67). When psychopaths say that it's wrong to hurt people, they are not expressing the same thing that normals do with the same sentence, since psychopaths are not motivated in the right way and thus their words mean something else. Rather, psychopaths use moral terms in an "inverted-commas" sense (Hare 1952). This inverted-commas response has been defended most vigorously by Smith, and it has generated a spirited debate (e.g., Brink 1997, Miller 1996, Smith 1994, 1996, 1997). I want to skirt most of the debate to consider a point at which the inverted-commas response joins an empirical issue.

It is important to be clear about exactly what the inverted-commas claim comes to. If the inverted-commas response is to insulate Conceptual Rationalism from the rational amoralist, then the claim cannot be that it is an empirical fact about psychopaths that they use moral terms in an inverted-commas sense. Rather, the claim must be that it is part of our *concept* of moral judgment that psychopaths do not really make moral judgments, but only 'moral' judgments. Conceptual Rationalism is, after all, supposed to characterize our ordinary moral concepts and intuitions. Indeed, as Smith develops it, Conceptual Rationalism is supposed to be a systematized set of platitudes that characterize the folk concept of morality. Although the project of systematizing the platitudes will presumably require serious analytic resources, the project also has substantive *empirical* checks since the platitudes themselves are supposed to be claims that most people would accept. Hence, an important initial question is, what *do* people think about moral judgments in psychopaths? Since both Conceptual Rationalists and their opponents are heavily invested in the debate, we should be wary of relying on their intuitions about what people think about psychopathic moral judgment. A less loaded alternative is to simply ask people who haven't been trained in the debate. In light of this, I carried out a preliminary study in which I presented philosophically unsophisticated undergraduates with questions about whether a given person really understands moral claims. Subjects were given the following probes:

John is a psychopathic criminal. He is an adult of normal intelligence, but he has no emotional reaction to hurting other people. John has hurt, and indeed killed, other people when he has wanted to steal their money. He says that he knows that hurting others is wrong, but that he just doesn't care if he does things that are wrong. Does John really understand that hurting others is morally wrong?

Bill is a mathematician. He is an adult of normal intelligence, but he has no emotional reaction to hurting other people. Nonetheless, Bill never hurts other people simply because he thinks that it is irrational to hurt others. He thinks that any rational person would be like him and not hurt other people. Does Bill really understand that hurting others is morally wrong?

The responses to these questions were striking – and they ran in exactly the opposite pattern from what Conceptual Rationalism would suggest. Most subjects (nearly 85%) maintained that the psychopath *did* really understand that hurting others is morally wrong, despite the absence of motivation. Neither was this due to an insipid reluctance to deny genuine moral judgment, for, surprisingly, a majority of subjects denied that the mathematician really understood that hurting others is morally wrong.[3] These responses suggest that, at least in some populations, the common conception of psychopaths is precisely that they *really* know the difference between right and wrong, but they don't care about doing what's right. *Prima facie*, this counts as evidence against the Conceptual Rationalist's inverted-commas gambit. For it seems to be a *platitude* that psychopaths really make moral judgments. And if it's a platitude that psychopaths really make moral judgments, it will be difficult to prove that Conceptual Rationalism captures the folk platitudes surrounding moral judgment. This is not to say that there are no responses available to the inverted-commas enthusiast. One might, for instance, maintain that a process of reflective equilibrium would lead people to reject the platitude about psychopathic moral judgment. However, it's important to note that this sort of response is yet another substantive empirical claim, which will not be persuasive without empirical evidence.

There is a more far-reaching empirical threat to Conceptual Rationalism from recent work on philosophical intuitions. Jonathan Weinberg, Steve Stich, and I explored epistemic intuitions in different cultures and socioeconomic groups. We found that there is considerable and surprising variation (both within and across cultures) in folk intuitions about standard epistemological thought experiments (Weinberg *et al.*, 2001). For instance, on a Gettier case, there was a significant difference between the responses of Western students and East Asian students. Although we do not yet have any cross-cultural data on intuitions about meta-ethics, the findings on epistemic intuitions obviously raise the possibility that there might also be considerable variation in intuitions about moral requirements. Thus, not only is it a substantive empirical assumption that the folk platitudes, when systematized, will exclude the platitude about psychopathic moral judgment, it is also a substantive empirical assumption that there is a stable and cross-culturally uniform set of intuitions or platitudes that comprise *the* folk concept of morality.

Thus, it is empirically dubious that there is a single, universal folk concept of morality according to which psychopaths do not make genuine moral judgment. As we will see, there is empirical evidence that indicates that the capacity for moral judgment is seriously disturbed in psychopaths, and they are plausibly regarded as using moral terms in an inverted-commas sense. However, this empirical evidence is of no help to the Conceptual Rationalist. For the problem psychopaths pose for Conceptual Rationalism concerns only the facts about our *concept* of psychopaths, not the facts about psychopaths themselves.

III.   Empirical Rationalism

In addition to rationalist claims about our moral concepts, there is another kind of rationalist claim, which I'll call *Empirical Rationalism*. The basic idea of Empirical Rationalism might be put as follows:

It is an empirical fact that moral judgment in humans is a kind of rational judgment; i.e., our moral judgments derive from our rational faculties or capacities.

In contrast to Conceptual Rationalism, Empirical Rationalism adverts to our actual rational capacities as the basis for our moral judgment, rather than anything about our concept of what a moral judgment is.

In recent years, Peter Singer has developed a version of Empirical Rationalism in the context of the evolutionary problem of how to explain the sense of responsibility:

How can evolutionary theory explain a sense of responsibility to make the entire world a better place? How could those who have such a sense avoid leaving fewer descendants, and thus, over time, being eliminated by the normal workings of the evolutionary process?

Here is one possible answer. Human beings lack the strength of the gorilla, the sharp teeth of the lion, the speed of the cheetah. Brain power is our specialty. The brain is a tool for reasoning, and a capacity to reason helps us to survive, to feed ourselves, and to safeguard our children . . . the ability to reason is a peculiar ability . . . it can take us to conclusions that we had no desire to reach. For reason is like an escalator, leading upwards and out of sight. . . . (Singer 1995, pp. 226–7).

Singer suggests that this natural capacity for reason enables us to "distance ourselves from our own point of view and take on, instead, a wider perspective, ultimately even the point of view of the universe" (Singer 1995, p. 229).

Although few other writers develop Empirical Rationalism in an evolutionary framework, there is reason to think that other rationalists also find Empirical Rationalism attractive. For instance, Thomas Nagel is concerned to dispel subjectivism, which he regards as an empirical hypothesis (1997, pp. 110–11). And Smith tries to explain the behavior of actual miscreants, like the successful criminal, by appealing to failures in the criminal's rational processes (1994, pp. 194–6). In effect, Smith suggests that those who actually exhibit persistent failings in moral judgment suffer from rational failings.

More broadly, rationalists often remark on the amount of actual agreement that is found in moral discourse, and they take this to support a rationalist claim. In discussing values, Nagel writes that "the degree to which agreement can be achieved and social prejudices transcended in the face of strong pressures suggests that something real is being investigated" (1986, p. 148). Similarly, Smith writes, "the empirical fact that moral argument tends to elicit the agreement of our fellows gives us reason to believe that there will be a convergence in our desires under conditions of full rationality. For the best explanation of that tendency is our convergence upon a set of extremely unobvious *a priori* moral truths" (1994, p. 187). These observations about actual agreement on moral issues are not about our *concept* of moral requirements; rather, they are claims about our actual and predicted moral judgments. Coming to agreement about moral issues is supposed to count as evidence that we arrive at our moral judgments through rational means. In this context, the analogy with mathematics is especially appealing. Smith exploits this analogy:

> Why not think . . . that if such a convergence emerged in moral practice then that would itself suggest that these particular moral beliefs, and the corresponding desires, *do* enjoy a privileged rational status? After all, something like such a convergence in mathematical practice lies behind our conviction that mathematical claims enjoy a privileged rational status. So why not think that a like convergence in moral practice would show that moral judgements enjoy the same privileged rational status?. . . . It remains to be seen whether sustained moral argument can elicit the requisite convergence in our moral beliefs, and corresponding desires to make the idea of a moral fact look plausible. . . . Only time will tell (Smith 1993, pp. 408–9).

By exploiting this analogy between moral judgment and mathematical judgment, we can offer a somewhat sharper characterization of Empirical Rationalism:

> The psychological capacities underlying moral judgment are, like the psychological capacities underlying mathematical judgment, rational mechanisms.

If this is right, then all rational creatures should eventually reach agreement about moral claims, as they do about mathematical claims.

According to Empirical Rationalism, then, human moral judgment is a product of reason, just as logic and mathematics are products of reason. That would provide ample justification for thinking that human morality is in fact objective. Because, if human moral judgment derives from our rational faculties, then creatures who have all of the rational faculties that we do (including aliens) should arrive at the same moral views that we do. It's worth emphasizing that this might be true quite independently of whether Conceptual Rationalism is true. It might turn out that our actual moral psychology really is akin in the relevant respects to our actual mathematical psychology, and this might be the case even if it's not part of our *concept* of moral requirement that moral requirements are requirements of rationality. Indeed, platitudes about psychopaths do not pose the slightest objection to the Empirical Rationalist claim that human morality derives from rational cognitive mechanisms. Rather, Empirical Rationalism is, I think, the most promising contender for securing moral objectivism.

IV. Empirical Rationalism and the Psychology of Psychopathy

Contrary to the Conceptual Rationalist claim, it is apparently a folk platitude that psychopaths understand that it is morally wrong to hurt others but don't care. However, recent evidence suggests that psychopaths really do have a defective understanding of moral violations. I'll argue that, ironically, this evidence poses a serious problem for the Empirical Rationalist. For psychopaths' moral judgment making is deeply disturbed, but this seems not to be the result of a defect in their rational capacities. So, while Conceptual Rationalism is at odds with our concept of psychopathy, Empirical Rationalism is at odds with the *psychology* of psychopathy.

Moral judgment in psychopaths

In order to explain the nature of the psychopath's deficit in moral judgment, we will need to review some recent work in moral psychology. In the empirical literature, the capacity for moral judgment has perhaps been most directly approached by exploring the basic capacity to distinguish moral violations (e.g., hitting another person) from conventional violations (e.g., playing with your food). This tradition in psychology began with the work of Elliot Turiel and has flourished over the last two decades (e.g., Turiel *et al.* 1987, Dunn & Munn 1987, Smetana & Braeges 1990, Nucci 1986). The easiest way to see the import of the data on moral judgment is to consider how subjects distinguish between prototypical examples of moral violations and protypical examples of conventional violations. Prototypical moral violations include pulling hair, pushing, and hitting. The examples of conventional violations that have been studied are much more varied. They include violations of school rules (e.g., talking out of turn), violations of etiquette (e.g., drinking soup out of a bowl), violations of family rules (e.g., not clearing one's dishes). What is striking about this literature is that, from a young age, children distinguish the cases of moral violations from the conventional violations on a number of dimensions. For instance, children tend to think that moral transgressions are generally less permissible and more serious than conventional transgressions. And the explanations for why moral transgressions are wrong are given in terms of fairness and harm to victims, whereas the explanation for why conventional transgressions are wrong is given in terms of social acceptability. Further, conventional rules, unlike moral rules, are viewed as dependent on authority. For instance, if the teacher at another school has no rule against chewing gum, children will judge that it's not wrong for a person to chew gum at that school; but even if the teacher at another school has no rule against hitting, children claim that it's still wrong for a person to hit at that school. Indeed, a fascinating study on Amish teenagers indicates that moral wrongs are not even regarded as dependent on *God's* authority. Nucci (1986) found that 100% of a group of Amish teenagers said that if God had made no rule against working on Sunday, it would not be wrong to work on Sunday. However, more than 80% of these subjects said that even if God had made no rule about hitting, it would still be wrong to hit.

R. James Blair has recently tested psychopaths and non-psychopathic control criminals on this basic capacity to distinguish moral and conven-tional violations (Blair 1995; see also Blair 1997). All the subjects were in prison at the time of the testing. To test the subjects' understanding of permissibility, they were asked,

"Was it O.K. for X to do Y?"

To test the subjects' judgment of seriousness, they were asked,

"Was it bad for X to do [the transgression]?" and

"On a scale of one to ten, how bad was it for X to do [the transgression]?"

The subjects were also asked,

"Why was it bad for X to do [the transgression]?"

to examine the subjects' justification categories. Finally, the subjects were asked:

"Now what if the teacher said before the lesson, before X did [the transgression], that 'At this school anybody can Y if they want to. Anybody can Y.'"

They were then asked,

"Would it be O.K. for X to do Y if the teacher says X can?"

This question tested whether the subjects viewed the rule as authority-dependent (Blair 1995, pp. 16–17). Blair found that control criminals, like normal adults and children, made a significant moral/conventional distinction on permissibility, seriousness, and authority contingence; psy-chopaths, on the other hand, didn't make a significant moral/conventional distinction on any of these dimensions. Furthermore, psy-chopaths were much less likely than the control criminals to justify rules with reference to the vic-tim's welfare. Rather, psychopaths typically gave conventional-type justifications for all transgres-sions (e.g., "it's not the done thing" [the subjects were British]). This failure to distinguish moral from conventional violations is illustrated in the remark taken from Ted Bundy at the beginning of Section II, where he notes that it is wrong to jaywalk, wrong to rob a bank, wrong to break into other people's houses, and wrong to drive without a license (Michaud & Aynesworth 1989, p. 116). Bundy doesn't seem to distinguish between the radically different kinds of wrongs involved here, mixing moral and conventional violations indiscriminately. It seems, then, that although there is a sense in which psychopaths do know right from wrong, they don't know (conventional) wrong from (moral) wrong. We would, in fact, have some justification in maintaining that they use moral terms only in an inverted-commas sense.

What's Wrong with Psychopaths?

The fact that the most celebrated class of amoralists have a defective capacity for moral judgment provides some support to the claim that moral judgment is closely linked with motivation. For we know that psychopaths aren't motivated by moral prohibitions the way normal people are. But one then needs to ask what the cognitive mechanisms are that produce this correlation between moral judgment and moral motivation, and what cognitive mechanisms are disrupted in psychopathy. It is at that point that we begin to see the problem posed for the Empirical Rationalist. For there is no easy way for Empirical Rationalists to explain the psychopath's deficit, but there is a non-rationalist explanation that has some independent support.

Rationalist accounts of the psychopath's deficit in moral judgment

One simple rationalist explanation of the problem with psychopaths would be that, although psychopaths have the relevant psychological faculties, they haven't been exposed to the right reasoning patterns. They just need to be convinced, presumably by argument, of the claims of morality. However, this option looks particularly unpromising, for it turns out that psychopathy is remarkably recalcitrant. Robert Hare, who devised the standard diagnostic measure for psychopathy, notes that

> many writers on the subject have commented that the shortest chapter in any book on psychopathy should be the one on treatment. A one-sentence conclusion such as, "No effective treatment has been found," or, "Nothing works," is the common wrap-up to scholarly reviews of the literature (Hare 1993, p. 194).

As a result, it would seem unduly optimistic to think that a course in moral philosophy would do the trick.

A more interesting line of rationalist response is that psychopaths really do lack some crucial faculty of reason that is intact in those who perform normally on the moral-judgment task. In order for the Empirical Rationalist to make this option plausible, he would need some principled account of what kind of rational abilities underlie the capacity for making the moral/conventional distinction, then show that those rational abilities are missing in the psychopath. The rationalist would also need to show that this rational defect is not present in groups that can make the moral/conventional distinction. This makes the rationalist's project particularly challenging. For the moral/conventional distinction is made by individuals with a wide range of cognitive abilities and disabilities. For instance, from a surprisingly young age, children are able to distinguish between moral and conventional violations. Smetana and Braeges (1990) claim that children appreciate the distinction around the third birthday. Recent research indicates that children with autism and children with Downs Syndrome, also make the moral/conventional distinction (Blair 1996). Further, as noted earlier, non-psychopathic criminals do make the moral/conventional distinction (Blair 1995).

The project of characterizing a rational deficit in psychopaths that might underlie a moral deficit has seldom been addressed directly, and there are few detailed proposals for a rational defect in psychopaths. However, there are some suggestions in the literature that might be interpreted as rationalist hypotheses. I'll consider three possibilities.

Perspective-taking abilities

One possibility is that moral understanding depends on perspective-taking abilities, which are commonly construed as rational cognitive abilities (e.g., Piaget 1966). Nagel seems to suggest something along these lines: "The principle of altruism . . . is connected with the conception of oneself as merely one person among others. It arises from the capacity to view oneself simultaneously as 'I' and as *someone* – an impersonally specifiable individual" (1970, p. 19). Elsewhere, he writes, "once the objective step is taken, the possibility is also open for the recognition of values and reasons that are independent of one's personal perspective and have force for anyone who can view the world impersonally, as a place that contains him" (1986, p. 140). So, perhaps the rationalist can maintain that the problem with psychopaths is that they have a defect in their ability to take a perspective that is not their own. However, there is no reason to think that psychopaths have such a deficit. Indeed, psychopaths seem to be quite capable of taking the perspective of others (e.g., Blair *et al.* 1996). That's presumably part of what makes them so successful at manipulating others. Furthermore, the fact that autistic children can make the moral/conventional distinction poses a further obstacle for the perspective-taking proposal. It's well known that autistic children have an impaired capacity for perspective taking. The most direct evidence for this comes from Baron-Cohen and colleagues (1985), who found that most autistic children have difficulty understanding that other people can have beliefs that differ from their own. Yet autistic children do *not* have the deficit in moral understanding found in psychopaths. So it seems that appealing to the capacity for perspective taking does not provide a good explanation for the psychopath's deficit in moral judgment.

General rational abilities

Another possible account of the problem with psychopaths is that they suffer from some general deficit in rationality. It is notoriously difficult to characterize rationality adequately, but in the literature in ethics, several writers have appealed to the idealization of a fully rational individual. Smith largely adopts Williams's (1981) account, according to which a fully rational agent must have no false beliefs, all relevant true beliefs, and the agent must deliberate correctly (1994, p. 156). Smith adds that correct deliberation must include the capacity to determine "whether our desires are *systematically justifiable.* . . . we can try to decide whether or not some particular underived desire that we have or might have is a desire to do something that is itself non-derivatively desirable" (1994, pp. 158–9). So, perhaps the rationalist might say that psychopaths deviate too far from the fully rational agent to understand morality.

Although it's *possible* that psychopaths have a general deficit in reasoning, to make this proposal plausible, one would need to characterize the general deficit in psychopathy and explain how this general deficit in reasoning is responsible for psychopaths' deficiencies in moral judgment. Again, this would have to be shown to be a general rational deficit in psychopaths that is not present in the groups that can draw the moral/conventional distinction. And it seems quite unlikely that psychopaths diverge from the ideal of the fully rational individual more than three-year-old children, children with autism, and children with Downs syndrome.

Intellectual arrogance

Smith does offer a more specific explanation of the rational defect in the successful criminal, which might be extended into a rationalist account of psychopathy. His suggestion is that the successful criminal suffers from "intellectual arrogance." Smith writes:

> the successful criminal thinks that he has a normative reason to gain wealth no matter what the cost to others, and he sticks with this opinion despite the fact that virtually everyone disagrees with him. Moreover, he does so without good reason. For he can give no account of why his own opinion about what fully rational creatures would want should be privileged over the opinion of others; he can give no account of why his opinion should be right, others' opinions should be wrong. He can give no such account because he rejects the very idea that the folk possess between them a stock of wisdom about such matters against which each person's opinions should be tested. And yet, ultimately, this is the only court of appeal there is for claims about what we have normative reason to do. The successful criminal thus seems to me to suffer from the all too common vice of *intellectual arrogance*. He therefore does indeed suffer from a 'failure to consider or appreciate certain arguments', for he doesn't feel the force of arguments that come from *others* at all (1994, pp. 195–6).

The claim that the successful criminal suffers from intellectual arrogance is a perfectly sensible hypothesis, but if this hypothesis is supposed to explain why psychopaths don't grasp the moral/conventional distinction, one would need to provide evidence that this kind of intellectual arrogance distinguishes psychopaths from non-psychopathic criminals, who do make the moral/conventional distinction. And there's little evidence on the issue. Certainly, there's no reason to think that psychopaths are intellectually arrogant in the sense that they won't rely on the knowledge of others. Psychopaths are perfectly willing to believe from their peers that arsenic is poison, that eating too much fat will make you over-weight, and so on. So to appeal to intellectual arrogance generally looks unprincipled. Furthermore, Blair's data themselves suggest that psychopaths do recognize that some things are right and some things are wrong. What psychopaths apparently fail to appreciate is that some prohibited actions (e.g., hitting another) have a different status than other prohibited actions (e.g., speaking out of turn). So they do seem to be capable of learning from their peers, and hence don't exhibit a general intellectual arrogance that would explain their deficit in moral judgment.

Affect-based accounts of the psychopath's deficit in moral judgment

The point of the foregoing was not to provide a knock-down argument against the possibility of finding a rational deficit in psychopaths that would explain their deficit in moral understanding. Rather, the point is to bring out the difficulty of such a project – the Empirical Rationalist needs to find a rational defect in psychopaths that explains their deficit in moral judgment; and this deficit should not be present in autistic individuals, young children, control criminals, and a host of other rationally idiosyncratic humans who don't share the psychopath's deficit in moral judgment. Now I'd like to present further reason to be skeptical that Empirical Rationalism can make a compelling response to the problem. For there are *affective* deficit accounts that are supported by independent evidence. And, if one of these accounts is shown to be right, then Empirical Rationalism will have been refuted.

It's difficult to find a rational defect that is present in psychopaths but absent in the groups of individuals that do draw the moral/conventional distinction. Recent research indicates that there is a salient psychological difference between psychopaths and the other groups, but it's not a difference in rational capacities. Rather, it's a difference in *affective response*. Blair and colleagues explored subjects' affective responses to cues of distress in others. They showed pictures of distressed faces and pictures of threatening faces to a wide range of subject populations. Over a series of studies, they found that normal children, autistic children and non-psychopathic criminals all show considerably heightened physiological response both to threatening stimuli and to cues that another is in distress; psychopaths, on the other hand, show considerably heightened physiological response to threatening stimuli, but show abnormally low responsiveness to distress cues (Blair *et al.* 1997; Blair 1999, see also Yirmiya *et al.* 1992). This finding of a distinctive affective deficit in psychopathy might provide the basis for explaining the psychopath's difficulties with the moral/conventional task.

Blair's own explanation of the psychopath's deficit in moral judgment appeals to what he calls a "Violence Inhibition Mechanism" or VIM (Blair 1995). The idea derives from Lorenz's (1966) proposal that social animals have evolved mechanisms to inhibit intra-species aggression. When a conspecific displays submission cues, the attacker stops. Blair suggests that there's something analogous in our cognitive systems, the VIM, and that this mechanism underlies both our response to distress cues and our capacity to distinguish moral from conventional violations. This mechanism is damaged in psychopathy, according to Blair, and this explains the psychopath's failure on the moral/conventional task. In normals, the VIM produces negative affect which generates moral judgment. Since psychopaths have a defective VIM, their moral judgment is correspondingly defective.

I think that there are a number of problems with Blair's VIM account of moral judgment and psychopathy (Nichols, 2002). On the model that I prefer, the capacity for drawing the moral/conventional distinction depends on two quite different mechanisms. First, there is a body of information, a normative "theory" that specifies a set of harm-based normative violations. But the data indicate that affect also plays a role in mediating performance on the moral/conventional task, and that affective response seems to infuse norms with a special status (Nichols, 2002). Since psychopaths have a deficiency in their affective response to harm in others, this plausibly explains why they fail to treat harm norms as distinctive (Nichols 2001, 2002).

There are serious questions about the relative merits of these two accounts of the capacities underlying moral judgment. However, for purposes of evaluating Empirical Rationalism, these issues don't need to be resolved. The important point is that on both of these accounts, an affective mechanism plays a critical role in the capacity for moral judgment. If anything much like these affect-based accounts is right, then it looks as though we have a non-rationalist explanation of the psychopath's deficit in moral judgment. For, on these accounts, the psychopath's deficit in moral judgment depends on a deficit in an affective mechanism, not on deficits in rationality. The evidence on psychopaths thus seems not to support Empirical Rationalism at all, but rather, rationalism's rival, sentimentalism. Apparently emotional responsiveness plays a key role in moral judgment after all.

V. Conclusion

Moral rationalism has seemed the most promising way to secure moral objectivism. I've suggested that rationalism can be developed in two quite different ways, as a conceptual claim or as an empirical claim, and psychopaths threaten both claims. Contrary to Conceptual Rationalist claims, psychopaths are commonly regarded as rational individuals who really make moral judgments but are not motivated by them. Recent evidence provides good reason to think that the common conception of psychopaths is wrong, for the capacity for moral judgment is apparently seriously disturbed in psychopathy. However, this provides no help to the Conceptual Rationalist and in fact seriously undermines Empirical Rationalism. For the defective capacity for moral judgment in psychopathy seems not to derive from a rational deficit, but rather from a deficit to an affective system.

There is a wicked irony in all this. The psychopath is often considered to be the epitome of evil, and now the facts about psychopaths seem to pose serious problems for the most promising avenues for securing moral objectivity. So, the

very individuals whose actions elicit our strongest condemnation provide evidence against theories that would allow us to regard moral violations as objectively wrong.

Notes

1   One might try to defend Conceptual Rationalism without committing oneself to the Practicality Requirement. However, the most prominent and influential versions of Conceptual Rationalism are tied to the Practicality Requirement, and I will simply assume in what follows that Conceptual Rationalism is committed to the Practicality Requirement.
2   A note is in order about Bundy's use of the third person at the beginning of the quotation. In his interviews with Michaud and Aynesworth (1989), Bundy initially refused to talk about the murders he was accused of committing. The interviewers suggested that, to avoid incriminating himself, Bundy use the third person to talk about the murders. Bundy agreed to this arrangement, and as a result, many of his statements are presented in the third person, even though they are presumably about Bundy himself.
3   A χ^2 goodness-of-fit test shows that the proportion of subjects saying that the psychopath did understand differs significantly from what would be expected by chance ($\chi^2(N = 26, df = 1) = 12.462, p < .001$, two-tailed). In addition, there was a statistically significant difference in subjects' responses to the psychopath and mathematician cases (which were counterbalanced) (McNemar's test, $N = 26, p < .025$, two-tailed).

References

Baron-Cohen, Simon, Leslie, Alan & Firth, Uta, 1985, "Does the Autistic Child Have a 'Theory of Mind'?" *Cognition*, 21, 37–46.
Blair, Robert James, 1995, "A Cognitive Developmental Approach to Morality: Investigating the Psychopath," *Cognition*, 57, 1–29.
Blair, Robert James, 1996, "Brief Report: Morality in the Autistic Child," *Journal of Autism and Developmental Disorders*, 26, 571–9.
Blair, Robert James, 1997, "Moral Reasoning and the Child with Psychopathic Tendencies," *Personality and Individual Differences*, 26, 731–9.
Blair, Robert James, 1999, "Psychophysiological Responsiveness to the Distress of Others in Children with Autism," *Personality and Individual Differences*, 26, 477–85.

Blair, Robert James; Jones, Lawrence; Clark, Fiona; Smith, Margaret, 1997, "The Psychopathic Individual: A lack of Responsiveness to Distress Cues?" *Psychophysiology*, 34, 192–98.

Blair, Robert James; Sellars, Carol; Strickland, Ian; Clark, Fiona; Williams, A.; Smith, Margaret & Jones, Lawrence, 1996, "Theory of Mind in the Psychopath," *Journal of Forensic Psychiatry*, 7, 15–25.

Brink, David, 1989, *Moral Realism and the Foundations of Ethics*, Cambridge University Press.

Brink, David, 1997, "Moral Motivation," *Ethics*, 108.

Darwall, Stephen, 1983, *Impartial Reason*, Ithaca, NY: Cornell University Press.

Dunn, Judy & Munn, Penny, 1987, "Development of Justification in Disputes with Mother and Sibling," *Developmental Psychology*, 23, 791–8.

Gewirth, Alan, 1978, *Reason and Morality*, University of Chicago Press.

Hare, Richard M., 1952, *The Language of Morals*, Oxford: Oxford University Press.

Hare, Robert D., 1993, *Without Conscience: The Disturbing World of the Psychopaths Among Us*, New York: Pocket Books.

Hume, David, 1777/1966, *Enquiry Concerning the Principles of Morals*, La Salle, IL: Open Court.

Korsgaard, Christine, 1986, "Skepticism About Practical Reason," *Journal of Philosophy*, 5–25.

Lewis, David, 1970, "How to Define Theoretical Terms," *Journal of Philosophy*, 427–46.

Lewis, David, 1972, "Psychophysical and Theoretical Identifications," *Australasian Journal of Philosophy*, 249–58.

Lorenz, Konrad, 1966, *On Aggression*, New York: Harcourt, Brace, Jovanovich.

Michaud, Stephen & Aynesworth, Hugh, 1989, *Ted Bundy: Conversations with a Killer*, New York: New American Library.

Miller, Alexander, 1996, "An Objection to Smith's Argument for Internalism," *Analysis* 56, 169–74.

Nagel, Thomas, 1970, *The Possibility of Altruism*, Princeton, NJ: Princeton University Press.

Nagel, Thomas, 1986, *The View from Nowhere*, Oxford University Press.

Nagel, Thomas, 1997, *The Last Word*, Oxford University Press.

Nichols, Shaun, 2001, "Mindreading and the Cognitive Architecture of Altruistic Motivation," *Mind & Language*, 16, 425–55.

Nichols, Shaun, 2002, "Norms with Feeling: Towards a Psychological Account of Moral Judgment," *Cognition*, 84, 221–36.

Nucci, Larry, 1986, "Children's Conceptions of Morality, Social Conventions and Religious prescription," in C. Harding, (ed.), *Moral Dilemmas: Philosophical and Psychological Reconsiderations of the Development of Moral Reasoning*. Chicago: Precedent Press.

Piaget, Jean, 1966, *The Psychology of Moral Development: The Nature and Validity of Moral Stages*, New York: Free Press.

Singer, Peter, 1995, *How Are We to Live*, Buffalo, NY: Prometheus Books.

Smetana, Judith & Braeges, Judith, 1990, "The Development of Toddlers' Moral and Conventional Judgements," *Merrill-Palmer Quarterly*, 36, 329–46.

Smith, Michael, 1993, "Realism," in P. Singer (ed.), *A Companion to Ethics*. Cambridge, MA: Blackwell, 399–410.

Smith, Michael, 1994, *The Moral Problem*, Oxford: Blackwell.

Smith, Michael, 1996, "The Argument for Internalism: Reply to Miller," *Analysis*, 56, 175–84.

Smith, Michael, 1997, "In Defense of *The Moral Problem*: A Reply to Brink, Copp, and Sayre-McCord," *Ethics*, 108, 84–119.

Stich, Stephen, 1992, "What is a Theory of Mental Representation?" *Mind*, 101, 243–61.

Turiel, Elliot, Killen, Melanie, & Helwig, Charles, 1987, "Morality: Its Structure, Functions, and Vagaries," in J. Kagan & S. Lamb (eds.), *The Emergence of Morality in Young Children*. Chicago: University of Chicago Press, 155–244.

Weinberg, Jonathan, Nichols, Shaun, and Stich, Stephen, 2001, "Normativity and Epistemic Intuitions," *Philosophical Topics*, 29, 429–60.

Williams, Bernard, 1981, "Internal and External Reasons," in his *Moral Luck*, Cambridge: Cambridge University Press.

Yirmiya, Nurit, Sigman, Marian, Kasari, Connie, & Mundy, Peter, 1992, "Empathy and Cognition in High-functioning Children with Autism," *Child Development*, 63, 150–60.

Part II
Altruism & Egoism

Introduction

Thomas Nadelhoffer and Shaun Nichols

On July 22, 2009, John McDonald stepped through the sunroof of a burning SUV to save a trapped child. McDonald wasn't a firefighter or a police officer. It wasn't his job to save people – McDonald is a furniture maker. Yet he risked his life to save a stranger. Why did he do this? His mother's explanation is simple and pleasing: "John loves people. He cares about people." A cynic might offer the much darker explanation that McDonald did it because he thought he would succeed unharmed and would reap the rewards of being labeled a hero. Acts like McDonald's are typically regarded as *altruistic*. We can think of altruism as "unselfish" concern for the welfare of others. But is such a thing possible? Can a person have a motive that isn't ultimately based in self-interest? And even if it's possible to have such a motive for others' welfare, do people actually have them? Finally, if we do have such unselfish motives, what is the psychological basis of them? These questions about altruistic motives are, fundamentally, questions about human nature.[1]

Plato (428–348 BCE) was one of the first philosophers to discuss the relationship between self-interest and moral behavior. In *The Republic*, he offers a striking thought experiment that bears on the issue. His character Glaucon recounts the myth of Gyges, who found a ring that could make him invisible. Gyges himself used this ring to take over the kingdom. What if you could make yourself invisible? Would you still behave fairly towards other people? Or would you only be interested in taking advantage of people? One interesting feature of Gyges' story is that it suggests that we are only nice to others because we either benefit from helping them or we are worried about what others will think of us if we don't help. After all, Glaucon claims that before Gyges found the ring, he was widely thought to be a kind and virtuous person. Yet, as soon as the ring of invisibility enabled Gyges to take advantage of others with impunity that is precisely what he did. Would the ring of invisibility have the same effect on you? At the end of the day, are you altruistic because you genuinely want to help others or do you help others only because something's in it for you?

Thomas Hobbes (1588–1679) is the philosopher most strongly identified with the stark view that there are no truly altruistic motives. Hobbes was an English philosopher with a bleak view of the human condition in general. By nature, Hobbes thought, each of us is inclined to engage in war with everyone else. Moreover, entering into community with other people is not intrinsically pleasing. Society forms because we want to avoid a terrible war of all against all. It is thus out of self-interest that we enter into civil society. I am willing to be in society with others only because it benefits *me*.

Some passages from Hobbes seem to say that *all* action is driven by self-interest. For instance, in an early work, Hobbes writes, "whatsoever is voluntarily done, is done for some good to him that wills it."[2] Such a claim is naturally associated with *psychological egoism*, the view that all of our motives are ultimately self-interested. Psychological egoism seems to exclude entirely the possibility of altruism. If all of my motives are ultimately about *me*, then it follows that none of them is about *you* (or anything other than myself).

Of course Hobbes is well aware that people sometimes help others, for example, in acts of charity. Hobbes has a range of explanations for such actions available to him. For instance, Hobbes notes that a person might give to charity because it expresses his power. But there are additional explanations too. Indeed, there's a revealing story from Hobbes' own life. Hobbes came upon a sick old man asking for alms, and Hobbes pulled money from his pocket, giving it to the old man. One of the witnesses of this event asked Hobbes to explain his charitable action, if all actions are driven by self-interest. Hobbes replied that he gave the old man money because, "I was in *pain* to consider the miserable condition of the old man; and now my alms, giving him some relief, doth also ease me."[3]

Joseph Butler (1692–1752) thoroughly rejects this picture of human motivation as entirely self-interested. First, he challenges Hobbes' attempt to explain emotions like compassion (and, by extension, charitable actions) in terms of self-interest. Then he goes on to challenge the very idea of psychological egoism. Butler acknowledges that self-interest ("self-love" is the term he uses) is part of our nature. But it's a confusion, he maintains, to think that all of our actions flow from self-interest. Of course every desire I have is *my* desire. That is a trivial, uninteresting fact (compare "every toe I have is my toe"). What is not trivial is the distinction between actions that are *directed at* one's own interests and actions that aren't. Sometimes my actions do spring from self-interest, as when I just want to do something because it will increase my wealth. But other times my actions do not seem to be directed at my self-interest. Butler uses the example of *revenge* to illustrate the point. I might seek revenge on someone even though I know that it will only deplete my resources and put me at risk of retaliation. In that case, my motive for revenge seems positively to go *against* my self-interest.

Even if Butler is right to reject psychological egoism, that does not yet show that people have motives in favor of the welfare of others. It might be that while we do have motives that aren't self-interested, none of those motives are directed at benefiting others. **Hutcheson** argues in favor of such warm motives towards others, providing a radically different picture than Hobbes. Hutcheson maintains that we behave kindly towards others because we have natural feelings of benevolence or love towards them. According to Hutcheson, benevolence is a kind of desire – one that is directed at the happiness of another. This desire can't be self-interested, else it doesn't even count as benevolence.

Why believe that we have such a disinterested desire for others' welfare? One important component here is the emotion of *compassion* that we feel towards other people. When we witness others' plight, we often feel compassion toward them, and that motivates us to help. At this juncture Hobbes might say that our motivation in such cases is purely to alleviate our own suffering. Hence, this again can be rendered consistent with a purely self-interested account of why we help. Hutcheson counters by saying if our sole intention were really just to relieve our own suffering, we could more easily do this by fleeing the offending scene. But, Hutcheson says, we don't do this, which suggests that the Hobbesian explanation is inadequate. Hutcheson goes on to give an ingenious thought experiment to push the point home. Imagine that you are distressed at the sight of someone suffering and God offers either to stop the person's suffering or to "blot out all memory of the person in distress." If your motive is simply to relieve your own pain, these should be equally attractive options. But, Hutcheson claims, of course we would ask that the person's suffering be stopped, and this shows that we do, in these cases, have a desire that really is directed at the welfare of the other person.

Hutcheson's defense of altruistic motives was done in the absence of any experimental evidence. But in the twentieth century, the social psychologist **Daniel Batson** ran experiments that bear directly on some of Hutcheson's speculations. In one experiment, Batson gave subjects the chance to help a classmate who had been in a car wreck. Recall Hutcheson's remark that if our motive to help others was entirely to relieve our own pain, then we should just run away from the scene. Batson's experiments exploit something very like this idea. For half of the people in Batson's experiment, it was easy to escape the situation without helping; for the other half, it was difficult to escape without helping. In addition, for some of the participants, Batson induced compassion or empathy for the victim (e.g., by having the participants imagine the perspective of the victim). As he had predicted, Batson found that for participants who felt empathy, it didn't matter whether it was easy or hard to escape. The vast majority offered to help. This fits perfectly with Hutcheson's view. Once our compassion is triggered, we will be motivated to help the other person, not primarily to get rid of our own pain, but because we have a genuine concern for the welfare of others.

In light of Batson's experiments, one might quite naturally want to understand how and why humans might have come to engage in altruistic behavior in the first place. After all, there are often serious costs and risks that are associated with helping others. So, while it is obvious why we might help our friends and family members, it is entirely unclear why we sometimes help strangers who we will likely never see again. From a biological perspective, humans are perhaps the most helpful creatures of all. We not only help strangers, but we also often help non-human animals. This kind of hyper-helpfulness cries out for an evolutionary explanation.

The anthropologist **Robert Trivers** developed one of the more important evolutionary models of altruistic behavior. In an effort to explain the biological tendency to help unrelated others in these contexts, Trivers developed the theory of reciprocal altruism according to which "under certain conditions natural selection favors . . . altruistic behaviors because in the long run they benefit the organism performing them." According to Trivers, altruists eventually tend to outperform non-altruists in terms of both reproduction and survival. On his view, by helping a stranger, I make it more likely that I will likewise be helped down the road when I find myself in a similar situation. After all, people are usually willing to help those who have helped them. Consider, for instance, the last time a friend asked you to help her move. If she was a helpful and dependable friend, you were likely inclined to help. If, on the other hand, she was generally selfish and unhelpful, you were likely not inclined to help.

One worry that arises on this front is that the kind of helping behavior that Trivers is trying to explain does not seem to comport with what moral philosophers traditionally had in mind when they talked about the possibility (or lack thereof) of altruism. On the one hand, we might be interested in whether a particular instance of helping behavior actually confers an advantage to the organism being helped while conferring a cost to the organism doing the helping. On the other hand, we might be interested in whether a person's *motives* for helping were driven by a genuine concern for the well-being of others rather than a self-interested desire to be helped downstream.

In *Unto Others*, philosophers **Elliott Sober** and **David Sloan Wilson** helpfully call these two kinds of altruism evolutionary altruism and psychological altruism, respectively. Having drawn this distinction, they then go on to argue that evolution has furnished humans with a tendency to engage in both kinds of altruistic behavior – that is, not only do we sometimes increase the fitness of non-relatives at a cost to ourselves, but we sometimes do so out of a genuine concern for their well-being. Moreover, they suggest that both types of altruism can be explained in terms of group selection – that is, the view that some traits or behaviors can spread in a population because of the benefits they bestow on the group, regardless of whether these traits enhance the fitness of any given individuals within the group.

According to Sober and Wilson, despite the fact that group selection started falling out of favor among evolutionary theorists in the 1960s, there is still some important explanatory work for it to do. As they say, "even if the gene is the unit of replication, it remains to be decided whether some genes evolve because they code for traits that benefit groups" (p. 189). On their view, group selection was a "strong force in human evolution" that operated via intergroup competition, warfare, and cultural transmission. Both the creation and the enforcement of social norms play an important role in Sober and Wilson's argument. By creating social norms and attaching costs to non-compliance, we are purportedly able to incentivize otherwise altruistic behavior. But given that compliance with the norm has thereby been rendered selfish, where does the altruism come into the picture? Sober and Wilson suggest that punishing non-compliance is itself altruistic since it imposes a cost on both those who punish and those who are punished. However, so long as this system of enforceable norms yields more benefits for the group than it does costs, groups that establish these norms will do better than those that do not. Sober and Wilson suggest this framework allows us to explain both evolutionary altruism and psychological altruism. On their view, group selection sheds lights on how humans were able to escape the clutches of egoism and embrace altruistic behavior. By eschewing the pure self-interestedness that was central to previous evolutionary models of morality, Sober and Wilson lay the groundwork for a rich and illuminating way of looking at human nature.

Psychologist **Barry Schwartz** is similarly interested in breaking the spell of what he calls "methodological individualism" and "psychological atomism" (p. 314). He observes that once scientists and philosophers adopt an egoistic framework, altruism becomes a puzzle that needs to be either explained or explained away. However, Schwartz suggests that we should resist the temptation to filter our view of human nature through the distorting lens of egoism. On his view, the well-worn strategy of trying to ferret out the selfish motives that purportedly undergird every otherwise altruistic act is a mistake that clouds our psychological, philosophical, and economic theories. Moreover, Schwartz suggests that not only does the assumption of egoism color our theories of human nature, but he also believes that it becomes a self-fulfilling prophecy – that is, the assumption of egoism tends to make us less altruistic. In an effort to beat back this creeping egoism, Schwartz sets out to highlight the important role that altruism plays in human behavior by examining the data from psychology. In short, Schwartz tries to establish that altruism is not a conceptual or empirical impossibility but rather a ubiquitous feature of human society. If he is right about this, then it turns out that the egoistic path that was first paved by Plato's Myth of Gyges and later elaborated upon by Hobbes and others may have actually misled philosophers and psychologists for the better part of two millennia.

Questions for Further Study

- Is it possible to do something altruistic if the action also gives you pleasure?
- If altruism is facilitated by empathy, what would this suggest about the extent to which people would be altruistic towards people in distant countries?
- If we have only weak altruistic motives towards people in distant countries, does this suggest that our moral obligations to those people are correspondingly weak?
- How does one bridge the gap between descriptive accounts of what human nature is like and "normative" accounts of our moral obligations?
- Is altruism really a puzzle to be explained away or is it a ubiquitous phenomenon?
- If altruism is relatively rare, in what ways might it still be important whether altruism exists at all?
- Is group selection a viable explanatory mechanism or is it undermined by the empirical and conceptual criticisms that have been put forward?
- Is altruism possible in the absence of enforceable social norms?

Notes

[1] There is a related issue in normative ethics concerning whether the morally correct action is always the one that benefits others, not oneself. However, even if there is an altruistic element in human nature, it is a separate question whether the right thing to do is always the altruistic one.

[2] Hobbes, *Philosophical Rudiments Concerning Government and Society* (1651) [originally published in Latin as *De Cive* (1642)], Chapter II, paragraph 8.

[3] Recounted in John Aubrey's *Brief Lives*.

Suggested Readings

Axelrod, R. (1981). The emergence of cooperation among egoists. *The American Political Science Review*, 75, 306–18.

Axelrod, R. (1984). *The Evolution of Cooperation*, New York: Basic Books.

Batson, C.D. (1987). Prosocial behavior: Is it ever truly altruistic? In L. Berkowitz (ed.), *Advances in*

Experimental Social Psychology. New York: Academic Press, pp. 65–122.

Binmore, K. (2005). *Natural Justice*. New York: Oxford University Press.

Boyd, R. and Lorberbaum, J. (1987). No pure strategy is evolutionarily stable in the repeated Prisoner's Dilemma game. *Nature*, 327, 58–9.

Broad, C.D. (1971). Egoism as a theory of human motives. In C.D. Broad, *Broad's Critical Essays in Moral Philosophy*, London: George Allen and Unwin.

Feinberg, J. (1978). Psychological egoism. In J. Feinberg, *Reason and Responsibility*, 4th (and other) edn. Belmont: Wadsworth.

Maynard Smith, J. (1978). The evolution of behavior. *Scientific American*, 239, 176–92.

Slote, M.A. (1964). An empirical basis for psychological egoism. *Journal of Philosophy*, 61, 530–7.

Wilson, D.S. and Sober, E. (1994). Reintroducing group selection to the human behavioral sciences. *Behavioral and Brain Sciences*, 17, 585–654.

10

Republic
Book II

Plato

Socrates – Glaucon

WITH these words I was thinking that I had made an end of the discussion; but the end, in truth, proved to be only a beginning. For Glaucon, who is always the must pugnacious of men, was dissatisfied at Thrasymachus' retirement; he wanted to have the battle out. So he said to me: Socrates, do you wish really to persuade us, or only to seem to have persuaded us, that to be just is always better than to be unjust?

I should wish really to persuade you, I replied, if I could.

Then you certainly have not succeeded. Let me ask you now: – How would you arrange goods – are there not some which we welcome for their own sakes, and independently of their consequences, as, for example, harmless pleasures and enjoyments, which delight us at the time, although nothing follows from them?

I agree in thinking that there is such a class, I replied.

Is there not also a second class of goods, such as knowledge, sight, health, which are desirable not only in themselves, but also for their results?

Certainly, I said.

And would you not recognize a third class, such as gymnastic, and the care of the sick, and the physician's art; also the various ways of money-making – these do us good but we regard them as disagreeable; and no one would choose them for their own sakes, but only for the sake of some reward or result which flows from them?

There is, I said, this third class also. But why do you ask?

Because I want to know in which of the three classes you would place justice?

In the highest class, I replied, – among those goods which he who would be happy desires both for their own sake and for the sake of their results.

Then the many are of another mind; they think that justice is to be reckoned in the troublesome class, among goods which are to be pursued for the sake of rewards and of reputation, but in themselves are disagreeable and rather to be avoided.

I know, I said, that this is their manner of thinking, and that this was the thesis which Thrasymachus was maintaining just now, when he censured justice and praised injustice. But I am too stupid to be convinced by him.

I wish, he said, that you would hear me as well as him, and then I shall see whether you and I agree.

From *The Republic* By Plato Written 360 B.C.E. Translated by Benjamin Jowett.

Moral Psychology: Historical and Contemporary Readings, edited by Thomas Nadelhoffer, Eddy Nahmias, and Shaun Nichols. © 2010 Blackwell Publishing Ltd except for editorial material and organization © 2010 Thomas Nadelhoffer, Eddy Nahmias, and Shaun Nichols.

For Thrasymachus seems to me, like a snake, to have been charmed by your voice sooner than he ought to have been; but to my mind the nature of justice and injustice have not yet been made clear. Setting aside their rewards and results, I want to know what they are in themselves, and how they inwardly work in the soul. If you, please, then, I will revive the argument of Thrasymachus. And first I will speak of the nature and origin of justice according to the common view of them. Secondly, I will show that all men who practise justice do so against their will, of necessity, but not as a good. And thirdly, I will argue that there is reason in this view, for the life of the unjust is after all better far than the life of the just – if what they say is true, Socrates, since I myself am not of their opinion. But still I acknowledge that I am perplexed when I hear the voices of Thrasymachus and myriads of others dinning in my ears; and, on the other hand, I have never yet heard the superiority of justice to injustice maintained by any one in a satisfactory way. I want to hear justice praised in respect of itself; then I shall be satisfied, and you are the person from whom I think that I am most likely to hear this; and therefore I will praise the unjust life to the utmost of my power, and my manner of speaking will indicate the manner in which I desire to hear you too praising justice and censuring injustice. Will you say whether you approve of my proposal?

Indeed I do; nor can I imagine any theme about which a man of sense would oftener wish to converse.

I am delighted, he replied, to hear you say so, and shall begin by speaking, as I proposed, of the nature and origin of justice.

Glaucon

They say that to do injustice is, by nature, good; to suffer injustice, evil; but that the evil is greater than the good. And so when men have both done and suffered injustice and have had experience of both, not being able to avoid the one and obtain the other, they think that they had better agree among themselves to have neither; hence there arise laws and mutual covenants; and that which is ordained by law is termed by them lawful and just. This they affirm to be the origin and nature of justice; – it is a mean or compromise, between the best of all, which is to do injustice and not be punished, and the worst of all, which is to suffer injustice without the power of retaliation; and justice, being at a middle point between the two, is tolerated not as a good, but as the lesser evil, and honoured by reason of the inability of men to do injustice. For no man who is worthy to be called a man would ever submit to such an agreement if he were able to resist; he would be mad if he did. Such is the received account, Socrates, of the nature and origin of justice.

Now that those who practise justice do so involuntarily and because they have not the power to be unjust will best appear if we imagine something of this kind: having given both to the just and the unjust power to do what they will, let us watch and see whither desire will lead them; then we shall discover in the very act the just and unjust man to be proceeding along the same road, following their interest, which all natures deem to be their good, and are only diverted into the path of justice by the force of law. The liberty which we are supposing may be most completely given to them in the form of such a power as is said to have been possessed by Gyges the ancestor of Croesus the Lydian. According to the tradition, Gyges was a shepherd in the service of the king of Lydia; there was a great storm, and an earthquake made an opening in the earth at the place where he was feeding his flock. Amazed at the sight, he descended into the opening, where, among other marvels, he beheld a hollow brazen horse, having doors, at which he stooping and looking in saw a dead body of stature, as appeared to him, more than human, and having nothing on but a gold ring; this he took from the finger of the dead and reascended. Now the shepherds met together, according to custom, that they might send their monthly report about the flocks to the king; into their assembly he came having the ring on his finger, and as he was sitting among them he chanced to turn the collet of the ring inside his hand, when instantly he became invisible to the rest of the company and they began to speak of him as if he were no longer present. He was astonished at this, and again touching the ring he turned the collet outwards and reappeared; he made several trials of the ring, and always with the same result-when he turned the collet inwards he became invisible, when outwards he reappeared. Whereupon he contrived to be chosen one of the messengers who were sent to the court; where as soon as he arrived he seduced the queen, and with her help conspired against the king and slew him, and took the kingdom. Suppose now that there were two such magic rings, and the just put on one of them and the unjust the other; no man can be imagined to be of such an iron nature that he would stand fast in justice. No man would keep his hands off what was not his own when he could safely take what he liked out of the market, or go into houses and lie with any one at his pleasure, or kill or release from prison whom he would, and in all respects be like a God among men. Then the actions of the just would be as the actions of the unjust; they would both come at last to the same point. And this we may truly affirm to be a great proof that a man is just, not willingly or because he thinks that justice is any good to him individually, but of necessity, for wherever any one thinks that he can safely be unjust, there he is unjust. For all men believe in their hearts that injustice is far more profitable to the individual than justice, and he who argues as I have been supposing, will say that they are right. If you could imagine any one obtaining this power of becoming invisible, and never doing any wrong or touching what was another's, he would be thought by the lookers-on to be a most wretched idiot, although they would praise him to one another's faces, and keep up appearances with one another from a fear that they too might suffer injustice. Enough of this.

Now, if we are to form a real judgment of the life of the just and unjust, we must isolate them; there is no other way; and how is the isolation to be effected? I answer: Let the unjust man be entirely unjust, and the just man entirely just; nothing is to be taken away from either of them, and both are to be perfectly furnished for the work of their respective lives. First, let the unjust be like other distinguished masters of craft; like the skilful pilot or physician, who knows intuitively his own powers and keeps within their limits, and who, if he fails at any point, is able to recover himself. So let the unjust make his unjust attempts in the right way, and lie hidden if he means to be great in his injustice (he who is found out is nobody): for

the highest reach of injustice is: to be deemed just when you are not. Therefore I say that in the perfectly unjust man we must assume the most perfect injustice; there is to be no deduction, but we must allow him, while doing the most unjust acts, to have acquired the greatest reputation for justice. If he have taken a false step he must be able to recover himself; he must be one who can speak with effect, if any of his deeds come to light, and who can force his way where force is required his courage and strength, and command of money and friends. And at his side let us place the just man in his nobleness and simplicity, wishing, as Aeschylus says, to be and not to seem good. There must be no seeming, for if he seem to be just he will be honoured and rewarded, and then we shall not know whether he is just for the sake of justice or for the sake of honours and rewards; therefore, let him be clothed in justice only, and have no other covering; and he must be imagined in a state of life the opposite of the former. Let him be the best of men, and let him be thought the worst; then he will have been put to the proof; and we shall see whether he will be affected by the fear of infamy and its consequences. And let him continue thus to the hour of death; being just and seeming to be unjust. When both have reached the uttermost extreme, the one of justice and the other of injustice, let judgment be given which of them is the happier of the two.

Socrates – Glaucon

Heavens! my dear Glaucon, I said, how energetically you polish them up for the decision, first one and then the other, as if they were two statues.

I do my best, he said. And now that we know what they are like there is no difficulty in tracing out the sort of life which awaits either of them. This I will proceed to describe; but as you may think the description a little too coarse, I ask you to suppose, Socrates, that the words which follow are not mine. – Let me put them into the mouths of the eulogists of injustice: They will tell you that the just man who is thought unjust will be scourged, racked, bound – will have his eyes burnt out; and, at last, after suffering every kind of evil, he will be impaled: Then he will understand that he ought to seem only, and not to be, just; the words of

Aeschylus may be more truly spoken of the unjust than of the just. For the unjust is pursuing a reality; he does not live with a view to appearances – he wants to be really unjust and not to seem only:

His mind has a soil deep and fertile,
Out of which spring his prudent counsels.

In the first place, he is thought just, and therefore bears rule in the city; he can marry whom he will, and give in marriage to whom he will; also he can trade and deal where he likes, and always to his own advantage, because he has no misgivings about injustice and at every contest, whether in public or private, he gets the better of his antagonists, and gains at their expense, and is rich, and out of his gains he can benefit his friends, and harm his enemies; moreover, he can offer sacrifices, and dedicate gifts to the gods abundantly and magnificently, and can honour the gods or any man whom he wants to honour in a far better style than the just, and therefore he is likely to be dearer than they are to the gods. And thus, Socrates, gods and men are said to unite in making the life of the unjust better than the life of the just.

Adeimantus – Socrates

I was going to say something in answer to Glaucon, when Adeimantus, his brother, interposed: Socrates, he said, you do not suppose that there is nothing more to be urged?

Why, what else is there? I answered.

11

Leviathan and *The Elements of Law Natural and Politic*

Thomas Hobbes

Leviathan

Of the Naturall Condition *of Mankind, as* Concerning Their Felicity, and Misery

Nature hath made men so equall, in the faculties of body, and mind; as that though there be found one man sometimes manifestly stronger in body, or of quicker mind then another; yet when all is reckoned together, the difference between man, and man, is not so considerable, as that one man can thereupon claim to himself any benefit, to which another may not pretend, as well as he. For as to the strength of body, the weakest has strength enough to kill the strongest, either by secret machination, or by confederacy with others, that are in the same danger with himself.

And as to the faculties of the mind, (setting aside the arts grounded upon words, and especially that skill of proceeding upon generall, and infallible rules, called science; which very few have, and but in few things; as being not a native faculty, born with us; nor attained, (as prudence,) while we look after somewhat else,) I find yet a greater equality amongst men, than that of strength. For prudence, is but experience; which equal time, equally bestowes on all men, in those things they equally apply themselves unto. That which may perhaps make such equality incredible, is but a vain conceipt of one's owne wisdom, which almost all men think they have in a greater degree, than the vulgar; that is, than all men but themselves, and a few others, whom by fame, or for concurring with themselves, they approve. For such is the nature of men, that howsoever they may acknowledge many others to be more witty, or more eloquent, or more learned; Yet they will hardly believe there be many so wise as themselves: For they see their own wit at hand, and other men's at a distance. But this proveth rather that men are in that point equall, than unequall. For there is not ordinarily a greater sign of the equall distribution of any thing, than that every man is contented with his share.

From this equality of ability, ariseth equality of hope in the attaining of our ends. And therefore if any two men desire the same thing, which neverthelesse they cannot both enjoy, they become enemies; and in the way to their end, (which is principally their owne conservation, and sometimes their delectation only,) endeavour to destroy, or subdue one an other. And from hence it comes to pass, that where an invader hath no more to fear, than an other man's single power; if one plant, sow, build, or possesse a convenient seat, others may probably be expected to come prepared with forces united, to dispossesse, and deprive him, not only of the fruit of his labour, but also of his life, or liberty. And the invader again is in the like danger of another.

From Thomas Hobbes, *Leviathan*. Text edited by A.R. Waller. Cambridge University Press, 1904. Excerpts from Chapters 11, 13, 14, and 15. pp 81–86, 97–103. Thomas Hobbes and Ferdinand Tonnies (ed.). *The Elements of Law Natural and Politic*. Simpkin, Marshall, and Co., 1889.

Moral Psychology: Historical and Contemporary Readings, edited by Thomas Nadelhoffer, Eddy Nahmias, and Shaun Nichols.

And from this diffidence of one another, there is no way for any man to secure himself, so reasonable, as anticipation; that is, by force, or wiles, to master the persons of all men he can, so long, till he see no other power great enough to endanger him: And this is no more than his own conservation requireth, and is generally allowed. Also because there be some, that taking pleasure in contemplating their own power in the acts of conquest, which they pursue farther than their security requires; if others, that otherwise would be glad to be at ease within modest bounds, should not by invasion increase their power, they would not be able, long time, by standing only on their defence, to subsist. And by consequence, such augmentation of dominion over men, being necessary to a man's conservation, it ought to be allowed him.

Again, men have no pleasure, (but on the contrary a great deale of griefe) in keeping company, where there is no power able to over-awe them all. For every man looketh that his companion should value him, at the same rate he sets upon himselfe: And upon all signs of contempt, or undervaluing, naturally endeavours, as far as he dares (which amongst them that have no common power to keep them in quiet, is far enough to make them destroy each other,) to extort a greater value from his contemners, by dommage; and from others, by the example.

So that in the nature of man, we find three principal causes of quarrell. First, Competition; secondly, Diffidence; thirdly, Glory.

The first, maketh men invade for gain; the second, for safety; and the third, for reputation. The first use violence, to make themselves masters of other men's persons, wives, children, and cattell; the second, to defend them; the third, for trifles, as a word, a smile, a different opinion, and any other signe of undervalue, either direct in their persons, or by reflexion in their kindred, their friends, their nation, their profession, or their name.

Hereby it is manifest, that during the time men live without a common power to keep them all in awe, they are in that condition which is called war; and such a war, as is of every man, against every man. For War, consisteth not in Battel onely, or the act of fighting; but in a tract of time, wherein the will to contend by Battel is sufficiently known: and therefore the notion of *time*, is to be considered in the nature of war; as it is in the nature of weather. For as the nature of foul weather, lyeth not in a showre or two of rain; but in an inclination thereto of many days together: So the nature of war, consisteth not in actual fighting; but in the known disposition thereto, during all the time there is no assurance to the contrary. All other time is Peace.

Whatsoever therefore is consequent to a time of war, where every man is enemy to every man; the same is consequent to the time, wherein men live without other security, than what their own strength, and their own invention shall furnish them withall. In such condition, there is no place for industry; because the fruit thereof is uncertain: and consequently no culture of the Earth; no navigation, nor use of the commodities that may be imported by sea; no commodious building; no instruments of moving, and removing such things as require much force; no knowledge of the face of the Earth; no account of time; no arts; no letters; no society; and which is worst of all, continual feare, and danger of violent death; And the life of man, solitary, poor, nasty, brutish, and short.

It may seem strange to some man, that has not well weighed these things; that Nature should thus dissociate, and render men apt to invade, and destroy one another: and he may therefore, not trusting to this inference, made from the passions, desire perhaps to have the same confirmed by experience. Let him therefore consider with himself, when taking a journey, he arms himself, and seeks to go well accompanied; when going to sleep, he locks his does; when even in his house he locks his chests; and this when he knowes there be laws, and public officers, armed, to revenge all injuries shall bee done him; what opinion he has of his fellow subjects, when he rides armed; of his fellow citizens, when he locks his does; and of his children, and servants, when he locks his chests. Does he not there as much accuse mankind by his actions, as I do by my words? But neither of us accuse man's nature in it. The desires, and other passions of man, are in themselves no sin. No more are the actions, that proceed from those passions, till they know a law that forbids them: which till laws be made they cannot know: nor can any law be made, till they have agreed upon the person that shall make it.

It may peradventure be thought, there was never such a time, nor condition of war as this; and I believe it was never generally so, over all the world: but there are many places, where they live so now. For the savage people in many places of *America*, except the government of small families, the concord whereof dependeth on natural lust, have no government at all; and live at this day in that brutish manner, as I said before. Howsoever, it may be perceived what manner of life there would be, where there were no common power to fear; by the manner of life, which men that have formerly lived under a peacefull government, use to degenerate into, in a civil warre.

But though there had never been any time, wherein particular men were in a condition of war one against another; yet in all times, Kings, and persons of soveraign authority, because of their independency, are in continuall jealousies, and in the state and posture of gladiators; having their weapons pointing, and their eyes fixed on one another; that is, their forts, garrisons, and guns upon the frontiers of their kingdoms; and continual spyes upon their neighbours; which is a posture of war. But because they uphold thereby, the industry of their subjects; there does not follow from it, that misery, which accompanies the liberty of particular men.

To this war of every man against every man, this also is consequent; that nothing can be unjust. The notions of right and wrong, justice and injustice have there no place. Where there is no common power, there is no law: where no law, no injustice. Force, and fraud, are in war, the two cardinall vertus. Justice, and injustice are none of the faculties neither of the body, nor mind. If they were, they might be in a man that were alone in the world, as well as his senses, and passions. They are qualities, that relate to men in society, not in solitude. It is consequent also to the same condition, that there be no propriety, no dominion, no *mine* and *thine* distinct; but only that to be every man's, that he can get; and for so long, as he can keep It. And thus much for the ill condition, which man by me nature is actually placed in; though with a possibility to come out of it, consisting partly in the passions, partly in his reason.

The passions that encline men to peace, are fear of death; desire of such things as are necessary to commodious living; and a hope by their industry to obtain them. And reason suggesteth convenient articles of peace, upon which men may be drawn to agreement. These articles, are they, which otherwise are called the laws of nature.

[. . .]

CHAP. XV.

Chapter XV: Of other laws of nature

From that law of nature, by which we are obliged to transfer to another, such rights, as being retained, hinder the peace of mankind, there followeth a third; which is this, *That men perform their covenants made:* without which, covenants are in vain, and but empty words; and the right of all men to all things remaining, wee are still in the condition of warre.

And in this law of nature, consisteth the fountain and originall of justice. For where no covenant hath preceded, there hath no right been transferred, and every man has right to every thing; and consequently, no action can be unjust. But when a covenant is made, then to break it is *unjust:* And the definition of injustice, is no other than *the not performance of covenant.* And whatsoever is not unjust, is *just.*

But because covenants of mutuall trust, where there is a fear of not performance on either part, (as hath been said in the former chapter,) are invalid; though the original of justice be the making of covenants; yet injustice actually there can be none, till the cause of such feare be taken away; which while men are in the naturall condition of warre, cannot be done. Therefore before the names of just, and unjust can have place, there must be some coercive power, to compell men equally to the performance of their covenants, by the terror of some punishment, greater than the benefit they expect by the breach of their covenant; and to make good that propriety, which by mutual contract men acquire, in recompence of the universal right they abandon: and such power there is none before the erection of a common-wealth. And this is also to be gathered out of the ordinary definition of justice in the schools: For they say, that *justice is the constant will of giving to every man his own.* And therefore where there is no *own,* that is, no propriety, there is no injustice; and where there is no coercive power erected, that is, where there is no common-wealth, there is no propriety; all men having right to all things: Therefore where there is no common-wealth, there nothing is unjust. So that the nature of justice, consisteth in keeping of valid covenants: but the validity of covenants begins not but with the constitution of a civill power, sufficient to compel men to keep them: And then it is also that propriety begins.

The fool hath said in his heart, there is no such thing as justice; and sometimes also with his tongue; seriously alleaging, that every man's conservation, and contentment, being committed to his own care, there could be no reason, why every man might not do what he thought conduced thereunto: and therefore also to make, or not make; keep, or not keep covenants, was not against reason, when it conduced to ones benefit. He does not therein deny, that there be covenants; and that they are sometimes broken, sometimes kept; and that such breach of them may be called injustice, and the observance of them justice: but he questioneth, whether injustice, taking away the feare of God, (for the same foole hath said in his heart there is no God,) may not sometimes stand with that reason, which dictateth to every man his own good; and particularly then, when it conduceth to such a benefit, as shall put a man in a condition, to neglect not onely the dispraise, and revilings, but also the power of other men. The Kingdom of God is gotten by violence: but what if it could be gotten by unjust violence? Were it against reason so to get it, when it is impossible to receive hurt by it? And if it be not against reason, it is not against justice: or else justice is not to be approved for good. From such reasoning as this, successfull wickednesse hath obtained the name of vertu: and some that in all other things have disallowed the violation of faith; yet have allowed it, when it is for the getting of a kingdom. And the Heathen that believed, that *Saturn* was deposed by his son *Jupiter*, believed neverthelesse the same *Jupiter* to be the avenger of injustice: Somewhat like to a piece of law in *Cokes* Commentaries on *Litleton*; where he says, If the right heire of the Crown be attainted of treason; yet the Crown shall descend to him, and *to instante* the attender be void: From which instances a man will be very prone to infer; that when the heir apparent of a Kingdome, shall kill him that is in possession, though his father; you may call it injustice, or by what other name you will; yet it can never be against reason, seeing all the voluntary actions of men tend to the benefit of themselves; and those actions are most reasonable, that conduce most to their ends. This specious reasoning is nevertheless false.

For the question is not of promises mutual, where there is no security of performance on either side; as when there is no civil power erected over the parties promising; for such promises are no covenants: But either where one of the parties has performed already; or where there is a power to make him performe; there is the question whether it be against reason, that is, against the benefit of the other to performe, or not. And I say it is not against reason. For the manifestation whereof, we are to consider; First, that when a man doth a thing, which notwithstanding any thing can be foreseen, and reckoned on, tendeth to his own destruction, howsoever some accident which he could not expect, arriving may turn it to his benefit; yet such events do not make it reasonably or wisely done. Secondly, that in a condition of war, wherein every man to every man, for want of a common power to keep them all in awe, is an enemy, there is no man can hope by his own strength, or wit, to defend himselfe from destruction, without the help of confederates; where every one expects the same defence by the confederation, that any one else does: and therefore he which declares he thinks it reason to deceive those that help him, can in reason expect no other means of safety, than what can be had from his own single power. He therefore that breaketh his Covenant, and consequently declareth that he thinks he may with reason do so, cannot be received into any society, that unite themselves for peace and defence, but by the error of them that receive him; nor when he is received, be retained in it, without seeing the danger of their error; which errors a man cannot reasonably reckon upon as the means of his security: and therefore if he be left, or cast out of society, he perisheth; and if he live in society, it is by the errors of other men, which he could not foresee, nor reckon upon; and consequently against the reason of his preservation; and so, as all men that contribute not to his destruction, forbear him onely out of ignorance of what is good for themselves.

As for the instance of gaining the secure and perpetuall felicity of Heaven, by any way; it is frivolous: there being but one way imaginable; and that is not breaking, but keeping of covenant.

And for the other instance of attaining soveraignty by rebellion; it is manifest, that though the event follow, yet because it cannot reasonably be expected, but rather the contrary; and because by gaining it so, others are taught to gain the same in like manner, the attempt thereof is against reason. Justice therefore, that is to say, keeping of covenant, is a rule of reason, by which we are forbidden to do any thing destructive to our life; and consequently a law of nature.

There be some that proceed further; and will not have the law of nature, to be those rules which conduce to the preservation of mans life on earth; but to the attaining of an eternall felicity after death; to which they think the breach of covenant may conduce; and consequently be just and reasonable; (such are they that think it a work of merit to kill, or depose, or rebell against, the soveraigne power constituted over them by their own consent.) But because there is no natural knowledge of man's estate after death; much less of the reward that is then to be given to breach of faith; but only a belief grounded upon other mens saying, that they know it supernaturally, or that they know those, that knew them, that knew others, that knew it supernaturally; Breach of faith cannot be called a precept of reason, or nature.

Others, that allow for a law of nature, the keeping of faith, do neverthelesse make exception of certain persons; as heretiques, and such as use not to performe their covenant to others: And this also is against reason. For if any fault of a man, be sufficient to discharge our covenant made; the same ought in reason to have been sufficient to have hindered the making of it.

The names of just, and injust, when they are attributed to men, signify one thing; and when they are attributed to actions, another. When they are attributed to men, they signify conformity, or inconformity of manners, to reason. But when they are attributed to actions, they signify the conformity, or inconformity to reason, not of manners, or manner of life, but of particular actions. A just man therefore, is he that taketh all the care he can, that his actions may be all just: and an unjust man, is he that neglecteth it. And such men are more often in our language stiled by the names of righteous, and unrighteous; then just, and unjust; though the meaning be the same. Therefore a righteous man, does not lose that title, by one, or a few unjust actions, that proceed from sudden passion, or mistake of things, or persons: nor does an unrighteous man, lose his

character, for such actions, as he does, or forbeares to do, for feare: because his will is not framed by the justice, but by the apparent benefit of what he is to do. That which gives to humane actions the relish of justice, is a certain noblenesse or gallantnesse of courage, (rarely found,) by which a man scorns to be beholding for the contentment of his life, to fraud, or breach of promise. This justice of the manners, is that which is meant, where justice is called a vertu; and injustice a vice.

But the justice of actions denominates men, not just, but *guiltless*: and the injustice of the same, (which is also called injury,) gives them but the name of *guilty*.

Again, the injustice of manners, is the disposition, or aptitude to do injurie; and is injustice before it proceed to act; and without supposing any individual person injured. But the injustice of an action, (that is to say injury,) supposeth an individual person injured; namely him, to whom the covenant was made: and therefore many times the injury is received by one man, when the dammage redoundeth to another. As when the master commandeth his servant to give mony to a stranger; if it be not done, the injury is done to the master, whom he had before covenanted to obey; but the damage redoundeth to the stranger, to whom he had no obligation; and therefore could not injure him. And so also in common-wealths, private men may remit to one another their debts; but not robberies or other violences, whereby they are endamaged; because the detaining of debt, is an injury to themselves; but robbery and violence, are injuries to the person of the common-wealth.

Whatsoever is done to a man, conformable to his own will signified to the doer, is no injury to him. For if he that doeth it, hath not passed away his originall right to do what he please, by some antecedent covenant, there is no breach of covenant; and therefore no injury done him. And if he have; then his will to have it done being signified, is a release of that covenant: and so again there is no injury done him.

Justice of actions, is by writers divided into *commutative*, and *distributive*: and the former they say consisteth in proportion arithmetical; the later in proportion geometrical. Commutative therefore, they place in the equality of value of the things contracted for; and distributive, in the distribution of equall benefit, to men of equall merit. As if it were injustice to sell dearer than we buy; or to give more to a man than he merits. The value of all things contracted for, is measured by the appetite of the contractors: and therefore the just value, is that which they be contented to give. And merit (besides that which is by covenant, where the performance on one part, meriteth the performance of the other part, and falls under justice commutative, not distributive,) is not due by justice; but is rewarded of grace onely. And therefore this distinction, in the sense wherein it useth to be expounded, is not right. To speak properly, commutative justice, is the justice of a contractor; that is, a performance of covenant, in buying, and selling; hiring, and letting to hire; lending, and borrowing; exchanging, bartering, and other acts of contract.

And distributive justice, the justice of an arbitrator; that is to say, the act of defining what is just. Wherein, (being trusted by them that make him arbitrator,) if he perform his trust, he is said to distribute to every man his own: and this is indeed Just distribution, and may be called (though improperly) distributive justice; but more properly equity; which also is a law of nature, as shall be shown in due place.

[. . .]

[N]o man giveth, but with intention of Good to himself; because gift is voluntary; and of all voluntary acts, the object is to every man his own good; of which if men see they shall be frustrated, there will be no beginning of benevolence, or trust; nor consequently of mutuall help; nor of reconciliation of one man to another; and therefore they are to remain still in the condition of *war*.

The Elements of Law Natural and Politic

Part I, Chapter 9

10. Pity is imagination or fiction of future calamity to ourselves, proceeding from the sense of another man's present calamity; but when it lighteth on such as we think have not deserved the same, the compassion is the greater, because then there appeareth the more probability that the same may happen to us. For the evil that happeneth to an innocent man, may happen to every man. But when we see a man suffer for great crimes, which we cannot easily think will fall upon ourselves, the pity is the less.

[. . .]

17. There is yet another passion sometimes called love, but more properly good will or Charity. There can be no greater argument to a man of his own power, than to find himself able, not only to accomplish his own desires, but also to assist other men in theirs: and this is that conception wherein consisteth charity. In which, first, is contained that natural affection of parents to their children, which the Greeks call Storgi, as also that affection wherewith men seek to assist those that adhere unto them. But the affection wherewith men many times bestow their benefits on strangers, is not to be called charity, but either contract, whereby they seek to purchase friendship; or fear, which maketh them to purchase peace.

12

Human Nature and Other Sermons

Excerpts from Sermon 5
"Upon Compassion"; and Sermon 11
"Upon the Love of Our Neighbour"

Joseph Butler

Sermon V: Upon Compassion

Romans xii. 15.
Rejoice with them that do rejoice, and
weep with them that weep.

[. . .]

When we rejoice in the prosperity of others and compassionate their distresses, we, as it were, substitute them for ourselves, their interest for our own, and have the same kind of pleasure in their prosperity, and sorrow in their distress, as we have from reflection upon our own. Now, there is nothing strange, or unaccountable, in our being thus carried out, and affected towards the interests of others. For, if there be any appetite, or any inward principle besides self-love; why may there not be an affection to the good of our fellow creatures, and delight from that affection being gratified, and uneasiness from things going contrary to it?[1]

Sermon XI: Upon the Love of Our Neighbor

Preached on Advent Sunday

Romans xiii. 9.
And if there be any other commandment,
it is briefly comprehended in this
sayings, namely, Thou shalt love
thy neighbor as thyself.

It is commonly observed, that there is a disposition in men to complain of the viciousness and corruption of the age in which they live, as greater than that of former ones; which is usually followed with this further observation, that mankind has been in that respect much the same in all times. Now, to determine whether this last be not contradicted by the accounts of history; thus much can scarce be doubted, that vice and folly takes different turns, and some particular kinds of it are

From Joseph Butler, *Fifteen sermons preached at the Rolls Chapel*, excerpts from Sermon 1 "Upon Human Nature"; Sermon 5 "Upon Compassion"; and Sermon 11 "Upon the Love of Our Neighbor." London: printed by W. Botham, for James and John Knapton, 1729. pp. 78–79, 147–164.

Moral Psychology: Historical and Contemporary Readings, edited by Thomas Nadelhoffer, Eddy Nahmias, and Shaun Nichols. © 2010 Blackwell Publishing Ltd except for editorial material and organization © 2010 Thomas Nadelhoffer, Eddy Nahmias, and Shaun Nichols.

more open and avowed in some ages than in others: and, I suppose, it may be spoken of as very much the distinction of the present, to profess a contracted spirit, and greater regards to self-interest, than appears to have been done formerly. Upon this account it seems worth while to inquire, whether private interest is likely to be promoted in proportion to the degree in which self-love engrosses us, and prevails over all other principles; "or whether the contracted affection may not possibly be so prevalent as to disappoint itself, and even contradict its own end, private good ?"

And since, further, there is generally thought to be some peculiar kind of contrariety, between self-love and the love of our neighbor, between the pursuit of public and of private good; insomuch, that when you are recommending one of these, you are supposed to be speaking against the other; and from hence arises a secret prejudice against, and frequently open scorn of all talk of public spirit, and real good will to our fellow creatures; it will be necessary to "inquire, what respect benevolence hath to self-love, and the pursuit of private interest to the pursuit of public?" Or whether there be any thing of that peculiar inconsistence and contrariety between them, over and above what there is between self-love and other passions and particular affections, and their respective pursuits?

These inquiries, it is hoped, may be favorably attended to; for there shall be all possible concessions made to the favorite passion, which hath so much allowed to it, and whose cause is so universally pleaded: it shall be treated with the utmost tenderness, and concern for its interests.

In order to this, as well as to determine the forementioned questions, it will be necessary to consider the nature, the object, and end of that self-love, as distinguished from other principles or affections in the mind and their respective objects.

Every man hath a general desire of his own happiness; and likewise a variety of particular affections, passions, and appetites, to particular external objects. The former proceeds from, or is, self-love; and seems inseparable from all sensible creatures, who can reflect upon themselves and their own interest or happiness, so as to have that interest and object to their minds: what is to be said of the latter is, that they proceed from, or together make up, that particular nature, according to which man is made. The object the former pursues is somewhat internal, our own happiness, enjoyment, satisfaction; whether we have, or have not, a distinct particular perception what it is, or wherein it consists: the objects of the latter are this or that particular external thing, which the affections tend towards, and of which it hath always a particular idea or perception. The principle we call self-love never seeks any thing external for the sake of the thing, but only as a means of happiness or good: particular affections rest in the external things themselves. One belongs to man as a reasonable creature reflecting upon his own interest or happiness; the other, though quite distinct from reason, are as much a part of human nature.

That all particular appetites and passions are towards *external things themselves*, distinct from the *pleasure arising from them*, is manifested from hence, that there could not be this pleasure, were it not for that prior suitableness between the object and the passion: There could be no enjoyment or delight for one thing more than another, from eating food more than from swallowing a stone, if there were not an affection or appetite to one thing more than another.

Every particular affection, even the love of our neighbor, is as really our own affection, as self-love; and the pleasure arising from its gratification is as much my own pleasure, as the pleasure self-love would have from knowing I myself should be happy some time hence, would be my own pleasure. And if, because every particular affection is a man's own, and the pleasure arising from its gratification his own pleasure, or pleasure to himself, such particular affection must be called self-love; according to this way of speaking, no creature whatever can possibly act but merely from self-love; and every action and every affection whatever is to be resolved up into this one principle. But then this is not the language of mankind: or, if it were, we should want words to express the difference between the principle of an action, proceeding from cool consideration that it will be to my own advantage; and an action, suppose of revenge, or of friendship, by which a man runs upon certain ruin, to do evil or good to another. It is manifest the principles of these actions are totally different, and so want different words to be distinguished by. All that they agree in is, that they both proceed from, and are done to gratify an inclination in a man's self. But the principle or inclination in one case is self-love; in the other, hatred, or love of another. There is then a distinction between the cool principle of self-love, or general desire of our own happiness, as one part of our nature, and one principle of action; and the particular affections towards particular external objects, as another part of our nature, and another principle of action. How much soever, therefore, is to be allowed to self-love, yet it cannot be allowed to be the whole of our inward constitution; because, you see, there are other parts or principles which come into it.

Further, private happiness or good is all which self-love can make us desire, or be concerned about. In having this consists its gratification: it is an affection to ourselves; a regard to our own interest, happiness, and private good: and in the proportion a man hath this, he is interested, or a lover of himself. Let this be kept in mind; because there is commonly, I shall presently have occasion to observe, another sense put upon these words. On the other hand, particular affections tend towards particular external things: these are their objects; having these is their end; in this consists their gratification; no matter whether it be, or be not, upon the whole, our interest or happiness. An action, done from the former of these principles, is called an interested action. An action proceeding from any of the latter, has its denomination of passionate, ambitious, friendly, revengeful, or any other, from the particular appetite or affection from which it proceeds. Thus self love as one part of human nature, and the several particular principles as the other part, are themselves, their objects and ends, stated and shown.

From hence it will be easy to see, how far, and in what ways, each of these can contribute and be subservient to the private good of the individual. Happiness does not consist in self-love. The desire of happiness is no more the thing itself, than the desire of riches is the possession or enjoyment of them. People may love themselves with the most entire and unbounded affection, and yet be extremely miserable. Neither can self-love any way help them out, but by setting them on work to get rid of the causes of their misery, to gain or make use of those objects which are by nature adapted to afford satisfaction. Happiness or satisfaction consists only in the enjoyment of those objects, which are by nature suited to our

several particular appetites, passions, and affections. So that if self-love wholly engrosses us, and leaves no room for any other principle, there can be absolutely no such thing at all as happiness or enjoyment of any kind whatever; since happiness consists in the gratification of particular passions, which supposes the having of them. Self-love then does not constitute *this* or *that* to be our interest or good; but, our interest or good being constituted by nature and supposed, self-love only puts us upon obtaining and securing it. Therefore, if it be possible that self-love may prevail and exert itself in a degree or manner which is not subservient to this end; then it will not follow, that our interest will be promoted in proportion to the degree in which that principle engrosses us, and prevails over others. Nay further, the private and contracted affection, when it is not subservient to this end, private good, may, for any thing that appears, have a direct contrary tendency and effect. And if we will consider the matter, we shall see that it often really has. Disengagement is absolutely necessary to enjoyment: and a person may have so steady and fixed an eye upon his own interest, whatever he places it in, as may hinder him from attending to many gratifications within his reach, which others have their minds free and open to. Over fondness for a child is not generally thought to be for its advantage: and, if there be any guess to be made from appearances, surely that character we call *selfish* is not the most promising for happiness. Such a temper may plainly be, and exert itself in a degree and manner which may give unnecessary and useless solicitude and anxiety, in a degree and manner which may prevent obtaining the means and materials of enjoyment, as well as the making use of them. Immoderate self-love does very ill consult its own interest: and, how much soever a paradox it may appear, it is certainly true, that, even from self-love, we should endeavor to get over all inordinate regard to, and consideration of ourselves. Every one of our passions and affections hath its natural stint and bound, which may easily be exceeded; whereas our enjoyments can possibly be but in a determinate measure and degree. Therefore such excess of the affection, since it cannot procure any enjoyment, must in all cases be useless; but is generally attended with inconveniences, and often is downright pain and misery. This holds as much with regard to self-love as to all other affections. The natural degree of it, so far as it sets us on work to gain and make use of the materials of satisfaction, may be to our real advantage; but beyond or besides this, it is in several respects an inconvenience and disadvantage. Thus it appears, that private interest is so far from being likely to be promoted in proportion to the degree in which self-love engrosses us, and prevails over all other principles, that *the contracted affection may be so prevalent, as to disappoint itself, and even contradict its own end, private good.*

"But who, except the most sordidly covetous, ever thought there was any rivalship between the love of greatness, honor, power, or between sensual appetites, and self-love? No, there is a perfect harmony between them. It is by means of these particular appetites and affectious that self-love is gratified in enjoyment, happiness, and satisfaction. The competition and rivalship is between self-love and the love of our neighbor. That affection which leads us out of ourselves, makes us regardless of our own interest, and substitute that of another in its stead." Whether then there be any peculiar competition and contrariety in this case, shall now be considered.

Self-love and interestedness was stated to consist in or be an affection to ourselves, a regard to our own private good: it is, therefore, distinct from benevolence, which is an affection to the good of our fellow creatures. But that benevolence is distinct from, that is, not the same thing with self-love, is no reason for its being looked upon with any peculiar suspicion, because every principle whatever, by means of which self-love is gratified, is distinct from it: and all things, which are distinct from each other, are equally so. A man has an affection or aversion to another: that one of these tends to, and is gratified by doing good, that the other tends to, and is gratified by doing harm, does not in the least alter the respect which either one or the other of these inward feelings has to self-love. We use the word *property* so as to exclude any other person's having an interest in that, of which we say a particular man has the property: and we often use the word *selfish* so as to exclude in the same manner all regards to the good of others. But the cases are not parallel: for though that exclusion is really part of the idea of property; yet such positive exclusion, or bringing this peculiar disregard to the good of others

into the idea of self-love, is in reality adding to the idea, or changing it from what it was before stated to consist in, namely, in an affection to ourselves. This being the whole idea of self-love, it can no otherwise exclude good will or love of others, than merely by not including it, no otherwise than it excludes love of arts, or reputation, or of any thing else. Neither, on the other hand, does benevolence, any more than love of arts or of reputation, exclude self-love. Love of our neighbor, then, has just the same respect to, is no more distant from self-love, than hatred of our neighbor, or than love or hatred of any thing else. Thus the principles, from which men rush upon certain ruin for the destruction of an enemy, and for the preservation of a friend, have the same respect to the private affection, are equally interested, or equally disinterested: and it is of no avail, whether they are said to be one or the other. Therefore, to those who are shocked to hear virtue spoken of as disinterested, it may be allowed, that it is indeed absurd to speak thus of it; unless hatred, several particular instances of vice, and all the common affections and aversions in mankind, are acknowledged to be disinterested too. Is there any less inconsistence between the love of inanimate things, or of creatures merely sensitive, and self-love, than between self-love, and the love of our neighbor? Is desire of, and delight in the happiness of another any more a diminution of self-love, than desire of and delight in the esteem of another? They are both equally desire of and delight in somewhat external to ourselves; either both or neither are so. The object of self-love is expressed in the term self: and every appetite of sense, and every particular affection of the heart, are equally interested or disinterested, because the objects of them all are equally self or somewhat else. Whatever ridicule, therefore, the mention of a disinterested principle or action may be supposed to lie open to, must, upon the matter being thus stated, relate to ambition, and every appetite and particular affection, as much as to benevolence. And indeed all the ridicule, and all the grave perplexity, of which this subject hath had its full share, is merely from words. The most intelligible way of speaking of it seems to be this: that self-love, and the actions done in consequence of it, (for these will presently appear to be the same as to this question,) are interested; that particular affections towards external objects, and the actions done in consequence of those affections, are not so. But every one is at liberty to use words as he pleases. All that is here insisted upon is, that ambition, revenge, benevolence, all particular passions whatever, and the actions they produce, are equally interested or disinterested.

Thus it appears, that there is no peculiar contrariety between self-love and benevolence; no greater competition between these, than between any other particular affections and self-love. This relates to the affections themselves. Let us now see whether there be any peculiar contrariety between the respective courses of life which these affections lead to; whether there be any greater competition between the pursuit of private and of public good, than between any other particular pursuits and that of private good.

There seems no other reason to suspect that there is any such peculiar contrariety, but only that the course of action which benevolence leads to, has a more direct tendency to promote the good of others, than that course of action which love of reputation, suppose, or any other particular affection, leads to. But that any affection tends to the happiness of another, does not hinder its tending to one's own happiness too. That others enjoy the benefit of the air and the light of the sun, does not hinder but that these are as much one's own private advantage now, as they would be if we had the property of them exclusive of all others. So a pursuit which tends to promote the good of another, yet may have as great tendency to promote private interest, as a pursuit which does not tend to the good of another at all, or which is mischievous to him. All particular affections whatever, resentment, benevolence, love of arts, equally lead to a course of action for their own gratification, *i.e.* the gratification of ourselves; and the gratification of each gives delight: so far, then, it is manifest, they have all the same respect to private interest. Now, take into consideration further, concerning these three pursuits, that the end of the first is the harm, of the second, the good of another, of the last, somewhat indifferent; and is there any necessity, that these additional considerations should alter the respect, which we before saw these three pursuits had to private interest; or render any one of them less conducive to it than any other? Thus, one man's affection is to honor, as his end; in order to obtain which, he thinks no pains too great. Suppose

another, with such a singularity of mind, as to have the same affection to public good, as his end, which he endeavors with the same labor to obtain. In case of success, surely the man of benevolence hath as great enjoyment as the man of ambition; they both equally having the end their affections, in the same degree, tended to: but in case of disappointment, the benevolent man has clearly the advantage; since endeavoring to do good, considered as a virtuous pursuit, is gratified by its own consciousness, *i.e.* is in a degree its own reward.

And as to these two, or benevolence and any other particular passions whatever, considered in a further view, as forming a general temper, which more or less disposes us for enjoyment of all the common blessings of life, distinct from their own gratification: is benevolence less the temper of tranquillity and freedom, than ambition or covetousness? Does the benevolent man appear less easy with himself, from his love to his neighbor? Does he less relish his being? Is there any peculiar gloom seated on his face? Is his mind less open to entertainment, to any particular gratification? Nothing is more manifest, than that being in good humor, which is benevolence whilst it lasts, is itself the temper of satisfaction and enjoyment.

Suppose then a man sitting down to consider, how he might become most easy to himself, and attain the greatest pleasure he could; all that which is his real natural happiness: this can only consist in the enjoyment of those objects, which are by nature adapted to our several faculties. These particular enjoyments make up the sum total of our happiness; and they are supposed to arise from riches, honors, and the gratification of sensual appetites. Be it so: yet none profess themselves so completely happy in these enjoyments, but that there is room left in the mind for others, if they were presented to them: nay, these, as much as they engage us, are not thought so high, but that human nature is capable even of greater. Now there have been persons in all ages, who have professed that they found satisfaction in the exercise of charity, in the love of their neighbor, in endeavoring to promote the happiness of all they had to do with, and in the pursuit of what is just, and right, and good, as the general bent of their mind, and end of their life; and that doing an action of baseness or cruelty, would be as great violence to *their* self, as much breaking in upon their nature, as any external force. Persons of this character would add, if they might be heard, that they consider themselves as acting in the view of an infinite Being, who is in a much higher sense the object of reverence and of love, than all the world besides; and, therefore, they could have no more enjoyment from a wicked action done under his eye, than the persons to whom they are making their apology could, if all mankind were the spectators of it; and that the satisfaction of approving themselves to his unerring judgment, to whom they thus refer all their actions, is a more continued, settled satisfaction than any this world can afford; as also that they have, no less than others, a mind free and open to all the common innocent gratifications of it, such as they are. And, if we go no further, does there appear any absurdity in this? Will any one take upon him to say, that a man cannot find his account in this general course of life, as much as in the most unbounded ambition, and the excesses of pleasure? Or that such a person has not consulted so well for himself, for the satisfaction and peace of his own mind, as the ambitious or dissolute man? And though the consideration, that God himself will in the end justify their taste, and support their cause, is not formally to be insisted upon here; yet thus much comes in, that all enjoyments whatever are much more clear and unmixed, from the assurance that they will end well. Is it certain, then, that there is nothing in these pretensions to happiness? especially when there are not wanting persons, who have supported themselves with satisfactions of this kind in sickness, poverty, disgrace, and in the very pangs of death; whereas it is manifest all other enjoyments fail in these circumstances. This surely looks suspicious of having somewhat in it. Self-love, methinks, should be alarmed. May she not possibly pass over greater pleasures, than those she is so wholly taken up with?

The short of the matter is no more than this. Happiness consists in the gratification of certain affections, appetites, passions, with objects which are by nature adapted to them. Self-love may indeed set us on work to gratify these. But happiness or enjoyment has no immediate connexion with self-love, but arises from such gratifications alone. Love of our neighbor is one of those affections. This, considered as a virtuous principle, is gratified by a consciousness of endeavoring to promote the good of others; but, considered

as a natural affection, its gratification consists in the actual accomplishment of this endeavor. Now, indulgence or gratification of this affection, whether in that consciousness, or this accomplishment, has the same respect to interest, as indulgence of any other affection; they equally proceed from, or do not proceed from self-love; they equally include, or equally exclude, this principle. Thus it appears, that "benevolence and the pursuit of public good hath at least as great respect to self-love and the pursuit of private good, as any other particular passions, and their respective pursuits."

Neither is covetousness, whether as a temper or a pursuit, any exception to this. For if by covetousness is meant the desire and pursuit of riches for their own sake, without any regard to, or consideration of the uses of them; this hath as little to do with self-love, as benevolence hath. But by this word is usually meant, not such madness and total distraction of mind, but immoderate affection to and pursuit of riches, as possessions, in order to some further end: namely, satisfaction, interest, or good. This, therefore, is not a particular affection, or particular pursuit, but it is the general principle of self-love, and the general pursuit of our own interest; for which reason, the word *selfish* is by every one appropriated to this temper and pursuit. Now, as it is ridiculous to assert, that self-love and the love of our neighbor are the same; so neither is it asserted, that following these different affections hath the same tendency and respect to our own interest. The comparison is not between self-love and the love of our neighbor; between pursuit of our own interest, and the interest of others; but between the several particular affections in human nature towards external objects, as one part of the comparison: and the one particular affection to the good of our neighbor, as the one part of it: and it has been shown, that all these have the same respect to self-love and private interest.

There is indeed frequently an inconsistence, or interfering, between self-love or private interest, and the several particular appetites, passions, affections, or the pursuits they lead to. But this competition or interfering is merely accidental; and happens much oftener between pride, revenge, sensual gratifications, and private interest, than between private interest and benevolence. For nothing is more common, than to see men give themselves up to a passion or an affection to their known prejudice and ruin, and in direct contradiction to manifest and real interest, and the loudest calls of self-love: whereas the seeming competitions and interfering between benevolence and private interest, relate much more to the materials or means of enjoyment, than to enjoyment itself. There is often an interfering in the former, when there is none in the latter. Thus, as to riches: so much money as a man gives away, so much less will remain in his possession. Here is a real interfering. But though a man cannot possibly give without lessening his fortune, yet there are multitudes might give without lessening their own enjoyment; because they may have more than they can turn to any real use or advantage to themselves. Thus, the more thought and time any one employs about the interests and good of others, he must necessarily have less to attend his own; but he may have so ready and large a supply of his own wants, that such thought might be really useless to himself, though of great service and assistance to others.

The general mistake, that there is some greater inconsistence between endeavoring to promote the good of another and self-interest, than between self-interest and pursuing any thing else, seems, as hath already been hinted, to arise from our notions of property; and to be carried on by this property's being supposed to be itself our happiness or good. People are so very much taken up with this one subject, that they seem from it to have formed a general way of thinking, which they apply to other things that they have nothing to do with. Hence, in a confused and slight way, it might well be taken for granted, that another's having no interest in an affection, (*i.e.* his good not being the object of it) renders, as one may speak, the proprietor's interest in it greater; and that if another had an interest in it, this would render his less, or occasion that such affection could not be so friendly to self love, or conducive to private good, as an affection or pursuit which has not a regard to the good of another. This, I say, might be taken for granted, whilst it was not attended to, that the object of every particular affection is equally somewhat external to ourselves: and whether it be the good of another person, or whether it be any other external thing, makes no alteration with regard to its being one's own affection, and the gratification of it one's

own private enjoyment. And so far as it is taken for granted, that barely having the means and materials of enjoyment is what constitutes interest and happiness; that our interest or good consists in possessions themselves, in having the property of riches, houses, lands, gardens, not in the enjoyment of them; so far it will even more strongly be taken for granted, in the way already explained, that an affection's conducing to the good of another, must even necessarily occasion it to conduce less to private good, if not to be positively detrimental to it. For, if property and happiness are one and the same thing, as by increasing the property of another, you lessen your own property, so by promoting the happiness of another, you must lessen your own happiness. But whatever occasioned the mistake, I hope it has been fully proved to be one; as it has been proved, that there is no peculiar rivalship or competition between self-love and benevolence; that as there may be a competition between these two, so there may also between any particular affection whatever and self-love; that every particular affection, benevolence among the rest, is subservient to self-love, by being the instrument of private enjoyment; and that in one respect benevolence contributes more to private interest, *i.e.* enjoyment or satisfaction, than any other of the particular common affections, as it is in a degree its own gratification.

And to all these things may be added, that religion, from whence arises our strongest obligation to benevolence, is so far from disowning the principle of self-love, that it often addresses itself to that very principle, and always to the mind in that state when reason presides; and there can no access be had to the understanding, but by convincing men, that the course of life we would persuade them to is not contrary to their interest. It may be allowed, without any prejudice to the cause of virtue and religion, that our ideas of happiness and misery are, of all our ideas, the nearest and most important to us; that they will, nay, if you please, that they ought to prevail over those of order, and beauty, and harmony, and proportion, if there should ever be, as it is impossible there ever should be, any inconsistency between them; though these last, too, as expressing the fitness of actions, are real as truth itself. Let it be allowed, though virtue or moral rectitude does indeed consist in affection to and pursuit of what is right and good, as such: yet that, when we sit down in a cool hour, we can neither justify to ourselves this or any other pursuit, till we are convinced that it will be for our happiness, or, at least, not contrary to it.

Common reason and humanity will have some influence upon mankind, whatever becomes of speculations: but, so far as the interests of virtue depend upon the theory of it being secured from open scorn, so far its very being in the world depends upon its appearing to have no contrariety to private interest and self-love. The foregoing observations, therefore, it is hoped, may have gained a little ground in favor of the precept before us, the particular explanation of which shall be the subject of the next discourse.

I will conclude, at present, with observing the peculiar obligation which we are under to virtue and religion, as enforced in the verses following the text, in the epistle for the day, from our Saviour's coming into the world. "The night is far spent, the day is at hand; let us, therefore, cast off the works of darkness, and let us put on the armor of light," &c. The meaning and force of which exhortation is, that Christianity lays us under new obligations to a good life, as by it the will of God is more clearly revealed, and as it affords additional motives to the practice of it, over and above those which arise out of the nature of virtue and vice; I might add, as our Saviour has set us a perfect example of goodness in our own nature. Now, love and charity is plainly the thing in which he hath placed his religion; in which, therefore, as we have any pretence to the name of Christians, we must place ours. He hath at once enjoined it upon us by the way of command, with peculiar force; and by his example, as having undertaken the work of our salvation, out of pure love and good will to mankind. The endeavor to set home this example upon our minds, is a very proper employment of this season, which is bringing on the festival of his birth; which, as it may teach us many excellent lessons of humility, resignation, and obedience to the will of God; so there is none it recommends with greater authority, force, and advantage, than this of love and charity; since it was "for us men, and for our salvation, that he came down from heaven, and was incarnate, and was made man;" that he might teach us our duty, and more especially that he might enforce the practice of it, reform mankind, and finally bring us to that "eternal salvation, of which he is the Author to all those that obey him."

Note

1 There being manifestly this appearance of men's substituting others for themselves, and being carried out and affected towards them as towards themselves; some persons, who have a system which excludes every affection of this sort, have taken a pleasant method to solve it; and tell you, it is *not another* you are at all concerned about, but your *self only*, when you feel the affection called compassion: *i.e.* Here is a plain matter of fact, which men cannot reconcile with the general account they think fit to give of things; they, therefore, instead of *that* manifest fact, substitute *another*, which is reconcileable to their own scheme. For, does not every body by compassion mean, an affection the object of which is another in distress? Instead of this, but designing to have it mistaken for this, they speak of an affection, or passion, the object of which is ourselves, or danger to ourselves. Hobbs defines *pity, imagination, or fiction, of future calamity to ourselves, proceeding from the sense* (he means sight, or knowledge) *of another man's calamity.* Thus, fear and compassion would be the same idea, and a fearful and a compassionate man the same character, which every one immediately sees are totally different.

13

An Inquiry into the Original of our Ideas of Beauty and Virtue
Treatise II: Concerning Moral Good and Evil

Francis Hutcheson

Section II. Concerning the Immediate Motive to Virtuous Actions

The motives of human actions, or their immediate causes, would be best understood after considering the passions and affections; but here we shall only consider the springs of the actions which we call *virtuous*, as far as it is necessary to settle the general foundation of the moral sense.

I. Every action, which we apprehend as either morally good or evil, is always supposed to flow from some affection toward sensitive natures; and whatever we call *virtue* or *vice*, is either some such affection, or some action consequent upon it. Or it may perhaps be enough to make an action or omission, appear vicious, if it argues the want of such affection toward rational agents, as we expect in characters counted morally good. All the actions counted religious in any country, are supposed, by those who count them so, to flow from some affections toward the Deity; and whatever we call *social virtue*, we still suppose to flow from affections toward our fellow creatures: for in this all seem to agree, 'that external motions, when accompanied with no affections toward God or man, or evidencing no want of the expected affections toward either, can have no moral good or evil in them.'

Ask, for instance, the most abstemious hermit, if *temperance* of itself would be morally good, sup-

posing it showed no obedience toward the Deity, made us no fitter for devotion, or the service of mankind, or the search after truth, than luxury; and he will easily grant, that it would be no moral good, though still it might be naturally good or advantageous to health: and mere *courage*, or contempt of danger, if we conceive it to have no regard to the defence of the innocent, or repairing of wrongs or self-interest, would only entitle its possessor to bedlam. When such sort of courage is sometimes admired, it is upon some secret apprehension of a good intention in the use of it, or as a natural ability capable of an useful application. *Prudence*, if it was only employed in promoting private interest, is never imagined to be a virtue: and *justice*, or observing a strict equality, if it has no regard to the good of mankind, the preservation of rights, and securing peace, is a quality properer for its ordinary gestamen, a beam and scales, than for a rational agent. So that these four qualities, commonly called *cardinal virtues*, obtain that name, because they are dispositions universally necessary to promote public good, and denote affections toward rational agents; otherwise there would appear no virtue in them.

II. Now, if it can be made appear, that none of these affections which we approve as virtuous, are either self-love, or desire of private interest; since all virtue is either some such affections, or actions consequent upon them; it must neces-

From Francis Hutcheson, *An Inquiry into the Origin of our Ideas of Beauty and Virtue*, excerpts from Treatise II: An Inquiry concerning Moral Good and Evil. First printed, 1725. Text here is from revised 4th edition, London, 1738.

Moral Psychology: Historical and Contemporary Readings, edited by Thomas Nadelhoffer, Eddy Nahmias, and Shaun Nichols.

sarily follow, 'that virtue springs from some other affection than self-love, or desire of private advantage. And where self-interest excites to the same action, the approbation is given only to the disinterested principle.'

The affections which are of most importance in morals, are commonly included under the names *love* and *hatred*. Now in discoursing of love, we need not be cautioned not to include that love between the sexes, which, when no other affections accompany it, is only desire of pleasure, and is never counted a virtue. Love toward rational agents, is subdivided into *love of complacence* or *esteem*, and *love of benevolence*: and hatred is subdivided into *hatred of displicence* or *contempt*, and *hatred of malice*. *Complacence* denotes approbation of any person by our moral sense; and is rather a perception than an affection; though the affection of good-will is ordinarily subsequent to it. *Benevolence* is the desire of the happiness of another. Their opposites are called *dislike* and *malice*. Concerning each of these separately we shall consider, 'whether they can be influenced by motives of self-interest.'

Complacence, esteem, or good-liking, at first view appears to be disinterested, and so displicence or dislike; and are entirely excited by some moral qualities, good or evil, apprehended to be in the objects; which qualities the very frame of our nature determines us to approve or disapprove, according to the moral sense above explained.[1] Propose to a man all the rewards in the world, or threaten all the punishments, to engage him to esteem and complacence toward a person entirely unknown, or if known, apprehended to be cruel, treacherous, ungrateful; you may procure external obsequiousness, or good offices, or dissimulation; but real esteem no price can purchase. And the same is obvious as to contempt, which no motive of advantage can prevent. On the contrary, represent a character as generous, kind, faithful, humane, though in the most distant parts of the world, and we cannot avoid esteem and complacence. A bribe may possibly make us attempt to ruin such a man, or some strong motive of advantage may excite us to oppose his interest; but it can never make us disapprove him, while we retain the same opinion of his temper and intentions. Nay, when we consult our own hearts, we shall find, that we can scarce ever persuade ourselves to attempt any

mischief against such persons, from any motive of advantage; nor execute it without the strongest reluctance and remorse, until we have blinded ourselves into a false opinion about his temper.

III. As to the *love of benevolence*, the very name excludes self-interest. We never call that man *benevolent*, who is in fact useful to others, but at the same time only intends his own interest, without any ultimate desire of the good of others. If there be any benevolence at all, it must be disinterested; for the most useful action imaginable loses all appearance of benevolence, as soon as we discern that it only flowed from self-love, or interest. Thus, never were any human actions more advantageous, than the inventions of fire, and iron; but if these were casual, or if the inventor only intended his own interest in them, there is nothing which can be called *benevolent* in them. Wherever then benevolence is supposed, there it is imagined disinterested, and designed for the good of others. To raise benevolence, no more is required than calmly to consider any sensitive nature not pernicious to others. Gratitude arises from benefits conferred from good-will on ourselves, or those we love; complacence is a perception of the moral sense. Gratitude includes some complacence, and complacence still raises a stronger good-will than that we have toward indifferent characters, where there is no opposition of interests.

But it must be here observed, that as all men have self-love, as well as benevolence, these two principles may jointly excite a man to the same action; and then they are to be considered as two forces impelling the same body to motion; sometimes they conspire, sometimes are indifferent to each other, and sometimes are in some degree opposite. Thus, if a man have such strong benevolence, as would have produced an action without any views of self-interest; that such a man has also in view private advantage, along with public good, as the effect of his action, does no way diminish the benevolence of the action. When he would not have produced so much public good, had it not been for prospect of self-interest, then the effect of self-love is to be deducted, and his benevolence is proportioned to the remainder of good, which pure benevolence would have produced. When a man's benevolence is hurtful to himself, then self-love is opposite to benevolence, and the benevolence is proportioned to the sum of the good produced, added to the resistance of self-love surmounted by it. In most cases it is impossible for men to know how far their fellows are influenced by the one or other of these principles; but yet the general truth is sufficiently certain, that this is the way in which the benevolence of actions is to be computed.

IV. There are two ways in which some may deduce benevolence from self-love, the one supposing that 'we voluntarily bring this affection upon ourselves, whenever we have an opinion that it will be for our interest to have this affection, either as it may be immediately pleasant, or may afford pleasant reflection afterwards by our moral sense, or as it may tend to procure some external reward from God or man.' The other scheme alleges no such power in us of raising desire or affection of any kind by our choice or volition; but 'supposes our minds determined by the frame of their nature to desire whatever is apprehended as the means of any private happiness; and that the observation of the happiness of other persons, in many cases is made the necessary occasion of pleasure to the observer, as their misery is the occasion of his uneasiness: and in consequence of this connection, as soon as we have observed it, we begin to desire the happiness of others as the means of obtaining this happiness to ourselves, which we expect from the contemplation of others in a happy state. They allege it to be impossible to desire either the happiness of another, or any event whatsoever, without conceiving it as the means of some happiness or pleasure to ourselves; but own at the same time, that desire is not raised in us directly by any volition, but arises necessarily upon our apprehending any object or event to be conducive to our happiness.'

That the former scheme is not just, may appear from this general consideration, that 'neither benevolence nor any other affection or desire can be directly raised by volition.' If they could, then we could be bribed into any affection whatsoever toward any object, even the most improper: we might raise jealousy, fear, anger, love, toward any sort of persons indifferently by an hire, even as we engage men to external actions, or to the dissimulation of passions; but this every person will by his own reflection find to be impossible. The prospect of any advantage to arise to us from having any affection, may indeed turn our attention to those qualities in the object, which are naturally constituted the necessary causes or occasions of the advantageous affection; and if we find such qualities in the object, the affection will certainly arise. Thus indirectly the prospect of advantage may tend to raise any affection; but if these qualities be not found or apprehended in the object, no volition of ours, nor desire, will ever raise any affection in us.

But more particularly, that desire of the good of others, which we approve as virtuous, cannot be alleged to be voluntarily raised from prospect of any pleasure accompanying the affection itself: for it is plain that our benevolence is not always accompanied with pleasure; nay, it is often attended with pain, when the object is in distress. Desire in general is rather uneasy than pleasant. It is true, indeed, all the passions and affections justify themselves; while they continue, (as Malebranche expresses it) we generally approve our being thus affected on this occasion, as an innocent disposition, or a just one, and condemn a person who would be otherwise affected on the like occasion. So the sorrowful, the angry, the jealous, the compassionate, approve their several passions on the apprehended occasion; but we should not therefore conclude, that sorrow, anger, jealousy or pity are pleasant, or chosen for their concomitant pleasure. The case is plainly thus: the frame of our nature on the occasions which move these passions, determines us to be thus affected, and to approve our affection at least as innocent. Uneasiness generally attends our desires of any kind; and this sensation tends to fix our attention, and to continue the desire. But the desire does not terminate upon the removal of the pain accompanying the desire, but upon some other event: the concomitant pain is what we seldom reflect upon, unless when it is very violent. Nor does any desire or affection terminate upon the pleasure which may accompany the affection; much less is it raised by an act of our will, with a view to obtain this pleasure.

The same reflection will show, that we do not by an act of our will raise in ourselves that benevolence which we approve as virtuous, with a view to obtain future pleasures of self-approbation by our moral sense. Could we raise affections in this manner, we should be engaged to any affection by the prospect of an interest equivalent to this of self-approbation, such as wealth or sensual pleasure, which with many tempers are more powerful; and yet we universally own, that *that* disposition to do good offices to others, which is raised by these motives, is not virtuous: how can we then imagine, that the virtuous benevolence is brought upon us by a motive equally *selfish*?

But what will most effectually convince us of the truth on this point, is reflection upon our own hearts, whether we have not a desire of the good of others, generally without any consideration or intention of obtaining these pleasant reflections on our own virtue: nay, often this desire is strongest where we least imagine virtue, in natural affection toward offspring, and in gratitude to a great benefactor; the absence of which is indeed the greatest vice, but the affections themselves are not esteemed in any considerable degree virtuous. The same reflection will also convince us, that these desires or affections are not produced by choice with a view to obtain this private good.

[. . .]

V. The other scheme is more plausible: that benevolence is not raised by any volition upon prospect of advantage; but that we desire the happiness of others, as conceiving it necessary to procure some pleasant sensations which we expect to feel upon seeing others happy; and that for like reason we have aversion to their misery. This connection between the happiness of others and our pleasure, say they, is chiefly felt among friends, parents and children, and eminently virtuous characters. But this benevolence flows as directly from self-love as any other desire.

To show that this scheme is not true in fact, let us consider, that if in our benevolence we only desired the happiness of others as the means of this pleasure to ourselves, whence is it that no man approves the desire of the happiness of others as a means of procuring wealth or sensual pleasure to ourselves? If a person had wagered concerning the future happiness of a man of such veracity, that he would sincerely confess whether he were happy or not; would this wagerer's desire of the happiness of another, in order to win the wager, be approved as virtuous? If not, wherein does this desire differ from the former? Except that in one case there is one pleasant sensation expected, and in the other case other sensations: for by increasing or diminishing the sum wagered, the interest in this case may be made either greater or less than that in the other.

Reflecting on our own minds again will best discover the truth. Many have never thought upon this connection: nor do we ordinarily intend the obtaining of any such pleasure when we do generous offices. We all often feel delight upon seeing others happy, but during our pursuit of their happiness we have no intention of obtaining this delight. We often feel the pain of compassion; but were our sole ultimate intention or desire the freeing ourselves from this pain, would the Deity offer to us either wholly to blot out all memory of the person in distress, to take away this connection, so that we should be easy during the misery of our friend on the one hand, or on the other would relieve him from his misery, we should be as ready to choose the former way as the latter; since either of them would free us from our pain, which upon this scheme is the sole end proposed by the compassionate person. Don't we find in ourselves that our desire does not terminate upon the removal of our own pain? Were this our sole intention, we would run away, shut our eyes, or divert our thoughts from the miserable object, as the readiest way of removing our pain: this we seldom do, nay, we crowd about such objects, and voluntarily expose ourselves to this pain, unless calm reflection upon our inability to relieve the miserable, countermand our inclination, or some selfish affection, as fear of danger, overpower it.

To make this yet clearer, suppose that the Deity should declare to a good man that he should be suddenly annihilated, but at the instant of his exit it should be left to his choice whether his friend, his children, or his country should be made happy or miserable for the future, when he himself could have no sense of either pleasure or pain from their state. Pray would he be any more indifferent about their state now, that he neither hoped or feared anything to himself from it, than he was in any prior period of his life? Nay, is it not a pretty common opinion among us, that after our decease we know nothing of what befalls those who survive us? How comes it then that we do not lose, at the approach of death, all concern for our families, friends, or country? Can there be any instance given of our desiring anything only as the means of private good, as violently when we know that we shall not enjoy this good many minutes, as if we expected the possession of this good for many years? Is this the way we compute the value of annuities?

How the disinterested desire of the good of others should seem inconceivable, it is hard to account: perhaps it is owing to the attempts of some great men to give definitions of simple ideas. Desire, say they, is uneasiness, or uneasy sensation upon the absence of any good. Whereas desire is as distinct from uneasiness, as volition is from sensation. Don't they themselves often speak of our desiring to remove uneasiness? Desire then is different from uneasiness, however a sense of uneasiness accompanies it, as extension does the idea of colour, which yet is a very distinct idea. Now wherein lies the impossibility of desiring the happiness of another without conceiving it as the means of obtaining anything farther, even as we desire our own happiness without farther view? If any allege, that we desire our own happiness as the means of removing the uneasiness we feel in the absence of happiness, then at least the desire of removing our own uneasiness is an ultimate desire: and why may we not have other ultimate desires?

'But can any being be concerned about the absence of an event which gives it no uneasiness?' Perhaps superior natures desire without uneasy sensation. But what if we cannot? We may be uneasy while a desired event is in suspense, and yet not desire this event only as the means of removing this uneasiness: nay, if we did not desire the event without view to this uneasiness, we should never have brought the uneasiness upon ourselves by desiring it. So likewise we may feel delight upon the existence of a desired event, when yet we did not desire the event only as the means of obtaining this delight; even as we often receive delight from events which we had an aversion to.

[. . .]

VII. As to malice, human nature seems scarce capable of malicious disinterested hatred, or a sedate ultimate desire of the misery of others, when we imagine them no way pernicious to us, or opposite to our interest: and for that hatred which makes us oppose those whose interests are opposite to ours, it is only the effect of self-love, and not of disinterested malice. A sudden passion may give us wrong representations of our fellow-creatures, and for a little time represent them as absolutely evil; and during this imagination perhaps we may give some evidences of disinterested malice: but as soon as we reflect upon human nature, and form just conceptions, this unnatural passion is allayed, and only self-love remains, which may make us, from self-interest, oppose our adversaries.

[. . .]

X. Having removed these false springs of virtuous actions, let us next establish the true one, viz. some determination of our nature to study the good of others; or some instinct, antecedent to all reason from interest, which influences us to the love of others; even as the moral sense, above explained,[2] determines us to approve the actions which flow from this love in ourselves or others. This disinterested affection, may appear strange to men impressed with notions of self-love, as the sole spring of action, from the pulpit, the schools, the systems, and conversations regulated by them: but let us consider it in its strongest and simplest kinds; and when we see the possibility of it in these instances, we may easily discover its universal extent.

An honest farmer will tell you, that he studies the preservation and happiness of his children, and loves them without any design of good to himself. But say some of our philosophers, 'The happiness of their children gives parents pleasure, and their misery gives them pain; and therefore to obtain the former, and avoid the latter, they study, from self-love, the good of their children.' Suppose several merchants joined in partnership of their whole effects; one of them is employed abroad in managing the stock of the company; his prosperity occasions gain to all, and his losses give them pain for their share in the loss: is this then the same kind of affection with that of parents to their children? Is there the same tender, personal regard? I fancy no parent will say so. In this case of merchants there is a plain conjunction of interest; but whence the conjunction of interest between the parent and child? Do the child's sensations give pleasure or pain to the parent? Is the parent hungry, thirsty, sick, when his children are so? No; but his naturally implanted desire of their good, and aversion to their misery, makes him be affected with joy or sorrow from their pleasures or pains. This desire then is antecedent to the conjunction of interest, and the cause of it, not the effect: it then must be disinterested. 'No, says another sophist, children are parts of ourselves, and in loving them we but love ourselves in them.' A very good answer! Let us carry it as far as it will go. How are they parts of ourselves? Not as a leg or an arm: we are not conscious of their sensations. 'But their bodies were formed from parts of ours.' So is a fly, or a maggot, which may breed in any discharged blood or humour: very dear insects surely! There must be something else then which makes children parts of ourselves; and what is this but that affection, which *nature* determines us to have toward them? This love makes them parts of ourselves, and therefore does not flow from their being so before. This is indeed a good metaphor; and wherever we find a determination among several rational agents to mutual love, let each individual be looked upon as a part of a great whole, or system, and concern himself in the public good of it.

But a later author observes, 'That natural affection in parents is weak, till the children begin to give evidences of knowledge and affections.' Mothers say they feel it strong from the very first: and yet I could wish, for the destruction of his hypothesis, that what he alleges was true; as I fancy it is in some measure, though we may find in some parents an affection toward idiots.

The observing of understanding and affections in children, which make them appear moral agents, can increase love toward them without prospect of *interest*; for I hope, this increase of love is not from prospect of advantage from the knowledge or affections of children, for whom parents are still toiling, and never intend to be refunded their expenses, or recompensed for their labour, but in cases of extreme necessity. If then the observing a moral capacity can be the occasion of increasing love without self interest, even from the frame of our nature; pray, may not this be a foundation of weaker degrees of love, where there is no preceding tie of parentage, and extend it to all mankind?

Notes

Taken from the revised 4th edition (1738). Spelling has been adjusted and original footnotes eliminated. Italics and initial capital letters have been minimized.

1 See *An Inquiry Concerning Moral Good and Evil*, Section I, pp. xx–xx in this volume.
2 See *An Inquiry Concerning Moral Good and Evil*, Section I, pp. xx–xx in this volume.

14

How Social an Animal?
The Human Capacity for Caring

C. Daniel Batson

It has been said that we are social animals. Aristotle said it. Charles Darwin said it. Elliot Aronson said it. Given this lineup of expert witnesses, I am not about to suggest otherwise. We *are* social animals. We spend an incredible proportion of our waking hours with other people – in appointments, classes, and committee meetings; on highways or mass transportation; with family, friends, and lovers. And when we are alone, we are rarely really alone. We read, listen to the radio, or watch TV; others are still there. Even on a solitary walk, we almost always take others with us; our thoughts are on this or that social interaction: What did she mean by that? What should I say to him?

But how social are we really? We live in a social arena; virtually all of our actions are directed toward or are responses to others. Yet to what end? In our interactions with others do we ever really care about them, or is the real target of our concern always, exclusively ourselves?

If we really care about them – if we desire certain outcomes for others because of what these outcomes mean for them and not simply because of what they mean for us – then we are very social animals indeed. But if the real target of our concern is always, exclusively ourselves, then we are far less social. True, we operate in a social arena, with others almost always on our minds. They are on our minds because they are necessary for us

to reach our goals, and they can be very hard to control. It can be a full-time job trying to bend the will of others, all seeking their own ends, so that they enable us to reach our ends. From this perspective other people, however dear, are simply complex objects in our environment – important sources of stimulation and gratification, of facilitation and inhibition – as we each pursue self-interest. We care for them only insofar as their welfare affects ours.

Perhaps the clearest way to phrase the question I am raising is by borrowing Milton Rokeach's (1973) distinction between terminal and instrumental values. Each of us values at least some other people. But do we value these others for their own sake – a terminal value – or for ours – an instrumental value? This is what it means to ask how social we really are.

Psychology's Explicit Response: Discreet Silence

Psychology, especially in recent years, has shied away from directly confronting this rather fundamental question about human nature. In spite of Gordon Allport's (1968) claim that understanding our social nature is "the key problem of social psychology" (p. 1), this problem has become a taboo topic – like sex for the Victorians – that we

How Social an Animal: the Human Capacity for Caring, from Dan Batson (March, 1990). How social an animal: The human capacity for caring. *American Psychologist*, 45, 3. American Psychological Association, Inc. (pp. 336, 339–46).

social psychologists politely avoid, especially in public. Our strategy has been to stay closer to the surface and address more circumspect, specific issues, assuming perhaps that the embarrassing problem of our social nature will disappear. Yet, if Allport is right that understanding our social nature is the key problem, then if it disappears, does not social psychology also disappear?

Psychology's Implicit Response: Social Egoism

There is, however, another possibility. Perhaps the reason that social psychologists have spent little time on the question of our social nature is because they already know the answer. As Donald Campbell (1975) and the Wallachs (Wallach & Wallach, 1983) have pointed out, the question of whether we care for others or only for ourselves is one of the few to which psychologists of all stripes, researchers and practitioners, implicitly give a common answer.

Psychology's implicit answer is that the only persons we are capable of caring about, ultimately, are ourselves. We value others instrument-ally; we care for their welfare only to the degree that it affects ours. Our behavior may be highly social; our thoughts may be highly social; but in our hearts, we live alone. *Altruism*, the view that we are capable of valuing and pursuing another person's welfare as an ultimate goal, is pure fantasy. We are *social egoists*.

[. . .]

The suggestion that we are in any degree capable of truly altruistic motives, of valuing and desiring another's welfare for his or her sake and not ours, has rarely even been entertained. Yet I believe that there is now considerable evidence that this latter view is right, that the human capacity for caring is far greater than we have thought. The main arena for recent debate of this issue has been analysis of the nature of the motivation underlying the empathy-helping relationship.

The empathy-helping relationship. Obviously, we humans can and do help each other. Our helpful acts range from the numerous small kindnesses and favors that we do for each other every day, to the great acts of self-sacrifice of the Albert Schweitzers and Mother Teresas, acts that win Carnegie Hero Fund Commission awards. Moreover, considerable research suggests that we are more likely to help someone in need when we "feel for" that person, when we feel emotions like empathy, sympathy, compassion, and tenderness (see Coke, Batson, & McDavis, 1978; Eisenberg & Miller, 1987). This relationship between feeling for and helping a person in need is what I mean by the empathy-helping relationship. As far as I know, there is now no doubt or debate that this relationship exists. There is, however, consider-able doubt and debate over why it exists and over what it tells us about our social nature.

Possible motives underlying the empathy-helping relationship: Egoism and altruism? Researchers approaching the evidence of an empathy-helping relationship from the perspective of social egoism have been quick to point out possible self-benefits of this helping. After all, when we feel empathy for someone in distress, does that not make us feel distress too? Maybe we act to relieve their distress simply as an instrumental means to the ultimate goal of relieving our own distress (Piliavin & Piliavin, 1973). Or maybe we anticipate feeling especially ashamed and guilty if we do not help someone for whom we feel empathy. Or maybe we anticipate feeling especially good about our-selves if we help such a person. Any of these three explanations – aversive-arousal reduction, punishment avoidance, or reward seeking – can account for the empathy-helping relationship within the context of social egoism. None requires that we care for anyone other than ourselves, except as instrumental means to our own self-serving ends.

But is any of these three egoistic explanations of the empathy-helping relationship correct? Rather than simply assuming one or more must be, we need to consider this question carefully. Admittedly, it is a difficult question, because it is not a question about behavior but about the motivation underlying behavior. At issue is the helper's ultimate goal. Social egoism claims that benefiting the person in need is an instrumental goal on the way to the ultimate goal of benefiting oneself. Altruism argues back that simply to show that self-benefits follow from benefiting the other does not prove that the self-benefits are the helper's goal. It is at least logically possible that the self-benefits are unintended consequences of the helper's reaching his or her ultimate goal of

Table 14.1   Formal Structure of the Altruism Question

	Outcomes of helping	
Explanations of why we help	We relieve the other's suffering	And as a result we receive self-benefits
Egoistic account	Instrumental goal	Ultimate goal
Altruistic account	Ultimate goal	Unintended consequence

benefiting the other. If this is the case, then the motivation is altruistic, not egoistic.

Distinguishing Between Egoistic and Altruistic Motives

The formal structure of the problem is depicted in Table 14.1. To determine whether empathy broadens the scope of the human capacity to care so that it includes at least some others, we must determine whether the empathically aroused helper (a) benefits the other as an instrumental goal on the way to reaching some self-benefit as an ultimate goal (egoism) or (b) benefits the other as an ultimate goal, with any resulting self-benefits being unintended consequences (altruism).

But if helping benefits both the person in need and the helper, how are we to know which is the ultimate goal? More generally, if multiple goals are reached by the same behavior, how are we ever to know which goal is ultimate? This problem has led many researchers to give up on the altruism question, concluding that it cannot be answered empirically. I think this surrender is premature. I think we can empirically ascertain people's ultimate goals; indeed, I think we do it all the time. Consider the following example.

Ascertaining a person's ultimate goal. Suzie and Frank work together. One morning, music-loving Suzie is unusually attentive to homely but well-heeled Frank. Frank wonders, "Have my prayers been answered? Has Suzie finally discovered my charms? Or is she broke and wanting me to take her to the concert this weekend?" Frank is questioning Suzie's ultimate goal. As matters stand, he lacks the information to make a clear inference, although wishful thinking may provide one. But what if Suzie, returning from lunch, finds in her mail two concert tickets sent by her father? If she coolly passes Frank on her way to invite John, then Frank can infer with considerable

confidence – and chagrin – the ultimate goal of her earlier attentions.

This simple example highlights three principles that are important when drawing inferences about a person's ultimate goal: First and most obviously, we do not observe another person's goals or intentions directly; we infer them from the person's behavior. Second, if we observe only a single behavior that has different potential ultimate goals, the true ultimate goal cannot be discerned. It is like having one equation with two unknowns; a clear answer is impossible. Third, we can draw reasonable inferences about a person's ultimate goal if we can observe the person's behavior in different situations that involve a change in the relation between the potential ultimate goals. Behavior should always be directed toward the true ultimate goal.

Everyday use of this strategy for inferring the motives underlying other people's behavior has been discussed in some detail by attribution theorists like Heider (1958) and Jones and Davis (1965). We use it to infer when a student is really interested or only seeking a better grade (e.g., what happens to the student's interest after the grades are turned in?), why a friend chose one job over another, and whether politicians mean what they say or are only seeking votes. This strategy also underlies much dissonance (Festinger, 1957) and reactance (Brehm, 1966) research.

Employing the example of Suzie and Frank as a model, two steps are necessary to infer the nature of a person's motivation from his or her behavior. First, we must conduct a conceptual analysis of the various potential alternative goals for the person's action. Unless we have some idea that a given goal may have been the person's aim, there is little likelihood of concluding that it was. Frank realized that Suzie actually might be interested in the concert and not in him. Second, we need to observe the person's behavior in systematically varying circumstances. Specifically, the circumstances need to be varied in a way that disentangles the relationship between potential ultimate goals, making it possible for the person to obtain one without having to obtain the other – just as after lunch Suzie could get to the concert without Frank. The person's behavioral choices in these situations should prove diagnostic, telling us which of the goals is ultimate, because the behavior should always be directed toward the ultimate goal. These two steps provide an empirical basis for inferring the nature of a person's motivation.

Possible egoistic goals of empathy-induced helping. My colleagues and I have applied this logic to the problem of the nature of the motivation underlying the empathy-helping relationship. We first sought to identify possible egoistic goals of empathically induced helping. The three we identified are the ones I have already mentioned: (a) reducing the aversive empathic arousal, (b) avoiding social and self-punishments such as shame and guilt, and (c) seeking social and self-rewards (see Batson, 1987). To account for the empathy-helping relationship, the arousal, punishments, or rewards must, of course, be empathy specific. They must exist, or at least exist to a greater degree, among individuals feeling a higher degree of empathy for the person in need.

Second, we sought techniques for systematically varying a helping situation so that for some individuals one or more of these possible egoistic goals could be obtained only by helping, whereas for others these goals could be obtained without having to endure the costs of helping. If this variation eliminated the empathy-helping relationship, then we would have evidence that the self-benefit – not benefit to the person in need – is the ultimate goal of the prosocial motivation associated with empathy. If this variation did not eliminate the empathy-helping relationship, then we would have evidence that the self-benefit is not the ultimate goal, suggesting that the motivation might be altruistic.

Using this strategy, we and other researchers have conducted over 20 experiments during the past decade to test one or more of the three proposed egoistic explanations of the empathy-helping relationship. In each experiment, the egoistic explanation(s) predicted a different pattern of results than did the *empathy-altruism hypothesis*, the hypothesis that empathy evokes truly altruistic motivation. A sketch of the logic

and results of these experiments will give you an idea of why I no longer believe that our capacity for caring is limited to ourselves. (For more complete reports, see Batson, 1987, 1991; Batson et al., 1988, Batson et al., 1989.)

Testing the Egoistic Alternatives to the Empathy-Altruism Hypothesis

1. *Aversive-arousal reduction.* The most frequently proposed egoistic explanation of the empathy-helping relationship is aversive-arousal reduction. Martin Hoffman (1981) put it in a nutshell: "Empathic distress is unpleasant and helping the victim is usually the best way to get rid of the source" (p. 52). According to this explanation, empathically aroused individuals help in order to benefit themselves by reducing their empathic arousal; benefiting the victim is simply a means to this self-serving end.

To test this aversive-arousal reduction explanation against the empathy-altruism hypothesis, experiments have been conducted varying the ease of escaping further exposure to a suffering victim without helping. Because empathic arousal is a result of witnessing the victim's suffering, either terminating this suffering by helping or terminating exposure to it by escaping should serve to reduce the arousal. Escape is not, however, a viable means of reaching the altruistic goal of relieving the victim's distress; it does nothing to promote that end.

The difference in viability of escape as a means to these two goals produces competing predictions in an Escape (easy vs. difficult) × Empathy (low vs. high) design. Among individuals experiencing low empathy for the person in need, both the aversive-arousal reduction explanation and the empathy-altruism hypothesis predict more helping when escape is difficult than when it is easy. This is because both assume that the motivation of individuals feeling low empathy will be egoistic. Among individuals feeling high empathy, the aversive-arousal reduction explanation predicts a similar (perhaps even greater) difference; it assumes that empathically induced motivation is also egoistic. But the empathy-altruism hypothesis predicts high helping even when escape is easy among individuals feeling high empathy. Across the four cells of an Escape × Empathy design, then, the aversive-arousal reduction explanation predicts less helping under easy escape in each empathy condition; the empathy-altruism hypothesis predicts a 1 versus 3 pattern: relatively low helping in the easy-escape/low empathy cell and high helping in the other three cells. These competing predictions are presented in Table 14.2.

Over half a dozen experiments have now been run using this Escape × Empathy design. In a typical procedure, participants observe a "worker" whom they believe is reacting badly to a series of uncomfortable electric shocks; they are then given a chance to help the worker by taking the shocks themselves. To manipulate ease of escape, some participants are informed that if they do not help, they will continue observing the worker take the shocks (difficult escape); others are informed that they will observe no more (easy escape). Empathy has been both manipulated and measured.

Results of these experiments have consistently conformed to the pattern in the bottom half of Table 14.2 predicted by the empathy–altruism hypothesis, not to the pattern in the top half predicted by the aversive-arousal reduction explanation. Only among individuals experiencing a predominance of personal distress rather than empathy (i.e., feeling relatively anxious, upset, distressed, and the like) does the chance for easy escape reduce helping. In spite of the popularity of the aversive-arousal reduction explanation of the empathy–helping relationship, a popularity that continues in a number of social psychology textbooks, this explanation appears to be wrong.

2. *Empathy-specific punishment.* The second egoistic explanation of the empathy-helping relationship claims that we have learned through socialization that an additional obligation to help, and so additional shame and guilt for failure to help, is attendant on feeling empathy for someone in need. As a result, when we feel empathy, we are faced with impending social or self-censure above and beyond any general punishment associated with not helping. We say to ourselves, "What will others think – or what will I think of myself – if I don't help when I feel like this?," and we help out of an egoistic desire to avoid these empathy-specific punishments. Eighteenth-century British social philosopher Bernard Mandeville (1714/1732) summarized this explanation prosaically:

> There is no merit in saving an innocent babe ready to drop into the fire: The action is neither good nor bad, and what benefit soever the infant received, we only obliged our selves; for to have seen it fall, and not strove to hinder it, would have caused a pain, which self-preservation compelled us to prevent. (p. 42)

Several different techniques have been used to test this empathy-specific punishment explanation against the empathy-altruism hypothesis. Let me discuss just one: providing justification for not helping. The logic behind this technique is that if a person is helping to avoid shame and guilt, then if we provide information that increases the justification for not helping, the rate of helping should drop. But if a person is helping out of an altruistic desire to reduce the other's suffering, then even with increased justification, the rate of helping should remain high. Therefore, the empathy-specific punishment explanation and the empathy-altruism hypothesis predict a different pattern of helping across the four cells of a Justification for Not Helping (low vs. high) × Empathy (low vs. high) design. These different predictions are presented in Table 14.3.

In the last five years, my colleagues and I have conducted three studies employing different versions of this Justification × Empathy design (Batson et al., 1988, Studies 2–4). In the first, justification was provided by information about the inaction of other potential helpers. We reasoned that if most people asked have said no to a request for help, then one should feel more justified in saying no as well. Individuals feeling either low or high empathy for a young women in

Table 14.2 Predictions From Aversive-Arousal Reduction Explanation and Empathy-Altruism Hypothesis for Rate of Helping in Escape × Empathy Design

	Empathy	
Escape	Low	High
Aversive-arousal reduction explanation		
Easy	Low	Low
Difficult	High	High/very high
Empathy-altruism hypothesis		
Easy	Low	High
Difficult	High	High

Table 14.3 Predictions From Empathy-Specific Punishment Explanation and Empathy-Altruism Hypothesis for Rate of Helping in Justification × Empathy Design

Justification for not helping	Empathy	
	Low	High
Empathy-Specific Punishment Explanation		
Low	Moderate	High
High	Low	Low
Empathy-Altruism Hypothesis		
Low	Moderate	High
High	Low	High

need were given an opportunity to pledge time to help her. Information on the pledge form about the responses of previously asked peers indicated that either 5 of 7 had pledged (low justification for not helping) or 2 of 7 had pledged (high justification). The young woman's plight was such that others' responses did not affect her need for help. As depicted in Table 14.3, the empathy-specific punishment explanation predicted more helping in the low-justification condition than in the high by individuals feeling high empathy. In contrast, the empathy-altruism hypothesis predicted high helping by these individuals in both justification conditions. The latter pattern was found. Only among individuals feeling low empathy were those in the high-justification condition less likely to help than those in the low-justification condition.

In the second study, justification was provided by attributional ambiguity. We reasoned that if individuals can attribute a decision not to help to helping-irrelevant features of the decision, then they should be less likely to anticipate social or self-punishment. Individuals feeling either low or high empathy for a peer they thought was about to receive electric shocks were given a chance to work on either or both of two task options. For each correct response on Option A, they would receive one raffle ticket for a $30 prize for themselves; for each correct response on Option B, they would reduce by one the shocks the peer was to receive. Information about helping-irrelevant attributes of the two task options indicated either that the two tasks were quite similar and neither was preferred (low justification for not helping)

or that one task involved numbers, the other letters, and most people preferred to work on the number (letters), whichever was paired with the non-helpful Option A (high justification). Once again, competing predictions were those in Table 14.3, and once again, results patterned as predicted by the empathy-altruism hypothesis, not as predicted by the empathy-specific punishment explanation.

In the third study, justification for not helping was provided by information about the difficulty of the performance standard on a qualifying task. We reasoned that if potential helpers knew that even if they volunteered to help they would only be allowed to do so if they met the performance standard on a qualifying task, then performance on the qualifying task would provide a behavioral measure of motivation to reduce the victim's suffering (which requires qualifying) or to avoid social and self-punishment (which does not). This should be true, however, only if poor performance could be justified. Poor performance could be justified if the performance standard on the qualifying task was so difficult that most people fail. If the standard was this difficult, a person could not be blamed for not qualifying – either by the self or others. In this case, individuals motivated to avoid self-punishment should either (a) decline to help because of the low probability of qualifying or (b) offer to help but not try very hard on the qualifying task, ensuring that they did not qualify. Bluntly put, they should take a dive.

In the study, then, individuals feeling either low or high empathy for a peer who they believed was reacting badly to a series of uncomfortable electric shocks were given a chance to help the peer by taking the remaining shocks themselves. But even if they volunteered, they had to meet the performance standard on the qualifying task to be eligible to help. Information about the difficulty of the standard indicated either that most college students qualify (low justification for not helping) or most do not (high justification).

Once more, results supported the empathy-altruism hypothesis. Helping again followed the pattern predicted in the bottom half of Table 14.3. The performance measure also followed the pattern predicted by the empathy-altruism hypothesis: Performance of low-empathy individuals was lower when the qualifying standard was difficult than when it was easy; performance of high-empathy individuals was higher when the qualifying standard was difficult. This inter-action pattern suggested that the motivation of low-empathy individuals was at least in part dir-ected toward avoiding self-punishment; whereas, contrary to the empathy-specific punishment explanation, the motivation of high-empathy individuals was not. The motivation of high-empathy individuals appeared to be directed toward the altruistic goal of relieving the other's suffering.

In all three studies, results conformed to the pattern predicted by the empathy-altruism hypothesis, not to the pattern predicted by the empathy-specific punishment explanation. Results of these studies, as well as highly consistent results from other studies using different tech-niques to test the empathy-specific punishment explanation, converge to suggest that this second egoistic explanation of the empathy-helping rela-tionship is also wrong.

[. . .]

If the empathy-altruism hypothesis is true, then I think we must radically revise our views of the human capacity for caring. For to say that we are capable of being altruistically motivated is to say that we can care about others' welfare as a terminal not just an instrumental value. We can seek their welfare for their sakes and not simply for our own. If this is true, then we are far more social animals than our psychological theories, including our most social social-psychological theories, would lead us to believe.

References

Allport, G. W. (1968). The historical background of social psychology. In G. Lindzey & E. Aronson (eds.), *The handbook of social psychology* (vol. 1, pp. 1–80). Reading, MA: Addison-Wesley.

Batson, C. D. (1987). Prosocial motivation: Is it ever truly altruistic? In L. Berkowitz (ed.), *Advances in experimental social psychology* (vol. 20, pp. 65–122). New York: Academic Press.

Batson, C. D. (1991). *The altruism question: Toward a social-psychological answer*. Hillsdale, NJ: Erlbaum.

Batson, C. D., Batson, J. G., Griffitt, C. A., Barrientos, S., Brandt, J. R., Sprengelmeyer, P., & Bayly, M. J. (1989). Negative-state relief and the empathy-altruism hypothesis. *Journal of Personality and Social Psychology, 56*, 922–33.

Batson, C. D., Dyck, J. L., Brandt, J. R., Batson, J. G., Powell, A. L., McMaster, M. R., & Griffitt, C. (1988). Five studies testing two new egoistic alternatives to the empathy-altruism hypothesis. *Journal of Personality and Social Psychology, 55*, 52–77.

Brehm, J. W. (1966). *A theory of psychological reactance*. New York: Academic Press.

Campbell, D. T. (1975). On the conflicts between biological and social evolution and between psychology and moral tradition. *American Psychologist, 30*, 1103–26.

Coke, J. S., Batson, C. D., & McDavis, K. (1978). Empathic mediation of helping: A two-stage model. *Journal of Personality and Social Psychology, 36*, 752–66.

Eisenberg, N., & Miller, P. (1987). Empathy and pro-social behavior. *Psychological Bulletin, 101*, 91–19.

Festinger, L. (1957). *A theory of cognitive dissonance*. Stanford, CA: Stanford University Press.

Heider, F. (1958). *The psychology of interpersonal relations*. New York: Wiley.

Hoffman, M. L. (1981). The development of empathy. In J. P. Rushton & R. M. Sorrentino (eds.), *Altruism and helping behavior: Social, personality, and developmental perspectives* (pp. 41–63). Hillsdale, NJ: Erlbaum.

Jones, E. E., & Davis, K. E. (1965). From acts to disposi-tions: The attribution process in person perception. In L. Berkowitz (ed.), *Advances in experimental social psychology* (vol. 2, pp. 219–66). New York: Academic Press.

Mandeville, B. (1732). *The fable of the bees: Or, private vices, public benefits*. London: J. Tonson. (Original work published 1714)

Piliavin, J. A., & Piliavin, I. M. (1973). *The Good Samaritan: Why does he help?* Unpublished manu-script, University of Wisconsin.

Rokeach, M. (1973). *The nature of human values*. New York: Free Press.

Wallach, M. A., & Wallach, L. (1983). *Psychology's sanction for selfishness: The error of egoism in theory and therapy*. San Francisco, CA: Freeman.

15

The Evolution of Reciprocal Altruism

Robert L. Trivers

Introduction

Altruistic behavior can be defined as behavior that benefits another organism, not closely related, while being apparently detrimental to the organism performing the behavior, benefit and detriment being defined in terms of contribution to inclusive fitness. One human being leaping into water, at some danger to himself, to save another distantly related human from drowning may be said to display altruistic behavior. If he were to leap in to save his own child, the behavior would not necessarily be an instance of "altruism"; he may merely be contributing to the survival of his own genes invested in the child.

Models that attempt to explain altruistic behavior in terms of natural selection are models designed to take the altruism out of altruism. For example, Hamilton (1964) has demonstrated that degree of relationship is an important parameter in predicting how selection will operate, and behavior which appears altruistic may, on knowledge of the genetic relationships of the organisms involved, be explicable in terms of natural selection: those genes being selected for that contribute to their own perpetuation, regardless of which individual the genes appear in. The term "kin selection" will be used in this paper to cover instances of this type – that is, of organisms being selected to help their relatively close kin.

The model presented here is designed to show how certain classes of behavior conveniently denoted as "altruistic" (or "reciprocally altruistic") can be selected for even when the recipient is so distantly related to the organism performing the altruistic act that kin selection can be ruled out. The model will apply, for example, to altruistic behavior between members of different species. It will be argued that under certain conditions natural selection favors these altruistic behaviors because in the long run they benefit the organism performing them.

The Model

One human being saving another, who is not closely related and is about to drown, is an instance of altruism. Assume that the chance of the drowning man dying is one-half if no one leaps in to save him, but that the chance that his potential rescuer will drown if he leaps in to save him is much smaller, say, one in twenty. Assume that the drowning man always drowns when his rescuer does and that he is always saved when the rescuer survives the rescue attempt. Also assume that the energy costs involved in rescuing are trivial compared to the survival probabilities. Were this an isolated event, it is clear that the rescuer should not bother to save the drowning man.

The Evolution of Reciprocal Altruism, from Robert Trivers (March, 1971). The evolution of reciprocal altruism. *Quarterly Review of Biology*, 46, 1. The University of Chicago Press. pp. 35–9, 45, 47–57.

But if the drowning man reciprocates at some future time, and if the survival chances are then exactly reversed, it will have been to the benefit of each participant to have risked his life for the other. Each participant will have traded a one half chance of dying for about a one-tenth chance. If we assume that the entire population is sooner or later exposed to the same risk of drowning, the two individuals who risk their lives to save each other will be selected over those who face drowning on their own. Note that the benefits of reciprocity depend on the unequal cost/benefit ratio of the altruistic act, that is, the benefit of the altruistic act to the recipient is greater than the cost of the act to the performer, cost and benefit being defined here as the increase or decrease in chances of the relevant alleles propagating themselves in the population. Note also that, as defined, the benefits and costs depend on the age of the altruist and recipient (see *Age-dependent changes* below). (The odds assigned above may not be unrealistic if the drowning man is drowning because of a cramp or if the rescue can be executed by extending a branch from shore.)

Why should the rescued individual bother to reciprocate? Selection would seem to favor being saved from drowning without endangering oneself by reciprocating. Why not cheat? ("Cheating" is used throughout this paper solely for convenience to denote failure to reciprocate; no conscious intent or moral connotation is implied.) Selection will discriminate against the cheater if cheating has later adverse affects on his life which outweigh the benefit of not reciprocating. This may happen if the altruist responds to the cheating by curtailing all future possible altruistic gestures to this individual. Assuming that the benefits of these lost altruistic acts outweigh the costs involved in reciprocating, the cheater will be selected against relative to individuals who, because neither cheats, exchange many altruistic acts.

This argument can be made precise. Assume there are both altruists and non-altruists in a population of size N and that the altruists are characterized by the fact that each performs altruistic acts when the cost to the altruist is well below the benefit to the recipient, where cost is defined as the degree to which the behavior retards the reproduction of the genes of the altruist and benefit is the degree to which the behavior increases the rate of reproduction of the genes of

the recipient. Assume that the altruistic behavior of an altruist is controlled by an allele (dominant or recessive), a_2, at a given locus and that (for simplicity) there is only one alternative allele, a_1, at that locus and that it does not lead to altruistic behavior. Consider three possibilities: (1) the altruists dispense their altruism randomly throughout the population; (2) they dispense it nonrandomly by regarding their degree of genetic relationship with possible recipients; or (3) they dispense it nonrandomly by regarding the altruistic tendencies of possible recipients.

(1) Random dispensation of altruism

There are three possible genotypes: a_1a_1, a_2a_1, and a_2a_2. Each allele of the heterozygote will be affected equally by whatever costs and benefits are associated with the altruism of such individuals (if a_2 is dominant) and by whatever benefits accrue to such individuals from the altruism of others, so they can be disregarded. If altruistic acts are being dispensed randomly throughout a large population, then the typical a_1a_1 individual benefits by $(1/N)\sum b_i$, where b_i is the benefit of the ith altruistic act performed by the altruist. The typical a_2a_2 individual has a net benefit of $(1/N)\sum b_i - (1/N)\sum c_j$, where c_j is the cost to the a_2a_2 altruist of his jth altruistic act. Since $-(1/N)\sum c_j$ is always less than zero, allele a_1 will everywhere replace allele a_2.

(2) Nonrandom dispensation by reference to kin

This case has been treated in detail by Hamilton (1964), who concluded that if the tendency to dispense altruism to close kin is great enough, as a function of the disparity between the average cost and benefit of an altruistic act, then a_2 will replace a_1. Technically, all that is needed for Hamilton's form of selection to operate is that an individual with an "altruistic allele" be able to distinguish between individuals with and without this allele and discriminate accordingly. No formal analysis has been attempted of the possibilities for selection favoring individuals who increase their chances of receiving altruistic acts by appearing as if they were close kin of altruists, although selection has clearly sometimes favored such parasitism (e.g., Drury and Smith, 1968).

*(3)   Nonrandom dispensation by reference
to the altruistic tendencies of the recipient*

What is required is that the net benefit accruing to
a typical a_2a_2 altruist exceed that accruing to an
a_1a_1 non-altruist, or that

$$(1/p^2)(\sum b_k - \sum c_j) > (1/q^2)\sum b_m,$$

where b_k is the benefit to the a_2a_2 altruist of the kth
altruistic act performed toward him, where c_j is
the cost of the jth altruistic act by the a_2a_2 altruist,
where b_m is the benefit of the mth altruistic act to
the a_1a_1 nonaltruist, and where p is the frequency
in the population of the a_2 allele and q that of the
a_1 allele. This will tend to occur if $\sum b_m$ is kept
small (which will simultaneously reduce $\sum c_j$).
And this in turn will tend to occur if an altruist
responds to a "nonaltruistic act" (that is, a failure
to act altruistically toward the altruist in a situation in which so doing would cost the actor less
than it would benefit the recipient) by curtailing
future altruistic acts to the non-altruist.

Note that the above form of altruism does not
depend on all altruistic acts being controlled by
the same allele at the same locus. Each altruist
could be motivated by a different allele at a different locus. All altruistic alleles would tend to be
favored as long as, for each allele, the net average
benefit to the homozygous altruist exceeded the
average benefit to the homozygous nonaltruist;
this would tend to be true if altruists restrict their
altruism to fellow altruists, regardless of what allele
motivates the other individual's altruism. The
argument will therefore apply, unlike Hamilton's
(1964), to altruistic acts exchanged between
members of different species. It is the *exchange*
that favors such altrium, not the fact that the
allele in question sometimes or often directly
benefits its duplicate in another organism.

If an "altruistic situation" is defined as any in
which one individual can dispense a benefit to a
second greater than the cost of the act to himself,
then the chances of selecting for altruistic beha-
vior, that is, of keeping $\sum c_j + \sum b_m$ small, are greatest
(1) when there are many such altruistic situations
in the lifetime of the altruists, (2) when a given
altruist repeatedly interacts with the same small
set of individuals, and (3) when pairs of altruists
are exposed "symmetrically" to altruistic situations,
that is, in such a way that the two are able to ren-

der roughly equivalent benefits to each other at
roughly equivalent costs. These three conditions
can be elaborated into a set of relevant biological
parameters affecting the possibility that reciprocally altruistic behavior will be selected for.

(1) *Length of lifetime.* Long lifetime of individuals of a species maximizes the chance that any
two individuals will encounter many altruistic
situations, and all other things being equal one
should search for instances of reciprocal altruism
in long-lived species.

(2) *Dispersal rate.* Low dispersal rate during
all or a significant portion of the lifetime of individuals of a species increases the chance that an
individual will interact repeatedly with the same
set of neighbors, and other things being equal one
should search for instances of reciprocal altruism
in such species. Mayr (1963) has discussed some
of the factors that may affect dispersal rates.

(3) *Degree of mutual dependence.* Interdepend-
ence of members of a species (to avoid predators,
for example) will tend to keep individuals near
each other and thus increase the chance they will
encounter altruistic situations together. If the
benefit of the mutual dependence is greatest when
only a small number of individuals are together,
this will greatly increase the chance that an individual will repeatedly interact with the same small
set of individuals. Individuals in primate troops,
for example, are mutually dependent for protection from predation, yet the optimal troop size
for foraging is often small (Crook, 1969). Because
they also meet the other conditions out lined
here, primates are almost ideal species in which
to search for reciprocal altruism. Cleaning symbioses provide an instance of mutual dependence
between members of different species, and this
mutual dependence appears to have set the stage
for the evolution of several altruistic behaviors
discussed below.

(4) *Parental care.* A special instance of mutual
dependence is that found between parents and
offspring in species that show parental care. The
relationship is usually so asymmetrical that few or
no situations arise in which an offspring is capable
of performing an altruistic act for the parents
or even for another offspring, but this is not
entirely true for some species (such as primates)
in which the period of parental care is unusually
long. Parental care, of course, is to be explained
by Hamilton's (1964) model, but there is no

reason why selection for reciprocal altruism cannot operate between close kin, and evidence is presented below that such selection has operated in humans.

(5) *Dominance hierarchy.* Linear dominance hierarchies consist by definition of asymmetrical relationships; a given individual is dominant over another but not vice versa. Strong dominance hierarchies reduce the extent to which altruistic situations occur in which the less dominant individual is capable of performing a benefit for the more dominant which the more dominant individual could not simply take at will. Baboons (*Papio cynocephalus*) provide an illustration of this. Hall and DeVore (1965) have described the tendency for meat caught by an individual in the troop to end up by preemption in the hands of the most dominant males. This ability to preempt removes any selective advantage that food-sharing might otherwise have as a reciprocal gesture for the most dominant males, and there is no evidence in this species of any food-sharing tendencies.

[...]

(6) *Aid in combat.* No matter how dominance-oriented a species is, a dominant individual can usually be aided in aggressive encounters with other individuals by help from a less dominant individual. Hall and DeVore (1965) have described the tendency for baboon alliances to form which fight as a unit in aggressive encounters (and in encounters with predators). Similarly, vervet monkeys in aggressive encounters solicit the aid of other, often less dominant, individuals (Struhsaker, 1967). Aid in combat is then a special case in which relatively symmetrical relations are possible between individuals who differ in dominance.

The above discussion is meant only to suggest the broad conditions that favor the evolution of reciprocal altruism. The most important parameters to specify for individuals of a species are how many altruistic situations occur and how symmetrical they are, and these are the most difficult to specify in advance. Of the three instances of reciprocal altruism discussed in this paper only one, human altruism, would have been predicted from the above broad conditions.

The relationship between two individuals repeatedly exposed to symmetrical reciprocal situations is exactly analogous to what game

theorists call the Prisoner's Dilemma (Luce and Raiffa, 1957; Rapoport and Chammah, 1965), a game that can be characterized by the payoff matrix in Figure 15.1.

	A_2	C_2
A_1	R, R	S, T
C_1	T, S	P, P

Figure 15.1

Where $S < P < R < T$ and where A_1 and A_2 represent the altruistic choices possible for the two individuals, and C_1 and C_2, the cheating choices (the first letter in each box gives the payoff for the first individual, the second letter the payoff for the second individual). The other symbols can be given the following meanings: R stands for the reward each individual gets from an altruistic exchange if neither cheats; T stands for the temptation to cheat; S stands for the sucker's payoff that an altruist gets when cheated; and P is the punishment that both individuals get when neither is altruistic (adapted from Rapoport and Chammah, 1965).

Iterated games played between the same two individuals mimic real life in that they permit each player to respond to the behavior of the other. Rapoport and Chammah (1965) and others have conducted such experiments using human players, and some of their results are reviewed below in the discussion of human altruism.

W. D. Hamilton (pers. comm.) has shown that the above treatment of reciprocal altruism can be reformulated concisely in terms of game theory as follows. Assuming two altruists are symmetrically exposed to a series of reciprocal situations with identical costs and identical benefits, then after $2n$ reciprocal situations, each has been "paid" nR. Were one of the two a nonaltruist and the second changed to a nonaltruistic policy after first being cheated, then the initial altruist would be paid $S + (n - 1)P$ (assuming he had the first opportunity to be altruistic) and the non-altruist would receive $T + (n - 1)P$. The important point here is that unless $T \gg R$, then even with small n, nR should exceed $T + (n - 1)P$. If this holds, the nonaltruistic type, when rare, cannot start to spread. But there is also a barrier to the spread of altruism when altruists are rare, for P > S implies nP > S + (n − 1)P. As n increases, these two total payoffs tend to equality, so the barrier to the spread of altruism is weak if n is large. The barrier will be overcome if the advantages gained by exchanges between altruists outweigh the initial losses to non-altruistic types.

Reciprocal altruism can also be viewed as a symbiosis, each partner helping the other while he helps himself. The symbiosis has a time lag, however; one partner helps the other and must then wait a period of time before he is helped in turn. The return benefit may come directly, as in human food-sharing, the partner directly returning the benefit after a time lag. Or the return may come indirectly, as in warning calls in birds, where the initial help to other birds (the warning call) sets up a causal chain through the ecological system (the predator fails to learn useful information) which redounds after a time lag to the benefit of the caller. The time lag is the crucial factor, for it means that only under highly specialized circumstances can the altruist be reasonably guaranteed that the causal chain he initiates with his altruistic act will eventually return to him and confer, directly or indirectly, its benefit. Only under these conditions will the cheater be selected against and this type of altruistic behavior evolve.

Although the preconditions for the evolution of reciprocal altruism are specialized, many species probably meet them and display this type of altruism. This paper will limit itself, however, to three instances. The first, behavior involved in cleaning symbioses, is chosen because it permits a clear discrimination between this model and that based on kin selection (Hamilton, 1964). The second, warning calls in birds, has already been elaborately analyzed in terms of kin selection; it is discussed here to show how the model presented above leads to a very different interpretation of these familiar behaviors. Finally, human reciprocal altruism is discussed in detail because it represents the best documented case of reciprocal altruism known, because there has apparently been strong selection for a very complex system regulating altruistic behavior, and because the above model permits the functional interpretation of details of the system that otherwise remain obscure.

[...]

Human Reciprocal Altruism

Reciprocal altruism in the human species takes place in a number of contexts and in all known cultures (see, for example, Gouldner, 1960). Any complete list of human altruism would contain the following types of altruistic behavior:

1 helping in times of danger (e.g. accidents, predation, intraspecific aggression);
2 sharing food;
3 helping the sick, the wounded, or the very young and old;
4 sharing implements; and
5 sharing knowledge.

All these forms of behavior often meet the criterion of small cost to the giver and great benefit to the taker.

During the Pleistocene, and probably before, a hominid species would have met the preconditions for the evolution of reciprocal altruism: long lifespan; low dispersal rate; life in small, mutually dependent, stable, social groups (Lee and DeVore, 1968; Campbell, 1966); and a long period of parental care. It is very likely that dominance relations were of the relaxed, less linear form characteristic of the living chimpanzee (Van Lawick-Goodall, 1968) and not of the more rigidly linear form characteristic of the baboon (Hall and DeVore, 1965). Aid in intraspecific combat, particularly by kin, almost certainly reduced the stability and linearity of the dominance order in early humans. Lee (1969) has shown that in almost all Bushman fights which are initially between two individuals, others have joined in. Mortality, for example, often strikes the secondaries rather than the principals. Tool use has also probably had an equalizing effect on human dominance relations, and the Bushmen have a saying that illustrates this nicely. As a dispute reaches the stage where deadly weapons may be employed, an individual will often declare: "We are none of us big, and others small; we are all men and we can fight; I'm going to get my arrows," (Lee, 1969). It is interesting that Van Lawick-Goodall (1968) has recorded an instance of strong dominance reversal in chimpanzees as a function of tool use. An individual moved from low in dominance to the top of the dominance hierarchy when he discovered the intimidating effects of throwing a metal tin around. It is likely that a diversity of talents is usually present in a band of hunter-gatherers such that the best maker of a certain type of tool is not often the best maker of a different sort or the best user of the tool. This contributes to the symmetary of relationships, since altruistic acts can be traded with reference to the special talents of the individuals involved.

[. . .]

The Psychological System Underlying Human Reciprocal Altruism

Anthropologists have recognized the importance of reciprocity in human behavior, but when they have ascribed functions to such behavior they have done so in terms of group benefits, reciprocity cementing group relations and encouraging group survival. The individual sacrifices so that the group may benefit. Recently psychologists have studied altruistic behavior in order to show what factors induce or inhibit such behavior. No attempt has been made to show what function such behavior may serve, nor to describe and interrelate the components of the psychological system affecting altruistic behavior. The purpose of this section is to show that the above model for the natural selection of reciprocally altruistic behavior can readily explain the function of human altruistic behavior and the details of the psychological system underlying such behavior. The psychological data can be organized into functional categories, and it can be shown that the components of the system complement each other in regulating the expression of altruistic and cheating impulses to the selective advantage of individuals. No concept of group advantage is necessary to explain the function of human altruistic behavior.

There is no direct evidence regarding the degree of reciprocal altruism practiced during human evolution nor its genetic basis today, but given the universal and nearly daily practice of reciprocal altruism among humans today, it is reasonable to assume that it has been an important factor in recent human evolution and that the underlying emotional dispositions affecting altruistic behavior have important genetic components. To assume as much allows a number of predictions.

(1) *A complex, regulating system.* The human altruistic system is a sensitive, unstable one. Often it will pay to cheat: namely, when the partner will not find out, when he will not discontinue his altruism even if he does find out, or when he is unlikely to survive long enough to reciprocate adequately. And the perception of subtle cheating may be very difficult. Given this unstable character of the system, where a degree of cheating is adaptive, natural selection will rapidly favor a complex psychological system in each individual regulating both his own altruistic and cheating tendencies and his responses to these tendencies in others. As selection favors subtler forms of cheating, it will favor more acute abilities to detect cheating. The system that results should simultaneously allow the individual to reap the benefits of altruistic exchanges, to protect himself from gross and subtle forms of cheating, and to practice those forms of cheating that local conditions make adaptive. Individuals will differ not in being altruists or cheaters but in the degree of altruism they show and in the conditions under which they will cheat.

The best evidence supporting these assertions can be found in Krebs' (1970) review of the relevant psychological literature. Although he organizes it differently, much of the material supporting the assertions below is taken from his paper. All references to Krebs below are to this review. Also, Hartshorne and May (1928–1930) have shown that children in experimental situations do not divide bimodally into altruists and "cheaters" but are distributed normally; almost all the children cheated, but they differed in how much and under what circumstances. ("Cheating" was defined in their work in a slightly different but analogous way).

(2) *Friendship and the emotions of liking and disliking.* The tendency to like others, not necessarily closely related, to form friendships and to act altruistically toward friends and toward those one likes will be selected for as the immediate emotional rewards motivating altruistic behavior and the formation of altruistic partnerships. (Selection may also favor helping strangers or disliked individuals when they are in particularly dire circumstances). Selection will favor a system whereby these tendencies are sensitive to such

parameters as the altruistic tendencies of the liked individual. In other words, selection will favor liking those who are themselves altruistic.

Sawyer (1966) has shown that all groups in all experimental situations tested showed more altruistic behavior toward friends than toward neutral individuals. Likewise, Friedrichs (1960) has shown that attractiveness as a friend was most highly correlated among undergraduates with altruistic behavior. Krebs has reviewed other studies that suggest that the relationship between altruism and liking is a two-way street: one is more altruistic toward those one likes and one tends to like those who are most altruistic (e.g., Berkowitz and Friedman, 1967; Lerner and Lichtman, 1968).

Others (Darwin, 1871; Williams, 1966; and Hamilton, 1969) have recognized the role friendship might play in engendering altruistic behavior, but all have viewed friendship (and intelligence) as prerequisites for the appearance of such altruism. Williams (1966), who cites Darwin (1871) on the matter, speaks of this behavior as evolving

> in animals that live in stable social groups and have the intelligence and other mental qualities necessary to form a system of personal friendships and animosities that transcend the limits of family relationships (p. 93).

This emphasis on friendship and intelligence as prerequisites leads Williams to limit his search for altruism to the Mammalia and to a "minority of this group." But according to the model presented above, emotions of friendship (and hatred) are not prerequisites for reciprocal altruism but may evolve *after* a system of mutual altruism has appeared, as important ways of regulating the system.

(4) *Moralistic aggression.* Once strong positive emotions have evolved to motivate altruistic behavior, the altruist is in a vulnerable position because cheaters will be selected to take advantage of the altruist's positive emotions. This in turn sets up a selection pressure for a protective mechanism. Moralistic aggression and indignation in humans was selected for in order

(a)   to counteract the tendency of the altruist, in the absence of any reciprocity, to continue

to perform altruistic acts for his own emotional rewards;

(b)   to educate the unreciprocating individual by frightening him with immediate harm or with the future harm of no more aid; and

(c)   in extreme cases, perhaps, to select directly against the unreciprocating individual by injuring, killing, or exiling him.

Much of human aggression has moral overtones. Injustice, unfairness, and lack of reciprocity often motivate human aggression and indignation. Lee (1969) has shown that verbal disputes in Bushmen usually revolve around problems of gift-giving, stinginess, and laziness. DeVore (pers. commun.) reports that a great deal of aggression in hunter-gatherers revolves around real or imagined injustices – inequities, for example, in food-sharing (see, for example, Thomas, 1958; Balikci, 1964; Marshall, 1961). A common feature of this aggression is that it often seems out of all proportion to the offenses committed. Friends are even killed over apparently trivial disputes. But since small inequities repeated many times over a lifetime may exact a heavy toll in relative fitness, selection may favor a strong show of aggression when the cheating tendency is discovered. Recent discussions of human and animal aggression have failed to distinguish between moralistic and other forms of aggression (e.g., Scott, 1958; Lorenz, 1966; Montague, 1968; Tinbergen, 1968; Gilula and Daniels, 1969). The grounds for expecting, on functional grounds, a highly plastic developmental system affecting moralistic aggression is discussed below.

(4) *Gratitude, sympathy, and the cost/benefit ratio of an altruistic act.* If the cost/benefit ratio is an important parameter in determining the adaptiveness of reciprocal altruism, then humans should be selected to be sensitive to the cost and benefit of an altruistic act, both in deciding whether to perform one and in deciding whether, or how much, to reciprocate. I suggest that the emotion of gratitude has been selected to regulate human response to altruistic acts and that the emotion is sensitive to the cost/benefit ratio of such acts. I suggest further that the emotion of sympathy has been selected to motivate altruistic behavior as a function of the plight of the recipient of such behavior; crudely put, the greater the potential benefit to the recipient, the greater

the sympathy and the more likely the altruistic gesture, even to strange or disliked individuals. If the recipient's gratitude is indeed a function of the cost/benefit ratio, then a sympathetic response to the plight of a disliked individual may result in considerable reciprocity.

[. . .]

(5) *Guilt and reparative altruism.* If an organism has cheated on a reciprocal relationship and this fact has been found out, or has a good chance of being found out, by the partner and if the partner responds by cutting off all future acts of aid, then the cheater will have paid dearly for his misdeed. It will be to the cheater's advantage to avoid this, and, providing that the cheater makes up for his misdeed and does not cheat in the future, it will be to his partner's benefit to avoid this, since in cutting off future acts of aid he sacrifices the benefits of future reciprocal help. The cheater should be selected to make up for his misdeed and to show convincing evidence that he does not plan to continue his cheating sometime in the future. In short, he should be selected to make a reparative gesture. It seems plausible, furthermore, that the emotion of guilt has been selected for in humans partly in order to motivate the cheater to compensate his misdeed and to behave reciprocally in the future, and thus to prevent the rupture of reciprocal relationships.

[. . .]

(6) *Subtle cheating: the evolution of mimics.* Once friendship, moralistic aggression, guilt, sympathy, and gratitude have evolved to regulate the altruistic system, selection will favor mimicking these traits in order to influence the behavior of others to one's own advantage. Apparent acts of generosity and friendship may induce genuine friendship and altruism in return. Sham moralistic aggression when no real cheating has occurred may nevertheless induce reparative altruism. Sham guilt may convince a wronged friend that one has reformed one's ways even when the cheating is about to be resumed. Likewise, selection will favor the hypocrisy of pretending one is in dire circumstances in order to induce sympathy-motivated altruistic behavior. Finally, mimicking sympathy may give the appearance of helping in order to induce reciprocity, and mimicking gratitude may mislead an individual into expecting he will be reciprocated. It is worth emphasizing that a mimic need not necessarily be conscious of the deception; selection may favor feeling genuine moralistic aggression even when one has not been wronged if so doing leads another to reparative altruism.

[. . .]

(7) *Detection of the subtle cheater: trustworthiness, trust, and suspicion.* Selection should favor the ability to detect and discriminate against subtle cheaters. Selection will clearly favor detecting and countering sham moralistic aggression. The argument for the others is more complex. Selection may favor distrusting those who perform altruistic acts without the emotional basis of generosity or guilt because the altruistic tendencies of such individuals may be less reliable in the future. One can imagine, for example, compensating for a misdeed without any emotional basis but with a calculating, self-serving motive. Such an individual should be distrusted because the calculating spirit that leads this subtle cheater now to compensate may in the future lead him to cheat when circumstances seem more advantageous (because of unlikelihood of detection, for example, or because the cheated individual is unlikely to survive). Guilty motivation, in so far as it evidences a more enduring commitment to altruism, either because guilt teaches or because the cheater is unlikely not to feel the same guilt in the future, seems more reliable. A similar argument can be made about the trustworthiness of individuals who initiate altruistic acts out of a calculating rather than a generous-hearted disposition or who show either false sympathy or false gratitude. Detection on the basis of the underlying psychological dynamics is only one form of detection. In many cases, unreliability may more easily be detected through experiencing the cheater's inconsistent behavior. And in some cases, third party interactions (as discussed below) may make an individual's behavior predictable despite underlying cheating motivations.

[. . .]

It is worth mentioning that a classic problem in social science and philosophy has been whether to define altruism in terms of motives (e.g., real vs. "calculated" altruism) or in terms of behavior, regardless of motive (Krebs, 1970). This problem reflects the fact that, wherever studied, humans seem to make distinctions about altruism partly on the basis of motive, and this tendency is consistent with the hypothesis that such discrimination is relevant to protecting oneself from cheaters.

(8) *Setting up altruistic partnerships.* Selection will favor a mechanism for establishing reciprocal relationships. Since humans respond to acts of altruism with feelings of friendship that lead to reciprocity, one such mechanism might be the performing of altruistic acts toward strangers, or even enemies, in order to induce friendship. In short, do unto others as you would have them do unto you.

The mechanism hypothesized above leads to results inconsistent with the assumption that humans always act more altruistically toward friends than toward others. Particularly toward strangers, humans may initially act more altruistically than toward friends. [. . .]

(9) *Multiparty interactions.* In the close-knit social groups that humans usually live in, selection should favor more complex interactions than the two-party interactions so far discussed. Specifically, selection may favor learning from the altruistic and cheating experiences of others, helping others coerce cheaters, forming multiparty exchange systems, and formulating rules for regulated exchanges in such multiparty systems.

(i) *Learning from others.* Selection should favor learning about the altruistic and cheating tendencies of others indirectly, both through observing interactions of others and, once linguistic abilities have evolved, by hearing about such interactions or hearing characterizations of individuals (e.g., "dirty, hypocritical, dishonest, untrustworthy, cheating louse"). One important result of this learning is that an individual may be as concerned about the attitude of onlookers in an altruistic situation as about the attitude of the individual being dealt with.

(ii) *Help in dealing with cheaters.* In dealing with cheaters selection may favor individuals helping others, kin or non-kin, by direct coercion against the cheater or by everyone refusing him reciprocal altruism. One effect of this is that an individual, through his close kin, may be compensated for an altruistic act even after his death. An individual who dies saving a friend, for example, may have altruistic acts performed by the friend to the benefit of his offspring. Selection will discriminate against the cheater in this situation, if kin of the martyr, or others, are willing to punish lack of reciprocity.

(iii) *Generalized altruism.* Given learning from others and multiparty action against cheaters, selection may favor a multiparty altruistic system in which altruistic acts are dispensed freely among more than two individuals, an individual being perceived to cheat if in an altruistic situation he dispenses less benefit for the same cost than would the others, punishment coming not only from the other individual in that particular exchange but from the others in the system.

(iv) *Rules of exchange.* Multiparty altruistic systems increase by several-fold the cognitive difficulties in detecting imbalances and deciding whether they are due to cheating or to random factors. One simplifying possibility that language facilitates is the formulation of rules of conduct, cheating being detected as inraction of such a rule. In short, selection may favor the elaboration of norms of reciprocal conduct.

[. . .]

(10) *Developmental plasticity.* The conditions under which detection of cheating is possible, the range of available altruistic trades, the cost/benefit ratios of these trades, the relative stability of social groupings, and other relevant parameters should differ from one ecological and social situation to another and should differ through time in the same small human population. Under these conditions one would expect selection to favor developmental plasticity of those traits regulating altruistic and cheating tendencies and responses to these tendencies in others. For example, developmental plasticity may allow the growing organism's sense of guilt to be educated, perhaps partly by kin, so as to permit those forms of cheating that local conditions make adaptive and to discourage those with more dangerous consequences. One would not expect any simple system regulating the development of altruistic behavior. To be adaptive, altruistic behavior must be dispensed with regard to many characteristics of the recipient (including his degree of relationship, emotional makeup, past behavior, friendships, and kin relations), of other members of the group, of the situation in which the altruistic behavior takes place, and of many other parameters, and no simple developmental system is likely to meet these requirements.

[. . .]

It is worth emphasizing that some of the psychological traits analyzed above have applications outside the particular reciprocal altruistic system being discussed. One may be suspicious, for example, not only of individuals likely to cheat on the altruistic system, but of any individual likely to harm oneself; one may be suspicious of the known tendencies toward adultery of another male or even of these tendencies in one's own mate. Likewise, a guilt-motivated show of reparation may avert the revenge of someone one has harmed, whether that individual was harmed by cheating on the altruistic system or in some other way. And the system of reciprocal altruism may be employed to avert possible revenge. The Bushmen of the Kalahari, for example, have a saying (Marshall, 1959) to the effect that, if you wish to sleep with someone else's wife, you get him to sleep with yours, then neither of you goes after the other with poisoned arrows. Likewise, there is a large literature on the use of reciprocity to cement friendships between neighboring groups, now engaged in a common enterprise (e.g., Lee and DeVore, 1968).

The above review of the evidence has only begun to outline the complexities of the human altruistic system. The inherent instability of the Prisoner's Dilemma, combined with its importance in human evolution, has led to the evolution of a very complex system. For example, once moralistic aggression has been selected for to protect against cheating, selection favors sham moralistic aggression as a new form of cheating. This should lead to selection for the ability to discriminate the two and to guard against the latter. The guarding can, in turn, be used to counter real moralistic aggression: one can, in effect, *impute* cheating motives to another person in order to protect one's own cheating. And so on. Given the psychological and cognitive complexity the system rapidly acquires, one may wonder to what extent the importance of altruism in human evolution set up a selection pressure for psychological and cognitive powers which partly contributed to the large increase in hominid brain size during the Pleistocene.

[. . .]

References

Balikci, A. 1964. Development of basic socioeconomic units in two Eskimo communities. National Museum of Canada Bulletin No. 202, Ottawa.

Berkowitz, L., and P. Friedman. 1967. Some social class differences in helping behavior. *J. Personal. Soc. Psychol.*, 5: 217–25.

Campbell, B. 1966. *Human Evolution*. Aldine, Chicago.

Crook, J. H. 1969. The socio-ecology of primates. In J. H. Crooke (ed.), *Social Behavior in Birds and Mammals*, p. 103–66. Academic Press, London.

Darwin, C. 1871. *The Descent of Man and Selection in Relation to Sex*. Random House, NY.

Drury, W. H., and W. J. Smith. 1968. Defense of feeding areas by adult herring gulls and intrusion by young. *Evolution*, 22: 193–201.

Friedrichs, R. W. 1960. Alter versus ego: an exploratory assessment of altruism. *Am. Sociol. Rev.*, 25: 496–508.

Gilula, M. F., and D. N. Daniels. 1969. Violence and man's struggle to adapt. *Science*, 164: 395–405.

Gouldner, A. 1960. The norm of reciprocity: a preliminary statement. *Am. Sociol. Rev.*, 47: 73–80.

Hall, K. R. L., and I. DeVore. 1965. Baboon social behavior. In I. DeVore (ed.), *Primate Behavior: Field Studies of Monkeys and Apes*, p. 53–110. Holt, Rhinehart and Winston, NY.

Hamilton, W. D. 1964. The genetical evolution of social behavior. *J. Theoret. Biol.*, 7: 1–52.

Hamilton, W. D. 1966. The moulding of senescence by natural selection. *J. Theoret. Biol.*, 12: 12–45.

Hamilton, W. D. 1969. Selection of selfish and altruistic behavior in some extreme models. Paper presented at "Man and Beast Symposium" (in press, Smithsonian Institution).

Hartshorne, H., and M. A. May. 1928–1930. *Studies in the Nature of Character. vol. 1, Studies in Deceit; vol. 2, Studies in Self-Control; vol. 3, Studies in the Organization of Character*. Macmillan, NY.

Krebs, D. 1970. Altruism — an examination of the concept and a review of the literature. *Psychol. Bull.*, 73: 258–302.

Lee, R. 1969. IKung Bushman violence. Paper presented at meeting of American Anthropological Association, Nov. 1969.

Lee, R., and I. DeVore. 1968. *Man the Hunter*. Aldine, Chicago.

Lerner, M. J., and R. R. Lichtman. 1968. Effects of perceived norms on attitudes and altruistic behavior toward a dependent other. *J. Personal. Soc. Psychol.*, 9: 226–32.

Lorenz, K. 1966. *On Aggression*. Harcourt, Brace and World, NY.

Luce, R. D., and H. Raiffa. 1957. *Games and Decisions*. Wiley, NY.

Marshall, L. K. 1959. Marriage among IKung Bushmen. *Africa*, 29: 335–65.

Marshall, L. K. 1961. Sharing, talking and giving: relief of social tension among IKung Bushmen. *Africa*, 31: 231–49.

Mayr, E. 1963. *Animal Species and Evolution*. Belknap Press, Cambridge.

Montagu, F. M. A. 1968. *Man and Aggression*. Oxford University Press, NY.

Rapoport, A., and A. Chammah. 1965. *Prisoner's Dilemma*. University of Michigan Press, Ann Arbor.

Sawyer, J. 1966. The altruism scale: a measure of cooperative, individualistic, and competitive inter-personal orientation. *Am. J. Social.* 71: 407–16.

Scott, J. P. 1958. *Aggression*. University of Chicago Press, Chicago.

Struhsaker, T. 1967. Social structure among vervet monkeys (*Cercopithecus aethiops*). *Behavior*, 29: 83–121.

Thomas, E. M. 1958. *The Harmless People*. Random House, NY.

Tinbergen, N. 1968. On war and peace in animals and man. *Science*, 160: 1411–18.

VanLawick-Goodall, J. 1968. A preliminary report on expressive movements and communication in the Gombe Stream chimpanzees. In P. Jay (ed.), *Primates*, p. 313–74 Holt, Rhinehart and Winston, NY.

Williams, G. C. 1966. *Adaptation and Natural Selection*. Princeton University Press, Princeton, NJ.

16

Summary of *Unto Others: The Evolution and Psychology of Unselfish Behavior*

Elliott Sober and David Sloan Wilson

The hypothesis of group selection fell victim to a seemingly devastating critique in 1960s evolutionary biology. In *Unto Others* (1998), we argue to the contrary, that group selection is a conceptually coherent and empirically well documented cause of evolution. We suggest, in addition, that it has been especially important in human evolution. In the second part of *Unto Others*, we consider the issue of psychological egoism and altruism – do human beings have ultimate motives concerning the well-being of others? We argue that previous psychological and philosophical work on this question has been inconclusive. We propose an evolutionary argument for the claim that human beings have altruistic ultimate motives.

I. Introduction

Part One of *Unto Others* (Sober & Wilson, 1998) addresses the biological question of whether evolutionary altruism exists in nature and, if so, how it should be explained. Part Two concerns the psychological question of whether any of our ultimate motives involves an irreducible concern for the welfare of others. Both questions are descriptive, not normative. And neither, on the surface, even mentions the topic of morality. How, then,

do these evolutionary and psychological matters bear on issues about morality? And what relevance do these descriptive questions have for normative ethical questions? These are problems we'll postpone discussing until we have outlined the main points we develop in *Unto Others*.

A behaviour is said to be altruistic in the evolutionary sense of that term if it involves a fitness cost to the donor and confers a fitness benefit on the recipient. A mindless organism can be an evolutionary altruist. It is important to recognize that the costs and benefits that evolutionary altruism involves come in the currency of reproductive success. If we give you a package of contraceptives as a gift, this won't be evolutionarily altruistic if the gift fails to enhance your reproductive success. And parents who take care of their children are not evolutionarily altruistic if they rear more children to adulthood than do parents who neglect their children. Evolutionary altruism is not the same as helping.

The concept of psychological altruism is, in a sense, the mirror image of the evolutionary concept. Evolutionary altruism describes the fitness effects of a behaviour, not the thoughts or feelings, if any, that prompt individuals to produce those behaviours. In contrast, psychological altruism concerns the motives that cause a behavior, not its actual effects. If your treatment

Summary of *Unto Others: The Evolution and Psychology of Unselfish Behavior*, from Eliot Sober and David Wilson (2000). Summary of *Unto Others: The Evolution and Psychology of Unselfish Behavior. Journal of Consciousness Studies*, 1–2. Center for Consciousness Studies at the University of Arizona, pp. 185–9, 194–206.

of others is prompted by your having an ultimate, noninstrumental concern for their welfare, this says nothing as to whether your actions will in fact be beneficial. Similarly, if you act only to benefit yourself, it is a further question what effect your actions will have on others. Psychological egoists who help because this makes them feel good may make the world a better place. And psychological altruists who are misguided, or whose efforts miscarry, can make the world worse.

Although the two concepts of altruism are distinct, they often are run together. People sometimes conclude that if genuine evolutionary altruism does not exist in nature, then it would be mere wishful thinking to hold that psychological altruism exists in human nature. The inference does not follow.

II.   Evolutionary Altruism – Part One of *Unto Others*

1.   The problem of evolutionary altruism and the critique of group selection in the 1960s

Evolutionary altruism poses a fundamental problem for the theory of natural selection. By definition, altruists have lower fitness than the selfish individuals with whom they interact. It therefore seems inevitable that natural selection should eliminate altruistic behaviour, just as it eliminates other traits that diminish an individual's fitness. Darwin saw this point, but he also thought that he saw genuinely altruistic characteristics in nature. The barbed stinger of a honey bee causes the bee to die when it stings an intruder to the nest. And numerous species of social insects include individual workers who are sterile. In both cases, the trait is good for the group though deleterious for the individuals who have it. In addition to these examples from nonhuman species, Darwin thought that human moralities exhibit striking examples of evolutionary altruism. In *The Descent of Man*, Darwin (1871) discusses the behaviour of courageous men who risk their lives to defend their tribes when a war occurs. Darwin hypothesized that these characteristics cannot be explained by the usual process of natural selection in which individuals compete with other individuals in the same group. This led him to advance the hypothesis of *group selection*. Barbed

stingers, sterile castes, and human morality evolved because groups competed against other groups. Evolutionarily selfish traits evolve if selection occurs exclusively at the individual level. Group selection makes the evolution of altruism possible.

Although Darwin invoked the hypothesis of group selection only a few times, his successors were less abstemious. Group selection became an important hypothesis in the evolutionary biologist's toolkit during the heyday of the Modern Synthesis (c. 1930–60). Biologists invoked individual selection to explain some traits, such as sharp teeth and immunity to disease; they invoked group selection to explain others, such as pecking order and the existence of genetic variation within species. Biologists simply used the concept that seemed appropriate. Discussion of putative group adaptations were not grounded in mathematical models of the group selection process, which hardly existed. Nor did naturalists usually feel the need to supply a mathematical model to support the claim that this or that phenotype evolved by individual selection.

All this changed in the 1960s when the hypothesis of group selection was vigorously criticized. It was attacked not just for making claims that are empirically false, but for being conceptually confused. The most influential of these critiques was George C. Williams' 1966 book, *Adaptation and Natural Selection*. Williams argued that traits don't evolve because they help groups; and even the idea that they evolve because they benefit individual organisms isn't quite right. Williams proposed that the right view is that traits evolve because they promote the replication of genes.

Williams' book, like much of the literature of that period, exhibits an ambivalent attitude towards the idea of group selection. Williams was consistently against the hypothesis; what he was ambivalent about was the grounds on which he thought the hypothesis should be rejected. Some of Williams' book deploys empirical arguments against group selection. For example, he argues that individual selection and group selection make different predictions about the sex ratio (the proportion of males and females) that should be found in a population; he claimed that the observations are squarely on the side of individual selection. But a substantial part of Williams' book advances somewhat *a priori* arguments against group selection. An example is his contention that the gene is the unit of selection because genes persist through many generations, whereas groups, organisms, and gene complexes are evanescent. Another example is his contention that group selection hypotheses are less parsimonious than hypotheses of individual selection, and so should be rejected on that basis.

The attack on group selection in the 1960s occurred at the same time that new mathematical models made it seem that the hypothesis of group selection was superfluous. W.D. Hamilton published an enormously influential paper in 1964, which begins with the claim that the classical notion of Darwinian fitness – an organism's prospects of reproductive success – can explain virtually none of the helping behaviour we see in nature. It can explain parental care, but when individuals help individuals who are not their offspring, a new concept of fitness is needed to explain why. This led Hamilton to introduce the mathematical concept of *inclusive fitness*. The point of this concept was to show how helping a relative and helping one's offspring can be brought under the same theoretical umbrella – both evolve because they enhance the donor's inclusive fitness. Many biologists concluded that helping behaviour directed at relatives is therefore an instance of selfishness, not altruism. Helping offspring and helping kin are both in one's genetic self-interest, because both allow copies of one's genes to make their way into the next generation. Behaviours that earlier seemed instances of altruism now seemed to be instances of genetic selfishness. The traits that Darwin invoked the hypothesis of group selection to explain apparently can be explained by 'kin selection' (the term that Maynard Smith, 1964, suggested for the process that Hamilton described), which was interpreted as an instance of individual selection. Group selection wasn't needed as a hypothesis; it was 'unparsimonious'.

Another mathematical development that pushed group selection further into the shadows was evolutionary game theory. Maynard Smith, one of the main architects of evolutionary game theory, wanted to provide a sane alternative to sloppy group selection thinking. Konrad Lorenz and others had suggested, for example, that animals restrain themselves in intraspecific combat because this is good for the species. Maynard Smith and Price (1973) developed their game of hawks versus doves to show how restraint in combat can result from purely individual selec-

tion. Each individual in the population competes with one other individual, chosen at random, to determine which will obtain some fitness benefit. Each plays either the hawk strategy of all-out fighting or the dove strategy of engaging in restrained and brief aggression. When a hawk fights a hawk, one of them gets the prize, but each stands a good chance of serious injury or death. When a hawk fights a dove, the hawk wins the prize and the dove beats a hasty retreat, thus avoiding serious injury. And when two doves fight, the battle is over quickly; there is a winner and a loser, but neither gets hurt. In this model, which trait does better depends on which trait is common and which is rare. If hawks are very common, a dove will do better than the average hawk – the average hawk gets injured a lot, but the dove does not. On the other hand, if doves are very common, a hawk will do better than the average dove. The evolutionary result is a polymorphism. Neither trait is driven to extinction; both are represented in the population. What Lorenz tried to explain by invoking the good of the species, Maynard Smith and Price proposed to explain purely in terms of individual advantage. Just as was true in the case of Hamilton's work on inclusive fitness, the hypothesis of group selection appeared superfluous. You don't *need* the hypothesis to explain what you observe. Altruism is only an appearance. Dovishness isn't present because it helps the group; the trait is maintained in the population because individual doves gain an advantage from not fighting to the death.

Another apparent nail in the coffin of group selection was Maynard Smith's (1964) 'haystack model' of group selection. Maynard Smith considered the hypothetical situation in which field mice live in haystacks. The process begins by fertilized females each finding their own haystacks. Each gives birth to a set of offspring who then reproduce among themselves, brothers and sisters mating with each other. After that, the haystack holds together for another generation, with first cousins mating with first cousins. Each haystack contains a group of mice founded by a single female that sticks together for some number of generations. At a certain point, all the mice come out of their haystacks, mate at random, and then individual fertilized females go off to found their own groups in new haystacks. Maynard Smith analyzed this process mathematically and concluded that altruism can't evolve by group selection. Group selection is an inherently weak force, unable to overcome the countervailing and stronger force of individual selection, which promotes the evolution of selfishness.

The net effect of the critique of group selection in the 1960s was that the existence of adaptations that evolve because they benefit the group was dismissed from serious consideration in biology. The lesson was that the hypothesis of group selection doesn't have to be considered as an empirical possibility when the question is raised as to why this or that trait evolved. You know *in advance* that group selection is not the explanation. Only those who cling to the illusion that nature is cuddly and hospitable could take the hypothesis of group adaptation seriously.

2.   Conceptual arguments against group selection

In *Unto Others*, we argue that this seemingly devastating critique of group selection completely missed the mark. The purely conceptual arguments against group selection show nothing. And the more empirical arguments also are flawed.

Let us grant that genes – not organisms or groups of organisms – are the *units of replication*. By this we mean that they are the devices that insure heredity. Offspring resemble parents because genes are passed from the latter to the former. However, this establishes nothing about why the adaptations found in nature have evolved. Presumably, even if the gene is the unit of replication, it still can be true that some genes evolve because they code for traits that benefit individuals – this is why sharp teeth and immunity from disease evolve. But the same point holds for groups: even if the gene is the unit of replication, it remains to be decided whether some genes evolve because they code for traits that benefit groups. The fact that genes are *replicators* is entirely irrelevant to the units of *selection* problem.

The idea that group selection should be rejected because it is unparsimonious also fails to pass muster. Here's an example of how the argument is deployed, in Williams (1966), in Dawkins (1976), and in many other places. Why do crows exhibit sentinel behaviour? Group selection was sometimes invoked to explain this as an instance of altruism. A crow that sights an approaching predator and issues a warning cry places itself at risk by attracting the predator's attention; in addition, the sentinel confers a benefit on the other crows in the group by alerting them to danger. Interpreted in this way, a group selection explanation may seem plausible. However, an alternative possibility is that the sentinel behaviour is not really altruistic at all. Perhaps the sentinel cry is difficult for the predator to locate, and maybe the cry sends the other crows in the group into a frenzy of activity, thus permitting the sentinel to beat a safe retreat. If the behaviour is selfish, no group selection explanation is needed. At this point, one might think that two empirical hypotheses have been presented and that observations are needed to test which is better supported. However, the style of parsimony argument advanced in the anti-group selection literature concludes without further ado that the group selection explanation should be rejected, just because an individual selection explanation has been *imagined*. Data aren't needed, because parsimony answers our question. In *Unto Others*, we argue that this is a spurious application of the principle of parsimony. Parsimony is a guide to how observations should be interpreted; it is not a substitute for performing observational tests.

[...]

5.   Group selection and human evolution

In *Unto Others*, we develop the conjecture that group selection was a strong force in human evolution. Group selection includes, but is not confined to, direct intergroup competition such as warfare. But, just as individual plants can compete with each other in virtue of the desert conditions in which they live (some being more drought-resistant than others), so groups can compete with each other without directly interacting (e.g., by some groups fostering co-operation more than others). In addition, cultural variation in addition to genetic variation can provide the mechanisms for phenotypic variation and heritability at the group level (see also Boyd and Richerson, 1985).

As noted earlier, the evolution of altruism depends on altruists interacting preferentially with each other. Kin selection is a powerful idea because interaction among kin is a pervasive pattern across many plant and animal groups. However, in many organisms, including especially human beings, individuals *choose* the individuals with whom they interact. If altruists seek out other altruists, this promotes the evolution of altruism. Although kin selection is a kind of group selection, there can be group selection that isn't kin selection; this, we suspect, is especially important in the case of human evolution. However, it isn't *uniquely* human – for example, even so-called lower vertebrates such as guppies can choose the social partners with which they interact.

An additional factor that helps altruism to evolve, which may be uniquely human, is the existence of cultural norms that impose social controls. Consider a very costly act, such as donating ten per cent of your food to the community. Since this act is very costly, a very strong degree of correlation among interactors will be needed to get it to evolve. However, suppose you live in a society in which individuals who make the donation are rewarded, and those who do not are punished. The act of donation has been transformed. It is no longer altruistic to make the donation, but selfish. Individuals in your group who donate do better than individuals who do not. However, it would be wrong to conclude from this that the existence of social controls make the hypothesis of group selection unnecessary. For where did the existence and enforcement of the social sanctions come from? Why do some individuals enforce the penalty for non-donation? This costs them something. A free-rider could enjoy the benefits without paying the costs of having a norm of donation enforced. Enforcing the requirement of donation is altruistic, even if donation is no longer altruistic. But notice that the cost of being an enforcer may be slight. It may not cost you anything like ten per cent of your food supply to help enforce the norm of donation. This means that the degree of correlation among interactors needed to get *this* altruistic behaviour to evolve is much less.

We believe that this argument may explain how altruistic behaviours were able to evolve in the genetically heterogeneous groups in which our ancestors lived. Human societies, both ancient and modern, are nowhere near as genetically uniform as bee hives and ant colonies. How, then, did co-operative behaviour manage to evolve in them? Human beings, we believe, did something that no other species was able to do. Social norms convert highly altruistic traits into traits that are selfish. And enforcing a social norm can involve a smaller cost than the required behaviour would have imposed if there were no norms. Social norms allow social organization to evolve by reducing its costs. Here again, it is important to recognize that culture allows a form of selection to occur whose elements may be found in the absence of culture. Bees 'police' the behaviour of other bees. What is uniquely human is the harnessing of socially shared values.

In addition to these rather 'theoretical' considerations, *Unto Others* also presents some observations that support the hypothesis that human beings are a group selected species. We randomly sampled twenty-five societies from the Human Relations Area File, an anthropological database, consulting what the files say about social norms. The actual contents of these norms vary enormously across our sample – for example, some societies encourage innovation in dress, while others demand uniformity. In spite of this diversity, cultural norms almost always require individuals to avoid conflict with each other and to behave benevolently towards fellow group members. Such constraints are rarely present with respect to outsiders, however. It also was striking how closely individuals can monitor the behaviour of group members in most traditional societies. Equally impressive is the emphasis on egalitarianism (among males – not, apparently, between males and females) found in many traditional societies; the norm was not that there should be complete equality, but that inequalities are permitted only when they enhance group functioning.

In addition to this survey data, we also describe a 'smoking gun' of cultural group selection – the conflict between the Nuer and Dinka tribes in East Africa. This conflict has been studied extensively by anthropologists for most of this century. The Nuer have gradually eroded the territory and resources of the Dinka, owing to the Nuer's superior group organization. The transformation was largely underwritten by people in Dinka villages defecting to the Nuers and being absorbed into their culture. We conjecture that this example has countless counterparts in the human past, and that the process of cultural group selection that it exemplifies has been an important influence on cultural change.

We think that Part I of *Unto Others* provides a solid foundation for the theory of group selection and that we have presented several well-documented cases of group selection in non-human species. Our discussion of human group selection is more tentative, but nonetheless we are prepared to claim that human beings have been strongly influenced by group selection processes.

III.   Psychological Altruism – Part Two of *Unto Others*

Psychological egoism is a theory that claims that all of our ultimate desires are self-directed. Whenever we want others to do well (or badly), we have these other-directed desires only instrumentally; we care about what happens to others only because we think that the welfare of others has ramifications for ourselves. Egoism has exerted a powerful influence in the social sciences and has made large inroads in the thinking of ordinary people. In Part Two of *Unto Others*, we review the philosophical and psychological arguments that have been developed about egoism, both *pro* and *con*. We contend that these arguments are inconclusive. A new approach is needed; in Chapter 10, we present an evolutionary argument for thinking that some of our ultimate motives are altruistic.

It is easy to invent egoistic explanations for even the most harrowing acts of self-sacrifice. The soldier in a foxhole who throws himself on a grenade to save the lives of his comrades is a fixture in the literature on egoism. How could this act be a product of self-interest, if the soldier knows that it will end his life? The egoist may answer that the soldier realizes in an instant that he would rather die than suffer the guilt feelings that would haunt him if he saved himself and allowed his friends to perish. The soldier prefers to die and have no sensations at all rather than live and suffer the torments of the damned. This reply may sound *forced*, but this does not show that it must be *false*. And the fact that an egoistic explanation can be *invented* is no sure sign that egoism is *true*.

1.   Clarifying egoism

When egoism claims that all our ultimate desires are self-directed, what do 'ultimate' and 'self-directed' mean?

There are some things that we want for their own sakes; other things we want only because we think they will get us something else. The crucial relation that we need to define is this:

> *S* wants *m* solely as a means to acquiring *e* if and only if *S* wants *m*, *S* wants *e*, and *S* wants *m* only because she believes that obtaining *m* will help her obtain *e*.

An ultimate desire is a desire that someone has for reasons that go beyond its ability to contribute instrumentally to the attainment of something else. Consider pain. The most obvious reason that people want to avoid pain is simply that they dislike experiencing it. Avoiding pain is one of our ultimate goals. However, many people realize that being in pain reduces their ability to concentrate, so they may sometimes take an aspirin in part because they want to remove a source of distraction. This shows that the things we want as ends in themselves we also may want for instrumental reasons.

When psychological egoism seeks to explain why one person helped another, it isn't enough to show that *one* of the reasons for helping was self-benefit; this is quite consistent with there being another, purely altruistic, reason that the individual had for helping. Symmetrically, to refute egoism, one need not cite examples of helping in which *only* other-directed motives play a role. If people sometimes help for both egoistic and altruistic ultimate reasons, then psychological egoism is false.

Egoism and altruism both require the distinction between self-directed and other-directed desires, which should be understood in terms of a desire's propositional content. If Adam wants the apple, this is elliptical for saying that Adam wants it to be the case that *he has the apple*. This desire is purely self-directed, since its propositional content mentions Adam, but no other agent. In contrast, when Eve wants *Adam to have the apple*, this desire is purely other-directed; its propositional content mentions another person, Adam, but not Eve herself. Egoism claims that all of our ultimate desires are self-directed; altruism, that some are other-directed.

A special version of egoism is psychological hedonism. The hedonist says that the only ultimate desires that people have are attaining pleasure and avoiding pain. Hedonism is some-times criticized for holding that pleasure is a single type of sensation – that the pleasure we get from the taste of a peach and the pleasure we get from seeing those we love prosper somehow boil down to the same thing (Lafollette, 1988). However, this criticism does not apply to hedon-ism as we have described it. The salient fact about hedonism is its claim that people are *motivational solipsists*; the only things they care about ulti-mately are states of their own consciousness. Although hedonists must be egoists, the reverse isn't true. For example, if people desire their own survival as an end in itself, they may be egoists, but they are not hedonists.

Some desires are neither purely self-directed nor purely other-directed. If Phyllis wants to be famous, this means that she wants others to know who she is. This desire's propositional content involves a relation between self and others. If Phyllis seeks fame solely because she thinks this will be pleasurable or profitable, then she may be an egoist. But what if she wants to be famous as an end in itself? There is no reason to cram this possibility into either egoism or altruism. So let us recognize *relationism* as a possibility distinct from both. Construed in this way, egoism avoids the difficulty of having to explain why the theory is compatible with the existence of some relational ultimate desires, but not with others (Kavka, 1986).

With egoism characterized as suggested, it obviously is not entailed by the truism that people act on the basis of their own desires, nor by the truism that they seek to have their desires satisfied. The fact that Joe acts on the basis of Joe's desires, not on the basis of Jim's, tells us *whose* desires are doing the work; it says nothing about whether the ultimate desires in Joe's head are *purely self-directed*. And the fact that Joe wants his desires to be satisfied means merely that he wants their propositional contents to come true (Stampe, 1994). If Joe wants it to rain tomorrow, then his desire is satisfied if it rains, whether or not he notices the weather. To want one's desires satisfied is not the same as wanting the feeling of satisfaction that sometimes accompanies a satisfied desire.

Egoism is sometimes criticized for attributing too much calculation to spontaneous acts of helping. People who help in emergency situations often report doing so 'without thinking' (Clark and Word, 1974). However, it is hard to take such reports literally when the acts involve a precise series of complicated actions that are well-suited to an apparent end. A lifeguard who rescues a struggling swimmer is properly viewed as having a goal and as selecting actions that advance that goal. The fact that she engaged in no ponderous and self-conscious calculation does not show that no means/end reasoning occurred. In any case, actions that really do occur without the mediation of beliefs and desires fall outside the scope of both egoism and altruism.

A related criticism is that egoism assumes that people are more rational than they really are. However, recall that egoism is simply a claim about the ultimate desires that people have. As such, it says nothing about how people decide what to do on the basis of their beliefs and desires. The assumption of rationality is no more a part of psychological egoism than it is part of *motiva-tional pluralism* – the view that people have both egoistic and altruistic ultimate desires.

2. Psychological arguments

It may strike some readers that deciding between egoism and motivational pluralism is easy. Indi-viduals can merely gaze within their own minds and determine by introspection what their ultimate motives are. The problem with this easy solution is that there is no independent reason to think that the testimony of introspection is to be trusted in this instance. Introspection is misleading or incomplete in what it tells us about other facets of the mind; there is no reason to think that the mind is an open book with respect to the issue of ultimate motives.

In *Unto Others*, we devote most of Chapter 8 to the literature in social psychology that seeks to test egoism and motivational pluralism experi-mentally. The most systematic attempt in this regard is the work of Batson and co-workers, summarized in Batson (1991). Batson tests a hypothesis he calls the *empathy-altruism hypo-thesis* against a variety of egoistic explanations. The empathy-altruism hypothesis asserts that empathy causes people to have altruistic ultimate desires. We argue that Batson's experiments succeed in refuting some simple forms of egoism, but that the perennial problem of refuting egoism remains – when one version of egoism is refuted by a set of observations, another can be invented that fits the data. We also argue that even if Batson's experiments show that empathy causes helping, they don't settle whether empathy brings about this result by triggering an altruistic ultimate motive. We don't conclude from this that experimental social psychology will never be able to answer the question of whether psychological egoism is true. Our negative conclusion is more modest – empirical attempts to decide between egoism and motivational pluralism have not yet succeeded.

3. A bevy of philosophical arguments

Egoism has come under fire in philosophy from a number of angles. In Chapter 9 of *Unto Others*, we review these arguments and conclude that none of them succeeds. Here, briefly, is a sampling of the arguments we consider, and our replies:

* Egoism has been said to be *untestable*, and thus not a genuine scientific theory at all. We reply that if egoism is untestable, so is motivational pluralism. If it is true that when one egoistic explanation is discredited, another can be invented in its stead, then the same can be said of pluralism. The reason that egoism and pluralism have this sort of flexibility is that both make claims about the *kinds* of explanations that human behaviour has; they do not provide a detailed explanation of any particular behaviour. Egoism and pluralism are *isms*, which are notorious for the fact that they are not crisply falsifiable by a single set of observations.
* Joseph Butler (1692–1752) is widely regarded as having refuted psychological hedonism (Broad, 1965; Feinberg, 1984; Nagel, 1970). His argument can be outlined as follows:
  1. People sometimes experience pleasure.
  2. When people experience pleasure, this is because they had a desire for some external thing, and that desire was satisfied.
  ∴ Hedonism is false.
  We think the second premise is false. It is overstated; although some pleasures are the result of a desire's being satisfied, others are not (Broad, 1965, p. 66). One can enjoy the smell of violets without having formed the desire to

smell a flower, or something sweet. Since desires are propositional attitudes, forming a desire is a cognitive achievement. Pleasure and pain, on the other hand, are sometimes cognitively mediated, but sometimes they are not. This defect in the argument can be repaired; Butler does not need to say that desire satisfaction is the one and only road to pleasure. The main defect in the argument occurs in the transition from premises to conclusion. Consider the causal chain from a *desire* (the desire for food, say), to an *action* (eating), to a *result* – pleasure. Because the pleasure traces back to an antecedently existing desire, it will be false that the resulting pleasure caused the desire (on the assumption that cause must precede effect). However, this does not settle how two *desires* – the *desire for food* and the *desire for pleasure* – are related. Hedonism says that people desire food *because* they want pleasure (and think that food will bring them pleasure). Butler's argument concludes that this causal claim is false, but for no good reason. The crucial mistake in the argument comes from confusing two quite different items – the *pleasure* that results from a desire's being satisfied and the *desire for pleasure*. Even if the occurrence of pleasure presupposed that the agent desired something besides pleasure, nothing follows about the relationship between the *desire for pleasure* and the desire for something else (Sober, 1992; Stewart, 1992). Hedonism does not deny that people desire external things; rather, the theory tries to explain why that is so.
* We also consider the argument against egoism that Nozick (1974) presents by his example of an 'experience machine', the claim that hedonism is a paradoxical and irrational motivational theory, and the claim that egoism has the burden of proof. We conclude that none of these attacks on egoism is decisive.

There is one philosophical argument that attempts to support egoism, not refute it. This is the claim that egoism is preferable to pluralism because the former theory is more parsimonious. Egoism posits one type of ultimate desire whereas pluralism says there are two. We have two criticisms. First, this parsimony argument measures a theory's parsimony by counting the kinds of

ultimate desires it postulates. The opposite conclusion would be obtained if one counted *causal
beliefs*. The pluralist says that people want others
to do well and that they also want to do well themselves. The egoist says that a person wants others
to do well only because he or she *believes* that this
will promote self-interest. Pluralism does not
include this belief attribution. Our second objection is that parsimony is a reasonable tie-breaker
when all other considerations are equal; it remains
to be seen whether egoism and pluralism are
equally plausible on all other grounds. In Chapter 10, we propose an argument to the effect that
pluralism has greater evolutionary plausibility.

4. An evolutionary approach

Psychological motives are *proximate mechanisms*
in the sense of that term used in evolutionary
biology. When a sunflower turns towards the
sun, there must be some mechanism inside the
sunflower that causes it to do so. Hence, if photo-
tropism evolved, a proximate mechanism that
causes that behaviour also must have evolved.
Similarly, if certain forms of helping behaviour
in human beings are evolutionary adaptations,
then the motives that cause those behaviours in
individual human beings also must have evolved.
Perhaps a general perspective on the evolution
of proximate mechanisms can throw light on
whether egoism or motivational pluralism was
more likely to have evolved.

Pursuing this evolutionary approach does not
presuppose that every detail of human behaviour,
or every act of helping, can be explained completely by the hypothesis of evolution by natural
selection. In Chapter 10, we consider a single
fact about human behaviour, and our claim is
that selection is relevant to explaining it. The
phenomenon of interest is that human parents
take care of their children; the average amount
of parental care provided by human beings is
strikingly greater than that provided by parents in
many other species. We will assume that natural
selection is at least part of the explanation of why
parental care evolved in our lineage. This is not to
deny that human parents vary; some take better
care of their children than others, and some even
abuse and kill their offspring. Another striking
fact about individual variation is that mothers, on
average, expend more time and effort on parental

care than fathers. Perhaps there are evolutionary explanations for these individual differences
as well; the question we want to address here,
however, makes no assumption as to whether this
is true.

In Chapter 10, we describe some general principles that govern how one might predict the
proximate mechanism that will evolve to cause a
particular behaviour. We develop these ideas by
considering the example of a marine bacterium
whose problem is to avoid environments in which
there is oxygen. The organism has evolved a
particular behaviour – it tends to swim away from
greater oxygen concentrations and towards areas
in which there is less. What proximate mechanism might have evolved that allows the organism
to do this?

First, let's survey the range of possible design
solutions that we need to consider. The most
obvious solution is for the organism to have an
oxygen detector. We call this the *direct solution* to
the design problem; the organism needs to avoid
oxygen and it solves that problem by detecting the
very property that matters.

It isn't hard to imagine other solutions to the
design problem that are less direct. Suppose that
areas near the pond's surface contain more oxygen
and areas deeper in the pond contain less. If so,
the organism could use an up/down detector to
make the requisite discrimination. This design
solution is *indirect*; the organism needs to distinguish high oxygen from low and accomplishes
this by detecting another property that happens
to be correlated with the target. In general, there
may be many indirect design solutions that the
organism could exploit; there are as many indirect solutions as there are correlations between
oxygen level and other properties found in the
environment. Finally, we may add to our list
the idea that there can be *pluralistic* solutions to
a design problem. In addition to the monistic
solution of having an oxygen detector and the
monistic solution of having an up/down detector,
an organism might deploy both.

Given this multitude of possibilities, how might
one predict which of them will evolve? Three
principles are relevant – *availability, reliability*,
and *efficiency*.

Natural selection acts only on the range of variation that exists ancestrally. An oxygen detector
might be a good thing for the organism to have,

144 ALTRUISM & EGOISM

but if that device was never present as an ancestral variant, natural selection cannot cause it to evolve. So the first sort of information we'd like to have concerns which proximate mechanisms were *available* ancestrally.

Let's suppose for the sake of argument that both an oxygen detector and an up/down detector are available ancestrally. Which of them is more likely to evolve? Here we need to address the issue of *reliability*. Which device does the more reliable job of indicating where oxygen is? Without further information, not much can be said. An oxygen detector may have any degree of reliability, and the same is true of an up/down detector. There is no *a priori* reason why the direct strategy should be more or less reliable than the indirect strategy. However, there is a special circumstance in which they will differ. It is illustrated by Figure 16.1.

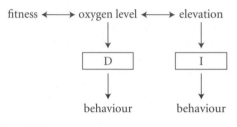

Figure 16.1

The double arrows [in Figure 16.1] indicate correlation; avoiding oxygen is correlated with fitness, and elevation is correlated with oxygen level. In the diagram, there is no arrow from elevation to fitness except the one that passes through oxygen level. This means that elevation is correlated with fitness *only because* elevation is correlated with oxygen, and oxygen is correlated with fitness. There is no *a priori* reason why this should be true. For example, if there were more predators at the bottom of ponds than at the top, then elevation would have two sorts of relevance for fitness. However, if oxygen level 'screens off' fitness from elevation in the way indicated, we can state the following principle about the reliability of the direct device D and the indirect device I:

(D/I) If oxygen level and elevation are less than perfectly correlated, and if D detects oxygen level at least as well as I detects elevation, then D will be more reliable than I.

This is the Direct/Indirect Asymmetry Principle. Direct solutions to a design problem aren't always more reliable, but they are more reliable in this circumstance.

A second principle about reliability also can be extracted from this diagram. Just as scientists do a better job of discriminating between hypotheses if they have more evidence rather than less, so it will be true that the marine bacterium we are considering will make more reliable discriminations about where to swim if it has two sources of information rather than just one:

(TBO) If oxygen level and elevation are less than perfectly correlated, and if D and I are each reliable, though fallible, detectors of oxygen concentration, then D and I working together will be more reliable than either of them working alone.

This is the Two-is-Better-than-One Principle. It requires an assumption – that the two devices do not interfere with each other when both are present in an organism.

The D/I Asymmetry and the TBO Principle pertain to the issue of reliability. Let us now turn to the third consideration that is relevant to predicting which proximate mechanism will evolve, namely *efficiency*. Even if an oxygen detector and an elevation detector are both available, and even if the oxygen detector is more reliable, it doesn't follow that natural selection will favour the oxygen detector. It may be that an oxygen detector requires more energy to build and maintain than an elevation detector. Organisms run on energy no less than automobiles do. Efficiency is relevant to a trait's overall fitness just as much as its reliability is.

With these three considerations in hand, let's return to the problem of predicting which motivational mechanism for providing parental care is likely to have evolved in the lineage leading to human beings. The three motivational mechanisms we need to consider correspond to three different rules for selecting a behaviour in the light of what one believes:

(HED) Provide parental care if, and only if, doing so will maximize pleasure and minimize pain.

(ALT) Provide parental care if, and only if, doing so will advance the welfare of one's children.

(PLUR)   Provide parental care if, and only if, doing so will either maximize pleasure and minimize pain, or will advance the welfare of one's children.

(ALT) is a relatively direct, and (HED) is a relatively indirect, solution to the design problem of getting an organism to take care of its offspring. Just as our marine bacterium can avoid oxygen by detecting elevation, so it is possible in principle for a hedonistic organism to provide parental care; what is required is that the organism be so constituted that providing parental care is the thing that usually maximizes its pleasure and minimizes its pain (or that the organism believes that this is so).

Let's consider how reliable these three mechanisms will be in a certain situation. Suppose that a parent learns that its child is in danger. Imagine that your neighbour tells you that your child has just fallen through the ice on a frozen lake. Figure 16.2 shows how (HED) and (ALT) will do their work:

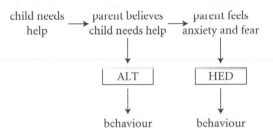

Figure 16.2

The altruistic parent will be moved to action just by virtue of believing that its child needs help. The hedonistic parent will not; rather, what moves the hedonistic parent to action are the feelings of anxiety and fear that are caused by the news. It should be clear from this diagram that the (D/I) Asymmetry Principle applies, (ALT) will be more reliable than (HED). And by the (TBO) Principle, (PLUR) will do better than both. In this example, hedonism comes in last in the three-way competition, at least as far as reliability is concerned.

The important thing about this example is that the feelings that the parent has are *belief mediated*. The only reason the parent *feels* anxiety and fear is that the parent *believes* that its child is in trouble. This is true of many of the situations that egoism and hedonism are called upon to explain, but it is not true of all. For example, consider the situation

in Figure 16.3 in which pain is a direct effect, and belief a relatively indirect effect, of bodily injury:

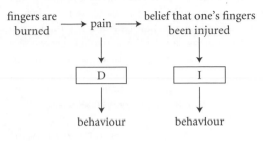

Figure 16.2

In this case, hedonism is a direct solution to the design problem; it would be a poor engineering solution to have the organism be unresponsive to pain and to have it withdraw its fingers from the flame only after it forms a belief about bodily injury. In this situation, *belief is pain-mediated* and the (D/I) Asymmetry Principle explains why a hedonistic focus on pain makes sense. However, the same principle indicates what is misguided about hedonism as a design solution when *pain is belief-mediated*, which is what occurs so often in the context of parental care.

If hedonism is less reliable than both pure altruism and motivational pluralism, how do these three mechanisms compare when we consider their availability and efficiency? With respect to availability, we make the following claim: *if hedonism was available ancestrally, so was altruism*. The reason is that the two motivational mechanisms differ in only a modest way. Both require a belief/desire psychology. And both the hedonistic and the altruistic parent want their children to do well; the only difference is that the hedonist has this propositional content as an instrumental desire while the altruist has it as an ultimate desire. If altruism and pluralism did not evolve, this was not because they were unavailable as variants for selection to act upon.

What about efficiency? Does it cost more calories to build and maintain an altruistic or a pluralistic organism than it does to build and maintain a hedonist? We don't see why. What requires energy is building the hardware that implements a belief/desire psychology. However, we doubt that it makes an energetic difference whether the organism has one ultimate desire rather than two. People with more beliefs apparently don't need to eat more than people with fewer. The same point seems to apply to the issue of how many, or which, ultimate desires one has.

In summary, pure altruism and pluralism are both more reliable than hedonism as devices for delivering parental care. And, with respect to the issues of availability and efficiency, we find no difference among these three motivational mechanisms. This suggests that natural selection is more likely to have made us motivational pluralists than to have made us hedonists.

From an evolutionary point of view, hedonism is a bizarre motivational mechanism. What matters in the process of natural selection is an organism's ability to survive and be reproductively successful. Reproductive success involves not just the production of offspring, but the survival of those offspring to reproductive age. So what matters is the survival of one's own body and the bodies of one's children. Hedonism, on the other hand, says that organisms care ultimately about the states of their own consciousness, and about that alone. Why would natural selection have led organisms to care about something that is peripheral to fitness, rather than have them set their eyes on the prize? If organisms were unable to conceptualize propositions about their own bodies and the bodies of their offspring, that might be a reason. After all, it might make sense for an organism to exploit the indirect strategy of deciding where to swim on the basis of elevation rather than on the basis of oxygen concentration, if the organism cannot detect oxygen. But if an organism is smart enough to form representations about itself and its offspring, this justification of the indirect strategy will not be plausible. The fact that we evolved from ancestors who were cognitively less sophisticated makes it unsurprising that avoiding pain and attaining pleasure are two of our ultimate goals. But the fact that human beings are able to form representations with so many different prepositional contents suggests that evolution supplemented this list of what we care about as ends in themselves.

IV.   Evolutionary Altruism, Psychological Altruism, and Ethics

The study of ethics has a *normative* and a *descriptive* component. Normative ethics seeks to say what is good and what is right; it seeks to identify what we are obliged to do and what we are permitted to do. Descriptive ethics, on the other hand, is neutral on these normative questions; it attempts to *describe* and *explain* morality as a cultural phenomenon, not *justify* it. How does morality vary within and across cultures, and through time? Are there moral ideas that constitute cultural universals? And how is one to explain this pattern of variation?

Although we think our work on evolutionary and psychological altruism bears on these questions, we also think that it is important not to blur the problems. Psychological altruism is not the same as morality. And an explanation of why human beings hold a moral principle is not, in itself, a justification (or a refutation) of that principle.

We say that psychological altruism is not the same as morality because individuals can have concerns about the welfare of specific others without their formulating those concerns in terms of ethical principles. A mother chimp may want her offspring to have some food, but this does not mean that she thinks that all chimps should be well-fed, or that all mothers should take care of their offspring. Egoistic and altruistic desires are both desires about specific individuals. Having self-directed preferences is not sufficient for having a morality; the same goes for other-directed preferences.

Why, then, did morality evolve? People can have specific likes and dislikes without this producing a socially shared moral code. And if everyone dislikes certain things, what is the point of there being a moral code that says that those things should be shunned? If everyone hates sticking pins in their toes, what is the point of an ethic that tells people that it is wrong to stick pins in their toes? And if parents invariably love their children, what would be the point of having a moral principle that tells parents that they ought to love their children? Behaviours that people do spontaneously by virtue of their own desires don't need to have a moral code laid on top of them. The obvious suggestion is that the social function of morality is to get people to do things that they would not otherwise be disposed to do, or to strengthen dispositions that people already have in weaker forms. Morality is not a mere redundant overlay on the psychologically altruistic motives we may have.

Functionalism went out of style in anthropology and other social sciences in part because it was hard to see what feedback mechanism might make institutions persist or disappear. Even if religion promotes group solidarity, how would that explain the persistence of religion? The idea of selection makes this question tractable. We hope that *Unto Others* will allow social scientists to explore the hypothesis that morality is a group adaptation. We do not deny that moral principles have functioned as ideological weapons, allowing some individuals to prosper at the expense of others in the same group. However, the hypothesis that moralities sometimes persist and spread because they benefit the group is not mere wishful thinking. Darwin's idea that features of morality can be explained by group selection needs to be explored.

What, if anything, do the evolutionary and psychological issues we discuss in *Unto Others* contribute to normative theory? Every normative theory relies on a conception of human nature. Sometimes this is expressed by invoking the *ought implies can principle*. If people ought to do something, then it must be possible for them to do it. Human nature circumscribes what is possible. We do not regard human nature as unchangeable. In part, this is because evolution isn't over. Genetic and cultural evolution will continue to modify the capacities that people have. But if we want to understand the capacities that people *now* have, surely an understanding of our evolutionary past is crucial. One lesson that may flow from the evolutionary and psychological study of altruism is that prisoners' dilemmas are in fact rarer than many researchers suppose. Decision theory says that it is irrational to co-operate (to act altruistically) in one-shot prisoners' dilemmas. However, perhaps some situations that appear to third parties to be prisoners' dilemmas really are not. Payoffs are usually measured in dollars, or in other tangible commodities. But if people sometimes care about each other, and not just about money, they are not irrational when they choose to co-operate in such interactions. Narrow forms of egoism make such behaviours appear irrational. Perhaps the conclusion to draw is not that people *are* irrational, but that the assumption of egoism needs to be rethought.

References

Batson, C. Daniel (1991), *The Altruism Question: Toward A Social-Psychological Answer* (Hillsdale, NJ: Lawrence Erlbaum Associates).

Boyd, Robert and Richerson, Peter (1985), *Culture and the Evolutionary Process* (Chicago: University of Chicago Press).

Broad, C.D (1965), *Five Types of Ethical Theory* (Totowa, NJ: Littlefield, Adams).

Clark, R.D. and Word, L.E. (1974), 'Where is the apathetic bystander? Situational characteristics of the emergency', *Journal of Personality and Social Psychology*, 29, pp. 279–87.

Darwin, Charles (1871), *The Descent of Man and Evolution in Relation to Sex* (London: Murray).

Dawkins, Richard (1976), *The Selfish Gene* (New York: Oxford University Press).

Feinberg, J. (1984), 'Psychological egoism', in *Reason at Work*, ed. S. Cahn, P. Kitcher and G. Sher (San Diego, Calif.: Harcourt Brace and Jovanovich), pp. 25–35.

Hamilton, W.D. (1964), 'The Genetical evolution of social behaviour I and II', *Journal of Theoretical Biology*, 7, pp. 1–16, pp. 17–52.

Kavka, Gregory (1986), *Hobbesian Moral and Political Theory* (Princeton, NJ: Princeton University Press).

Lafollette, Hugh (1988), 'The truth in psychological egoism', in *Reason and Responsibility*, 7th edn., ed. J. Feinberg (Belmont, Calif.: Wadsworth), pp. 500–7.

Maynard Smith, John (1964), 'Group selection and kin selection', *Nature*, 201, pp. 1145–6.

Maynard Smith, John and Price, George (1973), 'The logic of animal conflict', *Nature*, 246, pp. 15–18.

Nagel, Thomas (1970), *The Possibility of Altruism* (Oxford: Oxford University Press).

Nozick, Robert (1974), *Anarchy, State, and Utopia* (New York: Basic Books).

Sober, Elliott (1992), 'Hedonism and Butler's stone', *Ethics*, 103, pp. 97–103.

Sober, Elliott and Wilson, David Sloan (1998), *Unto Others: The Evolution and Psychology of Unselfish Behavior* (Cambridge, MA: Harvard University Press).

Stampe, Dennis (1994), 'Desire', in *A Companion to the Philosophy of Mind*, ed. S. Guttenplan (Cambridge, Mass.: Basil Blackwell), pp. 244–50.

Stewart, R.M. (1992), 'Butler's argument against psychological hedonism', *Canadian Journal of Philosophy*, 22, pp. 211–21.

Williams, George C. (1966), *Adaptation and Natural Selection* (Princeton, NJ: Princeton University Press).

17

Why Altruism Is Impossible . . . and Ubiquitous

Barry Schwartz

Historically, psychology has been guided by several theoretical presumptions that are so deep and pervasive that they are rarely noticed. These presumptions can be identified as methodological individualism, psychological atomism, egoism, and naturalism. Together, these presumptions imply that the proper unit for scientific analysis is the individual (methodological individualism), that the boundaries between different individuals are clear and distinct (psychological atomism), that individuals are interested primarily, if not exclusively, in themselves (egoism), and that all of this is "natural," is nature's way. Although psychology is certainly not unique among the human sciences in these presumptions, there is virtually no major area of psychology that is untouched by them.[1] These presumptions figure prominently when psychologists confront the phenomenon of altruism. The apparent fact that people will (sometimes, often, occasionally) act to serve the interests of others, even at substantial cost to themselves, becomes a puzzle that demands investigation and explanation. The very definition of altruism ("devotion to the interests of others; opposed to egoism," as one dictionary has it) depends on these theoretical presumptions. If people were not psychological atoms, dedicated to their own interests – if the boundaries between self and other were not clear and distinct – altruism as a distinct phenomenon might not even exist. But because of these presumptions, it does exist and so must be explained.

Or better, it must be explained away. In biology, it may be explained away by means of the "selfish gene" and the concepts of kin selection, inclusive fitness, and reciprocal altruism that accompany selfish-gene theory.[2] In economics, it may be explained away by the tautological notion of "preference maximization," which assumes that all choices maximize the preferences of the individuals who make them so that "it is ordinarily both convenient and reasonable for economics to . . . treat the individual as satisfying his preferences widiout dealing explicitly with the possibility that his preferences include a taste for helping other people."[3] In psychology, it may be explained away by appeal to similarly tautological notions such as mutual reinforcement. In all such cases, the operating principle is that for altruism to occur, there simply must be something in it for the altruist and, further, that something must be not merely an incidental byproduct of the altruistic act but its cause. Said another way, it is not good enough to claim that when individuals engage in altruistic acts, they also produce benefits for themselves. Instead, the claim must be that when people behave altruistically, it is because of the personal benefits derived from these acts. In the oft-quoted words of Michael Ghiselin, "Scratch an altruist and watch a hypocrite bleed."[4]

From Barry Schwartz (Sep. 1993). Why Altruism is Impossible . . . and Ubiquitous. *The Social Service Review*, 67, 3. The University of Chicago Press, pp. 314–26, 337–43.

Moral Psychology: Historical and Contemporary Readings, edited by Thomas Nadelhoffer, Eddy Nahmias, and Shaun Nichols. © 2010 Blackwell Publishing Ltd except for editorial material and organization © 2010 Thomas Nadelhoffer, Eddy Nahmias, and Shaun Nichols.

The net result of these views in the various human sciences is to make the presumption of egoism virtually unfalsifiable. Empirical evidence to document claims of egoism is rarely required. Reinterpretations of apparently altruistic acts in terms of their "real" egoistic causes are generated without constraint and accepted without careful scrutiny. Coupled with a more general cultural attitude that identifies cynicism with realism and sophistication, this orientation of the human sciences virtually guarantees that acts of altruism will not be accepted on their face.[5] Explanation of any social phenomenon that stops at altruism without unpacking the egoistic motives underlying it will be regarded as incomplete at best.

Within psychology, research on altruism is usually consistent with the theoretical presumptions I have identified. When examples of apparent altruism (e.g., children helping one another in play settings, adults coming to the aid of a stranger in distress) are subjected to research scrutiny, one of a handful of strategies is usually employed. Perhaps researchers attempt to uncover the "actual" selfish motives that the altruistic acts serve. Failing that, they attempt to uncover some mechanism (socialization, Freudian defense) that underlies it because it could not be the result, say, of rational deliberation on the part of the actor. Failing that, this act may be accepted on its face, but regarded as developmentally primitive, something immature that the actors will outgrow.[6] Finally, failing that, the very concept of altruism in general may be subjected to an analysis in terms of some self-interested concept like reinforcement.[7]

As a result of these strategies for explaining away altruism, a significant phenomenon is submerged. And as the presumptions and theories from the human sciences become the intellectual currency of the culture at large, little effort is made to appeal to altruistic motives or social concerns in efforts to get people to do the right thing in their day to day life. Instead, appeals are made that show how one or another seemingly altruistic act will serve the long-term interests of the actors. Appeals are made for social support for prenatal care for poor women not because it is right, but because it will cost less than later intensive medical care for their infants. Appeals are made to combat child and wife abuse not because they are evil, but because domestic abuse costs employers millions of dollars in absenteeism and lowered job productivity. Appeals are made to improve urban education not because everyone in a society like ours should be literate, but because illiteracy costs all of us in welfare payments, unemployment benefits, and high crime rates.[8] When appeals to self-interest are believed to be the only appeals that have any legitimacy, people begin to evaluate their own options and possibilities from within an egoistic calculus. The result is that the calculus of self-interest becomes self-fulfilling. As Jerome Kagan has said, "So many people have come to accept the truth of that assumption [of self-interest as the only interest] that the average person now treats it as a natural law."[9]

I intend to challenge some of these presumptions by taking altruism seriously. I will review briefly the empirical research and theoretical claims of others who take altruism seriously, and I will outline what is known about the social conditions that seem to promote altruism. In the course of this article, it should become apparent that under a different set of presumptions – presumptions that challenge individualism, atomism, and egoism – altruism becomes not impossible but ubiquitous.

Examples of Altruism

The phenomena that provoke discussions of altruism range from the dramatic to the mundane. In the former category are examples of people who put themselves in great physical danger to assist others, whether to save them from drowning or to pull them from a burning building. One recent account of such dramatic altruists is Samuel Oliner and Pearl Oliner's discussion of people who helped hide and save Jews during the Nazi holocaust.[10] A striking finding is that these life-saving altruists typically did not think they were doing anything unusual or heroic; they were doing what anyone would do. Also in the "dramatic" category is a voluminous line of research provoked by a failure of altruism. This research, on bystander intervention and bystander apathy, was begun as a result of a well-publicized incident in New York in which a woman was beaten to death as dozens of neighbors looked on from their apartment windows. Bibb Latane and John Darley, among others, attempted to bring this phenomenon into the laboratory to determine the variables that affect the likelihood of intervention.[11] They found that the likelihood of intervention decreases as the number of people who might intervene increases, as the physical proximity of the victim decreases, as the anonymity of the observers increases, as the familiarity of the victim decreases, and as the similarity of the victim to the observer decreases. People are much more likely to help in small towns than in big cities, they are much more likely to help people they know than strangers, they are much more likely to help people who are like them (in race, class, ethnicity) than people who are not, and they are much more likely to help if they are the only ones around. What is sometimes lost in all this analytical detail, however, is that most of the time, people do help. For example, in one series of studies that investigated the likelihood that young children and adolescents would come to the aid of an injured victim, fully 80 percent of subjects provided help.[12] So although people do not always help, they usually do.

In the category of more mundane acts of altruism are instances of giving to charity. Survey data indicate that more than 90 percent of Americans give to charity (more than 20 million American families give 5% or more of their incomes), and almost 50 percent do some kind of volunteer work.[13] In what may be the classic study of giving, Richard Titmuss surveyed 4,000 blood donors in England and found that only a small percentage of the donors expected to get anything – eidier directly or indirecdy – in return. The language they used to explain their behavior was a moral language emphasizing responsibility and obligation rather than interest or egoism. Titmuss also observed that in nations like the United States, where "donors" could sell their blood rather than giving it, the language of interest came to replace the language of responsibility.[14]

In addition to these examples of altruism, there are many examples of related phenomena – of sharing resources and cooperating on projects when neither is required by the situation, indeed even when the situation mitigates against cooperation or sharing. A classic example of a situation that pits cooperation against self-interest is found in game theory, specifically in what is called the Prisoner's Dilemma. In a classic Prisoner's Dilemma, each of two players may choose either to cooperate or to defect, and points are awarded to each based on his or her choices. Each player will do best if he or she defects and the other cooperates, and both players will do better if they both cooperate than if they both defect. The logic of the game dictates that unless the game has multiple turns, so that players can retaliate for defections, the only rational move for either player is defection. The result is that both players end up worse off than they would if they had cooperated.

In a game with multiple turns, however, cooperation can emerge as the dominant (i.e., most successful) strategy. Studies of the Prisoner's Dilemma have been used by Robert Axelrod and others to suggest the structural conditions necessary (principally, the possibility of retaliation for noncooperation) for cooperation to emerge among self-interested individuals.[15] However, recent research shows that many of these conditions are actually unnecessary. In Prisoner's Dilemma–like situations, subjects cooperated even when the games involved only one turn and their own choices were made anonymously. They cooperated even when cooperation could gain them nothing and could cost them substantially. The critical determinant of whether cooperation occurred was whether the people playing the game had an opportunity to communicate with one another prior to making their choices. Even brief group discussion was sufficient to engender in most subjects enough group identification and group solidarity that they felt bound to choose with group, not individual, interests in mind.[16] What this recent finding suggests is that Prisoner's Dilemma defections will reliably occur only when participants in a game are deprived of any opportunity to form any social bond. The presumptions of individualism, atomism, and egoism may have blinded previous investigators to the powerful effects of social solidarity and led to experiments conducted in a context in which solidarity could not possibly form. It appears that if solidarity can form, it will, and the logic of self-interest will be submerged as a result.

Much of the research that has been done on cooperation and sharing has been done with children in school settings. Although results tend to vary widi age, children do a substantial amount of spontaneous cooperating and sharing, and it is not very difficult to induce children to cooperate and share still more.[17] Because the typical classroom is not set up to encourage cooperation (children are required to work independently, social interaction among students is regarded as disruptive behavior, and teachers often use competitive incentives), it is all the more remarkable that it appears.

Studies of cooperation, of sharing, and of helping even among pre-school children, done both in the laboratory and in the home, demonstrate high frequencies of cooperation and sharing. In one such study, children between the ages of 3 and 7 were observed in play situations in which opportunities to help, comfort, or share with another child were possible. In the laboratory, more than half of the children studied displayed at least one of these prosocial behaviors during a 40-minute observation period. During a similar observation period in the home, almost 90 percent of the children acted selflessly.[18] Several other studies have produced similar results.[19]

Taken together, these phenomena, and many others like them, make it clear that altruistic behavior, whether dramatic or mundane, is not the least bit unusual. Helping, comforting, sharing, and cooperating occur among children and adults. They occur in school and in the home. They occur among acquaintances and among strangers. Akhough such behavior does not always occur, it occurs sufficiendy frequently, in sufficiently diverse settings, that to deny the existence of genuine altruism requires extraordinary acts of creative interpretation.

With all these diverse examples, I have yet to mention the class of altruistic behavior that is most pervasive – the behavior that occurs among members of a family. The subdiscipline of evolutionary biology known as sociobiology was essentially created to explain how these blatant and ubiquitous acts of self-sacrifice among family members can be reconciled with a general theory (natural selection) whose logic seems to demand selfishness.[20] Selfish genes, inclusive fitness, and kin selection are all postulated to show that deep down, self-sacrifice is really selfish. Sociobiology has been subject to substantial scrutiny and criticism, especially when it is applied to human behavior, but this is not the place to rehearse the arguments.[21] Leaving debates about sociobiology aside, if altruism is understood to mean "devotion to the interests of others," one glance at the behavior of families should convince us that it is everywhere.

Variables Affecting Altruism

Given that altruism does indeed occur, what can be said about the variables that influence its occurrence? Research on this topic has looked both at the individual and at the social context. It has explored whether altruism might be related to traits of character or personality and how it is affected by transient emotional or motivational states. It has examined in detail the socialization process for factors in the process of social development that might promote altruism. The literature is too voluminous to review here.[22] Thus, my discussion will be cursory, with an emphasis in the next section on what research in social development suggests are the necessary ingredients of altruism and the socialization experiences that promote it.

One variable that seems positively related to altruism and other forms of prosocial behavior is self-esteem. Although the literature is equivocal, most research has found that people – adults and children – with a positive self-concept are more likely to be helpful than people whose self-esteem is weak.[23] If one is sure of oneself, it seems easier to extend oneself to others. However, there are exceptions to this generalization. People with an extremely high opinion of themselves may feel no need to be connected to others, and people with a low opinion of themselves may be helpful just to garner social approval.[24] Thus, it seems that just the right amount of self esteem (whatever that might be) promotes altruism.

Still less clear is the relation of gender to altruism. In recent years, research on moral reasoning has led to the view that whereas men tend to be guided in their reasoning by an ethic of "rights," women tend to be guided by an ethic of "care, connection, and responsibility."[25] This difference in the criteria used for making moral judgments might lead one to suspect that women are more likely to be altruistic than men. However, research does not bear this expectation out. There are some studies in which women are more likely to help than men, but there are also studies in which the reverse is true, and there are many studies in which there seems to be no effect of gender.[26] And importandy, in one study of preschoolers, children who are presumably too young to have strongly developed gender roles, there were no observable gender differences in either helping, sharing, or moral reasoning.[27]

Two other variables that may be related to altruism are political and religious affiliation. In the political domain, there is some evidence that liberals score higher than conservatives on tests of moral reasoning, and that conservatives are more likely than liberals to hold the "just-world" view that people basically get what is coming to them.[28] These findings suggest potential differences in altruistic behavior, but I know of no studies that have found such differences. In the case of religion, many studies completed over the last 25 years have failed to find any relation between degree of religious conviction and a wide range of different kinds of altruistic activity.[29] One recent study, however, suggests that failures to find a relation between religious conviction and altruism may stem from measures of religious conviction that are too crude. Daniel Batson and colleagues distinguished among religious people those who see religion as a means to extrinsic ends, those who see it as an end in itself, and those who see it as a quest. Only among people in the latter group was helping positively related to religiosity.[30] Thus, if the relation between religious conviction and altruism is to be explored further, care must be taken to measure not only how religious individuals are, but what the content of their religious commitments is.

The only clear picture that emerges from the discussion thus far is that there is no clear picture. However, one variable that does seem to figure prominently in the degree of altruism people display is the extent to which potential altruists identify with the individuals or the group they will be helping. People are more inclined to help those who are perceived as similar to themselves than those who are perceived as different.[31] They are more likely to help members of their own racial or ethnic group than members of different groups.[32] Even when "groups" are established in the laboratory by means of a few minutes of discussion, the amount of group-serving, cooperative behavior is enhanced.[33] The anecdotal observation, confirmed by some empirical research, that people who live in small towns or rural settings are more likely to help than those who live in cities may in part be the result of group identification that small-town life makes possible and urban life prevents.[34] Altruistic acts that depend on group identification are susceptible to interpretations that suggest they are ultimately egoistic and self-interested, either by engendering future reciprocation (reciprocal altruism) or by deriving some benefits to one's social standing. Although there are several studies that have tried

with some success to rule these "ultimate self-interest" interpretations out, there seems to be an endless supply of new possibilities waiting in the wings to replace self-interest hypotheses that have been empirically eliminated.[35]

Altruism and Socialization

Whenever a claim is made that some characteristic or other is "human nature," attempts to evaluate the claim turn almost immediately to development. In light of the troika of presumptions about human nature with which I began this article – individualism, atomism, and egoism – researchers have paid a great deal of attention to the development of social behavior. If egoism is human nature, and positive social activity is a result of socialization, then we should expect to find that positive social behavior increases with development. If, however, there is something "natural" about positive social behavior, then we should see signs of it very early on. Although studies of development that have attempted to resolve this issue have been inconclusive, they have suggested what some of the requisite components of positive social behavior are, and what kinds of developmental experience seem to foster those components.[36]

In an influential account of the development of altruism, Martin Hoffman suggests that altruism has two requirements, one affective and one cognitive.[37] Genuine altruism requires empathy (affective) and perspective taking (cognitive). One's distress at the distress of another can be direct and immediate. It is painful, for example, to hear infants cry – even for other infants.[38] However, this empathy may not lead to altruism. Indeed, it may lead to escape if the affect is intense enough. For empathy to lead to altruism, it must be combined with perspective taking. To be able to feel what another is feeling (empathy) requires substantial understanding (perspective taking) of what the other is experiencing. Hoffman refers to this kind of affect combined with perspective taking as sympathy. According to Hoffman, children move from empathy to sympathy in stages as their cognitive sophistication increases.[39]

Although both empathy and perspective taking are necessary for altruism, neither is sufficient. One can experience intense distress at the distress of another, but without an accompanying under-standing of the source and nature of the distress, one might act only to relieve the distress in oneself (e.g., by escaping) or act to try to relieve the distress of the other in a way that is entirely inappropriate. Similarly, one can have a thorough understanding of the perspective of the other but use this only to serve one's own interests (e.g., by avoiding a similar situation oneself). To behave altruistically, one must both understand what the other is experiencing and want to do something about it.

As I indicated above, research on altruism in children, both in laboratory settings and in the home, suggests that it is abundant.[40] Most 18-month-olds will share something with another person, and most children between 18 and 24 months will respond positively to another's dis-tress. Thus, even before much of the requisite cognitive development has occurred, instances of altruism are common. However, there are also individual differences among children in altruism, and at least some evidence suggests that the different responses to others in distress when children are quite young can predict how these children will respond as much as 5 years later.[41] The existence of individual differences, together with the suggestion that early differences may be perpetuated, prompts one to investigate the socialization variables that may enhance or retard altruistic behavior.

The first place to look for socialization effects is at the relations between parents and children. Hoffman identified several child-rearing vari-ables that affect the degree of altruism displayed by children.[42] First, parents can enhance altruism by engaging in altruistic behavior themselves. Second, parents can enhance altruism by using certain disciplinary techniques when their chil-dren are responsible for another's distress. By using what Hoffman calls "inductive," as opposed to punitive, discipline, a parent can turn a child's transgressions to good effect. Inductive discipline stresses the effects of the child's behavior on others, emphasizing long-range, perhaps unfore-seen, effects, both psychological and physical, and steps that may be taken to ameliorate the consequences of the child's transgression. Such disciplinary techniques possess moral content; that is, the parent makes clear that the child's actions not only had unfortunate effects, but that

they were wrong. The constructive and reparative character of the induction seems to result in the child's internalization of the appropriate moral norm, making similar transgressions less likely in the future and spontaneous reparations more likely, should transgressions occur. In contrast with inductive discipline, discipline based on creating fear of future punishment, or discipline based on the assertion of parental power or on the direct withdrawal of parental love do not have salutary effects on the likelihood of future altruis-tic behavior. On Hoffman's account, inductive discipline succeeds in promoting altruism where other techniques fail because by emphasizing the plight of the victim the parent triggers empathic distress in the child. Other disciplinary techniques may also trigger distress, but the distress will be focused on the (future) plight of the self rather than on the victim. There is also some reason to believe that inductive discipline may promote altruism by encouraging children to reason about the moral significance of their actions, something that even young children seem able and willing to do.[43]

In addition to using inductive discipline, par-ents can promote altruism by providing whatever discipline they provide in a context of substan-tial parental affection. Persistent and abundant parental affection can reduce the child's focus or preoccupation with his or her own emotional needs, thus making it easier for sympathy and perspective taking to occur.

Although the home is certainly the central domain for socialization in childhood, it is not the only one. Much socialization occurs in the classroom. Cooperative learning and play settings in the classroom seem to enhance children's perspective-taking abilities.[44] They also seem to enhance self-esteem, which, as noted earlier, contributes to prosocial behavior.[45] Children with substantial experience cooperating in the classroom are more likely than other children to help others or to donate some of their resources to others.[46] Conversely, explicitly competitive classroom situations seem to reduce all of these prosocial effects.[47] There is also some evidence that in addition to providing opportunities for cooperation, schools can facilitate altruism by putting children into mixed-age groups.[48] Because children of different ages are expected to perform at different levels, mixing age groups discourages implicit competition. It also gives older children practice in perspective taking as they try to help the younger ones.

Friendship also positively influences prosocial behavior.[49] Studies of play in children from as young as 12 months to as old as 10 years indicate that turn taking and sharing are the rule. Despite the old Piagetian lore to the contrary, when young children speak as they play, the majority of their speech is social, not egocentric. The speech of each child is coordinated with the group's joint activities. As children get older (ages 6–7), friendships seem to be defined by strict reciprocity, but by the time they reach age 9 or 10, reciprocity is replaced by a richer understanding of mutual commitment and obligation in which children acknowledge a principle much like "from each according to his abilities and to each according to his needs." The friendship becomes a unit that is different from (more than) the individual needs and wants of the participants. At this age, children seem to realize that friendships take work and long-term commitment. The children seem no longer to see themselves (if they ever did) as the psychological atoms that most psychological theories presume.

None of these findings should come as much of a surprise. Millennia ago, in his *Nicomachean Ethics*, Aristotle observed that it is hard to be good – that being good takes practice. This practice occurs in the routine activities of daily life. If daily life is properly structured, being good becomes automatic. The literature on socialization and altruism confirms Aristotle's views by showing that when the home and the classroom are structured to give the child practice in prosocial behavior, such behavior becomes much more likely.

If practice at being good is a good thing, it seems natural to do whatever one can to encourage children to practice. This has led some investigators to study the effects of reward for prosocial behavior. Because rewards can be used effectively in general to strengthen desired behavior, it seems only natural to use them to encourage cooperation or altruism. It seems especially natural if one believes that such behavior occurs only when it serves the interests of the actor. A system of rewards for prosocial behavior can be seen as assuring that it will be in the individual's interests to be good.

The results of such studies paint a coherent picture. When rewards are contingent on various forms of prosocial behavior, they increase the frequency of the behavior – as long as the rewards continue to be present. If the rewards are withdrawn, the prosocial behavior decreases. Thus, unless one expects contingent rewards for prosocial behavior to be a permanent and ubiquitous part of the social scene, one cannot rely on them to be the primary source of prosocial behavior. We can understand such results from the framework provided by attribution theory.[50] Imagine a child who helps a playmate in distress. The child might seek to explain his or her helping behavior – to make a causal attribution. If no rewards are present, likely causal attributions would involve the state of distress of the victim, the understanding that helping is the right thing to do, and other explanations that focus on factors intrinsic to the act of helping. But the presence of rewards offers an alternative, and apparently dominant, causal candidate. "I did it for the reward," the child might say to him- or herself. With that understanding of his or her motivation, it would come as no surprise if altruistic acts were not forthcoming when rewards were not available. This is just a particular class of a much more general and well-documented phenomenon – the undermining of intrinsic motivation by extrinsic rewards.[51]

For example, in one study, second and third graders who were given rewards for helping were less likely to explain their own behavior in terms of intrinsic motivation to help than were children who did not receive rewards.[52] In another study, children were praised (social reward) or merely told that they were helpful people for making donations to another. Only in the latter case was the likelihood of donation high in a subsequent follow-up study.[53] In another study of elementary school children, it was found that their mothers' tendency to use rewards as socialization tools was negatively correlated with the likelihood that the children would help when unobserved in free-play settings.[54] Results similar to these have been obtained with adult subjects. The presence of extrinsic rewards decreased their perception of themselves as altruistic and decreased the likelihood that they would help again at a later time without rewards. Conversely, experimenter interventions that focused on the altruistic nature of the subjects increased the likelihood of future altruistic behavior.[55]

The literature on the use of rewards to promote altruism should remind the reader of where this article began. It began with a set of presumptions that, taken together, made genuine altruism seem impossible. Because of the inherently atomistic, self-interested character of human nature, there simply had to be something in it for the altruist. Not only that, but that "something" that served self-interest had to be the cause of the altruistic act. In other words, it would not do to suggest that although altruists get satisfaction from their altruistic acts, that is not the reason they do them – that they do them because they are the right things to do, and the satisfaction is a bonus. From within the presumptions of atomism and egoism, such an account is naive at best. The actors themselves may believe that their acts are motivated by obligation, responsibility, and commitment, but what really keeps them going is some kind of direct payoff. Thinking like this makes it perfectly natural to use extrinsic rewards to beef up the payoff for altruistic acts; extrinsic rewards are seen as making only a quantitative change in the incentive structure of a situation, not a qualitative one.

When theorists who hold the view that genuine altruism is impossible are presented with examples of altruism, they try to explain them by appealing to one or another mechanism of self-interest. Appeals to kin selection and inclusive fitness are the way sociobiology handles altruism toward offspring or other genetic relatives. Reciprocal altruism is one way sociobiologists (and other social scientists) handle the fact that altruism is much more likely among people who know one another or who are alike in some significant way. The rewarding power of praise and social approval is another way such acts of altruism are handled. And when empathy (or sympathy) is introduced as an essential ingredient of altruistic behavior, the atomists suggest that the altruist acts only to relieve the distress that is created by his or her empathy.

In principle, one could test these various self-interest-based alternatives to genuine altruism by creating experimental situations in which genuinely altruistic motives and self-interested motives will push people to behave differently. Batson and his associates have been doing pre-

cisely this for the last several years.[56] Thus, for example, Batson has provided evidence that empathy and personal distress at the plight of another are actually distinct and essentially independent affective states. This finding makes the claim that empathy-based altruism is really motivated by the relief of personal distress more difficult to sustain. He has also shown that the mood of altruistic actors is affected by whether or not the victim actually gains relief from his or her unfortunate situation and not by whether they happen to have been the agents responsible for that relief. This finding makes the claim that altruism is really only the pursuit of social approval and status more difficult to sustain.

Although careful, analytic experiments can be done to test particular egoistic explanations of altruistic behavior, there seems to be an endless supply of such explanations. Egoistic accounts of altruism will continue to sprout, like weeds, and investigators will face the task of evaluating and rejecting them, one by one, indefinitely unless the ground can be replowed and some of the presumptions that dominate the human sciences be replaced.

[...]

Conclusion: The Fragility of Altruism

Amartya Sen has argued that there is a source of concern for fairness that the logic of egoism cannot encompass, indeed, that sometimes leads to actions in direct violation of the logic of egoism.[57] He calls this source of concern "commitment" and suggests that it cannot be incorporated within the atomistic, egoistic framework. To act out of commitment is to do what one thinks is right, what will promote the public welfare, quite apart from whether it promotes one's own. It is to act out of a sense of responsibility as a citizen. Acts of commitment include voting in large, general elections. They include doing one's job to the best of one's ability – going beyond the terms of the contract, even if no one is watching and there is nothing to be gained from it. They include refusing to charge what the traffic will bear for necessities during times of shortage, refusing to capitalize on fortuitous circumstances at the expense of others.

Acts of commitment like these occur routinely. They are what holds society together. But they are

ALTRUISM & EGOISM

a problem for the logic of egoism. As Sen says, "Commitment ... drives a wedge between personal choice and personal welfare, and much of traditional economic theory relies on the identity of the two." He continues:

> The economic theory of utility ... is sometimes criticized for having too much structure; human beings are alleged to be "simpler" in reality ... precisely the opposite seems to be the case: traditional theory has *too little* structure. A person is given *one* preference ordering, and as and when the need arises, this is supposed to reflect his interests, represent his welfare, summarize his idea of what should be done, and describe his actual choices and behavior. Can one preference ordering do all these things? A person thus described may be "rational" in the limited sense of revealing no inconsistencies in his choice behavior, but if he has no use for this distinction between quite different concepts, he must be a bit of a fool. The *purely* economic man is indeed close to being a social moron.[58]

The existence of commitment casts the egoistic presumptions of social science in a whole new light. True, when making economic decisions, people will presumably choose that alternative that maximizes self-interest. But before they can do this, they have to make another choice. They have to choose to make an economic decision that is based on self-interest as against, say, a moral one that is based on commitment. In addition to having a set of preferences among commodities, people must be understood to have a set of preferences among their interests. Preferring one preference hierarchy over another amounts to preferring to be one kind of person over another, preferring to have one kind of character over another. Any thorough analysis of the logic of egoism must include an account of how people choose their preferences and how culture contributes to the set of preferences among which people choose. Much of modern social science takes this most fundamental aspect of human preference and choice as a given.

Fiske points out that most societies are heterogeneous in the rule systems they apply to the regulation of social life, although one may be more dominant than the others. In our own society, despite the dominance of market pricing, virtually all people have social relations guided by each type of rule. Indeed, one's relations with the same person may follow one rule system in one domain and a different rule system in another. Imagine two friends who share completely and indiscriminately their science fiction novels (communal sharing) and at the same time work at a task (patching and painting an apartment) in which one is the expert ordering the other around (authority ranking), who divide precisely their expenses and driving time for a crosscountry vacation (equality matching), and agree for one to buy the other's old car at the going market price. It may be that what we identify as essentially unlimited personal freedom in modern America is, in part, the freedom to apply whichever rule system we like to whatever domains of life we like, subject only to the agreement of the people with whom we will be interacting. If this is true, then, in effect, each of us has the power to decide whether to have an independent self or an interdependent one, whether to live by the rules of the market or to live by the rules of community, whether to obviate altruism by connecting our interests to the interests of others, or to obviate it by creating a system in which only the egoists can survive.

Notes

1. Charles B. MacPherson, *The Political Theory of Possessive Individualism: Hobbes to Locke* (New York: Oxford University Press, 1962); Michael A. Wallach and Lise Wallach, *Psychology's Sanction for Selfishness: The Error of Egoism in Theory and Therapy* (San Francisco: Freeman, 1983).
2. Robert D. Alexander, *The Biology of Moral Systems* (Hawthorne, N.Y.: Aldine de Gruyter, 1987); Richard Dawkins, *The Selfish Gene* (Oxford: Oxford University Press, 1976). For an alternative view, see Herbert I. Simon, "A Mechanism for Social Selection and Successful Altruism," *Science* 250 (1990): 1665–68.
3. Howard Margolis, *Selfishness, Altruism, and Rationality* (Cambridge: Cambridge University Press, 1982), pp. 11–12 (cited in Alfie Kohn, *The Brighter Side of Human Nature* [New York: Basic, 1990]).
4. Michael Ghiselin, *The Economy of Nature and the Evolution of Sex* (Berkeley: University of California Press, 1976), p. 247.
5. Teresa M. Amabile, "Brilliant but Cruel: Perceptions of Negative Evaluators," *Journal of Experimental Social Psychology* 18 (1983): 1–22.

[6] S. B. Dreman and Charles W. Greenbaum, "Altruism or Reciprocity: Sharing Behavior in Israeli Kindergarten Children," *Child Development* 44 (1973): 61–8.

[7] James H. Bryan and Perry London, "Altruistic Behavior by Children," *Psychological Bulletin* 73 (1970): 200–11.

[8] Kohn, *The Brighter Side of Human Nature* (n. 3 above).

[9] Jerome Kagan, *Unstable Ideas: Temperament, Cognition, and the Self* (Cambridge, Mass.: Harvard University Press, 1989).

[10] Samuel P. Oliner and Pearl M. Oliner, *The Altruistic Personality: Rescuers of Jews in Nazi Europe* (New York: Free Press, 1988).

[11] John Darley and Bibb Latane, "Bystander Intervention in Emergencies: Diffusion of Responsibility," *Journal of Personality and Social Psychology* 8 (1968): 377–83; Bibb Latane and John Darley, *The Unresponsive Bystander: Why Doesn't He Help?* (New York: Appleton-Century-Crofts, 1970).

[12] Elizabeth Midlarsky and M. E. Hannah, "Competence, Reticence, and Helping by Children and Adolescents," *Developmental Psychology* 21 (1985): 534–41.

[13] Virginia A. Hodgkinson, *Motivations for Giving and Volunteering: A Selected Review* (New York: Foundation Center, 1991).

[14] Richard M. Titmuss, *The Gift Relationship: From Human Blood to Social Policy* (New York: Pantheon, 1971).

[15] Robert Axelrod, *The Evolution of Cooperation* (New York: Basic, 1984).

[16] Linda R. Caporael, Robin M. Dawes, John M. Orbell, and Alphons J. C. van de Kragt, "Selfishness Examined: Cooperation in the Absence of Egoistic Incentives," *Behavioral and Brain Sciences* 12 (1989): 683–739; Robin M. Dawes, Alphons J. C. van de Kragt, and John M. Orbell, "Cooperation for the Benefit of Us – Not Me, or My Conscience," in *Beyond Self-interest*, ed. Jane J. Mansbridge (Chicago: University of Chicago Press, 1990), pp. 97–110.

[17] Alfie Kohn, *No Contest: The Case against Competition* (Boston: Houghton Mifflin, 1986).

[18] Marian Radke-Yarrow and Carolyn Zahn-Waxler, "Dimensions and Correlates of Prosocial Behavior in Young Children," *Child Development* 47 (1976): 118–25.

[19] Nancy Eisenberg-Berg and Michael Hand, "The Relationship of Preschoolers' Reasoning about Prosocial Moral Conflicts to Prosocial Behavior," *Child Development* 50 (1979): 356–63; Marian Radke-Yarrow and Carolyn Zahn-Waxler, "Roots, Motives, and Patterns in Children's Prosocial Behavior," in *Development and Maintenance of Prosocial Behavior*, ed. Ervin Staub, Daniel Bar-Tal, Jerzy Karylowski, and Janusz Reykowski (New York: Plenum, 1984), pp. 81–99; Linda Stanhope, Richard Q. Bell, and Nina Y. Parker-Cohen, "Temperament and Helping Behavior in Preschool Children," *Developmental Psychology* 23 (1987): 347–53.

[20] Edward O. Wilson, *Sociobiology* (Cambridge, Mass.: Harvard University Press, 1975).

[21] Philip Kitcher, *Vaulting Ambition* (Cambridge, Mass.: MIT Press, 1985); Marshall Sahlins, *The Use and Abuse of Biology* (Ann Arbor: University of Michigan Press, 1976); Barry Schwartz, *The Battle for Human Nature: Science, Morality, and Modern Life* (New York: Norton, 1986).

[22] For one such review, see Marian Radke-Yarrow, Carolyn Zahn-Waxler, and Michael Chapman, "Childrens' Prosocial Dispositions and Behavior," in *Handbook of Child Psychology*, ed. Paul H. Mussen (New York: Wiley, 1983), 4:495–536.

[23] David E. Barrett and Marian Radke-Yarrow, "Prosocial Behavior, Social Inferential Ability, and Assertiveness in Children," *Child Development* 48 (1977): 475–81; Ervin Staub, "A Conception of the Determinants and Development of Altruism and Aggression: Motives, the Self, and the Environment," in *Altruism and Aggression: Biological and Social Origins*, ed. Carolyn Zahn-Waxler, E. Mark Cummings, and Ronald Iannotti (Cambridge: Cambridge University Press, 1986), pp. 135–64.

[24] Nancy Eisenberg, *Altruistic Emotion, Cognition, and Behavior* (Hillsdale, N.J.: Erlbaum, 1986); Seymour Feshbach and Norma Feshbach, "Aggression and Altruism: A Personality Perspective," in Zahn-Waxler et al., eds. (n. 23 above), pp. 189–217.

[25] Carol Gilligan, *In a Different Voice: Psychological Theory and Women's Development* (Cambridge, Mass.: Harvard University Press, 1982); Lawrence Kohlberg, *The Philosophy of Moral Development: Moral Stages and the Idea of Justice* (San Francisco: Harper & Row, 1981).

[26] Daniel Bar-Tal, *Prosocial Behavior: Theory and Research* (Washington, D.C.: Hemisphere, 1976); Alice H. Eagly and Maureen Crowley, "Gender and Helping Behavior: A Meta-analytic Review of the Social Psychological Literature," *Psychological Bulletin* 100 (1986): 283–308; Latane and Darley (n. 11 above); Diane M. Tice and Roy F. Baumeister, "Masculinity Inhibits Helping in Emergencies: Personality Does Predict the Bystander Effect," *Journal of Personality and Social Psychology* 49 (1985): 420–8.

[27] Eisenberg-Berg and Hand (n. 19 above).

[28] Eisenberg (n. 24 above); Zick Rubin and Anne Peplau, "Belief in a Just World and Reactions to Another's Lot: A Study of Participants in the National Draft Lottery," *Journal of Social Issues* 29 (1973): 73–93.

[29] Lawrence V. Annis, "Emergency Helping and Religious Behavior," *Psychological Reports* 39 (1976): 151–58; Victor B. Cline and James M. Richards, Jr., "A Factor-analytic Study of Religious Belief and Behavior," *Journal of Personality and Social Psychology* 1 (1965): 569–78; Sharon Georgianna, "Is a Religious Neighborhood a Good Neighborhood?" *Humboldt Journal of Social Relations* 11 (1984): 1–16; Charles Y. Glock, Benjamin B. Ringer, and Earl R. Babbie, *To Comfort and to Challenge* (Berkeley: University of California Press, 1967).

[30] C. Daniel Batson, Kathryn C. Oleson, Joy L. Weeks, Sean P. Healy, Penny J. Reeves, Patrick Jennings, and Thomas Brown, "Religious Prosocial Motivation: Is It Altruistic or Egoistic?" *Journal of Personality and Social Psychology* 57 (1989): 873–84.

[31] Latane and Darley (n. 11 above); Herman E. Mitchell and Donn Byrne, "The Defendant's Dilemma: Effects of Jurors' Attitudes and Authoritarianism on Judicial Decisions," *Journal of Personality and Social Psychology* 25 (1973): 123–29.

[32] Norma Feshbach, "Studies of Empathic Behavior in Children," in *Progress in Experimental Personality Research*, ed. Brendan Maher (New York: Academic Press, 1978), 8:157–84.

[33] Caporael, Dawes, Orbell, and van de Kragt (n. 16 above); Dawes, van de Kragt, and Orbell (n. 16 above).

[34] Linden L. Nelson and Spencer Kagan, "Competition: The Star-spangled Scramble," *Psychology Today* (September 1972), pp. 53–56, 90–91; Harold Takooshian, Sandra Haber, and David J. Lucido, "Who Wouldn't Help a Lost Child?" *Psychology Today* (February 1977), pp. 67–8, 88. The importance of group identification to altruism raises an interesting theoretical issue that requires careful analysis and empirical investigation. The conception of justice that seems to dominate modern American thinking on the subject might be termed "universalist." That is, we are encouraged to aspire to a norm by which all people are treated fairly and equally, independent of their race, ethnicity, class, or gender. The great "melting pot" is one in which particularist attachments and loyalties are meant to be dissolved. We all know that, both as individuals and as a society, we have failed to meet this norm. However, the appropriateness of the norm is rarely questioned. What research on group identification and altruism suggests is the possibility that the norm may be not just unattainable, but undesirable. If people are required to treat all others equally, we may expect that they will treat them all equally badly. Universalism may leave us no alternative but egoism. If all people have an equal claim on our time, attention, and assistance, we have no time for anyone. Novelist Graham Greene may have had this in mind when he observed that while it is possible to love people, it is not possible to love humanity. A pluralistic culture that legitimates various ties to particular groups may foster altruism in a way that a melting pot does not.

[35] C. Daniel Batson, "Prosocial Behavior: Is It Ever Truly Altruistic?" In *Advances in Experimental Social Psychology*, ed. Leonard Berkowitz (New York: Academic Press, 1987), 20:65–122; C. Daniel Batson, Janine Dyck, J. Brandt, Judy Batson, Anne Powell, Rosalie McMaster, and Cari Griffit, "Five Studies Testing Two New Egoistic Alternatives to the Empathy-Altruism Hypothesis," *Journal of Personality and Social Psychology* 55 (1988): 52–77.

[36] Eisenberg (n. 24 above); Nancy Eisenberg and Paul A. Miller, "The Relation of Empathy to Prosocial and Related Behaviors," *Psychological Bulletin* 101 (1987): 91–119; Radke-Yarrow and Zahn-Waxler, "Roots, Motives, and Patterns in Children's Prosocial Behavior" (n. 19 above); Radke-Yarrow, Zahn-Waxler, and Chapman (n. 22 above).

[37] Martin L. Hoffman, "Altruistic Behavior and the Parent-Child Relationship," *Journal of Personality and Social Psychology* 31 (1975): 937–43, "Developmental Synthesis of Affect and Cognition and Its Implications for Altruistic Motivation," *Developmental Psychology* 11 (1975): 607–22, "The Development of Empathy," in *Altruism and Helping Behavior: Social, Personality, and Developmental Perspectives*, ed. J. Philippe Rushton and Richard Sorrentino (Hillsdale, N.J.: Erlbaum, 1981), pp. 245–77, "Affective and Cognitive Processes in Moral Internalization," in *Social Cognition and Social Development: A Socio-cultural Perspective*, ed. E. Tory Higgins, Diane Ruble, and Willard Hartup (New York: Cambridge University Press, 1983), pp. 236–74, "The Contribution of Empathy to Justice and Moral Development," in *Empathy and Its Development*, ed. Nancy Eisenberg and Janet Strayer (New York: Cambridge University Press, 1987), pp. 86–113, and "Empathy, Social Cognition, and Moral Action," in *Moral Behavior and Development: Advances in Theory, Research and Applications*, ed. William M. Kurtines and Jacob L. Gewirtz (Hillsdale, NJ: Erlbaum, 1989), pp. 106–43.

[38] Grace B. Martin and Russell D. Clark III, "Distress Crying in Neonates: Species and Peer Specificity," *Developmental Psychology* 18 (1982): 3–9; Abraham Sagi and Martin L. Hoffman, "Empathic Distress in the Newborn," *Developmental Psychology* 12 (1976): 175–76; James Youniss, "Development in Reciprocity through Friendship," in Zahn-Waxler et al., eds. (n. 23 above), pp. 86–106; Carolyn Zahn-Waxler, Ronald Iannotti, and Mark Chapman, "Peers and Prosocial Development," in *Peer Relationships and Social Skills in Childhood*, ed.

K. Rubin and H. Ross (New York: Springer-Verlag, 1982), pp. 133–62.

[39] Martin L. Hoffman, "Interaction of Affect and Cognition in Empathy," in *Emotions, Cognitions, and Behavior*, ed. Carol Izard, Jerome Kagan, and Robert Zajonc (Cambridge: Cambridge University Press, 1984), pp. 103–31.

[40] E. Mark Cummings, Barbara Hollenbeck, Ronald Iannotti, Marion Radke-Yarrow, and Carolyn Zahn-Waxler, "Early Organization of Altruism and Aggression: Developmental Patterns and Individual Differences," in Zahn-Waxler et al., eds. (n. 23 above), pp. 165–88; Carolyn Zahn-Waxler and Marian Radke-Yarrow, "The Development of Altruism: Alternative Research Strategies," in *The Development of Prosocial Behavior*, ed. Nancy Eisenberg (New York: Academic Press, 1982), pp. 25–52.

[41] Cummings et al. (n. 40 above).

[42] Hoffman, "Altruistic Behavior and the Parent-Child Relationship" (n. 37 above), "Affective and Cognitive Processes in Moral Internalization" (n. 37 above); see also Carolyn Zahn-Waxler, Marian Radke-Yarrow, and Robert A. King, "Child Rearing and Children's Prosocial Inclinations toward Victims of Distress," *Child Development* 50 (1979): 319–30.

[43] Eisenberg-Berg and Hand (n. 19 above).

[44] David W. Johnson and Roger T. Johnson, "The Socialization and Achievement Crisis: Are Cooperative Learning Experiences the Solution?" in *Applied Social Psychology Annual*, ed. L. Bickman (Beverly Hills, Calif.: Sage, 1983), 4:103–37; David W. Johnson and Roger T. Johnson, *Cooperation and Competition* (Edina, Minn.: Interaction Book Co., 1989).

[45] Kohn, *No Contest* (n. 17 above).

[46] David W. Johnson, Roger T. Johnson, Jeannette Johnson, and Douglas Anderson, "Effects of Cooperative versus Individualized Instruction on Student Prosocial Behavior, Attitudes toward Learning, and Achievement," *Journal of Educational Psychology* 68 (1976): 446–52.

[47] Mark A. Barnett and James H. Bryan, "Effects of Competition with Outcome Feedback on Children's Helping Behavior," *Developmental Psychology* 10 (1974): 838–42; Mark A. Barnett, Karen A. Matthews, and Charles B. Corbin, "The Effect of Competitive and Cooperative Instructional Sets on Children's Generosity," *Personality and Social Psychology Bulletin* 5 (1979): 91–94; in adults, see John T. Lanzetta and Basil G. Englis, "Expectations of Cooperation and Competition and Their Effects on Observers' Vicarious Emotional Responses," *Journal of Personality and Social Psychology* 56 (1989): 543–54.

[48] Aharon Bizman, Yoel Yinon, Esther Mivtzari, and Rivka Shavit, "Effects of the Age Structure of the Kindergarten on Altruistic Behavior," *Journal of School Psychology* 16 (1978): 154–60.

[49] James Youniss, "Development in Reciprocity through Friendship," in Zahn-Waxler et al., eds. (n. 23 above), pp. 88–107.

[50] Harold H. Kelley, "Attribution Theory in Social Psychology," in *Nebraska Symposium on Motivation*, ed. David Levine (Lincoln: University of Nebraska Press, 1967), pp. 192–238.

[51] Mark R. Lepper and David Greene, eds., *The Hidden Costs of Rewards* (Hillsdale, N.J.: Erlbaum, 1978); Barry Schwartz, "The Creation and Destruction of Value," *American Psychologist* 45 (1990): 7–15.

[52] David Gelfand and Donald Hartmann, "Response Consequences and Attributions," in Eisenberg, ed. (n. 40 above), pp. 176–96.

[53] Joan E. Grusec and Theodore Dix, "The Socialization of Prosocial Behavior: Theory and Reality," in Zahn-Waxler et al., eds. (n. 23 above), pp. 218–37; Joan E. Grusec and Erica Redler, "Attribution, Reinforcement, and Altruism: A Developmental Analysis," *Developmental Psychology* (1980): 525–34.

[54] Richard A. Fabes, Jim Fultz, Nancy Eisenberg, Traci May-Plumlee, and F. Scott Christopher, "Effects of Reward on Children's Prosocial Motivation: A Socialization Study," *Developmental Psychology* 25 (1989): 509–15.

[55] C. Daniel Batson, Jay S. Coke, M. L. Jasnoski, and Michael Hanson, "Buying Kindness: Effect of an Extrinsic Incentive for Helping on Perceived Altruism," *Personality and Social Psychology Bulletin* 4 (1978): 86–91; Delroy L. Paulhus, David R. Shaffer, and Leslie L. Downing, "Effects of Making Blood Donor Motives Salient upon Donor Retention: A Field Experiment," *Personality and Social Psychology Bulletin* 3 (1977): 99–102; Miron Zuckerman, Michelle M. Lazzaro, and Diane Waldgeir, "Undermining Effects of the Foot-in-the-Door Technique with Extrinsic Rewards," *Journal of Applied Social Psychology* 9 (1979): 292–96.

[56] Batson (n. 35 above); C. Daniel Batson, Judy G. Batson, Can A. Griffitt, Sergio Barrientos, J. Randall Brandt, Peter Sprengelmeyer, and Michael J. Bayly, "Negative-State Relief and the Empathy-Altruism Hypothesis," *Journal of Personality and Social Psychology* 56 (1989): 922–33; C. Daniel Batson and Jay S. Coke, "Empathy: A Source of Altruistic Motivation for Helping," in Rushton and Sorrentino, eds. (n. 37 above), pp. 167–87; Batson et al. (n. 35 above).

[57] Amartya Sen, "Rational Fools," *Philosophy and Public Affairs* 6 (1976): 317–44.

[58] Ibid., p. 329.

Part III
Virtue & Character

Introduction

Eddy Nahmias

In Part I on "Reason & Passion" a central question involved whether moral judgments and actions derive from a person's rational or emotional processes. Another dimension to this question is the extent to which moral actions derive from a person's character traits or their situations. For instance, if both Jim and Ray come across a car accident with victims in need of help, what would best explain why Ray stops to help while Jim walks past? Is it that Ray has the traits of compassion or courage while Jim is selfish or cowardly? One tradition that suggests that such character traits explain moral behavior is virtue ethics, which says that moral actions derive from the virtues, a person's dispositions to reason and act consistently and appropriately in response to situations calling for moral behavior. This theory of ethics and moral psychology was prominent in Greek philosophy (as well as some non-Western philosophies, such as Confucianism). It was largely displaced by Kantian and utilitarian theories, but it was revitalized in the late twentieth century by philosophers such as Alasdair MacIntyre, G.E.M. Anscombe, and Philippa Foot. One reason for this revitalization was the claim that virtue ethics provides a more realistic moral psychology than its Kantian and utilitarian competitors. For instance, it seems more plausible that humans' moral behavior is driven by their character traits than by their consideration of whether an action accords with Kant's categorical imperative or whether it maximizes overall utility. It also seems more realistic to suppose that we can

educate people to behave morally by inculcating certain character traits in them than by teaching them to consider their actions in light of abstract duties or overall consequences (of course, these may be overly simplistic ways of characterizing a developed theory of Kantian or utilitarian moral psychology).

Whether virtue ethics actually offers a realistic moral psychology, however, is a largely empirical issue. And some have argued that the evidence does not support this purported advantage of virtue ethics over its competitors because recent research in social psychology suggests that human behavior, including moral behavior, is caused primarily by situational factors rather than robust character traits. This research suggests, for instance, that the best explanation for Ray's altruistic behavior and Jim's seemingly callous behavior may be that when Ray witnessed the accident he was the only person present, whereas when Jim walked by there were several other inactive bystanders. Numerous experiments have suggested that these sorts of situational variables (e.g., the presence of bystanders) may account for our behavior more than differences in people's personality or character.

The central questions discussed in this Part include:

- What are character traits? What are virtues?
- How stable are character traits across various situations and how unified are the different virtues?

Moral Psychology: Historical and Contemporary Readings, edited by Thomas Nadelhoffer, Eddy Nahmias, and Shaun Nichols. © 2010 Blackwell Publishing Ltd except for editorial material and organization © 2010 Thomas Nadelhoffer, Eddy Nahmias, and Shaun Nichols.

- How do people develop character traits and virtues?
- What factors lead people to act "out of character"?

Plato and Aristotle developed influential accounts of the virtues, such as courage, justice, self-control, and wisdom, and argued that, in the virtuous person, these character traits are both *robust* across various situations and *interrelated* among each other. In the dialogue *Protagoras*, **Plato** (428–348 BCE) presents Socrates' argument that the virtues are unified – that is, they are all forms of the single virtue of wisdom. Protagoras agrees that the virtues are related to each other, as parts of a face are related to the whole, but claims that they are not unified in any stronger way. Socrates first disputes this claim by arguing that the opposite of wisdom is folly and that the opposite of temperance is folly, and since everything can have only one opposite, wisdom and temperance must be unified. Later, Socrates rejects Protagoras' claim that a courageous person can be unjust or unwise, arguing instead that courage and wisdom are unified, because the ignorant go into danger foolishly, not courageously, whereas the wise understand the dangers they take on: "in that case the wisest are also the most confident, and being the most confident are also the bravest, and upon that view again wisdom will be courage."

Plato's student **Aristotle** (384–322 BCE) also argues that the virtues are interrelated in that they all require practical wisdom – if you have one virtue, you have them all – though he does not agree that they are all simply forms of the unified virtue of wisdom. In *Nicomachean Ethics*, Aristotle argues that character traits are developed by habituation and that the virtues are inculcated in people as they mature by leading them to perform the right actions. But doing the right thing is not enough to be virtuous. One must also choose to do it *because* it is the right thing, and "the act must spring from a firm and unchangeable character". Virtues are, hence, stable and robust, not subject to the vagaries of one's impulses or irrelevant features of one's situation. Finally, practical wisdom is required to discern what is virtuous – namely, the *mean* between the extremes of a given character trait. Courage, for instance, is the mean between recklessness and cowardice. Aristotle sums up his account of

virtue by saying that "virtue or excellence is a characteristic involving choice, and that it consists in observing the mean relative to us, a mean which is defined by a rational principle, such as a man of practical wisdom would use to determine it".

Plato and Aristotle laid the foundation for a virtue theoretic account of character traits, upon which later philosophers built. In the twentieth century, however, an apparent empirical challenge to this picture emerged. One important and representative line of research came from the psychologist Stanley **Milgram** (1933–84). Milgram explored the extent to which people would be willing to obey an experimenter in a psychology study and provide increasingly intense electric shocks to another subject in a memory test, the "learner." The results were surprising, and disconcerting. Two-thirds of the subjects would continue to administer shocks beyond the point where the learner complained of chest pains, demanded to be released, and even stopped responding, appearing to go unconscious. Milgram also showed that the proportion of people who would continue to obey the experimenter depended on situational factors, such as the proximity of the learner to the subject. These results were consistent across a diverse range of participants and cultures, raising questions about whether people have the consistent character trait of compassion. Furthermore, the results suggest that people can end up behaving in ways that they would not predict or desire, of themselves or others, because of situational factors of which they are unaware.

Milgram's experiment is just one of many in the *situationist* tradition of social psychology suggesting that people's behavior is better explained by features of their external environment, including their social situation, than by internal character traits. Psychologists Lee **Ross** and Richard **Nisbett** offer an overview of situationism, arguing that consistency of behavior has more to do with consistency in people's environment than consistency of personality traits. Furthermore, our ordinary psychological explanations are based on over-emphasizing character traits and under-emphasizing situational factors. Among numerous studies supporting this theory, this selection includes a discussion of experiments on the bystander intervention effect, which have shown that whether people help someone in need depends largely on the presence or absence of (inactive) bystanders, as suggested in the example of Jim and Ray above, as well as the "Good Samaritan study," which showed that whether people help depends largely on whether they are in a hurry or not. These situational effects appear to make a larger difference to one's behavior than any measured character traits.

Philosopher John **Doris** brings this situationist research to bear on questions about moral theory, notably the challenge it poses to the conception of character required by virtue ethics. The situationist research suggests that humans do not have the robust character traits that virtue theorists, inspired by Plato and Aristotle, claim are required for virtuous behavior – or at least, that such virtuous persons are extremely rare. If virtue ethics accepts this empirical limitation on virtue, then it may not offer some of its purported advantages over other ethical theories, such as providing useful methods for moral education. Doris argues that, if virtue ethics suggests that people should guide their behavior in various situations by contemplating what the (rare) virtuous person would do, then it may be less effective than the guidance offered by a conception of character that recognizes the instability of character and the strength of situational influences on behavior. Reflection on a situationist conception of moral psychology, he argues, provides a type of self-knowledge that would foster ethical behavior more effectively than virtue ethics' "characterological moral thought," which "may have substantial pitfalls, in so far as it may foster a dangerous neglect of situational influences."

The philosopher Rachana **Kamtekar** argues that virtue ethics has the resources to deal with the challenge posed by situationist research. This is because, she argues, the conception of character traits actually employed by virtue ethics is simply not the one that situationism calls into question. She emphasizes that virtue ethicists, such as Aristotle, conceive of virtues as dispositions to respond appropriately in a given situation. Virtue begins with habituation but is eventually based on effectual practical reasoning, and Kamtekar suggests that such reasoning can be usefully informed by empirical psychology. Virtues may be relatively rare and difficult to exercise, as they require overcoming various cognitive limitations.

Indeed, most people do not have the virtues, but rather have character traits that are, as situationism suggests, inconsistent, because they derive from the conflicting demands of one's culture. Kamtekar also suggests that the presence or absence of character traits cannot be inferred based on action or inaction in one situation. The key situationist experiments, such as Milgram's, involve conflicting traits, such as compassion and obedience, so subjects' behavior in one experiment cannot inform us about whether, in general, subjects have such traits or not. In the end, Kamtekar suggests that the viability of virtue ethics depends more on our abilities to be effective practical reasoners than on the consistency of character traits as they are measured in social psychology. One might then wonder whether the social psychology research suggests a direct challenge to our practical reasoning capacities and hence a significant limitation on the degree to which people can attain the capacities required to be virtuous according to virtue theory. This potential challenge to practical reasoning thereby suggests a potential challenge to our ability to be autonomous and responsible agents, the topic of Part IV (see Nahmias 2007 and Doris 2002, chs. 4 and 6).

Finally, philosopher Maria **Merritt** develops a Humean account of the virtues that she argues is more empirically justified, given the situationist research, than neo-Aristotelian accounts of the virtues. Merritt suggests that the main lesson of the situationist research is that behavior is generated largely by social relationships and settings rather than robust character traits that operate independently of these external social contributions. But this lesson is entirely consistent with a type of virtue theory, like Hume's, that emphasizes the importance of dependable social relationships and external conditions to encourage virtuous behavior. The emphasis is on establishing social settings likely to secure human cooperation and basic goods rather than establishing (perhaps) unrealistic capacities in individuals to behave virtuously regardless of their situation.

Questions for Further Study

- Does virtue ethics require a conception of character that is unrealistic given the results of situationist social psychology?

- Is it consistent with the empirical evidence that some of the people in the social psychology experiments were in fact virtuous people in the sense Plato and Aristotle had in mind?
- Are there good reasons to accept the view that both character traits and situations are critical determinants of moral behavior? If so, would such a hybrid view count as a defense or a retreat for virtue ethics?
- If the evidence shows that character traits exert less influence on behavior than we might have expected, might those weaker effects still be crucial in some moral domains?

Suggested Readings

Anscombe, G.E.M. (1958). Modern moral philosophy. *Philosophy*, 33, 1–19.

Brandt, R.B. (1988). The structure of virtue. *Midwest Studies in Philosophy*, 13, 64–82.

Burnyeat, M. (1999). Aristotle on learning to be good. In N. Sherman (ed.), *Aristotle's Ethics: Critical Essays*. Lanham, MD: Rowman and Littlefield, pp. 205–30.

Driver, J. (2001). *Uneasy Virtue*, New York: Cambridge University Press.

Foot, P. (1978). *Virtues and Vices*. Oxford: Blackwell.

Harman, G. (1999). Moral philosophy meets social psychology: Virtue ethics and the fundamental attribution error. *Proceedings of the Aristotelian Society*, New Series vol. CXIX, 316–31.

Hursthouse, R. (1999). *On Virtue Ethics*. Oxford: Oxford University Press.

MacIntyre, A. (1985). *After Virtue*, 2nd edn. London: Duckworth.

McDowell, J. (1979). Virtue and reason. *Monist*, 62, 331–50.

Nisbett, R. and Wilson, T. (1977). Telling more than we can know: Verbal reports on mental processes. *Psychological Review* 84, 3, 231–59.

Sabini, J. and Silver, M. (2005). Lack of character? Situationism critiqued. *Ethics*, 115, 535–62.

Sreenivasan, G. (2002). Errors about errors: Virtue theory and trait attribution. *Mind*, 111, January, 47–68.

Wilson, T. (2004). *Strangers to Ourselves: Discovering the Adaptive Unconsciousness*. Cambridge: Harvard University Press.

References

Doris, J.M. 2002. *Lack of Character: Personality and Moral Behavior*. New York: Cambridge University Press.

Nahmias, E. (2007). Autonomous agency and social psychology. In M. Marraffa, M. Caro, and F. Ferretti (eds.), *Cartographies of the Mind: Philosophy and Psychology in Intersection*. Dordrecht: Springer, pp. 169–85.

18

Protagoras

Plato

SOCRATES: Now I, Protagoras, want to ask of you a little question, which if you will only answer, I shall be quite satisfied. You were saying that virtue can be taught; that I will take upon your authority, and there is no one to whom I am more ready to trust. But I marvel at one thing about which I should like to have my mind set at rest. You were speaking of Zeus sending justice and reverence to men; and several times while you were speaking, justice, and temperance, and holiness, and all these qualities, were described by you as if together they made up virtue. Now I want you to tell me truly whether virtue is one whole, of which justice and temperance and holiness are parts; or whether all these are only the names of one and the same thing: that is the doubt which still lingers in my mind.

PROTAGORAS: There is no difficulty, Socrates, in answering that the qualities of which you are speaking are the parts of virtue which is one.

And are they parts, I said, in the same sense in which mouth, nose, and eyes, and ears, are the parts of a face; or are they like the parts of gold, which differ from the whole and from one another only in being larger or smaller?

I should say that they differed, Socrates, in the first way; they are related to one another as the parts of a face are related to the whole face.

And do men have some one part and some another part of virtue? Of if a man has one part, must he also have all the others?

By no means, he said; for many a man is brave and not just, or just and not wise.

You would not deny, then, that courage and wisdom are also parts of virtue?

Most undoubtedly they are, he answered; and wisdom is the noblest of the parts.

And they are all different from one another? I said.

Yes.

And has each of them a distinct function like the parts of the face; the eye, for example, is not like the ear, and has not the same functions; and the other parts are none of them like one another, either in their functions, or in any other way? I want to know whether the comparison holds concerning the parts of virtue. Do they also differ from one another in themselves and in their functions? For that is clearly what the simile would imply.

Yes, Socrates, you are right in supposing that they differ.

Then, I said, no other part of virtue is like knowledge, or like justice, or like courage, or like temperance, or like holiness?

No, he answered.

Well then, I said, suppose that you and I enquire into their natures. And first, you would agree with me that justice is of the nature of a thing, would you not? That is my opinion: would it not be yours also?

Mine also, he said.

From Plato, Benjamin Jowett (trans.) and Maurice Francis Egan (introduction), *Dialogues of Plato: Containing the Apology of Socrates, Crito, Phaedo, and Protagoras*, Revised Edition. (The Colonial Press 1900). Pp. 154–179, 194–197, 207–208.

Moral Psychology: Historical and Contemporary Readings, edited by Thomas Nadelhoffer, Eddy Nahmias, and Shaun Nichols.
© 2010 Blackwell Publishing Ltd except for editorial material and organization © 2010 Thomas Nadelhoffer, Eddy Nahmias, and Shaun Nichols.

And suppose that some one were to ask us, saying, "O Protagoras, and you, Socrates, what about this thing which you were calling justice, is it just or unjust?" and I were to answer, just: would you vote with me or against me?

With you, he said.

Thereupon I should answer to him who asked me, that justice is of the nature of the just: would not you?

Yes, he said.

And suppose that he went on to say: "Well now, is there also such a thing as holiness?" we should answer, "Yes," if I am not mistaken?

Yes, he said.

Which you would also acknowledge to be a thing – should we not say so?

He assented.

"And is this a sort of thing which is of the nature of the holy, or of the nature of the unholy?" I should be angry at his putting such a question, and should say, "Peace, man; nothing can be holy if holiness is not holy." What would you say? Would you not answer in the same way?

Certainly, he said.

And then after this suppose that he came and asked us, "What were you saying just now? Perhaps I may not have heard you rightly, but you seemed to me to be saying that the parts of virtue were not the same as one another." I should reply, "You certainly heard that said, but not, as you imagine, by me; for I only asked the question; Protagoras gave the answer." And suppose that he turned to you and said, "Is this true, Protagoras? and do you maintain that one part of virtue is unlike another, and is this your position?" – how would you answer him?

I could not help acknowledging the truth of what he said, Socrates.

Well then, Protagoras, we will assume this; and now supposing that he proceeded to say further, "Then holiness is not of the nature of justice, nor justice of the nature of holiness, but of the nature of unholiness; and holiness is of the nature of the not just, and therefore of the unjust, and the unjust is the unholy": how shall we answer him? I should certainly answer him on my own behalf that justice is holy, and that holiness is just; and I would say in like manner on your behalf also, if you would allow me, that justice is either the same with holiness, or very nearly the same; and above all I would assert that justice is like holiness and holiness is like

justice; and I wish that you would tell me whether I may be permitted to give this answer on your behalf, and whether you would agree with me.

He replied, I cannot simply agree, Socrates, to the proposition that justice is holy and that holiness is just, for there appears to me to be a difference between them. But what matter? if you please I please; and let us assume, if you will I, that justice is holy, and that holiness is just.

Pardon me, I replied; I do not want this "if you wish" or "if you will" sort of conclusion to be proven, but I want you and me to be proven: I mean to say that the conclusion will be best proven if there be no "if."

Well, he said, I admit that justice bears a resemblance to holiness, for there is always some point of view in which everything is like every other thing; white is in a certain way like black, and hard is like soft, and the most extreme opposites have some qualities in common; even the parts of the face which, as we were saying before, are distinct and have different functions, are still in a certain point of view similar, and one of them is like another of them. And you may prove that they are like one another on the same principle that all things are like one another; and yet things which are like in some particular ought not to be called alike, nor things which are unlike in some particular, however slight, unlike.

And do you think, I said in a tone of surprise, that justice and holiness have but a small degree of likeness?

Certainly not; any more than I agree with what I understand to be your view.

Well, I said, as you appear to have a difficulty about this, let us take another of the examples which you mentioned instead. Do you admit the existence of folly?

I do.

And is not wisdom the very opposite of folly?

That is true, he said.

And when men act rightly and advantageously they seem to you to be temperate?

Yes, he said.

And temperance makes them temperate?

Certainly.

And they who do not act rightly act foolishly, and in acting thus are not temperate?

I agree, he said.

Then to act foolishly is the opposite of acting temperately?

He assented.

And foolish actions are done by folly, and temperate actions by temperance?

He agreed.

And that is done strongly which is done by strength, and that which is weakly done, by weakness?

He assented.

And that which is done with swiftness is done swiftly, and that which is done with slowness, slowly?

He assented again.

And that which is done in the same manner, is done by the same; and that which is done in an opposite manner by the opposite?

He agreed.

Once more, I said, is there anything beautiful?

Yes.

To which the only opposite is the ugly?

There is no other.

And is there anything good?

There is.

To which the only opposite is the evil?

There is no other.

And there is the acute in sound?

True.

To which the only opposite is the grave?

There is no other, he said, but that.

Then every opposite has one opposite only and no more?

He assented.

Then now, I said, let us recapitulate our admissions. First of all we admitted that everything has one opposite and not more than one?

We did so.

And we admitted also that what was done in opposite ways was done by opposites?

Yes.

And that which was done foolishly, as we further admitted, was done in the opposite way to that which was done temperately?

Yes.

And that which was done temperately was done by temperance, and that which was done foolishly by folly?

He agreed.

And that which is done in opposite ways is done by opposites?

Yes.

And one thing is done by temperance, and quite another thing by folly?

Yes.

And in opposite ways?

Certainly.

And therefore by opposites: then folly is the opposite of temperance?

Clearly.

And do you remember that folly has already been acknowledged by us to be the opposite of wisdom?

He assented.

And we said that everything has only one opposite?

Yes.

Then, Protagoras, which of the two assertions shall we renounce? One says that everything has but one opposite; the other that wisdom is distinct from temperance, and that both of them are parts of virtue; and that they are not only distinct, but dissimilar, both in themselves and in their functions, like the parts of a face. Which of these two assertions shall we renounce? For both of them together are certainly not in harmony; they do not accord or agree: for how can they be said to agree if everything is assumed to have only one opposite and not more than one, and yet folly, which is one, has clearly the two opposites wisdom and temperance? Is not that true, Protagoras? What else would you say?

He assented, but with great reluctance.

Then temperance and wisdom are the same, as before justice and holiness appeared to us to be nearly the same. And now, Protagoras, I said, we must finish the enquiry, and not faint. Do you think that an unjust man can be temperate in his injustice?

I should be ashamed, Socrates, he said, to acknowledge this which nevertheless many may be found to assert.

And shall I argue with them or with you? I replied.

I would rather, he said, that you should argue with the many first, if you will.

Whichever you please, if you will only answer me and say whether you are of their opinion or not. My object is to test the validity of the argument; and yet the result may be that I who ask and you who answer may both be put on our trial.

[...]

And I would rather hold discourse with you [Protagoras] than with any one, because I think that no man has a better understanding of most things which a good man may be expected to understand, and in particular of virtue. For who is there, but you? who not only claim to be a good man and a gentleman, for many are this, and yet have not the power of making others good whereas you are not only good yourself, but also the cause of goodness in others. Moreover such confidence have you in yourself, that although other Sophists conceal their profession, you proclaim in the face of Hellas that you are a Sophist or teacher of virtue and education, and are the first who demanded pay in return. How then can I do otherwise than invite you to the examination of these subjects, and ask questions and consult with you? I must, indeed.

And I should like once more to have my memory refreshed by you about the questions which I was asking you at first, and also to have your help in considering them. If I am not mistaken the question was this: Are wisdom and temperance and courage and justice and holiness five names of the same thing? or has each of the names a separate underlying essence and corresponding thing having a peculiar function, no one of them being like any other of them? And you replied that the five names were not the names of the same thing, but that each of them had a separate object, and that all these objects were parts of virtue, not in the same way that the parts of gold are like each other and the whole of which they are parts, but as the parts of the face are unlike the whole of which they are parts and one another, and have each of them a distinct function. I should like to know whether this is still your opinion; or if not, I will ask you to define your meaning, and I shall not take you to task if you now make a different statement. For I dare say that you may have said what you did only in order to make trial of me.

I answer, Socrates, he said, that all these qualities are parts of virtue, and that four out of the five are to some extent similar, and that the fifth of them, which is courage, is very different from the other four, as I prove in this way: You may observe that many men are utterly unrighteous, unholy, intemperate, ignorant, who are nevertheless remarkable for their courage.

Stop, I said; I should like to think about that. When you speak of brave men, do you mean the confident, or another sort of nature?

Yes, he said; I mean the impetuous, ready to go at that which others are afraid to approach.

In the next place, you would affirm virtue to be a good thing, of which good thing you assert yourself to be a teacher.

Yes, he said; I should say the best of all things, if I am in my right mind.

And is it partly good and partly bad, I said, or wholly good?

Wholly good, and in the highest degree.

Tell me then; who are they who have confidence when diving into a well?

I should say, the divers.

And the reason of this is that they have knowledge?

Yes, that is the reason.

And who have confidence when fighting on horseback – the skilled horseman or the unskilled?

The skilled.

And who when fighting with light shields – the peltasts or the nonpeltasts?

The peltasts. And that is true of all other things, he said, if that is your point: those who have knowledge are more confident than those who have no knowledge, and they are more confident after they have learned than before.

And have you not seen persons utterly ignorant, I said, of these things, and yet confident about them?

Yes, he said, I have seen such persons far too confident.

And are not these confident persons also courageous?

In that case, he replied, courage would be a base thing, for the men of whom we are speaking are surely madmen.

Then who are the courageous? Are they not the confident?

Yes, he said; to that statement I adhere.

And those, I said, who are thus confident without knowledge are really not courageous, but mad; and in that case the wisest are also the most confident, and being the most confident are also the bravest, and upon that view again wisdom will be courage.

Nay, Socrates, he replied, you are mistaken in your remembrance of what was said by me. When you asked me, I certainly did say that the courageous are the confident; but I was never asked whether the confident are the courageous; if you had asked me, I should have answered "Not all of them": and what I did answer you have not proved to be false, although you proceeded to show that those who have knowledge are more courageous than they were before they had knowledge, and more courageous than others who have no knowledge, and were then led on to think that courage is the same as wisdom. But in this way of arguing you might come to imagine that strength is wisdom. You might begin by asking whether the strong are able, and I should say "Yes"; and then whether those who know how to wrestle are not more able to wrestle than those who do not know how to wrestle, and more able after than before they had learned, and I should assent. And when I had admitted this, you might use my admissions in such a way as to prove that upon my view wisdom is strength; whereas in that case I should not have admitted, any more than in the other, that the able are strong, although I have admitted that the strong are able. For there is a difference between ability and strength; the former is given by knowledge as well as by madness or rage, but strength comes from nature and a healthy state of the body. And in like manner I say of confidence and courage, that they are not the same; and I argue that the courageous are confident, but not all the confident courageous. For confidence may be given to men by art, and also, like ability, by madness and rage; but courage comes to them from nature and the healthy state of the soul.

[. . .]

Then as to the motive from which the cowards act, do you call it cowardice or courage?

I should say cowardice, he replied.

And have they not been shown to be cowards through their ignorance of dangers?

Assuredly, he said.

And because of that ignorance they are cowards?

He assented.

And the reason why they are cowards is admitted by you to be cowardice?

He again assented.

Then the ignorance of what is and is not dangerous is cowardice?

He nodded assent.

But surely courage, I said, is opposed to cowardice?

Yes.

Then the wisdom which knows what are and are not dangers is opposed to the ignorance of them?

To that again he nodded assent.

And the ignorance of them is cowardice?

To that he very reluctantly nodded assent.

And the knowledge of that which is and is not dangerous is courage, and is opposed to the ignorance of these things?

At this point he would no longer nod assent, but was silent.

And why, I said, do you neither assent nor dissent, Protagoras?

Finish the argument by yourself, he said.

I only want to ask one more question, I said. I want to know whether you still think that there are men who are most ignorant and yet most courageous?

You seem to have a great ambition to make me answer, Socrates, and therefore I will gratify you, and say, that this appears to me to be impossible consistently with the argument.

My only object, I said, in continuing the discussion, has been the desire to ascertain the nature and relations of virtue; for if this were clear, I am very sure that the other controversy which has been carried on at great length by both of us – you affirming and I denying that virtue can be taught – would also become clear.

[. . .]

Protagoras replied: Socrates, I am not of a base nature, and I am the last man in the world to be envious. I cannot but applaud your energy and your conduct of an argument. As I have often said, I admire you above all men whom I know, and far above all men of your age; and I believe that you will become very eminent in philosophy. Let us come back to the subject at some future time; at present we had better turn to something else.

By all means, I said, if that is your wish. [. . .] So the conversation ended, and we went our way

Note

Translation by Benjamin Jowett.

19

Nicomachean Ethics

Aristotle

Book I

13.   *The psychological foundations of the virtues*

Since happiness is a certain activity of the soul in conformity with perfect virtue, we must now examine what virtue or excellence is. For such an inquiry will perhaps better enable us to discover the nature of happiness. [. . .]

There can be no doubt that the virtue which we have to study is human virtue. For the good which we have been seeking is a human good and the happiness a human happiness. By human virtue we do not mean the excellence of the body, but that of the soul, and we define happiness as an activity of the soul. If this is true, the student of politics must obviously have some knowledge of the workings of the soul, just as the man who is to heal eyes must know something about the whole body. In fact, knowledge is all the more important for the former, inasmuch as politics is better and more valuable than medicine, and cultivated physicians devote much time and trouble to gain knowledge about the body. Thus, the student of politics must study the soul, but he must do so with his own aim in view, and only to the extent that the objects of his inquiry demand: to go into it in greater detail would perhaps be more laborious than his purposes require.

Some things that are said about the soul in our less technical discussions are adequate enough to be used here, for instance, that the soul consists of two elements, one irrational and one rational. Whether these two elements are separate, like the parts of the body or any other divisible thing, or whether they are only logically separable though in reality indivisible, as convex and concave are in the circumference of a circle, is irrelevant for our present purposes.

Of the irrational element, again, one part seems to be common to all living things and vegetative in nature: I mean that part which is responsible for nurture and growth. [. . .] We may pass by the nutritive part, since it has no natural share in human excellence or virtue.

In addition to this, there seems to be another integral element of the soul which, though irrational, still does partake of reason in some way. In morally strong and morally weak men we praise the reason that guides them and the rational element of the soul, because it exhorts them to follow the right path and to do what is best. Yet we see in them also another natural strain different from the rational, which fights and resists the guidance of reason. The soul behaves in precisely the same manner as do the paralyzed limbs of the body. When we intend to move the limbs to the right, they turn to the left, and similarly, the impulses of morally weak persons turn in the

From Aristotle, *Nicomachean Ethics*, Martin Ostwald (trans.) (Macmillan Publishing, 1962). Pp. 29–44, 170–173.

Moral Psychology: Historical and Contemporary Readings, edited by Thomas Nadelhoffer, Eddy Nahmias, and Shaun Nichols.

direction opposite to that in which reason leads them. However, while the aberration of the body is visible, that of the soul is not. But perhaps we must accept it as a fact, nevertheless, that there is something in the soul besides the rational ele ment, which opposes and reacts against it. In what way the two are distinct need not concern us here. But, as we have stated, it too seems to partake of reason; at any rate, in a morally strong man it accepts the leadership of reason, and is per haps more obedient still in a self-controlled and courageous man, since in him everything is in harmony with the voice of reason.

Thus we see that the irrational element of the soul has two parts: the one is vegetative and has no share in reason at all, the other is the seat of the appetites and of desire in general and partakes of reason insofar as it complies with reason and accepts its leadership; it possesses reason in the sense that we say it is "reasonable" to accept the advice of a father and of friends, not in the sense that we have a "rational" understanding of math ematical propositions. That the irrational element can be persuaded by the rational is shown by the fact that admonition and all manner of rebuke and exhortation are possible. If it is correct to say that the appetitive part, too, has reason, it follows that the rational element of the soul has two subdivisions: the one possesses reason in the strict sense, contained within itself, and the other possesses reason in the sense that it listens to reason as one would listen to a father.

Virtue, too, is differentiated in line with this division of the soul. We call some virtues "intel lectual" and others "moral": theoretical wisdom, understanding, and practical wisdom are intel lectual virtues, generosity and self-control moral virtues. In speaking of a man's character, we do not describe him as wise or understanding, but as gentle or self-controlled; but we praise the wise man, too, for his characteristic, and praiseworthy characteristics are what we call virtues

Book II

1. Moral virtue as the result of habits

Virtue, as we have seen, consists of two kinds, intellectual virtue and moral virtue. Intellectual virtue or excellence owes its origin and develop ment chiefly to teaching, and for that reason

requires experience and time. Moral virtue, on the other hand, is formed by habit, *ethos*, and its name, *ēthikē*, is therefore derived, by a slight variation, from *ethos*. This shows, too, that none of the moral virtues is implanted in us by nature, for nothing which exists by nature can be changed by habit. For example, it is impossible for a stone, which has a natural downward movement, to become habituated to moving upward, even if one should try ten thousand times to inculcate the habit by throwing it in the air; nor can fire be made to move downward, nor can the direc tion of any nature-given tendency be changed by habituation. Thus, the virtues are implanted in us neither by nature nor contrary to nature: we are by nature equipped with the ability to receive them, and habit brings this ability to completion and fulfillment.

Furthermore, of all the qualities with which we are endowed by nature, we are provided with the capacity first, and display the activity afterward. That this is true is shown by the senses: it is not by frequent seeing or frequent hearing that we acquired our senses, but on the contrary we first possess and then use them; we do not acquire them by use. The virtues, on the other hand, we acquire by first having put them into action, and the same is also true of the arts. For the things which we have to learn before we can do them we learn by doing: men become builders by build ing houses, and harpists by playing the harp. Similarly, we become just by the practice of just actions, self-controlled by exercising self-control, and courageous by performing acts of courage.

This is corroborated by what happens in states. Lawgivers make the citizens good by inculcating (good) habits in them, and this is the aim of every lawgiver; if he does not succeed in doing that, his legislation is a failure. It is in this that a good constitution differs from a bad one.

Moreover, the same causes and the same means that produce any excellence or virtue can also destroy it, and this is also true of every art. It is by playing the harp that men become both good and bad harpists, and correspondingly with builders and all the other craftsmen: a man who builds well will be a good builder, one who builds badly a bad one. For if this were not so, there would be no need for an instructor, but everybody would be born as a good or a bad craftsman. The same holds true of the virtues: in our transactions with other men it is by action that some become just and others unjust, and it is by acting in the face of danger and by developing the habit of feeling fear or confidence that some become brave men and others cowards. The same applies to the appetites and feelings of anger: by reacting in one way or in another to given circumstances some people become self-controlled and gentle, and others self-indulgent and short-tempered. In a word, characteristics develop from corresponding activities. For that reason, we must see to it that our activities are of a certain kind, since any variations in them will be reflected in our characteristics. Hence it is no small matter whether one habit or another is inculcated in us from early childhood; on the contrary, it makes a considerable difference, or, rather, all the difference.

2. Method in the practical sciences

The purpose of the present study is not, as it is in other inquiries, the attainment of theoretical knowledge: we are not conducting this inquiry in order to know what virtue is, but in order to become good, else there would be no advantage in studying it. For that reason, it becomes necessary to examine the problem of actions, and to ask how they are to be performed. For, as we have said, the actions determine what kind of characteristics are developed.

That we must act according to right reason is generally conceded and may be assumed as the basis of our discussion. We shall speak about it later and discuss what right reason is and examine its relation to the other virtues. But let us first agree that any discussion on matters of action cannot be more than an outline and is bound to lack precision; for as we stated at the outset, one can demand of a discussion only what the subject matter permits, and there are no fixed data in matters concerning action and questions of what is beneficial, any more than there are in matters of health. And if this is true of our general discussion, our treatment of particular problems will be even less precise, since these do not come under the head of any art which can be transmitted by precept, but the agent must consider on each different occasion what the situation demands, just as in medicine and in navigation. But although such is the kind of discussion in which we are engaged, we must do our best.

First of all, it must be observed that the nature of moral qualities is such that they are destroyed by defect and by excess. We see the same thing happen in the case of strength and of health, to illustrate, as we must, the invisible by means of visible examples: excess as well as deficiency of physical exercise destroys our strength, and similarly, too much and too little food and drink destroys our health; the proportionate amount, however, produces, increases, and preserves it. The same applies to self-control, courage, and the other virtues: the man who shuns and fears everything and never stands his ground becomes a coward, whereas a man who knows no fear at all and goes to meet every danger becomes reckless. Similarly, a man who revels in every pleasure and abstains from none becomes self-indulgent, while he who avoids every pleasure like a boor becomes what might be called insensitive. Thus we see that self-control and courage are destroyed by excess and by deficiency and are preserved by the mean.

Not only are the same actions which are responsible for and instrumental in the origin and development of the virtues also the causes and means of their destruction, but they will also be manifested in the active exercise of the virtues. We can see the truth of this in the case of other more visible qualities, e.g., strength. Strength is produced by consuming plenty of food and by enduring much hard work, and it is the strong man who is best able to do these things. The same is also true of the virtues: by abstaining from pleasures we become self-controlled, and once we are self-controlled we are best able to abstain from pleasures. So also with courage: by becoming habituated to despise and to endure terrors we become courageous, and once we have become courageous we will best be able to endure terror.

3. Pleasure and pain as the test of virtue

An index to our characteristics is provided by the pleasure or pain which follows upon the tasks we have achieved. A man who abstains from bodily pleasures and enjoys doing so is self-controlled; if he finds abstinence troublesome, he is self-indulgent; a man who endures danger with joy, or at least without pain, is courageous; if he endures it with pain, he is a coward. For moral excellence is concerned with pleasure and pain; it is pleasure that makes us do base actions and pain that prevents us from doing noble actions. For that reason, as Plato says, men must be brought up from childhood to feel pleasure and pain at the proper things; for this is correct education.

Furthermore, since the virtues have to do with actions and emotions, and since pleasure and pain are a consequence of every emotion and of every action, it follows from this point of view, too, that virtue has to do with pleasure and pain. This is further indicated by the fact that punishment is inflicted by means of pain. For punishment is a kind of medical treatment and it is the nature of medical treatments to take effect through the introduction of the opposite of the disease. Again, as we said just now, every characteristic of the soul shows its true nature in its relation to and its concern with those factors which naturally make it better or worse. But it is through pleasures and pains that men are corrupted, i.e., through pursuing and avoiding pleasures and pains either of the wrong kind or at the wrong time or in the wrong manner, or by going wrong in some other definable respect. For that reason some people define the virtues as states of freedom from emotion and of quietude. However, they make the mistake of using these terms absolutely and without adding such qualifications as "in the right manner," "at the right or wrong time," and so forth. We may, therefore, assume as the basis of our discussion that virtue, being concerned with pleasure and pain in the way we have described, makes us act in the best way in matters involving pleasure and pain, and that vice does the opposite.

The following considerations may further illustrate that virtue is concerned with pleasure and pain. There are three factors that determine choice and three that determine avoidance: the noble, the beneficial, and the pleasurable, on the one hand, and on the other their opposites: the base, the harmful, and the painful. Now a good man will go right and a bad man will go wrong when any of these, and especially when pleasure is involved. For pleasure is not only common to man and the animals, but also accompanies all objects of choice: in fact, the noble and the beneficial seem pleasant to us. Moreover, a love of pleasure has grown up with all of us from infancy. Therefore, this emotion has come to be ingrained in our lives and is difficult to erase. Even in our actions we use, to a greater or smaller extent,

pleasure and pain as a criterion. For this reason, this entire study is necessarily concerned with pleasure and pain; for it is not unimportant for our actions whether we feel joy and pain in the right or the wrong way. Again, it is harder to fight against pleasure than against anger, as Heraclitus says; and both virtue and art are always concerned with what is harder, for success is better when it is hard to achieve. Thus, for this reason also, every study both of virtue and of politics must deal with pleasures and pains, for if a man has the right attitude to them, he will be good; if the wrong attitude, he will be bad.

We have now established that virtue or excellence is concerned with pleasures and pains; that the actions which produce it also develop it and, if differently performed, destroy it; and that it actualizes itself fully in those activities to which it owes its origin.

4. Virtuous action and virtue

However, the question may be raised what we mean by saying that men become just by performing just actions and self-controlled by practicing self-control. For if they perform just actions and exercise self-control, they are already just and self-controlled, in the same way as they are literate and musical if they write correctly and practice music.

But is this objection really valid, even as regards the arts? No, for it is possible for a man to write a piece correctly by chance or at the prompting of another: but he will be literate only if he produces a piece of writing in a literate way, and that means doing it in accordance with the skill of literate composition which he has in himself.

Moreover, the factors involved in the arts and in the virtues are not the same. In the arts, excellence lies in the result itself, so that it is sufficient if it is of a certain kind. But in the case of the virtues an act is not performed justly or with self-control if the act itself is of a certain kind, but only if in addition the agent has certain characteristics as he performs it: first of all, he must know what he is doing; secondly, he must choose to act the way he does, and he must choose it for its own sake; and in the third place, the act must spring from a firm and unchangeable character. With the exception of knowing what one is about, these considerations do not enter into the mastery of the arts; for the mastery of the virtues, however, knowledge is of little or no importance, whereas the other two conditions count not for a little but are all-decisive, since repeated acts of justice and self-control result in the possession of these virtues. In other words, acts are called just and self-controlled when they are the kind of acts which a just or self-controlled man would perform; but the just and self-controlled man is not he who performs these acts, but he who also performs them in the way just and self-controlled men do.

Thus our assertion that a man becomes just by performing just acts and self-controlled by performing acts of self-control is correct; without performing them, nobody could even be on the way to becoming good. Yet most men do not perform such acts, but by taking refuge in argument they think that they are engaged in philosophy and that they will become good in this way. In so doing, they act like sick men who listen attentively to what the doctor says, but fail to do any of the things he prescribes. That kind of philosophical activity will not bring health to the soul any more than this sort of treatment will produce a healthy body.

5. Virtue defined: the genus

The next point to consider is the definition of virtue or excellence. As there are three kinds of things found in the soul: (1) emotions, (2) capacities, and (3) characteristics, virtue must be one of these. By "emotions" I mean appetite, anger, fear, confidence, envy, joy, affection, hatred, longing, emulation, pity, and in general anything that is followed by pleasure or pain; by "capacities" I mean that by virtue of which we are said to be affected by these emotions, for example, the capacity which enables us to feel anger, pain, or pity; and by "characteristics" I mean the condition, either good or bad, in which we are, in relation to the emotions: for example, our condition in relation to anger is bad, if our anger is too violent or not violent enough, but if it is moderate, our condition is good; and similarly with our condition in relation to the other emotions.

Now the virtues and vices cannot be emotions, because we are not called good or bad on the basis of our emotions, but on the basis of our virtues and vices. Also, we are neither praised nor blamed

for our emotions: a man does not receive praise for being frightened or angry, nor blame for being angry pure and simple, but for being angry in a certain way. Yet we are praised or blamed for our virtues and vices. Furthermore, no choice is involved when we experience anger or fear, while the virtues are some kind of choice or at least involve choice. Moreover, with regard to our emotions we are said to be "moved," but with regard to our virtues and vices we are not said to be "moved" but to be "disposed" in a certain way.

For the same reason, the virtues cannot be capacities, either, for we are neither called good or bad nor praised or blamed simply because we are capable of being affected. Further, our capacities have been given to us by nature, but we do not by nature develop into good or bad men. We have discussed this subject before. Thus, if the virtues are neither emotions nor capacities, the only remaining alternative is that they are characteristics. So much for the genus of virtue.

6. Virtue defined: the differentia

It is not sufficient, however, merely to define virtue in general terms as a characteristic: we must also specify what kind of characteristic it is. It must, then, be remarked that every virtue or excellence (1) renders good the thing itself of which it is the excellence, and (2) causes it to perform its function well. For example, the excellence of the eye makes both the eye and its function good, for good sight is due to the excellence of the eye. Likewise, the excellence of a horse makes it both good as a horse and good at running, at carrying its rider, and at facing the enemy. Now, if this is true of all things, the virtue or excellence of man, too, will be a characteristic which makes him a good man, and which causes him to perform his own function well. To some extent we have already stated how this will be true; the rest will become clear if we study what the nature of virtue is.

Of every continuous entity that is divisible into parts it is possible to take the larger the smaller, or an equal part, and these parts may be larger, smaller, or equal either in relation to the entity itself, or in relation to us. The "equal" part is something median between excess and deficiency. By the median of an entity I understand a point equidistant from both extremes, and this point is one and the same for everybody. By the median relative to us I understand an amount neither too large nor too small, and this is neither one nor the same for everybody. To take an example: if ten is many and two is few, six is taken as the median in relation to the entity, for it exceeds and is exceeded by the same amount, and is thus the median in terms of arithmetical proportion. But the median relative to us cannot be determined in this manner: if ten pounds of food is much for a man to eat and two pounds little, it does not follow that the trainer will prescribe six pounds, for this may in turn be much or little for him to eat; it may be little for Milo and much for someone who has just begun to take up athletics. The same applies to running and wrestling. Thus we see that an expert in any field avoids excess and deficiency, but seeks the median and chooses it – not the median of the object but the median relative to us.

If this, then, is the way in which every science perfects its work, by looking to the median and by bringing its work up to that point – and this is the reason why it is usually said of a successful piece of work that it is impossible to detract from it or to add to it, the implication being that excess and deficiency destroy success while the mean safeguards it (good craftsmen, we say, look toward this standard in the performance of their work) – and if virtue, like nature, is more precise and better than any art, we must conclude that virtue aims at the median. I am referring to moral virtue: for it is moral virtue that is concerned with emotions and actions, and it is in emotions and actions that excess, deficiency, and the median are found. Thus we can experience fear, confidence, desire, anger, pity, and generally any kind of pleasure and pain either too much or too little, and in either case not properly. But to experience all this at the right time, toward the right objects, toward the right people, for the right reason, and in the right manner – that is the median and the best course, the course that is a mark of virtue.

Similarly, excess, deficiency, and the median can also be found in actions. Now virtue is concerned with emotions and actions; and in emotions and actions excess and deficiency miss the mark, whereas the median is praised and constitutes success. But both praise and success are signs of virtue or excellence. Consequently, virtue is a mean in the sense that it aims at the median. This is corroborated by the fact that there are many ways of going wrong, but only one way which is right – for evil belongs to the indeterminate, as the Pythagoreans imagined, but good to the determinate. This, by the way, is also the reason why the one is easy and the other hard; it is easy to miss the target but hard to hit it. Here, then, is an additional proof that excess and deficiency characterize vice, while the mean characterizes virtue: for "bad men have many ways, good men but one."

We may thus conclude that virtue or excellence is a characteristic involving choice, and that it consists in observing the mean relative to us, a mean which is defined by a rational principle, such as a man of practical wisdom would use to determine it. It is the mean by reference to two vices: the one of excess and the other of deficiency. It is, moreover, a mean because some vices exceed and others fall short of what is required in emotion and in action, whereas virtue finds and chooses the median. Hence, in respect of its essence and the definition of its essential nature virtue is a mean, but in regard to goodness and excellence it is an extreme.

Not every action nor every emotion admits of a mean. There are some actions and emotions whose very names connote baseness, e.g., spite, shamelessness, envy; and among actions, adultery, theft, and murder. These and similar emotions and actions imply by their very names that they are bad; it is not their excess nor their deficiency which is called bad. It is, therefore, impossible ever to do right in performing them: to perform them is always to do wrong. In cases of this sort, let us say adultery, rightness and wrongness do not depend on committing it with the right woman at the right time and in the right manner, but the mere fact of committing such action at all is to do wrong. It would be just as absurd to suppose that there is a mean, an excess, and a deficiency in an unjust or a cowardly or a self-indulgent act. For if there were, we would have a mean of excess and a mean of deficiency, and an excess of excess and a deficiency of deficiency. Just as there cannot be an excess and a deficiency of self-control and courage – because the intermediate is, in a sense, an extreme – so there cannot be a mean, excess, and deficiency in their respective opposites: their opposites are wrong regardless of how they are performed; for, in general, there is

no such thing as the mean of an excess or a deficiency, or the excess and deficiency of a mean.
   [. . .]

13. Practical wisdom and moral virtue

Accordingly, we must also re-examine virtue or excellence. Virtue offers a close analogy to the relation that exists between practical wisdom and cleverness. Just as these two qualities are not identical but similar, so we find the same relation between natural virtue and virtue in the full sense. It seems that the various kinds of character inhere in all of us, somehow or other, by nature. We tend to be just, capable of self-control, and to show all our other character traits from the time of our birth. Yet we still seek something more, the good in a fuller sense, and the possession of these traits in another way. For it is true that children and beasts are endowed with natural qualities or characteristics, but it is evident that without intelligence these are harmful. This much, to be sure, we do seem to notice: as in the case of a mighty body which, when it moves without vision, comes down with a mighty fall because it cannot see, so it is in the matter under discussion. If a man acts blindly, i.e., using his natural virtue alone, he will fail; but once he acquires intelligence, it makes a great difference in his action. At that point, the natural characteristic will become that virtue in the full sense which it previously resembled.

   Consequently, just as there exist two kinds of quality, cleverness and practical wisdom, in that part of us which forms opinions, (i.e., in the calculative element,) so also there are two kinds of quality in the moral part of us, natural virtue and virtue in the full sense. Now virtue in the full sense cannot be attained without practical wisdom. That is why some people maintain that all the virtues are forms of practical wisdom, and why Socrates' approach to the subject was partly right and partly wrong. He was wrong in believing that all the virtues are forms of wisdom, but right

in saying that there is no virtue without wisdom. This is indicated by the fact that all the current definitions of virtue, after naming the characteristic and its objects, add that it is a characteristic "guided by right reason." Now right reason is that which is determined by practical wisdom. So we see that these thinkers all have some inkling that virtue is a characteristic of this kind, namely, a characteristic guided by practical wisdom.

   But we must go a little beyond that. Virtue or excellence is not only a characteristic which is guided by right reason, but also a characteristic which is united with right reason; and right reason in moral matters is practical wisdom. In other words, while Socrates believed that the virtues *are* rational principles – he said that all of them are forms of knowledge – we, on the other hand, think that they are *united with* a rational principle.

   Our discussion, then, has made it clear that it is impossible to be good in the full sense of the word without practical wisdom or to be a man of practical wisdom without moral excellence or virtue. Moreover, in this way we can also refute the dialectical argument which might be used to prove that the virtues exist independently of one another. The same individual, it might be argued, is not equally well-endowed by nature for all the virtues, with the result that at a given point he will have acquired one virtue but not yet another. In the case of the natural virtues this may be true, but it cannot happen in the case of those virtues which entitle a man to be called good in an unqualified sense. For in the latter case, as soon as he possesses this single virtue of practical wisdom, he will also possess all the rest.

   It is now clear that we should still need practical wisdom, even if it had no bearing on action, because it is the virtue of a part of our soul. But it is also clear that it does have an important bearing on action, since no choice will be right without practical wisdom and virtue. For virtue determines the end, and practical wisdom makes us do what is conducive to the end.

20

Behavioral Study of Obedience

Stanley Milgram

Obedience is as basic an element in the structure of social life as one can point to. Some system of authority is a requirement of all communal living, and it is only the man dwelling in isolation who is not forced to respond, through defiance or submission, to the commands of others. Obedience, as a determinant of behavior, is of particular relevance to our time. It has been reliably established that from 1933–45 millions of innocent persons were systematically slaughtered on command. Gas chambers were built, death camps were guarded, daily quotas of corpses were produced with the same efficiency as the manufacture of appliances. These inhumane policies may have originated in the mind of a single person, but they could only be carried out on a massive scale if a very large number of persons obeyed orders.

Obedience is the psychological mechanism that links individual action to political purpose. It is the dispositional cement that binds men to systems of authority. Facts of recent history and observation in daily life suggest that for many persons obedience may be a deeply ingrained behavior tendency, indeed, a prepotent impulse overriding training in ethics, sympathy, and moral conduct. C. P. Snow (1961) points to its importance when he writes:

When you think of the long and gloomy history of man, you will find more hideous crimes have been committed in the name of obedience than have ever been committed in the name of rebellion. If you doubt that, read William Shirer's "Rise and Fall of the Third Reich." The German Officer Corps were brought up in the most rigorous code of obedience . . . in the name of obedience they were party to, and assisted in, the most wicked large scale actions in the history of the world [p. 24].

While the particular form of obedience dealt with in the present study has its antecedents in these episodes, it must not be thought all obedience entails acts of aggression against others. Obedience serves numerous productive functions. Indeed, the very life of society is predicated on its existence. Obedience may be ennobling and educative and refer to acts of charity and kindness, as well as to destruction.

General Procedure

A procedure was devised which seems useful as a tool for studying obedience (Milgram, 1961). It consists of ordering a naive subject to administer electric shock to a victim. A simulated shock generator is used, with 30 clearly marked voltage levels that range from 15 to 450 volts. The instrument bears verbal designations that range

Abridged version of 'Behavioural study of obedience' by Stanley Milgram (2001) in *Conflict, Order and Actions: Readings in Sociology*, Edward Ksenych and David Liu, Canadian Scholars Press inc. Reprinted with kind permission of Alexandra Milgram.

Moral Psychology: Historical and Contemporary Readings, edited by Thomas Nadelhoffer, Eddy Nahmias, and Shaun Nichols.

from Slight Shock to Danger: Severe Shock. The responses of the victim, who is a trained confederate of the experimenter, are standardized. The orders to administer shocks are given to the naive subject in the context of a "learning experiment" ostensibly set up to study the effects of punishment on memory. As the experiment proceeds the naive subject is commanded to administer increasingly more intense shocks to the victim, even to the point of reaching the level marked Danger: Severe Shock. Internal resistances become stronger, and at a certain point the subject refuses to go on with the experiment. Behavior prior to this rupture is considered "obedience," in that the subject complies with the commands of the experimenter. The point of rupture is the act of disobedience. A quantitative value is assigned to the subject's performance based on the maximum intensity shock he is willing to administer before he refuses to participate further. Thus for any particular subject and for any particular experimental condition the degree of obedience may be specified with a numerical value. The crux of the study is to systematically vary the factors believed to alter the degree of obedience to the experimental commands.

The technique allows important variables to be manipulated at several points in the experiment. One may vary aspects of the source of command, content and form of command, instrumentalities for its execution, target object, general social setting, etc. The problem, therefore, is not one of designing increasingly more numerous experimental conditions, but of selecting those that best illuminate the *process* of obedience from the socio-psychological standpoint.

The inquiry [. . .] derives, in the first instance, from direct observation of a social fact; the individual who is commanded by a legitimate authority ordinarily obeys. Obedience comes easily and often. It is a ubiquitous and indispensable feature of social life.

Method

Subjects

The subjects were 40 males between the ages of 20 and 50, drawn from New Haven and the surrounding communities.[1] Subjects were obtained by a newspaper advertisement and direct mail solicitation. Those who responded to the appeal believed they were to participate in a study of memory and learning at Yale University. A wide range of occupations is represented in the sample. Typical subjects were postal clerks, high school teachers, salesmen, engineers, and laborers. Subjects ranged in educational level from one who had not finished elementary school, to those who had doctorate and other professional degrees. They were paid $4.50 for their participation in the experiment. However, subjects were told that payment was simply for coming to the laboratory, and that the money was theirs no matter what happened after they arrived.

Personnel and Locale

The experiment was conducted on the grounds of Yale University in the elegant interaction laboratory. (This detail is relevant to the perceived legitimacy of the experiment. In further variations, the experiment was dissociated from the university, with consequences for performance.) The role of experimenter was played by a 31-year-old high school teacher of biology. His manner was impassive, and his appearance somewhat stern throughout the experiment. He was dressed in a gray technician's coat. The victim was played by a 47-year-old accountant, trained for the role; he was of Irish-American stock, whom most observers found mild-mannered and likable.

Procedure

One naive subject and one victim (an accomplice) performed in each experiment. A pretext had to be devised that would justify the administration of electric shock by the naive subject. This was effectively accomplished by the cover story. After a general introduction on the presumed relation between punishment and learning, subjects were told:

> But actually, we know *very little* about the effect of punishment on learning, because almost no truly scientific studies have been made of it in human beings.
>
> For instance, we don't know how *much* punishment is best for learning – and we don't know how much difference it makes as to who is giving the punishment, whether an adult learns best from a younger or an older person than himself – or many things of that sort.

So in this study we are bringing together a number of adults of different occupations and ages. And we're asking some of them to be teachers and some of them to be learners.

We want to find out just what effect different people have on each other as teachers and learners, and also what effect *punishment* will have on learning in this situation.

Therefore, I'm going to ask one of you to be the teacher here tonight and the other one to be the learner.

Does either of you have a preference?

Subjects then drew slips of paper from a hat to determine who would be the teacher and who would be the learner in the experiment. The drawing was rigged so that the naive subject was always the teacher and the accomplice always the learner. (Both slips contained the word "Teacher.") Immediately after the drawing, the teacher and learner were taken to an adjacent room and the learner was strapped into an "electric chair" apparatus.

The experimenter explained that the straps were to prevent excessive movement while the learner was being shocked. The effect was to make it impossible for him to escape from the situation. An electrode was attached to the learner's wrist, and electrode paste was applied "to avoid blisters and burns." Subjects were told that the electrode was attached to the shock generator in the adjoining room.

In order to improve credibility the experimenter declared, in response to a question by the learner: "Although the shocks can be extremely painful, they cause no permanent tissue damage."

Learning task. The lesson administered by the subject was a paired-associate learning task. The subject read a series of word pairs to the learner, and then read the first word of the pair along with four terms. The learner was to indicate which of the four terms had originally been paired with the first word. He communicated his answer by pressing one of four switches in front of him, which in turn lit up one of four numbered quadrants in an answer-box located atop the shock generator.

Shock generator. The instrument panel consists of 30 lever switches set in a horizontal line. Each switch is clearly labeled with a voltage designation that ranges from 15 to 450 volts. There is a 15-volt increment from one switch to the next going from left to right. In addition, the following verbal designations are clearly indicated for groups of

four switches going from left to right: Slight Shock, Moderate Shock, Strong Shock, Very Strong Shock, Intense Shock, Extreme Intensity Shock, Danger: Severe Shock. (Two switches after this last designation are simply marked XXX.)

Upon depressing a switch: a pilot light corresponding to each switch is illuminated in bright red; an electric buzzing is heard; an electric blue light, labeled "voltage energizer," flashes; the dial on the voltage meter swings to the right; various relay clicks are sounded.

[. . .] No subject in the experiment suspected that the instrument was merely a simulated shock generator.

Sample shock. Each naive subject is given a sample shock on the shock generator, prior to beginning his run as teacher. This shock is always 45 volts, and is applied by pressing the third switch of the generator. The shock is applied to the wrist of the naive subject, and has its source in a 45-volt battery wired into the generator. This further convinces the subject of the authenticity of the generator.

Shock instructions. The subject is told to administer a shock to the learner each time he gives a wrong response. Moreover – and this is the key command – the subject is instructed to "move one level higher on the shock generator each time the learner flashes a wrong answer." He is also instructed to announce the voltage level before administering a shock. This serves to continually remind subjects of the increasing intensity of shocks administered to the learner.

[. . .]

The experimenter instructs the subject to,

start from 15 volts and increase the shock level one step each time the learner gives a wrong answer.

Feedback from the victim. In all conditions the learner gives a predetermined set of responses to the word pair test, based on a schedule of approximately three wrong answers to one correct answer. In the present experimental condition no vocal response or other sign of protest is heard from the learner until Shock Level 300 is reached. When the 300-volt shock is administered, the learner pounds on the wall of the room in which he is bound to the electric chair. The pounding can be heard by the subject. From this point on, the learner's answers no longer appear on the four-way panel.

At this juncture, subjects ordinarily turn to the experimenter for guidance. The experimenter instructs the subject to treat the absence of a response as a wrong answer, and to shock the subject according to the usual schedule. He advises the subjects to allow 5–10 seconds before considering no response as a wrong answer, and to increase the shock level one step each time the learner fails to respond correctly. The learner's pounding is repeated after the 315-volt shock is administered; afterwards he is not heard from, nor do his answers reappear on the four-way signal box.

Experimenter feedback. At various points in the experiment the subject may turn to the experimenter for advice on whether he should continue to administer shocks. Or he may indicate that he does not wish to go on. It was important to standardize the experimenter's responses to these inquiries and reactions.

If the subject indicated his unwillingness to go on, the experimenter responded with a sequence of "prods," using as many as necessary to bring the subject into line.

Prod 1: Please continue. *or* Please go on.
Prod 2: The experiment requires that you continue.
Prod 3: It is absolutely essential that you continue.
Prod 4: You have no other choice, you *must* go on.

The prods were always made in sequence: Only if Prod 1 had been unsuccessful, could Prod 2 be used. If the subject refused to obey the experimenter after Prod 4, the experiment was terminated. The experimenter's tone of voice was at all times firm, but not impolite. The sequence was begun anew on each occasion that the subject balked or showed reluctance to follow orders.

Special prods. If the subject asked if the learner was liable to suffer permanent physical injury, the experimenter said:

Although the shocks may be painful, there is no permanent tissue damage, so please go on. [Followed by Prods 2, 3, and 4 if necessary.]

If the subject said that the learner did not want to go on, the experimenter replied:

Whether the learner likes it or not, you must go on until he has learned all the word pairs correctly. So please go on. [Followed by Prods 2, 3, and 4 if necessary.]

Dependent Measures

The primary dependent measure for any subject is the maximum shock he administers before he refuses to go any further. In principle this may vary from 0 (for a subject who refuses to administer even the first shock) to 30 (for a subject who administers the highest shock on the generator). A subject who breaks off the experiment at any point prior to administering the thirtieth shock level is termed a *defiant* subject. One who complies with experimental commands fully, and proceeds to administer all shock levels commanded, is termed an *obedient* subject.

[. . .]

Interview and dehoax. Following the experiment, subjects were interviewed; open-ended questions, projective measures, and attitude scales were employed. After the interview, procedure were undertaken to assure that the subject would leave the laboratory in a state of well being. A friendly reconciliation was arranged between the subject and the victim, and an effort was made to reduce any tensions that arose as a result of the experiment.

Results

Preliminary Notions

Before giving an account of the experimental results, it is instructive to consider how persons predict others will perform when commanded to administer powerful shocks to another person. Fourteen Yale seniors, all psychology majors, were provided with a detailed description of the experimental situation. They were asked to reflect carefully on it, and to predict the behavior of 100 hypothetical subjects. More specifically, they were instructed to plot the distribution of obedience of "100 Americans of diverse occupations, and ranging in age from 20 to 50 years," who were placed in the experimental situation.

There was considerable agreement among the respondents on the expected behavior of hypothetical subjects. All respondents predicted that only an insignificant minority would go through to the end of the shock series. (The estimates ranged from 0 to 3%; i.e., the most "pessimistic" member of the class predicted that of 100 persons, 3 would continue through to the most potent shock available on the shock generator – 450 volts.) The class mean was 1.2%. The question was also posed informally to colleagues of the author, and the most general feeling was that few if any subjects would go beyond the designation Very Strong Shock.

Result of Experiment I

Subjects accept situation. With few exceptions subjects were convinced of the reality of the experimental situation, that they were administering shocks to another person, and the most potent shocks were extremely painful. In the post-experimental interview subjects were asked: "How painful to the learner were the last few shocks that you administered to him?" Subjects were instructed to indicate their answers on a printed 14-point scale ranging from "Not at all painful" to "Extremely painful." The modal response was 14 (Extremely painful) with the mean at 13.42.

Signs of extreme tension. Many subjects showed signs of nervousness in the experimental situation, and especially upon administering the more powerful shocks. In a large number of cases the degree of tension reached extremes that are rarely seen in sociopsychological laboratory studies. Subjects were observed to sweat, tremble, stutter, bite their lips, groan, and dig their fingernails into their flesh. These were characteristic rather than exceptional responses to the experiment.

One sign of tension was the regular occurrence of nervous laughing fits. Fourteen of the 40 subjects showed definite signs of nervous laughter and smiling. The laughter seemed entirely out of place, even bizarre. Full-blown, uncontrollable seizures were observed for 3 subjects. On one occasion we observed a seizure so violently convulsive that it was necessary to call a halt to the experiment. The subject, a 46-year-old encyclopedia salesman, was seriously embarrassed by his untoward and uncontrollable behavior. In the post-experimental interviews subjects took pains to point out that they were not sadistic types, and that the laughter did not mean they enjoyed shocking the victim.

Table 20.1 Distribution or Breakoff Points

Verbal designation and voltage indication	Number of subjects for whom this was maximum shock
Slight Shock	
15	0
30	0
45	0
60	0
Moderate Shock	
75	0
90	0
105	0
120	0
Strong Shock	
135	0
150	0
165	0
180	0
Very Strong Shock	
195	0
210	0
225	0
240	0
Intense Shock	
255	0
270	0
285	0
300	5
Extreme Intensity Shock	
315	4
330	2
345	1
360	1
Danger: Severe Shock	
375	1
390	0
405	0
420	0
XXX	
435	0
450	26

Distribution of scores. It had been conjectured that persons would not, in general, agree to administer shocks beyond the level designated as Very Strong Shock. The distribution of maximum shocks for this experiment is shown in Table 20.1. The obtained distribution of scores deviates radically from the prediction.

Upon command of the experimenter, each of the 40 subjects went beyond the expected breakoff point. No subject stopped prior to administering Shock Level 20. (At this level – 300 volts – the victim kicks on the wall and no longer provides answers to the teacher's multiple-choice questions.)

Of the 40 subjects, 5 refused to obey the experimental commands beyond the 300-volt level. Four more subjects administered one further shock, and then refused to go on. Two broke off at the 330-volt level, and 1 each at 345, 360, and 375 volts. Thus a total of 14 subjects defied the experimenter. It is instructive to reprint their remarks at the point of defiance, as transcribed from the tape recordings:

[0124] I think he's trying to communicate, he's knocking. . . . Well it's not fair to shock the guy . . . these are terrific volts. I don't think this is very humane. . . . Oh, I can't go on with this; no, this isn't right. It's a hell of an experiment. The guy is suffering in there. No, I don't want to go on. This is crazy. [Subject refused to administer more shocks.]

[0123] He's banging in there. I'm gonna chicken out. I'd like to continue, but I can't do that to a man. . . . I'm sorry I can't do that to a man. I'll hurt his heart. You take your check. . . . No really, I couldn't do it.

These subjects were frequently in a highly agitated and even angered state. Sometimes, verbal protest was at a minimum, and the subject simply got up from his chair in front of the shock generator, and indicated that he wished to leave the laboratory.

Of the 40 subjects, 26 obeyed the orders of the experimenter to the end, proceeding to punish the victim until they reached the most potent shock available on the shock generator. At that point, the experimenter called a halt to the session. (The maximum shock is labeled 450 volts, and is two steps beyond the designation: Danger: Severe Shock.) Although obedient subjects continued to administer shocks, they often did so under extreme stress. Some expressed reluctance to administer shocks beyond the 300-volt level, and displayed fears similar to those who defied the experimenter; yet they obeyed.

After the maximum shocks had been delivered, and the experimenter called a halt to the proceed-

ings, many obedient subjects heaved sighs of relief, mopped their brows, rubbed their fingers over their eyes, or nervously fumbled cigarettes. Some shook their heads, apparently in regret. Some subjects had remained calm throughout the experiment, and displayed only minimal signs of tension from beginning to end.[2]

Discussion

The experiment yielded two findings that were surprising. The first finding concerns the sheer strength of obedient tendencies manifested in this situation. Subjects have learned from childhood that it is a fundamental breach of moral conduct to hurt another person against his will. Yet, 26 subjects abandon this tenet in following the instructions of an authority who has no special powers to enforce his commands. To disobey would bring no material loss to the subject; no punishment would ensue. It is clear from the remarks and outward behavior of many participants that in punishing the victim they are often acting against their own values. Subjects often expressed deep disapproval of shocking a man in the face of his objections, and others denounced it as stupid and senseless. Yet the majority complied with the experimental commands. This outcome was surprising from two perspectives: first, from the standpoint of predictions made in the questionnaire described earlier. (Here, however, it is possible that the remoteness of the respondents from the actual situation, and the difficulty of conveying to them the concrete details of the experiment, could account for the serious underestimation of obedience.)

But the results were also unexpected to persons who observed the experiment in progress, through one-way mirrors. Observers often uttered expressions of disbelief upon seeing a subject administer more powerful shocks to the victim. These persons had a full acquaintance with the details of the situation, and yet systematically underestimated the amount of obedience that subjects would display.

The second unanticipated effect was the extraordinary tension generated by the procedures. One might suppose that a subject would simply break off or continue as his conscience dictated. Yet, this is very far from what happened. There were striking reactions of tension and emotional strain. One observer related:

> I observed a mature and initially poised businessman enter the laboratory smiling and confident. Within 20 minutes he was reduced to a twitching, stuttering wreck, who was rapidly approaching a point of nervous collapse. He constantly pulled on his earlobe, and twisted his hands. At one point he pushed his fist into his forehead and muttered: "Oh God, let's stop it." And yet he continued to respond to every word of the experimenter, and obeyed to the end.

Any understanding of the phenomenon of obedience must rest on an analysis of the particular conditions in which it occurs. The following features of the experiment go some distance in explaining the high amount of obedience observed in the situation.

1. The experiment is sponsored by and takes place on the grounds of an institution of unimpeachable reputation, Yale University. It may be reasonably presumed that the personnel are competent and reputable. The importance of this background authority is now being studied by conducting a series of experiments outside of New Haven, and without any visible ties to the university.

2. The experiment is, on the face of it, designed to attain a worthy purpose   advancement of knowledge about learning and memory. Obedience occurs not as an end in itself, but as an instrumental element in a situation that the subject construes as significant, and meaningful. He may not be able to see its full significance, but he may properly assume that the experimenter does.

3. The subject perceives that the victim has voluntarily submitted to the authority system of the experimenter. He is not (at first) an unwilling captive impressed for involuntary service. He has taken the trouble to come to the laboratory presumably to aid the experimental research. That he later becomes an involuntary subject does not alter the fact that, initially, he consented to participate without qualification. Thus he has in some dgeree incurred an obligation toward the experimenter.

4. The subject, too, has entered the experiment voluntarily, and perceives himself under obligation to aid the experimenter. He has made a commitment, and to disrupt the experiment is a repudiation of this initial promise of aid.

5. Certain features of the procedure strengthen the subject's sense of obligation to the experimenter. For one, he has been paid for coming to the laboratory. In part this is canceled out by the experimenter's statement that:

> Of course, as in all experiments, the money is yours simply for coming to the laboratory. From this point on, no matter what happens, the money is yours.

6. From the subject's standpoint, the fact that he is the teacher and the other man the learner is purely a chance consequence (it is determined by drawing lots) and he, the subject, ran the same risk as the other man in being assigned the role of learner. Since the assignment of positions in the experiment was achieved by fair means, the learner is deprived of any basis of complaint on this count. (A similar situation obtains in Army units, in which – in the absence of volunteers – a particularly dangerous mission may be assigned by drawing lots, and the unlucky soldier is expected to bear his misfortune with sportsmanship.)

7 There is, at best, ambiguity with regard to the prerogatives of a psychologist and the corresponding rights of his subject. There is a vagueness of expectation concerning what a psychologist may require of his subject, and when he is overstepping acceptable limits. Moreover, the experiment occurs in a closed setting, and thus provides no opportunity for the subject to remove these ambiguities by discussion with others. There are few standards that seem directly applicable to the situation, which is a novel one for most subjects.

8. The subjects are assured that the shocks administered to the subject are "painful but not dangerous." Thus they assume that the discomfort caused the victim is momentary, while the scientific gains resulting from the experiment are enduring.

9. Through Shock Level 20 the victim continues to provide answers on the signal box. The subject may construe this as a sign that the victim is still willing to "play the game." It is only after Shock Level 20 that the victim repudiates the rules completely, refusing to answer further.

These features help to explain the high amount of obedience obtained in this experiment. Many of the arguments raised need not remain matters of speculation, but can be reduced to testable propostions to be confirmed or disproved by further experiments.

The following features of the experiment concern the nature of the conflict which the subject faces.

10. The subject is placed in a position in which he must respond to the competing demands of two persons: the experimenter and the victim. The conflict must be resolved by meeting the demands of one or the other; satisfaction of the victim and the experimenter are mutually exclusive. Moreover, the resolution must take the form of a highly visible action, that of continuing to shock the victim or breaking off the experiment. Thus the subject is forced into a public conflict that does not permit any completely satisfactory solution.

11. While the demands of the experimenter carry the weight of scientific authority, the demands of the victim spring from his personal experience of pain and suffering. The two claims need not be regarded as equally pressing and legitimate. The experimenter seeks an abstract scientific datum; the victim cries out for relief from physical suffering caused by the subject's actions.

12. The experiment gives the subject little time for reflection. The conflict comes on rapidly. It is only minutes after the subject has been seated before the shock generator that the victim begins his protests. Moreover, the subject perceives that he has gone through but two-thirds of the shock levels at the time the subject's first protests are heard. Thus he understands that the conflict will have a persistent aspect to it, and may well become more intense as increasingly more powerful shocks are required. The rapidity with which the conflict descends on the subject, and

his realization that it is predictably recurrent may well be sources of tension to him.

13. At a more general level, the conflict stems from the opposition of two deeply ingrained behavior dispositions: first, the disposition not to harm other people, and second, the tendency to obey those whom we perceive to be legitimate authorities.

References

Milgram, S. Dynamics of obedience. Washington: National Science Foundation, 25 January 1961. (Mimeo)

Snow, C. P. Either-or. *Progressive*, 1961 (Feb.), 24.

Notes

1 Milgram and others ran numerous replications and variations of this experiment, including ones with more diverse subject populations, including women, and ones using subjects in other countries. The same basic pattern of results showed up across all of these variations. Indeed, it has been called "the one great unchanging result." See Milgram, S. (1974). *Obedience to Authority*. New York: Harper and Row.

2 In other variations of the experiment, the learner provided verbal feedback, such as, "Experimenter, get me out of here! I won't be in the experiment any more! I refuse to go on!" at 150 volts, "I can't stand the pain" at 180 volts, "an agonized scream" and complaints of chest pains at 270 volts, and refusal to respond after 300 volts. Nonetheless, the results remained basically the same, with roughly 2/3 of subjects continuing to shock all the way to 450 volts. In the "touch-proximity" variation, the learner was moved into the room with the subject, who had to hold the learner's hand down on a shock plate. Though obedience went down, nonetheless, almost 1/3 of subjects continued to shock all the way to 450 volts. See Milgram (1974).

21

The Person and the Situation

Lee Ross and Richard E. Nisbett

Undergraduates taking their first course in social psychology generally are in search of an interesting and enjoyable experience, and they rarely are disappointed. They find out many fascinating things about human behavior, some of which validate common sense and some of which contradict it. The inherent interest value of the material, amounting to high-level gossip about people and social situations, usually ensures that the students are satisfied consumers.

The experience of serious graduate students, who, over the course of four or five years, are immersed in the problems and the orientation of the field, is rather different. For them, the experience is an intellectually wrenching one. Their most basic assumptions about the nature and the causes of human behavior, and about the very predictability of the social world, are challenged. At the end of the process, their views of human behavior and society will differ profoundly from the views held by most other people in their culture. Some of their new insights and beliefs will be held rather tentatively and applied inconsistently to the social events that unfold around them. Others will be held with great conviction, and will be applied confidently. But ironically, even the new insights that they are most confident about will tend to have the effect of making them less certain than their peers about predicting social behavior and making inferences about particular individuals or groups. Social psychology rivals philosophy in its ability to teach people that they do not truly understand the nature of the world. This book is about that hard-won ignorance and what it tells us about the human condition.

[. . .]

The Weakness of Individual Differences

Consider the following scenario: While walking briskly to a meeting some distance across a college campus, John comes across a man slumped in a doorway, asking him for help. Will John offer it, or will he continue on his way? Before answering such a question, most people would want to know more about John. Is he someone known to be callous and unfeeling, or is he renowned for his kindness and concern? Is he a stalwart member of the Campus Outreach Organization, or a mainstay of the Conservative Coalition Against Welfare Abuse? In short, what kind of person is John and how has he behaved when his altruism has been tested in the past? Only with such information in hand, most people would agree, could one make a sensible and confident prediction.

In fact, however, nothing one is likely to know or learn about John would be of much use in helping predict John's behavior in the situation we've described. In particular, the type of infor-

From Lee Ross and Richard E. Nisbett. *The Person and the Situation: Perspectives of Social Psychology.* (Temple University Press, 1991). Pp. 1–8, 18–20, 30–35, 41–44, 48–50.

Moral Psychology: Historical and Contemporary Readings, edited by Thomas Nadelhoffer, Eddy Nahmias, and Shaun Nichols.

mation about personality that most laypeople would want to have before making a prediction would prove to be of relatively little value. A half century of research has taught us that in this situation, and in most other novel situations, one cannot predict with any accuracy how particular people will respond. At least one cannot do so using information about an individual's personal dispositions or even about that individual's past behavior.

Even scientists who are most concerned with assessing individual differences in personality would concede that our ability to predict how particular people will respond in particular situations is very limited. This "predictability ceiling" is typically reflected in a maximum statistical correlation of .30 between measured individual differences on a given trait dimension and behavior in a novel situation that plausibly tests that dimension. This ceiling, for example, would characterize our ability to predict on the basis of a personality test of honesty how likely different people will be to cheat in a game or on an exam, or to predict on the basis of a test of friendliness or extroversion how much sociability different individuals will show at a particular social gathering. Now a correlation of .30, as we will emphasize later, is by no means trivial. Correlations of this magnitude can be quite important for many prediction purposes. But a correlation of .30 still leaves the great bulk of variance in people's behavior unaccounted for. More importantly, a correlation of this magnitude is a good deal lower than it would have to be to provide the type of predictability that most laypeople anticipate when they make predictions about each other's behavior or make inferences about others' personal attributes. Moreover, the .30 value is an upper limit. For most novel behaviors in most domains, psychologists cannot come close to that. Certainly, as we will see, neither the professional nor the layperson can do that well when obliged to predict behavior in one particular new situation on the basis of actions in one particular prior situation.

Despite such evidence, however, most people staunchly believe that individual differences or traits can be used to predict how people will behave in new situations. Such "dispositionism" is widespread in our culture. What is more, most of us, scientists and laypeople alike, seem to find our dispositionism affirmed by our everyday social experience. The challenge of accounting for this discrepancy between beliefs about everyday experience on the one hand and empirical evidence on the other hand is one of the most important faced by psychologists.

The Power of Situations

While knowledge about John is of surprisingly little value in predicting whether he will help the person slumped in the doorway, details concerning the specifics of the situation would be invaluable. For example, what was the appearance of the person in the doorway? Was he clearly ill, or might he have been a drunk or, even worse, a nodding dope addict? Did his clothing make him look respectably middle class or decently working class, or did he look like a homeless derelict?

Such considerations are fairly obvious once they are mentioned, and the layperson, upon reflection, will generally concede their importance. But few laypeople would concede, much less anticipate, the relevance of some other, subtler, contextual details that empirical research has shown to be important factors influencing bystander intervention. Darley and Batson (1973) actually confronted people with a version of the situation we've described and found what some of these factors are. Their subjects were students in a religious seminary who were on their way to deliver a practice sermon. If the subjects were in a hurry (because they thought they were late to give a practice sermon), only about 10 percent helped. By contrast, if they were not in a hurry (because they had plenty of time before giving their sermon), about 63 percent of them helped.

Social psychology has by now amassed a vast store of such empirical parables. The tradition here is simple. Pick a generic situation; then identify and manipulate a situational or contextual variable that intuition or past research leads you to believe will make a difference (ideally, a variable whose impact you think most laypeople, or even most of your peers, somehow fail to appreciate), and see what happens. Sometimes, of course, you will be wrong and your manipulation won't "work." But often the situational variable makes quite a bit of difference. Occasionally, in fact, it makes nearly all the difference, and information about traits and individual differences that other people thought all-important proves all but trivial. If so, you have contributed a situationist classic destined to become part of our field's intellectual legacy. Such empirical parables are important because they illustrate the degree to which ordinary men and women are apt to be mistaken about the power of the situation – the power of particular situational features, and the power of situations in general.

People's inflated belief in the importance of personality traits and dispositions, together with their failure to recognize the importance of situational factors in affecting behavior, has been termed the "fundamental attribution error" (Ross, 1977; Nisbett & Ross, 1980; see also Jones, 1979; Gilbert & Jones, 1986). Together with many other social psychologists, we have directed our attention to documenting this conjoint error and attempting to track down its origins.

[. . .]

The Subtlety of Situations

There is another face to situationism. Not all situational factors prove to be powerful determinants of behavior, not even those that seem intuitively strong to both laypeople and social scientists. Some, in fact, prove to be astonishingly weak.

Nowhere is the weakness of apparently big situational factors more perplexing than in studies of the impact of various real-life events on important social outcomes. For some of these weak effects we can be grateful. For example, it turns out that in most cases the long term impact of physical and sexual abuse suffered in childhood is relatively slight (Widom, 1989), as is the long-term effect of teenage pregnancy on a young woman's life outcomes (Furstenberg, Brooks-Gunn, & Morgan, 1987), and even the long-term effect of P.O.W. camp indoctrination (Schein, 1956). Unfortunately, apparently positive events sometimes also prove to be surprisingly weak in their effect. For example, the lives of major lottery winners seem to be influenced far less by their windfalls than most of us would predict, especially when we imagine how much our own lives would be changed by a similar windfall (Brickman, Coates, & Janoff-Bulman, 1978).

A more sobering example of the weakness of apparently large, apparently positive events is to be found in what is perhaps the progenitor of modern social intervention experiments, the Cambridge-Somerville study of delinquency described by Powers and Whitmer (1951) with follow-ups by the McCords (J. McCord, 1978; J. McCord & W. McCord, 1959; W. McCord & J. McCord, 1959). The subjects in this noble experiment were both "delinquency prone" and "average" boys living in a lower socioeconomic status in a mostly Irish and Italian suburb of Boston in the 1940s. Some of the boys were assigned to an extremely ambitious and intensive experimental intervention condition in which, over roughly a 5-year period, they were exposed to a wide variety of social, psychological, and academic supports. Thus counselors provided two home visits per month to work on personal and family problems. Tutoring in academic subjects was made available. Many of the boys received psychiatric or medical help. Contact with Boy Scouts, YMCA, or other community programs was facilitated, and a substantial number of the boys were given the opportunity to attend summer camps. Despite this intensive and apparently favorable intervention, however, the boys in this experimental, or "treatment," condition proved to be no less likely to become delinquent than those in an "untreated" control group. Indeed, follow-ups conducted 30 years after the end of the program suggested that treated subjects may actually have fared slightly worse as adults, for example, in terms of rates for serious adult offenses, than those subjects whose outcomes were merely monitored.

Follow-up research on the nondelinquent boys in the Cambridge Somerville sample who received no treatment (Long & Vaillant, 1984) showed even more surprising noneffects – in this case, noneffects of apparently important social factors in the boys' family backgrounds. The boys were classified into four different categories depending on the degree of social health or pathology of their home life. At the lowest extreme were families with many serious problems – for example, an alcoholic or abusive father, a schizophrenic mother, a dependence on many social agencies for financial support, and so forth. At the opposite extreme were families that seemed for the most part to be models of the working poor – fathers were employed, mothers were serving as home-makers, there was no obvious pathology and no dependence on social agencies. The life outcomes of boys in these different categories were then examined in a follow-up study 40 years later. On indicator after indicator – for example, income, mental health, prison incarcerations, suicides, and the like – the status of the subjects' home situation as children made little if any difference.

What do we learn from these spectacular non-effects? Certainly not that situational factors are unimportant in the world outside the social psychology laboratory. Many real-world effects turn out to be huge – from the dramatic personal changes wrought by immersing conservative young women in highly liberal surroundings (Newcomb, 1943), to the pronounced effect of competition on group conflict (Sherif, Harvey, White, Hood, & Sherif, 1961). Conversely, it is not only in the "real world" that situational factors and manipulations sometimes prove to be surprisingly small or nonexistent. It is the studies with detectable effects that get published, and the subset of the studies with large and unanticipated effects that become well known. The others languish in file drawers. We wish we had a dollar for every failed laboratory manipulation that social psychologists have designed with the confident expectation that the effects in question would be significant. What we have learned, in short, is that situational effects can sometimes be far different from what our intuitions, or theories, or even the existing psychological literature tell us they should be. Some factors that we expect to be very important prove to be trivial in their impact; and some factors that we expect to be weak prove, at least in some contexts, to exert a very large influence indeed. Accounting for our poor "calibration" as to the size of the effects produced by situational factors is a major focus of the education of the social psychologist and a chief concern of this book.

The Predictability of Human Behavior

When we, the authors, were undergraduates, we were assured that the sharply limited abilities of social scientists to make accurate predictions had to do with the relative youth of the social sciences. We no longer share such beliefs nor resort to such defenses of our field. We now believe that ours is not a particularly immature science and that we have, in fact, already discovered and documented some very important things about human social

behavior. At the same time, we accept the fact that social psychology is never going to reach the point of predicting how any given individual (even one who is well known to us) is going to behave in a given novel situation. A corollary of this concession is that the application of social science knowledge is always going to be a risky business. When we try something new, even a new intervention that seems very reasonable on prior grounds, we are frequently going to discover that people respond quite differently than we had anticipated.

The roots of this fundamental unpredictability, we will argue, are very deep and perhaps akin to a source of similar unpredictability in phenomena in the physical and biological sciences (Gleick, 1987).

[. . .]

The Conflict Between the Lessons of Social Psychology and the Experience of Everyday Life

As we have seen, the evidence of empirical social psychology often conflicts sharply with what we "know" from everyday life. To be sure, we are sometimes surprised by the behavior of our fellow human beings, or by a genuinely unexpected act on the part of one of our children, or one of our friends, or some public figure. But for the most part the world seems an orderly, predictable place. It is extroverted Bill who dons the lamp shade at the party and not introverted Jill. Similarly, it is the pastor of the Church of the Good Shepherd who preaches charity and the Republican congressman from the wealthiest district in the state who preaches self-reliance and free enterprise. Moreover, soft answers do seem to turn away wrath. Sending a boy to do a man's job generally does result in disappointment. And, when it really counts, our best friends usually do come through for us, just as we had expected they would.

Earlier in their careers the authors seriously entertained the hypothesis that most of this seeming order was a kind of cognitive illusion. We believed that human beings are adept at seeing things as they believe them to be, at explaining away contradictions and, in particular, at perceiving people as more consistent than they really are. While we continue to believe that such biased processing of evidence plays an important role in perceptions of consistency, we now believe that the predictability of everyday life is, for the most part, real. At the same time, we believe that many of the principles and intuitions that people use to explain and predict behavior are unreliable. That is, people often make correct predictions on the basis of erroneous beliefs and defective prediction strategies.

We draw an analogy here between lay and professional physics. Lay physics (which is largely the same as Aristotelian and medieval physics) is undeniably mistaken in some of its main presumptions (Holland, Holyoak, Nisbett, & Thagard, 1986; McCloskey, 1983). In particular, lay physics, like lay psychology, errs in focusing on the properties of the object to the neglect of the field of forces in which that object exists. Moreover, the main interactional notion of lay physics – namely, the intuitive notion of "momentum" – is the utterly mistaken notion that a force applied to an object gives it a store of energy gradually dissipates. The correct notion (that of inertia) requires that objects at rest remain at rest and that objects in motion remain in motion, unless some other force is applied. Nevertheless, lay physics does a perfectly good job of getting us through our days. In a world where air, land, and water all offer resistance or friction, the notion that objects somehow lose their momentum is good enough. Only when we step outside the normal haunts of daily life, for example, when we venture into a physics laboratory or into outer space, does our lay physics get us into serious trouble.

And so it is for social psychology. Our intuitive ideas about people and the principles governing their responses to their environment are generally adequate for most purposes of the office and the home; but they are seriously deficient when we must understand, predict, or control behavior in contexts that lie outside our most customary experience – that is, when we take on new and different roles or responsibilities, encounter new cultures, analyze newly arisen social problems, or contemplate novel social interventions to address such problems. When we go from being students to being professionals, when we bargain with a street vendor 5,000 miles from home, or when our community begins a new program to deal with crack addiction or homelessness, the inadequacies of lay principles are likely to be revealed.

[. . .]

Prediction by Laypeople

We are even more interested in the implications of social psychology's basic tenets for the layperson's predictions than for those of social scientists. We wish to demonstrate that lay predictions are often both wrong and too confidently made. To begin with, people are apt to have exaggerated notions about the strength of individual differences and the role such differences play in producing behavior. Some of the reasons for this are essentially perceptual. The continuity in Ralph's physical appearance and personal style (for example, his imposing stature, deep voice, steady gaze, and habit of clenching his fist to emphasize his words) may blind us to the lack of any real consistency in the degree of dependency or aggressiveness he shows across different situations. Other factors are more cognitive. Inconsistent data typically are assimilated in a way that produces illusions of past behavioral consistency. Our first impression that Ellen is friendly leads us to interpret her sarcastic response to Bill's whispered remark as jocular, or a justifiable reaction to what Bill must have said, or perhaps the result of pressures she has been under at work; but not as evidence that our earlier impression was wrong, and that Ellen is simply variable in her friendliness.

Beyond discussing such sources of illusory consistency, we will emphasize the extent to which uncertainty in the way particular individuals construe particular situations, and the difficulty in predicting such construals, necessarily limit the amount of observable cross-situational consistency that ever *could* be demonstrated. Ellen's friendliness, or lack of it, in particular social situations will depend on the way she labels those situations and resolves any ambiguity about the meaning of any behavior directed toward her.

At the same time, we will contend that people do, in fact, manifest considerable predictability of a sort that observers can perceive and make use of in their everyday social dealings. The apparent conflict between the lessons of formal research and the lessons of everyday experience, we believe, results from the investigator's reliance upon research strategies designed to disentangle the separate contributions of person and situation by exposing some sample of individuals to a fixed, and identical, set of situations. This strategy, despite several undeniable advantages for the theoretician, can lead us to ignore some important realities about everyday life. Foremost is the fact that in everyday experience the characteristics of actors and those of the situations they face are typically confounded – in ways that contribute to precisely the consistency that we perceive and count on in our social dealings. People often choose the situations to which they are exposed; and people often are chosen for situations on the basis of their manifest or presumed abilities and dispositions. Thus, clerics and criminals rarely face an identical or equivalent set of situational challenges. Rather, they place themselves, and are placed by others, in situations that differ precisely in ways that induce clergy to look, act, feel, and think rather consistently like clergy and that induce criminals to look, act, feel, and think like criminals.

We also will explore the implications of the fact that people sometimes feel *obliged*, even committed, to act consistently. This may be because of their social roles, because of the real-world incentives and sanctions that await those who honor or violate such roles, because of promises they make to others or even because of demands they place upon themselves. The net result of these influences is that we correctly anticipate a predictable social world, one with consistent, or at least coherent, actors. This result, moreover, is especially likely to be true in the domains that we care about most and in which we have the most experience.

Finally, it should be noted that both consistencies and seeming inconsistencies in behavior can sometimes be reflections of individual differences in the construal processes that people bring to their understanding of their social environments. Here we follow a strain in personality theory that has its origins in Freud, was developed by George Kelly (1955), and finds its modern fruition in work by Mischel (1973), Markus (1977; Markus, Smith, & Moreland, 1985), and Cantor & Kihlstrom (1987). Each of these theorists has contended that the key to a more powerful conception of individual differences is to be found in the enduring motivational concerns and cognitive schemes that guide attention, interpretation, and the formulation of goals and plans. An important consequence of this contention is that behavioral consistencies, where they are found, may not be well captured by traditional personality traits. That is, individuals may behave in consistent ways that distinguish them from their peers not because of their enduring predispositions to be friendly, dependent, aggressive, or the like, but rather because they are pursuing consistent goals using consistent strategies, in light of consistent ways of interpreting their social world (cf. Cantor & Kihlstrom, 1987).

In short, our overall thesis, is that some of the layperson's most fundamental assumptions about personal consistency and predictability are validated by everyday experience, even though the basis for such consistency may be misunderstood by the perceiver. Thus, despite the demonstrable errors and biases of lay prediction, the world as it is experienced daily is, in fact, a reasonably predictable place. Lay psychology, like lay physics, generally gets the job done reasonably well using dramatically mistaken principles; and when it fails, it will generally be for reasons that rather deep principles of our discipline allow us to understand and sometimes even anticipate.

[. . .]

Inhibition of Bystander Intervention

Some of the best and most interesting studies in the situationist tradition established by Lewin derive, at least initially, not from broad theories but from careful analysis of real-world events. The classic bystander intervention studies conducted two decades ago by John Darley and Bibb Latané provide perhaps the best-known examples of this tradition.

The 1960s were filled with events that made many feel that America's social fabric was unraveling. What caught the eye of Darley and Latané, however, was a rash of attacks on women in which no one came to the victim's aid. One such incident in particular received great national attention. Over a 30-minute period in Kew Gardens, a middle-class section of Queens, New York, a woman named Kitty Genovese was stabbed repeatedly by an assailant. Though she shouted for help continually during that time, and despite the fact (as police later were able to establish) that at least 38 people heard her and were aware of the incident, no one intervened in any way. No one even called the police!

The news media, never at a loss to explain human behavior, were unanimous in attributing the neighbors' lack of intervention to increasing alienation and apathy among dwellers in the megalopolis. Darley and Latané, trained in the situationist and subjectivist traditions of their field, thought otherwise. They hypothesized that in this incident, and in scores of others in which groups of bystanders failed to help victims of accidents, illnesses, or crimes (even in circumstances that would have exposed them to no danger or other significant costs), potential altruists had been inhibited not by indifference but rather by important aspects of the social situation. In particular, they had been inhibited by the presence of other potential altruists, and by their apparent failure to intervene in the same situation.

Group situations Darley and Latané (1968) argued, can inhibit bystander intervention in two ways. First, and most obvious, is the dilution or diffusion of responsibility that each person feels because of the presence of others ("Why should I be the one to intervene, especially if no one else is? I'd be willing to do my share, but not to take on all the responsibility myself"). Second, and less obvious, is the construal or social definition problem. That is, to the extent that there is ambiguity either about the nature of the situation or the nature of the appropriate response to that situation, the failure of other people to act serves to support interpretations or construals that are consistent with nonintervention ("it must just be a domestic dispute," or "she must not be hurt as badly or be in as much danger as she seems,"; or alternatively, "I guess this must be one of those situations where it's inappropriate, maybe even dangerous, to get involved, the kind of situation that prudent and sophisticated people steer clear of!"). In a sense, a vicious circle is initiated. The presence of other people inhibits quick intervention, and that initial lack of intervention supports definitions of the situation that make intervention seem unnecessary, unwise, or inappropriate, which in turn prompts further reluctance and delays, and so forth. By contrast, if the bystander is alone, and there is no one else to share the responsibility to intervene or to help define the situation, this vicious cycle never begins.

Darley and Latané undertook a number of studies to confirm the strongest version of this hypothesis – that is, that a victim's chances of receiving help would be greater if there were only a single bystander available than if there were a whole group of such bystanders. In one study (Latané & Darley, 1968), male undergraduates at Columbia were left to fill out a questionnaire either by themselves, with two other subjects, or with two confederates of the experimenter instructed to remain impassive and continue working when the subsequent "emergency" occurred. This emergency consisted of a stream of "smoke" that began to pour into the room through a wall vent, eventually filling up the entire room. While 75 percent of the solitary bystanders left the room to report the smoke, only 10 percent of the bystanders who participated alongside the two impassive confederates, and only 38 percent of the three-person groups, ever intervened in this way.

In another Columbia study (Latané & Rodin, 1969), individuals working alone on a questionnaire, individuals working in the presence of an impassive confederate, or dyads consisting of two naive subjects, heard what they believed was the sound of the female experimenter taking a bad fall on the other side of a movable room divider. Once again, most of the solitary bystanders (70 percent), but very few of the bystanders who sat next to an impassive confederate (7 percent), intervened to offer assistance. It also turned out that the victim would have fared better if she had been at the mercy of a lone bystander (70 percent intervention) than a pair of strangers (40 percent intervention).

Finally, in a New York University study (Darley & Latané, 1968), subjects heard someone whom they believed to be a fellow participant in an experiment feign an epileptic seizure while talking to them over an intercom system. When subjects believed they were the only listener, 85 percent intervened; when they believed that there was one other listener, 62 percent intervened, and when they believed that there were four other listeners, 31 percent intervened. Furthermore (as in both of the studies we've discussed previously), subjects who believed themselves to be the only potential intervener offered help more quickly. Indeed, by the end of the first minute of the feigned seizure, 50 percent of the solitary listeners, but none of those believing themselves to be only one of five listeners, had come to the assistance of the victim.

By 1980, four dozen follow-up studies had been undertaken – some using feigned emergencies in the confines of the laboratory, others exposing unwitting bystanders to simulated accidents, illnesses, or thefts, occurring in the streets, stores, elevators, and subway cars. And in about 90 percent of the comparisons, lone bystanders proved more likely to help than did people in groups (Latané & Nida, 1981). Moreover, as Darley and Latané had found in their seminal studies in the late 1960s, the victim's overall chances of receiving assistance often proved to be better if there was only a single bystander to rely upon than if there were many.

Follow-up interviews with subjects have also served to confirm the hunch that potential intervention situations, if at all ambiguous, are construed differently by group members than by lone bystanders. Potentially dangerous smoke pouring through a vent was interpreted as a leak in the air-conditioning or as vapors from a chemistry lab. Cries and moans of an accident victim became complaints and curses of someone who had probably suffered a mild sprain. The prospect of intervening now became "barging in," perhaps to the embarrassment of all concerned. Interestingly, it also appears that group situations may have inhibited subjects from noticing the emergency in the first place. Solitary students in the "smoke study" tended to glance around the room frequently as they worked on their questionnaires, generally noticing the smoke within 5 seconds. Those in groups typically kept their eyes on their work and didn't notice the smoke until it was quite thick – about 20 seconds after the first puff came through the vent.

The lesson of the Darley and Latané studies is not a difficult one to grasp, but it is sometimes hard to remember in the face of tales of "big city" life. In the movie *Midnight Cowboy* a naive young man comes from the range to the streets of Manhattan. Just off the bus, and walking through great throngs of people, he comes across a man lying on the sidewalk. He starts to reach down to see what's wrong with the man, then looks around him at the people walking past. They steer around the man on the sidewalk as they might avoid a log lying on a trail. The young man expresses surprise, then consternation, then shrugs his shoulders and goes about his business like the others.

One cannot witness such a scene without being reminded of one's own experiences of apathy and indifference in the megalopolis. But it should be helpful to ask oneself if New Yorkers, or Bostonians, or Philadelphians seem any less moved than their compatriots in Sioux Falls, Iowa, by the sufferings of stray cats, or by the fate of miners trapped in cave-ins, or by the plight of an abused and neglected child, or by the struggle of a young athlete stricken with a deadly variety of cancer. In our experience the answer is no. People are no more callous about such matters in one place than in another. To explain why urbanites walk around unfortunates lying in the street, or why they fail to investigate or call the police when they hear screams from an adjacent apartment, we need to look to the specifics of the relevant social situations, including, of course, the behavioral norms that are explicitly and implicitly communicated as these intervention opportunities continually present themselves.

[. . .]

Time to Be a Good Samaritan

We have already discussed the Darley and Latané demonstration that one apparently trivial feature of the social setting – the presence or absence of other people – can markedly influence bystander intervention. Darley and Batson (1973) showed that another, seemingly even less consequential, feature of the social situation could exert almost as much influence on the potential bystander. Their experiment, they tell us, was inspired by the Good Samaritan parable, whereby the priest and the Levite, both important (and presumably busy) people, hurry by a stricken traveler leaving it for the lowly (and presumably far less busy) Samaritan to offer the necessary assistance. Reflecting on this parable, and deriving a decidedly situationist message from it, Darley and Batson decided to manipulate the "hurried" versus "unhurried" status of potential "Good Samaritans" – all of whom, by no means coincidentally, were students at Princeton Theological Seminary.

In an initial phase of the experiment, the young seminarians were told that they were to prepare themselves for a brief extemporaneous talk (which, for half of the participants, was on the Good Samaritan parable itself) to be recorded in a nearby building. After receiving directions from the experimenter, the seminarians in one condition were told "you're late; they were expecting you a few minutes ago, so you'd better hurry," while in the other condition they were told "it will be a few minutes before they're ready for you, but you might as well head on over." En route, the participants in both the "late" and "early" condition came upon a man slumped in a doorway, head down, coughing and groaning. As predicted, the late seminarians seldom helped; in fact, only 10 percent offered any assistance. By contrast, with ample time on their hands, 63 percent of the early participants helped.

Does this study prove that these seminarians were indifferent to worldly suffering, or that they placed the interests of the relatively high-status people waiting for them ahead of the lowly character who seemed to need their help? By now the reader should be able to anticipate that we think that these findings tell us little if anything about the personal dispositions of seminarians but a great deal about the situational determinants of altruism. Once again, incidentally, we suspect that some of the subtler details of the situational manipulation may have been important and would merit some emphasis. We suspect that the "late" manipulation employed by Darley and Batson not only made the young seminarians reluctant to stop, it also guaranteed that they would feel a little harried and nervous about their forthcoming talk – enough so, perhaps, to prevent them from paying attention to the victim. On the other hand, the "early" manipulation may have served to make the young seminarians walk more slowly, contemplate their surroundings more closely, and perhaps even welcome an excuse to tarry (rather than having to wait around awkwardly while the anonymous "they" got everything ready).

Such situational influences tend to be far greater than most people are willing to predict. We can also note that scores of studies have probed additional situational determinants of altruistic behavior (and quite a few have looked for the personality characteristics of the altruist). The results of some of these studies have been fairly intuitive. Bryan and Test (1967), for example, showed that the presence or absence of altruistic "models" (peers who rendered the sought-after assistance in similar or identical circumstances) produced corresponding increases or decreases both in subjects' willingness to help motorists in distress and in their generosity when faced with a Salvation Army collection kettle. Other studies have produced more surprising, and often more complicated, results. For example, many studies have shown that mood inductions, either of "guilt" (Carlsmith & Gross, 1968) or "happiness" (Isen, Clark, & Schwartz, 1976; Isen, Shalker, Clark, & Karp, 1978) can markedly increase subjects' willingness to comply with requests for help or to show other altruistic behaviors. But none, we believe, can drive home the situationist message in general, and the importance of channel factors in particular, as pointedly as Darley and Batson's simple study. As we contemplate the earnest young seminarian (who, no doubt, has devoted in the past and will devote again in the future many hours to helping various types of unfortunates) almost literally stepping over a distressed victim as he hurries off to preach his sermonette on Good Samaritanism, we grasp an essential message of the Lewinian tradition: There but for the sake of a facilitating channel factor go we.

References

Brickman, P., Coates, D., & Janoff-Bulman, R. J. (1978). Lottery winners and accident victims: Is happiness relative? *Journal of Personality and Social Psychology*, 36, 917–27.

Bryan, J. H., & Test, M. A. (1967). Models and helping: Naturalistic studies in aiding behavior. *Journal of Personality and Social Psychology*, 6, 400–7.

Cantor, N., & Kihlstrom, J. F. (1987). *Personality and social intelligence*. Englewood Cliffs, NJ: Prentice-Hall.

Carlsmith, J. M., & Gross, A. E. (1968). Some effects of guilt on compliance. *Journal of Personality and Social Psychology*, 11, 232–9.

Darley, J. M., & Batson, C. D. (1973). From Jerusalem to Jericho: A study of situational and dispositional variables in helping behavior. *Journal of Personality and Social Psychology*, 27, 100–19.

Darley, J. M., & Latané, B. (1968). Bystander intervention in emergencies: Diffusion of responsibility. *Journal of Personality and Social Psychology*, 8, 377–83.

Furstenberg, F. F., Jr., Brooks-Gunn, J., & Morgan, P. S. (1987). *Adolescent mothers in later life*. Cambridge: Cambridge.

Gilbert., D. T., & Jones, E. E. (1986). Perceiver-induced constraints: Interpretation of self-generated reality.

Journal of Personality and Social Psychology, 50, 269–80.

Gleick, J. (1987). *Chaos: Making a new science.* New York: Viking.

Holland, J. H., Holyoak, K. J., Nisbett, R. E., & Thagard, P. R. (1986). *Induction: Processes of inference, learning and discovery.* Cambridge, MA: Bradford Books/M.I.T.

Isen, A. M., Clark, M., & Schwartz, M. F. (1976). Duration of the effect of good mood on helping: Footprints on the sands of time. *Journal of Personality and Social Psychology, 34,* 385–93.

Isen, A. M., Shalker, T. E., Clark, M., & Karp, L. (1978). Affect, acccessibility of material in memory, and behavior: A cognitive loop. *Journal of Personality and Social Psychology, 36,* 1–12.

Jones, E. E. (1979). The rocky road from acts to dispositions. *American Psychologist, 34,* 107–17.

Kelly, G. A. (1955). *The psychology of personal constructs* (2 vols.). New York: Norton.

Latané, B., & Darley, J. M. (1968). Group inhibition of bystander intervention in emergencies, *Journal of Personality and Social Psychology, 10,* 215–21.

Latané, B., & Nida, S. (1981). Ten years of research on group size and helping. *Psychological Bulletin, 89,* 308–24.

Latané, B., & Rodin, J. (1969). A lady in distress: Inhibiting effects of friends and strangers on bystander intervention, *Journal of Personality and Social Psychology, 5,* 189–202.

Long, J. V. F., & Vaillant, G. E. (1984). Natural history of male psychological health XI: Escape from the underclass. *American Journal of Psychiatry, 14,* 341–6.

Markus, H. (1977). Self-schemata and processing information about the self. *Journal of Personality and Social Psychology, 35,* 63–78.

Markus, H., Smith, J., & Moreland, R. L. (1985). Role of the self-concept in the perception of others, *Journal of Personality and Social Psychology, 49,* 1495–1512.

McCloskey, M. (1983, April). Intuitive physics. *Scientific American, 248,* 122–30.

McCord, J. (1978). A thirty-year follow-up of treatment effects. *American Psychologist, 33,* 284–9.

McCord, J., & McCord, W. (1959). A followup report on the Cambridge-Somerville youth study. *Annals of the American Academy of Political and Social Science, 32,* 89–96.

McCord, W., & McCord, J. (1959). *Origins of crime.* New York: Columbia.

Mischel, W. (1973). Toward a cognitive social learning reconceptualization of personality. *Psychological Review, 80,* 252–83.

Newcomb, T. M. (1943). *Personality and social change.* New York: Dryden.

Nisbett, R. E., & Ross, L. (1980). *Human inference: Strategies and shortcomings of social judgment.* Englewood Cliffs, NJ: Prentice-Hall.

Powers, E., & Whitmer, H. (1951). *An experiment in the prevention of delinquency: The Cambridge-Somerville youth study.* New York: Columbia.

Ross, L. (1977). The intuitive psychologist and his shortcomings. In L. Berkowitz (ed.), *Advances in experimental social psychology* (vol. 10). New York: Academic.

Schein, E. H. (1956). The Chinese indoctrination program for prisoners of war: A study of attempted brainwashing. *Psychiatry, 19,* 149–72.

Sherif, M., Harvey, O. J., White, B. J., Hood, W. R., & Sherif, C. W. (1961). *Intergroup conflict and cooperation: The Robbers Cave experiment.* Norman: University of Oklahoma Book Exchange.

Vallone, R. P., Griffin, D. W., Lin, S., & Ross, L. (1990). Overconfident prediction of future actions and outcomes by self and others. *Journal of Personality and Social Psychology, 58,* 582–92.

Widom, C. S. (1989). The cycle of violence. *Science, 24.* 160–6.

22

Persons, Situations, and Virtue Ethics

John M. Doris

I. Characterological Psychology, Empirical Inadequacy

Imagine a person making a call in a suburban shopping plaza. As the caller leaves the phone booth, along comes Alice, who drops a folder full of papers that scatter in the caller's path. Will the caller stop and help before the only copy of Alice's magnum opus is trampled by the bargain-hungry throngs? Perhaps it depends on the person: Jeff, an entrepreneur incessantly scheming about fattening his real estate holdings, probably won't, while Nina, a political activist who takes in stray cats, probably will. Nina is the compassionate type; Jeff isn't. In these circumstances we expect their true colors to show. But this may be a mistake, as an experiment conducted by Isen and Levin (1972) shows. There, the paper-dropper was an experimental confederate. For one group of callers, a dime was planted in the phone's coin return slot; for the other, the slot was empty. Here are the results (after Isen and Levin 1972: 387):

	Helped	Did not help
Dime	14	2
No dime	1	24

If greedy Jeff finds the dime, he'll likely help; if caring Nina doesn't, she very likely won't. This finding exemplifies a 70-year "situationist" experimental tradition in social and personality psychology, a tradition which has repeatedly demonstrated that the behavioral reliability expected on standard theoretical constructions of personality is not revealed in the systematic observation of behavior. I will suggest that situationist research has revisionary implications for ethical thought, particularly for the neo-Aristotelian ethical theory prominent in moral philosophy for the past quarter century. For such a claim to be fairly earned, we would have to examine decades of research and debate in social and personality psychology, a project I undertake elsewhere.[1] Here, my ambitions are modest: I hope only to produce the beginnings of a suspicion that Aristotelian moral psychology may be more problematic than philosophers engaged in the ethics and character debate have thought.

In this section, I argue that Aristotelian approaches to ethics, in so far as they presuppose certain distinctive commitments in descriptive psychology, may be subject to damaging empirical criticisms. [. . .] "Ethics," as Stevenson (1963: 13) said, "must not be psychology." Results in descriptive psychology, taken by themselves, cannot be decisive factors in evaluating normative claims. Accordingly, after considering empirical difficulties facing Aristotelian descriptive psychology and sketching what I contend is a more empirically adequate situationist alternative, in sections two and three I consider how the competing moral psychologies fare on normative grounds. If I am right, the approach to moral

From John Doris (1998). Persons, situations, and virtue ethics. *Noûs*, 32, 4. Blackwell Publishers Inc., 1998, excerpts from pp. 504–30. Reprinted with permission of Wiley-Blackwell.

Moral Psychology: Historical and Contemporary Readings, edited by Thomas Nadelhoffer, Eddy Nahmias, and Shaun Nichols.

psychology suggested by situationism enjoys certain advantages over Aristotelianism as a foundation for normative thought. Moreover, while motivating this claim inevitably requires more than empirical assessment of the alternatives, it will emerge that the advantages of situationism as a grounding for normative reflection are, in substantial measure, a result of its more empirically adequate descriptive psychology. Ethics is not simply psychology, but in this instance there are interesting and important connections between the two endeavors. To begin, then, I must give a sense of the issues on the descriptive side.

We believe the person of good character is not easily swayed by circumstance, and we have a rich normative vocabulary reflecting this ideal: "steady," "dependable," "steadfast," "unwavering," "unflinching." Conversely, when a person's behavior disappoints, we are equipped with terms of abuse to mark what we take to be lack of character: "weak," "fickle," "disloyal," "unfaithful," "irresolute." Apparently, character is expected to have regular behavioral manifestations: we believe that the person of good character will behave appropriately, even in situations with substantial pressures to moral failure, and we are similarly confident that we would be foolish to rely on the person of bad character. This interpretative strategy presupposes that the attribution of a character trait allows us to predict an individual's behavior in novel circumstances; we may not have previously observed Jim's behavior on a foundering ship, but if we know he is courageous, we know that he will perform his office properly should such a situation arise. Unfortunately, experimental evidence of the sort just mentioned suggests that this approach, however common-place it may be, is inadequate to the facts of actual behavior: trait attribution is often surprisingly inefficacious in predicting behavior in particular novel situations, because differing behavioral outcomes often seem a function of situational variation more than individual disposition. To put things crudely, people typically lack character. But while characterological moral psychology is problematic from the perspective of empirical psychology, it enjoys an impeccable philosophical provenance – it is a faithful rendering of certain features of Aristotle's, and neo-Aristotelian, ethical thought.

For Aristotle, good character is "firm and unchangeable" (1984: 1105b1): the virtues are *hexeis* (1984: 1106a10–12), and a *hexis* is a disposition that is "permanent and hard to change" (1984: Categories, 8b25–9a9). Virtues are supposed to have reliable behavioral manifestations: although good people may suffer misfortunes that impede the activity of virtue, they will never (*oudepote*) behave viciously (1984: 1100b32–4; cf. 1128b29). In addition, Aristotle thinks that virtue is typified by the performance of right actions in the most difficult and demanding circumstances (1984: 1105a8–10; cf. 1115a25–6); the practically wise *phronimos* will follow the appropriate course of action *whatever* circumstance he is in (1984: 1100b33–1101a7, 1140a25–8; cf. Hardie 1980: 104; Broadie 1991: 58). I don't claim exegetical authority here, but it is evident that these themes have figured prominently in neo-Aristotelian moral psychology. According to McDowell (1978: 26), properly habituated character "silences" temptations to vice; as Hollis (1995: 172) understands Aristotelianism, character sets "boundary conditions" on the realm of behavioral options. As in Aristotle, contemporary discussions involve assurances not only concerning negative behaviors being precluded by the possession of virtue, but also concerning the positive behaviors virtue will effect: Dent (1975: 328) maintains that the virtuous person will "quite consistently and predictably" conduct herself appropriately in "ever-various and novel situations," while McDowell (1979: 332; cf. Blum 1994: 178–80) supposes that virtue "issues in nothing but right conduct." In sum, we can say that Aristotelian virtues are *robust*, or substantially resistant to contrary situational pressures, in their behavioral manifestations.

Aristotelians also tend to maintain some version of an *evaluative consistency* thesis, maintaining that in a given personality the occurrence of a trait with a particular evaluative valence is probabilistically related to the occurrence of other traits with similar evaluative valences.[2] For example, the expectation is that a generous person is more likely compassionate than callous; a compassionate and generous person is evaluatively consistent, while a callous and generous person is not. Then for the Aristotelian, good character is supposed to be an integrated association of robust traits.

What would count as evidence supporting the attribution of Aristotelian traits and personality structures? I submit that the evidence we require is observed *behavioral reliability* – behavior consistent with a trait or grouping of related traits across a range of relevant eliciting situations that may vary widely in their particulars. That is, we are justified in inferring the existence of an Aristotelian personality structure when a person's behavior reliably conforms to the patterns expected on postulation of that structure. In the psychological lexicon, we can say that trait attribution requires substantial *cross-situational consistency* in behavior (e.g., Mischel 1968; Ross and Nisbett 1991). If I am right about the experimental data, systematic observation typically reveals failures of cross-situational consistency; behavior is very often surprisingly unreliable. We have good reason to consider an alternative, more empirically adequate, conception of moral personality.

Situationist social psychology suggests such an alternative. Situationism's three central theses concern behavioral variation, the nature of traits, and trait organization in personality structure:

(i) Behavioral variation across a population owes more to situational differences than dispositional differences among persons. Individual dispositional differences are not as strongly behaviorally individuating as we might have supposed; to a surprising extent we are safest predicting, for a particular situation, that a person will behave pretty much as most others would.

(ii) Empirical evidence problematizes the attribution of robust traits. Whatever behavioral reliability we do observe may be readily short-circuited by situational variation: in a run of trait-relevant situations with diverse features, an individual to whom we have attributed a given trait will often behave inconsistently with regard to the behavior expected on attribution of that trait. Note that this is not to deny the possibility of temporal stability in behavior; the situationist acknowledges that individuals may exhibit behavioral regularity over time across a run of substantially similar situations (Ross and Nisbett 1991: 101; Wright and Mischel 1987: 1161–2; Shoda, Mischel, and Wright 1994: 681–3).

(iii) Personality structure is not typically evaluatively consistent. For a given person, the

dispositions operative in one situation may have a very different evaluative status than those manifested in another situation – evaluatively inconsistent dispositions may "cohabitate" in a single personality.[3]

This situationist conception of personality is not an unrepentant skepticism about personological determinants of behavior such as that associated with Skinnerian behaviorism; although the situationist rejects the notion of robust traits effecting cross-situationally consistent behavior, she allows the possibility of temporally stable, situation-particular, "local" traits that may reflect dispositional differences among persons. These local traits may be extremely fine-grained: a person might be reliably helpful in iterated trials of the same situation (such as when she finds a dime in a mall phone booth and someone drops a pile of papers in her path), and reliably unhelpful in other, often surprisingly similar, circumstances (say when confronted with the same dropped papers when her search for change is disappointed). The difficulty for the Aristotelian is that local traits are not likely to produce the patterns of behavior expected on broad trait categories like "compassionate" or "courageous:" even seemingly insignificant variations in situation may "tap" different dispositions, effecting inconsistent behavior. We might say that systematically observed behavior, rather than suggesting evaluatively consistent personality structures, suggests instead *fragmented* personality structures – evaluatively inconsistent associations of large numbers of local traits. Thus, virtue-theoretic conceptions of moral personality, such as Geach's (1977) inventory of seven cardinal virtues, or Aristotle's somewhat less parsimonious inventory of twelve virtues of character and eight intellectual virtues, will seem too roughly hewn in light of the many and various moral dispositions people actually possess.

But we are not forced to choose between overly parsimonious characterological accounts and "fragmented" constructions of personality so theoretically unwieldy as to be useless in the explanation and prediction of behavior; situationism allows that a suitably fine-grained inventory of local traits may provide an account of personality that is both empirically adequate and theoretically useful. Were we in possession of a reasonably complete inventory of an individual's local traits, we would know quite a bit about how we could expect that individual to behave, although the expected behavior would not be consistent with regard to broad trait categories. Further, there is no empirical reason to deny that some individuals may possess constellations of local traits that are more or less conducive to success in their particular life circumstances; a person may possess an association of traits, albeit an evaluatively fragmented one, that better serves her in the life she has chosen, or fallen into.

It is important to notice that situationism is not embarrassed by the considerable behavioral regularity we do observe: because the preponderance of our life circumstances may involve a relatively structured range of situations, behavioral patterns are not, for the most part, haphazard (see Mischel 1968: 281). Still, we have reason to doubt that behavioral regularity is as substantial as casual observation – which even when directed at our intimates may occur on occasions limited in both number and diversity – may suggest. Every person, in the course of his or her life, exhibits a multitude of behaviors; since social observation is usually piecemeal and unsystematic, we should be hesitant to take our limited sampling of behaviors as evidence for confident interpretations of personality. At bottom, the question is whether the behavioral regularity we observe is to be primarily explained by reference to robust dispositional structures or situational regularity. The situationist insists that the striking variability of behavior with situational variation favors the latter hypothesis.

To summarize: According to the first situationist thesis, behavioral variation among individuals often owes more to distinct circumstances than distinct personalities; the difference between the person who behaves honestly and the one who fails to do so, for example, may be more a function of situation than character. Moreover, behavior may vary quite radically when compared with that expected on the postulation of a given trait. We have little assurance that a person to whom we attributed a trait will consistently behave in a trait-relevant fashion across a run of trait-relevant situations with variable pressures to such behavior; the putatively "honest" person may very well not consistently display honest behavior across a diversity of situations where honesty is appropriate.[4] This is just what we would expect on the second situationist thesis, which rejects notions of robust traits. Finally, as the third thesis suggests, expectations of evaluative consistency are likely to be disappointed. Behavioral evidence suggests that personality is comprised of evaluatively fragmented trait-associations rather than evaluatively integrated ones: e.g., for a given person, a local disposition to honesty will often be found together with local dispositions to dishonesty.

Some care is required, because the salience of situationist criticism depends on how characterological psychology is interpreted. Personality and social psychologists (e.g., Brody 1988: 31; Pervin 1994: 108) standardly treat personality traits as dispositions productive of behavior, and philosophers have typically understood virtues along the same lines.[5] As Hardie (1980: 107) reads Aristotle, a virtue is a "dispositional property" defined in terms of "hypothetical statements mentioning the conditions of [its] manifestations." On this *dispositionalist* account, to attribute a virtue is to (implicitly) assert a subjunctive conditional: if a person possesses a virtue, she will exhibit virtue-relevant behavior in a given virtue-relevant eliciting condition with some markedly above chance probability p. Just as with dispositional interpretations of properties in other areas, we want more of a story than the conditional provides, lest our account seem uninformative or trivial, but whatever further story we tell, the conditional does reflect the behavioral reliability that is a central characteristic of virtue. For my purposes the problem is that, even if we add the probabilistic qualification, the conditional is too strong: trait attribution does not ground confident predictions of particular behaviors (with probabilities markedly above chance, or approaching certainty), especially in situations where the behavior is outside the population norm for that situation.[6] If dispositionalism is committed to confident predictions of particular behaviors, it is subject to empirical difficulty.

Here it may be argued that a second approach to Aristotelian moral psychology can escape empirical difficulty, because it does not insist, as dispositionalist interpretations do, on a highly reliable connection between virtue and overt behavior. On an *intellectualist* account, virtue consists in a distinctive "way of seeing" – appropriate habits of moral perception, not reliable dispositions to action, are what distinguish the virtuous person. For example, on McDowell's interpretation virtue consists in a "perceptual capacity," or "reliable sensitivity" to morally salient features of one's environment. In calling this approach "intellectualist," I do not mean to suggest that moral sensitivity excludes less cognitively elaborated psychological mechanisms; of course the Aristotelian may wish to emphasize the importance of emotion or affect in moral understanding. The point is simply that while the dispositionalist stresses "overt" behaviors, the intellectualist emphasizes goings-on "within the head." Then the intellectualist virtue theorist may respond to my empirical challenge as follows: situationist experiments do show that dispositions may be "overridden" by situational factors, even surprisingly "insignificant" ones, but this is only to highlight something we knew all along – the activity of virtue is in many cases going to be very difficult. What typifies the virtuous person is a distinctive outlook, or way of seeing (and feeling about) the world, and nothing the situationist has said shows that this cannot be reliable, even if she has shown that its overt behavioral manifestations may not be. The cognitions and affects appropriate to virtue may be highly reliable despite the fact that dispositions to virtuous actions are not. When the nature of virtue is properly understood, its psychological realizability is not something the situationist experiments should cause us to doubt.

But if intellectualism de-emphasizes the importance of overt behavior too much, it begins to sound a little strange: "his ethical perceptions were unfailingly admirable, although he behaved only averagely" is not the most inspiring epitaph. An attractive account of virtue should be concerned not only with cognitive and affective patterns, but also with patterns of overt behavior; the ethical quality of a life is determined by actions as well as psychological states. If so, intellectualism can at most weaken the dispositionalist behavioral requirement, which would at best partially diffuse the empirical critique. I'm inclined to take intellectualism as a complement, not as an alternative, to dispositionalism, in so far as it may be understood as an explication of the psychological mechanisms which ground

behavioral regularity. In any event, we shall see momentarily that even a "pure" intellectualism that entirely eschewed predictions of overt behavior would be subject to empirical difficulty.

The situationist data can itself be read in two ways, corresponding to our two readings of Aristotelianism. In Darley and Batson's (1973) study demonstrating that increasing subjects' "degree of hurry" diminished the likelihood of helping behavior, it may appear that time pressures swamped subjects' dispositions to help someone they perceived to be in need of assistance. This interpretation is also applicable to Milgram's (1974) infamous obedience experiments. There, subjects who reluctantly consented to torture the recalcitrant "victim" with dangerous-seeming simulated "shocks" appear to have had appropriate attitudes towards compassion, but their dispositions to act on these attitudes were overridden by misguided feelings of obligation, or perhaps intimidation, generated by the experimenter's insistence on their continued participation in the "learning experiment." Their moral sensitivities appeared intact, but dispositions to act on them were overwhelmed by the demands of the experimental situation. Here, dispositionalist accounts face difficulty: the variability of behavior with situational manipulation suggests that dispositions to moral behavior are not robust in the requisite sense. So far, however, intellectualism remains a viable option; indeed, the empirical difficulties facing dispositionalism may tempt us to think that intellectualism was what the virtue theorist had in mind all along.

But another interpretation of the data problematizes the intellectualist account, by suggesting that the requisite "sensitivity" is itself highly variable with situational variation. This interpretation is recommended by Darley and Batson: apparently, some "hurried" non-helpers failed to help not because haste somehow overwhelmed helping dispositions, but because their haste apparently dampened the awareness required to notice that someone was in need of their assistance. Such a reading is also possible for Milgram: perhaps experimental pressures prevented some of his subjects from recognizing their situation as one where moral demands for compassion towards the victim should override their obligation to help the experimenter. In these cases, the failure apparently has more to do with a shortcoming of sensitivity than insufficiently robust dispositions to action. More generally, although situationists have typically agreed that cognitive capacities exhibit greater cross-situational consistency than do personality traits (e.g., Mischel 1968: 15), there is some cause to doubt that cognitive ability exhibits a high degree of reliability. Ceci (1993, 1993a) has recently urged a "contextualist" theory of intelligence to account for the often-demonstrated failure of cognitive ability in a particular area "transfer" to closely related areas: mathematical acuity in the classroom, for example, may not strongly correlate with ability to apply similar computations in work-related settings. The cognitive capacities requisite for "moral sensitivity" may exhibit surprising situational variability, just as other capacities and dispositions do. Then both the dispositionalist and intellectualist readings of Aristotelianism are subject to charges of empirical inadequacy. Aristotelian moral psychology, if it is construed as a descriptive psychology, emerges as deeply problematic.

At this juncture, the Aristotelian may charge that my arguments have missed the mark: she can allow that situationist research problematizes notions of personality in psychology, together with certain philosophical and lay conceptions of character, and still deny that it makes trouble for her conception of virtue. The psychology literature I rely on concerns personality traits generically construed, with relatively little self-conscious attention to traits we might be tempted to count as virtues, and I have apparently taken the liberty of relating results from that literature to the particular case of the virtues. Like many other writers on ethics, I believe a dispositional analysis applies to virtues as well as other traits. But I have neglected to discuss one important regard in which virtues are not "generic" traits; it may be argued that the virtues are extremely rare, not widely instantiated, traits. If so, the Aristotelian can argue as follows: the situationist research may show that the ordinary person's character is not as sturdy as we might hope, but it cannot rule out the possibility that there is some small percentage of people who are truly virtuous. The fact that many people failed morally in the observed situations tells us little about the adequacy of Aristotelian descriptive psychology, since such disappointing demographics are exactly what

the virtue theorist would expect. Indeed, a virtue-based approach can explain the situationist data: it is precisely because so few people are truly virtuous that we see the results that we do. On this reading, the Aristotelian's empirical claims are modest enough to be unembarrassed by the data; the account is only committed to the existence of a few exemplary individuals, by reference to which we guide our conduct.[7] For example, Blum's (1994: 94–6) virtue ethic does not require commitments regarding the general realizability of virtue: "it is given to very few to be moral exemplars," he says, regardless of "how conscientiously one sets oneself to become anything like the moral paragons one admires." Blum's (1994: 95–6) claim is not that many of us, or even any of us, can successfully emulate Aristotelian ideals of character, but rather that reflecting on these ideals can help us become people who are, and do, better: through reflection on moral exemplars, we may improve our own character and conduct. If the practical efficacy of emulation is not undercut by the extreme difficulty of the object of emulation being fully realized, emulation is not problematized by situationism.

This argument deserves to be taken seriously, but it is worth noting that such "empirically modest" accounts may deprive Aristotelianism of a substantial measure of its traditional appeal. Aristotelians have typically emphasized moral development and education (Aristotle 1984: e.g., 1099b29–32; 1103b21–31; McDowell: 1979: 333); the ideal of virtue, it is tempting to think, is a sort of model for the condition actual persons (with the right sort of nurturing) might achieve, or at least closely approximate. Recent philosophical writing on moral development and character (e.g., McDowell 1996, Herman 1996) is naturally read as emphasizing the sort of character agents may inculcate, rather than the advantages of reflection on a rarefied ideal. Moreover, it has commonly been held that virtues are to be appealed to in the explanation of behavior (e.g., Brandt 1988: 64); MacIntyre (1984: 199) goes so far as to argue that virtue theory is a necessary element in behavioral science. Perhaps these claims are compatible with an empirically modest moral psychology; perhaps developmental and explanatory appeals to virtue are meant to be of extremely limited empirical applicability. But it seems to me that such assertions are not typically qualified in ways that suggest empirical caution. Indeed, we may wonder if an empirically modest reading of Aristotelianism can account for its recent popularity, a popularity that appears to owe much to the promise of an engaging and lifelike moral psychology. So if we push the "argument from rarity" too far, it becomes uncertain what the distinctive attractions of Aristotelianism are supposed to be. But again, as I said at the outset, an empirically compelling moral psychology is not the only *desideratum* for ethical theory. So I must join the question directly: to what extent does reflection on a few extraordinary individuals facilitate ethically desirable behavior? Or more broadly: what exactly are the practical advantages enjoyed by ideals of virtue?

Such questions are asked with a certain prejudice – they assume that ethical reflection is a substantially practical endeavor, aimed at helping to secure ethically desirable behavior. This prejudice may seem quite a reasonable one: isn't it obvious that ethical reflection has much to do with questions regarding how to live, and so, in many instances, with questions regarding what to do (see Sher 1998: 15–17)? Yet it might be argued that philosophical ethics is properly more theoretical than practical – the aim of ethical theory is a theoretical account of what constitutes right action, perhaps, rather than to provide an approach to reflection that facilitates such action. Questions regarding the proper aims of ethical theory are complex, and I cannot resolve them here. Fortunately, in the context of Aristotelian ethics, it is not obvious that I need to do so, for it seems plain that a practical conception of ethics is Aristotelian in spirit. Aristotle (1984: 1103b28–9) insists that his project in the *Ethics* is not theoretical: "we are inquiring not in order to know what excellence is, but in order to become good, since otherwise our inquiry would have been of no use." Virtue ethics in the Aristotelian tradition, I submit, should have something to say about practical questions; while there may be interesting formulations of virtue ethics that reject the practical conception, I address my discussion of the normative issues to those who accept it. In what follows, I begin to develop the suggestion that situationist moral psychology may fare better than Aristotelian alternatives with respect to important practical concerns.

II.   Empirical Inadequacy and Ethical Revisionism

[. . .]

Even if I am on track so far, characterological discourse may yet be thought to ground central forms of ethical evaluation. First, characterological psychology may be central to the ethical evaluation of actions: Aristotle (1984: 1105a28–b1) insists that for an action to be considered truly virtuous it must be determined by the appropriately developed character of the agent. Second, in a line derived from Hume, judgments of moral responsibility may be thought to presuppose character assessments, because an agent may be thought fully morally responsible only for those actions which are judged to be legitimate expressions of her character. If these points go through, skepticism about character may emerge as radically, and not conservatively, revisionary, problematizing not only moral-psychological assessment of the agent, but assessment of the moral quality of actions and the assignment of responsibility quite generally. Adequate discussion of these topics requires more involved treatment than the present space allows; I must here be content with two brief observations.

First, the claim that an Aristotelian characterological approach is uniquely able to provide a rich account of responsibility is contentious; there is a substantial Kantian literature on responsibility, for example, and however attractive we may ultimately find such approaches, it is far from obvious that they must involve Aristotelian characterological discourse, or that they entail impoverished notions of responsibility. Second, a skepticism about Aristotelian notions of character does not commit one to an implausibly empiricist, non-psychologic account of responsibility and action assessment; my account has room for psychological notions like intention and motivation that may be requisite in such contexts. Situationism does not suggest a skepticism about the "inner states," that concern us in moral assessment, but only a skepticism regarding a conception of character as an integrated association of robust traits.

However, there remain a variety of contexts in which the Aristotelian may insist that we cannot get on, or get on as well, without characterological discourse. As I've said, I will limit sustained discussion to one area where such claims of practical indispensability might be made, first-personal ethical deliberation. I will say in advance that I have been unable to uncover considerations of this kind that unequivocally favor the Aristotelian approach. Indeed, it appears that situationist moral psychology is practically indispensable in important instances of ethical deliberation.

III. Character and Deliberation

If I am right, situationism suggests a certain redirection of our ethical attention. Rather than striving to develop characters that will determine our behavior in ways significantly independent of circumstance, we should invest more of our energies in attending to the features of our environment that impact behavioral outcomes. It may seem as though, in accepting this emphasis, we would be abdicating our status as persons – autonomous agents who can, in some deep sense, chart the courses of our own lives. While this way of putting the concern is overstated, I agree that my approach requires revision of heuristics that may be deeply entrenched in our self-conceptions, in so far as these conceptions have Aristotelian characterological underpinnings. But evaluation of ethical theories, like any problem in theory choice, involves determining the most attractive combination of costs and benefits; no theory, least of all in ethics, comes for free. In concluding, I'll try to show that the discomfort we experience in embracing a situationist moral psychology may be at least partly ameliorated by the promise of substantial advantages in the practice of deliberation.

Reflection on situationism has an obvious benefit in deliberation: it may serve to remind us that, for people like us, the world is a morally dangerous place. In an attitude study related to his obedience experiments, Milgram (1974:27–31) asked respondents to predict the maximum intensity shock they would deliver were the subjects "required" to punish the confederate "victim" with incrementally increasing shocks: the mean prediction was around 150 volts (level 10), and no subject said they would go beyond 300 volts (level 20). When these subjects were asked to predict the behavior of others, they predicted that

at most 1 or 2% of subjects would deliver the maximum shock of 450 volts (level 30). In fact, for a standard permutation of the experiment (version 5; Milgram 1974: 56–61), the mean maximum shock was 360 (level 24), and 65% continued to the highest possible shock of 450 volts (level 30). The usual expectation seems to be that behavior is much more situation-independent than it actually is; apparently, we tend to see character traits as substantially robust, with typical dispositions to moral decency serving as guarantors against destructive behavior even in circumstances like the Milgram experiment where the situational pressures to moral failure are relatively intense. Milgram's study indicates that perception and reality are markedly discrepant in this regard.[8] The consequence of this discrepancy, I contend, is an increased probability of moral failure; many times our confidence in character is precisely what puts us at risk in morally dangerous situations.[9] Far from being practically indispensable, characterological discourse is a heuristic we may often have very good reason to dispense with in our deliberations.

Take a prosaic example. Imagine that a colleague with whom you have had a long flirtation invites you for dinner, offering enticement of sumptuous food and fine wine, with the excuse that you are temporarily orphaned while your spouse is out of town. Let's assume the obvious way to read this text is the right one, and assume further that you regard the infidelity that may result as a morally undesirable outcome. If you are like one of Milgram's respondents, you might think that there is little cause for concern; you are, after all, a morally upright person, and a spot of claret never did anyone a bit of harm. On the other hand, if you take the lessons of situationism to heart, you avoid dinner like the plague, because you know that you may not be able to predict your behavior in a problematic situation on the basis of your antecedent values. You do not doubt that you sincerely value fidelity; you simply doubt your ability to act in conformity with this value once the candles are lit and the wine begins to flow. Relying on character once in the situation is a mistake, you agree; the way to achieve the ethically desirable result is to recognize that situational pressures may all too easily overwhelm character, and avoid the dangerous situation. I don't think it wild speculation to claim that this is a better strategy than donning your most fetching clothes and dropping by for a "harmless" evening, secure in the knowledge of your righteousness.

The way to get things right more often, I suggest, is by attending to the determinative features of situations. We should try, so far as we are able, to avoid "near occasions for sin" – morally dangerous circumstances. At the same time, we should seek near occasions for happier behaviors – situations conducive to ethically desirable conduct. This means that the determinants of moral success or failure may emerge earlier in an activity than we might think. In our example, the difficulty to be addressed lies less in an exercise of will after dinner than in deciding to engage the situation in the first place, a decision that may occur in a lower pressure, relatively "cool" context where even exquisitely situation-sensitive creatures such as ourselves may be able to act in accordance with their values. For instance, it may be easier to "do the right thing" over the phone than it would be in the moral "hot zone" of an intimate encounter. Then condemnation for ethical failure might very often be directed, not at a particular failure of the will in action, but at a certain culpable naiveté, or insufficiently careful attention to situations. The implication of this is that our duties may be surprisingly complex, involving not simply obligations to particular actions, but a sort of "cognitive responsibility" to attend, in our deliberations, to the determinative features of situations. If it is true that this cognitive responsibility may frequently be exercised in "cooler" decision contexts, this approach might effect a considerable reliability in ethical behavior.

Unfortunately, I doubt our optimism here should be unbounded. Those with knowledge of the Milgram paradigm, for example, are relatively unlikely to be obedient dupes in highly similar situations, but this knowledge may be difficult to apply in different circumstances. Further, many morally dangerous features of situations will have a degree of subtlety that will make them difficult to unmask, however we try; they may seem as innocuous as not finding change in the coin return, or running a few minutes late for an appointment. In short, we may often be in "Milgram situations" without being so aware – at a seminar, or in a meeting. So my approach cannot offer guarantees. But it can, I submit, focus our ethical attention where it may do the most good: deliberation contexts where reflection on our values may be most likely to make a difference.

The virtue theorist may now object that she and I are simply talking about different things. The examples I have given concern the *description* of herself under which the agent deliberates and acts, while virtue theory concerns the *ideal* the agent deliberates and acts according to. The virtue theorist may grant that a situationist account of personality is often the most effective descriptive psychology for guiding our deliberations, since it will increase our sensitivity to moral risk. But the question remains as to what regulative ideal should guide our conduct, and the virtue theorist might charge that I have said nothing that should cause us to reject the ideal of virtue in this role. There is the possibility, as we have seen Blum suggest (pp. 511–12 above), that the agent is best served by attempting to emulate an exemplar – perhaps looking to such ideals is the most effective way to facilitate ethically desirable conduct. It is crucial to see that this has the look of an empirical claim concerning the ways in which actual persons interact with ideals; whatever the empirical commitments of the background moral psychology, on this approach our choice of normative theories is impacted by empirical considerations regarding the influence of ideals on conduct. At this point we should require some compelling speculation in order to conclude that these considerations favor virtue-theoretic ideals over other sorts of ethical considerations. In what ways are ideals of virtue better suited to facilitating ethically desirable conduct than other ideals (e.g., Kantian, utilitarian), especially if the virtue theorist should agree that the most helpful descriptive psychology might very well be situationist?

Perhaps this depends on how we construe ideals of virtue. The account I have been assuming to date is an *emulation* model, which urges us to approximate the psychology and behavior of the moral exemplar. But there is also the possibility of an *advice* model, where deliberation involves consulting the advice of the ideally virtuous agent. A distinction like this is suggested by Smith (1995: 109–12) as an explication of practical rationality. According to Smith, the desirability of an agent performing an action depends on whether she would perform it were she fully rational. But if the fully rational self is to be emulated by the actual self, there is difficulty.[10] Suppose that my fully rational self would shake his opponent's hand after losing a hard game of squash. But my actual self, in his actual circumstances, will likely beat his opponent about the head in a fit of unsporting rage if he attempts the polite course. However, if he forces a grin and immediately departs the scene, no such calamity will ensue. It is clear, Smith thinks, that this latter course is what my fully rational self would recommend for my actual self, even though my fully rational self would pursue the more sporting course with no mishap. What my fully rational self would deem rational for my actual self is in part determined by the actual condition of my actual self; what my idealized self advises for my actual self is not necessarily what my idealized self would do in my actual self's circumstances.

This model of practical rationality may be applied to virtue theory. The guidance of the ideally virtuous advisor, like the fully rational self, must take into account the circumstances and capacities of actual, less-than-fully-virtuous agents in determining what they should do. In the case of our dangerous dinner invitation, the ideally virtuous advisor must take into account that actual persons, unlike herself, are susceptible to inappropriate sexual temptation. Although she can attend the dinner without risk, an ordinary person cannot; emulation in this case could have disastrous results. Because actual agents typically cannot attain, or closely approximate, the psychology of an ideally virtuous agent, they cannot, in many instances, safely pursue the course the ideal agent would favor for herself. With a little imagination we can see that there may be many such cases – morally dangerous circumstances where the virtuous can tread without fear, but the rest of us cannot. If so, emulation may often prove the wrong approach in particular decision contexts. Instead, what effective deliberation requires is advice based on the best understanding of our situational liabilities, and this understanding will be aided by familiarity with the deliverances of situationism. Then if consultation with the ideally virtuous advisor is to help secure desirable conduct, the ideally virtuous advisor must be a situationist psychologist

– reference to situationism is here practically indispensable.

We may wonder whether an advice model can be genuinely virtue-theoretic, since the distinctive emphasis of virtue theory is very plausibly thought to involve emulation of the virtuous rather than merely consulting their advice regarding particular behaviors. However, it may be that distinctively virtue-theoretic emulation account can incorporate the insights of the advice model. Ethical emulation is not slavish imitation. We needn't follow the moral exemplar in every respect – one needn't be snub-nosed to emulate Socrates. Nor must we engage in emulation on every occasion; it may be that in some instances securing the ethically desirable result requires another approach, such as that suggested by the advice model. This does not suggest that emulation is never appropriate, but only that on a suitably sophisticated account, emulation is selective. We should emulate the exemplar only in ethically significant respects, and only on those occasions when doing so would be conducive to ethically admirable behavior. Perhaps, then, the virtue theorist should favor some combination of the advice and emulation models. This certainly seems reasonable. But notice what sorts of considerations will help us decide when emulation is appropriate. In many cases, reflection on our situational liabilities is required to determine whether the situation at hand is an appropriate occasion for emulation; we should reflect on our own liability to sexual temptation before following the example of Socrates at a dinner party. And again, as I have been urging, situationist research is an invaluable source of information regarding situational liabilities. So if emulation is to be selective, this selectivity requires reference to situationist moral psychology. Then both the emulation and advice models will profit from situationism.

What I take myself to have shown, so far, is that situationist moral psychology may help ground desirable habits of ethical deliberation. Indeed, we have seen that situationist moral psychology may figure prominently even in virtue-based deliberation. I have also shown, by reflecting on Milgram's experiments and an example of my own, that characterological moral thought may have substantial pitfalls, in so far as it may foster a dangerous neglect of situational influences.

Still, there may be situations where characterological reflection, properly understood, is the best approach to ethical deliberation. But this is a claim in need of an argument, especially given the attractions of the situationist approach. [. . .]

If virtues are to be understood as deliberative ideals along the lines we have been considering, the familiar Williams-Stocker speculation concerning alienation does not tell in favor of virtue ethics, because worries about "theoretical mediation"[11] are re introduced on the idealized conception. One attraction of character-based approaches is that they appear to escape worries about what we might call the "creepiness" of theory-driven moral reflection; the decreased spontaneity and authenticity, and increased alienation, that are supposed to afflict "theoretical" approaches to morality (Stocker 1976; Williams 1973: 116, 131; 1985: 54–70). Virtue ethics, if it provides a way of inculcating appropriate dispositions and outlooks, might escape this worry; the properly habituated person behaves as she should, without reference to theory, and so escapes the alienating effects of theoretical mediation. But suppose, again, that we eschew descriptive-psychological accounts of virtues, and instead construe virtue discourse as pointing to ideals that inform the practice of deliberation. Now worries about theoretical mediation may recur, if ethical practice consists in regulating behavior by reference to an ideal of virtue, instead of simply acting from virtuous dispositions. In this scenario, what room is there for helping someone because one hates to see them suffer, or because one has compassionate dispositions? I do not deny that the virtue theorist can answer this question. Indeed, I have no interest in denying that competitors like the Kantian and utilitarian may have their own compelling answers to such charges. The point is that on the conception of virtues as regulative ideals the virtue theorist is as much in need of an argument as her opponents. Theoretical mediation through an ideal of virtue is no less obviously problematic than through an ideal of rationality, duty, or maximizing happiness, and alienation, if it is a genuine difficulty, may plague character-based ideals no less than other ideals.

In closing, let me review the dialectic: Aristotelian virtue ethics, when construed as invoking a generally applicable descriptive psychology, may appear more attractive than competitors such as Kantianism and consequentialism, in that characterological moral psychology might allow a more compelling account of moral development and agency. But understood this way, character-based approaches are subject to damaging empirical criticism. If, on the other hand, virtue theory is reformed as a normative theory concerned with regulative ideals more than empirically-constrained psychology, the empirical critique is disarmed, but virtue theory no longer has the selling point of a compelling descriptive psychology. At this juncture the virtue theorist must offer argument to the effect that her favored regulative ideals (however, exactly, they are to be construed), are better suited to effecting morally desirable conduct than alternatives offered by her competitors. I have argued that characterological ideals are not obviously indispensable in some central areas of normative practice, and also noted some attractions of the situationist alternative. This does not suggest that virtue theory is no longer in the running; but it does suggest that it is not, without further argument, out in front of the pack.[12]

Notes

1 The present version of this paper omits, for reasons of space, some of the references and qualifications found in the original version. A much fuller rendering of the argument gestured at here appeared in Doris (2002). Flanagan (1991) provided the first sustained account of situationism in philosophy; although our conclusions differ, the present discussion is indebted to his.

2 See Flanagan (1991: 283–90). Aristotle (1984: 1144b30–1145a2) apparently maintains a reciprocity thesis: because of their common origin in practical reason, possession of one particular virtue entails possession of all the virtues (for explication of Aristotle's argument, see Irwin 1988: 67–71). Some contemporary followers of Aristotle maintain a unity thesis; McDowell claims that the virtues are not independent capacities, but different manifestations of a "single complex sensitivity" (1979: 333; cf. Murdoch 1970: 57–8).

3 Many observers of the Holocaust have noted the "paradoxical" levels of inconsistency exhibited by genocidal killers; brutality can coexist all too comfortably, it seems, with compassion (Levi 1989: 56; Lifton 1986, e.g., 337; Todorov 1996: 141). The

208

virtuous no less than the vicious exemplify this paradox; in this age of unstinting biography, we repeatedly find that moral heroes as well as moral monsters exhibit gross inconsistencies in moral personality (Flanagan 1991: 6–12).

4 Some of the genocidal Nazi doctors at Auschwitz behaved decently, and even admirably, before the death camp; prior to his appointment at Auschwitz, the war criminal Wirths surreptitiously treated Jews after it had become illegal to do so (Lifton 1986: 386). Note that such "transformation" was not necessarily a function of situational factors that are readily construed as coercive; Lifton (1986: 198) maintains that it was possible for Auschwitz doctors to avoid perpetrating atrocities "without repercussions."

5 For this approach in the ethics literature see Alderman (1982: 134), Beauchamp and Childress (1983: 261–5), Blum (1994: 179), Brandt (1970: 27; 1988: 64), Foot (1978: 9–11), Frankena (1973: 65), Jardine (1995: 36), Rawls (1971: 192), Rorty and Wong (1990: 19n1), and Williams (1985: 8–9, 35). Flanagan (1991: 282) takes the view that "virtues are psychological dispositions *productive* of behavior" to be one of "the basic psychological premises of virtue theory."

6 Predictions by laypersons appear substantially overconfident in this regard. In one study, Kunda and Nisbett (1986: 210–11) found that subjects' estimated probability that an individual they rated as more honest than another in one situation would retain the same ranking in the next observed situation was typically around .8. This probability reflects an estimated correlation of approximately .81, while the relevant empirical study found the correlation to be .23, which translates into a probability of under .6, not highly above chance.

7 See McDowell 1978: 15, 21, 23, 28–9; 1979: 332–3, 343–6; cf. Murdoch 1970: 64–70.

8 This is also suggested by Zimbardo's (1973: 53–6) "prison experiment:" some "guards" in his simulated penitentiary rapidly descended into barbaric behavior despite their initial confidence that they were not the sort of person who would do such things.

9 As Zimbardo (1974: 566) suggested in his comments on Milgram's (1974) book, "the reason we can be so readily manipulated is precisely because we maintain an illusion of personal invulnerability and personal control."

10 The following example is Watson's (1982), put to this use by Smith (1995: 111–2).

11 The phrase is Railton's (1984: 137).

12 Versions of this paper were presented at Carnegie Mellon University; Ohio State University; Southern Methodist University; The University of Michigan, Ann Arbor; The University of Texas, Austin; and The University of California, Santa Cruz. Thanks to all of these audiences for helpful questions. Special thanks to Lawrence Becker, Justin D'Arms, Stephen Darwall, Stephen Everson, Allan Gibbard, David Hills, Nadeem Hussain, Manyul Im, Jim Joyce, Richard Nisbett, Ann Silvio, and Mike Weber.

Alderman, H. 1982. "By Virtue of a Virtue." *Review of Metaphysics* 36.

Aristotle. 1984. *The Complete Works of Aristotle, Oxford Revised Translation.* Edited by J. Barnes. Princeton: Princeton University Press.

Beauchamp, T. L., and Childress, J. F. 1983. *Principles of Biomedical Ethics* (2nd edn.). New York: Oxford University Press.

Blum, L. A. 1994. *Moral Perception and Particularity.* Cambridge: Cambridge University Press.

Brandt, R. B. 1970. "Traits of Character: A Conceptual Analysis." *American Philosophical Quarterly* 7.

Brandt, R. B. 1988. "The Structure of Virtue." *Midwest Studies in Philosophy* 13.

Broadie, S. 1991. *Ethics with Aristotle.* Oxford: Oxford University Press.

Brody, N. 1988. *Personality: In Search of Individuality.* New York: Academic.

Ceci, S. J. 1993. "Teaching for Transfer: The 'Now-You-See-It-Now-You-Don't' Quality of Intelligence in Context." In H. Rosselli (ed.), *The Edyth Bush Symposium on Intelligence.* Orlando, FL: Academic Press.

Ceci, S. J. 1993a. "Contextual Trends in Intellectual Development." *Developmental Review* 13.

Darley, J. M., and Batson, C. D. 1973. "From Jerusalem to Jericho: A Study of Situational and Dispositional Variables In Helping Behavior." *Journal of Personality and Social Psychology* 27.

Dent, N. J. H. 1975. "Virtues and Actions." *The Philosophical Quarterly* 25.

Doris, J. M. 2002. *Lack of Character: Personality and Moral Behavior.* Cambridge: Cambridge University Press.

Flanagan, O. 1991. *Varieties of Moral Personality.* Cambridge, MA.: Harvard University Press.

Foot, P. 1978. *Virtues and Vices.* Berkeley and Los Angeles: University of California Press.

Frankena, W. K. 1973. *Ethics* (2nd edn.). Englewood Cliffs, NJ: Prentice Hall.

Geach, P. T. 1977. *The Virtues.* Cambridge: Cambridge University Press.

Hardie, W. F. R. 1980. *Aristotle's Ethical Theory* (2nd edn.). Oxford: Oxford University Press.

Herman, B. 1996. "Making Room for Character." In S. Engstrom and J. Whiting (eds.), *Aristotle, Kant, and the Stoics: Rethinking Happiness and Duty*. Cambridge: Cambridge University Press.

Hollis, M. 1995. "The Shape of a Life." In J. E. J. Altham and R. Harrison (eds.), *World, Mind, and Ethics: Essays on the Ethical Philosophy of Bernard Williams*. Cambridge: Cambridge University Press.

Irwin, T. H. 1988. "Disunity in the Aristotelian Virtues." *Oxford Studies in Ancient Philosophy: Supplementary Volume*, 1988.

Isen, A. M. and Levin, H. 1972. "Effect of Feeling Good on Helping: Cookies and Kindness." *Journal of Personality and Social Psychology* 21.

Jardine, N. 1995. "Science, Ethics, and Objectivity." In J. E. J. Altham and R. Harrison (eds.), *World, Mind, and Ethics: Essays on the Ethical Philosophy of Bernard Williams*. Cambridge: Cambridge University Press.

Kunda, Z., and Nisbett, R. N. 1986. "The Psychometrics of Everyday Life." *Cognitive Psychology* 18.

Levi, P. 1989. *The Drowned and the Saved*. Translation by R. Rosenthal. New York: Vintage Books.

Levi, P. 1996. *Survival in Auschwitz*. Translation S. Woolf. New York: Touchstone Books. Originally published, 1958.

Lifton, R. J. 1986. *The Nazi Doctors*. New York: Basic Books.

MacIntyre, A. 1984. *After Virtue* (2nd. edn.). Notre Dame: University of Notre Dame Press.

McDowell, J. 1978. "Are Moral Requirements Hypothetical Imperatives?" *Proceedings of the Aristotelian Society Supplementary Volume 52*.

McDowell, J. 1979. "Virtue and Reason." *Monist* 62.

McDowell, J. 1996. "Deliberation and Moral Development in Aristotle's Ethics." In S. Engstrom and J. Whiting (eds.), *Aristotle, Kant, and the Stoics: Rethinking Happiness and Duty*. Cambridge: Cambridge University Press.

Milgram, S. 1974. *Obedience to Authority*. New York: Harper and Row.

Mischel, W. 1968. *Personality and Assessment*. New York: John J. Wiley and Sons.

Murdoch, I. 1970. *The Sovereignty of Good*. London: Routledge and Kegan Paul.

Pervin, L. A. 1994. "A Critical Analysis of Current Trait Theory." *Psychological Inquiry* 5.

Railton, P. 1984. "Alienation, Consequentialism and the Demands of Morality." *Philosophy and Public Affairs* 13.

Rawls, J. 1971. *A Theory of Justice*. Cambridge, MA: Harvard University Press.

Rorty, A. O., and Wong, D. 1990. "Aspects of Identity and Agency." In O. Flanagan and A. O. Rorty (eds.), *Identity, Character and Morality: Essays in Moral Psychology*. Cambridge, MA: MIT Press.

Ross, L., and Nisbett, R. E. 1991. *The Person and the Situation*. Philadelphia: Temple University Press.

Sher, G. 1998. "Ethics, Character, and Action." *Social Philosophy and Policy* 15.

Shoda, Y., Mischel, W., and Wright, J. C. 1994. "Intraindividual Stability in the Organization and Patterning of Behavior: Incorporating Psychological Situations Into the Idiographic Analysis of Personality." *Journal of Personality and Social Psychology* 67.

Smith, M. 1995. "Internal Reasons." *Philosophy and Phenomenological Research* 55.

Stevenson, C. L. 1963. "The Emotive Meaning of Ethical Terms." In C. L. Stevenson, *Facts and Values*. New Haven: Yale University Press. Originally published, 1937.

Stocker, M. 1976. "The Schizophrenia of Modern Moral Theories." *Journal of Philosophy* 73.

Todorov, T. 1996. *Facing the Extreme: Moral Life in the Concentration Camps*. New York: Metropolitan Books.

Watson, G. 1982. "Free Agency." In G. Watson (ed.), *Free Will*. Oxford: Oxford University Press.

Williams, B. A. O. 1973. "A Critique of Utilitarianism." In *Utilitarianism: For and Against*, by J. J. C. Smart and B. A. O. Williams. Cambridge: Cambridge University Press.

Williams, B. A. O. 1985. *Ethics and the Limits of Philosophy*. Cambridge, MA: Harvard University Press.

Wright, J. C., and Mischel, W. 1987. "A Conditional Approach to Dispositional Constructs: The Local Predictability of Social Behavior." *Journal of Personality and Social Psychology* 53.

Zimbardo, P. 1973. "The Mind is a Formidable Jailer: A Pirandellian Prison." *The New York Times Magazine*, April 8, 1973.

Zimbardo, P. 1974. "On 'Obedience to Authority.'" *American Psychologist* 29.

23

Situationism and Virtue Ethics on the Content of Our Character

Rachana Kamtekar

1. Introduction

According to situationist social psychologists, information about people's distinctive character-traits, opinions, attitudes, values, or past behavior is less useful for determining what they will do than is information about their situations. Although we might expect that the possessor of a given character-trait (such as helpfulness) would behave consistently (helpfully) across situations that are similar in calling for the relevant (helping) behavior, under experimental conditions, people's behavior turns out not to be cross-situationally consistent (the correlation between a person's behaving helpfully on one occasion and behaving helpfully on another is hardly above chance). Instead, across a range of situations, an individual's behavior tends to converge on the behavioral norm for those situations. If behavior does not co-vary with character-traits but with situations, then people's situations must explain why different people behave differently. Laypeople, in trying to explain and predict people's behaviors by their characters rather than their situations, routinely commit a "fundamental attribution error".[1]

Some moral philosophers argue that situationism has radical implications for moral philosophy. According to Harman 2000, the psychologists' research calls into question not only folk psychology, but also virtue ethics. For a character-trait is a "relatively stable and long-term disposition to act in distinctive ways," but "[e]mpirical studies designed to test whether people behave differently in ways that might reflect their having different character traits have failed to find relevant differences" (166). Thus, "ordinary attributions of character-traits to people may be deeply misguided, and it may even be the case that there is no such thing as character . . ." (165). And "[i]f there is no such thing as character, then there is no such thing as character building" (177). So moral philosophers ought to abandon character-based virtue ethics (176). Doris's (1998, 2002) less incendiary and perhaps more illuminating view is that the social psychology shows that our dispositions to distinctive behaviors are narrow rather than broad – our behavior is consistent in very similar situations but not across the range of trait-relevant-behavior-eliciting situations – and that these narrow dispositions are not integrated. Doris's conclusions about the implications for moral philosophy, however, are about the same as Harman's: since experimental psychology shows us that the broad dispositions of character-based virtue ethics are not to be had, moral philosophy should turn away from virtue ethics and seek a moral theory and practical ideals that are possible for creatures like us.

This chapter argues that the character-traits conceived of and debunked by situationist social psychological studies have very little to do with character as it is conceived of in classical virtue ethics – that is, by Plato, Aristotle, and the Stoics.[2] Traditional virtue ethics offers a conception of

From Rachana Kamtekar (2004). Situationism and virtue ethics on the content of our character. *Ethics* 114. The University of Chicago, April 2004. Reprinted with permission of The University of Chicago Press.

Moral Psychology: Historical and Contemporary Readings, edited by Thomas Nadelhoffer, Eddy Nahmias, and Shaun Nichols. © 2010 Blackwell Publishing Ltd except for editorial material and organization © 2010 Thomas Nadelhoffer, Eddy Nahmias, and Shaun Nichols.

character far superior to the one under attack by situationism; this chapter clarifies the differences and suggests ways in which social psychology might investigate character on the virtue ethics conception. Briefly, the so-called character-traits that the situationist experiments test for are independently-functioning dispositions to behave in stereotypical ways, dispositions that are isolated from how people reason. By contrast, the conception of character in virtue ethics is holistic and inclusive of how we reason: it is a person's character as a whole (rather than isolated character-traits) that explains her actions, and this character is a more-or-less consistent, more-or-less integrated, set of motivations, including the person's desires, beliefs about the world, and ultimate goals and values. The virtuous character that virtue ethics holds up as an ideal is one in which these motivations are organized so that they do not conflict, but support one another. Such an organization would be an achievement of practical reason, and its behavioral manifestation would be cross-situational consistency (although appreciating this might require insight into the virtuous person's reasons). Traditional virtue ethics explains behavioral inconsistency as a result of the cognitive and motivational obstacles to this achievement of practical reason rather than as the result of the absence of character-traits.

This is not to say that the social psychological findings are irrelevant to virtue ethics, however, for just as empirical social psychology can benefit from considering the superior conception of character in virtue ethics, so too, virtue ethics can benefit from considering the particular situational factors that social psychology identifies as having a profound influence on behavior. For the experiments in the situationist tradition teach us that the obstacles to living and acting virtuously are not only the ones that wear their moral relevance on their sleeve, such as temptation and insensitivity to others' feelings, but also, for example, the difficulty of figuring out when to rely on the social cues that usually stand us in good stead, and when to break away.

2.   The Experiments

My discussion focuses on the four experiments that figure most prominently in situationists' discussions: Milgram (1963, 1974); Darley and Batson (1973), Isen and Levin (1972), and Hartshorne and May (1928). Since previous readings [chapters 20–22 in this volume] describe and give situationist interpretations for three of these, I summarize only Hartshorne and May (1928) and then turn to what the experiments assume about character-traits.

2a.   Cheating, stealing, lying

Over 8,000 schoolchildren aged 8 to 16 were placed in moderately tempting situations where they had opportunities (1) to cheat on tests (by copying from a key, adding more answers after time was called, peeping, and faking a solution to a puzzle), (2) to cheat, on homework, or by faking a record in athletic contests, or by faking, peeping or stealing in party games, (3) to steal money from a box used in a test, (4) to lie, about their conduct in general or about cheating on tests in (1) above. The correlation between behaviors listed within any one of the groups (1)–(4) was quite high – for example, between behaviors in (1) it was .721, but the correlation across behavior-types (1), (2), (3) and (4) was only .227 (Hartshorne and May 1928, 122–5).

Situationists point out that we call a person who cheats on exams "a cheat" or "dishonest," expecting (they claim) that she will also pocket any money she finds and lie. The honesty studies falsify this expectation; instead, they find that people do behave consistently across situations that are very alike: the correlation between cheating on an exam and cheating on another exam is quite high; higher still is the correlation between cheating in a particular way on one cheating occasion (e.g., sneaking a look at the answer key) and doing so again. This kind of consistency at most licenses us to attribute to people "narrow" dispositions or traits such as "cheat on exams," or "answer-key-peep," but our ordinary character-attributions are not so situation-specific: upon discovering that someone has cheated on an exam, we are likely to say that he is a cheat, or dishonest.

3.   What's In and Out of Character on the Situationist Conception

Mischel (1968, 5–6) surveys the various senses in which psychologists speak of a "character-trait": as a "summary label for observed stable

individual differences in behavior"; as "a construct or abstraction to account for enduring
behavioral consistencies and differences"; finally,
as a real existence in a person which determines,
and can be inferred from, distinctive and consistent behavior. Although Harman (2000, 166)
and Doris (2002, 15–18) take this conception of
a character-trait to be the same as Aristotle's, it
is not. To see this, let us turn to situationists'
assumptions about character-traits.

3a.   Character traits are distinctive

In saying that behavior covaries more with
situation than with character, situationists are
not denying that the individual agent (as opposed
to her external environment) determines her
behavior, nor are they minimizing the individual
agent's contribution to her behavior. On the
situationist definition of character, *individuals*
may contribute a great deal to their actions
without their *character*-traits contributing to these
actions; this is because of the stipulation that
character-traits are distinctive (cf. Harman 2000,
175). So the claim that situation rather than character is explanatorily powerful is the claim that
behavior covaries with situational variables rather
than (putative) character variables: variations in
what the situation is, or is taken to be, result
in much greater behavioral *variation* than do
variations in who is responding to the situation;
what each individual contributes to behavior,
even if it is a great deal, is pretty much what any
other individual contributes.

Harman's (2000, 171) rhetorical questions
about Milgram's subjects, "can we really attribute
a 2 to 1 majority response to a character defect?
And what about the fact that *all* subjects were
willing to go at least to the 300-volt level? Does
everyone have this character defect?" tacitly assume
that character-traits must be distinctive. But
traditional virtue ethicists does not, and we ought
not, subscribe to the view that one person's
possession of a character-trait depends on most
other people's non-possession of that trait. If
a character-trait is by definition something that
distinguishes one individual and her behavior
from others and their behavior, then a successful
program of virtue inculcation, such as those
described in the political writings of Plato and
Aristotle, would have the odd consequence of

eliminating those character-traits they set out to
inculcate. A less paradoxical supposition is that
the distinctiveness of a given character-trait is an
empirical matter, dependent on such things as the
education and social pressure to develop that trait
(Milgram 1974 enumerates various such factors
responsible for the prevalence of obedience).

3b.   Character traits are broad-based

The distinctive situationist conclusion from
Hartshorne and May (1928) is that although
people behave consistently across situations that
are very like each other (e.g., cheating on tests
given opportunities to cheat), such narrow dispositions do not count as character-traits and are
difficult to distinguish from strategies developed
in a specific situation and then repeated (cf.
Harman 2000, 175). Character-traits must be
broad-based; that is, they must produce consistent behavior across the range of situations
presupposed by the character-term: the honest
person not only does not cheat on tests, but does
not lie or steal either.

Although we use a single word, "honest," to
describe the behaviors of not lying, not cheating,
and not stealing, it is not obvious what these
three have in common. It may be that underlying
this single word are three distinct and unrelated
dispositions, the first a disposition not to lie,
supported by the thought that respecting others
requires one to tell them the truth; the second a
disposition not to cheat, on the grounds that in
cheating one exploits a system that one should
uphold; the third a disposition not to steal, for
the reason that people should be able to enjoy
secure possession of their property. We should be
open to abandoning folk-psychological character-
traits if they predict cross-situational consistency
where there is no reason to, and to replacing them
in our thinking with dispositions like honesty
with respect to property. Alternatively, if people
are narrowly consistent because they re-use the
strategies they have developed in previous very
similar situations, we might build broader, cross-
situationally consistent, dispositions by extending these strategies to less similar cases. So, for
example, one might stop cheating upon realizing
that it involves a kind of deception of other people
importantly like the deception one objects to in
lying. If this is right, then there may in fact be

some sort of unity to honesty, but discovering this unity, and developing a disposition to honesty in general, may take a fair amount of work. Extending one's non-deceptive response across dissimilar situations may require strong interests in not deceiving, and may pose significant cognitive challenges.

3c. Subjective construal

Ross and Nisbett (1991, 12–13) say that it is not the situation as it is objectively that allows us to predict and explain behavior, but rather the actor's construal of the situation – how he or she interprets the situation. Laypeople, operating with the tools of folk psychology, "consistently fail to make sufficient allowance for the role that construal plays in determining behavior": we don't recognize the degree to which anyone's understanding of any situation is the result of a constructive process; we don't appreciate the variability of subjective construals among persons; finally, when we are surprised by someone's behavior, we tend to conclude that she is different from other ordinary people, rather than that she and we may be construing her situation differently. Factors determining subjective construal seem to include past experiences, goals, abilities, and temperaments (cf. Harman 1999).

These complaints against laypeople may also be levied against situationists' interpretations of the experiments. Supposedly inconsistent behavior may be consistent from the experimental subjects' point of view if, having different information from the experimenter, they construe the situation differently.[3] Sreenivasan 2002, 58 illustrates: "Suppose ... that Homer believes in 'finders keepers' and so does not consider pocketing some stray change to count as *stealing*. Then he will regard pocketing the change as perfectly consistent with his conventionally honest behavior in, say, the cheating situation. For their part, however, Hartshorne and May count *not* taking the change as the 'honest' response in this situation."[4]

Including subjective construal as part of the situation blurs the intuitive sharpness of the distinction between situation and character. One might wonder: if subjective construal is taken to be part of our situation rather than an effect of our character, hasn't the notion of character been so emptied that there is nothing left in character

for behavior to correlate to? Don't we ordinarily suppose character to include patterns of perception and reasoning, values, goals and beliefs – and hence subjective construal? And what is one construing, if one's situation includes how one construes one's situation? Perhaps situationists think that since behavior lacks the distinctiveness and cross-situational consistency we expect from character, and since behavior is determined by subjective construal, subjective construal lacks the distinctiveness and cross-situational consistency of character. Unfortunately, situationists are not at all clear whether subjective construals are or are not distinctive and consistent across situations. For example, Ross and Nisbett (1991, 63) illustrate one kind of subjective construal, the "framing effect," which is the effect on one's judgment of the comparison class one uses in making the judgment by saying, "For example, the vegetable soup you taste now is compared with the vegetable soup you had last week, the minestrone you had last month, the canned vegetable soup you had as a child, and so on." Depending on the comparison class against which every stimulus is judged (memories from the distant past?), construals may turn out to be quite distinctive and cross-situationally consistent.

Traditional virtue ethicists identify people's characters and explain their behaviors in terms of their distinctive ultimate goals. For example, Plato explains that the oligarchic character steals from orphans because of his single-minded pursuit of wealth (*Republic* 554a-55a) – rather than because of some orphan-robbing disposition, or even some general robbing disposition. And because the timocratic character's overarching goal is to win honor, he is like the oligarch in that he hoards his wealth, but unlike him in that he does so in secret (548b). The situationist's difference with the virtue ethicist here may be over the relative contribution to behavior of short vs. long-term goals, or situation-driven vs. value-based goals. Darley and Batson (1973) recorded as the "character variable" the seminarians' religious goals (whether they saw religion as a quest, means, or end) but found no correlation between these goals and the students' stopping to help a person in distress; what determined their stopping to help or not was how much time they thought they had before the lecture they had been told to give. Presumably a situationist would say that the seminarians' immediate goal of giving the requested lecture influenced their actions, but their long-term or ultimate or defining religious goals did not. This would be an interesting result, but because of its failure to investigate subjective construal – that is, how the seminarians saw the relationship between their religious goals and their actions – the experiment fails to establish it. Since Christianity enjoins Christians to do good works whether they value Christianity as an end, as a means to salvation, or as the meaning of life, if a difference in behavior between people with these different religious goals was to be found, it would have to lie in something other than their helping or not. Since the dependent variable was helping or not helping, it looks as if the point of the experiment was to show that even seminarians, to whom Christianity (and hence good works?) is a fundamental value, are governed primarily by how much time they have. But what is the contrast? What percentage of non-seminarians stop to help someone in trouble when they're in a hurry vs. when they're not?

3d. Further features of the situationist conception of character

Another assumption about character-traits comes to light when we examine experiments involving conflicting motivations. For example, Milgram (1963) supposedly reveals that most people do not have robust dispositions to avoid inflicting pain on unwilling and innocent persons. But if most people had walked out of the experiment rather than shock the learner, the study would have revealed that most people do not have robust dispositions to cooperativeness or obedience – whereas surely what is psychologically likely is that people have *both* kinds of dispositions. Again, the seminarians in Darley and Batson (1973) were faced with competing demands for help, from the experimenters and from the person in the doorway: it was in the course of helping the experimenters that they were called upon to help the person in the doorway. Whomever they helped, they would also have been failing to help someone, and so displaying inconsistently helpful behavior.

A person in a situation has to choose one course of action, sometimes among bad alternatives. But although one can ultimately act in only one way in

a situation, one can feel a number of different, even conflicting, ways about that action: one might think little of it, or feel torn, or wholeheartedly endorse it. Subjects' feelings about their actions go unmentioned in situationist conclusions – even though a number of studies record subjects' post-experiment reflections on what they did. Milgram (1974) documents the stress experienced by many of his experimental subjects, suggesting that defiant subjects experienced less stress even before the moment of defiance than did compliant subjects. Attention to actions alone can mask information that might further the understanding of why people act as they do.

In their exclusive attention to behavior, the psychological studies implicitly conceive of a character-trait as something that *will*, if present, manifest itself in characteristic behavior, and will do so no matter what else there is in the situation for the person to respond to – in other words, the character-trait will determine behavior in *isolation* from other character-traits, thoughts, concerns, etc. a person might have in a given situation. Whatever the origins of the character-traits being tested for (our ordinary discourse and practices, personality and social psychology or even virtue ethics), the experiments treat all the traits on the model of aggression: people who possess a given trait are expected, to the extent that they possess the trait, to behave spontaneously and unreflectively in ways that manifest it on every occasion.

This is an unreasonable expectation, and its unreasonableness points out that Darley and Batson (1973) teaches us very little about the helpfulness or lack thereof of the Princeton seminarians, or about the existence or non-existence of helpfulness. For consider: one could not be a very helpful person if one always allowed one's helping activity to be interrupted by new calls for help. Further, imagine someone who is *always* a good Samaritan, where this means helping in every situation where help is needed, and as much as is needed. Middle class adults (such as Darley and Batson's subjects) who have adapted to life in modern societies have to learn to filter out or somehow disregard the needs of others when responding to them would be too costly: the exceptionlessly good Samaritan not only will not make it to her talks on time; she had better give up any thoughts of a life-plan other than helping when needed. (Membership in a monastic order *might* provide the institutional support for a policy of helping whenever needed, but even that is not clear.) Many people to whom it is important to be helpful to those in need formulate policies – e.g., to give generously to established relief organizations but to refuse panhandlers, or to give to the first person who asks one for money each day but none thereafter, or to devote Saturday afternoons, but only Saturday afternoons, to charity work. It is true that some people at some times might adhere to such policies too rigidly, but it looks as though even quite moderate adherents to such policies would be counted inconsistently helpful by the criteria of the experiments, and could be adduced as evidence to support the assertion that the trait of helpfulness does not exist.

Even our lay understanding of character doesn't ordinarily lead us to expect that someone whom we may legitimately call helpful will display actions of the helpful type (whatever that type of action is) on every occasion, and so we wouldn't conclude from one failure to help that a person lacks the character-trait of helpfulness. We should not (and I think do not) expect even a very helpful person to stop to help a person in distress if she thinks that doing so will interfere with her doing something else she considers to be very important; we should only expect that the very helpful person will stop often, and more often than the not-so-helpful person, because she has judged that helping is important. And, as Ross and Nisbett (1991, 111, 116–17) acknowledge, predictions of *relative* likelihood (especially of extreme behaviors) are facilitated by observations of past (especially extreme) behaviors – in other words, although knowing how someone has behaved in the past doesn't allow us to predict accurately whether she will behave in the same way in a particular instance, it does enable us to predict accurately how much *more* likely she is to behave in this way than are other people whose past behavior was different.

Putting the traits that dispose us to act into their proper deliberative context explains why the expectation that a character-trait can operate in isolation is so implausible. Rather than isolating character-variables and testing for their manifestations in behavior, social psychologists need to engage in more painstaking research that takes into account how the considerations experimental subjects will have in mind in a given situation might involve various character-traits and how these might interact. Unlike Harman and Doris, who conclude from the psychologists' empirical findings that we should dispense with character, Ross and Nisbett (1991, 102–3) take it that we need a better conception of character. They advocate an "idiographic" approach, according to which we should only expect individuals to behave consistently with traits which they deem important to have, or in areas in which consistent behavior matters to them – rather than expecting them to have every trait to some extent. (One reason someone might cheat on tests but not steal money might be that she doesn't have much respect for tests but does care that people or institutions be secure in the possession of their property; we should expect this person not to steal, but we should not expect her to avoid cheating on tests.) Further, in determining which behaviors are relevant to consistency with a trait, we should be guided by the individuals themselves (a person might cheat on tests even if she cares to be honest across the board because she doesn't think how she behaves on tests has anything to do with being honest – she might think tests reward the educationally privileged, reinforce pernicious assumptions about innate differences in ability, etc.). Once we have identified the particular traits and behaviors relevant to particular individuals, we may test for consistency correlations between traits and behaviors and among behaviors across situations.[5] Far from denying the existence of character or individual differences, Ross and Nisbett's (1991, 20, cf. 162–8) conclusion is that "the key to a more powerful conception of individual differences is to be found in the enduring motivational concerns and cognitive schemes that guide attention, interpretations, and the formulation of goals and plans."

4. Virtue Ethics

The experiments that find character-traits to correlate poorly with behavior rely on a conception of a character-trait as an isolable and non-rational disposition to manifest a given stereotype behavior that differs from the behavior of others and is fairly situation-insensitive; however, social

psychologists who are on the lookout for a better conception of character-traits will find it in
traditional virtue ethics. According to traditional
virtue ethicists, *virtues* are not dispositions to perform stereotype actions popularly associated with
a given trait, but rather dispositions to respond
appropriately – in judgment, feeling, and action
– to one's situation. Such responses require the
active involvement of the agent's powers of reasoning. Below, I give a schematic account of the
traditional virtue ethics conception of character.

Before I turn to virtue ethics, however, a caveat:
situationists see the notion of character and
character-traits as an explanatory construct in
folk science, and criticize it as bad science (cf.
Nisbett and Ross 1980, 3ff). But we use character-
attributions evaluatively as well as well as explanatorily. Alive to this aspect of our character-talk,
Aristotle (2002) observes that we call one and the
same person "ambitious" and "unambitious,"
depending on which term we're using as a term
of praise (*Nicomachean Ethics* 1107b30 ff., cf.
1125b11 ff.) and that we consider meanness the
vice opposed to liberality because meanness is a
greater evil than prodigality and because most
people are naturally prone to meanness rather
than prodigality (1122a14–16). The best way to
understand our character-terms is, in Bernard
Williams' (1985, 129–31, 141–2) expression, as
"thick ethical concepts": notions that are at the
same time descriptive, or world-guided, and prescriptive, or action-guiding. Bearing in mind
the evaluative aspect of character-talk explains
some of what situationists can only see as our mistakes: for example, when we describe the cheat on
tests as a "cheat" rather than as a "cheat on tests,"
we may not (or not only) be overgeneralizing
on the basis of too little evidence, but instead
(or also) focusing attention on what is wrong
with the behavior – the fact that it is cheating
(where the fact that it is on a test is incidental) – so
as to direct the cheat on tests not to cheat again,
whether on a test or in another situation.

4a.   A disposition, with respect to actions and feelings, issuing in decisions

According to Aristotle, a virtue is "a disposition
issuing in decisions, depending on the inter-
mediacy of the kind relative to us, this being
determined by rational prescription and in the

way in which the wise person would determine it"
(1106b36–1107a2). A virtuous disposition is a
disposition to act and feel in particular ways in
response to rational considerations; it is expressed
in our decisions, which are determined through
rational deliberation (1104b3–13, 1105b20–
1106a13, 1106b18, cf. 25, 35 ff., 1112a18–1113a14,
1151b34–1152a4). The object of a decision is some
concrete action that will bring about some end
that the agent has, or some good according to the
agent's conception of the good. Because Aristotelian
vices are also dispositions issuing in decisions, we
should understand them, too, as dispositions of
our rational and appetitive faculties. Aristotle
does not treat virtues and vices as necessitating
particular kinds of behavior, but rather as inclin-
ing us to behave as we do. So, for example, the
prodigal tends to give away more than he has, and
to borrow so that he can keep spending, but this
is not a behavior beyond his control; indeed, in
conditions of poverty he can turn himself around
(1119b30–1121b15). Further, Aristotle does not
treat such dispositions as by themselves explanatory of behavior: the explanation of the prodigal's
behavior will ultimately refer to his beliefs about
what the good life is, and how to achieve it.

Aristotle insists that it is not possible to
have virtue without practical wisdom, which is
the disposition to deliberate well about what
conduces to the good life in general (1140a25 ff.,
1144b2–1145a5). He has many reasons for this
view: the intermediate, at which virtue arrives, is
in each case determined by right reason (1138b20;
1103b32; 1144b20–30); decision involves deliberation, and so an agent's decision will be good
only if her reasoning is true and her desire right
(1139a21 ff.). But the deepest reason is that virtue,
as a disposition to act and feel in response to
reasons, is an excellence of a rational creature,
something that puts its possessor and user in a good
condition (1106a15–25). We are interested in
virtue as something good for us, because we want
what is good for us. And so we are interested in a
condition that guides us well, not simply one that
disposes us to perform certain sorts of actions.
The condition that interests us will have to be
intelligent, if it is to guide us in all the different
situations life presents us. So it will have to
include practical wisdom.

The centrality of practical wisdom to virtuous
character leads Aristotle to distinguish between

virtue, properly speaking, and what he calls "natural virtue." Natural virtue is a disposition to be moved in a certain way, but without practical wisdom: even animals and children can have natural virtue, such as the passion that drives wild animals to face a danger when they are distressed or hungry. But animals and children do not face danger for the sake of the noble. Aristotle compares possessors of natural virtue to blind people with heavy or powerful bodies – they may always be able to move in a certain way, but since their movement is not guided by sight, they may also in some cases come crashing down. Similarly, natural virtue without practical wisdom can be harmful for its possessor because it is not directed at the right objects. So, Aristotle says, he agrees with Socrates in believing that the virtues require knowledge (1144b5–22, cf. 1116b24–1117a1).

On this picture, the virtues (properly speaking) cannot be dispositions merely to face danger, or to give aid to others, or to resist temptations, because what Aristotle and his audience are interested in are dispositions to do these things with the right goal in mind, in relation to the right objects, in the right manner, and so on. So practical wisdom will be a condition that by its presence makes the natural virtues genuine virtues (1145a1–2). Aristotle individuates the virtues by enumerating the various domains in our lives which call for practical wisdom: in relation to dangers (courage), in relation to temptations (moderation), in relation to wealth, generosity (or on a larger scale, magnificence), in relation to honor, due pride (or magnanimity), and so on. But although the virtues of friendliness, truthfulness, wittiness, justice, are all virtues in the domain of our relations to other people, their individuation is more fine-grained, according to different types of relationships and social situations. Aristotle's practice here suggests flexibility in the individuation of the particular virtues – a flexibility allowed him because he conceives of virtue as one condition guided by practical wisdom. It seems open, then, to an Aristotelian to admit as new domains for practical attention those features of situations that social psychology identifies as particularly consequential for action: for example, in the domain of group effects, there might be a virtue of taking appropriate account of the judgments of others.

An examination of Aristotle's account of the early stages of virtue-acquisition suggests how this global condition, practical wisdom, might enter into a person's character. According to Aristotle, we begin to acquire the virtues of character by a process of habituation (1103a17). Under the guidance of someone else, we repeatedly perform certain actions and thereby come to have the corresponding virtue or vice: we become just by doing just actions, unjust by doing unjust actions, and so on (1103b20–25, 1105a16–1106a13). But this should not be understood as a process of conditioning in which a malleable soul is impressed by models of just any act-type, leading her to perform acts of that type: one consequence of Aristotle's assumption that we desire our own good is that not just any repeated action will stamp itself on the soul; rather, if it is to engage our motivation, we must see the action as good for us. Aristotelian habituation involves the discovery of (some of) the intrinsic value of virtuous actions in doing them; this is why Aristotle says that the virtuous person takes pleasure in acting virtuously. So, for example, the experience of facing danger for the sake of a noble cause allows the agent to appreciate the value of acting courageously and so to take pleasure in acting courageously. Aristotle says that habituation provides a starting point for knowledge (1098b4); as Burnyeat (1980) sums up the view, Aristotle's point is that "practice has cognitive powers, in that it is the way we learn what is noble or just" (73). It is in a soul that has come to see the pleasantness of virtuous actions that practical wisdom takes hold, illuminating the reasons why these actions are noble and virtuous, and enhancing the agent's capacity to discern what is the virtuous action in novel situations and hard cases.

The social psychological observation that our stable traits tend to be narrow may be explained by this account of how virtue is acquired by practice and then completed by practical wisdom. By performing actions of a certain type, I can see some of what is of value in so acting, in that situation. I develop narrow dispositions easily. But what I need is the ability to respond correctly in situations for which my narrow traits are inadequate: they may give me no guidance, or conflicting guidance, or just the wrong guidance. And for this, I need to reflect on what makes the responses guided by my narrow traits appropriate

for the situations in which I found them appropriate, and how similarities and differences in new
circumstances will bear on the appropriateness
of acting similarly or differently. Presumably I
need to engage in this kind of reflection in both
real-life and imagined situations, and with a view
to consistently responding well. (It is a further
question whether there is anything for reflection
to discover, and if so, whether what it discovers is
only what cultures regard as appropriate.)

4b. Consistency

Situationist reports of our cross-situational
inconsistency purport to be paradoxical; moral
philosophers suggest that among the orthodoxies
swept away by situationism is virtue ethics. So it is
striking how frequently traditional virtue ethicists
complain that most of us are unstable and inconsistent. Plato, for example, says that non-virtuous
people are "never alike, not even to themselves.
They are impulsive and unstable . . ." (Plato, 1997,
Lysis 214d); the person who lacks the virtue of
justice is "not of one mind" (*Republic* 352a) but
"shifts back and forth" (*Gorgias* 481e). Similarly,
the Stoic Epictetus chides his audience, "you
are frequently bewildered and disturbed by your
external impressions, and overcome by their
persuasive character; and at one moment you
consider these things good, and then again you
consider them, though the very same, evil, and
later on as neither good nor evil; and, in a word,
you are subject to pain, fear, envy, turmoil, and
change . . ." (*Discourses* 2.22.6, cf. 25)

   Yet virtue ethicists do not deny that non-
virtuous people have characters, indeed, some of
them engage in classifying vicious people into various character-types. Plato describes four defective
characters corresponding to the four defective
constitutions: the timocrat, oligarch, democrat,
and tyrant (*Republic* 544d-579d). In *Characters*,
Aristotle's student Theophrastus sketches various
vicious character-types according to the formula,
"The X is the sort of person who x1, x2, x3" where
x1, x2, x3 are stereotype actions that an X sort
of person does. These two thoughts – that the
majority of us, who lack virtue, are unstable and
inconsistent, and that we nevertheless fall into
various character types – are squared by the
idea that most people's characters are produced
and sustained by their societies, through such

mechanisms as familial and peer pressure
(cf. *Republic* 549c–550b), which usually involve
conflicting ideals, so that most people lack consistent guides to behavior (thus Plato's ideal society
would strictly monitor its stories about gods
and heroes.) Guaranteeing that the behavior of
ordinary people (who lack philosophical wisdom)
consistently conforms to virtue requires manipulating their situations – not only the environment
in which people are brought up, but also the
situations in which they are called upon to act as
adults. But such consistency and conformity to
virtue is fragile: Plato points out that those of
us who are not firmly enough anchored in our
opinions about virtue may lose these opinions
as a result of dialectical arguments we cannot
respond to (535 ff.).

   So in the absence of wisdom our characters are
dispositions to behave reliably in those situations
for which our upbringing has prepared us; our
characters are limited in stability and consistency
and in their ability to guide us; our judgments
are swayed by appearances and irrelevant effects
of context and perspective (cf. *Protagoras* 356ce).
Overcoming the inconsistency of our appear-
ance-led judgments requires ethical knowledge.
Knowledge can stabilize our characters and make
our judgments and actions consistent because we
want to live well, virtue enables us to live well, and
knowledge enables us to identify and do things
that are conducive to virtue and living well.
What this knowledge consists in varies among the
different formulations of traditional virtue ethics:
Plato characterizes it variously as a science by
which to measure pleasure and pain, as knowledge of how to use assets like health and wealth
correctly, as a grasp of standards approximated by
things in the world, as an account of the reason
why. For the Stoics, it is the knowledge that only
virtue is good and only vice evil, and that of the
"indifferent" remainder, such-and-such are to be
pursued as according to nature, others avoided
as contrary to it. For Aristotle, the knowledge is
a discriminative ability to judge where the right
response lies in each particular case.

   I am not suggesting that traditional virtue
ethicists were the first situationists except for
their higher hopes for ethical knowledge. The
inconsistency they diagnose (rather than observe)
is specifically inconsistency in a person's evaluations or judgments of what is good or bad, right

or wrong, to-be-done or not-to-be-done. And the consistency they recommend is consistency across one's evaluations, and across the whole of one's life – rather than on a single trait-dimension. Indeed, some inconsistency on a single trait-dimension would seem to be necessary for consistency in doing well in a practically rational creature. If one has found that helping one's close associates brings benefits (praise, returns in kind, and so on) whereas helping strangers brings high costs (overwhelming responsibilities, fear, uncertainty as to what to do next, reproof from one's family or friends), surely it is rational to be wary of helping strangers (cf. Mischel 1973, 258–9: a child who is rewarded for cuddly behavior by his preschool teacher but punished for the same behavior by his peers will and should be cuddly with his preschool teacher but not his peers; absolute behavioral consistency would be maladaptive).

It may be objected that the experiments find people inconsistent in situations where behavioral consistency would not be maladaptive, or particularly difficult: it is easy to see, and the virtuous person would surely see, that one should defy the experimenter rather than continuing to shock an experimental subject, or that one should assist someone who is in distress rather than make it on time to give a talk. I do not doubt that the virtuous person would see her way to the right course of action, but the experiments show that it is *not* easy to see what one should do in these situations. Perhaps there were only a few virtuous persons among the subjects of these experiments, but if virtue requires practical wisdom, it stands to reason that virtuous persons would be rare. That we can easily say what is the thing to do upon hearing or reading a description of the experimental situation testifies to the difference between observer and participant construals of the situations and to observer insensitivity to factors to which participants are oversensitive. One conclusion to draw from situationist research may be that we should not confuse our conviction that some behavior is correct with the virtuous person's reasoned judgment that that behavior is correct: these judgments might converge, but the reasoning behind them may be very different.

The difference between the situationist concern with behavioral consistency and the virtue ethics concern with consistent success raises the

question: relative to what standard of consistency ought people to be judged consistent or not? If one's purpose is to evaluate folk psychology, then it is reasonable to take ordinary people's expectations as the standard. But if one's purpose is to evaluate virtue ethics, then the standard will have to be different, and to take account of the fact that we are thinking, goal-oriented creatures. It is possible to ask people not only what they consider to be behavior relevant to or consistent with the trait under examination, but also what they hope to accomplish by their action, what they think are the constraints under which they are acting, and what the relevant options are. No doubt this will not be the whole story because there are things about what we do that are unavailable to us, but that is no reason for ignoring what is available.

4c. Traits and virtues

The role of practical wisdom in the Aristotelian conception of virtue suggests some important differences between many of the character-traits social psychology tests for (e.g., honesty, rigidity, avoidance, conditionability, dependency, and aggression) and the traditional virtues (wisdom or prudence, courage, moderation, justice, piety and their derivatives.) While one *might* think that how aggressive, helpful, friendly, or honest one is has little or nothing to do with how one reasons, traditional virtue ethics assumes that because we want to live well, and because the virtues enable us to live well, the virtues must enable one to make the right judgments about what to value and do and so must involve reasoning. The relationship between being virtuous and living well is also why traditional virtue ethics claims that the virtues require one another, and why virtue ethics is willing to revise ordinary conceptions of what behavior flows from a given virtue. For virtue to enable one to live well, the intellectual component of a virtue must be both relatively unrestricted and situation-sensitive; that would be what enables the virtuous person to get it right in a range of circumstances.

5. Strategies

If consistency of character requires ethical knowledge, and such knowledge is very demanding, how fruitful is it for people like us to attempt character-building? Later Stoic philosophers, in particular, are very concerned with how we can make progress towards consistency. For example, Marcus Aurelius urges, "Wipe out your external impression. Stay the movement of the puppet-strings" (7.29). One strategy is the adoption of a personal role-model as one's ideal. Epictetus suggests in his manual, "When you are about to meet somebody, in particular when it is one of those men who are held in very high esteem, propose to yourself the question, 'What would Socrates or Zeno have done under these circumstances?' and you will not be at a loss to make proper use of the occasion" (33.12–13). Critics who complain that this is useless advice because Socrates or Zeno wouldn't be in these circumstances or because if one could figure out what Socrates or Zeno would do, then one wouldn't need to think of their response at all, are missing the point. Socrates and Zeno also find themselves in difficult situations (in love with Alcibiades, shipwrecked), and thinking of Socrates or Zeno or whoever else can put one in mind of possibilities for action that wouldn't otherwise have occurred to one.

Another strategy is to imagine yourself in situations that will test your commitment to your values – imagine losing your child, or finding out you are about to die – and think of how you want to respond.[6] This kind of vivid imagining would be hard work – it is not mere daydreaming about heroism, but thinking in detail through all of the possible features of our situation, and all of the consequences of particular responses to these features. This should prepare us for situations we may encounter so that if they come to pass we will not find as many surprises as we would if we had never thought through them. Yet another strategy is to analyze what is happening to you into what is "given" and what is your contribution. When one faces a conflict, one can accomplish this by thinking through one's various possible responses to the situation and their consequences. (If I stop to help this person, I might end up losing the day, or longer, dealing with him. On the other hand, I might just be late for and be disqualified from the experiment, in which case I'd lose $1.50 and wouldn't be part of the data. Also, the experimenters might be annoyed with me. If I don't stop, he might die. Or maybe someone else, with

more time to spare, will find him – is anyone else likely to come by?)

It may seem that the kinds of ethical deliberation recommended here involve too much theoretical mediation and lead to alienation from the sorts of motives or reasons for action one would want a virtuous or decent and healthy person to have.[7] The recommendations indeed require alienation, but this much alienation is necessary to avoid complacency, crowd-following, accepting the constraints on one's action generated by others' expectations of one and other such social cues, and in general inappropriately unreflective behavior. Further, the recommended strategies are not recommended for situations in which one's default dispositions are just fine (where engaging in the strategies might cost one valuable time, for example), but rather, for situations in which one feels conflicted, or unsure as to what one should do (as did Milgram's and Darley and Batson's subjects). Finally, an agent might have recourse to these kinds of deliberation as a check on the choices motivated by her default dispositions – rather than her action being motivated by the thought, "I want to be like the Good Samaritan, and helping this person get up is what the Good Samaritan would have done, so I'll do it" (which does seem self-absorbed), she would be acting on a disposition to help people in trouble when she can, and then checking, against her ideal conception of virtue: is this what the Good Samaritan would have done, or would he have done something else?' There seems nothing objectionably alienated about this.

The Stoics say that the goal of life is living consistently. Consistency in all areas of one's life may be psychologically easier to achieve than being consistent in just one area. For it takes into account the feedbacks to behavior that do and don't support consistency, and makes use of the feedbacks that do support it. For example, suppose resolve not to be wasteful. It will be hard for me to achieve this on the strength of will-power alone, especially if everything else (such as the social and financial costs, my sense of self-worth) is pitted against my will. My resolve can be strengthened by reflection on how my non-wasteful behavior supports my ideals for myself (I want to be environmentally responsible), how it supports consequences I value (my son is less likely to be wasteful if he doesn't see me being wasteful), and so on. I will be more likely not to waste if I can see not wasting as consistent with and supportive of other things that I value, rather than on the strength of my resolve alone. And to do this I will need to think about not only what consistent non-wastefulness demands, but also about how not wasting fits in with the other things I think I should be doing (like protecting my son from the scorn of his peers, and so allowing him new clothes instead of endlessly patching his old ones, even if buying new clothes is a bit more wasteful). I will also have to think about what impediments I face towards behaving non-wastefully (such as the opinions of others who think nothing of being wasteful) in particular, and behaving well in general.

In giving such practical suggestions, the Stoics are not displaying their notorious hubris; they are responding to a practical question, one even the most convinced situationist surely faces: what can I do so that I'm not just pulled by the puppet-strings? It is perhaps not the job of social psychologists to answer this question, but it is the job of moral philosophers to notice that there is this question, and that it is not answered by recommending social policies to change situations (which the social psychologists admit is dangerous). Nor is it answered by the recommendation that we avoid situations that will tempt us to behave in ways we do not want to.[8] How can I avoid situations in which I'm in a hurry and come across someone needing help? Or situations in which I might be able to obtain something I want by lying or cheating or stealing? Or situations in which I have to choose whether to do as some higher-up tells me or follow my own sense of right and wrong? As individual agents, we can't just rig our situations or wait for our situations to be changed, we have to act in and upon the situations we find ourselves in. It may turn out that some of the ancient strategies are unworkable, but the ancients provide, at the very least, a rich resource of strategies to be considered.

A second point: from the agent perspective, the social psychologists' own studies suggest that the character-traits we believe we have exert an influence on our behavior (although it is unclear how much contrary pressure such beliefs would allow us to withstand). Nisbett and Ross cite a study in which children who were told they were neat and concerned about keeping their environment clean cleaned up after themselves and others far more and for far longer than children who were merely encouraged to clean up, or children who were told nothing. Similarly, children who were told they were good or hardworking at mathematics improved in mathematics to a greater extent and for a longer time than did children who were told that they should be good at mathematics or should try harder at mathematics.[9] It is not easy to say why attributions would have this effect: perhaps attributions affect our self-conceptions, which we try to live in accordance with; or perhaps attributions lead us to feel that others expect certain sorts of behavior from us and so to behave as expected. Whatever the exact mechanism(s), this study does not simply testify to the power of the situation (on the grounds that the attribution is situational); for the attributions obviously "stuck" and were internalized by the children. If attributions can have a profound influence on behavior, perhaps self-attributions can as well. We have good reason to suppose self-attributions can affect behavior, because self-attributions need not simply be self-descriptions; they are often also resolutions.[10]

An intelligent practical response to the situationist findings is to identify the factors in one's environment that support the behavior one wants and then to see to the preservation of these factors. One instance of this among ancient virtue ethicists is their emphasis on how much our friends and associates influence what we are willing to do and urge us to attend to whom we associate with (e.g. Plato, Gorgias, 481c–82c, 510a–e). But the ancients do think that the result of following their recommendations is a character that can be counted on even when the sustaining situational contribution is gone (e.g., when one's peer group isn't looking – although perhaps not forever, because a character can be destroyed.) Studies as old as Sherif (1937) documenting the internalization of group norms support the thought that attitudes formed in the context of one peer-group can withstand pressures from other peer-groups and other changes in situation (although the question is of course, how much).

Perhaps, if situationism is true, then the answer to the practical question "what can I do to take charge of my situation?" is "nothing" – the features of situations that determine behavior are so subtle and surprising that no ordinary rational strategies could enable us to be masters of our situations. But such pessimism is premature, and if it were ever to become warranted, then it is not only virtue ethics and the notion of character that we would have to jettison, but the power of practical reasoning.

Notes

1   See Ross and Nisbett, 1991, ch. 21 of this volume.
2   This is noted by Kupperman 2001 and Sreenivasan 2002, but neither spells out the virtue ethics conception of character in detail.
3   These points are noted in Mischel 1973, 268, and Mischel 1990, 118–20.
4   Sreenivasan's methodological point is right, but to their credit, Hartshorne and May explicitly consider the issue whether their tests measure what they claim to measure, and one of their methods for ascertaining this was to ask the children how they understood what they had done. So, for example, they asked the students who had had an opportunity to cheat "whether or not they used the answer sheets wrongly or got help at home and whether they regarded this as cheating." Of the 2,141 answers they document, 91% answered the question, and 88% of these said that copying from answer keys was cheating. They are sure that 44% of the 2,141 did copy from answer keys, and of these, 89% answered the question and 82% of them said that copying from answer keys was cheating (1928, 139).
5   See Bem and Allen 1974. Mischel and Peake 1982 describe a study of conscientiousness on 63 Carleton College students, using 19 behavioral measures supplied by the students and recording the students' own assessment of their conscientiousness. They found that the students who described themselves as consistently conscientious were more consistently conscientious on what they saw as prototypic behaviors for conscientiousness than were students who described themselves as variably conscientious. Across situations (prototypic and nonprototypic), however, there was no difference between the consistency of those who described themselves as consistently conscientious and those who described themselves as variably conscientious.
6   Marcus 1930, 2.11, 2.5, 2.2, 7.69, cf. Epictetus, *Manual* sec. 21, Seneca *Letters* 93, 6, 101, 7. Marcus also recommends concentrating on the present moment: 7.54, 8.36, 12.1, 3.10.1; separating oneself from what others say: 12.3.1; taking an objective view, namely, realizing that all things change and dissolve: 3.11, 6.13, 10.11, 10.18.

7   For a perspicuous framing of the problem, including an acknowledgement of the proper place of alienation in moral life, see Railton 1984.
8   Doris 1998, 516–17, 2002, 147–8.
9   Miller, Brickman, and Bolen 1975; the neatness study is discussed in Ross and Nisbett 1991, 228–30.
10 On self-attributions as resolutions, see Kupperman 2001, 248.

References

Aristotle 2002. *Nicomachean Ethics*. Tr. C. Rowe and S. Broadie. Oxford: Oxford University Press.

Bem, D. and Allen, A. 1974. "On Predicting Some of the People Some of the Time: The Search for Cross-situational Consistencies in Behavior." *Psychological Review*, 81, pp. 506–20.

Burnyeat, M.F. 1980. "Aristotle on learning to be good" in A. Rorty (ed.) *Essays on Aristotle's Ethics*. Berkeley: University of California Press.

Darley, J.M. and Batson, C.D. 1973. ' "From Jerusalem to Jericho": A Study of Situational and Dispositional Variables in Helping Behavior,' *Journal of Personality and Social Psychology*, 27: 1, pp. 100–8.

Doris, J. 1998. "Persons, Situations, and Virtue Ethics," *Nous* 32, pp. 504–30.

Doris, J. 2002. *Lack of Character: Personality and Moral Behavior*. Cambridge: Cambridge University Press.

Epictetus, *The Discourses as Reported by Arrian, the Manual, and Fragments*, Discourse (trans. W.A. Oldfather, Cambridge: Harvard University Press, 1952–6).

Harman, G. 1999. "Virtue Ethics Without Character Traits." http://www.princeton.edu/~harman/Papers/Thomson.html

Harman, G. 2000. "Moral Philosophy Meets Social Psychology: Virtue Ethics and the Fundamental Attribution Error," in *Explaining Value and Other Essays in Moral Philosophy*. Oxford: Oxford University Press, pp. 165–78.

Hartshorne, H. and May, M.A. 1928. *Studies in the Nature of Character*, vol 1: *The Nature of Deceit*. New York: Macmillan.

Isen, A.M. and Levin, P.F. 1972. "Effect of Feeling Good on Helping: Cookies and Kindness," *Journal of Personality and Social Psychology*, 21: 3, pp. 384–8.

Kupperman, J. 2001, "The Indispensability of Character," *Philosophy*, 76, pp. 239–50.

Marcus Aurelius. 1930. *Meditations*. trans. C.R. Haines. Cambridge: Harvard University Press.

Milgram, S. 1963. "Behavioral Study of Obedience," *Journal of Abnormal and Social Psychology*, 67, pp. 371–8.

Milgram, S. 1974. *Obedience to Authority*. New York: Harper and Row.

Miller, R.L., Brickman, P., and Bolen, D. 1975. "Attribution versus persuasion as a means for modifying behavior," *Journal of Personality and Social Psychology*, 31, pp. 430–41.

Mischel, W. 1968. *Personality and Assessment*. New York: Wiley.

Mischel, W. 1973. "Toward a cognitive social learning reconceptualization of personality," *Psychological Review*, 80: 4.

Mischel, W. and Peake, P.K. 1982. "Beyond Déjà vu in the Search for Cross-situational Consistency". *Psychological Review*, 89: 6, pp. 730–55.

Mischel, W. 1990. "Personality dispositions revisited and revised," in L.A. Pervin (ed.), *Handbook of Personality*. New York: Guilford Press.

Nisbett, R.E. and Ross, L. 1980. *Human Inference: Strategies and Shortcomings of Social Judgment*. Englewood Cliffs: Prentice-Hall.

Plato. 1997. *Complete Works*. ed. J.M.C. Cooper and D. Hutchinson. Indianapolis: Hackett.

Railton, P. 1984. "Alienation, Consequentialism and the Demands of Morality," *Philosophy and Public Affairs*, 13: 2, pp. 134–71.

Ross, L. and Nisbett, R.E. 1991. *The Person and the Situation*, Philadelphia: Temple University Press.

Seneca 1925–34. *Letters to Lucillus*. tr. Richard M. Gummere, Cambridge: Harvard University Press.

Sherif, M. 1937. "An Experimental Approach to the Study of Attitudes," *Sociometry*, 1, pp. 90–8.

Sreenivasan, G. 2002. "Errors about Errors: Virtue Theory and Trait Attribution," *Mind*, 111, pp. 47–68.

Theophrastus, 1960. *Characters* ed. R.G. Ussher, New York: Macmillan.

Williams, B.A.O. 1985. *Ethics and the Limits of Philosophy*. Cambridge, MA: Harvard University Press.

24

Virtue Ethics and Situationist Personality Psychology

Maria Merritt

The Problem

A deflationary view of personal traits is now widely accepted in the field of social psychology. Following standard practice, I call this deflationary view situationism. Situationism challenges the belief that the behavioral consistencies we encounter in others and ourselves are accurately explained by the attribution of robust personal traits, such as friendliness, aggressiveness, generosity, and honesty.

To conceive of a personal disposition as a robust trait is to expect that it will reliably give rise to the relevant kind of behavior, across the full range of situations in which the behavior would be appropriate, including situations that exert contrary pressures.[1] For example, to attribute to someone a robust trait of generosity is to expect him to give freely of his attention and resources, when doing so is an action reasonably available to him and will do someone else significant good in proportion to what it costs him.

The expectation is that relatively arbitrary factors, such as whether the 'generous' person is in a good mood, whether he is in a hurry, or whether anyone else is around, will have minimal impact on his appropriate performance of generous actions. But in the results of experimental studies, generous behavior is most consistently correlated with precisely such ethically arbitrary situational factors.[2] The general thesis of situationism is that in reality, personal dispositions are highly situation-specific, with the consequence that we are in error to interpret behavioral consistencies in terms of robust traits. The preponderance of evidence drawn from systematic experimental observation, situationists say, supports the conclusion that individual behavior varies with situational variation in ways that familiar concepts of robust traits fail dismally to register.[3]

Moral philosophers have recently taken an interest in situationism because it seems to present a challenge to virtue ethics.[4] Virtue ethics employs ideals of ethically admirable personal dispositions, the virtues, in the principled articulation of normative standards concerning the conduct of life.[5] The experimental findings cited in support of situationism confront us with empirical claims that seem to undermine our beliefs about the role of personal dispositions in governing individual conduct, thereby undermining too our beliefs about the psychological nature of the virtues.

Let's assume for the sake of argument that situationist descriptive psychology is correct. Now what implications does it have for philosophical virtue ethics? That depends. We must have in hand a clear account of the distinctive philosophical commitments of 'virtue ethics' before we can assess situationism's impact on it. But in fact there

From Maria Merritt (2000). Virtue ethics and situationist personality psychology. *Ethical Theory and Moral Practice* 3. Kluwer Academic Publishers, Netherlands, 2000. (excerpt from pp. 365–7, 369–83).

Moral Psychology: Historical and Contemporary Readings, edited by Thomas Nadelhoffer, Eddy Nahmias, and Shaun Nichols. © 2010 Blackwell Publishing Ltd except for editorial material and organization © 2010 Thomas Nadelhoffer, Eddy Nahmias, and Shaun Nichols.

is no single, uncontroversial conception of what virtue ethics is and what resources it purports to offer us. On the contrary, there are multiple conceptions of virtue ethics, each with its own sense of how ideals of virtue should contribute to ethical reflection and practice.

[. . .]

What Is Virtue Ethics For?

As I understand virtue ethics, the form of its principal normative claim is this: the life that offers the surest chance of being, from the point of view of the person who lives it, a very good life, is the life of having the virtues [. . .]

If we think of virtue ethics as taking the form of a theory, how one should live is what it can most powerfully be a theory about.[6] This is the context of reflection in which I think virtue ethics still has the most to offer us today. And this is the arena in which its capacity to accommodate situationist descriptive psychology is most importantly tested.

[. . .]

Let's now assume that the primary and most interesting problem addressed by virtue ethics *is* the problem of how one should live. Then a necessary (though not sufficient) condition for the viability of a particular theory in virtue ethics is that, if a person adopts it, it tends to enhance his or her ability to live the life that the theory itself characterizes as a good life. At the very least, it should certainly not hinder the person's ability to do so. When it comes to the question of how well a particular theory in virtue ethics can accommodate situationist personality psychology, then, here is what we have to ask. Can a practically interested, fairly reflective person do all the following at once: (1) undertake to follow in practice the theory's recommendation to have the virtues, where that includes taking to heart its normative ideal of the recommended qualities; (2) accept a descriptive moral psychology that seems, in light of the evidence, to be closest to the truth; and (3) succeed in living as one should live by the lights of the theory? So far as situationist psychology causes difficulty for any particular version of virtue ethics, it will be through presenting obstacles to meeting this test. In the next section, I explain how such obstacles might arise.

Situationist Psychology and the Recommendation to Have the Virtues

[. . .]

Our everyday expectations of behavioral consistency, even if they are based on erroneous attributions of robust personal traits, often turn out to be successful in practice. The larger goal of situationist psychology is to reconcile the results of systematic observation with this experience. The claim is that ordinary behavioral consistency, which looks to us for all the world as though it is produced by robust traits, has quite other sources, whose effects on individual behavior mimic the expected manifestation of robust traits.

The basic principle of this situationist 'error theory' is that for the typical case in which we are inclined to explain behavioral consistency by attributing a robust personal trait to someone, a better explanation is available. The better explanation works by identifying a certain kind of situational factor on the one hand, and on the other hand a highly situation-specific disposition on the part of the person, such that when she encounters situational factors of that kind, she will tend to act consistently with respect to the relevant situation-specific disposition. Such interactions between situational factors and highly situation-specific personal dispositions, according to the situationist, account for the better part of all the behavioral consistencies we ever witness. We normally witness episodes of behavior in a quite restricted range of circumstances, in which common situational regularities recur over and over again. According to the error theory, then, it is not any robust personal trait that accounts for the consistencies we usually observe, but rather the repetition of certain situational regularities, in combination with relevant situation-specific dispositions of the persons whom we normally encounter in those situations.[7]

This opens the door to a new understanding of how our dispositions to make ethically good choices hold up (when they do) under many circumstances, not just how they appear to break down under some circumstances. In my view the most significant challenge to virtue ethics from the quarter of situationism arises from such alternative explanations of ordinary behavioral consistency. This is because they implicate not only consistency in behavior from one occasion to the next, but the very possession over time of dispositions to make ethically good choices.

Here's how. First, some of the situation-specific dispositions that seem to do the most explanatory work in accounting for behavioral consistency are directed most immediately toward the particular social relationships and settings that hold importance in a person's life. Second, these sorts of dispositions are remarkably subject to alteration and modification, depending on the social expectations that are most palpably in force for a person over a given period of time. For instance, a particular relationship or setting may decline in importance in a person's life, to the point where the situation-specific dispositions supported by his participation in it cease to be active or even cease to exist. Or in the opposite case, increased importance of a particular relationship or setting in a person's life could bring into being, or strengthen, related situation-specific dispositions. I call this the *sustaining social contribution* to character.

What threatens to cause difficulty for philosophical virtue ethics is reflective acknowledgment of the sustaining social contribution. The alternative model of personality portrays dispositions to make ethically admirable choices as being, for each person, elements in a highly individualized profile of situation-specific personal dispositions, which are potentially alterable with changes in important social relationships and settings. To be sure, this model does not rule out the possibility that some ethically admirable dispositions in some individuals are in fact firmly resistant to alteration. It can still make sense to speak of some people as rock-solid with respect to, say, physical courage or fidelity to trust, or any other specific virtue, when compelling evidence is everywhere at hand in the way they have led their lives. But the challenging conclusion to be drawn from the alternative model is that dispositions to make ethically admirable choices are for the most part socially sustained in most people – even in most of us who understand ourselves as caring seriously and consistently about ethical considerations. Once we admit into reflective self-awareness a conception of such dispositions as socially sustained, we must reckon with the understanding of our own ethical character as dependent, in an ongoing way and in maturity (not just during early development), upon our involvements in social life.

It then makes a difference whether avoiding such dependence is something we care deeply about. Some normative ideals of virtue encourage

more serious concern about this than others. Philosophical conceptions of virtue vary with respect to the strength of what I call their ideals of *motivational self-sufficiency of character* (MSC for short). The strength of such an ideal is a matter of the degree to which it calls for the possession of the motivational structure of virtue to be, in maturity and under normal circumstances, independent of factors outside oneself, such as particular social relationships and settings. Acknowledging a sustaining social contribution to ethical character has damaging consequences for, at most, conceptions of virtue that include a very strong ideal of MSC. What situationist psychology makes problematic is not as such the recommendation to have the virtues, but the normative ideal of the virtues as qualities that must be possessed in a strongly self-sufficient form.

The Advantage of Humean Virtue Ethics over Aristotelean Virtue Ethics

Now we are in a position to see more clearly just how situationist psychology presents a problem for virtue ethics in the Aristotelean tradition. [. . .]

The ethical philosophy of Aristotle's *Nicomachean Ethics* advances a very strong ideal of MSC. Aristotle requires that genuine virtues be firmly secured in one's own individual constitution, in such a way that one's reliability in making good practical choices depends as little as possible on contingent external factors.[8] So anyone who wants to follow Aristotle's recommendation to have the virtues should take to heart the requirement that the acts of the truly virtuous person must "proceed from a firm and unchangeable character" (1105a). Now let's assume for the sake of argument that situationist personality psychology is closest to the truth. Then, I want to argue, if you accept this as a descriptive moral psychology while at the same time taking to heart the Aristotelean normative ideal of virtue, you will encounter serious psychological strains in your attempt to live the life of the Aristotelean virtuous person.

Let me emphasize that as I see this problem, it is not simply that is hard to live up to an extremely demanding standard. To point out that an ethical ideal is extremely demanding is not by itself a very powerful objection to the ideal. The problem is rather that once you accept a situationist descriptive psychology, this generates an *internal* tension within the effort to adopt Aristotelean virtue ethics in practice. When an awareness of the likely role of the sustaining social contribution is added to a very strong ideal of MSC, the effect is to remove even the mature agent, at least in imaginative self-understanding, to a starting-point quite a long way back from the goal. Even if you appear to yourself and others to be a good virtuous agent, it becomes an open question whether your disposition to make virtuous choices is 'firm and unchangeable,' as the Aristotelean ideal of character requires. The aspiration to realize a strong ideal of MSC would then tend to make you extremely vigilant against the possible dependence of your good character upon contingent social factors. But such vigilance would tend to be counterproductive for purposes of otherwise living the life of the Aristotelean ideal: the life of directing practical attention primarily toward the real goods and evils to which the virtuous person should be sensitive.

[. . .]

Now, if you were anxious to realize a very strong ideal of MSC, it looks as though there are in principle some things you could try to do about it. You could try to figure out how the specific social relationships and settings that are important to you might be what support you in responding appropriately to various ethical considerations. You could then try somehow to substitute your own self-sufficient resources for those supportive contributions. But because the sustaining social contribution involves, cumulatively, the most important aspects of your life as a social being, it would be at best counterproductive and at worst hardly sane to seek motivational independence from all, or even most, of its many particular instances.[9]

[. . .]

An undertaking more sensible than the attempt to make your character as independent as possible of all particular social settings or relationships, would be the exercise of care in your choice of them, and so far as possible in how you allow yourself to be affected by them.[10] That is at least doable to some extent, and worth trying to do, because some particular social influences may be discernibly more effective and reliable than others at supporting your ethically admirable dispositions.

By contrast with Aristotelean virtue ethics, it is possible to recommend having and acting from the virtues, but at the same time to invoke a normative conception of them that remains uncommitted to any strong ideal of MSC. This is close to David Hume's position in the *Treatise of Human Nature*, as I read him. What is important for Hume's purposes is that one's possession of the virtues, which he characterizes as socially or personally beneficial qualities of mind, should be relatively stable over time somehow or other, not that it should be stable through taking a special, self-sufficiently sustained psychological form. A Humean approach leaves us plenty of room to say that if an otherwise admirable structure of motivation were stable in a person only because it was in large part socially sustained, it would be no less a genuine virtue for that. In this case the aspiration to have the virtues is not put under strain by reflective acknowledgment of the sustaining social contribution to character.

How is it that Aristotelean virtue ethics values MSC – motivational self-sufficiency of character – so highly, and Humean virtue ethics does not? We can account for this difference between the two in terms of their fundamentally different perspectives on the value of the virtues.

In the Aristotelean perspective, having the virtues is the way to be fully capable of getting it right, throughout one's life, about what is truly worthwhile among objects of choice. The value of the virtues is in their securing this enduring capability for their possessor. An essential constituent of each specific virtue is a conviction about the comparative worth of the type of good the virtue is concerned with. This is not just any sort of strongly felt conviction, but a conviction understood by the possessor of virtue to be true or correct and held for the right reasons, reasons that she is able to understand and affirm for herself. Moreover they are reasons such that to succeed in grasping them is to be unsusceptible to forgetting them or losing sight of them, except under conditions of global psychological debilitation, or perhaps other kinds of extreme misfortune that strike at the deepest roots of psychological well-being. So far as a person's stability in holding the relevant convictions is subject to more ordinarily contingent factors of social life, she falls short of the level of rational self-possession required for genuine virtue in the Aristotelean perspective.

The Humean perspective is centered on the recognition of elementary human problems and goods, with respect to which personal reliability in various kinds of conduct produces welcome effects: hence the value of the virtues.[11] From this point of view, seeking to live well involves comparatively modest aspirations: at minimum, to belong to a society where conventions of cooperation allow us to live more peacefully and prosperously than we could in their absence; beyond this, to cultivate the fruits of advanced social organization and the enjoyments of private life. An acquaintance with history, and with conditions prevailing in much of the world even today, reminds us that these aspirations are not so modest in the practical sense of being easy to fulfill. But they are anyway ethically modest in that they do not require a sage-like perfection of personal character. They are also philosophically modest. The Humean conception of how to live carries no commitment to defend a positive account of what ends are of genuine worth in life, and what priorities we should establish for ourselves among these ends. It focuses on avoiding human disaster and securing the basic goods of cooperative society.

Accordingly, what the Humean normative ideal of the virtuous person presents us with is the figure of someone with whom it would be reasonable to want to live in every kind of cooperative social relation[12] – as opposed to the Aristotelean figure of someone who has mastered a set of correct, rationally well-founded attitudes governing practical choice. With that ideal of the virtuous person in view, it makes sense to think of Humean normative judgment as primarily sensitive simply to the stability over time of ethically important qualities of mind, however it may come about.

[. . .]

Humean virtue ethics as I have sketched it does invite some critical questions. [. . .] If we decline to be committed to a strong ideal of MSC, are we abandoning something crucial to the idea of an ethically admirable life?

It could be argued that we need the virtues most, precisely when social support fails us. They are called for, and sometimes displayed, under circumstances where most or all the sources of the sustaining social contribution have completely broken down. Think of people who endure years of hostile captivity as prisoners of war or prisoners of conscience, never breaking with their earlier standards of conduct. Someone might reasonably think: that's what it is to be genuinely virtuous. The reasonableness of this characterization of genuine virtue represents a watershed point for Humean virtue ethics. The Humean might take either of two positions.

One position would be to agree that instances like these set the standard of stability for genuine virtue. [. . .]

The other position would be to point to the statistical rarity of individuals who, absent social support, remain capable of that impressive degree of stability, while allowing that despite its rarity and difficulty it stands for something desirable in the possession of virtue. But what it stands for is, simply, the importance of stability, however that may be secured. It would still be counterproductive, for the same kinds of reasons I gave above in discussing the practice of Aristotelean virtue ethics, to aspire to a stability that is at all times totally independent of social support – at least for those of us fortunate enough to spend most of our time in ethically supportive social environments. For us, what it makes most sense to concentrate on is making sure stability of virtue is supported in us somehow or other.

I favor this latter position. The fact that some extreme situations make the highest degree of MSC necessary for stability in virtuous qualities does not, by itself, give us a good reason to resist dependence on social support in the (fortunately non-extreme) greater part of our lives. What we do have good reason to do is to take an active, discriminating interest in the climates of social expectation we inhabit. We must come to grips with psychological reality in understanding and explaining what kinds of things can possibly bring about stability in the possession of virtuous qualities, including stability that approaches or achieves the incontrovertible. It is an expression of bad faith, or wishful thinking, just to hold out a blank ideal of perfect stability without also offering a realistic account of how it could come about. When we do begin to develop such an account, we will find it very rare indeed for virtuous qualities to become so firmly fixed in individual character as to be impervious to climates of social expectation. Then what remains is to pay attention to the ways in which climates of social expectation can engage deeply enough with individual character to produce effects approaching incontrovertible stability: as for instance when they engage with normatively charged emotions like pride, shame, guilt, and the sense of integrity.

Notes

1   In adopting this characterization of robustness I follow Doris (1998) [chapter 22].

2   For instance, see Darley and Batson (1973), and Isen and Levin (1972).

3   The best available interpretative survey of the psychological evidence supporting situationism is Ross and Nisbett (1991) [chapter 21].

4   The work of philosophy that first opened the question of situationism's impact on philosophical virtue ethics is Flanagan (1991).

5   A note on terminology. Roger Crisp, following Julia Driver, has suggested a useful distinction between the terms 'virtue ethics' and 'virtue theory': 'Virtue theory is the area of enquiry concerned with the virtues in general; virtue ethics is narrower and prescriptive, and consists primarily in the advocacy of the virtues.' See Crisp (1996, p. 5) and Driver (1996, p. 111). Someone could, for instance, theorize about the psychological nature of the virtues and so advance positive claims in virtue theory, but at the same time reject the normative principle that having the virtues holds great ethical importance, and so be opposed to virtue ethics. Many authors seem to use the terms 'virtue ethics' and 'virtue theory' more or less interchangeably to mean what Driver and Crisp mean by 'virtue ethics'. I find that the Driver/Crisp distinction adds clarity to discussion of the virtues, and my own usage will be in accordance with it.

6   See Annas (1998).

7   See Bandura (1986), Cantor and Kihlstrom (1987), Mischel and Shoda (1995).

8   For instance, as Aristotle remarks at 1100b in the Nichomachean Ethics,

> [Durability], then, will belong to the happy man [who is also the virtuous man], and he will be happy throughout his life; for always, or by preference to everything else, he will do and contemplate what is excellent, and he will bear the chances of life most nobly and altogether decorously. . . .

9   On a plausible reading of Aristotle himself, this problem would never have come up for his intended listeners, because it is assumed that their good

upbringing and life experiences have already supplied them with something close to virtuous character in a very motivationally self-sufficient form, and they know it. An important difference between us and Aristotle's intended listeners is that we now have to accommodate a descriptive psychology that, applied to ourselves, places us a long way from the enduringly stable character they were supposed to be able to take for granted in their own case.

10   Or in the case of what must be unchosen, such as standing in the relationship of child to a particular parent, you can still make some choices about how much and what kind of importance to give the relationship.

11   Despite its sensitivity to the welcome effects of choices made by possessors of the virtues, Humean virtue ethics is not a form of consequentialism: it involves no attempt to reduce all human goods and problems to the terms of a uniform ethical calculus, and no belief in the ultimate commensurability of values. On this point see Sayre-McCord (1996).

12   "And 'tis a most certain rule, that if there be no relation of life, in which I cou'd not wish to stand to a particular person, his character must so far be allow'd to be perfect. If he be as little wanting to himself as to others, his character is entirely perfect. This is the ultimate test of merit and virtue" (Hume, A Treatise of Human Nature, p. 606).

References

Annas, J., Virtue and Eudaimonism, Social Philosophy and Policy 15(1) (1998), pp. 37–55.

Aristotle, The Nicomachean Ethics, tr. David Ross, revised by J.L. Ackrill and J.O. Urmson. Oxford: Oxford University Press, 1988.

Bandura, A., Social Foundations of Thought and Action: A Social Cognitive Theory. Englewood Cliffs, NJ: Prentice Hall, 1986.

Cantor, N., and Kihlstrom, J.F., Personality and Social Intelligence. Englewood Cliffs, NJ: Prentice Hall. Prentice Hall, 1987.

Crisp, R., Modern Moral Philosophy and the Virtues, in R. Crisp (ed.), How Should One Live? Essays on the Virtues. Oxford: Oxford University Press, 1996, pp. 1–18.

Darley, J.M., and Batson, C.D., From Jerusalem to Jericho: A Study of Situational and Dispositional Variables in Helping Behavior, Journal of Personality and Social Psychology 27(1) (1973), pp. 100–8.

Doris, J.M., Persons, Situations, and Virtue Ethics, Nous 32 (1998), pp. 504–30.

Driver, J., The Virtues and Human Nature, in R. Crisp (ed.) *How Should One Live? Essays on the Virtues.* Oxford: Oxford University Press, 1996, pp. 111–29.

Flanagan, O., *Varieties of Moral Personality: Ethics and Psychological Realism.* Cambridge, Mass.: Harvard University Press, 1991.

Hume, D., in L.A. Selby-Bigge (eds.), *A Treatise of Human Nature, 1739–40*, 2nd edn. revised by P.H. Nidditch. Oxford: Oxford University Press 1978.

Isen, A.M. and Levin, H., Effect of Feeling Good on Helping: Cookies and Kindness, *Journal of Personality and Social Psychology* 21(3) (1972), pp. 384–8.

Mischel, W. and Shoda, Y., A Cognitive-Affective System Theory of Personality: Reconceptualizing the Invariances in Personality and the Role of Situations, *Psychological Review* 102(2) (1995), pp. 246–68.

Ross, L. and Nisbett, R., *The Person and the Situation: perspectives of social psychology.* Philadelphia: Temple University Press, 1991.

Sayre-McCord, G., Hume and the Bauhaus Theory of Ethics, in P.A. French, T.E. Uehling and H.K. Wettstein (eds.), *Midwest Studies in Philosophy*, vol. XX. Notre Dame, Indiana: University of Notre Dame Press, 1996, pp. 280–98.

Part IV
Agency & Responsibility

Introduction

Eddy Nahmias

There are a host of questions in moral psychology about the nature of agency and the conditions required for moral responsibility, such as the nature of intentional action, practical reasoning, deliberation, self-knowledge, weakness of will, and the mind-body relation. The selections here focus on the types of freedom and control required for agents to be morally responsible, whether such agency is conceptually possible, and whether discoveries in psychology and neuroscience explain, or conversely, explain *away*, human freedom and responsibility. As the sciences of the mind tell us more and more about how human beings work, do they thereby suggest that we have less and less free will and responsibility for our actions?

The two central questions of this Part are:

1 How should we understand free will and moral responsibility?
2 What do the empirical facts suggest about whether humans are free and responsible agents?

This Part's readings reflect a long-running controversy about the type of agency required for moral responsibility. One tradition focuses on the cognitive and volitional capacities that allow us to deliberate and reason about what to do, and then to decide and act in accord with that reasoning. On this view, responsible agency requires that we have the various capacities involved in rational self-control. But it does not require that we ultimately control what reasons we have, nor that our acts of will (or intention formation) are uncaused. This view is associated with *compatibilism* in the traditional debates about free will, because the abilities it identifies with free and responsible agency are compatible with the truth of *determinism* (the thesis that, given conditions in the past and the laws of nature, there is only one physically possible future). More generally, this view is consistent with a broadly naturalistic view of human agency according to which all events, including human decisions, are part of the natural causal order governed by the laws of nature. On this view, free will and moral responsibility are possible as long as what we do properly derives from our reasoning and character, even if we are not *ultimately* responsible for our reasons or character and even if we do not initiate new causal chains when we make decisions.

The other tradition is associated with the theory of *agent causation* (one form of *libertarianism* in the traditional free will debates). According to this view, in addition to the capacities for rational self-control, moral responsibility requires that an agent must also be able to initiate new causal chains when she makes decisions, such that she can be ultimately responsible for her actions. Her alternatives for choice are *influenced* by external circumstances and by her own desires and reasons, but ultimately the agent's choice is not entirely determined by these factors. A modern proponent of agent causation, Roderick Chisholm,

Moral Psychology: Historical and Contemporary Readings, edited by Thomas Nadelhoffer, Eddy Nahmias, and Shaun Nichols. © 2010 Blackwell Publishing Ltd except for editorial material and organization © 2010 Thomas Nadelhoffer, Eddy Nahmias, and Shaun Nichols.

puts the basic idea as follows: "If we are responsible, . . . then we have a prerogative which some
would attribute only to God: each of us, when we
act, is a prime mover unmoved. In doing what
we do, we cause certain events to happen, and
nothing – or no one – causes us to cause those
events to happen" (1964: 34). This is an *incompat-
ibilist* theory because agent causation is incompatible with the truth of determinism. Such a view
also seems to suggest that the existence of free
will and responsibility is incompatible with a
naturalistic theory of human agency.

These two competing conceptions of responsible agency will be challenged or supported by
different sorts of evidence from the empirical sciences. Hence, the answer to the second question
above – whether humans are free and responsible
– depends largely on one's answer to the first
question. It is essential, then, to determine which
conception of free and responsible agency is
the correct one. This interesting question gets
answered in different ways by different philosophers, as demonstrated in the chapters in this
Part. Many of them (as well as scientists writing
about these issues) tend to rely in some way
on ordinary intuitions and conceptual usage to
support their position. Recently, "experimental
philosophers" have carried out empirical studies
to try to determine more systematically what people's intuitions and conceptions of free will and
moral responsibility actually are (e.g., Nahmias,
Morris, Nadelhoffer, and Turner 2006; Nichols
and Knobe 2007).

Indeed, **Aristotle** (384–322 BCE), often began
with commonsense cases and ordinary usage to
develop his systematic account of the moral
psychology of agency and responsibility. In the
Nicomachean Ethics, Aristotle distinguishes voluntary from involuntary actions, and also offers
an important intermediary category of "non-
voluntary" actions based on the agent's ignorance
of relevant facts. He then examines choice and
deliberation, connecting these functions of human
psychology to practical reasoning and virtue.
Finally, Aristotle explains the conditions for
moral responsibility. While some have suggested
that Aristotle's account includes an agent-causal
component, most of the focus is on the compatibilist conditions of rational self-control.
Aristotle also emphasizes that we are responsible
for habitual actions that derive from our character

traits (see also the Aristotle selection in Part III).
He suggests that we are responsible for our
choices, assuming we have proper knowledge of
what we are doing, because our choices are caused
by our character traits, and we are responsible for
our character traits because they initially derive
from our choices. Some philosophers, however,
see a problematic circularity here and suggest
that the only way to break out of it is to posit
something like agent causation.

Thomas **Reid** (1710–96) represents one such
proponent of agent causation and incompatibilism about determinism and responsibility.
Reid, along with his compatibilist contemporary
David Hume, played a central role in the Scottish
Enlightenment. Reid was noted for his defense of
"common sense," his view that we are constructed
so that certain truths are evident to us and that the
burden of proof lies with those who challenge
common sense. Reid argues that one of these
commonsense truths is that we have an active
power as agents to initiate causal chains whenever
we make decisions and that this is required to be
responsible and free, to have what he calls "moral
liberty." Reid does not fully explain how agent
causation works, though he suggests that it is
clearly conceivable – indeed, that our experience
of agency makes our agent causal powers more
evident to us than the causal relations we attribute
to events in the external world. Others, however,
have found the idea of agent causation, as well as
the sense of ultimate responsibility it is supposed
to sustain, incoherent – even pernicious. This is
the view of Frederich Nietzsche.

In the two short excerpts here, **Nietzsche**
(1844–1900) presents derisive attacks on a particular conception of free agency and responsibility,
the self-moved mover (or *causa sui*) that he
identifies with philosophers like Reid and with the
Judeo-Christian worldview. Though Nietzsche
appears here to be a skeptic about free will, he may
also be read as a skeptic *only* about what he takes
to be the exaggerated agent-causal view required
to undergird the retributive punishment of the
Judeo-Christian tradition. His scathing attack on
agent-causal freedom is consistent with accepting
the alternative compatibilist view of agency and
with adopting a new sense of personal responsibility. As Nietzsche says, "The 'unfree will' is
mythology: in real life it is only a matter of *strong*
and *weak* will" (BGE 21). A more realistic view of

agency is attainable, while the agent causal view is not. This two-sided view of philosophical discussions of agency is captured by his claim that willing is "*complicated*, something that is a unit only as a word" (BGE 19).[1] Nietzsche's attack on agent causation, as well as his explanation for our illusory experience of conscious will, foreshadows work by twentieth-century psychologists which has provided a novel set of empirical challenges to free will and moral responsibility.

For instance, B.F. **Skinner** (1904–90), a leading figure in behaviorist psychology, maintains that human behavior is caused not by inner mental states or character traits but by environmental stimuli and a person's history of behavioral reinforcement. Understanding human behavior – and manipulating it – is not improved by reference to "autonomous man," an inner originator of uncaused choices, and Skinner suggests we can and should eliminate reference to such inner goal-directed processes in psychology, as we have in physics and biology. Indeed, just as modern physicists and biologists no longer look to the theories of Socrates and Aristotle, Skinner argues that modern psychology must also leave behind these outdated thinkers. Skinner recognizes that his theory challenges our sense of freedom and dignity and that we are strongly motivated to hold onto our view of ourselves as free and unique. However, he claims that a theory of human nature cannot change what we actually are, and he believes that his behaviorist theory will help us improve our world with a "technology of man." (It is useful to compare Skinner's behaviorism to the situationist social psychology represented in Part III and consider whether they may pose similar challenges to freedom and responsibility.)

Skinner's behaviorism was eventually replaced by cognitive psychology, which examines the internal mental processes that interact and mediate the relations between stimuli and behavior. Does this reintroduction of the "inner mind" allow a place for free and responsible agents whose conscious will can influence their bodily actions? Psychologists Daniel **Wegner** and Thalia **Wheatley** suggest that the answer is "no." They argue that our experience of our thoughts or intentions causing our actions is an illusion. Instead, non-conscious processes generate both our actions and our experience of willing those actions. We interpret conscious thoughts as causing action because of three factors: (1) we experience the thoughts as *consistent* with the action, (2) the thought immediately *precedes* the action, and (3) we experience no competing causes of the action (*exclusivity*). Wegner and Wheatley marshal evidence supporting this "theory of apparent mental causation" with experiments showing that the experience of conscious will can be manipulated by varying any of these three factors and with cases where people experience themselves as causing actions they do not in fact control and cases where people experience no control over actions they do in fact cause. Wegner and other psychologists have concluded that such evidence shows that our sense of agency, and indeed free will, is an illusion.

Another interpretation of such evidence is that these cases represent not the rule but the *exception* to the normal cases in which conscious intentions do play a causal role in action. The fact that our experiences of consciously willing our actions *can* be mistaken does not show that they are *always* illusory any more than visual illusions show that our eyes always deceive us. The philosopher Eddy **Nahmias** develops this and other responses to Daniel Wegner's interpretation of the psychological research as demonstrating that conscious will is an illusion. Nahmias offers reasons to think that Wegner's criteria for experiencing conscious will – consistency, priority, and exclusivity – are neither necessary nor sufficient for our experience of agency and authorship of our actions. Nahmias then analyzes two different ways Wegner's conclusion might be interpreted, highlighting the difference between illusory experiences and mistaken theories. First, it might be interpreted as a challenge to a dualistic conception of agency, as suggested by agent causation, but then it would be nothing new (cf. Nietzsche) and it is unclear what the psychological evidence adds to the debate. Rather, this evidence is more clearly relevant to a second interpretation, the testable empirical claim that the neural processes involved in conscious intention formation are not causally relevant to action generation. Nahmias argues that this interpretation is *not* supported by the evidence, especially if we consider the role of conscious planning and deliberation in the formation of (distal) intentions to act at a later time or in the formation of non-conscious habitual patterns of behavior (cf. Aristotle).

These roles for consciousness in agency high-light the compatibilist theory that defines free will in terms of rational planning and self-control. This theory is further developed by psychologist Roy **Baumeister**. He recognizes that psychologists are not in a good position to settle conceptual debates about free will, so he stipulates a meaning that he thinks psychologists *are* in a good position to study, one that he also thinks captures much of what ordinary people associate with free will – namely, the processes involved in rational delib-eration, choice, and self-control. He offers an evolutionary account of these capacities in terms of their role in our complex social interactions. Perhaps Baumeister's most interesting discovery is that these processes associated with free will all appear to draw from a common and limited source of energy. For instance, when people have to concentrate on solving a difficult problem, they are subsequently less able to restrain them-selves from eating. Unlike Skinner and Wegner, Baumeister does not argue that science is dis-covering that free will is an illusion, but his research does suggest that free will may be a limited resource and that exercising it can be hard work. Baumeister also discusses recent research that suggests that when people are told that free will is an illusion, it can make them behave worse, reminding us that what people believe about free will matters.

Philosopher Alfred **Mele** emphasizes the import-ance of conceptual clarity when considering the relevance of scientific research to questions about human agency and responsibility. Mele discusses both the work of Wegner and research by the neuroscientist Benjamin Libet which has also been interpreted as showing that conscious intentions never play a role in producing corresponding actions. Libet's research suggests that non-conscious activity in the brain ("RPs") precede conscious awareness of the intention to move, such that consciousness must occur too late to do any causal work. Mele argues that this research does not tell us whether the RPs are best under-stood as the subjects' decisions or intentions, as Libet suggests, or rather, as urges or causal precursors to conscious decisions. Furthermore, neither Libet's nor Wegner's research general-izes, since they focus on decisions to do things immediately, and say nothing about the role of conscious *distal* intentions to act at a later time. Furthermore, Wegner neglects the possibility that intentional actions may be produced in different ways, so that his cases of actions produced without conscious intentions do not show that conscious intentions never produce actions. Mele also offers several examples of cases where it is highly implausible to think that conscious deci-sions make no difference to behavior. He concludes by comparing the "magical or supernatural" con-ception of free will used by Wegner and other scientists, who suggest that free will is an illusion, with the conception used by Baumeister, which allows that science can fruitfully study the nature of free will.

Questions for Further Study

- How should we understand free will? What powers must humans have to be free and respon-sible agents? Is something like agent causation necessary for freedom and responsibility?
- What evidence about human decision-making and action is relevant to answering questions about whether humans are free and responsible agents?
- Is it possible that humans entirely lack free will and are not truly morally responsible for any of their actions? What philosophical arguments or scientific evidence could demonstrate this seemingly radical conclusion?
- Is it possible that humans have *less* free will – or are less morally responsible for their actions – than they tend to think? What arguments or scientific evidence could demonstrate this?

Note

1 For further complications in Nietzsche's view of free will, see his discussion of the "sovereign individual" in *Geneology of Morals* II, 2.

Suggested Readings

Baer, J., Kaufman, J.C., & Baumeister, R. (eds.) (2008). *Are We Free? Psychology and Free Will.* New York: Oxford University Press.

Bargh, J. and Ferguson, M. (2000). Beyond behaviorism: On the automaticity of higher mental processes. *Psychological Bulletin*, 126, 925–45.

Dennett, D. (1984). *Elbow Room: The Varieties of Free Will Worth Wanting*. Cambridge: MIT Press.

Fischer, J. and Ravizza, M. (1998). *Responsibility and Control: A Theory of Moral Responsibility*. Cambridge: Cambridge University Press.

Frankfurt, H. (1988). *The Importance of What We Care About*. Cambridge: Cambridge University Press.

Kane, R. (1996). *The Significance of Free Will*. New York: Oxford University Press.

Pereboom, D. (2001). *Living Without Free Will*. Cambridge: Cambridge University Press.

Strawson, P. (1962). Freedom and resentment. In G. Watson (ed.) (1982), *Free Will*. New York: Oxford University Press, pp. 59–80.

van Inwagen, P. (1983). *An Essay on Free Will*. Oxford: Oxford University Press.

References

Chisholm, R. (1964). Human freedom and the self. In G. Watson (ed.) (2003), *Free Will*, 2nd edn. New York: Oxford University Press, pp. 26–37.

Nahmias, E., Morris, S., Nadelhoffer, T. and Turner, J. (2006). Is incompatibilism intuitive? *Philosophy and Phenomenological Research*, 73: 28–53.

Nichols, S. and Knobe, J. (2007). Moral responsibility and determinism: The cognitive science of folk intuitions. *Nous*, 41: 663–85.

25

Nicomachean Ethics

Aristotle

Book III

1. Actions voluntary and involuntary

Virtue or excellence is, as we have seen, concerned with emotions and actions. When these are voluntary we receive praise and blame; when involuntary, we are pardoned and sometimes even pitied. Therefore, it is, I dare say, indispensable for a student of virtue to differentiate between voluntary and involuntary actions, and useful also for lawgivers, to help them in meting out honors and punishments.[1]

It is of course generally recognized that actions done under constraint or due to ignorance are involuntary. An act is done under constraint when the initiative or source of motion comes from without. It is the kind of act in which the agent or the person acted upon contributes nothing. For example, a wind might carry a person somewhere he did not want to go, or men may do so who have him in their power. But a problem arises in regard to actions that are done through fear of a greater evil or for some noble purpose, for instance, if a tyrant were to use a man's parents or children as hostages in ordering him to commit a base deed, making their survival or death depend on his compliance or refusal. Are actions of this kind voluntary or involuntary? A similar problem also arises when a cargo is jettisoned in a storm. Considering the action itself, nobody would voluntarily throw away property; but when it is a matter of saving one's own life and that of his fellow passengers, any sensible man would do so. Actions of this kind are, then, of a mixed nature, although they come closer to being voluntary than to being involuntary actions. For they are desirable at the moment of action; and the end for which an action is performed depends on the time at which it is done. Thus the terms "voluntary" and "involuntary" are to be used with reference to the moment of action. In the cases just mentioned, the agent acts voluntarily, because the initiative in moving the parts of the body which act as instruments rests with the agent himself; and where the source of motion is within oneself, it is in one's power to act or not to act. Such actions, then, are voluntary, although in themselves they are perhaps involuntary, since nobody would choose to do any one of them for its own sake.

That actions of this kind are considered as voluntary is also shown by the fact that sometimes people are even praised for doing them, for example, if they endure shameful or painful treatment in return for great and noble objectives. If the opposite is the case, reproach is heaped upon them, for only a worthless man would endure utter disgrace for no good or reasonable purpose. There are some instances in which such actions elicit forgiveness rather than praise, for example, when a man acts improperly under a strain

From Aristotle, *Nicomachean Ethics*, Martin Ostwald (trans.) (Macmillan Publishing, 1962). Pp. 52–68.

greater than human nature can bear and which no one could endure. Yet there are perhaps also acts which no man can possibly be compelled to do, but rather than do them he should accept the most terrible sufferings and death. Thus, the circumstances that compel Alcmaeon in Euripides' play to kill his own mother are patently absurd. In making a choice, it is sometimes hard to decide what advantages and disadvantages should be weighed against one another, and what losses we should endure to gain what we want; but it is even harder to abide by a decision once it is made. For as a rule, what we look forward to is painful and what we are forced to do is base. It is because of this difficulty that praise or blame depends on whether or not a man successfully resists compulsion.

What kind of actions can we say, then, are done under constraint? To state the matter without qualification, are all actions done under constraint of which the cause is external and to which the agent contributes nothing? On the other hand, actions which are in themselves involuntary, yet chosen under given circumstances in return for certain benefits and performed on the initiative of the agent – although such actions are involuntary considered in themselves, they are nonetheless voluntary under the circumstances, and because benefits are expected in return. In fact, they have a greater resemblance to voluntary actions. For actions belong among particulars, and the particular act is here performed voluntarily. But it is not easy to lay down rules how, in making a choice, two alternatives are to be balanced against one another; there are many differences in the case of particulars.

There is a conceivable objection to this definition of "voluntary." Suppose someone were to assert that pleasant and noble acts are performed under constraint because the pleasant and the noble are external to us and have a compelling power. But on this view, all actions would be done under constraint: for every man is motivated by what is pleasant and noble in everything he does. Furthermore, it is painful to act under constraint and involuntarily, but the performance of pleasant and noble acts brings pleasure. Finally, it is absurd to blame external circumstances rather than oneself for falling an easy prey to such attractions, and to hold oneself responsible for noble deeds, while pleasure is held responsible for one's base deeds.

It appears, thus, that an act done under constraint is one in which the initiative or source of motion comes from without, and to which the person compelled contributes nothing.

Turning now to acts due to ignorance, we may say that all of them are non-voluntary, but they are involuntary only when they bring sorrow and regret in their train: a man who has acted due to ignorance and feels no compunction whatsoever for what he has done was not a voluntary agent, since he did not know what he was doing, nor yet was he involuntary, inasmuch as he feels no sorrow. There are, therefore, two distinct types of acts due to ignorance: a man who regrets what he has done is considered an involuntary agent, and a man who does not may be called a non-voluntary agent; for as the two cases are different, it is better to give each its own name.

There also seems to be a difference between actions *due to* ignorance and acting *in* ignorance. A man's action is not considered to be due to ignorance when he is drunk or angry, but due to intoxication and anger, although he does not know what he is doing and is in fact acting in ignorance.

Now every wicked man is in a state of ignorance as to what he ought to do and what he should refrain from doing, and it is due to this kind of error that men become unjust and, in general, immoral. But an act can hardly be called involuntary if the agent is ignorant of what is beneficial. Ignorance in moral choice does not make an act involuntary – it makes it wicked; nor does ignorance of the universal, for that invites reproach; rather, it is ignorance of the particulars which constitute the circumstances and the issues involved in the action. It is on these that pity and pardon depend, for a person who acts in ignorance of a particular circumstance acts involuntarily.

It might, therefore, not be a bad idea to distinguish and enumerate these circumstances. They are: ignorance of (1) who the agent is, (2) what he is doing, (3) what thing or person is affected, and sometimes also (4) the means he is using, e.g., some tool, (5) the result intended by his action, e.g., saving a life, and (6) the manner in which he acts, e.g., gently or violently.

Now no one except a madman would be ignorant of all these factors, nor can he obviously be ignorant of (1) the agent; for how could a man not know his own identity? But a person might be ignorant of (2) what he is doing. For example, he might plead that something slipped out of his mouth, or that he did not know that he was divulging a secret, as Aeschylus said when he was accused of divulging the Mysteries; or again, as a man might do who discharges a catapult, he might allege that it went off accidentally while he only wanted to show it. Moreover, (3) someone might, like Merope, mistake a son for an enemy; or (4) he might mistake a pointed spear for a foil, or a heavy stone for a pumice stone. Again, (5) someone might, in trying to save a man by giving him something to drink, in fact kill him; or, (6) as in sparring, a man might intend merely to touch, and actually strike a blow.

As ignorance is possible with regard to all these factors which constitute an action, a man who acts in ignorance of any one of them is considered as acting involuntarily, especially if he is ignorant of the most important factors. The most important factors are the thing or person affected by the action and the result. An action upon this kind of ignorance is called involuntary, provided that it brings also sorrow and regret in its train.

Since an action is involuntary when it is performed under constraint or through ignorance, a voluntary action would seem to be one in which the initiative lies with the agent who knows the particular circumstances in which the action is performed.

This implies that acts due to passion and appetite are voluntary. For it is perhaps wrong to call involuntary those acts which are due to passion and appetite. For on that assumption we would, in the first place, deny that animals or even children are capable of acting voluntarily. In the second place, do we perform none of the actions that are motivated by appetite and passion voluntarily? Or do we perform noble acts voluntarily and base acts involuntarily? The latter alternative is ridiculous, since the cause in both cases is one and the same. But it is no doubt also absurd to call those things which we ought to desire "involuntary." For in some cases we should be angry and there are some things for which we should have an appetite, as for example, health and learning. Moreover, we think of involuntary actions as painful, while actions that satisfy our appetite are pleasant. And finally, what difference is there, as far as involuntariness is concerned, between a wrong committed after calculation and a wrong

committed in a fit of passion? Both are to be avoided; but the irrational emotions are considered no less a part of human beings than reasoning is, and hence, the actions of a man which spring from passion and appetite are equally a part of him. It would be absurd, then, to count them as involuntary.

2. Choice

After this definition of voluntary and involuntary actions, our next task is to discuss choice. For choice seems to be very closely related to virtue and to be a more reliable criterion for judging character than actions are.

Choice clearly seems to be something voluntary, but it is not the same as voluntariness; voluntariness is a wider term. For even children and animals have a share in the voluntary, but not in choice. Also, we can describe an act done on the spur of the moment as a voluntary act, but not the result of choice.

It seems to be a mistake to identify choice, as some people do, with appetite, passion, wish, or some form of opinion. For choice is not shared by irrational creatures, whereas appetite and passion are. Moreover, the acts of a morally weak person are accompanied by appetite, but not by choice, while a morally strong person acts from choice, but not from appetite. Also, appetite can be opposed to choice, but not appetite to appetite. Again, appetite deals with what is pleasant and painful, while choice deals neither with the pleasant nor with the painful. The resemblance between choice and passion is even slighter. For an act due to passion hardly seems to be based on choice.

Choice is not even the same as wish, although the two seem to be close to one another. For choice does not have the impossible as its object, and if anyone were to assert that he was *choosing* the impossible, he would be considered a fool. But wish can be for the impossible, e.g., immortality. Wish has as its objects also those things which cannot possibly be attained through our own agency. We might, for instance, wish for the victory of a particular actor or a particular athlete. But no one chooses such things, for we choose only what we believe might be attained through our own agency. Furthermore, wish is directed at the end rather than the means, but choice at the means which are conducive to a given end. For example, we *wish* to be healthy and *choose* the things that will give us health. Similarly, we say that we *wish* to be happy and describe this as our wish, but it would not be fitting to say that we *choose* to be happy. In general, choice seems to be concerned with the things that lie within our power.

Again, choice cannot be identified with opinion. For opinion may refer to any matter, the eternal and the impossible no less than things within our power. Also, opinions are characterized by their truth or falsity, not by their moral goodness or badness, as choices are.

Now, perhaps no one identifies choice with opinion in general; but it would not even be correct to identify it with some particular opinion. For our character is determined by our choosing good or evil, not by the opinions we hold. We choose to take or avoid a good or an evil, but we hold opinions as to what a thing is, whom it will benefit, or how: but the decision to take or avoid is by no means an opinion. Also, a choice is praised for being directed to the proper object or for being correctly made, but opinions are praised for being true. Moreover, we make a choice of things which we definitely know to be good, whereas we form opinions about what we do not quite know. Nor does it seem that the same people make the best choices and also hold the best opinions: some hold rather good opinions, but because of a moral depravity they do not make the right choice. Whether opinion precedes or follows choice is immaterial; for we are not concerned with this problem, but only whether choice is to be identified with some some form of opinion.

Since choice, then, is none of the things mentioned, what is it or what kind of thing? As we have said, it clearly seems to be something voluntary, but not everything voluntary is the object of choice. Could it be the result of preceding deliberation? This is probably correct, for choice involves reason and thought. The very name "choice"[2] seems to suggest that it is something "chosen before" other things.

3.   *Deliberation*

To turn to deliberation: do people deliberate about everything? And is everything an object of deliberation? Or are there some things about which one cannot deliberate? Perhaps we ought to say that an object of deliberation is what a sensible man would deliberate about, but not a fool or madman. Now, nobody deliberates about the eternal, such as the order of the universe or the incommensurability of the diagonal and the side of the square. Nor, on the other hand, do we deliberate about things that are in motion if they always occur in the same way, whether by sheer necessity, by nature, or by some other cause: for example, we do not deliberate about solstices and sunrises. Neither do we deliberate about irregular occurrences, such as drought or rain, nor about chance events, such as the discovery of a treasure. We do not even deliberate about anything and everything that concerns man: no Spartan deliberates about what form of government would be best for the Scythians. For none of these things can happen through our agency.

But what we do deliberate about are things that are in our power and can be realized in action; in fact, these are the only things that remain to be considered. For in addition to nature, necessity, and chance, we regard as causal principles intelligence and anything done through human agency. But of course different groups of people deliberate only about what is attainable by their own actions. Also, there can be no deliberation in any science that is exact and self-contained, such as writing the letters of the alphabet: we have no differences of opinion as to how they are to be written. Rather, we deliberate about matters which are done through our own agency, though not always in the same manner, e.g., about questions of medicine or of acquiring wealth. We deliberate more about navigation than about physical training, because navigation is less exact as a discipline. The same principle can also be applied to the other branches of knowledge. But we deliberate more about the arts than about the sciences, since we have more differences of opinion about them. Deliberation, then, operates in matters that hold good as a general rule, but whose outcome is unpredictable, and in cases in which an indeterminate element is involved. When great issues are at stake, we distrust our own abilities as insufficient to decide the matter and call in others to join us in our deliberations.

We deliberate not about ends but about the means to attain ends: no physician deliberates whether he should cure, no orator whether he should be convincing, no statesman whether he should establish law and order, nor does any expert deliberate about the end of his profession. We take the end for granted, and then consider in what manner and by what means it can be realized. If it becomes apparent that there is more than one means by which it can be attained, we look for the easiest and best; if it can be realized by one means only, we consider in what manner it can be realized by that means, and how that means can be achieved in its turn. We continue that process until we come to the first link in the chain of causation, which is the last step in order of discovery. For when a man deliberates, he seems to be seeking something and to be analyzing his problem in the manner described, as he would a geometrical figure: the last step in the analysis is at once the first in constructing the figure. (By the way, it seems that not all investigation is deliberation – mathematical investigation is not – though every deliberation is an investigation.) Moreover, if in the process of investigation we encounter an insurmountable obstacle, for example, if we need money and none can be procured, we abandon our investigation; but if it turns out to be possible, we begin to act. By "possible" I mean those things which can be realized through our own agency: for even what our friends do for us is, in a way, done through our own agency, since the initiative is our own. Sometimes the object of our investigation is to find the instruments we need and sometimes to discover how to use them. The same is true of other matters, too: sometimes we have to find what the means are, and sometimes how they are to be used or through whom they can be acquired. To sum up our conclusions: (1) man is the source of his actions; (2) deliberation is concerned with things attainable by human action; and (3) actions aim at ends other than themselves. For we cannot deliberate about ends but about the means by which ends can be attained. Nor can we deliberate about particular facts, e.g., whether this is a loaf of bread or whether this loaf of bread has been properly baked: such facts are the object of sense perception. And if we continue deliberating each point in turn, we shall have to go on to infinity.

The object of deliberation and the object of choice are identical, except that the object of choice has already been determined, since it has been decided upon on the basis of deliberation.

For every man stops inquiring how he is to act when he has traced the initiative of action back to himself and to the dominant part of himself: it is this part that exercises choice. This may be illustrated by the ancient political systems represented in Homer, where the kings would make a choice and then proclaim it to the people.

Since, then, the object of choice is something within our power which we desire as a result of deliberation, we may define choice as a deliberate desire for things that are within our power: we arrive at a decision on the basis of deliberation, and then let the deliberation guide our desire. So much for an outline of choice, its objects, and the fact that it is concerned with means rather than ends.

[...]

5. Man as responsible agent

Now, since the end is the object of wish, and since the means to the end are the objects of deliberation and choice, it follows that actions concerned with means are based on choice and are voluntary actions. And the activities in which the virtues find their expression deal with means. Consequently, virtue or excellence depends on ourselves, and so does vice. For where it is in our power to act, it is also in our power not to act, and where we can say "no," we can also say "yes." Therefore, if we have the power to act where it is noble to act, we also have the power not to act where not to act is base, and conversely, if we have the power not to act where inaction is noble, we also have the power to act where action is base. But if we have the power to act nobly or basely, and likewise the power not to act, and if such action or inaction constitutes our being good and evil, we must conclude that it depends on us whether we are decent or worthless individuals. The saying, "No one is voluntarily wicked nor involuntarily happy," seems to be partly false and partly true. That no one is involuntarily happy is true, but wickedness is voluntary. If we do not accept that, we must contradict the conclusions at which we have just arrived, and must deny that man is the source and begetter of his actions as a father is of his children. But if our conclusions are accepted, and if we cannot trace back our actions to starting points other than those within ourselves, then all actions in which the initiative lies in ourselves are in our power and are voluntary actions.

These conclusions are corroborated by the judgment of private individuals and by the practice of lawgivers. They chastise and punish evildoers, except those who have acted under constraint or due to some ignorance for which they are not responsible, but honor those who act nobly; their intention seems to be to encourage the latter and to deter the former. Yet nobody encourages us to perform what is not within our power and what is not voluntary: there would be no point in trying to stop by persuasion a man from feeling hot, in pain, or hungry, and so forth, because we will go on feeling these conditions no less for that.

Even ignorance is in itself no protection against punishment if a person is thought to be responsible for his ignorance. For example, the penalty is twice as high if the offender acted in a state of drunkenness, because the initiative is his own: he had the power not to get drunk, and drunkenness was responsible for his ignorance. Moreover, punishment is inflicted for offenses committed in ignorance of such provisions of the law as the offender ought to have known or might easily have known. It is also inflicted in other cases in which ignorance seems to be due to negligence: it was in the offender's power not to be ignorant, it is argued, and he could have made sure had he wanted to.

But, it might be objected, carelessness may be part of a man's character. We counter, however, by asserting that a man is himself responsible for becoming careless, because he lives in a loose and carefree manner; he is likewise responsible for being unjust or self-indulgent, if he keeps on doing mischief or spending his time in drinking and the like. For a given kind of activity produces a corresponding character. This is shown by the way in which people train themselves for any kind of contest or performance: they keep on practicing for it. Thus, only a man who is utterly insensitive can be ignorant of the fact that moral characteristics are formed by actively engaging in particular actions.

Moreover, it is unreasonable to maintain that a man who acts unjustly or self-indulgently does not wish to be unjust or self-indulgent. If a man is not ignorant of what he is doing when he performs acts which will make him unjust, he will of course become unjust voluntarily; nor again, can wishing any more make him stop being unjust and become just than it can make a sick man healthy. Let us assume the case of a man who becomes ill voluntarily through living a dissolute life and disobeying doctors' orders. In the beginning, before he let his health slip away, he could have avoided becoming ill: but once you have thrown a stone and let it go, you can no longer recall it, even though the power to throw it was yours, for the initiative was within you. Similarly, since an unjust or a self-indulgent man initially had the possibilty not to become unjust or self-indulgent, he has acquired these traits voluntarily; but once he has acquired them it is no longer possible for him not to be what he is.

There are some cases in which not only the vices of the soul, but also those of the body are voluntary and are accordingly criticized. Nobody blames a man for being ugly by nature; but we do blame those who become ugly through lack of exercise and through taking no care of their person. The same applies to infirmities and physical handicaps: every one would pity rather than reproach a man who was blind by nature or whose blindness is due to disease or accident, but all would blame him if it were caused by drunkenness or some other form of self-indulgence. In other words, those bodily vices which depend on ourselves are blamed and those which do not are not blamed. This being so, we may conclude that other kinds of vice for which we are blamed also depend upon ourselves.

But someone might argue as follows: "All men seek what appears good to them, but they have no control over how things appear to them; the end appears different to different men." If, we reply, the individual is somehow responsible for his own characteristics, he is similarly responsible for what appears to him to be good. But if he is not so responsible, no one is responsible for his own wrongdoing, but everyone does wrong through ignorance of the proper end, since he believes that his actions will bring him the greatest good. However, the aim we take for the end is not determined by the choice of the individual himself, but by a natural gift of vision, as it were, which enables him to make correct judgments and to choose what is truly good: to be well endowed by nature means to have this natural gift. For to be well and properly provided by nature with the greatest and noblest of gifts, a gift which can be got or learned from no one else, but which is one's possession in the form in which nature has given it: that is the meaning of being well endowed by nature in the full and true sense of the word.

But if this theory is true, how will virtue be any more voluntary than vice? The end has been determined for, and appears to, a good man and a bad man alike by nature or something of that sort; and both will use the end thus determined as the standard for any actions they may undertake. Thus, whether the end that appears to be good to a particular person, whatever it may be, is not simply given to him by nature but is to some extent due to himself; or whether, though the end is given by nature, virtue is voluntary in the sense that a man of high moral standards performs the actions that lead up to the end voluntarily: in either case vice, too, is bound to be no less voluntary than virtue. For, like the good man, the bad man has the requisite ability to perform actions through his own agency, even if not to formulate his own ends. If, then, our assertion is correct, viz., that the virtues are voluntary because we share in some way the responsibility for our own characteristics and because the ends we set up for ourselves are determined by the kind of persons we are, it follows that the vices, too, are voluntary; for the same is true of them.

To sum up: we have described the virtues in general and have given an outline of the genus to which they belong, i.e., that they are means and that they are characteristics. We have stated that they spontaneously tend to produce the same kind of actions as those to which they owe their existence; that they are in our power and voluntary; and that they follow the dictates of right reason. However, our actions and our characteristics are not voluntary in the same sense: we are in control of our actions from beginning to end, insofar as we know the particular circumstances surrounding them. But we control only the beginning of our characteristics: the particular steps in their development are imperceptible, just as they are in the spread of a disease; yet since the power to behave or not to behave in a given way was ours in the first place, our characteristics are voluntary.

Let us resume our discussion of the various virtues: what are they? With what sort of thing do they deal? And how do they operate? The answer to these questions will also tell us how many virtues there are.

Notes

1 There is no clear equivalent in English to express *hekousion* and its opposite *akousion*, which form the theme of this chapter. An agent is described as *hekōn* when he has consented to perform the action which he is performing. This consent may range from mere passive acquiescence to intentional and deliberate conduct. The neuter *hekousion* is used to denote an action so performed. Conversely, an *akōn* is a man who has not given his consent to acting the way he does, regardless of whether he acts unconsciously, inadvertently, or even against his own will, and an *akousion* is an action performed by such a man.

2 *Proairesis*, literally "fore-choice" or "preference".

26

Essays on the Active Powers of Man, Essay IV: Of the Liberty of Moral Agents

Thomas Reid

Chapter I: The Notions of Moral Liberty and Necessity Stated

By the *liberty* of a moral agent, I understand, a power over the determinations of his own will.

If, in any action, he had power to will what he did, or not to will it, in that action he is free. But if, in every voluntary action, the determination of his will be the necessary consequence of something involuntary in the state of his mind, or of something in his external circumstances, he is not free; he has not what I call the liberty of a moral agent, but is subject to necessity.

This liberty supposes the agent to have understanding and will; for the determinations of the will are the sole object about which this power is employed; and there can be no will, without, at least, such a degree of understanding as gives the conception of that which we will.

The liberty of a moral agent implies, not only a conception of what he wills, but some degree of practical judgment or reason.

For, if he has not the judgment to discern one determination to be preferable to another, either in itself, or for some purpose which he intends, what can be the use of a power to determine? His determinations must be made perfectly in the dark, without reason, motive, or end. They ran neither be right nor wrong, wise nor foolish. Whatever the consequences may be, they cannot be imputed to the agent, who had not the capacity of foreseeing them, or of perceiving any reason for acting otherwise than he did.

We may perhaps be able to conceive a being endowed with power over the determinations of his will, without any light in his mind to direct that power to some end. But such power would be given in vain. No exercise of it could be either blamed or approved. As nature gives no power in vain, I see no ground to ascribe a power over the determinations of the will to any being who has no judgment to apply it to the direction of his conduct, no discernment of what he ought or ought not to do.

For that reason, in this essay, I speak only of the liberty of moral agents, who are capable of acting well or ill, wisely or foolishly, and this, for distinction's sake, I shall call *moral liberty*.

What kind, or what degree of liberty belongs to brute animals, or to our own species, before any use of reason, I do not know. We acknowledge that they have not the power of self-government. Such of their actions as may be called *voluntary*, seem to be invariably determined by the passion or appetite, or affection or habit, which is strongest at the time.

This seems to be the law of their constitution, to which they yield, as the inanimate creation does, without any conception of the law, or any intention of obedience.

From Thomas Reid, *Essays on the Active Powers of Man*. Book IV, Chapter 1 and 2. Originally published in 1788.

Moral Psychology: Historical and Contemporary Readings, edited by Thomas Nadelhoffer, Eddy Nahmias, and Shaun Nichols. © 2010 Blackwell Publishing Ltd except for editorial material and organization © 2010 Thomas Nadelhoffer, Eddy Nahmias, and Shaun Nichols.

But of civil or moral government, which are addressed to the rational powers, and require a conception of the law and an intentional obedience, they are, in the judgment of all mankind, incapable. Nor do I see what end could be served by giving them a power over the determinations of their own will, unless to make them intractable by discipline, which we see they are not.

The effect of moral liberty is, that it is in the power of the agent to do well or ill. This power, like every other gift of God, may be abused. The right use of this gift of God is to do well and wisely, as far as his best judgment can direct him, and thereby merit esteem and approbation. The abuse of it is to act contrary to what he knows, or suspects to be his duty and his wisdom, and thereby justly merit disapprobation and blame.

By *necessity*, I understand the want of that moral liberty which I have above defined.

If there can be a better and worse in actions on the system of necessity, let us suppose a man necessarily determined in all cases to will and to do what is best to be done, he would surely be innocent and inculpable. But, as far as I am able to judge, he would not be entitled to the esteem and moral approbation of those who knew and believed this necessity. What was, by an ancient author, said of Cato, might indeed be said of him *He was good because he could not be otherwise.* But this saying, if understood literally and strictly, is not the praise of Cato, but of his constitution, which was no more the work of Cato, than his existence.

On the other hand, if a man be necessarily determined to do ill, this case seems to me to move pity, but not disapprobation. He was ill, because he could not be otherwise. Who can blame him? Necessity has no law.

If he knows that he acted under this necessity, has he not just ground to exculpate himself? The blame, if there be any, is not in him, but in his constitution. If he be charged by his Maker with doing wrong, may he not expostulate with him, and say, why hast thou made me thus? I may be sacrificed at thy pleasure, for the common good, like a man that has the plague, but not for ill desert; for thou knowest that what I am charged with is thy work, and not mine.

Such are my notions of moral liberty and necessity, and of the consequences inseparably connected with both the one and the other.

This moral liberty a man may have, though it do not extend to all his actions, or even to all his voluntary actions. He does many things by instinct, many things by the force of habit without any thought at all. and consequently without will. In the first part of life, he has not the power of self-government any more than the brutes. That power over the determinations of his own will, which belongs to him in ripe years, is limited, as all his powers are; and it is perhaps beyond the reach of his understanding to define its limits with precision. We can only say, in general, that it extends to every action for which he is accountable.

This power is given by his Maker, and at his pleasure whose gift it is, it may be enlarged or diminished, continued or withdrawn. No power in the creature can be independent of the Creator.

Supposing it therefore to be true, that man is a free agent, it may be true, at the same time, that his liberty may be impaired or lost, by disorder of body or mind, as in melancholy, or in madness; it may be impaired or lost by vicious habits; it may, in particular cases, be restrained by divine interposition.

We call man a free agent in the same way as we call him a reasonable agent. In many things he is not guided by reason, but by principles similar to those of the brutes. His reason is weak at best. It is liable to be impaired or lost, by his own fault, or by other means. In like manner, he may be a free agent, though his freedom of action may have many similar limitations.

The liberty I have described has been represented by some philosophers as inconceivable, and as involving an absurdity.

"Liberty," they say, "consists only in a power to act as we will, and it is impossible to conceive in any being a greater liberty than this. Hence it follows, that liberty does not extend to the determinations of the will, but only to the notions consequent to its determination, and depending upon the will. To say that we have power to will such an action, is to say, that we may will it, if we will. This supposes the will to be determined by a prior will; and, for the same reason, that will must be determined by a will prior to it, and so on in an infinite series of wills, which is absurd. To act freely, therefore, can mean nothing more than to act voluntarily; and this is all the liberty that can be conceived in man, or in any being."

This reasoning, first I think, advanced by Hobbes, has been very generally adopted by the defenders of necessity. It is grounded upon a definition of liberty totally different from that which I have given, and therefore does not apply to moral liberty, as above defined.

But it is said that this is the only liberty that is possible, that is conceivable, that does not involve an absurdity.

It is strange indeed! if the word *liberty* has no meaning but this one. I shall mention three, all very common. The objection applies to one of them, but to neither of the other two.

Liberty is sometimes opposed to external force or confinement of the body. Sometimes it is opposed to obligation by law, or by lawful authority. Sometimes it is opposed to necessity.

First, it is opposed to confinement of the body by superior force. So we say a prisoner is set at liberty when his fetters are knocked off, and he is discharged from confinement. This is the liberty defined in the objection; and I grant that this liberty extends not to the will, neither does the confinement, because the will cannot be confined by external force.

Secondly, liberty is opposed to obligation, by law, or lawful authority. This liberty is a right to act one way or another, in things which the law has neither commanded nor forbidden; and this liberty is meant when we speak of a man's natural liberty, his civil liberty, his Christian liberty. It is evident that this liberty, as well as the obligation opposed to it, extends to the will: for it is the will to obey that makes obedience; the will to transgress that makes a transgression of the law. Without will there can be neither obedience nor transgression. Law supposes a power to obey or to transgress; it does not take away this power, but proposes the motives of duty and of interest, leaving the power to yield to them, or to take the consequence of transgression.

Thirdly, liberty is opposed to necessity, and in this sense it extends to the determinations of the will only, and not to what is consequent to the will.

In every voluntary action, the determination of the will is the first part of the action, upon which alone the moral estimation of it depends. It has been made a question among philosophers, whether, in every instance, this determination be the necessary consequence of the constitution of the person, and the circumstances in which he is placed; or whether he had not power, in many cases, to determine this way or that?

This has, by some, been called the *philosophical* notion of liberty and necessity; but it is by no means peculiar to philosophers. The lowest of the vulgar have, in all ages, been prone to have recourse to this necessity, to exculpate themselves or their friends in what they do wrong, though, in the general tenor of their conduct, they act upon the contrary principle.

Whether this notion of moral liberty be conceivable or not, every man must judge for himself. To me there appears no difficulty in conceiving it. I consider the determination of the will as an effect. This effect must have a cause which had power to produce it; and the cause must be either the person himself, whose will it is, or some other being, the first is as easily conceived as the last. If the person was the cause of that determination of his own will, he was free in that action, and it is justly imputed to him, whether it be good or bad. But, if another being was the cause of this determination, either by producing it immediately, or by means and instruments under his direction, then the determination is the act and deed of that being, and is solely imputable to him.

But it is said, "That nothing is in our power but what depends upon the will, and therefore the will itself cannot be in our power."

I answer, that this is a fallacy arising from taking a common saying in a sense which it never was intended to convey, and in a sense contrary to what it necessarily implies.

In common life, when men speak of what is, or is not, in a man's power, they attend only to the external and visible effects, which only can be perceived, and which only can affect them. Of these, it is true, that nothing is in a man's power, but what depends upon his will, and this is all that is meant by this common saying.

But this is so far from excluding his will from being in his power, that it necessarily implies it. For to say that what depends upon the will is in a "man's power," but the will is not in his power, is to say that the end is in his power, but the means necessary to that end are not in his power, which is a contradiction.

In many propositions which we express universally, there is an exception necessarily implied, and therefore always understood. Thus when we say that all things depend upon God, God himself is necessarily excepted. In like manner, when we say, that all that is in our power depends upon the will, the will itself is necessarily excepted; for if the will be not, nothing else can be in our power. Every effect must be in the power of its cause. The determination of the will is an effect, and therefore must be in the power of its cause, whether that cause be the agent himself, or some other being.

From what has been said in this chapter, I hope the notion of moral liberty will be distinctly understood, and that it appears that this notion is neither inconceivable, nor involves any absurdity or contradiction.

Chapter II: Of the Words Cause and Effect, Action and Active Power

The writings upon liberty and necessity have been much darkened by the ambiguity of the words used in reasoning upon that subject. The words *cause* and *effect*, *action* and *active power*, *liberty* and *necessity*, are related to each other: the meaning of one determines the meaning of the rest. When we attempt to define them, we can only do it by synonymous words which need definition as much. There is a strict sense in which those words must be used, if we speak and reason clearly about moral liberty; but to keep to this strict sense is difficult, because, in all languages, they have, by custom, got a great latitude of signification.

As we cannot reason about moral liberty, without using those ambiguous words, it is proper to point out, as distinctly as possible, their proper and original meaning, in which they ought to be understood in treating of this subject, and to show from what causes they have become so ambiguous in all languages, as to darken and embarrass our reasonings upon it.

Everything that begins to exist, must have a cause of its existence, which had power to give it existence. And every thing that undergoes any change, must have some cause of that change.

That neither existence, nor any mode of existence, can begin without an efficient cause, is a principle that appears very early in the mind of man; and it is so universal, and so firmly rooted in human nature, that the most determined skepticism cannot eradicate it.

It is upon this principle that we ground the rational belief of a Deity. But that is not the only use to which we apply it. Every man's conduct is governed by it every day, and almost every hour of his life. And if it were possible for any man to root out this principle from his mind, he must give up everything that is called common prudence and be fit only to be confined as insane.

From this principle it follows, that every thing which undergoes any change, must either be the efficient cause of that change in itself or it must be changed by some other being.

In the *first* case it is said to have *active power*, and to *act*, in producing that change. In the *second* case it is merely *passive*, or is *acted upon* and the active power is in that being only which produces the change.

The name of a *cause* and of an *agent*, is properly given to that being only, which by its active power, produces some change in itself, or in some other being. The change, whether it be of thought, of will, or of motion, is the *effect*. Active power, therefore, is a quality in the cause, which enables it to produce the effect. And the exertion of that active power in producing the effect, is called *action, agency, efficiency*.

In order to the production of any effect, there must be in the cause, not only power, but the exertion of that power: for power that is not exerted produces no effect.

All that is necessary to the production of any effect, is power in an efficient cause to produce the effect, and the exertion of that power: for it is a contradiction to say, that the cause has power to produce the effect, and exerts that power, and yet the effect is not produced. The effect cannot be in his power unless all the means necessary to its production be in his power.

It is no less a contradiction to say, that a cause has power to produce a certain effect, but that he cannot exert that power: for power which cannot be exerted is no power, and is a contradiction in terms.

To prevent mistake, it is proper to observe, that a being may have a power at one time which it has not at another. It may commonly have a power, which, at a particular time, it has not. Thus, a man may commonly have power to walk or to run; but he has not this power when asleep, or when he is confined by superior force. In common language, he may be said to have a power which he cannot then exert. But this popular expression means only that he commonly has this power, and will have it when the cause is removed which at present deprives him of it: for, when we speak strictly and philosophically, it is a contradiction to say that he has this power, at that moment when he is deprived of it.

These, I think, are necessary consequences from the principle first mentioned, that every change which happens in nature must have an efficient cause which had power to produce it.

Another principle, which appears very early in the mind of man, is, that we are efficient causes in our deliberate and voluntary actions.

We are conscious of making an exertion, sometimes with difficulty, in order to produce certain effects. An exertion made deliberately and voluntarily, in order to produce an effect, implies a conviction that the effect is in our power. No man can deliberately attempt what he does not believe to be in his power. The language of all mankind, and their ordinary conduct in life, demonstrate, that they have a conviction of some active power in themselves to produce certain motions in their own and in other bodies, and to regulate and direct their own thoughts. This conviction we have so early in life, that we have no remembrance when, or in what way we acquired it.

[. . .]

It is very probable, that the very conception or idea of active power, and efficient causes, is derived from our voluntary exertions in producing effects; and that, if we were not conscious of such exertions, we should have no conception at all of a cause, or of active power, and consequently no conviction of the necessity of a cause of every change which we observe in nature.

It is certain that we can conceive no kind of active power but what is similar or analogous to that which we attribute to ourselves; that is, a power which is exerted by will and with understanding. Our notion, even of Almighty power, is derived from the notion of human power, by removing from the former those imperfections and limitations to which the latter is subjected.

It may be difficult to explain the origin of our conceptions and belief concerning efficient causes and active power. The common theory, that all our ideas are ideas of sensation or reflection, and that all our belief is a perception of the agreement or the disagreement of those ideas, appears to be repugnant, both to the idea of an efficient cause, and to the belief of its necessity.

An attachment to that theory has led some philosophers to deny that we have any conception of an efficient cause, or of active power, because efficiency and active power are not ideas, either of sensation or reflection. They maintain, therefore, that a cause is only something prior to the effect, and constantly conjoined with it. This is Mr. Hume's notion of a cause, and seems to be adopted by Dr. Priestly, who says, "That a cause cannot be defined to be any thing, but *such previous circumstances as are constantly followed by a certain effect*, the constancy of the result making us conclude, that there must be a *sufficient reason*, in the nature of the things, why it should be produced in those circumstances."

But theory ought to stoop to fact, and not fact to theory. Every man who understands the language knows, that neither priority, nor constant conjunction, nor both taken together, imply efficiency.

The very dispute, whether we have the conception of an efficient cause, shows that we have. For though men may dispute about things which have no existence, they cannot dispute about things of which *they* have no conception.

What has been said in this chapter is intended to show, that the conception of causes, of action, and of active power, in the strict and proper sense of these words, is found in the minds of all men very early, even in the dawn of their rational life. It is therefore probable, that, in all languages, the words by which these conceptions were expressed were at first distinct and unambiguous, yet it is certain, that, among the most enlightened nations, these words are applied to so many things of different natures, and used in so vague a manner, that it is very difficult to reason about them distinctly.

This phenomenon, at first view, seems very unaccountable. But a little reflection may satisfy us, that it is a natural consequence of the slow and gradual progress of human knowledge.

And since the ambiguity of these words has so great influence upon our reasoning about moral liberty, and furnishes the strongest objections against it, it is not foreign to our subject to show whence it arises. When we know the causes that have produced this ambiguity, we shall be less in danger of being misled by it, and the proper and strict meaning of the words will more evidently appear.

27

Selections from *Beyond Good and Evil* and *Twilight of the Idols*

Friedrich Nietzsche

Beyond Good and Evil: Prelude to a Philosophy of the Future

Part 1: On the Prejudices of Philosophers

18

It is certainly not the least charm of a theory that it is refutable; it is precisely thereby that it attracts subtler minds. It seems that the hundred times refuted theory of a "free will" owes its persistence to this charm alone: again and again someone comes along who feels he is strong enough to refute it.

19

Philosophers are accustomed to speak of the will as if it were the best-known thing in the world; indeed, Schopenhauer has given us to understand that the will alone is really known to us, absolutely and completely known, without subtraction or addition. But again and again it seems to me that in this case, too, Schopenhauer only did what philosophers are in the habit of doing – he adopted a *popular prejudice* and exaggerated it. Willing seems to me to be above all something *complicated*, something that is a unit only as a

word – and it is precisely in this one word that the popular prejudice lurks, which has defeated the always inadequate caution of philosophers. So let us for once be more cautious, let us be "unphilosophical", let us say: in all willing there is, first, a plurality of sensations, namely, the sensation of the state "*away from which*," the sensation of the state "*towards which*," the sensation of this "from" and "towards" themselves, and then also an accompanying muscular sensation, which, even without our putting into motion "arms and legs," begins its action by force of habit as soon as we "will" anything. Therefore just as sensations (and indeed many kinds of sensation) are to be recognized as ingredients of the will, so, secondly, should thinking also: in every act of the will there is a ruling thought – let us not imagine it possible to sever this thought from the "willing," as if any will would then remain over! Third, the will is not only a complex of sensation and thinking, but it is above all an *affect*, and specifically the affect of command. That which is termed "freedom of the will" is essentially the affect of superiority in relation to him who must obey: "I am free, 'he' must obey" – this consciousness is inherent in every

Extracts from Poetry Translated by L A Magnus, New York Macmillan 1909 XV 268pp, *The Complete Works of Friedrich Nietzsche*, Volume 16 and *The Twilight of the Idols*, translated by Anthony M Ludovici, New York Macmillan 1911 Unwin 1899

Moral Psychology: Historical and Contemporary Readings, edited by Thomas Nadelhoffer, Eddy Nahmias, and Shaun Nichols.
© 2010 Blackwell Publishing Ltd except for editorial material and organization © 2010 Thomas Nadelhoffer, Eddy Nahmias, and Shaun Nichols.

will; and equally so the straining of the attention, the straight look that fixes itself exclusively on one aim, the unconditional evaluation that "this and nothing else is necessary now," the inward certainty that obedience will be rendered – and whatever else belongs to the position of the commander. A man who *wills*, commands something within himself that renders obedience, or that he believes renders obedience. But now let us notice what is strangest about the will – this manifold thing for which the people have only one word: inasmuch as in the given circumstances we are at the same time the commanding *and* the obeying parties, and as the obeying party we know the sensations of constraint, impulsion, pressure, resistance and motion, which usually begin immediately after the act of will, inasmuch as, on the other hand, we are accustomed to disregard this duality, and to deceive ourselves about it by means of the synthetic concept "I," a whole series of erroneous conclusions, and consequently of false evaluations of the will itself, has become attached to the act of willing – to such a degree that he who wills believes sincerely that willing *suffices* for action. Since in the great majority of cases there has been exercise of will only when the effect of the command – that is, obedience; that is, the action – was to be *expected*, the *appearance* has translated itself into the feeling, as if there were a *necessity of effect*. In short, he who wills believes with a fair amount of certainty that will and action are somehow one; he ascribes the success, the carrying out of the willing, to the will itself, and thereby enjoys an increase of the sensation of power which accompanies all success. "Freedom of the will" – that is the expression for the complex state of delight of the person exercising volition, who commands and at the same time identifies himself with the executor of the order – who, as such, enjoys also the triumph over obstacles, but thinks within himself that it was really his will itself that overcame them. In this way the person exercising volition adds the feeling of delight of his successful executive instruments, the useful "under-wills" or under-souls – indeed, our body is but a social structure composed of many souls – to his feelings of delight as commander. *L'effet c'est moi* [I am the effect]: what happens here is what happens in every well-constructed and happy commonwealth; namely, the governing class identifies itself with the successes of the commonwealth. In all willing it

is absolutely a question of commanding and obeying, on the basis, as already said, of a social structure composed of many "souls." Hence a philosopher should claim the right to include willing as such within the sphere of morals – morals being understood as the doctrine of the relations of supremacy under which the phenomenon of "life" comes to be.

[. . .]

21

The *causa sui* [cause of itself] is the best self-contradiction that has been conceived so far, it is a sort of rape and perversion of logic; but the extravagant pride of man has managed to entangle itself profoundly and frightfully with just this nonsense. The desire for "freedom of the will" in the superlative metaphysical sense, which still holds sway, unfortunately, in the minds of the half-educated; the desire to bear the entire and ultimate responsibility for one's actions oneself, and to absolve God, the world, ancestors, chance, and society involves nothing less than to be precisely this *causa sui* and, with more than Munchhausen's audacity, to pull oneself up into existence by the hair, out of the swamps of nothingness. Suppose someone were thus to see through the boorish simplicity of this celebrated concept of "free will" and put it out of his head altogether, l beg of him to carry his "enlightenment" a step further, and so put out of his head the contrary of this monstrous conception of "free will": I mean "unfree will," which amounts to a misuse of cause and effect. One should not wrongly *reify* "cause" and "effect" as the natural scientists do (and whoever, like them, now "naturalizes" in his thinking), according to the prevailing mechanical doltishness which makes the cause press and push until it "effects" its end; one should use "cause" and "effect" only as pure *concepts*, that is to say, as conventional fictions for the purpose of designation and communication – *not* for explanation. In the "in itself" there is nothing of "causal connections," of "necessity," or of "psychological non-freedom"; there the effect does *not* follow the cause, there is no rule of "law." It is *we* alone who have devised cause, sequence, for-each-other, relativity, constraint, number, law, freedom, motive, and purpose; and when we project and mix this symbol world into things as if it existed "in itself," we act once more as we have always acted, namely *mythologically*. The "unfree will" is mythology: in real life it is only a matter of *strong* and *weak* wills. – It is almost always a symptom of what is lacking in himself when a thinker senses in every "causal connection" and "psychological necessity" something of constraint, need, compulsion to obey, pressure, and unfreedom; it is suspicious to have such feelings – that person betrays himself. And in general, if I have observed correctly, the "unfreedom of the will" is regarded as a problem from two entirely opposite standpoints, but always in a profoundly *personal* manner: some will not give up their "responsibility," their belief in *themselves*, the personal right to *their* merits at any price (the vain races belong to this class); others, on the contrary, do not wish to be answerable for anything, or blamed for anything, and owing to an inward self-contempt, seek to *shift the blame* for themselves somewhere else. The latter, when they write books, are in the habit today of taking the side of criminals; a sort of socialist pity is their most attractive disguise. And as a matter of fact, the fatalism of the weak-willed embellishes itself surprisingly when it can pose as "*la religion de la souffrance humaine*" ["the religion of human suffering"]: that is *its* "good taste."

Twilight of the Idols: Or How One Philosophizes With a Hammer

The Four Great Errors

1

The error of confusing cause and effect. There is no more dangerous error than that *of mistaking the effect for the cause*: I call it the real corruption of reason. Yet this error belongs among the most ancient and recent habits of mankind: it is even hallowed among us and goes by the name of "religion" or "morality." *Every* single sentence which religion and morality formulate contains it; priests and legislators of moral codes are the originators of this corruption of reason. – I give an example. Everybody knows the book of the famous Cornaro in which he recommends his slender diet as a recipe for a long and happy life – a virtuous one too. Few books have been read so much; even now thousands of copies are sold in England every year. I do not doubt that scarcely any book (except the Bible, as is meet) has done as much harm, has *shortened* as many lives, as this well-intentioned *curiosum*. The reason: the mistaking of the effect for the cause. The worthy Italian thought his diet was the *cause* of his long life, whereas the precondition for a long life, the extraordinary slowness of his metabolism, the consumption of so little, was the cause of his slender diet. He was not free to eat little *or* much; his frugality was *not* a matter of "free will": he became sick when he ate more. But whoever is no carp not only does well to eat *properly*, but needs to. A scholar in *our* time, with his rapid consumption of nervous energy, would simply destroy himself with Cornaro's diet. *Crede experto.* – [Believe him who has tried.]

[. . .]

3

The error of a false causality. People have believed at all times that they knew what a cause is; but whence did we take our knowledge – or more precisely, our faith – that we had such knowledge? From the realm of the famous "inner facts," of which not a single one has so far proved to be factual. We believed ourselves to be causal in the act of willing: we thought that here at least we *caught causality in the act.* Nor did one doubt that all the antecedents of an act, its causes, were to be sought in consciousness and would be found there once sought – as "motives": else one would not have been free and responsible *for* it. Finally, who would have denied that a thought is caused? that the ego causes the thought? . . . Of these three "inward facts" which seem to guarantee causality, the first and most persuasive is that of the *will as cause.* The conception of a consciousness ("spirit") as a cause, and later also that of the ego as cause (the "subject"), are only afterbirths: first the causality of the will was firmly accepted as given, as *empirical* . . . Meanwhile we have thought better of it. Today we no longer believe a word of all this. The "inner world" is full of phantoms and will-o'-the-wisps: the will is one of them. The will no longer moves anything, hence does not explain anything either – it merely accompanies events; it can also be absent. The so-called *motive*: another error. Merely a surface phenomenon of consciousness, something along-side the deed that is more likely to cover up the antecedents of the deeds than to represent them. And as for the ego! That has become a fable, a fiction, a play on words: it has altogether ceased to think, feel, or will! . . . What follows from this? There are no mental causes at all! The whole of the allegedly empirical evidence for that has gone to the devil! *That* is what follows! And what a fine abuse we had perpetrated with this "empirical evidence"; we *created* the world on this basis as a world of causes, a world of will, a world of spirits. The most ancient and enduring psychology was at work here and did not do anything else: all that happened was considered a doing, all doing the effect of a will; the world became to it a multiplicity of doers; a doer (a "subject") was slipped under all that happened. It was out of himself that man projected his three "inner facts" – that in which he believed most firmly: the will, the spirit, the ego. He even took the concept of being from the concept of the ego; he posited "things" as being, in his image, in accordance with his concept of the ego as a cause. Is it any wonder that later he always found in things only that *which he had put into them*? – The thing itself, to say it once more, the concept of thing is a mere reflex of the faith in the ego as cause . . . And even your atom, my dear mechanists and physicists – how much error, how much rudimentary psychology is still residual in your atom! – Not to mention the "thing-in-itself," the *horrendum pudendum* of the metaphysicians! The error of the spirit as cause mistaken for reality! And made the very measure of reality! And called *God*!

[. . .]

7

The error of free will. Today we no longer have any pity for the concept of "free will": we know only too well what it is – the foulest of all theologians' artifices aimed at making mankind "responsible" in their sense, that is, *dependent upon them* . . .

Here I simply supply the psychology of all making-responsible. – Wherever responsibilities are sought, it is usually the instinct of *wanting to judge and punish* which is at work. Becoming has been deprived of its innocence when any being-such-and-such is traced back to will, to purposes, to acts of responsibility: the doctrine of the will has been invented essentially for the purpose of punishment, that is, because one *wanted to impute guilt*. The entire old psychology, the psychology of will, was conditioned by the fact that its originators, the priests at the head of ancient communities, wanted to create for themselves the *right* to punish – or wanted to create this right for God . . . Men were considered "free" so that they might be judged and punished – so that they might become *guilty*: consequently, every act *had to be* considered as willed, and the origin of every act had to be considered as lying within the consciousness (and thus the *most fundamental* counterfeit *in psychologicis* was made the principle of psychology itself . . .). Today, as we have entered into the *reverse* movement and we immoralists are trying with all our strength to take the concept of guilt and the concept of punishment out of the world again, and to cleanse psychology, history, nature, and social institutions and sanctions of them, there is in our eyes no more radical opposition than that of the theologians, who continue with the concept of a "moral world-order" to infect the innocence of becoming by means of "punishment" and "guilt." Christianity is a metaphysics of the hangman . . .

8

What alone can be *our* doctrine? – That no one *gives* man his qualities – neither God, nor society, nor his parents and ancestors, nor he *himself* (the nonsense of the last idea was taught as "intelligible freedom" by Kant – perhaps by Plato already). *No one* is responsible for man's being there at all, for his being such-and-such, or for his being in these circumstances or in this environment. The fatality of his essence is not to be disentangled from the fatality of all that has been and will be. Man is *not* the effect of some special purpose, of a will, an end; *nor* is he the object of an attempt to attain an "ideal of humanity" or an "ideal of happiness" or an "ideal of morality" – it is absurd to wish to *devolve* one's essence on some end or other. *We* have invented the concept of "end": in reality *there is no* end . . . One is necessary, one is a piece of fatefulness, one belongs to the whole, one *is* in the whole; there is nothing which could judge, measure, compare, or sentence our being, for that would mean judging, measuring, comparing, or sentencing the whole . . . *But there is nothing besides the whole*! – That nobody is held responsible any longer, that the mode of being may not be traced back to a *causa prima*, that the world does not form a unity either as a sensorium or as "spirit" – *that alone is the great liberation*; with this alone is the *innocence* of becoming restored . . . The concept of "God" was until now the greatest *objection* to existence . . . We deny God, we deny the responsibility in God: only *thereby* do we redeem the world.

28

Beyond Freedom and Dignity

B.F. Skinner

1. A Technology of Behavior

Twenty-five hundred years ago it might have been said that man understood himself as well as any other part of his world. Today he is the thing he understands least. Physics and biology have come a long way, but there has been no comparable development of anything like a science of human behavior. Greek physics and biology are now of historical interest only (no modern physicist or biologist would turn to Aristotle for help), but the dialogues of Plato are still assigned to students and cited as if they threw light on human behavior. Aristotle could not have understood a page of modern physics or biology, but Socrates and his friends would have little trouble in following most current discussions of human affairs. And as to technology, we have made immense strides in controlling the physical and biological worlds, but our practices in government, education, and much of economics, though adapted to very different conditions, have not greatly improved.

We can scarcely explain this by saying that the Greeks knew all there was to know about human behavior. Certainly they knew more than they knew about the physical world, but it was still not much. Moreover, their way of thinking about human behavior must have had some fatal flaw.

[. . .]

It is easy to conclude that there must be something about human behavior which makes a scientific analysis, and hence an effective technology, impossible, but we have not by any means exhausted the possibilities. There is a sense in which it can be said that the methods of science have scarcely yet been applied to human behavior. We have used the instruments of science; we have counted and measured and compared; but something essential to scientific practice is missing in almost all current discussions of human behavior. It has to do with our treatment of the causes of behavior.

Man's first experience with causes probably came from his own behavior: things moved because he moved them. If other things moved, it was because someone else was moving them, and if the mover could not be seen, it was because he was invisible. The Greek gods served in this way as the causes of physical phenomena. They were usually outside the things they moved, but they might enter into and "possess" them. Physics and biology soon abandoned explanations of this sort and turned to more useful kinds of causes, but the step has not been decisively taken in the field of human behavior. Intelligent people no longer believe that men are possessed by demons but human behavior is still commonly attributed to in-dwelling agents. [. . .]

Careless references to purpose are still to be found in both physics and biology, but

From B.F. Skinner, *Beyond Freedom and Dignity*. Alfred A. Knopf, New York, 1989. Pp. 5–9, 10–22, 198–201, 205–206, 211–215.

Moral Psychology: Historical and Contemporary Readings, edited by Thomas Nadelhoffer, Eddy Nahmias, and Shaun Nichols.

good practice has no place for them; yet almost everyone attributes human behavior to intentions, purposes, aims, and goals. If it is still possible to ask whether a machine can show purpose, the question implies, significantly, that if it can it will more closely resemble a man.

[...] Biology continued for a long time to appeal to the *nature* of living things, and it did not wholly abandon vital forces until the twentieth century. Behavior, however, is still attributed to human nature, and there is an extensive "psychology of individual differences" in which people are compared and described in terms of traits of character, capacities, and abilities.

[...]

It is usually supposed that the "behavioristic" objection to ideas, feelings, traits of character, will, and so on concerns the stuff of which they are said to be made. Certain stubborn questions about the nature of mind have, of course, been debated for more than twenty-five hundred years and still go unanswered. How, for example, can the mind move the body? As late as 1965 Karl Popper could put the question this way: "What we want is to understand how such nonphysical things as *purposes, deliberations, plans, decisions, theories, tensions,* and *values* can play a part in bringing about physical changes in the physical world." And, of course, we also want to know where these non-physical things come from.

[...]

The world of the mind steals the show. Behavior is not recognized as a subject in its own right. In psychotherapy, for example, the disturbing things a person does or says are almost always regarded merely as symptoms, and compared with the fascinating dramas which are staged in the depths of the mind, behavior itself seems superficial indeed. In linguistics and literary criticism what a man says is almost always treated as the expression of ideas or feelings. In political science, theology, and economics, behavior is usually regarded as the material from which one infers attitudes, intentions, needs, and so on. For more than twenty-five hundred years close attention has been paid to mental life, but only recently has any effort been made to study human behavior as something more than a mere by-product.

The conditions of which behavior is a function are also neglected. The mental explanation brings curiosity to an end. We see the effect in casual discourse. If we ask someone, "Why did you go to the theater?" and he says, "Because I felt like going," we are apt to take his reply as a kind of explanation. It would be much more to the point to know what has happened when he has gone to the theater in the past, what he heard or read about the play he went to see, and what other things in his past or present environments might have induced him to go (as opposed to doing something else), but we accept "I felt like going" as a sort of summary of all this and are not likely to ask for details.

The professional psychologist often stops at the same point. A long time ago William James corrected a prevailing view of the relation between feelings and action by asserting, for example, that we do not run away because we are afraid but are afraid because we run away. In other words, what we feel when we feel afraid is our behavior – the very behavior which in the traditional view expresses the feeling and is explained by it. But how many of those who have considered James's argument have noted that no antecedent event has in fact been pointed out? Neither "because" should be taken seriously. No explanation has been given as to why we run away *and* feel afraid.

[...]

Unable to understand how or why the person we see behaves as he does, we attribute his behavior to a person we cannot see, whose behavior we cannot explain either but about whom we are not inclined to ask questions. We probably adopt this strategy not so much because of any lack of interest or power but because of a longstanding conviction that for much of human behavior there *are* no relevant antecedents. The function of the inner man is to provide an explanation which will not be explained in turn. Explanation stops with him. He is not a mediator between past history and current behavior, he is a *center* from which behavior emanates. He initiates, originates, and creates, and in doing so he remains, as he was for the Greeks, divine. We say that he is autonomous – and, so far as a science of behavior is concerned, that means miraculous.

The position is, of course, vulnerable. Autonomous man serves to explain only the things we are not yet able to explain in other ways. His existence depends upon our ignorance, and he naturally loses status as we come to know more about behavior. The task of a scientific analysis is to explain how the behavior of a person as a physical system is related to the conditions under which the human species evolved and the conditions under which the individual lives. Unless there is indeed some capricious or creative intervention, these events must be related, and no intervention is in fact needed. The contingencies of survival responsible for man's genetic endowment would produce tendencies to *act* aggressively, not feelings of aggression. The punishment of sexual behavior changes sexual *behavior,* and any feelings which may arise are at best by-products. Our age is not suffering from anxiety but from the accidents, crimes, wars, and other dangerous and painful things to which people are so often exposed. Young people drop out of school, refuse to get jobs, and associate only with others of their own age not because they feel alienated but because of defective social environments in homes, schools, factories, and elsewhere.

We can follow the path taken by physics and biology by turning directly to the relation between behavior and the environment and neglecting supposed mediating states of mind. Physics did not advance by looking more closely at the jubilance of a falling body, or biology by looking at the nature of vital spirits, and we do not need to try to discover what personalities, states of mind, feelings, traits of character, plans, purposes, intentions, or the other perquisites of autonomous man really are in order to get on with a scientific analysis of behavior.

There are reasons why it has taken us so long to reach this point. The things studied by physics and biology do not behave very much like people, and it eventually seems rather ridiculous to speak of the jubilance of a falling body or the impetuosity of a projectile; but people do behave like people, and the outer man whose behavior is to be explained could be very much like the inner man whose behavior is said to explain it. The inner man has been created in the image of the outer.

A more important reason is that the inner man seems at times to be directly observed. We must infer the jubilance of a falling body, but can we not *feel* our own jubilance? We do, indeed, feel things inside our own skin, but we do not feel the things which have been invented to explain behavior. The possessed man does not feel the possessing *demon* and may even deny that one exists. The juvenile delinquent does not feel his

disturbed personality. The intelligent man does not feel his *intelligence* or the introvert his *introversion.* (In fact, these dimensions of mind or character are said to be observable only through complex statistical procedures.) The speaker does not feel the *grammatical rules* he is said to apply in composing sentences, and men spoke grammatically for thousands of years before anyone knew there were rules. The respondent to a questionnaire does not feel the *attitudes* or *opinions* which lead him to check items in particular ways. We do feel certain states of our bodies associated with behavior, but as Freud pointed out, we behave in the same way when we do not feel them; they are by-products and not to be mistaken for causes.

There is a much more important reason why we have been so slow in discarding mentalistic explanations: it has been hard to find alternatives. Presumably we must look for them in the external environment, but the role of the environment is by no means clear. The history of the theory of evolution illustrates the problem. Before the nineteenth century, the environment was thought of simply as a passive setting in which many different kinds of organisms were born, reproduced themselves, and died. No one saw that the environment was responsible for the fact that there *were* many different kinds (and that fact, significantly enough, was attributed to a creative Mind). The trouble was that the environment acts in an inconspicuous way: it does not push or pull, it *selects.* For thousands of years in the history of human thought the process of natural selection went unseen in spite of its extraordinary importance. When it was eventually discovered, it became, of course, the key to evolutionary theory.

The effect of the environment on behavior remained obscure for an even longer time. We can see what organisms do to the world around them, as they take from it what they need and ward off its dangers, but it is much harder to see what the world does to them. It was Descartes who first suggested that the environment might play an active role in the determination of behavior, and he was apparently able to do so only because he was given a strong hint. He knew about certain automata in the Royal Gardens of France which were operated hydraulically by concealed valves. As Descartes described it, people entering the gardens "necessarily tread on certain tiles or plates, which are so disposed that if they approach a bathing Diana, they cause her to hide in the rosebushes, and if they try to follow her, they cause a Neptune to come forward to meet them, threatening them with his trident." The figures were entertaining just because they behaved like people, and it appeared, therefore, that something very much like human behavior could be explained mechanically. Descartes took the hint: living organisms might move for similar reasons. (He excluded the human organism, presumably to avoid religious controversy.)

The triggering action of the environment came to be called a "stimulus" – the Latin for goad – and the effect on an organism a "response," and together they were said to compose a "reflex." Reflexes were first demonstrated in small decapitated animals, such as salamanders, and it is significant that the principle was challenged throughout the nineteenth century because it seemed to deny the existence of an autonomous agent – the "soul of the spinal cord" – to which movement of a decapitated body had been attributed. When Pavlov showed how new reflexes could be built up through conditioning, a full-fledged stimulus-response psychology was born, in which all behavior was regarded as reactions to stimuli. One writer put it this way: "We are prodded or lashed through life." The stimulus-response model was never very convincing, however, and it did not solve the basic problem, because something like an inner man had to be invented to convert a stimulus into a response. Information theory ran into the same problem when an inner "processer" had to be invented to convert input into output.

The effect of an eliciting stimulus is relatively easy to see, and it is not surprising that Descartes' hypothesis held a dominant position in behavior theory for a long time, but it was a false scent from which a scientific analysis is only now recovering. The environment not only prods or lashes, it *selects*. Its role is similar to that in natural selection, though on a very different time scale, and was overlooked for the same reason. It is now clear that we must take into account what the environment does to an organism not only before but after it responds. Behavior is shaped and maintained by its consequences. Once this fact is recognized, we can formulate the interaction between organism and environment in a much more comprehensive way.

There are two important results. One concerns the basic analysis. Behavior which operates upon the environment to produce consequences ("operant" behavior) can be studied by arranging environments in which specific consequences are contingent upon it. The contingencies under investigation have become steadily more complex, and one by one they are taking over the explanatory functions previously assigned to personalities, states of mind, feelings, traits of character, purposes, and intentions. The second result is practical: the environment can be manipulated. It is true that man's genetic endowment can be changed only very slowly, but changes in the environment of the individual have quick and dramatic effects. A technology of operant behavior is, as we shall see, already well advanced, and it may prove to be commensurate with our problems.

That possibility raises another problem, however, which must be solved if we are to take advantage of our gains. We have moved forward by dispossessing autonomous man, but he has not departed gracefully. He is conducting a sort of rear-guard action in which, unfortunately, he can marshal formidable support. He is still an important figure in political science, law, religion, economics, anthropology, sociology, psychotherapy, philosophy, ethics, history, education, child care, linguistics, architecture, city planning, and family life. These fields have their specialists, and every specialist has a theory, and in almost every theory the autonomy of the individual is unquestioned. The inner man is not seriously threatened by data obtained through casual observation or from studies of the structure of behavior, and many of these fields deal only with groups of people, where statistical or actuarial data impose few restraints upon the individual. The result is a tremendous weight of traditional "knowledge," which must be corrected or displaced by a scientific analysis.

Two features of autonomous man are particularly troublesome. In the traditional view, a person is free. He is autonomous in the sense that his behavior is uncaused. He can therefore be held responsible for what he does and justly punished if he offends. That view, together with its associated practices, must be re-examined when a scientific analysis reveals unsuspected controlling relations between behavior and environment. A certain amount of external control can be tolerated. Theologians have accepted the fact that man must be predestined to do what an omniscient God knows he will do, and the Greek dramatist took inexorable fate as his favorite theme. Soothsayers and astrologers often claim to predict what men will do, and they have always been in demand. Biographers and historians have searched for "influences" in the lives of individuals and peoples. Folk wisdom and the insights of essayists like Montaigne and Bacon imply some kind of predictability in human conduct, and the statistical and actuarial evidences of the social sciences point in the same direction.

Autonomous man survives in the face of all this because he is the happy exception. Theologians have reconciled predestination with free will, and the Greek audience, moved by the portrayal of an inescapable destiny, walked out of the theater free men. The course of history has been turned by the death of a leader or a storm at sea, as a life has been changed by a teacher or a love affair, but these things do not happen to everyone, and they do not affect everyone in the same way. Some historians have made a virtue of the unpredictability of history. Actuarial evidence is easily ignored; we read that hundreds of people will be killed in traffic accidents on a holiday weekend and take to the road as if personally exempt. Very little behavioral science raises "the specter of predictable man." On the contrary, many anthropologists, sociologists, and psychologists have used their expert knowledge to prove that man is free, purposeful, and responsible. Freud was a determinist – on faith, if not on the evidence – but many Freudians have no hesitation in assuring their patients that they are free to choose among different courses of action and are in the long run the architects of their own destinies.

This escape route is slowly closed as new evidences of the predictability of human behavior are discovered. Personal exemption from a complete determinism is revoked as a scientific analysis progresses, particularly in accounting for the behavior of the individual. Joseph Wood Krutch has acknowledged the actuarial facts while insisting on personal freedom: "We can predict with a considerable degree of accuracy how many people will go to the seashore on a day when the temper-

ature reaches a certain point, even how many will jump off a bridge . . . although I am not, nor are you, compelled to do either." But he can scarcely mean that those who go to the seashore do not go for good reason, or that circumstances in the life of a suicide do not have some bearing on the fact that he jumps off a bridge. The distinction is tenable only so long as a word like "compel" suggests a particularly conspicuous and forcible mode of control. A scientific analysis naturally moves in the direction of clarifying all kinds of controlling relations.

By questioning the control exercised by autonomous man and demonstrating the control exercised by the environment, a science of behavior also seems to question dignity or worth. A person is responsible for his behavior, not only in the sense that he may be justly blamed or punished when he behaves badly, but also in the sense that he is to be given credit and admired for his achievements. A scientific analysis shifts the credit as well as the blame to the environment, and traditional practices can then no longer be justified. These are sweeping changes, and those who are committed to traditional theories and practices naturally resist them.

There is a third source of trouble. As the emphasis shifts to the environment, the individual seems to be exposed to a new kind of danger. Who is to construct the controlling environment and to what end? Autonomous man presumably controls himself in accordance with a built-in set of values; he works for what he finds good. But what will the putative controller find good, and will it be good for those he controls? Answers to questions of this sort are said, of course, to call for value judgments.

Freedom, dignity, and value are major issues, and unfortunately they become more crucial as the power of a technology of behavior becomes more nearly commensurate with the problems to be solved. The very change which has brought some hope of a solution is responsible for a growing opposition to the kind of solution proposed.

[. . .]

9. What is Man?

[. . .]

It is in the nature of an experimental analysis of human behavior that it should strip away the functions previously assigned to autonomous man and transfer them one by one to the controlling environment. The analysis leaves less and less for autonomous man to do. But what about man himself? Is there not something about a person which is more than a living body? Unless something called a self survives, how can we speak of self-knowledge or self-control? To whom is the injunction "Know thyself" addressed?

[. . .]

The picture which emerges from a scientific analysis is not of a body with a person inside, but of a body which *is* a person in the sense that it displays a complex repertoire of behavior. The picture is, of course, unfamiliar. The man thus portrayed is a stranger, and from the traditional point of view he may not seem to be a man at all. "For at least one hundred years," said Joseph Wood Krutch, "we have been prejudiced in every theory, including economic determinism, mechanistic behaviorism, and relativism, that reduces the stature of man until he ceases to be man at all in any sense that the humanists of an earlier generation would recognize." Matson has argued that "the empirical behavioral scientist . . . denies, if only by implication, that a unique being, called Man, exists." "What is now under attack," said Maslow, "is the 'being' of man." C. S. Lewis put it quite bluntly: Man is being abolished.

There is clearly some difficulty in identifying the man to whom these expressions refer. Lewis cannot have meant the human species, for not only is it not being abolished, it is filling the earth. (As a result it may eventually abolish itself through disease, famine, pollution, or a nuclear holocaust, but that is not what Lewis meant.) Nor are individual men growing less effective or productive. We are told that what is threatened is "man *qua* man," or "man in his humanity," or "man as Thou not It," or "man as a person not a thing." These are not very helpful expressions, but they supply a clue. What is being abolished is autonomous man – the inner man, the homunculus, the possessing demon, the man defended by the literatures of freedom and dignity.

His abolition has long been overdue. Autonomous man is a device used to explain what we cannot explain in any other way. He has been constructed from our ignorance, and as our understanding increases, the very stuff of which he is composed vanishes. Science does not dehumanize man, it de-homunculizes him, and it must do so if it is to prevent the abolition of the human species. To man *qua* man we readily say good riddance. Only by dispossessing him can we turn to the real causes of human behavior. Only then can we turn from the inferred to the observed, from the miraculous to the natural, from the inaccessible to the manipulable.

It is often said that in doing so we must treat the man who survives as a mere animal. "Animal" is a pejorative term, but only because "man" has been made spuriously honorific. Krutch has argued that whereas the traditional view supports Hamlet's exclamation, "How like a god!," Pavlov, the behavioral scientist, emphasized "How like a dog!" But that was a step forward. A god is the archetypal pattern of an explanatory fiction, of a miracle-working mind, of the metaphysical. Man is much more than a dog but like a dog he is within range of a scientific analysis.

[. . .]

A scientific analysis of behavior dispossesses autonomous man and turns the control he has been said to exert over to the environment. The individual may then seem particularly vulnerable. He is henceforth to be controlled by the world around him, and in large part by other men. Is he not then simply a victim? Certainly men have been victims, as they been victimizers, but the word is too strong. It implies despoliation, which is by no means an essential consequence of interpersonal control. But even under benevolent control is the individual not at best a spectator who may watch what happens but is helpless to do anything about it? Is he not "at a dead end in his long struggle to control his own destiny"?

It is only autonomous man who has reached a dead end. Man himself may be controlled by his environment, but it is an environment which is almost wholly of his own making. The physical environment of most people is largely man-made. The surfaces a person walks on, the walls which shelter him, the clothing he wears, many of the foods he eats, the tools he uses, the vehicles he moves about in, most of the things he listens to and looks at are human products. The social environment is obviously man-made – it generates the language a person speaks, the customs he follows, and the behavior he exhibits with respect to the ethical, religious, governmental, economic, educational, and psychotherapeutic institutions which control him. The evolution of a culture is in fact a kind of gigantic exercise in self-control. As the individual controls himself by manipulating the world in which he lives, so the human species has constructed an environment in which its members behave in a highly effective way. Mistakes have been made, and we have no assurance that the environment man has constructed will continue to provide gains which outstrip the losses, but man as we know him, for better or for worse, is what man has made of man.

[. . .]

Science has probably never demanded a more sweeping change in a traditional way of thinking about a subject, nor has there ever been a more important subject. In the traditional picture a person perceives the world around him, selects features to be perceived, discriminates among them, judges them good or bad, changes them to make them better (or, if he is careless, worse), and may be held responsible for this action and justly rewarded or punished for its consequences. In the scientific picture a person is a member of a species shaped by evolutionary contingencies of survival, displaying behavioral processes which bring him under the control of the environment in which he lives, and largely under the control of a social environment which he and millions of others like him have constructed and maintained during the evolution of a culture. The direction of the controlling relation is reversed: a person does not act upon the world, the world acts upon him.

It is difficult to accept such a change simply on intellectual grounds and nearly impossible to accept its implications. The reaction of the traditionalist is usually described in terms of feelings. One of these, to which the Freudians have appealed in explaining the resistance to psychoanalysis, is wounded vanity. Freud himself expounded, as Ernest Jones has said, "the three heavy blows which narcissism or self-love of mankind had suffered at the hands of science. The first was cosmological and was dealt by Copernicus; the second was biological and was dealt by Darwin; the third was psychological and was dealt by Freud." (The blow was suffered by the belief that something at the center of man knows all that goes on within him and that an instrument called will power exercises command and control over the rest of one's personality.)

[. . .]

These reactions to a scientific conception of man are certainly unfortunate. They immobilize men of good will, and anyone concerned with the future of his culture will do what he can to correct them. No theory changes what it is a theory about. Nothing is changed because we look at it, talk about it, or analyze it in a new way. Keats drank confusion to Newton for analyzing the rainbow, but the rainbow remained as beautiful as ever and became for many even more beautiful. Man has not changed because we look at him, talk about him, and analyze him scientifically. His achievements in science, government, religion, art, and literature remain as they have always been, to be admired as one admires a storm at sea or autumn foliage or a mountain peak, quite apart from their origins and untouched by a scientific analysis. What does change is our chance of doing something about the subject of a theory. Newton's analysis of the light in a rainbow was a step in the direction of the laser.

The traditional conception of man is flattering; it confers reinforcing privileges. It is therefore easily defended and can be changed only with difficulty. It was designed to build up the individual as an instrument of counter-control, and it did so effectively but in such a way as to limit progress. We have seen how the literatures of freedom and dignity, with their concern for autonomous man, have perpetuated the use of punishment and condoned the use of only weak nonpunitive techniques, and it is not difficult to demonstrate a connection between the unlimited right of the individual to pursue happiness and the catastrophes threatened by unchecked breeding, the unrestrained affluence which exhausts resources and pollutes the environment, and the imminence of nuclear war.

Physical and biological technologies have alleviated pestilence and famine and many painful, dangerous, and exhausting features of daily life, and behavioral technology can begin to alleviate other kinds of ills. In the analysis of human behavior it is just possible that we are slightly beyond Newton's position in the analysis of light, for we are beginning to make technological applications. There are wonderful possibilities – and all the more wonderful because traditional approaches have been so ineffective. It is hard to imagine a world in which people live together without quarreling, maintain themselves by producing the food, shelter, and clothing they need, enjoy themselves and contribute to the enjoyment of others in art, music, literature, and games, consume only a reasonable part of the resources of the world and add as little as possible to its pollution, bear no more children than can be raised decently, continue to explore the world around them and discover better ways of dealing with it, and come to know themselves accurately and, therefore, manage themselves effectively. Yet all this is possible, and even the slightest sign of progress should bring a kind of change which in traditional terms would be said to assuage wounded vanity, offset a sense of hopelessness or nostalgia, correct the impression that "we neither can nor need to do anything for ourselves," and promote a "sense of freedom and dignity" by building "a sense of confidence and worth." In other words, it should abundantly reinforce those who have been induced by their culture to work for its survival.

An experimental analysis shifts the determination of behavior from autonomous man to the environment – an environment responsible both for the evolution of the species and for the repertoire acquired by each member. Early versions of environmentalism were inadequate because they could not explain how the environment worked, and much seemed to be left for autonomous man to do. But environmental contingencies now take over functions once attributed to autonomous man, and certain questions arise. Is man then "abolished"? Certainly not as a species or as an individual achiever. It is the autonomous inner man who is abolished, and that is a step forward. But does man not then become merely a victim or passive observer of what is happening to him? He is indeed controlled by his environment, but we must remember that it is an environment largely of his own making. The evolution of a culture is a gigantic exercise in self-control. It is often said that a scientific view of man leads to wounded vanity, a sense of hopelessness, and nostalgia. But no theory changes what it is a theory about; man remains what he has always been. And a new theory may change what can be done with its subject matter. A scientific view of man offers exciting possibilities. We have not yet seen what man can make of man.

29

Apparent Mental Causation
Sources of the Experience of Will

Daniel M. Wegner and Thalia Wheatley

Conscious will is a pervasive human experience. We all have the sense that we do things, that we cause our acts, that we are agents. As William James (1890) observed, "the whole sting and excitement of our voluntary life . . . depends on our sense that in it things are *really being decided* from one moment to another, and that it is not the dull rattling off of a chain that was forged innumerable ages ago" (p. 453). And yet, the very notion of the will seems to contradict the core assumption of psychological science. After all, psychology examines how behavior is caused by mechanisms – the rattling off of genetic, unconscious, neural, cognitive, emotional, social, and yet other chains that lead, dully or not, to the things people do. If the things we do are caused by such mechanisms, how is it that we nonetheless experience willfully doing them?

Our approach to this problem is to look for yet another chain – to examine the mechanisms that produce the experience of conscious will itself. In this article, we do this by exploring the possibility that the experience of will is a result of the same mental processes that people use in the perception of causality more generally. Quite simply, it may be that *people experience conscious will when they interpret their own thought as the cause of their action*. This idea means that people can experience conscious will quite independent of any actual causal connection between their thoughts and actions (cf. Brown, 1989; Harnad, 1982; Kirsch & Lynn, 1997; Langer, 1975; Libet, 1985; Spanos, 1982; Spence, 1996). Reductions in the impression that there is a link between thought and action may explain why people get a sense of involuntariness during motor automatisms, hypnosis, and some psychological disorders. Inflated perceptions of this link, in turn, may explain why people experience conscious will at all – when psychological science suggests that all behavior can be ascribed to mechanisms that transcend human agency.

The Experience of Will

Conscious will is an experience like the sensation of the color red, the perception of a friend's voice, or the enjoyment of a fine spring day. David Hume (1739/1888) appreciated the will in just this way, defining it as "nothing but *the internal impression we feel and are conscious of, when we knowingly give rise to any new motion of our body, or new perception of our mind*" (p. 399). Hume realized that the will, like causal force more generally, is not a thing that inheres in objects or people, but rather is a perception that follows from the constant conjunction of events:

From Daniel Wegner and Thalia Wheatley (1999). Apparent mental causation: Sources of the experience of will. *American Psychologist*, 54, 7. American Psychological Association, pp. 480–92. Reprinted with permission of the American Psychological Association.

Some have asserted, that we feel an energy, or power, in our own mind. . . . But to convince us how fallacious this reasoning is, we need only consider, that the will being here consider'd as a cause, has no more a discoverable connexion with its effects, than any material cause has with its proper effect. . . . In short, the actions of the mind are, in this respect, the same with those of matter. We perceive only their constant conjunction; nor can we ever reason beyond it. No internal impression has an apparent energy, more than external objects have. (pp. 400–1)

The person experiencing will, in this view, is in the same position as someone perceiving causation as one billiard ball strikes another. Causation is inferred from the conjunction of ball movements, and will is inferred from the conjunction of events that lead to action. In the case of billiard balls, however, the players in the causal analysis are quite simple: one ball and the other ball. What are the items that seem to click together in our minds to yield the perception of will? One view of this was provided by Ziehen (1899), who suggested that thinking of self before action yields the sense of agency. He proposed that "we finally come to regard the ego-idea as the cause of our actions because of its very frequent appearance in the series of ideas preceding each action" (p. 296). Current evidence indicates that self-attention may indeed be associated with perceived control or responsibility for action (Duval & Wicklund, 1973, Gibbons, 1990), but this effect seems to be a general feature of a more specific process.

This specific process is the perception of a causal link between one's own thought and action. It makes sense that we would tend to see ourselves as the authors of an act primarily when we had experienced relevant thoughts about the act at an appropriate interval in advance, and so could infer that our own mental processes had set the act in motion. Actions we perform that are not presaged in our minds, in turn, would appear not to be caused by our minds, In essence, then, this view suggests a connection between what Michotte (1963) identified as the two forms of conscious evidence we have for the causality of self in any action: "The first is our ability to foresee the result before it actually takes place, the second the presence of a feeling of 'activity'" (p. 10). The feeling of activity may derive from the perception of our own foresight.

The important point in this analysis is that the will is not a psychological force that causes action. Rather, as a perception that results from interpretation, it is a conscious experience that may only map rather weakly, or perhaps not at all, onto the actual causal relationship between the person's cognition and action. Thus, as Searle (1983) has put it,

It is always possible that something else might actually be causing the bodily movement we think the experience [of acting] is causing. It is always possible that I might think I am raising my arm when in fact some other cause is raising it. So there is nothing in the experience of acting that actually guarantees that it is causally effective. (p. 130)

In essence, then, this is an example of the basic disconnection between mental process and the perception and verbal report of that process. As Nisbett and Wilson (1977) have observed, the occurrence of a mental process does not guarantee the individual any special knowledge of the mechanism of this process, and instead it may be that the individual commonly uses a priori causal theories to account for his or her own psychological operations. The conscious will may arise from a theory designed to account for the regular relationship between thought and action.

The possibility that the conscious will does not reflect an actual causal link has been captured in several research findings. Perhaps the most compelling are Libet's (1985) studies of the role of unconscious cerebral initiative in voluntary action. He took advantage of the finding that a brain readiness potential (RP), a scalp-recorded slow negative shift in electrical potential, begins up to a second or more before a self-paced, apparently voluntary motor act (Kornhuber & Deecke, 1965). In spontaneous, intentional finger movement, Libet found that this RP preceded the movement (measured electromyographically) by a minimum of about 550 milliseconds. This finding by itself indicates only that some sort of brain activity reliably precedes the onset of voluntary action. The further step Libet took was to ask participants to recall the position of a clock at their initial awareness of intending to move their finger. The awareness of intention followed the RP by about 350–400 milliseconds, even when adjustment was made for the time it took people to monitor the clock. So, although the conscious intention preceded the finger movement, it occurred well after whatever brain events were signaled by the RP. These findings are compatible with the idea that brain events cause intention and action, whereas conscious intention itself may not cause action.

[. . .]

There are a variety of other findings that lend themselves to similar interpretations. The striking absence of the experience of will in the case of motor automatisms such as table-turning, Ouija-board spelling, automatic writing, pendulum divining, and the like (cf. Ansfield & Wegner, 1996; Carpenter, 1888; Spitz, 1997; Wegner, 2002; Wegner & Fuller, 1999), for example, suggests that there are circumstances that can produce actions with all the signs of voluntariness – but that nonetheless feel unwilled. There also exist neuropsychological anomalies in which people perform voluntary actions while reporting no intention or feeling of will. In the case of alien hand syndrome, for example, a person may experience one hand as acting autonomously, often at cross purposes with conscious intention. Banks et al. (1989) reported such a patient whose "left hand would tenaciously grope for and grasp any nearby object, pick and pull at her clothes, and even grasp her throat during sleep. . . . She slept with the arm tied to prevent nocturnal misbehavior. She never denied that her left arm and hand belonged to her, although she did refer to her limb as though it were an autonomous entity" (p. 456). The sense of will, in short, is a variable quantity that is not tied inevitably to voluntary action – and so must be accounted for as a distinct phenomenon.

A model of a mental system for the production of an experience of conscious will that is consistent with these various findings is shown in Figure 29.1. The model represents the temporal flow of events (from left to right) leading up to a voluntary action. In this system, unconscious mental processes give rise to conscious thought about the action (e.g., intention, expectation), and other unconscious mental processes give rise to the voluntary action.[1] There may or may not be links between these underlying unconscious systems (as designated by the bidirectional unconscious potential path), but this is irrelevant to the perception of the apparent path from conscious thought to action. There need be no actual path

here, as it is the perception of the apparent path that gives rise to the experience of will: When we think that our conscious intention has caused the voluntary action that we find ourselves doing, we feel a sense of will. We have willfully done the act.

The degree of correspondence between the perceived conscious will and the actual mechanisms linking thought and behavior is, of course, an essential problem in its own right, the topic of intriguing theorizing (e.g., Brown, 1989; Dennett, 1984; Libet, 1985; Spence, 1996). But the degree of conscious will that is experienced for an action is not a direct indication of any causal link between mind and action. Rather, our analysis suggests that conscious will results from a causal illusion that is the psychological equivalent of the third-variable problem in causal analysis. We can never be sure that *A* causes *B*, as there could always be a third variable, *C*, that causes both of them. In the same sense, we can never be sure that our thoughts cause our actions, as there could always be unconscious causes that have produced them both. The impression that a thought has caused an action rests on a causal inference that is always open to question – yet this impression is the basis of the experience of will.

Sources of Experienced Will

Imagine for a moment that you are in a park, looking at a tree. It is a windless day, and yet you get the idea that a particular limb you are gazing at is going to move at just a certain moment. Then it does. Zowie. You look away and then a bit later you look back at the limb and think it is going to move again – and darn it, the thing moves again just in the way you thought it would. At this point, you would probably have the distinct feeling that you are somehow moving the limb. With a tree limb, of course, all this would be quite strange, but in fact, this is the very position we are in with regard to our own limbs, not to mention the rest of our bodies and even our minds. We get ideas of what they are going to do, and when we find that these doings actually occur, we perceive that we have willed the actions.

There are important limits to this effect. If the magic limb moved before we thought of it moving, for example, there would be nothing unusual and we would experience no sense of willful

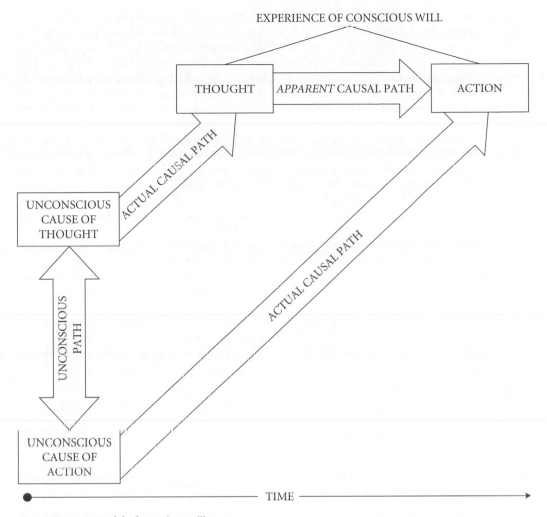

Figure 29.1   A model of conscious will

Note. Will is experienced to the degree that an apparent causal path is inferred from thought to action.

action. The thought of movement would simply be a memory or a perception of what had happened. If we thought of the tree limb moving and then something different moved (say, a nearby chicken dropped to its knees), again there would be no experience of will. The thought would be irrelevant. And if we thought of the tree limb moving but noticed that something other than our thoughts had moved it (say, a passing lumberjack), no will would be sensed. There would be only the perception of an external causal event. These observations point to three sources of the experience of conscious will – the *priority*, *consistency*, and *exclusivity* of the thought we have about

the action. The thought should occur before the action, be consistent with the action, and not be accompanied by other potential causes.

Studies of how people perceive physical events (Michotte, 1963) indicate that the perception of causality is highly dependent on these features of the relationship between the potential cause and potential effect. The candidate for the role of cause must come first or at least at the same time as the effect, it must yield movement that is consistent with its own movement, and it must be unaccompanied by rival causal events. The absence of any of these conditions tends to undermine the perception that causation has occurred. [. . .]

Priority: The thought should precede the action at a proper interval

Causal events precede their effects, usually in a timely manner. So, for example, in Michotte's (1963) studies of cause perception, when one object moves along and appears to strike another, which then immediately begins to move in the same direction, people perceive a causal event. The first object has launched the second. If the second object sits there for a bit after the first has touched it, however, and only then begins moving, the sense that this is a causal event is lost, and the second object is perceived to have started moving on its own. Then again, if the second object begins to move before the first even comes to touch it, the perception of causation is also absent. To be perceived as a truly worthy cause, the event can't start too soon or start too late – it has to be on time just before the effect.

These observations suggest that the experience of will may also depend on the timely occurrence of thought prior to action. Thought that occurs too far in advance of an action is not likely to be seen as the cause of it; a person who thinks of dumping a bowl of soup on her boss's head, for example, and then never thinks about this again until doing it some days later during a quiet dinner party is not likely to experience the action as willful. Thought that occurs well after the relevant action is also not prone to cue an experience of will. The person who discovers having done an act that was not consciously considered in advance – say, getting in the car on a day off and absently driving all the way to work – would also feel little in the way of conscious will.

Somewhere between these extreme examples exist cases in which conscious will is regularly experienced. Little is known about the parameters of timing that might maximize this experience, but it seems likely that thoughts occurring just a few seconds before an action would be most prone to support the perception of willfulness.
 [. . .]
This brief window reminds us that even long-term planning for an action may not produce an experience of will unless the plan reappears in mind just as the action is performed. Although thinking of an action far in advance of doing it would seem to be a signal characteristic of a premeditated action (cf. Brown, 1996; Vallacher &

Wegner, 1985), our analysis suggests that such distant foresight yields less will perception than does immediately prior apprehension of the act. In the absence of thought about the action that occurs just prior to its performance, even the most distant foresight would merely be premature and would do little to promote the feeling that one had willed the action. In line with this suggestion, Gollwitzer (1993) has proposed that actions intended far in advance to correspond with a triggering event (e.g., "I'll go when the light turns green") may then tend to occur automatically without conscious thought, and thus without a sense of volition, when the triggering event ensues.

The priority principle also indicates that thoughts coming after action will not prompt the experience of will. But again, it is not clear just how long following action the thought would need to occur for will not to be experienced. One indication of the lower bound for willful experience is Libet's (1985) observation that in the course of a willed finger movement, conscious intention precedes action by about 200 milliseconds. Perhaps if conscious thought of an act occurs past this time, it is perceived as following the act, or at least as being too late, and so is less likely to be seen as causal.
 [. . .]

Consistency: The thought should be compatible with the action

When a billiard ball strikes another, the struck ball moves in the same general direction that the striking ball was moving. We do not perceive causality very readily if the second ball takes off in a direction that, by the laws of physics, is inconsistent with the movement of the first (Michotte, 1963). In the social attribution realm, too, consistency is evident in the inclination perceivers have to attribute causality for behaviors to people whose personalities are seen as consistent with the behaviors (e.g., Jones & Davis, 1965). Causes consistent with effects are more likely to be perceived as causal (Einhorn & Hogarth, 1986; Nisbett & Ross, 1980).

The principle of consistency in the experience of will draws on the observation that the thoughts that serve as potential causes of actions typically have semantic associations with the actions.

A thought that is perceived to cause an act is often the name of the act or an image of its stimulus, execution, or consequence (Vallacher & Wegner, 1985). Consistency of thought and act depends on a cognitive process whereby the thoughts occurring prior to the act are compared with the act as subsequently perceived. When people do what they think they were going to do, there exists consistency between thought and act, and the experience of will is enhanced. When they think of one thing and do another – and this inconsistency is observable to them – their action does not feel as willful.

[...]

The consistency principle also extends to more arcane and puzzling cases of the loss of will. Motor automatisms such as dowsing, for example, appear to derive their lack of perceived voluntariness from the inconsistency of thought and action. [...]

The Chevreul pendulum is another automatism that depends on obscuring the relationship between intention and action. When people hold a bob on a chain in one hand, they often get the sense that the pattern or frequency of the pendulum movement is occurring without their volition (Ansfield & Wegner, 1996; Carpenter, 1888).

[...] The lack of consistency between intention and action of the pendulum promotes the sense that the pendulum's movement is not controlled by the will. The involuntariness of a variety of the motor automatisms appears traceable to movement confusion that interferes with perceptions of consistency (Wegner, 2002).

The consistency principle also offers a way of understanding the experiences of involuntariness reported by people with some forms of schizophrenia. Phenomena of alien control such as thought insertion and auditory hallucinations that can occur in schizophrenia involve thoughts, images, and actions that occur with marked feelings of unintendedness. In the case of hearing voices, for example, although neuropsychological evidence indicates that the voices are self-generated (e.g., McGuire, Shah, & Murray, 1993), schizophrenic patients with this symptom describe the voices as coming from someone other than themselves. Hoffman (1986) has proposed that this experience occurs when people find that their thoughts do not match their current conscious

goals for thinking. The thoughts come to mind without a clear preview, and in fact may be highly discordant with the person's thoughts of what to think or say next. In the context of a conversation about the weather, for example, the person might experience the thought "Eat the wax fruit." The inconsistency produces such a strong sense that the self did not will the thought that the thought is judged to be the action of an outside agent – and so is heard as a "voice."

[...]

Exclusivity: The thought should be the only apparent cause of action

A basic principle of causal inference is that we tend to discount the causal influence of one potential cause if there are others available (Kelley, 1972; McClure, 1998). So, for instance, in the case of those well-worn billiard balls, the causal influence of one on another can be called into question by the arrival of a third just at the time of impact. Applied to the experience of will, this principle suggests that people will be particularly sensitive to the possibility that there are other causes of an action besides their own thoughts. When their own thoughts do not appear to be the exclusive cause of their action, they experience less conscious will. And when other plausible causes are less salient, in turn, they experience more conscious will.

The causes that compete with thoughts are of two kinds – internal and external. The plausible internal causes for an action might include one's emotions, habits, traits, or other unconscious action tendencies. Whenever we become aware of one of these unconscious tendencies, we may lose some of the sense of will even though we have a prior, consistent thought of the action. Knowing that we are going to eat a large bag of potato chips may not contribute to the sense that this is willful when we do it, for example, if we also realize that we are big, fat, compulsive chip-hounds. At the same time, if a thought not to eat those chips occurs and does predict effective abstinence, the precedence of this thought over our disposition toward free feeding may lead us to feel that a special surge of will has caused our successful self-control. The experience of will may arise both in thoughts that initiate behaviors and in thoughts that stop them – and may be particularly strong when we find that thoughts consistent with stopping a behavior seem to have overridden a pressing impulse and kept the behavior from occurring.

The exclusivity of thought as a cause of action can also be challenged by external causes. Plausible external causes for an action might include other people or external forces that impinge on us even when we are thinking of the action in advance. The extensive contemporary literature on causal attribution in social situations (e.g., Gilbert, 1995) has suggested that the presence of others and of situational forces provides an intricate causal context that could influence the individual's experience of will in a variety of ways. Other people with whom we interact, of course, are also thinking and acting, so our perceptions of the causal relations between their thoughts and actions can enter into our interpretation of their willfulness, which may, then, have implications for the degree to which our behavior in interaction with them is interpreted as willful as well.

The interplay of these factors in the experience of will is illustrated in the phenomenon of action projection (Wegner & Fuller, 1999). Action projection occurs when a person performs a voluntary action and yet believes that this action was done by someone else. Although such an error sounds bizarre, it turns out the effect can be produced readily. The initial indications of this effect were found in the practice of facilitated communication, a technique of helping people with communication disorders to communicate by holding or bracing their hands while they are at a computer keyboard. Although such facilitation does not actually promote accurate communication (Jacobson, Mulick, & Schwartz, 1995; Spitz, 1997; Twachtman-Cullen, 1997), it does leave people who have served as facilitators with the profound sense that they have helped someone to communicate – even though the content that is communicated is fully traceable to the facilitator (Burgess et al. 1998).

[. . .]

Ambiguous exclusivity may also underlie the sense of involuntariness that occurs in hypnosis. As a rule, there is a common sensation among people who are hypnotized that their suggested behaviors occur without conscious will (Lynn, Rhue, & Weekes, 1990). When people are induced to experience arm levitation ("Your arm feels very light, and it is rising up, rising up"), for example, in addition to the arm actually rising, people often report that it does so without benefit of their conscious will. Although people who experience involuntariness indeed have thoughts of what their arm will do that are consistent with their action and prior to their action, they may well be having trouble discerning whether those thoughts are the exclusive cause of the action.

People in hypnosis consent to follow instructions from the hypnotist, so their thoughts do not appear as the exclusive cause of their actions. But unlike everyday social interaction, in which people typically can follow instructions without losing the sense of will, it seems that the process of hypnosis undermines will perception. To understand this, it is useful to note that in hypnotic induction, the hypnotist suggests a series of actions, many of which are difficult to perceive in oneself (e.g., "try to relax") and many of which are so innocuous that the person sees no difficulty in complying (e.g., "close your eyes"). Each time the hypnotist gives an instruction, the person then thinks about that action and subsequently performs the action or receives no bodily feedback to the contrary. Over the course of several repetitions, it could be that the hypnotist's suggestions come to be interpreted as the primary causes of the person's behavior, and the person's thoughts as only echoes of what the hypnotist has said.

[. . .]

The problem of understanding "whodunit" is an important one in social life more generally, and it often amounts to sorting out matters of exclusivity. As long as there are other possible agents around, whether real or imagined, one's actions may at times be attributed to them, and fluctuations in the sense of one's own will may follow. This is what Milgram (1974) was speaking of in his suggestion that obedience to authority is accompanied by an *agentic shift*, a change in the perceived source of agency for actions that occur when one obeys another. A further complication arising in dyads and groups is that a group level of agency may also be constructed, such that there are things "we" do independent of what "you" do or what "I" do. One might experience the will of one's group rather than that of the self, for example, as a result of knowing that the group was thinking of doing something and that the group action had ensued. The computation of will in social life begins with the principle of exclusivity, but then blossoms into a variety of interesting formats quite beyond the basic sense of self as agent.

An Illustrative Experiment: The *I Spy* Study

If will is an experience fabricated from perceiving a causal link between thought and action, it should be possible to lead people to experience willful action when in fact they have done nothing. We conducted an experiment to learn whether people will feel they willfully performed an action that was actually performed by someone else when conditions suggest their own thought may have caused the action. The study focused on the role of priority of thought and action when there is consistency between the thought and action and when the exclusivity of thought as a cause of action is ambiguous. To create this circumstance, we were inspired by the ordinary household Ouija board. We tested whether people would feel they had moved a Ouija-like pointer if they simply thought about where it would go just in advance of its movement – even though the movement was in fact produced by another person.

Undergraduates (23 men and 28 women) from the University of Virginia participated in exchange for credit in introductory psychology. Each arrived for the experiment at about the same time as a confederate who was posing as another participant. Both were greeted by the experimenter and seated facing each other across a small table. On the table between them was a 12-centimeter square board, mounted atop a computer mouse. Both participant and confederate were asked to place their fingertips on the side of the board closest to them so that they could move the mouse together. They were asked to move the mouse in slow sweeping circles and, by doing so, to move a cursor around a computer screen, which was visible to both. The screen showed a photo called 'Tiny Toys" from the book *I Spy* (Marzollo & Wick, 1992), picturing about 50 small objects (e.g., plastic dinosaur, swan, car).

The experimenter explained that the study would investigate people's feelings of intention for acts and how these feelings come and go. It was explained that the pair were to stop moving the mouse every 30 seconds or so and that they would rate each stop they made for personal intentionality. That is, they each would rate how much they had intended to make each stop, independent of their partner's intentions. The participant and confederate made these ratings on scales, which they kept on clipboards in their laps. Each scale consisted of a 14-centimeter line with endpoints *I allowed the stop to happen* and *I intended to make the stop*, and marks on the line were converted to percentage intended (0–100).

The participant and confederate were told that they would hear music and words through headphones during the experiment. Each trial would involve a 30-second interval of movement, after which they would hear a 10-second clip of music, which would indicate that they should make a stop. They were told that they would be listening to two different tracks of an audio tape, but that they would hear music at about the same times and should wait a few seconds into their music before making the stops to make sure they both were ready. Participant and confederate were also told that they would hear words over the headphones, ostensibly to provide a mild distraction and that the reason for the separate audio tracks was so that they would hear different words. To emphasize this point, the experimenter played a few seconds of the tape and asked the participant and confederate which word they heard in their headphones. The confederate always reported hearing a different word from the participant. Thus, participants were led to believe that the words they heard were not heard by the confederate.

The words served to prime thoughts about items on the screen for the participant (e.g., "swan"), and one was presented for each trial. The confederate, on the other hand, heard neither words nor music, but instead heard instructions to make particular movements at particular times. For four of the trials, the confederate was instructed to move to an object on the screen. A countdown followed until the time the confederate was to stop on the object. These forced stops were timed to occur midway through the participant's music. Each of these stops (e.g., to land on the swan) was timed to occur at specific intervals from when the participant heard the corresponding word (i.e., "swan"). The participant heard the word consistent with the stop either 30 seconds before, 5 seconds before, 1 second before, or 1 second after the confederate stopped on the object. By varying the timing, we thus manipulated priority. Each of these four stops was on a different object. These forced stops were embedded in a series of other trials for which the confederate simply let the participant make the stops. For these unforced stops, the participant heard a word 2 seconds into the music, whereas the confederate did not hear a word. The word corresponded to an object on the screen for about half of these trials, and was something not on screen for the others.

[...] Simply hearing words did not cause participants to stop on the items. The forced stops created by the confederate were thus not likely to have been abetted by movement originated by the participant.

On the forced stops, a pattern of perceived intention emerged as predicted by the priority principle. Although there was a tendency overall for participants to perceive the forced stops as intended $(M = 52\%, SD = 23.95)$, there was a marked fluctuation in this perception depending on when the prime word occurred. As shown in Figure 29.2, perceived intentionality was lower when the prime word appeared 30 seconds before the forced stop, increased when the word occurred 5 seconds or 1 second before the stop, and then dropped again to a lower level when the

word occurred 1 second following the stop. [...] Compared with trials when thought consistent with the forced action was primed 30 seconds before or 1 second after the action, there was an increased experience of intention when the thought was primed 1–5 seconds before the forced action. The mean percentage of intention reported on all the unforced stops – when participants were indeed free to move the cursor anywhere – was 56.09 $(SD = 11.76)$, a level in the same range as that observed for the forced stops in the 1-second and 5-second priming trials.

[...] We do not know from these data just what feature of having the object in mind prior to the forced stop produced the sense of will, but it is clear that the timing of the thought in relation to the action is important. When participants were reminded of an item on the screen just 1 or 5 seconds before they were forced to move the cursor to it, they reported having performed this movement intentionally. Such reminding a full 30 seconds before the forced movement or 1 second after the movement, in turn, yielded less of this sense of intentionality. The parallel observation that participants did not move toward primed objects on unforced trials suggests that participants were unlikely to have contributed to the movement on the forced trials. Apparently, the experience of will can be created by the manipulation of thought and action in accord with the principle of priority, and this experience can

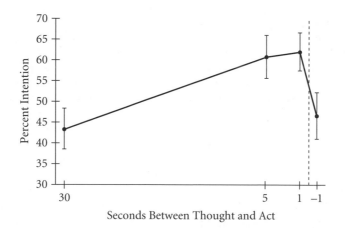

Figure 29.2 Mean Percentage of Intentionality Rated for Forced Stops on Objects Primed 30 Seconds Before, 5 Seconds Before, 1 Second Behre, or 1 Second After the Stop
Note. Error bars are standard errors.

occur even when the person's thought cannot have created the action.

Conclusion: Real and Apparent Mental Causation

The experience of will is like magic. As Harold Kelley (1980) observed, a magic trick involves disguising a real causal sequence (e.g., a rabbit is placed in the hat when the audience is looking elsewhere) and presenting instead an apparent causal sequence (i.e., a nice floppy-eared bunny is extracted from an empty hat). The magician creates the illusion by managing events so that the apparent causal sequence is far more conspicuous than the real one. The experience of conscious will is a comparable illusion produced by the perception of an apparent causal sequence relating one's conscious thought to one's action. In reality, this may not be the causal mechanism at all.

The real and apparent causal sequences relating thought and action probably do tend to correspond with each other some proportion of the time. After all, people are pretty good information processors when given access to the right information. The occurrence of conscious intention prior to action provides a fine clue as to how things that are on the person's mind might pertain to what the person does. In fact, the mental system that introduces thoughts of action to mind and keeps them coordinated with the actions is itself an intriguing mechanism. However, if as we suggest, conscious will is an experience that arises from the interpretation of cues to cognitive causality, then apparent mental causation is generated by an interpretive process that is fundamentally separate from the mechanistic process of real mental causation. The experience of will can be an indication that mind is causing action, especially if the person is a good self-interpreter, but it is not conclusive.

The experience of will is the way our minds portray their operations to us, then, not their actual operation. Because we have thoughts of what we will do, we can develop causal theories relating those thoughts to our actions on the basis of priority, consistency, and exclusivity. We come to think of these prior thoughts as intentions, and we develop the strong sense that the intentions have causal force even though they are actually

just previews of what we may do. The real causal mechanism is the marvelously intricate web of causation that is the topic of scientific psychology. The sense of will is not directly connected to this web and instead is an expression of our tendency to take what Dennett (1987) has called an "intentional stance" toward people. The intentional stance involves viewing psychological causation not in terms of causal mechanism but rather in terms of agents who have desires and beliefs that cause their acts. Conscious will is part of the process of taking an intentional stance toward oneself.

This analysis suggests that the real causal mechanisms underlying behavior are never present in consciousness. Rather, the engines of causation are unconscious mechanisms of mind. Much of the recent research suggesting a fundamental role for automatic processes in everyday behavior (e.g., Bargh, 1997) can be understood in this light. The real causes of human action are unconscious, so it is not surprising that behavior could often arise – as in automaticity experiments – without the person having conscious insight into its causation. Conscious will arises from a set of processes that are not the same as those that cause the behavior to which the experience of will pertains, however, so even processes that are not automatic – mental processes described as "controlled" (Posner & Snyder, 1975) or "conscious" (Wegner & Bargh, 1998) – have no direct expression in a person's experience of will. These processes may be less efficient than automatic processes and require more cognitive resources, but even if they occur along with an experience of control or conscious will, this experience is not a direct indication of their real causal influence.[2]

The unique human convenience of conscious thoughts that preview our actions gives us the privilege of feeling we willfully cause what we do. In fact, unconscious and inscrutable mechanisms create both conscious thought about action and create the action as well, and also produce the sense of will we experience by perceiving the thought as the cause of action. So, although our thoughts may have deep, important, and unconscious causal connections to our actions, the experience of conscious will arises from a process that interprets these connections, not from the connections themselves. Believing that our conscious thoughts cause our actions is an error

based on the illusory experience of will – much
like believing that a rabbit has indeed popped out
of an empty hat.

Notes

1 Voluntary action is defined here not in terms of perceptions of voluntariness but instead as it is in the
animal literature – as behavior that can be initiated
or inhibited in response to instruction or reinforcement (e.g., Kimble & Perlmuter, 1970; Passingham,
1993).

2 The experience of conscious will may be more likely
to accompany inefficient processes than efficient
ones because there is more time available prior to
action for inefficient thoughts to become conscious,
so as to prompt the formation of causal inferences
linking thought and action. This might explain why
controlled or conscious processes are often linked
with feelings of will, whereas automatic processes
are not.

References

Ansfield, M. E., & Wegner, D. M. (1996). The feeling of
doing. In P. M. Gollwitzer & J. A. Bargh (eds.), *The
psychology of action: Linking cognition and motivation
to behavior* (pp. 482–506). New York: Guilford Press.

Banks, G., Short, P., Martinez, A. J., Latchaw, R.,
Ratcliff, G., & Boller, F. (1989). The alien hand syn-
drome clinical and postmortem findings. *Archives of
Neurology, 46,* 456–9.

Bargh, J. A. (1997). The automaticity of everyday life.
In R. S. Wyer, Jr. (ed.), *Advances in social cognition*
(vol. 10, pp. 1–61). Mahwah, NJ: Erlbaum.

Brown, J. W. (1989). The nature of voluntary action.
Brain and Cognition, 10, 105–20.

Brown, J. W. (1996). *Time, will, and mental process.*
New York: Plenum.

Burgess, C. A., Kirsch, I., Shane, H., Niederauer, K. L.,
Graham, S. M., & Bacon, A. (1998). Facilitated com-
munication as an ideomotor response. *Psychological
Science, 9,* 71–4.

Carpenter, W. B. (1888). *Principles of mental physiology.*
New York: Appleton.

Dennett, D. C. (1984). *Elbow room: The varieties of
free will worth wanting.* Cambridge, MA: Bradford
Books/The MIT Press.

Dennett, D. C. (1987). *The intentional stance.*
Cambridge, MA: Bradford Books/The MIT Press.

Duval, S., & Wicklund, R. A. (1973). Effects of objective
self-awareness on attribution of causality. *Journal of
Experimental Social Psychology, 9,* 17–31.

Einhorn, H. J., & Hogarth, R. M. (1986). Judging probable cause. *Psychological Bulletin, 99,* 3–19.

Gibbons, F. X. (1990). Self-attention and behavior: A
review and theoretical update. In M. Zanna (ed.),
Advances in experimental social psychology (Vol. 23,
pp. 249–303). San Diego, CA: Academic Press.

Gilbert, D. T. (1995). Attribution and interpersonal
perception. In A. Tesser (ed.), *Advanced social psychology* (pp. 98–147). New York: McGraw-Hill.

Gollwitzer, P. M. (1993). Goal achievement: The role
of intentions. In W. Stroebe & M. Hewstone (eds.),
European review of social psychology (pp. 141–85).
London: Wiley.

Harnad, S. (1982). Consciousness: An afterthought.
Cognition and Brain Theory, 5, 29–47.

Hoffman, R. E. (1986). Verbal hallucinations and
language production processes in schizophrenia.
Behavioral and Brain Sciences, 9, 503–48.

Hume, D. (1888). *A treatise on human nature* (L. A.
Selby-Bigge, ed.). London: Oxford University Press.
(original work published 1739)

Jacobson, J. W., Mulick, J. A., & Schwartz, A. A. (1995).
A history of facilitated communication: Science,
pseudoscience, and antiscience. *American Psychologist,
50,* 750–65.

James, W. (1890). *Principles of psychology.* New York:
Holt.

Jones, E. E., & Davis, K. E. (1965). From acts to dispositions: The attribution process in person perception.
In L. Berkowitz (ed.), *Advances in experimental
social psychology* (Vol. 2, pp. 219–66). New York:
Academic Press.

Kelley, H. H. (1972). Causal schemata and the attribution process. In E. E. Jones, D. E. Kanouse, H. H.
Kelley, R. E. Nisbett, S. Valins, & B. Weiner (eds.),
Attribution: Perceiving the causes of behavior (pp. 151
–74). Morristown, NJ: General Learning Press.

Kelley, H. H. (1980). Magic tricks: The management of
causal attributions. In D. Görlitz (ed.), *Perspectives
on attribution research and theory: The Bielefeld
Symposium* (pp. 19–35). Cambridge, MA: Ballinger.

Kimble, G. A., & Perlmuter, L. C. (1970). The problem
of volition. *Psychological Review, 77,* 361–84.

Kirsch, I., & Lynn, S. J. (1997). Hypnotic involuntariness and the automaticity of everyday life. *American
Journal of Clinical Hypnosis, 40,* 329–48.

Kornhuber, H. H., & Deecke, L. (1965). Hirnpotent-
ialandeerungen bei Wilkurbewegungen und passiv
Bewegungen des Menschen: Bereitschaftspotential und
reafferente Potentiale. *Pflugers Archiv fur Gesamte
Psychologie, 284,* 1–17.

Langer, E. J. (1975). The illusion of control. *Journal of
Personality and Social Psychology, 32,* 311–28.

Libet, B. (1985). Unconscious cerebral initiative and the
role of conscious will in voluntary action. *Behavioral
and Brain Sciences, 8,* 529–66.

Lynn, S. J., Rhue, J. W., & Weekes, J. R. (1990). Hypnotic involuntariness: A social cognitive analysis. *Psychological Review, 97*, 169–84.

Marzollo, J., & Wick, W. (1992). *I spy*. New York: Scholastic.

McClure, J. (1998). Discounting causes of behavior: Are two reasons better than one? *Journal of Personality and Social Psychology, 74*, 7–20.

McGuire, P. K., Shah, G. M. S., & Murray, R. M. (1993). Increased blood flow in Broca's area during auditory hallucinations in schizophrenia. *Lancet, 342*, 703–06.

Michotte, A. (1963). *The perception of causality* (T. R. Miles & Elaine Miles, Trans.). New York: Basic Books.

Milgram, S. (1974). *Obedience to authority*. New York: Harper & Row.

Nisbett, R. E., & Ross, L. (1980). *Human inference: Strategies and shortcomings of social judgment*. Englewood Cliffs, NJ: Prentice-Hall.

Nisbett, R. E., & Wilson, T. D. (1977). Telling more than we can know: Verbal reports on mental processes. *Psychological Review, 84*, 231–59.

Passingham, R. E. (1993). *The frontal lobes and voluntary action*. Oxford, England: Oxford University Press.

Posner, M. I., & Snyder, C. R. R. (1975). Attention and cognitive control. In R. L. Solso (ed.), *Information processing and cognition* (pp. 55–85). Hillsdale, NJ: Erlbaum.

Searle, J. R. (1983). *Intentionality: An essay in the philosophy of mind*. New York: Cambridge University Press.

Spanos, N. P. (1982). Hypnotic behavior: A cognitive, social psychological perspective. *Research Communications in Psychology, Psychiatry, and Behavior, 7*, 199–13.

Spence, S. A. (1996). Free will in the light of neuropsychiatry. *Philosophy, Psychiatry, & Psychology, 3*, 75–90.

Spitz, H. H. (1997). *Nonconscious movements: From mystical messages to facilitated communication*. Mahwah, NJ: Erlbaum.

Twachtman-Cullen, D. (1997). *A passion to believe: Autism and the facilitated communication phenomenon*. Boulder, CO: Westview.

Vallacher, R. R., & Wegner, D. M. (1985). *A theory of action identification*. Hillsdale, NJ: Erlbaum.

Wegner, D. M. (2002). *The illusion of conscious will*. Cambridge, MA: MIT Press.

Wegner, D. M. (2003). The mind's best trick: How we experience conscious will. *Trends in Cognitive Science, 7*, 65–9.

Wegner, D. M., & Bargh, J. A. (1998). Control and automaticity in social life. In D. Gilbert, S. T. Fiske, & G. Lindzey (eds.), *Handbook of social psychology* (4th edn, Vol. 1, pp. 446–96). New York: McGraw-Hill.

Wegner, D. M., & Fuller, V. A. (1999). *Clever hands: Action projection in facilitated communication*. Manuscript submitted for publication.

Ziehen, T. (1899). *Introduction to physiological psychology* (C. C. Van Liew & O. W. Beyer, Trans.). New York: Macmillan.

30

Agency, Authorship, and Illusion

Eddy Nahmias

1. Introduction

Daniel Wegner suggests that our experience of consciously willing our actions is an illusion.[1] This claim has important implications for our sense of ourselves as agents and as authors of our actions. At a minimum, it suggests that things are not as they seem regarding that aspect of the world most important to us, ourselves. It might, for instance, imply that we are not free and morally responsible in the way we think we are. As Wegner puts it, "The fact is, it seems to each of us that we have conscious will. It seems we have selves. It seems we have minds. It seems we are agents. It seems we cause what we do . . . It is sobering and ultimately accurate to call all this an illusion" (2002, pp. 341–2).

But to determine if these claims are accurate requires, first, some analysis of what the experience of willing an action is, as well as its relation to the experiences of agency and authorship, and second, some analysis of what it means to say that an experience is illusory. Each of these tasks is monumental, so I will have to be somewhat sketchy. After examining Wegner's "theory of apparent mental causation," I will argue that this theory gives us no reason to conclude that our relevant experiences of agency and authorship are illusory. More specifically, I will argue that: (1) having illusory experiences is not the same as having mistaken theories, (2) it would take a dif-

ferent sort of evidence than Wegner presents to show our experience of agency is illusory, and (3) the experience of *agency* or of willing an action is importantly different than the experience of *authorship* (or being the source of one's actions), so that in whatever sense the former *may* be shown to be mistaken, the latter need not be. Though my discussion will focus on Wegner's views, they may be applicable to other views that have a similar structure.[2]

2. The Theory of Apparent Mental Causation

Daniel Wegner's experiments are ingenious and the unusual phenomena he describes in his work raise important questions about the psychology of agency, including the sorely neglected topic of the phenomenology of agency. In general, Wegner focuses on two types of situations that suggest there are notable exceptions to the ostensible rule that our voluntary actions are caused by our conscious intentions to perform them. First, there are situations in which people perform an action that looks voluntary but they do not experience themselves, or their own thoughts, to be the cause of the action. Examples include automatisms, alien hand syndrome, facilitated communication, and schizophrenia's alien control. Conversely, there are situations in which

From Eddy Nahmias, (2005) Consciousness and Cognition, 14, pp. 771–785.

people experience relevant thoughts about performing an action but the action is *not* in fact caused by those thoughts. Wegner has developed experiments that induce in his subjects an enhanced sense of agency and authorship for actions they do not in fact bring about (or even perform) simply because they are prompted to have a conscious thought that corresponds with an observed action and that occurs just prior to it.

For instance, in the "helping hands" experiment, subjects look in a mirror at the movements of a confederate's arms which are placed under the subjects' arms to look like their own. When subjects hear a command for a certain type of arm movement (e.g., "make the OK sign") that occurs just prior to their seeing the arm of the confederate making that movement, the subjects report an increased sense of controlling or willing the action compared to those cases when the command subjects hear does *not* match the movement they see in the mirror (or that comes well before the movement). That is, some sense of agency or authorship can be induced for actions the subjects clearly did not perform.[3]

Such experiments and phenomena led Wegner to the conclusion that our experience of mental causation derives from an unconscious inferential mechanism. Using Hume's account of our perception of causation in general, Wegner suggests that we experience a conscious thought (usually an intention) to be the cause of an action to the extent that the content of the thought is *consistent* with the action and immediately *precedes* the action, and we perceive no other likely cause for the action (*exclusivity*). This is the theory of "apparent mental causation" – the idea that when our experiences satisfy these three conditions we unconsciously infer that our conscious thoughts caused our actions. As Wegner puts it, "the feeling that we consciously will our own actions is traceable to an inference we make from the match between our conscious thoughts and observed action" (Wegner et al., 2004, p. 839). Elsewhere, Wegner stresses that this inference issues in a "cognitive feeling" or "authorship emotion" (2004, p. 658) such that we feel like our conscious intentions cause our actions.

Below I will examine how one might interpret this theory to imply that our experiences are thereby *illusory*, which will require clarifying both what our experiences of agency are and what it means for an experience to be illusory. First,

however, let us look more closely at the three conditions – consistency, priority, and exclusivity – Wegner associates with our experiences of agency.

It is unlikely that these three conditions will generally be *sufficient* for us to experience our normal sense of agency, at least for bodily actions. In addition, other factors, such as proprioceptive and kinesthetic feedback, normally play an important role in our experience of full-fledged agency.[4] It is not just that our thoughts match our observed actions that produces an experience of agency, but we also have sensorimotor experiences of our body and its movements, and these experiences are part of a feedback loop between predicted and perceived movements which, if disrupted, diminishes one's experience of agency.

Sacks (1970) discusses the case of Chris, a woman who has lost her sense of proprioception. Eventually she learns to get around by coordinating her intentions with her visually observed movements – her intentions are then consistent with, temporally prior to, and perceived to be the exclusive causes of her actions. Yet, despite meeting these conditions of Wegner's model, she does *not* feel her normal sense of agency or self nor move as fluidly or efficiently. As she puts it, "It's like something has been scooped right out of me, right at the centre . . . see Chris, the first pithed human being [with] no sense of herself – disembodied Chris, the pithed girl!" (pp. 51–52). Chris' loss of the experience of her own body seems to disrupt her experience of herself as the source of her actions, even though she has the relevant experiences of priority, consistency, and exclusivity sufficient to *infer* that her intentions are the cause of her bodily movements.

It is likely that the missing proprioceptive feedback in Wegner's helping hands experiment also helps to explain why these subjects do *not* in fact report feeling that they controlled the relevant movements or acted intentionally in making the movements. Rather, they report a statistically significant higher degree of "vicarious control" when the consistency and priority conditions are met, but the absolute value of the increase is only about 1 point on a 7 point scale, with the reports remaining on average below 3 out of 7. That is, subjects did report that they experienced a slightly enhanced sense of control when priority and consistency were present, but *not* that they experienced themselves as controlling the action. Of course, in this experiment the exclusivity condition is not met. In the "I-Spy" experiment, where the exclusivity condition was made ambiguous, satisfying the priority and consistency conditions also raised subjects' judgments of "personal intention" for causing an action, but only from about 45% to about 60% (see Wegner & Wheatley, 1999 [chapter 29, figure 29.2]). That is, in these experiments Wegner is *not* in fact producing situations where subjects feel their actions are caused by their conscious intentions and demonstrating that this is not the case. Subjects do *not* report "having performed the movement intentionally" and it has not been shown that "the experience of will can be created by the manipulation of thought and action in accord with the principle of priority" (2002, p. 78).[5]

I also doubt Wegner's three conditions are *necessary* for us to feel like we are the authors of our actions. We often experience ourselves as the authors of our well-rehearsed automatic behaviors, as in athletic or musical performances, even when we experience no immediately preceding conscious thoughts (e.g., intentions) to perform the specific behaviors involved. Rather, we seem to have a general intention or plan to play well, perhaps to carry out some array of actions, and then we let our bodies take over, consciously monitoring our movements but not consciously forming intentions to carry out specific subsequent actions (indeed, forming such conscious intentions tends to trip us up). Nonetheless, we experience ourselves as the source of the resulting actions. Perhaps in certain cases of well-rehearsed actions we may experience a *reduced* sense of agency; actions that require an exercise of "willpower" or concentration may be accompanied by a greater sense of personal agency than skilled actions performed more effortlessly.[6] Nonetheless, unless the priority condition is interpreted to include a much longer span of time than the 1–5 s Wegner suggests, it does not seem necessary for us to experience ourselves as the authors of our actions. I'll return to this point in Section 5.[7]

Having raised these questions, I suggest that Wegner is nevertheless correct that the three conditions cited by his theory of apparent mental causation are surely significant *contributors* to our normal experience of agency, and he demonstrates as much with numerous experiments that show that manipulating the presence of these conditions does influence subjects' reports about the *degree* to which they experience control or authorship for their actions. For now, let us assume that the theory of apparent mental causation is a roughly accurate account of the inference mechanisms that produce our sense of consciously willing our actions. The question then is why this would then lead to the further and more disconcerting conclusion that our experience of agency is *illusory*.

3. Illusory Experiences

Wegner recognizes that his use of the word "illusion" to describe our experiences of agency, of authorship – of having a self at all – is controversial and would provoke criticism (see his 2004, p. 682). A legitimate criticism is that he never clarifies exactly what he means by calling these experiences an illusion or what he means by "the experience of conscious will."[8] For instance, he concludes his book by saying that it is an illusion "that we cause what we do" and "Our sense of being a conscious agent who does things comes at the cost of being technically wrong all the time" (2002, p. 342), but elsewhere he writes, "Questions of whether thought actually does cause action, for example, have been left in peace, and the role of consciousness in the causation of action has been ignored as well" (2005, p. 32). I will try to clarify the situation by explaining what I take it to mean for an experience to be illusory and then offering various ways of interpreting Wegner's claim that the experience of conscious will is illusory.[9]

An experience is illusory if the way it represents things is not the way things actually are. More precisely, a person's experience of X is illusory if the content of the experience includes that X has various features, but X does *not* in fact have those features. So, to show that an experience of X is illusory requires (1) showing that the content of the experience includes that X has certain features and (2) showing that X does *not* in fact have those features. It may also require (3) showing that even after the person comes to *believe* that X does not have the relevant features, she nevertheless continues to experience X as having those features (i.e., illusions are "cognitively impenetrable").[10] I will focus on the first two features for now.

So, what is the experience that Wegner is claiming is illusory – what is the "X" and what features does it *seem* to have that it does not *actually* have? To answer this question, it is just as important to understand the relevant phenomenology as it is to understand the relevant psychological and neurobiological facts. And the relevant phenomenology has not been adequately explored, by Wegner or anyone else.[11] It likely involves various experiences, including experiences of *mental* actions such as deliberating and making decisions, as well as various experiences of *bodily* actions, including acting "thoughtfully" (with one's intention in mind), acting "thoughtlessly" (without concurrent awareness of one's intention), exerting oneself in action, feeling in control, and acting directly in response to "triggering" stimuli (e.g., returning a shot in tennis).

Though all of these experiences likely involve the agent's feeling that she is importantly involved in the action, it is far from obvious that they all involve the agent's feeling that her *conscious* thoughts are causing her bodily movements. Wegner seems to have in mind those cases where an agent is consciously performing some action, and he takes the paradigmatic cases to involve "willpower" and the "exercise of self-control" (2003, p. 30). So, the experiences in question involve an agent's being aware of her intention to perform an action and being aware of performing that action. What then are the relevant *features* of these experiences that are supposed to be illusory?

Notice that the more substantial the purported experience (the "thicker" the phenomenology), the more plausible it will turn out to be illusory, and conversely, the less substantial the experience (the "thinner" the phenomenology), the less likely it will be illusory. More, and more detailed, features of experience mean there's more to get wrong. Hence, it would advance Wegner's conclusion if he could offer evidence that our experience of agency includes features that are unlikely (even impossible) to be true. Though, as I have suggested, he does not offer much evidence regarding the phenomenology, he may be read as suggesting our experience of agency includes a robust experience of a self, or homunculus, that is not mechanistic, suggestive of a Cartesian soul, and that directly causes our actions, perhaps even in an agent-causal way.[12] If our experience of agency is this robust, then Wegner is right that it is illusory. But I do not think that our experience includes, or commits us to believing in, anything as metaphysically sophisticated as a dualistic or agent-causal self.[13] In any case, if *this* is the illusion Wegner has in mind, then: (a) he would not be offering any new revelations and (b) the sort of evidence he presents would not be particularly relevant.

A slightly less robust, though still Cartesian, conception of the experience of agency includes the feature of being "self-knowing" or "self-luminous" (2004, p. 682) – that is, in consciously performing an action, the agent is directly aware of the *cause* of the action, specifically, that the agent or his intentions cause the action. Then, the claim is that this experience is illusory because we do *not* have direct access to the causes of our actions and we can be mistaken about them. To show that our experience is illusory in this sense, it is not enough to show that we are sometimes, or even often, mistaken about why we do what we do – a fact well-confirmed by some of Wegner's work, along with a long tradition of research in social psychology. It must also be established that we experience ourselves as being *infallible* about our own reasons for action, that the experience of action essentially includes awareness of the motivating causes of the action. I find it highly dubious that our experience of agency includes this experience of infallibility. Though we are likely overconfident about how much self-knowledge we have, we certainly seem to recognize what our friends, Freud, and a long literary tradition tell us – that sometimes we are wrong about why we do what we do – that sometimes our true intentions are not (easily) accessible to us. That we sometimes have to confabulate explanations for our actions (and sometimes know we have confabulated) offers some evidence that *during* action we do not have a "self-luminous" experience of mental causation.

Perhaps the illusion, then, derives not from the purported experience of infallibility but from the purported experience of *direct access* to the causes of our actions. That is, when we *do* feel we know why we are acting, we are conscious of our relevant mental states as the cause of our actions, but these mental states are not the causes of our action. As above, we might question whether we do experience our mental states as causing our actions.[14] I am inclined to say we do. But then the burden falls on Wegner to show that our mental states do not cause our actions. Sometimes Wegner suggests that our experience of agency is an illusion because we experience our conscious thoughts as the cause of our actions but we do not – perhaps cannot – experience the low-level mechanisms actually involved in producing both the thoughts and the actions. For instance, he writes, "The real causal sequence underlying human behavior involves a massively complicated set of mechanisms" (2002, p. 27), and "We should be surprised, after all, if cognitive creatures with our demonstrably fallible self-insight were capable of perceiving the deepest mechanisms of our own minds" (2003, p. 68).

But here it is more appropriate to describe our experiences as *incomplete* rather than illusory. We are quite lucky we do not experience most of what happens before and after we form our intentions, including all the neural work that goes on between the intention and the muscle movements, and also any unconscious inferential processes that inform our causal judgments. But this lack of direct introspection of what happens below the surface does not entail that our experiences are *illusory* any more than our lack of direct perception of the molecular activity that happens below the surface when one billiard ball strikes another entails that our experience of causation in that case is illusory. Rather, our experiences would be illusory in both cases only if there were no significant relationship (perhaps supervenience or identity) between the low-level processes and the interactions that occur at the level we *do* perceive. Unless, that is, we are willing to say that *all* of our experiences of causal interactions are illusory because we do not perceive the underlying causal mechanisms.[15]

Here is another way to put the point. Suppose the theory of apparent mental causation is accurate in that our experience of ourselves or our intentions as the cause of our actions is inferential. The fact that we experience such causation as *non*-inferential does not show the experience to be illusory unless the "conclusion" of the inference is systematically mistaken. So, it would have to be shown not merely that we do not know everything about the process by which we experience our actions as caused by our conscious intentions but that, in general, the intentions (or other relevant mental states) that we are

(sometimes) conscious of are *not* the causes of our actions. And, as I will discuss below in Section 4, this has not been established by Wegner nor could it be established by the sort of evidence he presents.

Perhaps, however, Wegner is better interpreted as suggesting not so much that our *experiences* of will and agency are mistaken, but that our *beliefs* about them are mistaken. That is, we may be radically *mistaken* about how the relevant causal processes work. Indeed, we may have *theories* about how causation, whether physical or psychological, works that are just dead wrong. For instance, we may have a mistaken theory about a force called "impetus" that moves from one ball to the other when they strike. And it is quite possible that lots of people have false *theories* about what happens when they act – they may, for instance, have a dualist *theory* of mind and believe that their intentions are non-physical causes of their actions. But a false theory is not best described as an *illusion* in part because of the fact that false theories or beliefs, unlike illusory experiences, lose their hold on us when they are corrected (this was my third claim about illusions above).[16] It should be no surprise that our folk psychological theories are not entirely correct, just as our folk physics and folk biology are not entirely correct. But these theories derive from more than our experiences, and our experiences are consistent with different (and more accurate) theories.

Sometimes Wegner seems to be suggesting this sort of approach to the psychological study of agency. That is, we should not take our experiences of agency or will to be any more indicative of the underlying nature and causal structure of ourselves, our minds, or our actions than we take our perceptual experiences to be indicative of the underlying nature and causal structure of the external world. For instance, Wegner writes, "The task of determining the causal relations between conscious representations and actions is a matter of inspection through scientific inquiry" because our experiences of such causal relations "can be misled by any number of circumstances that render invalid inferences" (2003, p. 68). This conclusion is an appropriate call for research. But who would disagree with it? Anyone studying the mind should be interested in the causal relations between consciously experienced mental states and bodily movements, and few cognitive scientists or philosophers would think that direct introspection is the best (or even primary) method for revealing those *causal* relations.[17] Any physicalist about the mind will also seek to understand the neural processes that are the subvenient base of our conscious mental states and the causal relations between these processes and bodily movements.[18]

Indeed, any satisfying *physicalist* theory of mind will have to explain our conscious experiences, including for instance, why we experience our intentional actions at the level of purposeful mental states rather than mechanistic interactions. But if the idea is that the existence of such explanations shows our experiences to be illusory, it is too hasty, because our experiences alone do not commit us to the belief that such explanations do not exist. Similarly, our ordinary perceptual experiences are not illusory just because there are complex neurobiological explanations for those experiences. Our *experiences* of agency are best viewed as theory-neutral. They are consistent with a variety of theories about the metaphysics of mental causation, including some forms of physicalism. Though some people's experience of agency may incline them towards a dualistic theory of mind, a committed physicalist does not stop experiencing herself as consciously willing her actions.[19]

Instead, for our experiences of agency to be an *illusion*, they must involve a genuinely misleading experience of what actually happens when we act, a misleading experience that can be explained away but cannot be corrected in the way a theory can. For this to be the case, it would require not just that our experiences are incomplete or our theories about mental causation are mistaken, but that our experiences are systematically misinformative. What would it mean for our experiences of agency and authorship to be misleading in this way?

4.   A One-Way Exit?

Wegner thinks that we experience our conscious intentions as the cause of our actions but they are *not* in fact the cause. Again, this does not follow from the fact that conscious intentions are not the *direct* cause of bodily movements without

intervening mechanisms or the fact that conscious intentions may be physically instantiated. Rather, our experiences of conscious will would be systematically misleading in this sense only if there were some (set of) causes for our behaviors that systematically bypass conscious intentions entirely.

Assuming a physicalist theory, the only way I can make sense of this claim is that the neural processes involved in our forming conscious intentions are not causally connected to our action-production system – those neural processes involved in causing behavior. Wegner suggests this picture with his diagram of "apparent mental causation" that has unconscious mental events producing both actions and thoughts about them, but the thoughts have no causal effects on the actions (there are no "actual causal path" arrows leading away from the "thought" box).[20] But Wegner's evidence for this view is not based on neurobiological discoveries that the two systems are in fact disconnected or that the system involving conscious intentions does not feed into the action-production system.[21] Rather, he seems to base his claim primarily on the fact that sometimes we experience an intention without the appropriate action following, and sometimes we perform what looks like voluntary movements without experiencing the appropriate intention. These exceptional cases are then taken to prove the rule that conscious intentions do not play any role in causing actions.

But of course the fact that events of type X sometimes occur without events of type Y, and vice versa, does not entail that when such events – in this case a conscious intention and the corresponding action – *do* occur together the X-type event is not the cause of Y-type event. All you need is the possibility of alternative effects of X-type events and of alternative causes of Y-type events for these exceptions to be possible and explicable.[22] For example, our experience of seeing an orange may be caused by a hologram (and, of course, a real orange may not cause an experience of seeing an orange), but these exceptions do not entail that the presence of an orange is not usually the cause of our experiences of seeing an orange. Similarly, my experience of willing to move my arm may not cause my anesthetized arm to move, and my arm's moving as I dribble a basketball may not be caused by *immediately* prior conscious intentions to move them, but these exceptions do not entail that my conscious intentions are *never* the cause of my arm's moving.

I put this in terms of *types* because doing so allows us to see that there may be *token* instances of causal factors other than *X*-type ones that can bring about a token *Y*-type event. And vice versa. But again, these token instances may represent exceptions to the rule that *X*'s typically cause *Y*'s. For instance, in the extension of Wegner's helping hands experiment I describe in footnote 5, we might induce in subjects a substantial sense of agency while we know that they are not causing any bodily movements at all. But in this case, as in *all* of the cases Wegner uses to show that we can experience some degree of agency without causing the relevant action, there is another causal source of the action as well as a causal explanation for the induced experience of agency. These exceptional cases certainly open up the *possibility* that our conscious intentions *never* play a role in action production, but they do not establish that possibility as actual.[23]

Rather, the evidence required to establish this generalization would involve showing that the neural processes that cause voluntary behavior are not regularly influenced by the neural processes that are the subvenient base for (or are identical to) our consciously forming our intentions. The intention-system would be, as it were, on a one-way exit from the action-production system, as suggested by Wegner's diagram. While this sort of epiphenomenalism is possible, it is not suggested by the exceptional cases Wegner discusses – since, again, in these cases there is always some explanation for the disconnect between the experience of agency and the cause of action. On the contrary, numerous other experiments suggest that conscious intentions are causally implicated in action.[24] Wegner's work effectively explains *when* our experience of agency is an illusion but not that such experiences are *always* illusions.

One final reason to reject the view that our experience of conscious will is illusory is that these experiences are clearly functional. They allow us to act effectively in the world in the same sense that our visual experiences represent the world in a way that allows us to act effectively. Our visual experiences are, of course, *incomplete*

in that they do not represent the micro-structure of the world but this tends to be a good thing as long as we are not doing physics (or perhaps metaphysics). Our visual experiences are also subject to illusions in that they sometimes misrepresent the *macro*-structure of the world. These illusions tend to occur, however, precisely because our visual systems evolved to represent the macro-world in a useful and accurate way. For instance, the environmental cues we use to perceive depth from a two-dimensional retinal image are the same cues that lead us to misperceive as unequal the equally long lines in the Müller–Lyer illusion and to misperceive a Necker cube as three dimensional.

Similarly, it should not be surprising that our experiences of willing our actions are *sometimes* subject to illusion in this sense. For instance, it is useful for us to interpret other agent's intelligent behavior in terms of the agent's beliefs and desires (this "theory of mind" system likely evolved in the context of our ancestors' complex social environments). But this system may lead us to attribute mental states to complex systems (like computers or even the weather) that do not have such mental states. Such misattributions do not, however, entail that *no* agents actually have mental states that cause their actions. Wegner (2002, chaps. 6–7) discusses such misattributions (including anthropomorphism) and suggests that our attribution of conscious mental states as causes is always illusory but allows us to "construct a virtual agent in which we can reside" (p. 269). But just as our visual illusions occur against a background of functional perceptions, it may be that our mistaken attributions of mental causation do not represent a rule that no such mental causation exists but rather occur against the background of generally functional and accurate perceptions of our own and others' actions being caused by the relevant mental states (some of which are conscious).[25]

The claim that conscious will is an illusion has the ring of a skeptical argument. Such arguments have this basic form: we know our experiences are *sometimes* misleading, so we cannot know that they are not *always* misleading. Such arguments are notoriously challenging in the context of philosophical debates about epistemology.[26] But luckily, in the context of empirical psychology, we can look to empirical data to explore the likelihood of systematic illusion. In the case of perception, we can discover the mechanisms responsible for our misperceptions and explain why they depend on the mechanisms responsible for our normally perceiving the world accurately. In the case of intentional action, we might similarly discover the mechanisms responsible for the cases Wegner discusses and explain why they depend on the mechanisms responsible for our normally perceiving ourselves accurately. Of course, we may discover that we *are* systematically misperceiving the role of conscious intentions because they really are epiphenomenal – in the sense of being causally cut off from behavior production. But demonstrating this would require neurobiological evidence beyond what Wegner discusses. Discovering that the neural processes involved in the formation of conscious intentions do not causally influence the behavior-production system is possible but, I think, highly unlikely. Here's one reason why.

5. Agency vs. Authorship

Suppose it did turn out that those conscious intentions that occur just prior to action are only effects, not causes, within the behavior-production system. Even this discovery would not show that conscious deliberation and intention formation are not causally implicated in our actions. This is because many of the intentions we form are not intentions to perform an action now but rather to perform various actions later. Here we must distinguish, first, *distal* intentions from *proximal* intentions (Mele, 1992) and, second, *conscious* intentions from *non-conscious* intentions. Distal intentions are intentions to perform an action at some future time, with varying degrees of specificity regarding the time to perform the action and how exactly to carry it out. And sometimes the intention is to perform an action in response to some predicted situation (or triggering stimulus). I may intend to go jogging sometime later today, or I may intend to offer a particular answer to the question I expect a student to ask in class. Distal intentions are often formed with conscious deliberation and we are usually conscious of them when we form them. However, we are often *not* conscious of these intentions just prior to acting on them. We are

also not conscious of many of our *proximal* intentions, those that occur just prior to action. If it were shown that, in those cases when we *are* conscious of our proximal intentions, our being conscious of them is not causally relevant to the action, this would not in itself show that our consciousness of our distal intentions plays no causal role in our performing the actions later.

These distinctions allow us to recognize that even if it turns out that our experience of *agency* were shown to be illusory in the sense that our conscious experience of proximal intentions is causally irrelevant to our action, this would not thereby show that our experience of *authorship* is illusory. Here, it is important to be clear about the relevant phenomenology. It seems right to say that often the experience of *agency* – especially the cases of "willpower" and self-control Wegner highlights – involves the feeling that one's conscious proximal intention to perform a specific movement is the cause of that movement. But the more general experience of being the *author* of our actions encompasses a much wider scope of intentions and actions. Reporting just my own phenomenology (I ask you to consult your own), I feel like I often carry out many complex actions without forming immediately prior conscious intentions to perform those acts. Rather, at some earlier time I formed a general plan or a set of distal intentions to carry out an array of actions, and later (sometimes significantly later) I carry out those actions automatically without forming conscious proximal intentions for each action.[27] I have in mind not just playing guitar or basketball "in the zone" (unconsciously, as it were), but also the various actions following a decision to walk to the fridge to get a beer, to drive home, or even to deliver a well-planned lecture. In such cases, even if my conscious thoughts are not proximal causes of my actions, they seem to be crucial distal causes.[28]

Wegner writes, "many of our most fluid, expert, and admirable acts are ones we do not experience consciously willing" and this leads to a "loss of the sense of authorship in skilled actions" which "do not feel willed as they unfold" (2005, p. 29). I do not think this is an accurate description of the relevant phenomenology. We do not experience our skilled actions as happening to us or as disconnected from our own intentions, plans, and goals, including some formed during conscious learning and conscious deliberation. Rather, we experience ourselves as the authors and sources of these actions, sometimes the more so precisely because of the earlier conscious effort we have put into them.

This explanation for our sense of authorship would offer an alternative explanation for certain cases of what Wegner calls "vicarious agency," our experience of authorship for others' actions. It is not that we feel "a twinge of authorship when our child wins an award . . . because our anticipatory thoughts of the glory made us vicarious agents in the action" (Wegner et al., 2004, p. 847). Rather, we may feel a twinge of authorship in such cases because we feel like we were important distal causes of our children's success; we raised them to be so successful! Similarly, I can feel some sense of authorship for the eventual effects of some of my actions, even when my actions are not the proximal causes of those effects. Authorship, like responsibility, can be experienced to different degrees and can be shared among various agents.

Finally, Wegner has given us no reason to believe that our conscious thoughts are not causal factors in our *mental* actions, such as concentrating, deliberating, or making decisions. And it is these mental actions involved in deliberation and the formation of general plans of action that seem most significant to our sense of authorship and responsibility for our later actions, many of which may be carried out without any experience of forming a proximal intention to perform them. If you jump to the aid of a person in need or keep silent in response to someone's degrading comment, you may feel responsible for your action or your omission even without forming conscious intentions to act (or not to act), because you may trace your response to earlier character-forming actions or to conscious considerations about what sort of person you want to be. We are authors of our actions in part because we are authors of our general plans and distal intentions.

It is *possible* that even these conscious deliberations leading to decisions and plans of action are just epiphenomenal effects of processes that could occur without input from the processes underlying conscious awareness, but I see no reason to think this is likely.[29] Rather, given the way the brain is interconnected, it is unlikely that any significant set of neural processes – including those involved in conscious mental states – is causally cut off from those involved in producing behavior. Thus, even if more evidence turned up to show that we are not quite the *agents* we think we are – because our conscious mental states are not the immediate causes of our actions – we could still be the *authors* we think we are – our conscious mental states being significant distal causal contributors to at least many of our decisions and actions.

6.   Conclusion: What Am I Afraid Of?

In his recent reply to commentaries, Wegner (2004) scoffs at my whimsical use of Jerry Fodor's oft-cited remark that if our beliefs and desires do not cause our actions, then "practically everything I believe about anything is false and it's the end of the world" (1990, p. 196 quoted in Nahmias, 2002, p. 539). Wegner suggests that anyone who reacts with such "shrill invective" against his views must be motivated by emotion – "a motor, an emotional basis that drives the rhetoric" (2004, p. 680). This response is reminiscent of the defense a Freudian might use against his opponent: "Of course, you don't accept my theory. You're repressing your sexuality."[30]

Well, I am motivated (perhaps even by my emotions!) to try to understand and find fault with the claim that our sense of self, agency, and will are all illusory, because these are significant claims, ones that may have an influence beyond the ivory tower on people's conception of themselves and of ethical, legal, and political issues. (Of course, I may have other motivations that I do not even know about – my experience of agency is not infallible.) But let me be clear about what is *not* the "emotional basis" of my critique. I am not afraid of the fact that our conscious experiences fail to provide a direct view into the workings of our brain. Introspection thankfully does not allow us to experience the low-level neural activity involved in our coming to form our intentions and actions. Nor is introspection an infallible guide to why we do what we do or whether our conscious intentions cause our actions. Wegner is right to call for more psychological research into the phenomenology of agency and the causal mechanisms involved in action and the experience of agency. Nor am I afraid that our naïve theories of mental causation may be mistaken in significant ways. I am a physicalist. So if our folk psychology tends to be dualist, I think it *is* radically mistaken. But I do not think our experiences of agency would be illusory if dualism is false because I think our experiences are consistent with a physicalist ontology.

As a physicalist I am also not afraid that we are, in some sense, complicated mechanisms that can be studied scientifically, though I *am* motivated by the worry that it is very easy to misinterpret – and to *misrepresent* – this truth to suggest, for instance, that it shows that we are not really agents, that we do not really have minds, that we lack free will or moral responsibility, or that our sense of self is illusory. Future scientific study of the mind may show that some of these claims are accurate, but doing so will require that we analyze more carefully what our phenomenology of agency actually is, what it would mean for it to be illusory, and what the underlying neurobiology is. Indeed, I *am* afraid that such scientific study might someday show that our conscious deliberations, decisions, and intentions are *not* causally relevant to our actions (or even that they are much less relevant than we think – e.g., because they have only a retrospective role in helping us take responsibility for what our bodies do). But, luckily, Wegner has not shown this yet.

Notes

1   See Wegner (2005, 2004), Wegner, Sparrow, and Winerman (2004), Wegner and Wheatley (1999, chapter 29 in this volume), and especially Wegner (2002).
2   See, for instance, Bargh (2005) and Prinz (2003), who writes, "There appears to be no support for the folk psychology notion that the act follows the will, in the sense that physical action is caused by mental events that precede them" (p. 26).
3   See Wegner et al. (2004). See also the 'I-Spy' experiment in Wegner and Wheatley (1999 [chapter 29]).
4   Wegner discusses some of these other factors in Wegner et al. (2004, pp. 838–9). The case of *mental* actions, such as calculating, deciding, or planning do not involve proprioception, so Wegner's three conditions are more likely to be sufficient in these cases. I discuss mental actions more fully in Section 5.
5   It would be interesting to develop a "helping hands" experiment that *did* create a sense in subjects of being the *exclusive* cause of the hands' movements.

Here's a possibility (though it may not pass the Human Subjects' Committee). First, numb subjects' arms, but let them see that they can still move their arms without proprioceptive feedback. Then, surreptitiously place them in a set-up like the helping hands scenario. Then, have a well-disguised confederate's arms carry out movements that match commands the subjects are asked to carry out (while the subjects' numbed arms are restrained without their feeling it). If the set-up is convincing, these subjects would, I predict, report they had moved their own arms. However, without proprioceptive feedback, I suspect they, like Christina, would *not* report a full-fledged feeling of agency, and it may be that their reports are based less on a normal experience of agency than on an inference that they must have moved their arms based on the exclusivity principle: "Who else could have moved my arm?" Wegner suggests, rather, that the normal experience of agency is always based on such a causal inference that produces a cognitive emotion of conscious will.

6   This is one place where the phenomenology is complex and under-explored. Some cases of skilled behavior seem to be accompanied by a *heightened* sense of one's self being engaged in and in control of the activity, while others seem to involve a diminished sense of agency (perhaps including "flow" experiences).
7   Coordinated actions, as in ballroom dancing, may also raise questions about the relation between the experience of agency and the exclusivity condition. There are real-life examples of situations like the helping hands scenario, in which people have thoughts consistent with and just prior to observed actions caused by another agent. I have in mind synchronized swimmers or ballet dancers. It would be interesting to probe the phenomenology of such agents to see if satisfying the same two conditions as in the helping hands experiment produces any enhanced sense of control or agency for their partners' actions.
8   Note that, assuming Wegner thinks that, by definition, our experiences are conscious, the phrase "the experience of conscious will" is itself very confusing. Is it that we are conscious of being conscious of willing (presumably a rare occurrence) or is there just an extra 'conscious' used so that it should read 'the experience of willing [or intending] an action'? And, as I will discuss below, the experience of willing an action may be importantly different from the (presumably more general) experiences of agency or of authorship.
9   For further discussion of various interpretations of Wegner's theses, see Nahmias (2002), Bayne (2006), and commentaries in Wegner (2004).

[10] Take, for example, our visual experience of Müller–Lyer lines: our experience includes the feature that the line with inward-pointing arrowheads is longer than the line with outward-pointing arrowheads, but the lines in fact do not have this feature, since they are equal in length. For most people the lines continue to appear unequal even after they come to believe they are equal in length. The most extreme cases of illusion involve experiences of something existing that does not actually exist (e.g., a hallucination). For agency and intention to be an illusion in this sense would require that agents and intentions do not exist at all. Wegner sometimes suggests this eliminativist position – e.g., "To be accurate, we must speak of apparent mental causation, or of virtual agency, rather than of intention or of a controller" (2005, p. 32).

[11] For some recent discussions, see Bayne and Levy (2006), Horgan, Tienson, and Graham (2003), Nahmias, Morris, Nadelhoffer, and Turner (2004).

[12] See Bayne (2006).

[13] See Nahmias et al. (2004) for discussion of the phenomenology of free will, including whether there is evidence that ordinary people have an experience of agent causation. See also Horgan et al. (2003).

[14] See Horgan et al. (2003, p. 225).

[15] It is somewhat ironic that Wegner cites Hume on causation since Hume *is* a skeptic about all causal relations (i.e., about our knowledge of any necessary relations between events), whereas Wegner is a skeptic about conscious will (mental causation) precisely because we do not experience the low-level mechanistic processes he dubs the "real causes of human action" (2002, p. 97). A consistent Humean about causation should be no less skeptical about mental causation than any other type of causation, so long as there are the requisite observed regularities (see below).

[16] See Jack and Robbins commentary on Wegner (2004).

[17] Even Cartesian dualists should want to study the causal interactions they think hold between (immaterial) conscious thoughts and bodily movements and understand when they are inaccurately perceived, though the difficulty of understanding what these mind–body causal interactions might be is a notorious problem for such dualists.

[18] Again, if Wegner's claim that conscious will is an illusion is just the claim that Cartesian interactionism is false, then it seems he presents the wrong kind of evidence. The right kind of evidence would be neurobiological evidence offering complete causal explanations of bodily movements by physical states (though this evidence would not be conclusive since overdetermination is a logical possibility).

[19] Of course, it is an empirical question whether most people in fact have a dualistic theory of the metaphysics of mental causation. I suspect that these theories are influenced more by people's culture and religion than by their phenomenology of agency.

[20] See diagram in Wegner and Wheatley (1999) [chapter 29, figure 29.1]).

[21] Wegner does discuss Benjamin Libet's experiments that purportedly show that actions are produced by brain activity that precedes conscious awareness of the intention to act, but there are important problems with interpreting Libet's work. For instance, Libet's data may only show that our *urge* to move precedes our awareness of the intention to move. Libet's data do *not* establish that the brain activity involved in our conscious intentions is not causally related to our actions. Wegner also references Penfield's work and theory of mind research to suggest that the intention-formation system may be a distinct 'module' from the action-production system (2002, chaps. 1–2), but even if they are distinct, that would not show that they are causally disconnected. See Nahmias (2002).

[22] Alternatively, causal activity in one system A may normally be caused by causal activity in another system B, but sometimes similar activity in A might be caused by activity that bypasses B. This would not show that B activity is not the usual cause of A activity.

[23] Note also that the cases Wegner describes of an agent's actions that look voluntary but are not experienced as consciously intended (e.g., automatisms, alien hand) do not show that the agent has an *illusory* sense of agency, since the agent does *not* have a sense of agency in these cases. That is, these agents are not mistaken in believing that their conscious intention did not cause their action, because they did not *have* a conscious intention to perform the action. They are, of course, mistaken if they believe that they (i.e., their bodies and brains) are not causally responsible for their movements.

[24] Consider the interesting research by neurobiologists at Duke University led by Miguel Nicolelis (see, e.g., Carmena et al., 2003, and "Monkeys Consciously Control a Robot Arm Using Only Brain Signals" at http://www.dukenews.duke.edu/2003/10/20031013.html). They record specific neural activity of monkeys moving a joystick so that a computer can read off such brain activity and then produce the corresponding movements before the monkeys do. The monkeys learn that they can simply form the intention to move and the computer will take over so that they do not have to carry out the movement of the joystick. Assuming the monkeys have conscious intentions (or that similar work could be done with humans), it appears that the

neural processes involved in forming such intentions are causally implicated in subsequent actions.

25 This is an appropriate place to refer the reader to Austin's response (1977) to the so-called "argument from illusion," in which he points out that the existence of perceptual illusions that are virtually indistinguishable from veridical experiences (cases of which are much rarer than suggested by advocates of the argument) does *not* suggest that there are no important differences between them. There is usually a straightforward explanation for the unusual experience. Similarly, there are explanations (though perhaps less straightforward) for the unusual experiences Wegner discusses or creates in the lab.

26 Challenging not because they force us to accept the conclusion but because they force us to analyze the concepts involved in the argument, such as "knowledge." The arguments, of course, are more complex and complete than the one above.

27 This is not to say that I do not have *intentions* to perform these actions since, as pointed out above, intentions can exist without our being conscious of them. It would be a mistake to say that we must be conscious of any intentions we have at the time we have them.

28 Indeed, there is research on the "causal primacy effect" to suggest that we generally attribute greater causality to earlier rather than later events in a causal chain, which would help to explain our experiences of authorship for actions caused in part by our prior intention formation.

29 I am here ignoring the philosophical arguments that pose problems for the causal efficacy of conscious mental properties in general (e.g., Kim, 1998), since such possibilities neither support, nor are supported by, Wegner's discussion. If the causal exclusion problem is the illusion Wegner is suggesting, then his evidence is not the sort needed to make his case. See Nahmias (2002).

30 Thanks to Neil Levy for this way of putting it.

References

Austin, J. L. (1977). In G. J. Warnock (ed.), *Sense and sensibilia*. New York: Oxford University Press.

Bargh, J. (2005). Bypassing the will: Towards demystifying behavioral priming effects. In R. Hassin, J. S. Uleman, & J. A. Bargh (eds.), *The new unconscious* (pp. 37–58). New York: Oxford University Press.

Bayne, T. (2006). Phenomenology and the feeling of doing: Wegner on the conscious will. In S. Pockett,

W.P. Banks, & S. Gallagher (eds.), *Does consciousness cause behavior? An investigation of the nature of volition* pp. 169–86. Cambridge: MIT Press.

Bayne, T., & Levy, N. (2006). The feeling of doing: Deconstructing the phenomenology of agency. In N. Sabanz & W. Prinz (Eds.), *Disorders of volition* pp. 49–68. Cambridge: MIT Press.

Carmena, J. M., Lebedev, M. A., Crist, R. E., O'Doherty, J. E., Santucci, D. M., Dimitrov, D. F., et al. (2003). Learning to control a brain–machine interface for reaching and grasping by primates. *PLoS Biology, 1*, 193–208.

Horgan, T., Tienson, J., & Graham, G. (2003). The phenomenology of first-person agency. In S. Walter & H. D. Heckmann (eds.), *Physicalism and mental causation: The metaphysics of mind and action*. Exeter: Imprint Academic.

Kim, J. (1998). *Mind in a physical world*. Cambridge: MIT Press.

Mele, A. (1992). *Springs of action: Understanding intentional behavior*. New York: Oxford University Press.

Nahmias, E. (2002). When consciousnes matters: A critical review of Daniel Wegner's. The illusion of conscious will. *Philosophical Psychology, 15*(4), 527–41.

Nahmias, E., Morris, S., Nadelhoffer, T., & Turner, J. (2004). The phenomenology of free will. *Journal of consciousness studies, 11*(7–8), 162–79.

Prinz, W. (2003). How do we know about our own actions? In S. Maasen, W. Prinz, & G. Roth (eds.), *Voluntary action: Brains, minds, and sociality* (pp. 21–33). New York: Oxford University Press.

Sacks, O. (1970/1987). *The man who mistook his wife for a hat*. New York: Harper & Row.

Wegner, D. M. (2002). *The illusion of conscious will*. Cambridge, MA: MIT Press.

Wegner, D. M. (2003). The mind's best trick: How we experience conscious will. *Trends in Cognitive Science, 7*, 65–9.

Wegner, D. M. (2004). Précis of *The illusion of conscious will* [and Commentaries]. *Behavioral and Brain Sciences, 27*(5), 634–92.

Wegner, D. M. (2005). Who is the controller of controlled processes? In R. Hassin, J. S. Uleman, & J. A. Bargh (eds.), *The new unconscious* (pp. 19–36). New York: Oxford University Press.

Wegner, D. M., & Wheatley, T. (1999). Apparent mental causation: Sources of the experience of will. *American Psychologist, 54*, 480–91.

Wegner, D. M., Sparrow, B., & Winerman, L. (2004). Vicarious agency: Experiencing control over the movements of others. *Journal of Personality and Social Psychology, 86*, 838–48.

31

Free Will in Scientific Psychology

Roy F. Baumeister

What shall I do? Why did you do that? Are people captains of their fate, or are they mere products of their times and victims of circumstances? Should they be held responsible for their actions? These and similar questions pertain to the psychological problem of free will, also known as freedom of action.

At the core of the question of free will is a debate about the psychological causes of action. That is, is the person an autonomous entity who genuinely chooses how to act from among multiple possible options? Or is the person essentially just one link in a causal chain, so that the person's actions are merely the inevitable product of lawful causes stemming from prior events, and no one ever could have acted differently than how he or she actually did?

My thesis is that free will can be understood in terms of the different processes that control human action and that, indeed, these differences correspond to what laypersons generally mean when they distinguish free from unfree action. To discuss free will in the terms of scientific psychology is therefore to invoke notions of self-regulation, controlled processes, behavioral plasticity, and conscious decisionmaking.

Background

[. . .] If free will is only occasional, whereas behavior is constantly occurring, then it is neces-

sary to posit two systems for guiding behavior: a default one that mostly runs the show and an occasional one that sometimes intervenes to make changes. Free will should be understood not as the starter or motor of action but rather as a passenger who occasionally grabs the steering wheel or even as just a navigator who says to turn left up ahead.

Objections to the Very Idea

Many psychologists disdain the idea of free will, for several reasons. First, some think that in order to be a scientist it is necessary to believe in determinism, because a scientist studies causality and cannot tolerate or accept exceptions. Second, and related to the first, free choice (especially the full, extreme case of total freedom) cannot seem to be explained in scientific terms. Causality is how the human mind generally (and the scientific mind particularly) understands events, and there is no way to explain a free action causally. In other words, even if free will exists, there is no use in scientists talking about it, because there would be no replicable patterns of behavior. (On this I disagree most emphatically – see below.) Third, and perhaps more formidably, plenty of research has by now shown that people are sometimes mistaken when they believe their actions to be free, insofar as factors outside their awareness do

From Free will in scientific psychology. *Perspectives on Psychological Science*, 3, 1. Association for Psychological Science, 2008. pp 14–19. Reprinted with permission of Wiley-Blackwell.

Moral Psychology: Historical and Contemporary Readings, edited by Thomas Nadelhoffer, Eddy Nahmias, and Shaun Nichols.

exert a causal influence on them (e.g., Bargh, 1994; Wegner, 2002; Wilson, 2002).

The fact that automatic, nonconscious processes are the direct causes of action (e.g., Libet, 1985, 1999) seems now well established and has dealt a severe blow to some theories of conscious free will. But new theories of action have separated the deciding from the initiating (Gollwitzer, 1999), and free conscious choosing may have its main role in the deciding (deliberative) stage. To illustrate, free will would have more to do with deciding (now) to walk to the store when the rain stops (later) than with directing each footstep during the actual trip. Modern research methods and technology have emphasized slicing behavior into milliseconds, but these advances may paradoxically conceal the important role of conscious choice, which is mainly seen at the macro level (Donald, 2002).

Meanwhile, there are several objections to the determinists too. To require scientists to believe in determinism seems unwarranted. After all, the deterministic hypothesis – that every event is fully and inevitably caused by prior events and nothing else than what happened was ever possible – is itself unproven and even unprovable, so it requires a big leap of faith. Determinism is also contrary to everyday experience (in which people do make choices, and they believe subjectively that more than one outcome is possible). Moreover, to say that scientific data and especially psychological data point to determinism is itself severely overstated. Most psychological experiments demonstrate probabilistic rather than deterministic causation: A given cause changes the odds of a particular response but almost never operates with the complete inevitability that deterministic causality would entail. These objections do not disprove determinism, but they certainly raise questions. It seems unreasonable to require that every scientist must believe something that is unproven, unprovable, contrary to daily experience, and incongruent with our data.

[. . .]

Psychology's Task

In my opinion, it would be a mistake for psychologists to argue about whether free will exists and to debate the conceptual details. Philosophers and others have already spent centuries refining the concepts through such argument, and repeating their work would not be a good use of time and effort. In comparison with philosophers, psychologists are amateurs at conceptual refinement and debate but are specialists at conducting experimental tests of causal hypotheses. Our expertise is thus not well suited for ascertaining the existence or nonexistence of free will, which is probably impossible to prove. Researchers such as Wegner (2002) and Bargh and Morsella (2008) may show that people are sometimes unaware of the causes of particular behaviors, but such findings are incapable of establishing that all behaviors are the result of firm causal processes of which people are unaware. Conversely, it seems equally impossible to prove that a given person could have acted differently than he or she did under exactly the same circumstances.

Psychology's contribution lies elsewhere. Psychologists should focus on what we do best: collecting evidence about measurable variance in behaviors and inner processes and identifying consistent patterns in them. With free will, it seems most productive for psychologists to start with the well-documented observation that some acts are freer than others. As already noted, dissonance, reactance, coping with stress, and other behaviors have been shown in the laboratory to depend on variations in freedom and choice. Hence, it is only necessary to assume that there are genuine phenomena behind those subjective and objective differences in freedom. In a nutshell, we should explain what happens differently between free and unfree actions.

Thus, the optimal agenda for psychology would be to find out what people mean when they use concepts of freedom, choice, and responsibility in their daily lives and then to illuminate the inner processes that produce those phenomena.

What Makes Action Free?

A starting point for psychology is to identify what aspects of an action make people regard it as free versus unfree. To be sure, some factors can contribute to a mistaken sense of freedom in one's own action. Wegner (2002) showed that when the thought of an event immediately precedes its actual occurrence, people believe they have caused it, even if in reality they have not. For example, when participants who were moving a cursor around a computer screen along with someone else (akin to having four hands on the pointer on a Ouija board) heard the name of some image mentioned and then the cursor stopped there 2 s later, they believed that they had intentionally caused the cursor to stop, even though the stopping was actually programmed by the apparatus (Wegner & Wheatley, 1999 [chapter 29]).

There are several ways to interpret these findings. One is to suggest that all conscious will and volition are illusions: From the observation that people are sometimes mistaken about conscious will, one could extrapolate that they are always mistaken. Another is to suggest that people do not have a direct, introspective way of knowing when they initiate action, and so they rely on salient cues to give them the feel and subjective impression of having acted or chosen, and this system of cues can be fooled.

Shifts in the social distribution of causality and agency are important to people, and these correspond to social phenomena that people have encountered for millennia. Power, for example, confers on one person the right to make decisions that may affect others (e.g., Keltner, Gruenfeld, & Anderson, 2003), and the long history of power struggles can be viewed as being about who gets to choose. Studies by Brehm (1966) and his colleagues have also shown that people are very sensitive to having their freedom of choice restricted by others. When an option is taken away from them, they respond by desiring that option more, by trying actively to reassert that freedom and take that option, and even by aggressing against whomever restricted their freedom. Such patterns seem hard to reconcile with the view that all free will and choice (in every sense) are illusions: Why would people care so much about something that is entirely inconsequential?

Another approach to understanding what people mean by free will is to have participants rate how free a stimulus person's actions are. Stillman, Sparks, Baumeister, and Tice (2006) had participants rate scenarios that varied systematically along several dimensions. Participants rated people's actions as freest when their choices were made after conscious deliberation, when their actions went against external pressure rather than going along with it, and when people acted against their short-term self-interest. Thus conscious, rational choice and self-control seem to be

integral parts of what people perceive as free. When people wrote autobiographical accounts of their own acts that felt free or unfree, pursuing long-term personal goals was central to the feeling of freedom. The difference suggests that people see free will in others as useful for restraining their socially undesirable impulses, but in themselves they see free will in the sustained pursuit of (enlightened) self-interest. As Dennett (1984, 2003) has argued, free will is hardly worth having unless it helps you get something you want.

The Evolution of Freedom

Several recent authors have argued that human freedom of action is a product of evolutionary processes (e.g., Dennett, 2003). I proposed that the defining thrust of human psychological evolution was selection in favor of cultural capability (Baumeister, 2005). That process might well have included a new, different way of controlling behavior, whose purpose was enabling the beast to function in a complex, information-based society. The hallmarks of this new form of behavioral control include personal responsibility, conscious deliberation, invoking abstract rules and principles to guide actions, autonomous initiative, and a capacity to resist urges that have earlier evolutionary roots but that may be incompatible with civilized life (e.g., eating any food you find when hungry, including what is on the plates of other restaurant patrons). Whether this pattern will satisfy the various theological and philosophical definitions of free will is hard to say, but it could well correspond to what ordinary people mean when they speak of free action.

The previous section noted that free will has to be useful for benefiting the person. Evolution has favored animals with psychological processes insofar as those processes help them pursue their goals. A more intelligent animal, for example, may be better able to find food and reproduce than a less intelligent one. In human cultural life, however, there is sometimes a tradeoff between short-term and long-term goals, and much of the success of the human species is based on our ability to sacrifice short-term goals for the long-term ones, as in delay of gratification (Mischel & Ayduk, 2004). For example, taking someone else's food may bring short-term benefits, but if it leads the other group members to imprison or expel the person, it could be self-defeating in the long run. Hence free will may be most useful in fostering the pursuit of enlightened self-interest. Were evolution working instead to enable the human animal to pursue what it wants right now to maximum effect, it might have promoted physical strength, speed, and ferocity rather than brainpower and social skills. But to succeed and live harmoniously in a cultural group, the animal is best served by being able to inhibit its impulses and desires. Perhaps ironically, free will is necessary to enable people to follow rules.

Let me focus briefly on two of the most important phenomena that are associated with the concept of free will: self-control and rational intelligent choice. The cultural-animal argument has the following assumptions. First, self-control and smart choice are much more highly developed in humans than in other animals and thus are among the most distinctively human traits. Second, these traits are highly conducive for living in a cultural society. Third, these traits are probably interrelated in the sense of sharing some inner processes and mechanisms, which suggests that one evolved first and the other piggy-backed on the first one's system.

My speculative evolutionary scenario is that self-control evolved first, because it is useful already in merely social (as opposed to cultural) groups. For example, it would be natural for hungry animals to eat food that they see and want, but in many social groups the alpha male would beat up any other who tries to take his food or usurp his other prerogatives. Therefore, in order to live in social groups, animals must develop the capacity to restrain their impulses and bring their behavior into line with externally imposed constraints. Moving from social to cultural groups substantially increases the importance of following rules, including moral principles, laws, commands, religious prescriptions, norms, and customs.

Rational intelligent choice, then, evolved later than self-control and was even more distinctively associated with culture. Culture is based on information, and the large amount of information in a culture creates great opportunities for reasoning powers to sort through it and draw action-relevant conclusions. Human decision making is far more complex and varied than that in other species. As Searle (2001) pointed out, rationality is widely regarded as a central human trait, but not all have noticed that rationality entails at least some limited concept of free will – at least to the extent that one can alter one's behavior on the basis of that reasoning. Put another way, self-control gives the capacity to alter your behavior to conform to the group's rules, and rationality enables you to work out your own rules and then behave accordingly.

This line of thought fits the view of free will as a sometime thing. People are incompletely rational and self-controlled. They have the capacity for acting for acting rationally and exerting self-control, but they only use it sometimes. This suggests the capacity is limited.

Why Free Will is Limited

Our research on ego depletion provides one way to understand why free will is at best an occasional phenomenon. In testing several competing theories about self-regulation, we consistently found that people performed relatively poorly at almost any self-control task if they had recently performed a different self-control task (Baumeister, Bratslavsky, Muraven, & Tice, 1998; Muraven & Baumeister, 2000). The implication is that some resource is used up by the first act of self-control, leaving less available for the second.

Choice may also deplete the same resource. Vohs et al. (2006) found that making a series of choices led to poorer self-control on subsequent, unrelated tasks, as compared with just thinking about items or answering questions about them without making choices among them. The fact that effortful choice uses the same resource as self-control links the two main forms of free will and supports the idea that they share a common underlying mechanism.

Thus, the traditional concept of "willpower" does appear to be a useful metaphor, insofar as both self-control and rational choice rely on some kind of power. To move beyond metaphor, Gailliot et al. (2007) began studying blood-glucose dynamics. Glucose is a chemical in the bloodstream that is the fuel for brain (and other) activities. Although all brain processes use glucose, some use much more than others, and self-control is a likely candidate to be one of these more expensive processes. Gailliot et al. (2007) found that acts of self-control caused reductions in the levels of glucose in the bloodstream, and that low levels of blood glucose after initial acts of self-control were strongly correlated with poor self-control on subsequent tasks. Moreover, experimental administrations of glucose counteracted some of the ego-depletion effects. That is, drinking a glass of lemonade with sugar enabled people to perform well at self-control even if they had recently gone through a depleting exercise of self-control. Lemonade made with a sugar substitute (thus not furnishing glucose) had no effect.

These findings suggest that human evolution developed a second, new, and expensive way of controlling action. It involved using relatively large quantities of the body's caloric energy to fuel complex psychological processes. If the cultural-animal argument is correct, then these processes should have improved biological success by enabling people to behave in more advantageous ways.

Ample evidence confirms that this second executive mode of action control has adaptive benefits and that when its resources are depleted or inadequate, behavior is less successful. Nondepleted persons outperform ego-depleted ones at making effective and unbiased decisions (Amir, Dhar, Pocheptsaya, & Baumeister, 2007), at logical reasoning and intelligent thought (Schmeichel, Vohs, & Baumeister, 2003), and at active coping with unexpected setbacks (Vohs & Baumeister, 2006). Self-control has multiple benefits, and people who are high on the trait end up more successful in work and school, are more popular and better liked, have healthier and more stable relationships, commit fewer crimes, and have less psychopathology (Duckworth & Seligman, 2005; Gottfredson & Hirschi, 1990; Mischel, Shoda, & Peake, 1988; Tangney, Baumeister, & Boone, 2004). And as for following rules generally, there is some cross-cultural evidence that countries with higher rule of law report significantly higher subjective well-being (Veenhoven, 2004).

Believing in Freedom

This brief article has argued that psychology's task is to find out what people perceive as free will and what genuine psychological phenomena underlie those perceptions. Such investigations will not establish whether free will exists according to some philosophical or theological definitions, and it remains possible that many laypersons' beliefs about free will are partly or wholly mistaken. If free will is entirely an illusion, however, then it becomes especially perplexing that people devote so much time and effort to sustaining those illusions. Belief in free will is highly relevant to many social, legal, and moral judgments. For example, if all actions are fully caused and therefore inevitable, why does the legal system spend so much time trying to establish whether a perpetrator was acting freely? "Heat of passion" crimes are just as fully caused as any other crimes, in that view, so it makes little sense for judges to award lighter sentences. Yet they do.

One possible explanation for the widespread social belief in free will is that it helps produce socially desirable and harmonious actions. To return to the cultural-animal framework, I am assuming that people evolved so as to be able to live and work in culture (Baumeister, 2005). Anything that makes people better able to do that, including improvements in cooperation and prosocial actions or reductions in antisocial actions, would therefore be beneficial. To speculate, cultures that believed in free will might have outreproduced and supplanted cultures that did not.

Belief in free will does support socially desirable actions, according to Vohs and Schooler (2008). They found that participants who had been induced to disbelieve in free will were subsequently more likely than a control group to cheat on a test. Further studies by Baumeister, Masicampo, and DeWall (2006) using the Vohs–Schooler methods found that inducing participants to disbelieve in free will made them more aggressive and less helpful toward others. If we combine the cheating, aggression, and helping findings, it seems reasonable to suggest that belief in free will is conducive to better, more harmonious social behavior.

Conclusion

The distinction between free choice and unfree action has enormous and widespread significance individually, socially, historically, and politically.

That distinction also seems so thoroughly woven into the fabric of human social life that it seems quixotic to try to imagine a society that had abandoned the concept so as to operate "beyond freedom and dignity," in Skinner's (1971 [chapter 28]) titular phrase. Psychology can explore and elucidate that difference between free and unfree action without having to resolve metaphysical questions. Conscious, controlled, and self-regulating processes seem likely to be important aspects of what people understand as free will.

A scientific approach to free will should perhaps start with the view that freedom of action evolved as a new, more sophisticated form of controlling behavior. Its two components, self-control and rational intelligent choice, conferred important advantages by enabling the human animal to function within a cultural society. Recent evidence about ego depletion and glucose dynamics suggests that this new, freer form of action control is biologically expensive, which may help explain why free will is only used occasionally. Nonetheless, even its occasional use may contribute greatly to increasing the flexibility and adaptive diversity of human behavior.

References

Amir, O., Dhar, R., Pocheptsaya, A., & Baumeister, R.F. (2007). *The fatigued decision maker: Ego depletion changes decision process and outcome.*

Bargh, J.A. (1994). The four horsemen of automaticity. Awareness, efficiency, intention, and control in social cognition. In R.S. Wyer Jr., & T.K. Srull (eds.), *Handbook of social cognition* (2nd edn., pp. 1–40). Hillsdale, NJ: Erlbaum.

Bargh, J.A., & Morsella, E. (2008). The primacy of the unconscious. *Perspectives on Psychological Science, 3*, 73–9.

Baumeister, R.F. (2005). *The cultural animal: Human nature, meaning, and social life.* New York: Oxford University Press.

Baumeister, R.F., Bratslavsky, E., Muraven, M., & Tice, D.M. (1998). Ego depletion: Is the active self a limited resource? *Journal of Personality and Social Psychology, 74*, 1252–65.

Baumeister, R.F., Masicampo, E.J., & DeWall, C.N. (2006). *Prosocial benefits of feeling free: Inducing disbelief in free will increases aggression and reduces helpfulness.*

Brehm, J. (1966). *A theory of psychological reactance.* New York: Academic Press.

Dennett, D.C. (1984). *Elbow room: The varieties of free will worth wanting.* Cambridge, MA: MIT Press.

Dennett, D.C. (2003). *Freedom evolves.* New York: Viking/Penguin.

Donald, M. (2002). *A mind so rare: The evolution of human consciousness.* New York: Norton.

Duckworth, A.L., & Seligman, M.E.P. (2005). Self-discipline outdoes IQ in predicting academic performance of adolescents. *Psychological Science, 16*, 939–44.

Gailliot, M.T., Baumeister, R.F., DeWall, C.N., Maner, J.K., Plant, E.A., Tice, D.M., et al. (2007). Self-control relies on glucose as a limited energy source: Willpower is more than a metaphor. *Journal of Personality and Social Psychology, 92*, 325–36.

Gollwitzer, P.M. (1999). Implementation intentions: Strong effects of simple plans. *American Psychologist, 54*, 493–503.

Gottfredson, M.R., & Hirschi, T. (1990). *A general theory of crime.* Stanford, CA: Stanford University Press.

Keltner, D., Gruenfeld, D.H., & Anderson, C. (2003). Power, approach, and inhibition. *Psychological Review, 110*, 265–84.

Libet, B. (1985). Unconscious cerebral initiative and the role of conscious will in voluntary action. *Behavior and Brain Sciences, 8*, 529–66.

Libet, B. (1999). Do we have free will? *Journal of Consciousness Studies, 6*, 47–57.

Mischel, W., & Ayduk, O. (2004). Willpower in a cognitive-affective processing system: The dynamics of delay of gratification. In R. Baumeister & K. Vohs (eds.), *Handbook of self-regulation: Research, theory, and applications* (pp. 99–129). New York: Guilford.

Mischel, W., Shoda, Y., & Peake, P.K. (1988). The nature of adolescent competencies predicted by preschool delay of gratification. *Journal of Personality and Social Psychology, 54*, 687–96.

Muraven, M.R., & Baumeister, R.F. (2000). Self-regulation and depletion of limited resources: Does self-control resemble a muscle? *Psychological Bulletin, 126*, 247–59.

Schmeichel, B.J., Vohs, K.D., & Baumeister, R.F. (2003). Intellectual performance and ego depletion: Role of the self in logical reasoning and other information processing. *Journal of Personality and Social Psychology, 85*, 33–46.

Searle, J.R. (2001). *Rationality in action.* Cambridge, MA: MIT Press.

Skinner, B.F. (1971). *Beyond freedom and dignity.* New York: Knopf.

Stillman, T.D., Sparks, E., Baumeister, R.F., & Tice, D.M. (2006). *What makes freedom? Situational factors that influence ratings of free will.*

Tangney, J.P., Baumeister, R.F., & Boone, A.L. (2004). High self-control predicts good adjustment, less pathology, better grades, and interpersonal success. *Journal of Personality, 72*, 271–322.

Veenhoven, R. (2004). *World database of happiness: Continuous register of scientific research on subjective appreciation of life.* Retrieved September 26, 2004, from http://www.eur.nl/fsw/research/happiness

Vohs, K.D., & Baumeister, R.F. (2006). *Does depletion promote passivity? Self-regulatory resources and active coping.*

Vohs, K.D., & Schooler, J.W. (2008). The value of believing in free will: Encouraging a belief in determinism increases cheating. *Psychological Science, 19*, 49–54.

Vohs, K.D., Baumeister, R.F., Nelson, N.M., Rawn, C.D., Twenge, J.M., Schmeichel, B.J., & Tice, D.M. (2006). *Making choices impairs subsequent self-control: A limited resource account of decision making, self-regulation, and active initiative.*

Wegner, D.M. (2002). *The illusion of conscious will.* Cambridge, MA: MIT Press.

Wegner, D.M., & Wheatley, T. (1999). Apparent mental causation: Sources of the experience of will. *American Psychologist, 54*, 480–91.

Wilson, T.D. (2002). *Strangers to ourselves: Discovering the adaptive unconscious.* Cambridge, MA: Harvard University Press.

32

Scientific Skepticism About Free Will

Alfred R. Mele

My topic is recent scientific skepticism about free will. A leading argument for such skepticism features the proposition – defended by Daniel Wegner (2002, 2008) and Benjamin Libet (1985, 2004) among others – that conscious intentions (and their physical correlates) never play a role in producing corresponding overt actions.[1] (Overt actions are actions that essentially involve peripheral bodily motion.)[2] This chapter examines alleged scientific evidence for the truth of this proposition. (For discussion of evidence that the proposition is false, see Mele 2009a, ch. 7.)

1. Introducing Libet's Work

Libet contends both that "the brain 'decides' to initiate or, at least, prepare to initiate [certain actions] before there is any reportable subjective awareness that such a decision has taken place" (1985, p. 536) and that "If the 'act now' process is initiated unconsciously, then conscious free will is not doing it" (2001, p. 62; see 2004, p. 136). He also claims that once we become aware of these decisions, we can exercise free will in vetoing them (2004, pp. 137–49). Some people follow Libet part of the way; they accept the thesis about when and how decisions are made but reject the window of opportunity for free will as illusory (Wegner 2002, p. 55, Hallett 2007).

Libet's findings are generated by an innovative series of studies (see Libet 1985 and 2004 for summaries). In some of the studies, subjects are regularly encouraged to flex a wrist whenever they wish. In subjects who do not report any advance planning of their movements, electrical readings from the scalp (EEGs) – averaged over at least 40 flexes for each subject – show a shift in readiness potentials (RPs) beginning about 550 milliseconds (ms) before the time at which an electromyogram (EMG) shows relevant muscular activity to begin. These are type II RPs. Subjects who are not regularly encouraged to aim for spontaneity or who report some advance planning produce RPs that begin about half a second earlier – type I RPs. The same is true of subjects instructed to flex at a prearranged time (Libet et al. 1982, p. 325). (According to a common use of "readiness potential," it is a measure of activity in the motor cortex that precedes voluntary muscle motion and, by definition, EEGs generated in situations in which there is no muscle motion do not count as RPs. Libet's use of the term is broader. For example, because there is no muscle motion in the veto experiment described later, some scientists would not refer to what Libet calls "the 'veto' RP" [1985, p. 538] as an RP.)

Subjects are also instructed to recall where a revolving spot was on a special clock when they first became aware of something, x, that Libet variously describes as a decision, intention, urge, wanting, will, or wish to move. (The spot on this Libet clock makes a complete revolution in less than three seconds.) On average, the onset of type

Moral Psychology: Historical and Contemporary Readings, edited by Thomas Nadelhoffer, Eddy Nahmias, and Shaun Nichols.
© 2010 Blackwell Publishing Ltd except for editorial material and organization © 2010 Thomas Nadelhoffer, Eddy Nahmias, and Shaun Nichols.

II RPs preceded what subjects reported to be the time of their initial awareness of x (time W) by 350 ms. Time W, then, preceded the beginning of muscle motion (a muscle burst) by about 200 ms. The results may be represented as follows.

Libet's results for type II RPs

−550 ms	−200 ms	0 ms
RP onset	reported time W	muscle begins to move

(Libet finds evidence of what he regards as an error in subjects' recall of the times at which they first become aware of sensations [1985, pp. 531, 534]. Correcting for it, time W is −150 ms.)

Again, in Libet's view, consciousness opens a tiny window of opportunity for free will in his subjects. If a subject becomes aware of his decision or intention at −150 ms, and if by −50 ms his condition is such that "the act goes to completion with no possibility of its being stopped by the rest of the cerebral cortex" (Libet 2004, p. 138), his window is open for 100 ms. Libet writes: "The role of conscious free will [is] not to initiate a voluntary act, but rather to control whether the act takes place. We may view the unconscious initiatives as 'bubbling up' in the brain. The conscious-will then selects which of these initiatives may go forward to an action or which ones to veto and abort" (1999, p. 54).

2.   Conceptual Background

Some conceptual background will prove useful for the purposes of assessing implications of Libet's findings. I start with the concept of deciding to do something – practical deciding. (Deciding that something is true – propositional deciding – is a distinct phenomenon.) Like many philosophers, I take *deciding* to A to be an action – as I see it, a momentary action of forming an intention to A (Mele 2003, ch. 9). Deliberating about what to do is not a momentary action, but it must be distinguished from an act of deciding that is based on deliberation.

This conception of practical deciding does not entail that all intentions are formed in acts of deciding. In fact, many intentions seem to be acquired without being so formed. For example, when Al unlocked his office door this morning, he

intended to unlock it. But because he is in the habit of unlocking his door in the morning and conditions were normal, nothing called for a decision to unlock it. *If* Al had heard a fight in his office, he might have paused to consider whether to unlock the door or walk away, and he might have decided to unlock it. But given the routine nature of his conduct, there is no need to posit an action of intention formation in this case. His intention to unlock the door may have arisen without having been actively formed. If, as I believe, all decisions about what to do are prompted partly by uncertainty about what to do (Mele 2003, ch. 9), in situations in which there is no such uncertainty, no decisions will be made. Even so, intentions may be acquired in these situations.

Some decisions and intentions are about things to do straightaway. They are *proximal* decisions and intentions. Others – *distal* decisions and intentions – are about things to do later. Ann's decision to phone Bob now is a proximal decision; her decision to phone Beth tomorrow evening is a distal decision. The scientific work on decisions and intentions to be discussed here focuses on the proximal kind.

Deciding to do something should be distinguished from wanting (or having an urge) to do it. Sometimes people want to do things that they decide not to do. And often, when people want to do each of two incompatible things – for example, meet some friends for lunch at noon and attend a lecture at noon – they settle matters by deciding which one to do. Just as deciding should be distinguished from wanting, so should intending. Intending to do something is more tightly connected to action than is merely wanting to do it.

The account of practical deciding sketched here is not the only account of it. For critiques of alternative accounts, see Mele 2003, ch. 9. A virtue of the account just sketched, for present purposes, is that it is consonant with Libet's apparent conception of practical deciding.

3.   Assessing Some Inferences

One inference Libet makes on the basis of his findings is that the brain produces a proximal decision or intention to flex about a third of a second before the subject becomes aware of that decision or intention. Is this inference warranted? One alternative hypothesis is that what the brain produces around −550 ms is a potential cause of a subsequent proximal decision or intention to flex and the decision or intention emerges significantly later.

How might one get evidence about whether the onset of the type II RPs at −550 ms is correlated with unconscious proximal decisions or intentions to flex or instead with potential causes of decisions or intentions? An apt question to ask in this connection is how long it takes a proximal intention to flex to generate a muscle burst. If, in fact, the brain produces proximal decisions or intentions in Libet's study about 550 ms before the muscle burst, then, in his subjects, it takes those decisions or intentions about 550 ms to produce a muscle burst. Is this a realistic figure?

Some reaction-time studies provide relevant evidence. In a study in which subjects were watching a Libet clock, the mean time between the sounding of the go signal and the muscle burst was 231 ms (Haggard and Magno 1999, p. 104). Subjects were instructed to respond as rapidly as possible to the go signal by pressing a button. If detection of the go signal produced a proximal intention to press the button, then the mean time between a subject's acquiring a proximal intention to press and the muscle burst was less than 231 ms. (Detecting a go signal takes time.) And notice how close this is to Libet's time W – his subjects' reported time of their initial awareness of something he variously describes as an intention, urge, wanting, decision, will, or wish to move (−200 ms). Even without putting much weight on the exact number (−231 ms), one can fairly observe that if proximal intentions to flex are acquired in Libet's studies, the finding just reported makes it look like a much better bet that they are acquired around time W than that they are acquired around −550 ms.

Someone might object that in reaction time studies of the kind described, muscle bursts and actions are not produced by proximal intentions but by something else. It may be claimed, for example, that the combination of subjects' *conditional* intentions to press whenever they detect the go signal together with their detection of it produces muscle bursts and pressings without the assistance of any proximal intentions to press. (A typical conditional intention has this form: "if

[or when] x happens, do y.") But if this claim is accepted, a parallel claim about Libet's studies should be taken seriously. The parallel claim is that, in Libet's studies, the muscle bursts and actions are not produced by proximal intentions but by the combination of subjects' conditional intentions to flex whenever they detect a conscious proximal urge to flex together with their detection of such an urge. Someone who makes this claim may hypothesize that the onset of the type II RPs at −550 ms is correlated with a potential cause of a conscious proximal urge to flex. Libet's findings do not contradict this hypothesis.

Even if Libet is wrong in claiming that the brain produces proximal intentions or decisions to flex at about −550 ms, his claim about the 100 ms window of opportunity for free will merits attention. Libet's idea is that free will can only be exercised consciously and, therefore, can only be exercised after his subjects become conscious of proximal intentions, decisions, or urges to flex (and before it is too late to stop what is in place from generating a muscle burst). He contends that free will can be exercised only in vetoing the decision, intention, or urge of which the person has become conscious. One alternative hypothesis is that Libet's subjects exercise free will in consciously deciding to flex rather than after they become conscious of such a decision (or intention or urge). Given that Libet's findings do not justify the inference that proximal decisions to flex are made before the subjects are conscious of any such decision, they do not contradict the present hypothesis.

Libet's findings are sometimes said to support the thesis that conscious intentions and decisions play no role in producing corresponding actions. It is claimed that they are caused by the same brain events that cause actions and that they are not themselves in the causal chain that results in action. Sometimes the following assertion is offered in support of the preceding one: Subjects' conscious proximal intentions to flex cannot be among the causes of their flexes because those intentions are caused by unconscious brain events (Pockett 2006, p. 21, Roediger, Goode and Zaromb 2008, p. 208). This assertion is misguided, as attention to the following analogous assertion shows: Burnings of fuses cannot be among the causes of explosions of firecrackers because burnings of fuses are caused by lightings of fuses. Obviously, both the lighting of its fuse and the burning of its fuse are among the causes of a firecracker's exploding in normal scenarios. Other things being equal, if the fuse had not been lit – or if the lit fuse had stopped burning early – there would have been no explosion. There is no reason to believe that the more proximal causes of firecracker explosions cannot themselves have causes. Analogously, there is no reason to believe that items that are among the relatively proximal causes of flexes cannot themselves have causes and cannot be caused by unconscious brain events.

Might it be that conscious proximal intentions to flex are part of the causal chain leading to the flexing actions of Libet's subjects? Someone who wishes to answer this question should first ask another: Is the brain activity registered by, for example, the first 300 ms of type II RPs – *type 300 activity*, for short – as tightly connected to subsequent flexes as lightings of firecracker fuses are to exploding firecrackers? In fact, no one knows. In the experiments that yield Libet's type II RPs, it is the muscle burst that triggers a computer to make a record of the preceding brain activity. In the absence of a muscle burst, there is no record of that activity. So, for all anyone knows, there were many occasions on which type 300 activity occurred in Libet's subjects and there were no associated flexes.

Libet mentions that some subjects encouraged to flex spontaneously report that they sometimes suppressed conscious proximal urges to flex (1985, p. 538). As he points out, because there was no muscle activation, there was no trigger to initiate the computer's recording of any RP that may have preceded the veto (2004, p. 141). So, for all anyone knows, type 300 activity was present before the urges were suppressed.

It is urges that these subjects are said to report and suppress. Might it be that type 300 activity is a potential cause of conscious urges to flex in Libet's subjects and that some subjects make no decision about when to flex – unconsciously or otherwise – until after the conscious urge emerges? And might it be that prior to the emergence of the conscious urge, subjects have no proximal intention to flex? That our urges often are generated by processes of which we are not conscious is not surprising. And if we sometimes make effective decisions about whether or not to act on a conscious urge, so much the better for

free will. Moreover, Libet's data do not show that subjects have unconscious proximal intentions to flex before they have conscious ones. The data do not contradict the hypothesis that what precedes these conscious proximal intentions is a causal process that includes no unconscious proximal decisions or intentions to flex.

Even if Libet's data do not warrant his claim that his subjects have proximal intentions to flex before they think they do, his idea that we have unconscious proximal intentions should not be lightly dismissed. Such intentions may be at work when, for example, experienced drivers flip their turn indicators to signal for turns they are about to make. In a study in which subjects are instructed to flex whenever they feel like it without also being instructed to report after flexing on when they first became aware of an intention, urge, or decision to flex, would they often be conscious of proximal intentions, urges, or decisions to flex? Might unconscious proximal intentions to flex – and, more specifically, proximal intentions of which they are *never* conscious – be at work in producing flexes in the imagined scenario?

Imagine that someone conducts the experiment just sketched and discovers (somehow) that the subjects were never or rarely conscious of proximal urges, intentions, or decisions to flex. Could it legitimately be inferred that, in Libet's own experiment, conscious urges, intentions, and decisions had no effect on the flexing actions? No. One possibility is that some of Libet's subjects treat their initial consciousness of an urge to flex as a go signal. If they do, the conscious urge seemingly has a place in the causal process that issues in the flexing. Another possibility is that some subjects treat the conscious urge as what may be called a *decide signal* – a signal calling for them consciously to decide right then whether to flex right away or to wait a while. If that is so, and if they consciously decide to flex and execute that decision, the conscious urge again seemingly has a place in the causal process, as does the conscious decision.

Perhaps it will be suggested that even if a subject treats a conscious urge to flex as a go or decide signal, that urge has no place in the causal process that issues in a flex because an unconscious brain event caused the conscious urge. But the inference here has the same form as the misguided assertion about conscious intention discussed earlier. An x can be among the causes of a y even if the x itself is caused (recall the firecracker example). Possibly, it will be claimed that by the time the conscious urge emerges it is too late for the subject to refrain from acting on it (something that Libet denies) and that is why the conscious urge should not be seen as part of the process at issue, even if subjects think they are treating the urge as a go or decide signal. One way to get evidence about this is to conduct an experiment in which subjects are instructed to flex at a time t unless they detect a stop signal – for example, a change in the color of the clock from white to red. (On stop signal experiments, see Logan 1994.) By varying the interval between the stop signal and the mean time of the completion of a full flex when there is no stop signal, experimenters can try to ascertain when subjects reach the point of no return. (Time t can be a designated point on a Libet clock, and brain activity can be measured backward from t.) Perhaps it will be discovered that that point is reached significantly later than time W. (Of course, some researchers worry about how seriously subjects' reports of their first awareness of a proximal urge or intention to flex – time W – should be taken. For discussion and references, see Mele 2009a, ch. 6.)

Libet offers two kinds of evidence to support his claim that subjects have time to veto proximal conscious urges to flex. One kind has already been mentioned: subjects say they did this. The other kind is produced by an experiment in which subjects are instructed to prepare to flex at a prearranged clock time but to refrain from actually flexing and "to veto the developing intention/preparation to act . . . about 100 to 200 ms before [that] time" (Libet 1985, p. 538).

The results of Libet's veto study suggest an interpretation of type I and type II RPs that is contrary to his own interpretation. As a first step toward seeing why, notice that Libet's claim that the subjects in this study veto "*intended* motor action" (1985, p. 38; emphasis added) is implausible (see Mele 1997, p. 322; 2009a, pp. 52–3). These subjects were instructed in advance *not* to flex, but to prepare to flex at the prearranged time and to "veto" this. The subjects intentionally complied with the request. They intended from the beginning *not* to flex at the appointed time. So what is indicated by what Libet refers to as "the 'veto' RP" before "about 150–250 ms before the

preset time" (Libet 1985, p. 538)? Presumably, not the acquisition or presence of an *intention* to flex; for then, at some point in time, subjects would have both an intention to flex at the prearranged time and an intention not to flex at that time. And how can a normal agent simultaneously be settled on A-ing at t and settled on not A-ing at t?[3]

A segment of "the 'veto' RP" resembles segments of type I RPs in cases in which subjects do flex, as Libet observes (1985, p. 538). Given that this segment of "the 'veto' RP" is not correlated with a proximal intention to flex, perhaps the similar segments of type I RPs (and of type II RPs) also are not correlated with proximal intentions to flex. Even so, they might be correlated with potential causes of such intentions.

This idea is developed in Mele 2006 and 2009a. The shape the idea takes there is based partly on the following possibilities about subjects in the veto experiment:

perhaps a subject's wanting to comply with the instructions – including the instruction to prepare to flex at the appointed time – together with his recognition that the time is approaching produces an unconscious urge to flex soon, a pretty reliable causal contributor to an urge to flex soon, or the motor preparedness typically associated with such an urge. Things of these kinds are potential causal contributors to the acquisition of proximal intentions to flex. A related possibility is suggested by the observation that "the pattern of brain activity associated with imagining making a movement is very similar to the pattern of activity associated with preparing to make a movement" (Spence and Frith 1999, p. 27 . . .).[4] The instructions given to [subjects in the veto experiment] would naturally elicit imagining flexing very soon, an event of a kind suitable, in the circumstances, for making a causal contribution to the emergence of a proximal urge to flex. (Mele 2009a, p. 55)

The suggestion is that these same items – as opposed to proximal intentions to flex – are candidates for what the pertinent segments of type I RPs signify and that *proximal intentions* to flex emerge later, both in the case of flexes associated with type I RPs and in the case of flexes associated with type II RPs (Mele 2009a, ch. 3). And again, the reaction time study discussed earlier provides independent evidence about when proximal intentions emerge that places their emergence much closer to the muscle burst than −550 ms.

I conclude this section with a simple observation about generalizing from findings like Libet's. To the extent that free will is being studied in these experiments, it is being studied in the sphere of proximal decisions or intentions about matters that do not normally call for decision making – for example, exactly when to flex a wrist. Generalizing from results obtained in this domain to a view about distal decisions made about important issues in situations of a very different kind would be rash, to say the least. Even so, Libet is inclined to generalize: "our overall findings do suggest some fundamental characteristics of the simpler acts that may be applicable to all consciously intended acts and even to responsibility and free will" (1985, p. 563).

4.   Introducing Wegner's Work

Daniel Wegner (2002, 2004) attempts to support his claim that conscious intentions are not among the causes of corresponding actions in two general ways. One line of argument features Libet's studies. The other, as Richard Holton interprets it, "is a version of the argument from illusion" (2004, p. 219). Because I discussed Libet's work in previous sections, I focus on Wegner's second line of argument here. If Wegner is right about conscious intentions, then if only beings whose conscious intentions sometimes are among the causes of corresponding actions are capable of acting freely, free will is an illusion.

Various studies provide evidence that, in some circumstances, people are not conscious of some of their actions; in others, people believe they intentionally did things that, in fact, they did not do; and in yet others, people do things "automatically" and for no good reason. This section reviews some such findings. Assessment of their implications is reserved for subsequent sections. Some background on epiphenomenalism sets the stage.

The thesis that although all mental events are caused by physical events, no mental events are among the causes of any physical events may be termed *philosophical epiphenomenalism*. Some scientists appeal to findings of the sort to be reviewed here to support what they call "epiphe-

nomenalism" about intentions. However, what they mean by this word in this connection is not what philosophers mean by it. Attention to the difference helps forestall confusion.

Let "proximal intentions*" name a collection composed of proximal intentions, their acquisition, and their persistence. Suppose that all proximal intentions* are caused by physical events but no proximal intentions* are among the causes of any physical events. Suppose also that physical correlates of proximal intentions* sometimes are among the causes of physical events – for example, bodily motions involved in overt intentional actions. Although this pair of suppositions does not contradict philosophical epiphenomenalism, it does contradict a *scientific epiphenomenalism* according to which neither proximal intentions* nor their physical correlates are among the causes of bodily motions. The scientific epiphenomenalism at issue here extends to the physical correlates of proximal intentions*: the claim at issue is that neither proximal intentions* nor their physical correlates are among the causes of physical events that proximal intentions* are thought to cause – those involved in corresponding overt intentional actions.

I turn to data. Some actions that people do not realize they are performing are detectable with sensitive devices (Wegner 2002, pp. 122–25). In one study, a person asked to think of an object to the left slowly moved a hand in that direction. A person asked to hide an object in a room slowly moved a hand in the direction of the object he hid when asked to think about it. And a person instructed to count a metronome's clicks made tiny hand movements that matched the rhythm.

Wegner discusses the practice of facilitated communication, which was designed to help people with a disorder that hampers speech (e.g., autism or cerebral palsy) express themselves (2002, pp. 195–201). A trained facilitator holds the hand of a client who is seated in front of a keyboard. Facilitators are supposed to help clients communicate without influencing which keys clients press, and there is considerable evidence that this is what many of the facilitators intended to do and believed they were doing. Often, people who had been uncommunicative apparently typed out sentences, paragraphs, or more. However, it was found that the facilitators were actually in control of what was being typed – without realizing that they were.

People suffering from a certain kind of damage to the frontal lobes display utilization behavior (Wegner 2002, p. 122). For example, a person whose hands were touched with several pairs of eyeglasses, put them all on and wore several pairs at once.

In some experimental situations, people are caused to believe (to some degree) that they intentionally did things they did not in fact do. In one study (Wegner and Wheatley 1999 [chapter 29]), a confederate and a subject, both of whom are wearing headphones, jointly operate a computer mouse on which "a 12-centimeter square board" is mounted (p. 487). About fifty tiny objects are displayed on a computer monitor, and the mouse controls the movement of a cursor over the display. Subjects are asked how much they "intended" to make a stop of the cursor on an image (p. 488). When subjects hear the name of an image in the display (e.g., "swan") very shortly before the cursor stops on that image, they give, on average, a higher "intended" rating to the stop than they do under other conditions, even though, in fact, the confederate is stopping the cursor on that image. (For an instructive critique of this study, see Mallé 2006, pp. 223–4.)

Studies and findings such as the ones described here are sometimes taken to support the claim that actions never have conscious proximal intentions* or their physical correlates among their causes. This is the thesis of *scientific epiphenomenalism* about conscious proximal intentions*. Now, it is true that the studies and findings indicate that people sometimes perform actions of which they are not conscious, sometimes do things for no good reason, and sometimes believe (to some degree) that they intentionally did things they did not actually do. But how are these truths supposed to lead to scientific epiphenomenalism about conscious proximal intentions*?

One route that Wegner maps features the proposition that all actions are caused in basically the same way (2002, p. 144). If some actions are performed in the absence of conscious intentions to perform them and all actions are caused in basically the same way, that basic way includes neither conscious intentions to perform the actions at issue nor the physical correlates of such intentions. (Only existing conscious intentions

have existing physical correlates.) Why then do we even have conscious intentions? Why did we evolve in such a way as to have them? Wegner's reply is that we have conscious intentions because they give us a sense of which of the things we do we are responsible for (2002, p. 341).

Whether all actions are caused in basically the same way depends on how "basically the same way" is to be read. For example, if what is meant is simply that all actions have brain events among their causes, the claim is true (in my opinion). But, of course, this leaves it open that some of the brain events that are among the causes of some actions are physical correlates of conscious intentions to perform actions of those kinds. Wegner means something much more specific – that just as people who unknowingly move a hand slowly in the direction of an object they are thinking about are caused to do so by automatic processes of which they are unaware, all actions are caused by, and only by, such processes. Wegner reports that his "analysis suggests that the real causal mechanisms underlying behavior are never present in consciousness" (2002, p. 97). As usual, he has the relatively proximal causes of behavior in mind. In the following passage, Wegner goes well beyond merely *suggesting*: "it has to be one way or the other. Either the automatisms are oddities against the general backdrop of conscious behavior causation in everyday life, or we must turn everything around quite radically and begin to think that behavior that occurs *with* a sense of will is somehow the odd case, an add on to a more basic underlying system" (p. 144)

5. Conscious Will and Scientific Epiphenomenalism

As Eddy Nahmias observes, Wegner's defense of his "illusion" thesis about "conscious will" is focused on *proximal* intentions (2002, p. 536). This is not surprising given Wegner's assertion that "*Intention* is normally understood as an idea of what one is going to do that appears in consciousness just before one does it" (2002, p. 18). This assertion plainly does not apply to distal intentions. (Nor does it identify a sufficient condition for something's being an intention. As you are driving, another driver cuts you off. The following idea of what you are "going to do . . .

appears in consciousness just before" you hit his car: "Oh no! I'm going to hit that car." The idea expresses a prediction, not an intention; and "intention" definitely is not normally understood in such a way that this idea is an intention.) If Wegner intends his "illusion" thesis to apply even to distal intentions, he has done little to support that application. In this section, the spotlight remains where Wegner shines it – on proximal intentions.[5]

Elisabeth Pacherie voices a common complaint: "Some authors, including Wegner himself on occasion, seem to think that the fact that the experience of conscious will can be non-veridical is evidence for the claim that conscious mental causation is an illusion. This inference [is not] compelling. To show that the experience of willing is not always errorless is certainly not to show that it is always in error" (2006, p. 163; also see Baumeister 2008). Recall Wegner's idea that "it has to be one way or the other" (2002, p. 144) – either unconscious automatic processes are what produce all of our actions or "conscious will" does it all. This stark formulation of the idea raises some questions. Does it really all have to be one way or the other? Do conscious proximal intentions* or decisions (or their physical correlates) sometimes benefit from automatic mechanisms in the causation of actions? What might count as evidence that conscious proximal intentions* or decisions (or their physical correlates) play a role in producing some actions?

Return to Libet's studies. Imagine a study of this kind in which subjects are explicitly instructed to make a *conscious decision* about when to flex a wrist and to flex in response to it. Can they comply with this instruction, literally interpreted? If they do comply, then it would seem that their conscious decisions (or their physical correlates) are among the causes of their flexing actions.

A scientific epiphenomenalist about conscious decisions may reply that these subjects would have flexed even if they had unconsciously decided (or intended) to flex and that the conscious decisions (and their physical correlates) therefore played no causal role in producing the flexes. (Wegner himself cannot offer this reply, if he is committed to the view that intentions and decisions are essentially conscious.) There is a serious problem with this reply. The reply

implicitly appeals to the following principle: If y would have happened even if x had not happened, then x is not among the causes of y. And this principle is false. Sally's mother drove her to school, and Sally arrived there at 8:00 a.m. What Sally's mother did was a cause of Sally's arriving at school when she did. This is true, even though, if Sally's mother had not driven her to school, Sally's father would have done so and delivered her there at the same time.

Might a scientific epiphenomenalist about conscious decisions claim that, in the imagined experiment, the subjects' conscious decisions were not among the causes of their flexes because the decisions themselves were caused by unconscious processes? A reader who is tempted to accept this claim has failed to absorb the moral of the firecracker analogy in an earlier section. The fact that x has a cause does not entail that x is not among the causes of y.

6.   Wegner on Free Will

In Wegner's view, conscious will is intimately related to free will. He reports that his discussion of conscious will "has actually been *about* the experience of free will, examining at length when people feel it and when they do not. The special idea we have been exploring is to explain the experience of free will in terms of deterministic or mechanistic processes" (2004, p. 656). Wegner writes:

> Experience of apparent mental causation renders the self magical because it does not draw on all the evidence. We don't have access to the myriad neural, cognitive, dispositional, biological, or social causes that have contributed to the action – nor do we have access to the similar array of causes that underlie the production of the thoughts we have about the action. Instead, we look at the two items our magic selves render visible to us – our conscious thought and our conscious perception of our act – and believe that these are magically connected by our will. In making this link, we take a mental leap over the demonstrable power of the unconscious to guide action . . . and conclude that the conscious mind is the sole player. (2008, p. 234)

Obviously, even people who believe that some of their conscious intentions play a role in causing some of their behavior should not believe that "the conscious mind is the sole player." After all, among the things that play a role in causing our intentions are events in the external world. And if, for example, conscious proximal intentions* play a role in causing overt actions, causal processes of which we are not conscious link them to bodily motions. So one should set aside the magical idea that the conscious mind or self is not itself causally influenced by anything and is a direct and complete cause of some of our actions. More realistic ideas are more worthy of attention: for example, the hypothesis that conscious intentions* or their physical correlates make a causal contribution to some behavior. Again, Wegner marshals evidence that, in some circumstances, people believe (to some degree) that they did things that, in fact, they did not do and, in others, people believe they did not do things that they actually did. But it is a long way from these findings to the conclusion that the hypothesis just formulated is false.

Do we ever act freely? That depends on how free action is to be understood. If acting freely requires the existence of something that does not exist – a supernatural, magical self – then we never act freely. But I know of no good reason to understand free action in that way. In my opinion, on any reasonable conception of free action, the studies and data reviewed here leave it open that we sometimes act freely. For a discussion of imaginary experimental results that would show that no one ever acts freely, see Mele 2009a, ch. 8.

7. Free Will

What does "free will" mean? Wegner is not alone among scientists in understanding its meaning to include something magical or supernatural. P. Read Montague, for example, writes:

Free will is the idea that we make choices and have thoughts independent of anything remotely resembling a physical process. Free will is the close cousin to the idea of the soul – the concept that "you," your thoughts and feelings, derive from an entity that is separate and distinct from the physical mechanisms that make up your body. From this perspective, your choices are not caused by physical events, but instead emerge wholly

formed from somewhere indescribable and outside the purview of physical descriptions. This implies that free will cannot have evolved by natural selection, as that would place it directly in a stream of causally connected events. (2008, p. 584)

When people read in newspapers that scientists have demonstrated the nonexistence of free will, do they take this to mean that scientists have shown that something supernatural or magical does not exist? Or do they – or most of them – understand the news differently?

Wegner and Montague offer no scientific evidence in support of their view of what "free will" means. But there are ways to get evidence about what lay people mean by "free will." One element in Roy Baumeister's multifaceted research project on free will is an attempt to understand how lay people conceive of free will. In Baumeister's view, when the topic is free will, "the optimal agenda for psychology would be to find out what people mean when they use the concepts of freedom, choice, and responsibility in their daily lives and then to illuminate the inner processes that produce those phenomena" (2008, p. 16 [chapter 31]). As he reports, lay people seem to understand free will in a way that features "conscious, rational choice and self-control" (p. 16, also see Stillman et al. forthcoming), and there is evidence that the majority of lay people do not understand free will as Wegner and Montague do (Monroe and Malle, in press, Nahmias et al. 2006).

Another part of Baumeister's project on free will investigates the effects of disbelief in free will. There is evidence that lowering people's subjective probability that they have free will increases misbehavior – for example, lying, cheating, stealing, and socially aggressive conduct (Baumeister et al. 2009, Vohs and Schooler 2008). This finding has provided skeptics like me about scientific argumentation for the thesis that free will is illusory with additional motivation to explain why the data fall well short of justifying this thesis (see Mele 2009a). My focus has been on alleged evidence for such theses as that all of our decisions about what to do are made unconsciously and that conscious intentions (and their physical correlates) never play a role in producing corresponding overt actions. The truth of such theses would threaten the existence of free will even given nonmagical conceptions of it. I have no inclination at all to resist the claim that when free will is understood as something magical or supernatural, there are good grounds for believing that no human beings have free will.

As I have said elsewhere (Mele 2008a), I believe that scientists embarking on work on free will ought to ask themselves *why* they think "free will" means whatever they think it means. Once they find an answer (or find themselves stumped), they should ask themselves another question: Why do people with a different conception of free will conceive of it as they do? The next step would be to reflect on the relative merits of one's own conception of free will and the various alternative conceptions one encounters. One may find that some of the conceptions are self-contradictory, that others are hopelessly magical or mysterious, and that yet others suggest potentially fruitful research programs. One would expect most scientists with an experimental interest in free will to be attracted to conceptions of the third kind. I look forward the results of future scientific work guided by such conceptions of free will.[6]

Notes

[1] Because the expression "neural correlate" is used in various senses in the literature, I avoid it here. "Physical correlate" is, I hope, an innocuous technical term. From a physicalist neuroscientific point of view, proof that the physical correlates of, for example, a particular intention were among the causes of a particular action constitutes proof that the intention was among the causes of the action. It is primarily philosophers who would worry about the metaphysical intricacies of the mind-body problem despite accepting the imagined proof about physical correlates, and the relevant argumentation would be distinctly philosophical. (Jackson 2000 is an excellent brief review of various relevant philosophical positions that highlights the metaphysical nature of the debate.)

[2] Libet maintains that once we become conscious of a decision to perform an overt action, we can exercise free will in "vetoing" it (1985, 1999, 2004, pp. 137–49). Neither the veto nor the associated refraining from acting on the vetoed decision is an overt action.

[3] Try to imagine that you intend to eat some cake now while also intending not to eat it now. What would you do? Would you reach for it with one hand and grab the reaching hand with your other hand?

People who suffer from anarchic hand syndrome sometimes display behavior of this kind. Sean Spence and Chris Frith suggest that these people "have conscious 'intentions to act' [that] are thwarted by . . . 'intentions' to which the patient does not experience conscious access" (1999, p. 24).

[4] James Kilner and coauthors produce evidence that, as they put it, "the readiness potential (RP) – an electrophysiological marker of motor preparation – is present when one is observing someone else's action" (2004, p. 1299).

[5] Powerful evidence that some conscious distal intentions play a role in producing corresponding intentional actions is discussed in Mele 2009a, ch. 7.

[6] Parts of this chapter derive from Mele 2008a, 2008b, 2009a, and 2009b.

References

Baumeister, R. (2008). Free will in scientific psychology. *Perspectives on Psychological Science*, 3, 14–19.

Baumeister, R., Masicampo, E., and DeWall, C. (2009). Prosocial benefits of feeling free: Disbelief in free will increases aggression and reduces helpfulness. *Personality and Social Psychology Bulletin*, 35, 260–8.

Haggard, P. and Magno, E. (1999). Localising awareness of action with transcranial magnetic stimulation. *Experimental Brain Research*, 127, 102–7.

Hallett, M. (2007). Volitional control of movement: The physiology of free will. *Clinical Neurophysiology*, 118, 1179–92.

Holton, R. (2004). Review of Wegner 2002. *Mind*, 113, 218–21.

Jackson, F. (2000). Psychological explanation and implicit theory. *Philosophical Explorations*, 3, 83–95.

Kilner, J., Vargas, C., Duval, S., Blakemore, S., and Sirigu, A. (2004). Motor activation prior to observation of a predicted movement. *Nature Neuroscience*, 7, 1299–1301.

Libet, B. (1985). Unconscious cerebral initiative and the role of conscious will in voluntary action. *Behavioral and Brain Sciences*, 8, 529–66.

Libet, B. (1999). "Do we have free will?" *Journal of Consciousness Studies*, 6, 47–57.

Libet, B. (2001). Consciousness, free action and the brain. *Journal of Consciousness Studies*, 8, 59–65.

Libet, B. (2004). *Mind Time*. Cambridge, MA: Harvard University Press.

Libet, B., Wright, E., and Gleason, C. (1982). Readiness potentials preceding unrestricted "spontaneous" vs. pre-planned voluntary acts. *Electroencephalography and Clinical Neurophysiology*, 54, 322–35.

Logan, G. (1994). On the ability to inhibit thought and action: A users' guide to the stop signal paradigm. In

E. Dagenbach and T. Carr (eds.), *Inhibitory Processes in Attention, Memory, and Language*. San Diego: Academic Press.

Malle, B. (2006). Of windmills and straw men: Folk assumptions of mind and action. In S. Pockett, W. Banks, and S. Gallagher (eds.), *Does Consciousness Cause Behavior? An Investigation of the Nature of Volition*. Cambridge, MA: MIT Press.

Mele, A. (1997). Strength of motivation and being in control: Learning from Libet. *American Philosophical Quarterly*, 34, 319–32.

Mele, A. (2003). *Motivation and Agency*. New York: Oxford University Press.

Mele, A. (2006). *Free Will and Luck*. New York: Oxford University Press.

Mele, A. (2008a). Psychology and free will: A commentary. In J. Baer, J.C. Kaufman, and R. Baumeister (eds.), *Are We Free: Psychology and Free Will*, Oxford: Oxford University Press, pp. 325–46.

Mele, A. (2008b). Recent work on free will and science. *American Philosophical Quarterly*, 45, 107–29.

Mele, A. (2009a). *Effective Intentions*. New York: Oxford University Press.

Mele, A. (2009b). "Free will." In W. Banks (ed.), *Encyclopedia of Consciousness*, vol. 1. Amsterdam: Elsevier.

Monroe, A., and Malle, B. (in press). From uncaused will to conscious choice: The need to study, not speculate about people's folk concept of free will. *Review of Philosophy and Psychology*.

Montague, P.R. (2008). Free will. *Current Biology Magazine*, 18, 14, R584–R585.

Nahmias, E. (2002). When consciousness matters. A critical review of Daniel Wegner's *The Illusion of Conscious Will*. *Philosophical Psychology*, 15, 527–41.

Nahmias, E., Morris, S., Nadelhoffer, T., and Turner, J. (2006). Is incompatibilism intuitive? *Philosophy and Phenomenological Research*, 73, 28–53.

Pacherie, E. (2006). Toward a dynamic theory of intentions. In S. Pockett, W. Banks, and S. Gallagher (eds.), *Does Consciousness Cause Behavior? An Investigation of the Nature of Volition*. Cambridge, MA: MIT Press.

Pockett, S. (2006). The neuroscience of movement. In S. Pockett, W. Banks, and S. Gallagher (eds.), *Does Consciousness Cause Behavior? An Investigation of the Nature of Volition*. Cambridge, MA: MIT Press.

Roediger, H., Goode, M. and Zaromb, F. (2008). "Free will and the control of action." In J. Baer, J.C. Kaufman, and R. Baumeister (eds.), *Are We Free: Psychology and Free Will*, Oxford: Oxford University Press, pp. 205–25.

Spence, S., and Frith, C. (1999). Towards a functional anatomy of volition. *Journal of Consciousness Studies*, 6, 11–29.

Stillman, T., Baumeister, R., and Mele, A. (forthcoming). Free will in everyday life: Autobiographical accounts of free and unfree actions. *Philosophical Psychology*.

Vohs, K., and Schooler, J. (2008). The Value of believing in free will: Encouraging a belief in determinism increases cheating. *Psychological Science*, 19, 49–54.

Wegner, D. (2002). *The Illusion of Conscious Will*. Cambridge, MA: MIT Press.

Wegner, D. (2004). Précis of *The Illusion of Conscious Will. Behavioral and Brain Sciences*, 27, 649–59.

Wegner, D. (2008). Self is magic. In J. Baer, J.C. Kaufman, and R. Baumeister (eds.), *Are We Free: Psychology and Free Will*, Oxford: Oxford University Press, pp. 226–47.

Wegner, D. and Wheatley, T. (1999). Apparent mental causation: Sources of the experience of will. *American Psychologist*, 54, 480–91.

Part V
Moral Intuitions

Introduction

Thomas Nadelhoffer

The history of moral philosophy is replete with what are variously called "thought experiments," "intuition pumps," or "vignettes." Consider, for instance, some of the moral scenarios that we have encountered thus far in this anthology. From Plato's Gyges Ring and Hobbes's State of Nature to Hume's Sensible Knave, we find hypothetical situations designed to elicit moral intuitions – that is, spontaneous judgments about particular moral cases. According to some philosophers, these intuitions provide us with evidentiary grounds for criticizing, rejecting, or accepting competing moral theories. On this view, intuitions about particular cases are to moral philosophy what empirical data are to the natural sciences. Given the evidentiary status often attributed to moral intuitions, it is unsurprising that they have recently received so much attention by both philosophers and psychologists alike. According to some moral psychologists, if our intuitions are going to continue to play a foundational role in moral philosophy, we need to make sure that we understand how and why we end up with the moral intuitions we happen to have.

One philosopher who focused extensively on the nature of moral intuition was the English philosopher **Henry Sidgwick** (1838–1900). On his view, "just as the generalizations of physical science rest on particular observations, so in ethics general truths can only be reached by induction from judgments or perceptions relating to the rightness or wrongness of particular acts" (B1 Chap. VIII). Sidgwick claims that the correct method of moral philosophizing involves trying to develop general moral propositions that "harmonize" with our intuitions. According to Sidgwick, our moral faculty makes it possible for us to have clear and distinct intuitions about general moral rules. Moreover, it is claimed that these general rules already tacitly exist in the minds of "ordinary men." However, while non-philosophers may have a loose grasp of these rules, it is the job of the moral philosopher – who has a "special habit of contemplating clearly and steadily abstract moral notions" – to state the moral rules with precision while using intuitions concerning the "truth and bindingness" of the rules as a guide.

Sidgwick suggests that the moral philosopher's task is a combination of abstract reflection, systematization, and conceptual clarification. The overall goal of this project is to capture the bulk of folk morality – that is, the "morality of common sense" – in a clear and conspicuous way. However, as Sidgwick points out, even if we are able to fish all of the salient rules out of the sea of moral intuition and both systematize and render them consistent, it would still be an open question whether the rules themselves were right or justified. As such, the moral philosopher must take her investigations one step further. On this view, the philosopher is to rely on her faculty of moral judgment to discern the even more basic

Moral Psychology: Historical and Contemporary Readings, edited by Thomas Nadelhoffer, Eddy Nahmias, and Shaun Nichols.
© 2010 Blackwell Publishing Ltd except for editorial material and organization © 2010 Thomas Nadelhoffer, Eddy Nahmias, and Shaun Nichols.

foundational rules that undergird folk morality. In the event that the beliefs of non-philosophers conflict with the more abstract and purportedly self-evident philosophical moral intuitions, the intuitions of laypersons ought to be revised. At the end of the day, Sidgwick's intuitionist approach is akin to the Socratic method – a philosophical tool which relies on folk beliefs and intuitions, tentative definitions, thought experiments, and counter-examples as a means of ferreting out the essential nature of morality.

But what kind of moral rules or obligation are likely to survive this dialectical process? *Sir William David Ross* (1877–1971) is another moral philosopher who provided a novel and influential answer to this question. On Ross' view, we can arrive at the truth about what to do, morally speaking, by directly reflecting on "what we really think" about particular cases. But once again, a skeptic might naturally want to ask why we ought to trust what we "really think." According to Ross, our trust in moral intuition is warranted. Indeed, on his view, that we have prima facie duties to be honest, grateful, and fair becomes "self-evident" once one has "reached sufficient mental maturity" and considered the underlying moral issues with sufficient care and thoroughness. Moreover, Ross suggests that the "moral order" that is represented by the prima facie duties is no less a part of the fabric of the natural universe than are the spatial and numerical values one finds in the axioms of geometry and arithmetic. In morality no less than in mathematics, Ross claims that there are some self-evident truths which cannot and need not be proved. As such, when we are deliberating about our actual moral obligations in particular cases, we must reflect on "the self-evident prima facie rightness of an individual act of a particular type." Having first identified all of the prima facie duties that apply in a particular case, we are to then rely on a process of "intuitive induction" to determine which of the duties is the most stringent in the context, which in turns gives us insight into what we are obligated to do.

But to see just how difficult it can be to sort out our moral intuitions in a coherent and satisfactory way, it is helpful to look at the much discussed work on the so-called Trolley Problem by philosopher **Judith Jarvis Thomson**. Thomson walks the reader through a series of related yet distinct thought experiments that push and pull our moral intuitions in competing directions. For instance, imagine that you have the ability to divert a run-away trolley in order to save five people but that doing so will cause the trolley to kill one person. Let's call this case the Bystander at the Switch. Under these circumstances, is it morally permissible for you to hit the switch, divert the trolley, save the five, and kill the one? Thomson maintains that intuitively, it seems morally *permissible* to sacrifice the one in order to save the five. Next, Thomson has us imagine that the only way you can save five people from a runaway trolley is by pushing someone off a bridge and into the path of the trolley. Let's call this case the Footbridge. Thomson maintains that in Footbridge, it seems morally *impermissible* to push the innocent bystander to her death. Subsequent research has revealed that most people share Thomson's competing intuitions about the two cases.

But what explains this intuitional asymmetry? After all, in both cases, sacrificing the one will save five others. As such, why is it that we feel so strongly that sacrificing one person to save five is permissible in Bystander at the Switch but not in Footbridge? Our first tendency is to insist that there must be some salient difference between the cases and then set about trying to ferret it out. Indeed, upon reflection, we notice that in Bystander at the Switch, the death of the individual on the side track is a side effect of saving the five whereas in Footbridge, the death of the individual is the actual means by which we intend to save the five. With the distinction between side effects and primary actions in hand, we can now try to explain our competing intuitions. But notice that this distinction is itself based on yet further intuitions and judgments that need to be justified. How are we to put a stop to this explanatory regress? We could opt for the kind of foundational intuitionism of Sidgwick and Ross whereby the regress terminates in self-evident moral rules, duties, and obligations. We could also question instead the epistemological framework that undergirds intuition-driven moral philosophy.

One philosopher who opts for this latter approach is **Peter Unger**. In order to motivate his deflationary stance towards moral intuitions, he introduces two cases that are supposed to generate competing intuitions despite the fact that the morally salient features are purportedly the same in each one. In the first scenario, you have the ability to save a child who is drowning in a pond but it will ruin your $100 pair of shoes. Unger suggests that most people would think that under these circumstances you are obligated to help. Indeed, if you don't help, people will judge that you are a moral monster. But now imagine that you have the chance to save 30 starving children by donating $100 to UNICEF. Are you similarly obligated to help under these circumstances? Unger claims that the most common intuitive response to this later case is that while saving the children would be a nice gesture, there is nothing wrong with choosing instead not to help. According to Unger, our intuitions in the former case are driven by morally salient features of the scenario – for example, the drowning child – whereas our intuitions in the latter case are being driven by morally irrelevant "distortional" features – for example, the distant location of the starving children. If he is right about this, then we cannot simply read off our moral commitments by examining our intuitions about particular cases since some of these intuitions do not reveal anything at all about these commitments. Given the distortional influences that purportedly undergird some of our intuitions, Unger cautions us against assuming that all of our intuitions are on the same footing, morally speaking.

Because our intuitions are amenable to scientific investigation, the issue Unger raises is an empirically tractable one. For instance, Jonathan Haidt is a psychologist who has made moral intuitions the central focus of his research. On Haidt's view, our immediate, unreflective moral intuitions play a much larger role in our moral psychology than our moral reasoning. Moreover, Haidt suggests that moral reasoning is ultimately an ex post facto process that we rely on to influence the intuitions and judgments of other people. Hence, the intuitionist part of Haidt's model is driven by his view of the source of our moral judgments and the social part of the model is driven by his view concerning the inherently interpersonal element of moral reasoning. Haidt goes on to suggest that while our moral judgments may result from reflection and ratiocination under ideal circumstances, they are usually formed as the result of spontaneous, non-inferential, affective cognitive processes. As such, it is often the case that we feel strongly that an act is morally unacceptable even though we might not be able to articulate why we feel thus. Haidt calls this commonplace phenomenon "moral dumbfounding" and he suggests that rationalist models have a hard time accommodating it. However, unlike Unger, Haidt does not disparage these automatic intuitions. Rather, he thinks that they are at the root of most of our moral reactions, and that the fact that they are not the product of reasoning is no basis for treating them with suspicion.

Not all researchers working in moral psychology are as conciliatory to intuitions as Haidt. Joshua Greene, a philosopher and a psychologist, has similarly tried to shed light on the nature and limitations of moral intuition, and his view about the philosophical import of moral intuitions is closer to Unger's. In a series of studies, Greene and colleagues attempted to explore the neural substrates of our moral intuitions. While participants were in an fMRI machine, they read versions of the aforementioned Trolley Problem. In light of the findings, Greene claims that the main difference between Bystander at the Switch case and Footbridge is that while our intuitive response to the former is driven by sophisticated "higher order" cognitive processes, our intuitive responses to the latter are driven primarily by emotion. Because the thought of physically pushing someone to her death produces a greater affective response than the thought of diverting a trolley onto someone, we end up arriving at competing judgments in the two cases. Greene suggests that the emotional responses that generate the "no" response to Footbridge are crude alarm bells. We should discount these reactions, Greene maintains, since they are manifestly insensitive to broader ethical considerations. By contrast, Greene maintains that the intuition that it is permissible to divert the train in Bystander is driven by the kinds of more deliberative and reflective cognitive processes that are purportedly characteristic of consequentialist reasoning.

Based on these and similar data, Greene suggests that the philosophical tradition of deontological ethics is ultimately based on the alarm-like emotions that drive responses to Footbridge. Moreover, Greene goes on to suggest that deontological theories can helpfully be construed as a kind of post hoc moral confabulation. On this view, deontology is a story that philosophers have cleverly made up in order to explain their pre-potent emotional responses to harm. Consequentialist intuitions, on the other hand, are purportedly the result of inherently aggregative and context-sensitive moral cost benefit analyses that are driven by more sophisticated cognitive processes than their deontological counterparts. As such, Greene concludes that consequentialism is a more reliable guide to morality than deontology. However, discussing the merits of the final step in Greene's argument – which is admittedly controversial – would take us too far afield for present purposes. Instead, we need to briefly examine the arguments contained in the final reading of this section.

Walter Sinnott-Armstrong is yet another researcher working at the cross-roads of philosophy and psychology. In a series of recent papers, Sinnott-Armstrong has used findings in social psychology to put pressure on the kind of intuitionism one finds in Sidgwick and Ross. Just to take one example, Sinnott-Armstrong notes that people have different intuitions about trolley cases depending on the order in which the cases are presented. In light of the gathering data from moral psychology, Sinnott-Armstrong suggests that our intuitions are "partial, controversial, emotional, subject to illusion, and explicable by dubious sources." As such, he claims that before we are warranted in trusting the moral intuitions we happen to have, we need some sort of confirmation. In short, moral intuitions are not in and of themselves sufficient for justified moral beliefs. Rather, justified moral beliefs will necessarily be inferential beliefs. But if Sinnott-Armstrong is right about this, the attempt by Sidgwick, Ross, and others to ground morality on non-inferential moral intuitions is on a shaky epistemological footing.

Keep in mind that the targets of Sinnott-Armstrong's criticisms are versions of moral intuitionism whereby our intuitions provide us with access to self-evident truths about morality. After all, only a variety of intuitionism that appeals to non-inferentially justified moral intuitions could in principle steer us away from the aforementioned regressive path towards moral skepticism. Thus, if we have both philosophical and psychological grounds for doubting that moral intuitions can be justified non-inferentially, we must devise a new strategy for avoiding the moral skeptic's grasp. Minimally, Sinnott-Armstrong

claims that simply assuming that our moral intuitions are (almost) always a reliable guide to the truth is no longer an empirically viable strategy for moral philosophy. At the end of the day, he suggests that much more work needs to be done at the cross-roads of moral philosophy and psychology before we can rest on our intuitive moral laurels.

Questions for Further Study

*   How do we get from descriptive claims concerning the cognitive underpinnings of our moral intuitions to criticisms of first order moral theories such as consequentialism, deontology, and the like?
*   How might one establish that moral intuitions are non-inferentially justified?
*   Even if we agree that not all intuitions are reliable guides to what morality requires, how should we go about distinguishing the reliable intuitions from the unreliable ones?
*   If we reject moral intuitionism, are we left with moral skepticism?
*   What would a moral theory that entirely eschewed moral intuitions look like?

Suggested Readings

Baron, J. (1994). Nonconsequentialist decisions. *Behavioral and Brain Sciences*, 17, 1–42.

Greene, J., Nystromm, L., Engell, A., Darley, J., and Cohen, J. (2004). The neural bases of cognitive conflict and control in moral judgment. *Neuron*, 44, 389–400.

Horowitz, T. (1998). Philosophical intuitions and psychological theory. In M. DePaul and W. Ramsey (eds.), *Rethinking Intuition: The Psychology of Intuition and its Role in Philosophical Inquiry*. Lanham, MD: Rowman and Littlefield.

Kamm, F.M. (1998). Moral intuitions, cognitive psychology, and the harming-versus-not-aiding distinction. *Ethics*, 108, 463–88.

Mikhail, J. (2007). Universal moral grammar: Theory, evidence, and the future. *Trends in Cognitive Sciences*, 11, 4, 143–52.

Moll, J., de Oliveira-Souza, R., Eslinger, P.J., Bramati, I.E., Mourao-Miranda, J., Andreiuolo, P.A., and Pessoa, L. (2002). The neural correlates of moral sensitivity: A functional magnetic resonance imaging investigation of basic and moral emotions. *Journal of Neuroscience*, 22, 2730–6.

Petrinovich, L. and O'Neill, P. (1996). Influence of wording and framing effects on moral intuitions. *Ethology and Sociobiology*, 17, 145–71.

Rawls, J. (1951). Outline of a decision procedure for ethics. *Philosophical Review*, 60, 177–97.

Sinnott-Armstrong, W. (2008). Framing moral intuitions. In W. Sinnott-Armstrong (ed.), *Moral Psychology, Volume 2: The Cognitive Science of Morality*. Cambridge: MIT Press, pp. 47–76.

Sunstein, C. (2005). Moral heuristics. *Behavioral and Brain Sciences*, 28, 4, 531–42.

Tversky, A. and Kahneman, D. (1981). The framing of decisions and the psychology of choice. *Science*, 211, 453–8.

33

The Methods of Ethics

Henry Sidgwick

Book I, Chapter VIII

Section 2

The common antithesis between 'intuitive' and
'inductive' morality is misleading [. . .] since a
moralist may hold the rightness of actions to be
cognisable apart from the pleasure produced by
them, while yet his method may be properly
called Inductive. For he may hold that, just as the
generalisations of physical science rest on particular observations, so in ethics general truths can
only be reached by induction from judgments or
perceptions relating to the rightness or wrongness
of particular acts.

For example, when Socrates is said by Aristotle
to have applied inductive reasoning to ethical
questions, it is this kind of induction which is
meant. He discovered, as we are told, the latent
ignorance of himself and other men: that is, that
they used general terms confidently, without
being able, when called upon, to explain the
meaning of those terms. His plan for remedying
this ignorance was to work towards the true
definition of each term, by examining and
comparing different instances of its application.
Thus the definition of Justice would be sought
by comparing different actions commonly judged
to be just, and framing a general proposition

that would harmonise with all these particular
judgments.

So again, in the popular view of Conscience it
seems to be often implied that particular judgments are the most trustworthy. 'Conscience' is
the accepted popular term for the faculty of moral
judgment, as applied to the acts and motives
of the person judging; and we most commonly
think of the dictates of conscience as relating to
particular actions. Thus when a man is bidden, in
any particular case, to 'trust to his conscience',
it commonly seen is to be meant that he should
exercise a faculty of judging morally this particular case without reference to general rules, and
even in opposition to conclusions obtained by
systematic deduction from such rules. And it is
on this view of Conscience that the contempt
often expressed for 'Casuistry' may be most easily
justified: for if the particular case can be satisfactorily settled by conscience without reference
to general rules, 'Casuistry', which consists in the
application of general rules to particular cases, is
at best superfluous. But then, on this view, we
shall have no practical need of any such general
rules, or of scientific Ethics at all. We may of
course form general propositions by induction
from these particular conscientious judgments,
and arrange them systematically: but any interest
which such a system may have will be purely

From Henry Sidgwick (1838–1900), *The Methods of Ethics*, Book I, Chapter VIII Sections 2,3, and 4, Book III, Chapter 1,
Sections 1,2, 4, and 5.

Moral Psychology: Historical and Contemporary Readings, edited by Thomas Nadelhoffer, Eddy Nahmias, and Shaun Nichols.

speculative. And this accounts, perhaps, for the indifference or hostility to systematic morality shown by some conscientious persons. For they feel that they can at any rate do without it: and they fear that the cultivation of it may place the mind in a wrong attitude in relation to practice, and prove rather unfavourable than otherwise to the proper development of the practically important faculty manifested or exercised in particular moral judgments.

The view above described may be called, in a sense, 'ultra-intuitional', since, in its most extreme form, it recognises simple immediate intuitions alone and discards as superfluous all modes of reasoning to moral conclusions: and we may find in it one phase or variety of the Intuitional method, – if we may extend the term 'method' to include a procedure that is completed in a single judgment.

Section 3

But though probably all moral agents have experience of such particular intuitions, and though they constitute a great part of the moral phenomena of most minds, comparatively few are so thoroughly satisfied with them, as not to feel a need of some further moral knowledge even from a strictly practical point of view. For these particular intuitions do not, to reflective persons, present themselves as quite indubitable and irrefragable: nor do they always find when they have put an ethical question to themselves with all sincerity, that they are conscious of clear immediate insight in respect of it. Again, when a man compares the utterances of his conscience at different times, he often finds it difficult to make them altogether consistent: the same conduct will wear a different moral aspect at one time from that which it wore at another, although our knowledge of its circumstances and conditions is not materially changed. Further, we become aware that the moral perceptions of different minds, to all appearance equally competent to judge, frequently conflict: one condemns what another approves. In this way serious doubts are aroused as to the validity of each man's particular moral judgments: and we are led to endeavour to set these doubts at rest by appealing to general rules, more firmly established on a basis of common consent.

And in fact, though the view of conscience above discussed is one which much popular language seems to suggest, it is not that which Christian and other moralists have usually given. They have rather represented the process of conscience as analogous to one of jural reasoning, such as is conducted in a Court of Law. Here we have always a system of universal rules given, and any particular action has to be brought under one of these rules before it can be pronounced lawful or unlawful. Now the rules of positive law are usually not discoverable by the individual's reason: this may teach him that law ought to be obeyed, but what law is must, in the main, be communicated to him from some external authority. And this is not unfrequently the case with the conscientious reasoning of ordinary persons when any dispute or difficulty forces them to reason: they have a genuine impulse to conform to the right rules of conduct, but they are not conscious, in difficult or doubtful cases, of seeing for themselves what these are: they have to inquire of their priest, or their sacred books, or perhaps the common opinion of the society to which they belong. In so far as this is the case we cannot strictly call their method Intuitional. They follow rules generally received, not intuitively apprehended. Other persons, however (or perhaps all to some extent), do seem to see for themselves the truth and bindingness of all or most of these current rules. They may still put forward 'common consent' as an argument for the validity of these rules: but only as supporting the individual's intuition, not as a substitute for it or as superseding it.

Here then we have a second Intuitional Method: of which the fundamental assumption is that we can discern certain general rules with really clear and finally valid intuition. It is held that such general rules are implicit in the moral reasoning of ordinary men, who apprehend them adequately for most practical purposes, and are able to enunciate them roughly; but that to state them with proper precision requires a special habit of contemplating clearly and steadily abstract moral notions. It is held that the moralist's function then is to perform this process of abstract contemplation, to arrange the results as systematically as possible, and by proper definitions and explanations to remove vagueness and prevent conflict. It is such a system as this which seems to be generally intended when Intuitive or *a priori* morality is mentioned, and which will chiefly occupy us in Book III.

Section 4

By philosophic minds, however, the 'Morality of Common Sense' (as I have ventured to call it), even when made as precise and orderly as possible, is often found unsatisfactory as a system, although they have no disposition to question its general authority. It is found difficult to accept as scientific first principles the moral generalities that we obtain by reflection on the ordinary thought of mankind, even though we share this thought. Even granting that these rules can be so defined as perfectly to fit together and cover the whole field of human conduct, without coming into conflict and without leaving any practical questions unanswered, – still the resulting code seems an accidental aggregate of precepts, which stands in need of some rational synthesis. In short, without being disposed to deny that conduct commonly judged to be right is so, we may yet require some deeper explanation *why* it is so. From this demand springs a third species or phase of Intuitionism, which, while accepting the morality of common sense as in the main sound, still attempts to find for it a philosophic basis which it does not itself offer: to get one or more principles more absolutely and undeniably true and evident, from which the current rules might be deduced, either just as they are commonly received or with slight modifications and rectifications.

The three phases of Intuitionism just described may be treated as three stages in the formal development of Intuitive Morality: we may term them respectively Perceptional, Dogmatic, and Philosophical. The last-mentioned I have only defined in the vaguest way: in fact, as yet I have presented it only as a problem, of which it is impossible to foresee how many solutions may be attempted: but it does not seem desirable to investigate it further at present, as it will be more satisfactorily studied after examining in detail the Morality of Common Sense.

It must not be thought that these three phases are sharply distinguished in the moral reasoning of ordinary men: but then no more is Intuitionism of any sort sharply distinguished from either species of Hedonism. A loose combination or confusion of methods is the most common type

of actual moral reasoning. Probably most moral men believe that their moral sense or instinct in any case will guide them fairly right, but also that there are general rules for determining right action in different departments of conduct: and that for these again it is possible to find a philosophical explanation, by which they may be deduced from a smaller number of fundamental principles. Still for systematic direction of conduct, we require to know on what judgments we are to rely as ultimately valid.

So far I have been mainly concerned with differences in intuitional method due to difference of generality in the intuitive beliefs recognised as ultimately valid. There is, however, another class of differences arising from a variation of view as to the precise quality immediately apprehended in the moral intuition. These are peculiarly subtle and difficult to fix in clear and precise language, and I therefore reserve them for a separate chapter.

Book III, Chapter I

Section 1

The effort to examine, closely but quite neutrally, the system of Egoistic Hedonism, with which we have been engaged in the last Book, may not improbably have produced on the reader's mind a certain aversion to the principle and method examined, even though (like myself) he may find it difficult not to admit the 'authority' of self-love, or the 'rationality' of seeking one's own individual happiness. In considering 'enlightened self-interest' as supplying a *prima facie* tenable principle for the systematisation of conduct, I have given no expression to this sentiment of aversion, being anxious to ascertain with scientific impartiality the results to which this principle logically leads. When, however, we seem to find on careful examination of Egoism (as worked out on a strictly empirical basis) that the common precepts of duty, which we are trained to regard as sacred, must be to the egoist rules to which it is only generally speaking and for the most part reasonable to conform, but which under special circumstances must be decisively ignored and broken, – the offence which Egoism in the abstract gives to our sympathetic and social nature adds force to the recoil from it caused by the perception of its occasional practical conflict with common notions of duty. But further, we are accustomed to expect from Morality clear and decisive precepts or counsels: and such rules as can be laid down for seeking the individual's greatest happiness cannot but appear wanting in these qualities. A dubious guidance to an ignoble end appears to be all that the calculus of Egoistic Hedonism has to offer. And it is by appealing to the superior certainty with which the dictates of Conscience or the Moral Faculty are issued, that Butler maintains the practical supremacy of Conscience over Self-love, in spite of his admission (in the passage before quoted) of theoretical priority in the claims of the latter. A man knows certainly, he says, what he ought to do: but he does not certainly know what will lead to his happiness.

In saying this, Butler appears to me fairly to represent the common moral sense of ordinary mankind, in our own age no less than in his. The moral judgments that men habitually pass on one another in ordinary discourse imply for the most part that duty is usually not a difficult thing for an ordinary man to *know*, though various seductive impulses may make it difficult for him to *do* it. And in such maxims as that duty should be performed 'advienne que pourra', that truth should be spoken without regard to consequences, that justice should be done 'though the sky should fall', it is implied that we have the power of seeing clearly that certain kinds of actions are right and reasonable in themselves, apart from their consequences; – or rather with a merely partial consideration of consequences, from which other consequences admitted to be possibly good or bad are definitely excluded. And such a power is claimed for the human mind by most of the writers who have maintained the existence of moral intuitions; I have therefore thought myself justified in treating this claim as characteristic of the method which I distinguish as Intuitional.

[. . .]

Section 4

But the question may be raised, whether it is legitimate to take for granted (as I have hitherto been doing) the existence of such intuitions? And, no doubt, there are persons who deliberately deny that reflection enables them to discover any such phenomenon in their conscious experience as the judgment or apparent perception that an act is in itself right or good, in any other sense than that of being the right or fit means to the attainment of some ulterior end. I think, however, that such denials are commonly recognised as paradoxical, and opposed to the common experience of civilised men: – at any rate if the psychological question, as to the *existence* of such moral judgments or apparent perceptions of moral qualities, is carefully distinguished from the ethical question as to their *validity*, and from what we may call the 'psychogonical' question as to their *origin*. The first and second of these questions are sometimes confounded, owing to an ambiguity in the use of the term 'intuition'; which has sometimes been understood to imply that the judgment or apparent perception so designated is *true*. I wish therefore to say expressly, that by calling any affirmation as to the rightness or wrongness of actions 'intuitive', I do not mean to prejudge the question as to its ultimate validity, when philosophically considered: I only mean that its truth is apparently known immediately, and not as the result of reasoning. I admit the possibility that any such 'intuition' may turn out to have an element of error, which subsequent reflection and comparison may enable us to correct; just as many apparent perceptions through the organ of vision are found to be partially illusory and misleading: indeed the sequel will show that I hold this to be to an important extent the case with moral intuitions commonly so called.

The question as to the validity of moral intuitions being thus separated from the simple question 'whether they actually exist', it becomes obvious that the latter can only be decided for each person by direct introspection or reflection. It must not therefore be supposed that its decision is a simple matter, introspection being always infallible: on the contrary, experience leads me to regard men as often liable to confound with moral intuitions other states or acts of mind essentially different from them, – blind impulses to certain kinds of action or vague sentiments of preference for them, or conclusions from rapid and half-unconscious processes of reasoning, or current opinions to which familiarity has given an illusory air of self-evidence. But any errors of this kind, due to careless or superficial reflection, can only be cured by more careful reflection. This may indeed be much aided by communication with other minds; it may also be aided, in a subordinate way, by an inquiry into the antecedents of the apparent intuition, which may suggest to the reflective mind sources of error to which a superficial view of it is liable. Still the question whether a certain judgment presents itself to the reflective mind as intuitively known cannot be decided by any inquiry into its antecedents or causes.

It is, however, still possible to hold that an inquiry into the Origin of moral intuitions must be decisive in determining their Validity. And in fact it has been often assumed, both by Intuitionists and their opponents, that if our moral faculty can be shown to be 'derived' or 'developed' out of other pre-existent elements of mind or consciousness, a reason is thereby given for distrusting it; while if, on the other hand, it can be shown to have existed in the human mind from its origin, its trustworthiness is thereby established. Either assumption appears to me devoid of foundation. On the one hand, I can see no ground for supposing that a faculty thus derived, is, as such, more liable to error than if its existence in the individual possessing it had been differently caused: to put it otherwise, I cannot see how the mere ascertainment that certain apparently self-evident judgments have been caused in known and determinate ways, can be in itself a valid ground for distrusting this class of apparent cognitions. I cannot even admit that those who affirm the truth of such judgments are bound to show in their causes a tendency to make them true: indeed the acceptance of any such *onus probandi* would seem to me to render the attainment of philosophical certitude impossible. For the premises of the required demonstration must consist of caused beliefs, which as having been caused will equally stand in need of being proved true, and so on *ad infinitum*: unless it be held that we can find among the premises of our reasonings certain apparently self-evident judgments which have had no antecedent causes, and that these are therefore to be accepted as valid without proof. But such an assertion would be an extravagant paradox: and, if it be admitted that all beliefs are equally in the position of being effects of antecedent causes, it seems evident that this characteristic alone cannot serve to invalidate any of them.

I hold, therefore, that the *onus probandi* must be thrown the other way: those who dispute the validity of moral or other intuitions on the ground of their derivation must be required to show, not merely that they are the effects of certain causes, but that these causes are of a kind that tend to produce invalid beliefs. Now it is not, I conceive, possible to prove by any theory of the derivation of the moral faculty that the fundamental ethical conceptions 'right' or 'what ought to be done', 'Good' or 'what it is reasonable to desire and seek', are invalid, and that consequently *all* propositions of the form 'X is right' or 'good' are untrustworthy: for such ethical propositions, relating as they do to matter fundamentally different from that with which physical science or psychology deals, cannot be inconsistent with any physical or psychological conclusions. They can only be shown to involve error by being shown to contradict each other; and such a demonstration cannot lead us cogently to the sweeping conclusion that all are false. It may, however, be possible to prove that some ethical beliefs have been caused in such a way as to make it probable that they are wholly or partially erroneous: and it will hereafter be important to consider how far any Ethical intuitions, which we find ourselves disposed to accept as valid, are open to attack on such psychogonical grounds. At present I am only concerned to maintain that no general demonstration of the derivedness or developedness of our moral faculty can supply an adequate reason for distrusting it.

On the other hand, if we have been once led to distrust our moral faculty on other grounds — as (e.g.) from the want of clearness and consistency in the moral judgments of the same individual, and the discrepancies between the judgments of different individuals – it seems to me equally clear that our confidence in such judgments cannot properly be re-established by a demonstration of their 'originality'. I see no reason to believe that the 'original' element of our moral cognition can be ascertained; but if it could, I see no reason to hold that it would be especially free from error.

Section 5

How then can we hope to eliminate error from our moral intuitions? One answer to this question was briefly suggested in a previous chapter where the different phases of the Intuitional Method were discussed. It was there said that in order to settle the doubts arising from the uncertainties and discrepancies that are found when we compare our judgments on particular cases, reflective persons naturally appeal to general rules or formulae: and it is to such general formulae that Intuitional Moralists commonly attribute ultimate certainty and validity. And certainly there are obvious sources of error in our judgments respecting concrete duty which seem to be absent when we consider the abstract notions of different kinds of conduct; since in any concrete case the complexity of circumstances necessarily increases the difficulty of judging, and our personal interests or habitual sympathies are liable to disturb the clearness of our moral discernment. Further, we must observe that most of us feel the need of such formulae not only to correct, but also to supplement, our intuitions respecting particular concrete duties. Only exceptionally confident persons find that they always seem to see clearly what ought to be done in any case that comes before them. Most of us, however unhesitatingly we may affirm rightness and wrongness in ordinary matters of conduct, yet not unfrequently meet with cases where our unreasoned judgment fails us; and where we could no more decide the moral issue raised without appealing to some general formula, than we could decide a disputed legal claim without reference to the positive law that deals with the matter.

And such formulae are not difficult to find: it only requires a little reflection and observation of men's moral discourse to make a collection of such general rules, as to the validity of which there would be apparent agreement at least among moral persons of our own age and civilisation, and which would cover with approximate completeness the whole of human conduct. Such a collection, regarded as a code imposed on an individual by the public opinion of the community to which he belongs, we have called the Positive Morality of the community: but when regarded as a body of moral truth, warranted to be such by the *consensus* of mankind, – or at least of that portion of mankind which combines adequate intellectual enlightenment with a serious concern

for morality – it is more significantly termed the morality of Common Sense.

When, however, we try to apply these currently accepted principles, we find that the notions composing them are often deficient in clearness and precision. For instance, we should all agree in recognising Justice and Veracity as important virtues; and we shall probably all accept the general maxims, that 'we ought to give every man his own' and that 'we ought to speak the truth': but when we ask (1) whether primogeniture is just, or the disendowment of corporations, or the determination of the value of services by competition, or (2) whether and how far false statements may be allowed in speeches of advocates, or in religious ceremonials, or when made to enemies or robbers, or in defence of lawful secrets, we do not find that these or any other current maxims enable us to give clear and unhesitating decisions. And yet such particular questions are, after all, those to which we naturally expect answers from the moralist. For we study Ethics, as Aristotle says, for the sake of Practice: and in practice we are concerned with particulars.

Hence it seems that if the formulae of Intuitive Morality are really to serve as scientific axioms, and to be available in clear and cogent demonstrations, they must first be raised – by an effort of reflection which ordinary persons will not make – to a higher degree of precision than attaches to them in the common thought and discourse of mankind in general. We have, in fact, to take up the attempt that Socrates initiated, and endeavour to define satisfactorily the general notions of duty and virtue which we all in common use for awarding approbation or disapprobation to conduct. This is the task upon which we shall be engaged in the nine chapters that follow. I must beg the reader to bear in mind that throughout these chapters I am not trying to prove or disprove Intuitionism, but merely by reflection on the common morality which I and my reader share, and to which appeal is so often made in moral disputes, to obtain as explicit, exact, and coherent a statement as possible of its fundamental rules.

34

The Right and the Good

W.D. Ross

Chapter 2: What Makes Right Acts Right?

[. . .]

I suggest 'prima facie duty' or 'conditional duty' as a brief way of referring to the characteristic (quite distinct from that of being a duty proper) which an act has, in virtue of being of a certain kind (e.g. the keeping of a promise), of being an act which would be a duty proper if it were not at the same time of another kind which is morally significant. Whether an act is a duty proper or actual duty depends on *all* the morally significant kinds it is an instance of. The phrase 'prima facie duty' must be apologized for, since

1 it suggests that what we are speaking of is a certain kind of duty, whereas it is in fact not a duty, but something related in a special way to duty. Strictly speaking, we want not a phrase in which duty is qualified by an adjective, but a separate noun.

2 'Prima' facie suggests that one is speaking only of an appearance which a moral situation presents at first sight, and which may turn out to be illusory; whereas what I am speaking of is an objective fact involved in the nature of the situation, or more strictly in an element of its nature, though not, as duty proper does, arising from its whole nature.

[. . .]

There is nothing arbitrary about these *prima facie* duties. Each rests on a definite circumstance which cannot seriously be held to be without moral significance. Of *prima facie* duties I suggest, without claiming completeness or finality for it, the following division.[1]

1 Some duties rest on previous acts of my own. These duties seem to include two kinds,
   A those resting on a promise or what may fairly be called an implicit promise, such as the implicit undertaking not to tell lies which seems to be implied in the act of entering into conversation (at any rate by civilized men), or of writing books that purport to be history and not fiction. These may be called the duties of fidelity.
   B Those resting on a previous wrongful act. These may be called the duties of reparation.
2 Some rest on previous acts of other men, i.e. services done by them to me. These may be loosely described as the duties of gratitude.[2]
3 Some rest on the fact or possibility of a distribution of pleasure or happiness (or of the means thereto) which is not in accordance with the merit of the persons concerned; in such cases there arises a duty to upset or prevent such a distribution. These are the duties of justice.

From W.D. Ross (1930). *The Right and the Good*, Chapter 2. Clarendon Press, 1930.

4 Some rest on the mere fact that there are beings in the world whose condition we can make better in respect of virtue, or of intelligence, or of pleasure. These are the duties of beneficence.
5 Some rest on the fact that we can improve our own condition in respect of virtue or of intelligence. These are the duties of self-improvement.
6 I think that we should distinguish from (4) the duties that may be summed up under the title of 'not injuring others'. No doubt to injure others is incidentally to fail to do them good; but it seems to me clear that non-maleficence is apprehended as a duty distinct from that of beneficence, and as a duty of a more stringent character.

It will be noticed that this alone among the types duty has been stated in a negative way. An attempt might no doubt be made to state this duty, like the others, in a positive way. It might be said that it is really the duty to prevent ourselves from acting either from an inclination to harm others or from an inclination to seek our own pleasure, in doing which we should incidentally harm them. But on reflection it seems clear that the primary duty here is the duty not to harm others, this being a duty whether or not we have an inclination that if followed would lead to our harming them; and that when we have such an inclination the primary duty not to harm others gives rise to a consequential duty to resist the inclination. The recognition of this duty of non-maleficence is the first step on the way to the recognition of the duty of beneficence; and that accounts for the prominence of the commands

'thou shalt not kill',
'thou shalt not commit adultery',
'thou shalt not steal',
'thou shalt not bear false witness',

in so early a code as the Decalogue. But even when we have come to recognize the duty of beneficence, it appears to me that the duty of non-maleficence is recognized as a distinct one, and as *prima facie* more binding. We should not in general consider it justifiable to kill one person in order to keep another alive, or to steal from one in order to give alms to another.

[. . .]

One or two other comments must be made on this provisional list of the divisions of duty.

(1) The nomenclature is not strictly correct. For by 'fidelity' or 'gratitude' we mean, strictly, certain states of motivation; and, as I have urged, it is not our duty to have certain motives, but to do certain acts. By 'fidelity', for instance, is meant, strictly, the disposition to fulfil promises and implicit promises *because we have made them*. We have no general word to cover the actual fulfilment of promises and implicit promises *irrespective of motive*; and I use 'fidelity', loosely but perhaps conveniently, to fill this gap. So too I use 'gratitude' for the returning of services, irrespective of motive. The term 'justice' is not so much confined, in ordinary usage, to a certain state of motivation, for we should often talk of a man as acting justly even when we did not think his motive was the wish to do what was just simply for the sake of doing so. Less apology is therefore needed for our use of 'justice' in this sense. And I have used the word 'beneficence' rather than 'benevolence', in order to emphasize the fact that it is our duty to do certain things, and not to do them from certain motives.

(2) If the objection be made, that this catalogue of the main types of duty is an unsystematic one resting on no logical principle, it may be replied, first, that it makes no claim to being ultimate. It is a *prima facie* classification of the duties which reflection on our moral convictions seems actually to reveal. And if these convictions are, as I would claim that they are, of the nature of knowledge, and if I have not misstated them, the list will be a list of authentic conditional duties, correct as far as it goes though not necessarily complete. The list of *goods* put forward by the rival theory is reached by exactly the same method – the only sound one in the circumstances – viz. that of direct reflection on what we really think. Loyalty to the facts is worth more than a symmetrical architectonic or a hastily reached simplicity. If further reflection discovers a perfect logical basis for this or for a better classification, so much the better.

(3) It may, again, be objected that our theory that there are these various and often conflicting types of *prima facie* duty leaves us with no principle upon which to discern what is our actual duty in particular circumstances. But this objection is not one which the rival theory is in a position

to bring forward. For when we have to choose between the production of two heterogeneous goods, say knowledge and pleasure, the 'ideal utilitarian' theory can only fall back on an opinion, for which no logical basis can be offered, that one of the goods is the greater; and this is no better than a similar opinion that one of two duties is the more urgent. And again, when we consider the infinite variety of the effects of our actions in the way of pleasure, it must surely be admitted that the claim which *hedonism* sometimes makes, that it offers a readily applicable criterion of right conduct, is quite illusory.

I am unwilling, however, to content myself with an *argumentum ad hominem*, and I would contend that in principle there is no reason to anticipate that every act that is our duty is so for one and the same reason. Why should two sets of circumstances, or one set of circumstances, not possess different characteristics, any one of which makes a certain act our *prima facie* duty? When I ask what it is that makes me in certain cases sure that I have a *prima facie* duty to do so and so, I find that it lies in the fact that I have made a promise; when I ask the same question in another case, I find the answer lies in the fact that I have done a wrong. And if on reflection I find (as I think I do) that neither of these reasons is reducible to the other, I must not on any *a priori* ground assume that such a reduction is possible.

[. . .]

Something should be said of the relation between our apprehension of the *prima facie* rightness of certain types of act and our mental attitude towards particular acts. It is proper to use the word 'apprehension' in the former case and not in the latter. That an act, *qua* fulfilling a promise, or *qua* effecting a just distribution of good, or *qua* returning services rendered, or *qua* promoting the good of others, or *qua* promoting the virtue or insight of the agent, is *prima facie* right, is self-evident, not in the sense that it is evident from beginning of our lives, or as soon as we attend to the proposition for the first time, but in the sense that when we have reached sufficient mental maturity and have given sufficient attention to the proposition it is evident without any need of proof, or of evidence beyond itself. It is self-evident just as a mathematical axiom, or the validity of a form of inference, is evident. The moral order expressed in these propositions is just as much part of the fundamental nature of the universe (and, we may add, of any possible universe in which there were moral agents at all) as is the spatial or numerical structure expressed in the axioms of geometry or arithmetic. In our confidence that these propositions are true there is involved the same trust in our reason that is involved in our confidence in mathematics; and we should have no justification for trusting it in the latter sphere and distrusting it in the former. In both cases we are dealing with propositions that cannot be proved, but that just as certainly need no proof.

Some of these general principles of *prima facie* duty may appear to be open to criticism. It may be thought, for example, that the principle of returning good for good is a falling off from the Christian principle, generally and rightly recognized as expressing the highest morality, of returning good for evil. To this it may be replied that I do not suggest that there is a principle commanding us to return good for good and forbidding us to return good for evil, and that I do suggest that there is a positive duty to seek the good of all men. What I maintain is that an act in which good is returned for good is recognized as specially binding on us just because it is of that character, and that *ceteris paribus* any one would think it his duty to help his benefactors rather than his enemies, if he could not do both; just as it is generally recognised that *ceteris paribus* we should pay our debts rather than give our money in charity, when we cannot do both. A benefactor is not only a man, calling for our effort on his behalf on that ground, but also our benefactor, calling for our *special* effort on that ground.

Our judgements about our actual duty in concrete situations have none of the certainty that attaches to our recognition of the general principles of duty. A statement is certain, i.e. is an expression of knowledge, only in one or other of two cases: when it is either self-evident, or a valid conclusion from self-evident premises. And our judgements about our particular duties have neither of these characters. (1) They are not self-evident. Where a possible act is seen to have two characteristics, in virtue of one of which it is *prima facie* right, and in virtue of the other *prima-facie* wrong, we are (I think) well aware that we are not certain whether we ought or ought not to do it; that whether we do it or not, we are taking a moral risk. We come in the long run, after consideration, to think one duty more pressing than the other, but we do not feel certain that it is so. And though we do not always recognize that a possible act has two such characteristics, and though there may be cases in which it has not, we are never certain that any particular possible act has not, and therefore never certain that it is right, nor certain that it is wrong. For, to go no further in the analysis, it is enough to point out that any particular act will in all probability in the course of time contribute to the bringing about of good or of evil for many human beings, and thus have a *prima facie* rightness or wrongness of which we know nothing. (2) Again, our judgements about our particular duties are not logical conclusions from self-evident premises. The only possible premises would be the general principles stating their *prima facie* rightness or wrongness *qua* having the different characteristics they do have; and even if we could (as we cannot) apprehend the extent to which an act will tend on the one hand, for example, to bring about advantages for our benefactors, and on the other hand to bring about disadvantages for fellow men who are not our benefactors, there is no principle by which we can draw the conclusion that it is on the whole right or on the whole wrong. In this respect the judgement as to the rightness of a particular act is just like the judgement as to the beauty of a particular natural object or work of art. A poem is, for instance, in respect of certain qualities beautiful and in respect of certain others not beautiful; and our judgement as to the degree of beauty it possesses on the whole is never reached by logical reasoning from the apprehension of its particular beauties or particular defects. Both in this and in the moral case we have more or less probable opinions which are not logically justified conclusions from the general principles that are recognized as self-evident.

There is therefore much truth in the description of the right act as a fortunate act. If we cannot be certain that it is right, it is our good fortune if the act we do is the right act. This consideration does not, however, make the doing of our duty a mere matter of chance. There is a parallel here between the doing of duty and the doing of what will be to our personal advantage. We never *know* what act will in the long run be to our advantage. Yet it is certain that we are more likely in general

to secure our advantage if we estimate to the best of our ability the probable tendencies of our actions in this respect, than if we act on caprice. And similarly we are more likely to do our duty if we reflect to the best of our ability on the *prima facie* rightness or wrongness of various possible acts in virtue of the characteristics we perceive them to have, than if we act without reflection. With this greater likelihood we must be content.

Many people would be inclined to say that the right act for me is not that whose general nature I have been describing, viz. that which if I were omniscient I should see to be my duty, but that which on all the evidence available to me I should think to be my duty. But suppose that from the state of partial knowledge in which I think act A to be my duty, I could pass to a state of perfect knowledge in which I saw act B to be my duty, should I not say 'act B was the right act for me to do'? I should no doubt add 'though I am not to be blamed for doing act A'. But in adding this, am I not passing from the question 'what is right' to the question 'what is morally good'? At the same time I am not making the *full* passage from the one notion to the other; for in order that the act should be morally good, or an act I am not to be blamed for doing, it must not merely be the act which it is reasonable for me to think my duty; it must also be done for that reason, or from some other morally good motive. Thus the conception of the right act as the act which it is reasonable for me to think my duty is an unsatisfactory compromise between the true notion of the right act and the notion of the morally good action.

The general principles of duty are obviously not self-evident from the beginning of our lives. How do they come to be so? The answer is, that they come to be self-evident to us just as mathematical axioms do. We find by experience that this couple of matches and that couple make four matches, that this couple of balls on a wire and that couple make four balls: and by reflection on these and similar discoveries we come to see that it is of the nature of two and two to make four. In a precisely similar way, we see the *prima facie* rightness of an act which would be the fulfilment of a particular promise, and of another which would be the fulfilment of another promise, and when we have reached sufficient maturity to think in general terms, we apprehend *prima facie* rightness to belong to the nature of any fulfilment of promise. What comes first in time is the apprehension of the self-evident *prima facie* rightness of an individual act of a particular type. From this we come by reflection to apprehend the self-evident general principle of *prima facie* duty. From this, too, perhaps along with the apprehension of the self-evident *prima facie* rightness of the same act in virtue of its having another characteristic as well, and perhaps in spite of the apprehension of its *prima facie* wrongness in virtue of its having some third characteristic, we come to believe something not self-evident at all, but an object of probable opinion, viz. that this particular act is (not *prima facie* but) actually right.

In this respect there is an important difference between rightness and mathematical properties. A triangle which is isosceles necessarily has two of its angles equal, whatever other characteristics the triangle may have – whatever, for instance, be its area, or the size of its third angle. The equality of the two angles is a parti-resultant attribute.[3] And the same is true of all mathematical attributes. It is true, I may add, of *prima facie* rightness. But no act is ever, in virtue of falling under some general description, necessarily actually right; its rightness depends on its whole nature[4] and not on any element in it. The reason is that no mathematical object (no figure, for instance, or angle) ever has two characteristics that tend to give it opposite resultant characteristics, while moral acts often (as every one knows) and indeed always (as on reflection we must admit) have different characteristics that tend to make them at the same time *prima facie* right and *prima facie* wrong; there is probably no act, for instance, which does good to any one without doing harm to some one else, and *vice versa*.

|...|

In what has preceded, a good deal of use has been made of 'what we really think' about moral questions, a certain theory has been rejected because it does not agree with what we really think. It might be said that this is in principle wrong; that we should not be content to expound what our present moral consciousness tells us but should aim at a criticism of our existing moral consciousness in the light of theory. Now I do not doubt that the moral consciousness of men has in detail undergone a good deal of modification as regards the things we think right, at the hands of moral theory. But if we are told, for instance,

that we should give up our view that there is a special obligatoriness attaching to the keeping of promises because it is self-evident that the only duty is to produce as much good as possible, we have to ask ourselves whether we really, when we reflect, are convinced that this is self-evident, and whether we really can get rid of our view that promise-keeping has a bindingness independent of productiveness of maximum good. In my own experience I find that I cannot, in spite of a very genuine attempt to do so; and I venture to think that most people will find the same, and that just because they cannot lose the sense of special obligation, they cannot accept as self-evident, or even as true, the theory which would require them to do so. In fact it seems, on reflection, self-evident that a promise, simply as such, is something that *prima facie* ought to be kept, and it does note on reflection, seem self-evident that production of maximum good is the only thing that makes an act obligatory. And to ask us to give up at the bidding of a theory our actual apprehension of what is right and what is wrong seems like asking people to repudiate their actual experience of beauty, at the bidding of a theory which says 'only that which satisfies such and such conditions can be beautiful'. If what I have called our actual apprehension is (as I would maintain that it is) truly an apprehension, i.e. an instance of knowledge, the request is nothing less than absurd.

I would maintain, in fact, that what we are apt to describe as 'what we think' about moral questions contains a considerable amount that we do not think but know, and that this forms the standard by reference to which the truth of any moral theory has to be tested, instead of having itself to be tested by reference to any theory. I hope that I have in what precedes indicated what in my view these elements of knowledge are that are involved in our ordinary moral consciousness.

It would be a mistake to found a natural science on 'what we really think', i.e. on what reasonably thoughtful and well educated people think about the subjects of the science before they have studied them scientifically. For such opinions are interpretations, and often misinterpretations, of sense-experience; and the man of science must appeal from these to sense-experience itself, which furnishes his real data. In ethics no such appeal is possible. We have no more direct way of access to the facts about rightness and goodness and about what things are right or good, than by thinking about them; the moral convictions of thoughtful and well-educated people are the data of ethics just as sense-perceptions are the data of a natural science. Just as some of the latter have to be rejected as illusory, so have some of the former; but as the latter are rejected only when they are in conflict with other more accurate sense-perceptions, the former are rejected only when they are in conflict with other convictions which stand better the test of reflection. The existing body of moral convictions of the best people is the cumulative product of the moral reflection of many generations, which has developed an extremely delicate power of appreciation of moral distinctions; and this the theorist cannot afford to treat with anything other than the greatest respect. The verdicts of the moral consciousness of the best people are the foundation on which he must build; though he must first compare them with one another and eliminate any contradictions they may contain.

[. . .]

Notes

1   I should make it plain at this stage that I am *assuming* the correctness of some of our main convictions as to *prima facie* duties, or, more strictly, am claiming that we know them to be true. To me it seems as self-evident as anything could be, that to make a promise, for instance, is to create a moral claim on us in someone else. Many readers will perhaps say that they do nor know this to be true. If so, I certainly cannot prove it to them; I can only ask them to reflect again, in the hope that they will ultimately agree that they also know it to be true. The main moral conviction of the plain man seem to me to be, not opinions which it is for philosophy to prove or disprove, but knowledge from the start; and in my own case I seem to find little difficulty in distinguishing these essential convictions from other moral convictions which I also have, which are merely fallible opinions based on an imperfect study of the working for good or evil of certain institutions or types of action.

2   For a needed correction of this statement, cf. pp. 22–3 [in the original book].

3   Cf. pp. 28, 122–3 [in the original book].

4   To avoid complicating unduly the statement of the general view I am putting forwards I have here rather overstated it. Any act is the origination of a great variety of things many of which make no difference to its rightness or wrongness. But there are always many elements in its nature (i.e. in what it is the origination of) that make a difference to its rightness or wrongness, and no element in its nature can be dismissed without consideration as indifferent.

35

The Trolley Problem

Judith Jarvis Thomson

I

Some years ago, Philippa Foot drew attention to an extraordinarily interesting problem.[1] Suppose you are the driver of a trolley. The trolley rounds a bend, and there come into view ahead five track workmen, who have been repairing the track. The track goes through a bit of a valley at that point, and the sides are steep, so you must stop the trolley if you are to avoid running the five men down. You step on the brakes, but alas they don't work. Now you suddenly see a spur of track leading off to the right. You can turn the trolley onto it, and thus save the five men on the straight track ahead. Unfortunately, Mrs. Foot has arranged that there is one track workman on that spur of track. He can no more get off the track in time than the five can, so you will kill him if you turn the trolley onto him. Is it morally permissible for you to turn the trolley?

Everybody to whom I have put this hypothetical case says, Yes, it is.[2] Some people say something stronger than that it is morally permissible for you to turn the trolley: They say that morally speaking, you *must* turn it – that morality requires you to do so. Others do not agree that morality requires you to turn the trolley, and even feel a certain discomfort at the idea of turning it. But everybody says that it is true, at a minimum, that you *may* turn it – that it would not be morally wrong for you to do so.

Now consider a second hypothetical case. This time you are to imagine yourself to be a surgeon, a truly great surgeon. Among other things you do, you transplant organs, and you are such a great surgeon that the organs you transplant always take. At the moment you have five patients who need organs. Two need one lung each, two need a kidney each, and the fifth needs a heart. If they do not get those organs today, they will all die; if you find organs for them today, you can transplant the organs and they will all live. But where to find the lungs, the kidneys, and the heart? The time is almost up when a report is brought to you that a young man who has just come into your clinic for his yearly check-up has exactly the right blood-type, and is in excellent health. Lo, you have a possible donor. All you need do is cut him up and distribute *his* parts among the five who need them. You ask, but he says, "Sorry. I deeply sympathize, but no." Would it be morally permissible for you to operate anyway? Everybody to whom I have put this second hypothetical case says, No, it would not be morally permissible for you to proceed.

Here then is Mrs. Foot's problem: *Why* is it that the trolley driver may turn his trolley, though the surgeon may not remove the young man's

From Judith Jarvis Thompson (1985). "The Trolley Problem." *The Yale Law Journal*, Vol 94: 1395. The Yale Law Journal Company, 1985. Pp. 1395–1401, 1403–1406, 1409–1410.

Moral Psychology: Historical and Contemporary Readings, edited by Thomas Nadelhoffer, Eddy Nahmias, and Shaun Nichols.

lungs, kidneys, and heart?[3] In both cases, one will die if the agent acts, but five will live who would otherwise die – a net saving of four lives. What difference in the other facts of these cases explains the moral difference between them? I fancy that the theorists of tort and criminal law will find this problem as interesting as the moral theorist does.

II

Mrs. Foot's own solution to the problem she drew attention to is simple, straightforward, and very attractive. She would say: Look, the surgeon's choice is between operating, in which case he kills one, and not operating, in which case he lets five die; and killing is surely worse than letting die[4] – indeed, so much worse that we can even say

(I) Killing one is worse than letting five die.

So the surgeon must refrain from operating. By contrast, the trolley driver's choice is between turning the trolley, in which case he kills one, and not turning the trolley, in which case he does not *let five die*, he positively *kills* them. Now surely we can say

(II) Killing five is worse than killing one.

But then that is why the trolley driver may turn his trolley: He would be doing what is worse if he fails to turn it, since if he fails to turn it he kills five.

I do think that that is an attractive account of the matter. It seems to me that if the surgeon fails to operate, he does not kill his five patients who need parts; he merely lets them die. By contrast, if the driver fails to turn his trolley, he does not merely let the five track workmen die; he drives his trolley into them, and thereby kills them.

But there is good reason to think that this problem is not so easily solved as that.

Let us begin by looking at a case that is in some ways like Mrs. Foot's story of the trolley driver. I will call her case *Trolley Driver*; let us now consider a case I will call *Bystander at the Switch*. In that case you have been strolling by the trolley track, and you can see the situation at a glance: The driver saw the five on the track ahead, he stamped on the brakes, the brakes failed, so he fainted. What to do? Well, here is the switch, which you can throw, thereby turning the trolley

yourself. Of course you will kill one if you do. But I should think you may turn it all the same.[5]

Some people may feel a difference between these two cases. In the first place, the trolley driver is, after all, captain of the trolley. He is charged by the trolley company with responsibility for the safety of his passengers and anyone else who might be harmed by the trolley he drives. The bystander at the switch, on the other hand, is a private person who just happens to be there.

Second, the driver would be driving a trolley into the five if he does not turn it, and the bystander would not – the bystander will do the five no harm at all if he does not throw the switch.

I think it right to feel these differences between the cases.

Nevertheless, my own feeling is that an ordinary person, a mere bystander, may intervene in such a case. If you see something, a trolley, a boulder, an avalanche, heading towards five, and you can deflect it onto one, it really does seem that – other things being equal – it would be permissible for you to *take* charge, *take* responsibility, and deflect the thing, whoever you may be. Of course you run a moral risk if you do, for it might be that, unbeknownst to you, other things are not equal. It might be, that is, that there is some relevant difference between the five on the one hand, and the one on the other, which would make it morally preferable that the five be hit by the trolley than that the one be hit by it. That would be so if, for example, the five are not track workmen at all, but Mafia members in workmen's clothing, and they have tied the one workman to the right-hand track in the hope that you would turn the trolley onto him. I won't canvass all the many kinds of possibilities, for in fact the moral risk is the same whether you are the trolley driver, or a bystander at the switch.

Moreover, second, we might well wish to ask ourselves what exactly is the difference between what the driver would be doing if he failed to turn the trolley and what the bystander would be doing if he failed to throw the switch. As I said, the driver would be driving a trolley into the five; but what exactly would his driving the trolley into the five consist in? Why, just sitting there, doing nothing! If the driver does just sit there, doing nothing, then that will have been how come he drove his trolley into the five.

I do not mean to make much of that fact about what the driver's driving his trolley into the five would consist in, for it seems to me to be right to say that if he does not turn the trolley, he does drive his trolley into them, and does thereby kill them. (Though this does seem to me to be right, it is not easy to say exactly what makes it so.) By contrast, if the bystander does not throw the switch, he drives no trolley into anybody, and he kills nobody.

But as I said, my own feeling is that the bystander *may* intervene. Perhaps it will seem to some even less clear that morality requires him to turn the trolley than that morality requires the driver to turn the trolley; perhaps some will feel even more discomfort at the idea of the bystander's turning the trolley than at the idea of the driver's turning the trolley. All the same, I shall take it that he *may*.

If he may, there is serious trouble for Mrs. Foot's thesis (I). It is plain that if the bystander throws the switch, he causes the trolley to hit the one, and thus he kills the one. It is equally plain that if the bystander does not throw the switch, he does not cause the trolley to hit the five, he does not kill the five, he merely fails to save them – he lets them die. His choice therefore is between throwing the switch, in which case he kills one, and not throwing the switch, in which case he lets five die. If thesis (I) were true, it would follow that the bystander may not throw the switch, and that I am taking to be false.

III

I have been arguing that

(I) Killing one is worse than letting five die

is false, and a fortiori that it cannot be appealed to to explain why the surgeon may not operate in the case I shall call *Transplant*.

I think it pays to take note of something interesting which comes out when we pay close attention to

(II) Killing five is worse than killing one.

For let us ask ourselves how we would feel about *Transplant* if we made a certain addition to it. In telling you that story, I did not tell you why the surgeon's patients are in need of parts. Let us imagine that the history of their ailments is as follows. The surgeon was badly overworked last fall – some of his assistants in the clinic were out sick, and the surgeon had to take over their duties dispensing drugs. While feeling particularly tired one day, he became careless, and made the terrible mistake of dispensing chemical X to five of the day's patients. Now chemical X works differently in different people. In some it causes lung failure, in others kidney failure, in others heart failure. So these five patients who now need parts need them because of the surgeon's carelessness. Indeed, if he does not get them the parts they need, so that they die, he will have killed them. Does that make a moral difference? That is, does the fact that he will have killed the five if he does nothing make it permissible for him to cut the young man up and distribute his parts to the five who need them?

We could imagine it to have been worse. Suppose what had happened was this: The surgeon was badly overextended last fall, he had known he was named a beneficiary in his five patients' wills, and it swept over him one day to give them chemical X to kill them. Now he repents, and would save them if he could. If he does not save them, he will positively have murdered them. Does *that* fact make it permissible for him to cut the young man up and distribute his parts to the five who need them?

I should think plainly not. The surgeon must not operate on the young man. If he can find no other way of saving his five patients, he will *now* have to let them die – despite the fact that if he now lets them die, he will have killed them.

We tend to forget that some killings themselves include lettings die, and do include them where the act by which the agent kills takes time to cause death – time in which the agent can intervene but does not.

In the face of these possibilities, the question arises what we should think of thesis (II), since it *looks* as if it tells us that the surgeon ought to operate, and thus that he may permissibly do so, since if he operates he kills only one instead of five.

There are two ways in which we can go here. First, we can say: (II) does tell us that the surgeon ought to operate, and that shows it is false. Second, we can say: (II) does not tell us that the surgeon ought to operate, and it is true.

For my own part, I prefer the second. If Alfred kills five and Bert kills only one, then questions of motive apart, and other things being equal, what

Alfred did *is* worse than what Bert did. If the surgeon does not operate, so that he kills five, then it will later be true that he did something worse than he would have done if he had operated, killing only one – especially if his killing of the five was murder, committed out of a desire for money, and his killing of the one would have been, though misguided and wrongful, nevertheless a well-intentioned effort to save five lives. Taking this line would, of course, require saying that assessments of which acts are worse than which other acts do not by themselves settle the question what it is permissible for an agent to do.

But it might be said that we ought to by-pass (II), for perhaps what Mrs. Foot would have offered us as an explanation of why the driver may turn the trolley in *Trolley Driver* is not (II) itself, but something more complex, such as

(II′) If a person is faced with a choice between doing something *here and now* to five, by the doing of which he will kill them, and doing something else *here and now* to one, by the doing of which he will kill only the one, then (other things being equal) he ought to choose the second alternative rather than the first.

We may presumably take (II′) to tell us that the driver ought to, and hence permissibly may, turn the trolley in *Trolley Driver*, for we may presumably view the driver as confronted with a choice between here and now driving his trolley into five, and here and now driving his trolley into one. And at the same time, (II′) tells us nothing at all about what the surgeon ought to do in *Transplant*, for he is not confronted with such a choice. If the surgeon operates, he does do something by the doing of which he will kill only one; but if the surgeon does not operate, he does not do something by the doing of which he kills five; he merely fails to do something by the doing of which he would make it be the case that he has not killed five.

I have no objection to this shift in attention from (II) to (II′). But we should not overlook an interesting question that lurks here. As it might be put: *Why* should the present tense matter so much? Why should a person prefer killing one to killing five if the alternatives are wholly in front of him, but not (or anyway, not in every case) where

one of them is partly behind him? I shall come back to this question briefly later.

Meanwhile, however, even if (II′) can be appealed to in order to explain why the trolley driver may turn his trolley, that would leave it entirely open why the bystander at the switch may turn *his* trolley. For he does not drive a trolley into each of five if he refrains from turning the trolley; he merely lets the trolley drive into each of them.

So I suggest we set *Trolley Driver* aside for the time being. What I shall be concerned with is a first cousin of Mrs. Foot's problem, viz.: Why is it that the bystander may turn his trolley, though the surgeon may not remove the young man's lungs, kidneys, and heart? Since *I* find it particularly puzzling that the bystander may turn his trolley, I am inclined to call this The Trolley Problem. Those who find it particularly puzzling that the surgeon may not operate are cordially invited to call it The Transplant Problem instead.

[. . .]

V

Suppose the bystander at the switch proceeds: He throws the switch, thereby turning the trolley onto the right-hand track, thereby causing the one to be hit by the trolley, thereby killing him – but saving the five on the straight track. There are two facts about what he does which seem to me to explain the moral difference between what he does and what the agent in *Transplant* would be doing if *he* proceeded. In the first place, the bystander saves his five by making something that threatens them instead threaten one. Second, the bystander does not do that by means which themselves constitute an infringement of any right of the one's.

As is plain, then, my hypothesis as to the source of the moral difference between the cases makes appeal to the concept of a right. My own feeling is that solving this problem requires making appeal to that concept – or to some other concept that does the same kind of work.[6] Indeed, I think it is one of the many reasons why this problem is of such interest to moral theory that it does force us to appeal to that concept; and by the same token, that we learn something from it about that concept.

Let us begin with an idea, held by many friends of rights, which Ronald Dworkin expressed crisply in a metaphor from bridge: Rights "trump" utilities.[7] That is, if one would infringe a right in or by acting, then it is not sufficient justification for acting that one would thereby maximize utility. It seems to me that something like this must be correct.

Consideration of this idea suggests the possibility of a very simple solution to the problem. That is, it might be said (i) The reason why the surgeon may not proceed in *Transplant* is that if he proceeds, he maximizes utility, for he brings about a net saving of four lives, but in so doing he would infringe a right of the young man's.

Which right? Well, we might say: The right the young man has against the surgeon that the surgeon not kill him – thus a right in the cluster of rights that the young man has in having a right to life.

Solving this problem requires being able to explain also why the bystander may proceed in *Bystander at the Switch*. So it might be said (ii) The reason why the bystander may proceed is that if he proceeds, he maximizes utility, for he brings about a net saving of four lives, and in so doing he does *not* infringe any right of the one track workman's.

But I see no way – certainly there is no easy way – of establishing that these ideas are true.

Is it clear that the bystander would infringe no right of the one track workman's if he turned the trolley? Suppose there weren't anybody on the straight track, and the bystander turned the trolley onto the right-hand track, thereby killing the one, but not saving anybody, since nobody was at risk, and thus nobody needed saving. Wouldn't that infringe a right of the one workman's, a right in the cluster of rights that he has in having a right to life?

So should we suppose that the fact that there are five track workmen on the straight track who are in need of saving makes the one lack that right – which he would have had if that had not been a fact?

But then why doesn't the fact that the surgeon has five patients who are in need of saving make the young man also lack that right?

I think some people would say there is good (excellent, conclusive) reason for thinking that the one track workman lacks the right (given there are five on the straight track) lying in the fact that (given there are five on the straight track) it is morally permissible to turn the trolley onto him. But if your reason for thinking the one lacks the right is that it is permissible to turn the trolley onto him, then you can hardly go on to explain its being permissible to turn the trolley onto him by appeal to the fact that he lacks the right. It pays to stress this point: If you want to say, as (ii) does, that the bystander may proceed because he maximizes utility and infringes no right, then you need an independent account of what makes it be the case that he infringes no right – independent, that is, of its being the case that he may proceed.

There is *some* room for maneuver here. Any plausible theory of rights must make room for the possibility of waiving a right, and within that category, for the possibility of failing to have a right by virtue of assumption of risk; and it might be argued that that is what is involved here, i.e., that track workmen know of the risks of the job, and consent to run them when signing on for it.

But that is not really an attractive way of dealing with this difficulty. Track workmen certainly do not explicitly consent to being run down with trolleys when doing so will save five who are on some other track – certainly they are not asked to consent to this at the time of signing on for the job. And I doubt that they consciously assume the risk of it at that or any other time. And in any case, what if the six people involved had not been track workmen? What if they had been young children? What if they had been people who had been shoved out of helicopters? Wouldn't it all the same be permissible to turn the trolley?

So it is not clear what (independent) reason could be given for thinking that the bystander will infringe no right of the one's if he throws the switch.

I think, moreover, that there is *some* reason to think that the bystander will infringe a right of the one if he throws the switch, even though it is permissible for him to do so. What I have in mind issues simply from the fact that if the bystander throws the switch, then he does what will kill the one. Suppose the bystander proceeds, and that the one is now dead. The bystander's motives were, of course, excellent – he acted with a view to saving five. But the one did not volunteer his life so that the five might live; the bystander volunteered it for him. The bystander made him pay with his life for the bystander's saving of the five. This consideration seems to me to lend some weight to the idea that the bystander did do him a wrong – a wrong it was morally permissible to do him, since five were saved, but a wrong *to him* all the same.

Consider again that lingering feeling of discomfort (which, as I said, some people do feel) about what the bystander does if he turns the trolley. No doubt it is permissible to turn the trolley, but still . . . but still. . . . People who feel this discomfort also think that, although it is permissible to turn the trolley, it is not morally required to do so. My own view is that they are right to feel and think these things. We would be able to explain why this is so if we supposed that if the bystander turns the trolley, then he does do the one track workman a wrong – if we supposed, in particular, that he infringes a right of the one track workman's which is in that cluster of rights which the workman has in having a right to life.[8]

I do not for a moment take myself to have established that (ii) is false. I have wished only to draw attention to the difficulty that lies ahead of a person who thinks (ii) true, and also to suggest that there is some reason to think that the bystander would infringe a right of the one's if he proceeded, and thus some reason to think that (ii) is false. It can easily be seen that if there is some reason to think the bystander would infringe a right of the one's, then there is also some reason to think that (i) is false – since if the bystander does infringe a right of the one's if he proceeds, and may nevertheless proceed, then it cannot be the fact that the surgeon infringes a right of the young man's if *he* proceeds which makes it impermissible for *him* to do so.

Perhaps a friend of (i) and (ii) can establish that they are true. I propose that, just in case he can't, we do well to see if there isn't some other way of solving this problem than by appeal to them. In particular, I propose we grant that both the bystander and the surgeon would infringe a right of their ones, a right in the cluster of rights that the ones' have in having a right to life, and that we look for some *other* difference between the cases which could be appealed to to explain the moral difference between them.

Notice that accepting this proposal does not commit us to rejecting the idea expressed in that crisp metaphor of Dworkin's. We can still say that rights trump utilities – if we can find a further feature of what the bystander does if he turns the trolley (beyond the fact that he maximizes utility) which itself trumps the right, and thus makes it permissible to proceed.

[. . .]

VII

[. . .]

Consider a case – which I shall call *Fat Man* – in which you are standing on a footbridge over the trolley track. You can see a trolley hurtling down the track, out of control. You turn around to see where the trolley is headed, and there are five workmen on the track where it exits from under the footbridge. What to do? Being an expert on trolleys, you know of one certain way to stop an out-of-control trolley: Drop a really heavy weight in its path. But where to find one? It just so happens that standing next to you on the footbridge is a fat man, a really fat man. He is leaning over the railing, watching the trolley; all you have to do is to give him a little shove, and over the railing he will go, onto the track in the path of the trolley. Would it be permissible for you to do this? Everybody to whom I have put this case says it would not be. But why?

Suppose the agent proceeds. He shoves the fat man, thereby toppling him off the footbridge into the path of the trolley, thereby causing him to be hit by the trolley, thereby killing him – but saving the five on the straight track. Then it is true of this agent, as it is true of the agent in *Bystander at the Switch*, that he saves his five by making something which threatens them instead threaten one.

But *this* agent does so by means which themselves constitute an infringement of a right of the one's. For shoving a person is infringing a right of his. So also is toppling a person off a footbridge.

I should stress that doing these things is infringing a person's rights even if doing them does not cause his death – even if doing them causes him no harm at all. As I shall put it, shoving a person, toppling a person off a footbridge, are *themselves* infringements of rights of his. A theory of rights ought to give an account of what makes it be the case that doing either of these things is itself an infringement of a right of his. But I think we may take it to be a datum that it is, the job which confronts the theorist of rights being, not to establish that it is, but rather to explain why it is.

Consider by contrast the agent in *Bystander at the Switch*. He too, if he proceeds, saves five by making something that threatens them instead threaten one. But the means he takes to make that be the case are these: Turn the trolley onto the right-hand track. And turning the trolley onto the right-hand track is not *itself* an infringement of a right of anybody's. The agent would do the one no wrong at all if he turned the trolley onto the right-hand track, and by some miracle the trolley did not hit him.

We might of course have imagined it not necessary to shove the fat man. We might have imagined that all you need do to get the trolley to threaten him instead of the five is to wobble the handrail, for the handrail is low, and he is leaning on it, and wobbling it will cause him to fall over and off. Wobbling the handrail would be impermissible, I should think – no less so than shoving. But then there is room for an objection to the idea that the contrast I point to will help explain the moral differences among these cases. For it might be said that if you wobble the handrail, thereby getting the trolley to threaten the one instead of the five, then the means you take to get this to be the case are just these: Wobble the handrail. But doing that is not *itself* an infringement of a right of anybody's. You would do the fat man no wrong at all if you wobbled the handrail and no harm came to him in consequence of your doing so. In this respect, then, your situation seems to be exactly like that of the agent in *Bystander at the Switch*. Just as the means he would be taking to make the trolley threaten one instead of five would not constitute an infringement of a right, so also would the means you would be taking to make the trolley threaten one instead of five not constitute an infringement of a right.

What I had in mind, however, is a rather tighter notion of "means" than shows itself in this objection. By hypothesis, wobbling the handrail will cause the fat man to topple onto the track in the path of the trolley, and thus will cause the trolley to threaten him instead of the five. But the trolley will not threaten him instead of the five unless

wobbling the handrail does cause him to topple. Getting the trolley to threaten the fat man instead of the five *requires* getting him into its path. You get the trolley to threaten him instead of them by wobbling the handrail only if, and only because, by wobbling the handrail you topple him into the path of the trolley.

What I had in mind, then, is a notion of "means" which comes out as follows. Suppose you get a trolley to threaten one instead of five by wobbling a handrail. The means you take to get the trolley to threaten the one instead of the five include wobbling the handrail, *and* all those further things that you have to succeed in doing by wobbling the handrail if the trolley is to threaten the one instead of the five.

So the means by which the agent in *Fat Man* gets the trolley to threaten one instead of five include toppling the fat man off the footbridge; and doing that is itself an infringement of a right of the fat man's. By contrast, the means by which the agent in *Bystander at the Switch* gets the trolley to threaten one instead of five include no more than getting the trolley off the straight track onto the right-hand track; and doing that is not itself an infringement of a right of anybody's.

Notes

1. See P. Foot, *The Problem of Abortion and the Doctrine of the Double Effect*, in Virtues and Vices and Other Essays in Moral Philosophy 19 (1978).
2. I think it possible (though by no means certain) that John Taurek would say No, it is not permissible to (all simply) turn the trolley; what you ought to do is flip a coin. See Taurek, *Should the Numbers Count?*, 6 Phil. & Pub. Aff. 293 (1977). (But he is there concerned with a different kind of case, namely that in which what is in question is not whether we may do what harms one to avoid harming five, but whether we may or ought to choose to save five in preference to saving one.) For criticism of Taurek's article, see Parfit, *Innumerate Ethics*, 7 Phil. & Pub. Aff. 285 (1978).
3. I doubt that anyone would say, with any hope of getting agreement from others, that the surgeon ought to flip a coin. So even if you think that the trolley driver ought to flip a coin, there would remain, for you, an analogue of Mrs. Foot's problem, namely: Why ought the trolley driver flip a coin, whereas the surgeon may not?

4   Mrs. Foot speaks more generally of causing injury and failing to provide aid; and her reason for thinking that the former is worse than the latter is that the negative duty to refrain from causing injury is stricter than the positive duty to provide aid. *See* P. Foot, *supra* note 1, at 27–9.

5   A similar case (intended to make a point similar to the one that I shall be making) is discussed in Davis, *The Priority of Avoiding Harm*, in Killing and Letting Die 172, 194–5 (B. Steinbock ed. 1980).

6   I strongly suspect that giving an account of what makes it wrong to *use* a person [...] would also require appeal to the concept of a right.

7   R. Dworkin, Taking Rights Seriously ix (1977).

8   Many of the examples discussed by Bernard Williams and Ruth Marcus plainly call out for this kind of treatment. *See* B. Williams, *Ethical Consistency*, in Problems of the Self 166 (1973); Marcus, *Moral Dilemmas and Consistency*, 77 J. Phil. 121 (1980).

36

Living High and Letting Die
Our Illusion of Innocence

Peter Unger

Illusions of Innocence: an Introduction

Each year millions of children die from easy to beat disease, from malnutrition, and from bad drinking water. Among these children, about 3 million die from dehydrating diarrhea. As UNICEF has made clear to millions of us well-off American adults at one time or another, with a packet of oral rehydration salts that costs about 15 cents, a child can be saved from dying soon.

By sending checks earmarked for Oral Rehydration Therapy, or ORT, to the US Committee for UNICEF, we Americans can help save many of these children. Here's the full mailing address:

United States Committee for UNICEF
United Nations Children's Fund
333 East 38th Street
New York, NY 10016

Now, you can write that address on an envelope well prepared for mailing. And, in it, you can place a $100 check made out to the *US Committee for UNICEF* along with a note that's easy to write:

WHERE IT WILL HELP THE MOST, USE THE ENCLOSED FUNDS FOR ORT.

So, as is reasonable to believe, you can easily mean a big difference for vulnerable children.

Toward realistically thinking about the matter, I'll use a figure far greater than just 15 cents per child saved: Not only does the US Committee have overhead costs, but so does UNICEF itself; and, there's the cost of transporting the packets, and so on. Further, to live even just one more year, many children may need several saving interventions and, so, several packets. And, quite a few of those saved will die shortly thereafter, anyway, from some sadly common Third World cause. So, to be more realistic about what counts most, let's multiply the cost of the packet by 10, or, better, by 20!

For getting one more Third World youngster to escape death and live a reasonably long life, $3 is a more realistic figure than 15 cents and, for present purposes, it will serve as well as any. Truth to tell, in the light of searching empirical investigation, even this higher figure might prove too low. But, as nothing of moral import will turn on the matter, I'll postpone a hard look at the actual cost till quite late in the book.[1] As will become evident, for a study that's most revealing that's the best course to take.

With our $3 figure in mind, we do well to entertain this proposition: If you'd contributed $100 to one of UNICEF's most efficient lifesaving programs a couple of months ago, this month there'd be over thirty fewer children who, instead of painfully dying soon, would live reasonably long lives. Nothing here's special to the months

From Peter Unger, *Living High and Letting Die: Our Illusion of Innocence* (Oxford University Press, 1996). Pp. 3–13, 14–23.

Moral Psychology: Historical and Contemporary Readings, edited by Thomas Nadelhoffer, Eddy Nahmias, and Shaun Nichols.

just mentioned; similar thoughts hold for most of what's been your adult life, and most of mine, too. And, more important, unless we change our behavior, similar thoughts will hold for our future. That nonmoral fact moved me to do the work in moral philosophy filling this volume. Before presenting it, a few more thoughts about the current global life-and-death situation.

1.   Some widely available thoughts about many easily preventable childhood deaths

As I write these words in 1995, it's true that, in each of the past 30 years, well over 10 million children died from readily preventable causes. And, except for a lack of money aimed at doing the job, most of the deaths could have been prevented by using any one of many means.

Before discussing a few main means, it's useful to say something about the regions where the easily preventable childhood deaths have been occurring. First, there's this well-known fact: Over ninety percent of these deaths occur in the countries of the so-called Third World. By contrast, here's something much less widely known: Though almost all these needless deaths occur in the materially poorest parts of the world, poverty itself is hardly the whole story. For a good case in point, take the poverty-ridden Indian state of Kerala. While per capita income in this state of about thirty million is notably lower than in India as a whole, life expectancy in Kerala is higher than in *any other* Indian state. And, the childhood mortality rate is *much* lower than in India as a whole.[2] Why? Without telling a long historical story, most of the answer may be put like this: In this vibrantly democratic and responsive state, Kerala's millions have food security, safe drinking water and very basic health care. By contrast, many of the richer Indians *don't* have their basic needs met, and don't have their *children's* needs met. So, while often a factor, poverty itself hardly explains why millions of kids needlessly die each year.

In one direction, I'll amplify that remark.[3] As is well known, many millions of children don't get enough to eat. These related truths are less well known: First, for each child that dies in a famine, several die from *chronic malnutrition*. Second, even if she gets over eighty percent of the calories needed by a youngster of her age for excellent health, a child who regularly gets less than ninety percent is so malnourished that she'll have a dangerously inadequate immune system. Third, what happens to many such vulnerable children is that, because she's among the many millions who haven't been vaccinated against measles, when she gets measles she dies from it. So, fourth, each year mere measles still kills about a million Third World kids.[4]

Several means of reducing measles deaths are worth mentioning, including these: Semiannually, an underfed child can be given a powerful dose of Vitamin A, with capsules costing less than 10 cents. For that year, this will improve the child's immune system. So, if she hasn't been vaccinated, during this year she'll be better able to survive measles. What's more, from her two capsules, she'll get a big bonus: With her immune system improved, this year she'll have a better chance of beating the two diseases that take far more young lives than measles claims, pneumonia and diarrhea.

Though usually all that's needed to save a child from it is the administration of antibiotics that cost about 25 cents, pneumonia now claims about 3.5 million young lives a year, making it the leading child-killing disease. And, in the text's first paragraph, I've related the score for diarrhea. But, let's again focus on measles.

Having already said plenty about Vitamin A, I'll note that, for about $17 a head, UNICEF can vaccinate children against measles. On the positive side, the protection secured lasts a lifetime; with no need for semiannual renewal, there's no danger of failing to renew protection! What's more, at the same time each child can be vaccinated for lifetime protection against five other diseases that, taken together, each year kill about another million Third World kids: tuberculosis, whooping cough, diphtheria, tetanus and polio. Perhaps best of all, these vaccinations will be part of a worldwide immunization campaign that, over the years, is making progress toward *eliminating* these vaccine-preventable diseases, much as smallpox was eliminated only a decade or two ago. Indeed, with no incidence in the whole Western Hemisphere since 1991, polio is quite close to being eliminated; with good logistical systems in place almost everywhere, the campaign's success depends mainly on funding.[5]

Finally, the vast majority of the world's very vulnerable children live in lands with UNICEF programs operating productively, including all 13 developing countries lately (1992) ranked among the world's 20 most populous nations: China, India, Indonesia, Brazil, Pakistan, Bangladesh, Nigeria, Mexico, Vietnam, Philippines, Iran, Turkey and Thailand.[6] By now, we've seen the main point: Through the likes of UNICEF, it's well within your power, in the coming months and years, to lessen serious suffering.

For even modestly well-informed readers, what I've just related doesn't come as a big surprise. All they'll have learned are some particulars pertaining to what they've learned long ago: By directing donations toward the worthy end, well-off folks can be very effective in lessening serious suffering and loss. Indeed, so well accustomed are they to this thought that, when reading the presented particulars, the worldly individuals won't make any notable response. For far fewer readers, what I've related will be something completely new. From many of them, my remarks will evoke a very notable response, even if a fairly fleeting one, about how we ought to behave: The thought occurs that each of us ought to contribute (what's for her) quite a lot to lessen early deaths; indeed, it's *seriously* wrong not to do that.

But, soon after making such a strict response, the newly aware also become well accustomed to the thought about our power. And, then, they also make the much more lenient response that almost everyone almost always makes: While it's good for us to provide vital aid, it's *not even the least bit wrong* to do *nothing* to help save distant people from painfully dying soon. (The prevalence of the lenient response is apparent from so much passive behavior: Even when unusually good folks are vividly approached to help save distant young lives, it's very few who contribute anything.[7])

Which of these two opposite responses gives the more accurate indication of what morality requires? Is it really seriously wrong not to do anything to lessen distant suffering; or, is it quite all right to do nothing?

[. . .]

2. Singer's legacy: an inconclusive argument for an importantly correct conclusion

While directly concerned more with famine relief than with the children's health issues just highlighted, it was Peter Singer who first thought to argue, seriously and systematically, that it's the first response that's on target.[8] Both early on and recently, he offers an argument for the proposition that it's wrong for us not to lessen distant serious suffering. The argument's first premise is this general proposition:

> If we can prevent something bad without sacrificing anything of comparable significance, we ought to do it.[9]

So that it may help yield his wanted conclusion, Singer rightly has us understand this premise in a suitably strong sense, with its consequent, "we ought to do it," entailing "it's *wrong* for us *not* to do it," not just the likes of "it's better for us to do it than not." But, in such a strong sense, many think the premise to be unacceptable. Briefly, I'll explain why that's so.[10]

Wanting his first premise to find favor, Singer offers a compelling example that's an instance of the general proposition. Using his words, and some of my own, here's that justly famous case[11]:

> *The Shallow Pond.* The path from the library at your university to the humanities lecture hall passes a shallow ornamental pond. On your way to give a lecture, you notice that a small child has fallen in and is in danger of drowning. If you wade in and pull the child out, it will mean getting your clothes muddy and either cancelling your lecture or delaying it until you can find something clean and dry to wear. If you pass by the child, then, while you'll give your lecture on time, the child will die straightaway. You pass by and, as expected, the child dies.

Now, when responding to this example, almost everyone's intuitive moral judgment is that your conduct's abominable. Does this reflect a strong obligation to aid that's quite general? Needed for Singer's first premise, the thought that it does is a pretty plausible proposition. But, also pretty plausibly, many think our response to the Shallow Pond doesn't reflect anything very general at all.

What moves them most here is the fact that, to other cases with people in great need, our intuitive responses are markedly different. Indeed, from typical thoughts about UNICEF, there's suggested:

The Envelope. In your mailbox, there's something from (the US Committee for) UNICEF. After reading it through, you correctly believe that, unless you soon send in a check for $100, then, instead of each living many more years, over thirty more children will die soon. But, you throw the material in your trash basket, including the convenient return envelope provided, you send nothing, and, instead of living many years, over thirty more children soon die than would have had you sent in the requested $100.

To this example, almost everyone reacts that your conduct isn't even wrong at all. Just so, many hold that, well indicated by our disparate responses to the Shallow Pond and the Envelope, there's a big moral difference between the cases. As they pretty plausibly contend, rather than any general duty to aid folks in vital need, there are only more limited obligations, like, say, a duty to *rescue* certain people.

Since what I've just related has considerable appeal, there's no way that, by itself, any such general argument for Singer's importantly correct conclusion will convince those who'd give more weight to the response the Envelope elicits than they'd give his general reasoning's first premise, or any relevantly similar statement. So for many years, there's been a stand-off here, with little progress on the issue.[12]

Deciding this philosophical issue amounts to the same thing as deciding between our two quite opposite responses to the thought that it's within a well-off person's power to lessen serious suffering significantly, the strict response made when first aware of that thought and the lenient response regularly made later. This disagreement between philosophers mirrors a difference, then, that many experience without the benefit of philosophy. It's important to provide the discrepancy with a rational resolution.

3. Two approaches to our intuitions on particular cases: Preservationism and Liberationism

Toward that important end, we'll examine vigorously our moral reactions to many *particular cases*. And, we'll explore not only many cases where aiding's the salient issue, but also many other ethically interesting examples. Briefly, I'll explain

why: As we've observed, a few philosophers think that, while some of our responses to aiding examples are good indications of morality's true nature, like our strict reaction to the Shallow Pond, others are nothing of the kind, like our lenient reaction to the Envelope. And, as we've also observed, many other philosophers think that (almost) all our responses to aiding examples are good indications of morality's true nature, including our response to the Envelope. Rather than being narrow or isolated positions, when intelligently maintained each flows from a broad view of the proper philosophical treatment for (almost) all of morality. Thus, the majority thinks that, or has their morally substantive writing actually guided by the proposition that, not just for aiding, but right across the board, our untutored intuitions on cases (almost) always are good indications of conduct's true moral status; by contrast, we in the minority think that, and have our morally substantive writing guided by the proposition that, right across the board, even as our responses to particular cases *often are* good indications of behavior's moral status, so, also, they *often aren't* any such thing at all.

Though few of them may hold a view that's so very pure, those in the majority hold a position that's a good deal like what's well called *Preservationism:* At least at first glance, our moral responses to particular cases appear to reflect accurately our deepest moral commitments, or our *Basic Moral Values,* from which the intuitive reactions primarily derive; with all these case-specific responses, or almost all, the Preservationist seeks to *preserve* these appearances. So, on this view, it's only by treating all these various responses as valuable data that we'll learn much of the true nature of these Values and, a bit less directly, the nature of morality itself. And, so, in our moral reasoning, any more general thoughts must (almost) always accommodate these reactions.

To be sure, our intuitive responses to particular cases are a very complicated motley. So, for Preservationism, any interesting principle that actually embodies our Values, and that may serve to reveal these Values, will be extremely complex. But, at the same time, the view has the psychology of moral response be about as simple as possible. For now, so much for Preservationism's methodological aspect.

Just as the view itself has it, the morally substantive aspect of Preservationism is whatever's found by employing the method at the heart of the position. So, unlike the minority view we're about to encounter, it hasn't any antecedent morally substantive aspect. For now, so much for Preservationism.[13]

By contrast with Preservationists, we in the minority hold that insight into our Values, and into morality itself, won't be achieved on an approach to cases that's anywhere near as direct, or as accommodating, as what's just been described. On our contrasting *Liberationist* view, folks' intuitive moral responses to many specific cases derive from sources far removed from our Values and, so, they fail to reflect the Values, often even pointing in the opposite direction. So, even as the Preservationist seeks (almost) always to *preserve* the appearances promoted by these responses, the Liberationist seeks often to *liberate* us from such appearances.

Not by itself, nor even when combined with our intuitive judgments for the Envelope and for the Shallow Pond, will much of moral substance follow from the methodological aspect of Liberationism, barely sketched just above. But, that's certainly no problem with the view. To the contrary, it's the position's substantive side that, in the first place, moves Liberationists to be so skeptical of many of our case-specific responses. Just so, on the Liberationist view, a sensible methodology for treating our responses to examples will be guided by some morally substantive propositions, even as it will guide us toward further statements with moral substance. While our formulations of it are all fair game for much revision, most of the substantial moral core will be taken correctly to defeat any opposing propositions.[14]

Very briefly, here's a fallible formulation of a fair bit of Liberationism's substantive side[15]: Insofar as they need her help to have a decent chance for decent lives, a person must do a great deal for those few people, like her highly dependent children, to whom she has the most serious sort of special moral obligation. Insofar as it's compatible with that, which is often very considerably indeed, and sometimes even when it's not so compatible, she must do a lot for other innocent folks in need, so that they may have a decent chance for decent lives. For now,

so much for Liberationism's morally substantive side.

Just that much substance suffices to move the Liberationist to hold that, even as (in the morally most important respects) the Envelope's conduct is *at least as bad* as the Shallow Pond's behavior, so (in those most important respects) that conduct is seriously wrong.[16] Now, even if he merely judged the Envelope's conduct to be somewhat wrong, the Liberationist would want to provide a pretty ambitious account of why our response to the case is lenient. And, since he goes much further, the account he'll offer is so very ambitious as to run along these general lines: Not stemming from our Values, the Envelope's lenient response is generated by the work of *distortional* dispositions. But, concerning the very same moral matter, there are other cases, like the Shallow Pond, that don't encourage the working of those dispositions. Accurately reflecting our Values, and the true nature of morality, our responses to these other cases *liberate* us from the misleading appearances flowing from that distortional work.[17]

[. . .]

6. Morality, rationality and truth: on the importance of our Basic Moral Values

Starting in the next chapter, I'll try hard to make a strong case for Liberationism. Before that, it's useful to place to the side large matters that, in moments of confusion, might be thought greatly to affect my inquiry. By focusing on two of the very largest of those matters, and two that are most representative, in this section I'll try to show how usefully, and how safely, that may be done.

The first concerns the relation between morality and rationality. For millennia, philosophers have been concerned to show a strong connection between these two normative conceptions. In some instances, their belief has been that, unless morality has the backing of rationality, reasonable people, like them, and us, won't engage in morally decent behavior. But, since there's nothing to this thought, I needn't here inquire into the relation between morality and rationality. Briefly, I'll try to show that.

Consider the *Rival Heirs*, a case closely based on one from James Rachels[18]: You and your four-year-old cousin, a distant relation whom you've previously seen only twice, are the only heirs of the bachelor uncle, very old and very rich, to whom you're both related. Now, the old man has only a few months left. And, as his will states, if both of you are alive when he dies, then you'll inherit only one million dollars and the cousin, to whom the uncle's much more closely related, will inherit fully nine; but, if the order of deaths is first your cousin, and then your uncle, you'll inherit all of ten million dollars. Right now, you see that it's this cousin of yours who, even as she's the only other person anywhere about, is on the verge of drowning in a nearby shallow pond. As it happens, you can easily arrange for things to look like you were then elsewhere; so, if you let the child drown, you can get away with it completely. And, since you'd take a drug that would leave you with no memories of the incident at all, you'd never feel even the slightest guilt. So, in a short time, you'd then enjoy ten million dollars, not just one.

As is very clear, your letting the child drown is extremely immoral behavior. But, it might be asked, is it *irrational* behavior? Now, some philosophers will hold that it's also irrational. By contrast, others will hold that, on at least one sense of "rationality," your conduct *isn't* irrational: You care for this very distant cousin little more than for a perfect stranger; largely owing to the "wonder" drug, there won't be any significantly bad effects on your life; nine million ain't hay, and so on.

For the sake of the exposition, let's suppose that, as new arguments all conspire to show, the second group of philosophers is *completely* correct: Even in accordance with *the only* sense of "rationality", and of cognate terms, that highly immoral conduct is only very rational behavior and, further, your saving the child must be highly irrational. For good measure, let's suppose that, plenty reasonably enough, you've become quite certain of all that. With these strong suppositions firmly in mind, how many readers would let such a little rival drown?

Since I'm sure my readers are decent people, I'm also sure of this: Very few will be even so much as strongly disposed to behave in such a morally outrageous manner; fewer still would actually do it. So, for being a potent guide for our conduct, morality certainly doesn't need any help from whatever authority we may accord rationality. For my main purposes, it's quite enough to learn a lot about which conduct is really morally all right and, in contrast, which is morally horrible behavior. If the former also has rationality's backing, that's fine; but, if not, it's no big deal.

Properly placing to the side the very interesting question of how rationality relates to morality, I'll turn to the equally interesting question of how truth relates to morality. Now, various philosophers have been concerned to show that there are many significant moral truths and that, far from reducible to even the wisest people's most basic moral commitments, they're as fully objective as any truths. Truth to tell, I myself believe in such robust moral propositions. But, what I'll now be concerned to show is just that, given this inquiry's purposes, it's a distracting digression to investigate the issue.

Why do objectivists offer arguments for our metaethical position? Ranging from sheer intellectual impulses to religious convictions, the motivation behind the endeavors is very varied. But, it's just this worrisome one I'd best discuss here and now: What would happen if we believed there weren't any substantial moral truths? Mightn't all hell break loose? Rather than feeling constrained by our deepest moral commitments, mightn't even we decent folk be free to do just what we please, or what's to our advantage? For, if the Values don't point to some reality beyond themselves, then there's nothing to have us comport with them rather than even our most self-centered desires. And, then, there won't be much more point to learning about our Values than, say, our most refined preferences in food.

Though those thoughts have a certain appeal, they're deeply confused. Recall the Rival Heirs and, this time, suppose you've come to think there aren't any objective moral truths. Will that free you up to let your little rival drown? Not a chance; when clear that there's a great conflict between some conduct and our Values, we avoid it like the plague.

None of this is to deny the philosophical importance of investigating the relations among morality, truth and rationality; it's just to say that, whatever holds for those abstruse matters, investigating our Values may help us engage in more decent behavior. Just so, when speaking of certain moral propositions as being true, it's quite well that I'll address many who abjure such Realistic talk; in terms of their favorite treatment of moral discourse, they'll understand me, I'm sure, both easily and well.

Notes

1 In the summer of 1995, I fervently sought to learn how much it really costs, where the most efficient measures get their highest yield, to get vulnerable children to become adults. Beyond reading, I phoned experts at UNICEF, the Rockefeller Foundation, the Johns Hopkins School of Hygiene and Public Health and, finally, the World Bank. As I say in the text, nothing of moral import turns on my search's findings. For those to whom that isn't already clear, it will be made evident, I think, by the arguments of chapter 6. Partly for that reason, it's there that I'll present the best empirical estimates I found.

2 Most of what I say about Kerala was first inspired by reading Frances Moore Lappé and Rachel Schurman, *Taking Population Seriously*, the Institute for Food and Development Policy, 1988. Almost all is well documented in a more recent book from the Institute, entirely devoted to the Indian state: Richard W. Franke and Barbara H. Chasin, *Kerala: Radical Reform as Development in an Indian State*, 1989. Still more recently, these statements are confirmed by material on pages 18–19 of the United Nations Development Programme's *Human Development Report 1993*, Oxford University Press, 1993.

3 Much of what I'll say about causes of childhood death, and about the interventions that can nullify these causes, is systematically presented in James P. Grant's *The State of the World's Children 1993*, published for UNICEF by the Oxford University Press in 1993. To a fair extent, not more, I've cross-checked this against the (somewhat independent) material I've skimmed in the more massive *World Development Report 1993*, published for the World Bank by the OUP in 1993.

4 But, happily, UNICEF's worldwide immunization campaign has been making great strides against measles for years. So, while just a few years ago measles claimed over 1.5 million young lives, in the past year, 1994, it claimed about 1 million.

5 In "Polio Isn't Dead Yet," *The New York Times*, June 10, 1995, Hugh Downs, the chairman of the U.S. Committee, usefully writes, "The United States spends $270 million on domestic [polio] immunization each year. For about half that amount polio could be eliminated worldwide in just five years, according to experts from Unicef and the World Health Organization. If the disease is wiped off the earth, we would no longer need to immunize

American children and millions of dollars could be diverted to other pressing needs."

6 The widely available table I use is presented on page 135 of *The 1993 Information Please Almanac*, Houghton Mifflin, 1993. The statement that each of these countries has a well established UNICEF program in place, and that it's currently (1995) easy for the program to work well in large parts of the nation, was told me by a US Committee staffer.

7 In a typical recent year, 1993, the US Committee for UNICEF mailed out, almost every month, informative appeals to over 450,000 potential donors. As a Committee staffer informed me, the prospects were folks whose recorded behavior selected them as *well above* the national average in responding to humanitarian appeals. With only a small overlap between the folks in each mailing, during the year over 4 million "charitable" Americans were vividly informed about what just a few of their dollars would mean. With each mailing, a bit less than 1% donated anything, a pattern persisting year after year.

8 See his landmark essay, "Famine, Affluence and Morality," *Philosophy and Public Affairs*, 1972.

9 See page 169 of the original edition of his *Practical Ethics*, Cambridge University Press, 1979. Without any change, this first premise appears on page 230 in the book's Second Edition, published by the CUP in 1993.

10 Now, without departing from it's original spirit, the premise may be reformulated so that, at least at first sight, there are more appealing arguments for its importantly correct conclusion, that it's wrong for us not to lessen serious suffering, and even for the wanted stronger conclusion that it's *seriously* wrong. For example, one more appealing formulation has us replace Singer's original first premise with this proposition that, briefly, will be discussed in chapter 2, section 17:

> *Pretty Cheaply Lessening Early Death.* Other things being even nearly equal, if your behaving in a certain way will result in the number of people who *very prematurely lose their lives* being less than the number who'll do so if you don't so behave and *if even so you'll still be at least reasonably well off*, then it's seriously wrong for you not to so behave.

But, in any event, at least one of the argument's premises will be a general proposition many will think unacceptable.

11 The case first appears in "Famine, Affluence and Morality." The words I use come from the Second Edition of *Practical Ethics*.

12 For a complementary explanation of the impasse, see the subsection "The Methodological Objection,"

on pages 104–05 in Garrett Cullity's recent paper, "International Aid and the Scope of Kindness," *Ethics*, 1994. Taking the paper's text together with its footnotes, there's a useful overview of the discussion that, in the past couple of decades, pertains to Singer's contribution.

[13] Many contemporary ethicists are *pretty close* to being (pure) Preservationists, prominently including Frances M. Kamm, in papers and, more recently, in *Moralityl Mortality*, Oxford University Press, Volume 1, 1993 and Volume 2, 1996; Warren S. Quinn, in papers collected in *Morality and Action*, Cambridge University Press, 1993; and, Judith J. Thomson, in papers collected in *Rights, Restitution and Risk*, Harvard University Press, 1986 and, more recently, in *The Realm of Rights*, Harvard, 1990.

Whatever the *avowed* methodological stance, it's a radically rare ethicist who'll actually advocate, and continue to maintain, a morally substantive proposition that's strongly at odds with his reactions to more than a few cases he considers.

Of course, many gesture at the propositions presented in John Rawls' "Outline of a Decision Procedure for Ethics," *Philosophical Review*, 1951, fashionably uttering the words "reflective equilibrium". With the Liberationism this book develops, perhaps there's a step toward putting some meat on some such schematic bones; in any case, there's more than just a gesture.

[14] As I'll suppose, my fellow Liberationists, including Peter Singer, are reasonably flexible here.

[15] The Liberationism whose moral substance is now to be spelled out, very incompletely, is the sort I myself favor. Others, like Peter Singer, will profess somewhat different guiding substantive moral beliefs, or Values. While those differences are important in certain contexts, in the context of this inquiry they aren't.

[16] The expressions just bracketed in the text are to allow for certain nice ways these matters can be complicated by considerations of our *Secondary Basic Moral Values*, which Values aren't introduced in the text till the book's second chapter. For now, don't bother with that, but just note this: Even the staunchest Liberationist can establish semantic contexts in which it's *correct to say* that only the Shallow Pond's conduct is badly wrong, and even that the Envelope's isn't wrong at all. (It's not until the book's last chapter that I'll provide the sort of semantic account that supports this note's qualification.)

[17] On a third view, our responses to *both* cases fail to reflect anything morally significant: Just as it's all right not to aid in the Envelope, so, it's also perfectly all right in the Shallow Pond. Aptly named *Negativism*, this repellently implausible position has such very great difficulties that, in these pages, I'll scarcely ever consider it. To keep the text itself free from mentions of such a hopeless view, on the few occasions when Negativism's addressed at all, the brief notices will be confined to footnotes.

[18] I refer to the case of Jones, in his, "Active and Passive Euthanasia," *The New England Journal of Medicine*, 1975. Reprinted in several places, especially useful is an anthology edited by J. Fischer and M. Ravizza, *Ethics: Problems and Principles*, Harcourt Brace Jovanovich, 1992. There, the example appears on page 114. Rachels uses the case to discuss very different questions.

37

The Emotional Dog and Its Rational Tail

A Social Intuitionist Approach to Moral Judgment

Jonathan Haidt

Julie and Mark are brother and sister. They are traveling together in France on summer vacation from college. One night they are staying alone in a cabin near the beach. They decide that it would be interesting and fun if they tried making love. At the very least it would be a new experience for each of them. Julie was already taking birth control pills, but Mark uses a condom too, just to be safe. They both enjoy making love, but they decide not to do it again. They keep that night as a special secret, which makes them feel even closer to each other. What do you think about that? Was it OK for them to make love?

Most people who hear the above story immediately say that it was wrong for the siblings to make love, and they then begin searching for reasons (Haidt, Bjorklund, & Murphy, 2000). They point out the dangers of inbreeding, only to remember that Julie and Mark used two forms of birth control. They argue that Julie and Mark will be hurt, perhaps emotionally, even though the story makes it clear that no harm befell them. Eventually, many people say something like. "I don't know, I can't explain it, I just know it's wrong." But what model of moral judgment allows a person to know that something is wrong without knowing why?

Moral psychology has long been dominated by rationalist models of moral judgment (Figure 37.1). Rationalist approaches in philosophy stress "the power of a priori reason to grasp substantial truths about the world" (Williams, 1967, p. 69). Rationalist approaches in moral psychology, by extension, say that moral knowledge and moral judgment are reached primarily by a process of reasoning and reflection (Kohlberg, 1969; Piaget,

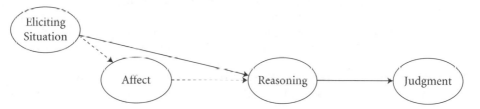

Figure 37.1 The rationalist model of moral judgment. Moral affects such as sympathy may sometimes be inputs to moral reasoning.

From The Emotional Dog and Its Rational Tail: A Social Intuitionist Approach to Moral Judgment, from Jonathan Haidt. *Psychological Review*, 108, 4. The American Psychological Association, Inc., 2001 (pp. 814–23, 828–34).

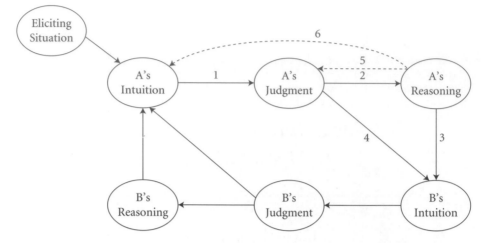

Figure 37.2 The social intuitionist model of moral judgment. The numbered links, drawn for Person A only, are (1) the intuitive judgment link, (2) the post hoc reasoning link, (3) the reasoned persuasion link, and (4) the social persuasion link. Two additional links are hypothesized to occur less frequently: (5) the reasoned judgment link and (6) the private reflection link.

1932/1965; Turiel, 1983). Moral emotions such as sympathy may sometimes be inputs to the reasoning process, but moral emotions are not the direct causes of moral judgments. In rationalist models, one briefly becomes a judge, weighing issues of harm, rights, justice, and fairness, before passing judgment on Julie and Mark. If no condemning evidence is found, no condemnation is issued.

This article reviews evidence against rationalist models and proposes an alternative: the social intuitionist model (Figure 37.2). Intuitionism in philosophy refers to the view that there are moral truths and that when people grasp these truths they do so not by a process of ratiocination and reflection but rather by a process more akin to perception, in which one "just sees without argument that they are and must be true" (Harrison, 1967, p. 72). Thomas Jefferson's declaration that certain truths are "self-evident" is an example of ethical intuitionism. Intuitionist approaches in moral psychology, by extension, say that moral intuitions (including moral emotions) come first and directly cause moral judgments (Haidt, 2003; Kagan, 1984; Shweder & Haidt, 1993; J. Q. Wilson, 1993). Moral intuition is a kind of cognition, but it is not a kind of reasoning.

The social part of the social intuitionist model proposes that moral judgment should be studied as an interpersonal process. Moral reasoning is usually an ex post facto process used to influence the intuitions (and hence judgments) of other people. In the social intuitionist model, one feels a quick flash of revulsion at the thought of incest and one knows intuitively that something is wrong. Then, when faced with a social demand for a verbal justification, one becomes a lawyer trying to build a case rather than a judge searching for the truth. One puts forth argument after argument, never wavering in the conviction that Julie and Mark were wrong, even after one's last argument has been shot down. In the social intuitionist model it becomes plausible to say, "I don't know, I can't explain it, I just know it's wrong."

The article begins with a brief review of the history of rationalism in philosophy and psychology. It then describes the social intuitionist model and recent relevant findings from a variety of fields. These findings offer four reasons for doubting the causality of reasoning in moral judgment: (a) There are two cognitive processes at work – reasoning and intuition – and the reasoning process has been overemphasized; (b) reasoning is often motivated; (c) the reasoning process constructs post hoc justifications, yet we experience the illusion of objective reasoning; and (d) moral action covaries with moral emotion more than with moral reasoning. Because much of this evidence is drawn from research outside of the domain of moral judgment, the social intuitionist model is presented here only as a plausible alternative approach to moral psychology, not as an established fact. The article therefore concludes with suggestions for future research and for ways of integrating the findings and insights of rationalism and intuitionism.

It must be stressed at the outset that the social intuitionist model is an antirationalist model only in one limited sense: It says that moral reasoning is rarely the direct cause of moral judgment. That is a descriptive claim, about how moral judgments are actually made. It is not a normative or prescriptive claim, about how moral judgments ought to be made. Baron (1998) has demonstrated that people following their moral intuitions often bring about nonoptimal or even disastrous consequences in matters of public policy, public health, and the tort system. A correct understanding of the intuitive basis of moral judgment may therefore be useful in helping decision makers avoid mistakes and in helping educators design programs (and environments) to improve the quality of moral judgment and behavior.

Philosophy and the Worship of Reason

Philosophers have frequently written about the conflict between reason and emotion as a conflict between divinity and animality. Plato's *Timaeus* (4th century BC/1949) presents a charming myth in which the gods first created human heads, with their divine cargo of reason, and then found themselves forced to create seething, passionate bodies to help the heads move around in the world. The drama of human moral life was the struggle of the heads to control the bodies by channeling the bodies' passions toward virtuous ends. The stoic philosophers took an even dimmer view of the emotions, seeing them as conceptual errors that bound one to the material world and therefore to a life of misery (R. C. Solomon, 1993). Medieval Christian philosophers similarly denigrated the emotions because of their link to desire and hence to sin. The 17th century's continental rationalists (e.g., Leibniz, Descartes) worshiped reason as much as Plato had, hoping to model all of philosophy on the deductive method developed by Euclid.

In the 18th century, however, English and Scottish philosophers (e.g., Shaftesbury, Hutcheson, Hume, and Smith) began discussing alternatives to rationalism. They argued that people have a built-in moral sense that creates pleasurable feelings of approval toward benevolent acts and corresponding feelings of disapproval toward evil and vice. David Hume in particular proposed that moral judgments are similar in form to aesthetic judgments: They are derived from sentiment, not reason, and we attain moral knowledge by an "immediate feeling and finer internal sense," not by a "chain of argument and induction" (Hume, 1777/1960, p. 2). His most radical statement of this position was that "we speak not strictly and philosophically when we talk of the combat of passion and of reason. Reason is, and ought only to be the slave of the passions, and can never pretend to any other office than to serve and obey them"[1] (Hume. 1739–40/1969, p. 462).

The thrust of Hume's attack on rationalism was that reason alone cannot accomplish the magnificent role it has been given since Plato. Hume saw reason as a tool used by the mind to obtain and process information about events in the world or about relations among objects. Reason can let us infer that a particular action will lead to the death of many innocent people, but unless we care about those people, unless we have some *sentiment* that values human life, reason alone cannot advise against taking the action. Hume argued that a person in full possession of reason yet lacking moral sentiment would have difficulty choosing any ends or goals to pursue and would look like what we now call a psychopath (Cleckley, 1955; Hume, 1777/1960).

Hume's emotivist approach to ethics was not well received by philosophers. Kant's (1785/1959) rationalist ethical theory[2] was created as an attempt to refute Hume, and Kant has had a much larger impact than Hume on modern moral philosophers (e.g., R. M. Hare, 1981; Rawls, 1971), many of whom have followed Kant in attempting to deduce a foundation for ethics from the meaning of rationality itself.

[. . .]

Questioning the causality of reasoning

People undeniably engage in moral reasoning. But does the evidence really show that such reasoning is the cause, rather than the consequence, of moral judgment? Turiel, Hildebrandt, and Wainryb (1991) examined young adults' reasoning about issues of abortion, homosexuality, pornography, and incest. They found that people who judged the actions to be moral violations also talked about harmful consequences, whereas people who thought the actions were not wrong generally cited no harmful consequences. Turiel et al. (1991) interpreted these findings as showing the importance of "informational assumptions"; for example, people who thought that life begins at conception were generally opposed to abortion, whereas people who thought that life begins later were generally not opposed to abortion. In making this interpretation, however, Turiel et al. made a jump from correlation to causation. The correlation they found between judgment and supporting belief does not necessarily mean that the belief caused the judgment. An intuitionist interpretation is just as plausible: The anti-abortion judgment (a gut feeling that abortion is bad) causes the belief that life begins at conception (an ex post facto rationalization of the gut feeling).

Haidt, Koller, and Dias (1993) found evidence for such an intuitionist interpretation. They examined American and Brazilian responses to actions that were offensive yet harmless, such as eating one's dead pet dog, cleaning one's toilet with the national flag, or eating a chicken carcass one has just used for masturbation. The stories were carefully constructed so that no plausible harm could be found, and most participants directly stated that nobody was hurt by the actions in question, yet participants still usually said the actions were wrong, and universally wrong. They frequently made statements such as, "It's just wrong to have sex with a chicken." Furthermore, their affective reactions to the stories (statements that it would bother them to witness the action) were better predictors of their moral judgments than were their claims about harmful consequences. Haidt and Hersh (2001) found the same thing when they interviewed conservatives and liberals about sexual morality issues, including homosexuality, incest, and unusual forms of masturbation. For both groups, affective reactions were good predictors of judgment, whereas perceptions of harmfulness were not. Haidt and Hersh also found that participants were often "morally dumbfounded" (Haidt et al., 2000); that is, they would stutter, laugh, and express surprise at their inability to find supporting reasons, yet they would not change their initial judgments of condemnation.

It seems, then, that for affectively charged events such as incest and other taboo violations, an intuitionist model may be more plausible than a rationalist model. But can an intuitionist model handle the entire range of moral judgment? Can it accommodate the findings from rationalist research programs while also explaining new phenomena and leading to new and testable predictions? The social intuitionist model may be able to do so.

The Social Intuitionist Model

The central claim of the social intuitionist model is that moral judgment is caused by quick moral intuitions and is followed (when needed) by slow, ex post facto moral reasoning. Clear definitions of moral judgment, moral intuition, and moral reasoning are therefore needed.

Moral judgment

Moral philosophers have long struggled to distinguish moral judgments from other kinds of judgments (e.g., aesthetics, skill, or personal taste). Rather than seeking a formal definition that lists the necessary and sufficient features of a moral judgment, the present article takes a more empirical approach, starting from a behavioral fact about human beings: that in every society, people talk about and evaluate the actions of other people, and these evaluations have consequences for future interactions (Boehm, 1999). Many of these evaluations occur against the backdrop of specific cultural practices, in which one praises or criticizes the skills or talents of an individual (e.g., "she is a daring chef"). However, an important subset of these evaluations are made with respect to virtues or goods that are applied to everyone in the society (e.g., fairness, honesty, or piety in some cultures), or to everyone in a certain social category (e.g., chastity for young women in some cultures or generosity for lineage heads). These virtues are obligatory in that everyone (within the relevant categories) is expected to strive to attain them. People who fail to embody these virtues or whose actions betray a lack of respect for them are subject to criticism, ostracism, or some other punishment. It is this subset of evaluations that is at issue in the present article. (For more on moral goods, see Ross, 1930; Shweder & Haidt, 1993.)

Moral judgments are therefore defined as evaluations (good vs. bad) of the actions or character of a person that are made with respect to a set of virtues held to be obligatory by a culture or subculture. This definition is left broad intentionally to allow a large gray area of marginally moral judgments. For example, "eating a low-fat diet" may not qualify as a moral virtue for most philosophers, yet in health-conscious subcultures, people who eat cheeseburgers and milkshakes are seen as morally inferior to those who eat salad and chicken (Stein & Nemeroff, 1995).

Moral reasoning

Everyday moral reasoners are sometimes said to be like scientists, who learn by forming and testing hypotheses, who build working models of the social world as they interact with it, and who consult these models when making moral judgments (Turiel, 1983). A key feature of the scientist metaphor is that judgment is a kind of inference made in several steps. The reasoner searches for relevant evidence, weighs evidence, coordinates evidence with theories, and reaches a decision (Kuhn, 1989; Nisbett & Ross, 1980). Some of these steps may be performed unconsciously and any of the steps may be subject to biases and errors, but a key part of the definition of reasoning is that it has steps, at least a few of which are performed consciously. Galotti (1989), in her definition of everyday reasoning, specifically excludes "any one-step mental processes" such as sudden flashes of insight, gut reactions, or other forms of "momentary intuitive response" (p. 333).

Building on Galotti (1989), *moral reasoning* can now be defined as conscious mental activity that consists of transforming given information about people in order to reach a moral judgment. To say that moral reasoning is a conscious process means that the process is intentional, effortful, and controllable and that the reasoner is aware that it is going on (Bargh, 1994).

Moral intuition

Commentators on intuition have generally stressed the fact that a judgment, solution, or other conclusion appears suddenly and effortlessly in consciousness, without any awareness by the person of the mental processes that led to the outcome (Bastick, 1982; Simon, 1992). Bruner (1960) said that intuition does not advance in careful steps; rather, it involves "manoeuvers based seemingly on an implicit perception of the total problem. The thinker arrives at an answer, which may be right or wrong, with little if any awareness of the process by which he reached it" (p. 57). It must be stressed that the contrast of intuition and reasoning is not the contrast of emotion and cognition. Intuition, reasoning, and the appraisals contained in emotions (Frijda, 1986; Lazarus, 1991) are all forms of cognition. Rather, the words *intuition* and *reasoning* are intended to capture the contrast made by dozens of philosophers and psychologists between two kinds of cognition. The most important distinctions (see Table 37.1) are that intuition occurs quickly, effortlessly, and automatically, such that the outcome but not the process is accessible to consciousness, whereas reasoning occurs more slowly, requires some effort, and involves at least some steps that are accessible to consciousness.

Building on Bastick (1982), Bruner (1960), Simon (1992), and others, *moral intuition* can be defined as the sudden appearance in consciousness of a moral judgment, including an affective valence (good–bad, like–dislike), without any conscious awareness of having gone through steps of searching, weighing evidence, or inferring a conclusion. Moral intuition is therefore the psychological process that the Scottish philosophers talked about, a process akin to aesthetic judgment: One sees or hears about a social event and one instantly feels approval or disapproval.

The links in the model

The social intuitionist model is composed of four principal links or processes, shown as solid arrows in Figure 37.2. The existence of each link is well established by prior research in some domains of judgment, although not necessarily in the domain of moral judgment. The model is therefore presented as a proposal to spur thinking and new research on moral judgment.

1. The intuitive judgment link. The model proposes that moral judgments appear in consciousness automatically and effortlessly as the

Table 37.1 General features of the two systems

The intuitive system	The reasoning system
Fast and effortless	Slow and effortful
Process is unintentional and runs automatically	Process is intentional and controllable
Process is inaccessible; only results enter awareness	Process is consciously accessible and viewable
Does not demand attentional resources	Demands attentional resources, which are limited
Parallel distributed processing	Serial processing
Pattern matching; thought is metaphorical, holistic	Symbol manipulation; thought is truth preserving, analytical
Common to all mammals	Unique to humans over age 2 and perhaps some language-trained apes
Context dependent	Context independent
Platform dependent (depends on the brain and body that houses it)	Platform independent (the process can be transported to any rule following organism or machine)

Note. These contrasts are discussed in Bruner (1986), Chaiken (1980), Epstein (1994), Freud (1900/1976), Margolis (1987), Metcalfe and Mischel (1999), Petty and Cacioppo (1986), Posner and Snyder (1975), Pyszczynski and Greenberg (1987), Reber (1993), Wegner (1994), T. D. Wilson (2004), and *Zajonc (1980)*.

result of moral intuitions. Examples of this link in nonmoral cognition include Zajonc's (1980) demonstrations that affectively valenced evaluations are made ubiquitously and rapidly, before any conscious processing has taken place. More recent examples include findings that much of social cognition operates automatically and implicitly (Bargh & Chartrand, 1999; Greenwald & Banaji, 1995).

2. The post hoc reasoning link. The model proposes that moral reasoning is an effortful process, engaged in after a moral judgment is made, in which a person searches for arguments that will support an already-made judgment. Nisbett and Wilson (1977) demonstrated such post hoc reasoning for causal explanations. Kuhn (1991), Kunda (1990), and Perkins, Farady, and Bushey (1991) found that everyday reasoning is heavily marred by the biased search only for reasons that support one's already-stated hypothesis.

3. The reasoned persuasion link. The model proposes that moral reasoning is produced and sent forth verbally to justify one's already-made moral judgment to others. Such reasoning can sometimes affect other people, although moral discussions and arguments are notorious for the rarity with which persuasion takes place. Because moral positions always have an affective component to them, it is hypothesized that reasoned persuasion works not by providing logically compelling arguments but by triggering new affectively

valenced intuitions in the listener. The importance of using affective persuasion to change affectively based attitudes has been demonstrated by Edwards and von Hippel (1995) and by Shavitt (1990).

4. The social persuasion link. Because people are highly attuned to the emergence of group norms, the model proposes that the mere fact that friends, allies, and acquaintances have made a moral judgment exerts a direct influence on others, even if no reasoned persuasion is used. Such social forces may elicit only outward conformity (Asch, 1956), but in many cases people's privately held judgments are directly shaped by the judgments of others (Berger & Luckman, 1967; Davis & Rusbult, 2001; Newcomb, 1943; Sherif, 1935).

These four links form the core of the social intuitionist model. The core of the model gives moral reasoning a causal role in moral judgment but only when reasoning runs through other people. It is hypothesized that people rarely override their initial intuitive judgments just by reasoning privately to themselves because reasoning is rarely used to question one's own attitudes or beliefs (see the motivated reasoning problem, below).

However, people are capable of engaging in private moral reasoning, and many people can point to times in their lives when they changed their minds on a moral issue just from mulling the matter over by themselves. Although some of these cases may be illusions (see the post hoc reasoning problem, below), other cases may be real, particularly among philosophers, one of the few groups that has been found to reason well (Kuhn, 1991). The full social intuitionist model therefore includes two ways in which private reasoning can shape moral judgments.

5. *The reasoned judgment link.* People may at times reason their way to a judgment by sheer force of logic, overriding their initial intuition. In such cases reasoning truly is causal and cannot be said to be the "slave of the passions." However, such reasoning is hypothesized to be rare, occurring primarily in cases in which the initial intuition is weak and processing capacity is high. In cases where the reasoned judgment conflicts with a strong intuitive judgment, a person usually has a "dual attitude" (T. D. Wilson, Lindsey, & Schooler, 2000) in which the reasoned judgment may be expressed verbally yet the intuitive judgment continues to exist under the surface.

6. *The private reflection link.* In the course of thinking about a situation a person may spontaneously activate a new intuition that contradicts the initial intuitive judgment. The most widely discussed method of triggering new intuitions is role-taking (Selman, 1971). Simply by putting oneself into the shoes of another person, one may instantly feel pain, sympathy, or other vicarious emotional responses. This is one of the principal pathways of moral reflection according to Piaget (1932/1965), Kohlberg (1969, 1971), and other cognitive developmentalists. A person comes to see an issue or dilemma from more than one side and thereby experiences multiple competing intuitions. The final judgment may be determined either by going with the strongest intuition or by allowing reason to choose among the alternatives on the basis of the conscious application of a rule or principle. This pathway amounts to having an inner dialogue with oneself (Tappan, 1997), obviating the need for a discourse partner.

Rationalist models focus on Links 5 and 6. In the social intuitionist model, in contrast, moral judgment consists primarily of Links 1–4, although the model allows that Links 5 and 6 may sometimes contribute (such as during a formal moral judgment interview). The next section of this article reviews four problems for rationalist models. For each problem, a social intuitionist reinterpretation of the evidence is offered, relying primarily on Links 1–4.

Four Reasons to Doubt the Causal Importance of Reason

1.   The dual process problem: there is a ubiquitous and under-studied intuitive process at work

It is now widely accepted in social and cognitive psychology that two processing systems are often at work when a person makes judgments or solves problems (see Table 37.1; see also Chaiken & Trope, 1999). Because these two systems typically run in parallel and are capable of reaching differing conclusions, these models are usually called *dual process* models. Dual process models have thus far had little impact on moral judgment research because most researchers have focused their efforts on understanding the reasoning process (but see Eisenberg, Shea, Carlo, & Knight, 1991; Gibbs, 1991). There is evidence, however, that moral judgment works like other kinds of judgment, in which most of the action is in the intuitive process.

[. . .]

Automatic moral judgment. Moral judgments typically involve more complex social stimuli than the simple words and visual objects used in automatic evaluation studies. Could moral judgments be made automatically as well? The emerging view in social cognition is that *most* of our behaviors and judgments are in fact made automatically (i.e., without intention, effort, or awareness of process; Bargh, 1994; Bargh & Chartrand, 1999; Greenwald & Banaji, 1995).

The literature most relevant to moral judgment is the literature on attitudes, where a central question has been how people form attitudes about other people. The evidence indicates that attitude formation is better described as a set of automatic processes than as a process of deliberation and reflection about the traits of a person. People form first impressions at first sight (Albright, Kenny, & Malloy, 1988), and the impressions that they form from observing a "thin slice" of behavior (as little as 5 s) are almost identical to the impressions they form from much longer and more leisurely observation and deliberation (Ambady & Rosenthal, 1992). These first impressions alter subsequent evaluations, creating a halo effect (Thorndike, 1920), in which positive evaluations of nonmoral traits such as attractiveness lead to beliefs that a person possesses corresponding moral traits such as kindness and good character (Dion, Berscheid, & Walster, 1972). People also categorize other people instantly and automatically, applying stereotypes that often include morally evaluated traits (e.g., aggressiveness for African Americans; Devine, 1989). All of these findings illustrate the operation of the intuitive judgment link (Link 1 in Figure 37.2), in which the perception of a person or an event leads instantly and automatically to a moral judgment without any conscious reflection or reasoning.

[. . .] A particularly important heuristic for the study of moral judgment is the "I agree with people I like" heuristic (Chaiken, 1980). If your friend is telling you how Robert mistreated her, there is little need for you to think systematically about the good reasons Robert might have had. The mere fact that your friend has made a judgment affects your own intuitions directly, illustrating the social persuasion link (Link 4). Only if the agreement heuristic leads to other conflicts (e.g., if Robert is a friend of yours) will your sufficiency threshold be raised above your actual level of confidence, triggering effortful systematic processing (Links 5 and 6) to close the gap.

However, the social intuitionist model posits that moral reasoning is usually done interpersonally rather than privately. If Robert is in fact a friend of yours, then you and your friend might present arguments to each other (Link 3, the reasoned persuasion link) in the hope of triggering new intuitions, getting the other to see Robert's actions in a better or worse light. Moral discussions can then be modeled as a repeated cycle through Links 1, 2, and 3 in Person A, then in Person B, then in Person A, and so on. Link 4 would exert a constant pressure toward agreement if the two parties were friends and a constant pressure against agreement if the two parties disliked each other. If at least one of the parties began without a strong initial intuition, then some degree of convergence would be likely. Davis and Rusbult (2001) recently documented this convergence process, which they called *attitude alignment*. However, if both parties began with strongly felt opposing intuitions (as in a debate over abortion), then reasoned persuasion would be likely to have little effect, except that the post *hoc* reasoning triggered in the other person could lead to even greater disagreement, a process labeled "attitude polarization" by Lord, Ross, and Lepper (1979).

[. . .]

The social intuitionist solution. The social intuitionist model is fully compatible with modern dual process theories. Like those theories, the model posits that the intuitive process is the default process, handling everyday moral judgments in a rapid, easy, and holistic way. It is primarily when intuitions conflict, or when the social situation demands thorough examination of all facets of a scenario, that the reasoning process is called upon. Reasoning can occur privately (Links 5 and 6), and such solitary moral reasoning may be common among philosophers and among those who have a high need for cognition (Cacioppo & Petty, 1982). Yet ever since Plato wrote his *Dialogues*, philosophers have recognized that moral reasoning naturally occurs in a social setting, between people who can challenge each other's arguments and trigger new intuitions (Links 3 and 4). The social intuitionist model avoids the traditional focus on conscious private reasoning and draws attention to the role of moral intuitions, and of other people, in shaping moral judgments.

2. The motivated reasoning problem: the reasoning process is more like a lawyer defending a client than a judge or scientist seeking truth

It appears, then, that a dual process model may be appropriate for a theory of moral judgment. If so, then the relationship between the two processes must be specified. Is the reasoning process the "smarter" but more cognitively expensive process, called in whenever the intuitive process is unable to solve a problem cheaply? Or is the relationship one of master and servant, as Hume suggested, in which reason's main job is to formulate arguments that support one's intuitive conclusions? Research on both motivated reasoning and everyday reasoning suggests that the post hoc reasoning link (Link 2) is more important than the reasoned judgment and private reflection links (Links 5 and 6).

Two major classes of motives have been shown to bias and direct reasoning. The first class can be called *relatedness motives*, for it includes concerns about impression management and smooth interaction with other people. The second class can be called *coherence motives*, for it includes a variety of defensive mechanisms triggered by cognitive dissonance and threats to the validity of one's cultural worldview.

Relatedness motives. From an evolutionary perspective, it would be strange if our moral judgment machinery was designed principally for accuracy, with no concern for the disastrous effects of periodically siding with our enemies and against our friends. Studies of attitudes, person perception, and persuasion show that desires for harmony and agreement do indeed have strong biasing effects on judgments. Chaiken and her colleagues incorporated *impression motivation* into the heuristic-systematic model, which is described as "the desire to hold attitudes and beliefs that will satisfy current social goals" (Chen & Chaiken, 1999, p. 78). Chen, Shechter, and Chaiken (1996) found that people who expected to discuss an issue with a partner whose views were known expressed initial attitudes, before the interaction, that were shifted toward those of their anticipated partner. More broadly, Darley and Berscheid (1967) found that people rate a description of a person's personality as more likable if they expect to interact with the person than if they do not expect to interact.

[...]

Coherence motives. Psychologists since Freud have argued that people construct views of themselves and of the world and that they experience potentially crippling anxiety when these constructions are threatened (Moskowitz, Skurnik, & Galinsky, 1999). Research on cognitive dissonance (Festinger, 1957; Wicklund & Brehm, 1976) showed just how readily people change their thinking and beliefs to avoid the threat of internal contradictions. More recently, Chaiken, Giner-Sorolla, and Chen (1996) defined *defense motivation* as "the desire to hold attitudes and beliefs that are congruent with existing self definitional attitudes and beliefs" (p. 557). Self-definitional attitudes include values and moral commitments. When defense motivation is triggered, both heuristic and systematic thinking work to preserve self-definitional attitudes.

[...]

Mechanisms of bias. Studies of everyday reasoning reveal the mechanisms by which relatedness and coherence motivations make people act like lawyers. Kuhn (1991) found that most people

have difficulty understanding what evidence is, and when pressed to give evidence in support of their theories they generally give anecdotes or illustrative examples instead. Furthermore, people show a strong tendency to search for anecdotes and other "evidence" exclusively on their preferred side of an issue, a pattern that has been called the "my-side bias" (Baron, 1995; Perkins et al., 1991). Once people find supporting evidence, even a single piece of bad evidence, they often stop the search, since they have a "makes-sense epistemology" (Perkins, Allen, & Hafner, 1983) in which the goal of thinking is not to reach the most accurate conclusion but to find the first conclusion that hangs together well and that fits with one's important prior beliefs.

[...]

This review is not intended to imply that people are stupid or irrational. It is intended to demonstrate that the roots of human intelligence, rationality, and ethical sophistication should not be sought in our ability to search for and evaluate evidence in an open and unbiased way. Rather than following the ancient Greeks in worshiping reason, we should instead look for the roots of human intelligence, rationality, and virtue in what the mind does best: perception, intuition, and other mental operations that are quick, effortless, and generally quite accurate (Gigerenzer & Goldstein, 1996; Margolis, 1987).

The social intuitionist solution. The reasoning process in moral judgment may be capable of working objectively under very limited circumstances: when the person has adequate time and processing capacity, a motivation to be accurate, no a priori judgment to defend or justify, and when no relatedness or coherence motivations are triggered (Forgas, 1995; Wegner & Bargh, 1998). Such circumstances may be found in moral judgment studies using hypothetical and unemotional dilemmas. Rationalist research methods may therefore *create* an unusual and nonrepresentative kind of moral judgment. However, in real judgment situations, such as when people are gossiping or arguing, relatedness motives are always at work. If more shocking or threatening issues are being judged, such as abortion, euthanasia, or consensual incest, then coherence motives also will be at work. Under these more realistic circumstances, moral reasoning is not left free to search for truth but is likely to be hired out like a lawyer by various motives, employed only to seek confirmation of preordained conclusions.

3.   The post hoc problem: the reasoning process readily constructs justifications of intuitive judgments, causing the illusion of objective reasoning

When people are asked to explain the causes of their judgments and actions, they frequently cite factors that could not have mattered and fail to recognize factors that did matter. Nisbett and Schachter (1966), for example, asked participants to take electric shocks, either with or without a placebo pill that was said to produce the same symptoms as electric shock. Participants in the pill condition apparently attributed their heart palpitations and butterflies in the stomach to the pill and were able to take four times as much shock as those who had no such misattribution available for their symptoms. However, when the placebo condition participants were asked if they had made such an attribution, only 25% of them said that they had. The remaining participants denied that they had thought about the pill and instead made up a variety of explanations for their greater shock tolerance, such as, "Well, I used to build radios and stuff when I was 13 or 14, and maybe 1 got used to electric shock" (Nisbett & Wilson, 1977, p. 237).

Nisbett and Wilson (1977) interpreted such causal explanations as post hoc constructions. When asked to explain their behaviors, people engage in an effortful search that may feel like a kind of introspection. However, what people are searching for is not a memory of the actual cognitive processes that caused their behaviors, because these processes are not accessible to consciousness. Rather, people are searching for plausible theories about why they might have done what they did. People turn first to a "pool of culturally supplied explanations for behavior," which Nisbett and Wilson (1977) refer to as "a priori causal theories" (p. 248). When asked why he enjoyed a party, a person turns first to his cultural knowledge about why people enjoy parties, chooses a reason, and then searches for evidence that the reason was applicable. The search is likely to be a one-sided search of memory for supporting evidence only (Kunda, 1990; Pyszczynski & Greenberg, 1987).

Additional illustrations of post hoc causal reasoning can be found in studies in which hypnosis (Zimbardo, LaBerge, & Butler, 1993) and subliminal presentation (Kunst-Wilson & Zajonc, 1980) were used to make people perform actions. When asked to explain their actions or choices, people readily made up reasons that sounded plausible but were false. Split-brain patients show this effect in its most dramatic form. When the left hand, guided by the right brain, performs an action, the verbal centers in the left brain readily make up stories to explain it (Gazzaniga, Bogen, & Sperry, 1962). The language centers are so skilled at making up post hoc causal explanations that Gazzaniga (1985) speaks of an "interpreter" module. He argues that behavior is usually produced by mental modules to which consciousness has no access but that the interpreter module provides a running commentary anyway, constantly generating hypotheses to explain why the self might have performed any particular behavior.

Post hoc moral reasoning. The idea that people generate causal explanations out of a priori causal theories is easily extended into the moral domain. In a moral judgment interview, a participant is asked to decide whether an action is right or wrong and is then asked to explain why she thinks so. However, if people have no access to the processes behind their automatic initial evaluations then how do they go about providing justifications? They do so by consulting their a priori moral theories. *A priori moral theories* can be defined as a pool of culturally supplied norms for evaluating and criticizing the behavior of others. A priori moral theories provide acceptable reasons for praise and blame (e.g., "unprovoked harm is bad"; "people should strive to live up to God's commandments"). Because the justifications that people give are closely related to the moral judgments that they make, prior researchers have assumed that the justificatory reasons caused the judgments. But if people lack access to their automatic judgment processes then the reverse causal path becomes more plausible.

[. . .]

The illusions of moral judgment. If moral reasoning is generally a post hoc construction intended to justify automatic moral intuitions, then our moral life is plagued by two illusions. The first illusion can be called the *wag-the-dog illusion*: We believe that our own moral judgment (the dog) is driven by our own moral reasoning (the tail). The second illusion can be called the *wag-the-other-dog's-tail illusion*: In a moral argument, we expect the successful rebuttal of an opponent's arguments to change the opponent's mind. Such a belief is like thinking that forcing a dog's tail to wag by moving it with your hand will make the dog happy.

The wag-the-dog illusion follows directly from the mechanics of the reasoning process described above. Pyszczynski and Greenberg (1987) point out that by going through all the steps of hypothesis testing, even though every step can be biased by self-serving motivations, people can maintain an "illusion of objectivity" about the way they think. The wag-the-dog illusion may therefore be one of the mechanisms underlying naive realism (Griffin & Ross, 1991; Robinson, Keltner, Ward, & Ross, 1995), the finding that people think that they see the world as it is whereas their opponents in a moral dispute are biased by ideology and self-interest.

The bitterness, futility, and self-righteousness of most moral arguments can now be explicated. In a debate about abortion, politics, consensual incest, or what my friend did to your friend, both sides believe that their positions are based on reasoning about the facts and issues involved (the wag-the-dog illusion). Both sides present what they take to be excellent arguments in support of their positions. Both sides expect the other side to be responsive to such reasons (the wag-the-other-dog's-tail illusion). When the other side fails to be affected by such good reasons, each side concludes that the other side must be closed minded or insincere. In this way the culture wars over issues such as homosexuality and abortion can generate morally motivated players on both sides who believe that their opponents are not morally motivated (Haidt & Hersh, 2001; Robinson et al., 1995).

The social intuitionist solution. People have quick and automatic moral intuitions, and when called on to justify these intuitions they generate post hoc justifications out of a priori moral theories. They do not realize that they are doing this, so they fall prey to two illusions. Moral arguments are therefore like shadow-boxing matches: Each contestant lands heavy blows to the opponent's shadow, then wonders why she doesn't fall down.

Thus, moral reasoning may have little persuasive power in conflict situations, but the social intuitionist model says that moral reasoning can be effective in influencing people before a conflict arises. Words and ideas do affect friends, allies, and even strangers by means of the reasoned-persuasion link. If one can get the other person to see the issue in a new way, perhaps by reframing a problem to trigger new intuitions, then one can influence others with one's words. Martin Luther King Jr.'s "I Have a Dream" speech was remarkably effective in this task, using metaphors and visual images more man prepositional logic to get White Americans to see and thus feel that racial segregation was unjust and un-American (see Lakoff, 1996, on the role of metaphor in political persuasion).

[. . .]

Integrating Rationalism and Intuitionism

The debate between rationalism and intuitionism is an old one, but the divide between the two approaches may not be unbridgeable. Both sides agree that people have emotions and intuitions, engage in reasoning, and are influenced by each other. The challenge, then, is to specify how these processes fit together. Rationalist models do this by focusing on reasoning and then discussing the other processes in terms of their effects on reasoning. Emotions matter because they can be inputs to reasoning. Social settings and social interactions matter because they encourage or retard the development of reasoning, in part by providing or blocking opportunities for role-taking. However, if researchers want to get at the heart of the process, the place where most of the variance is located, they should focus on moral reasoning.

The social intuitionist model proposes a very different arrangement, one that fully integrates reasoning, emotion, intuition, and social influence. The discussion thus far may have given the impression that the model dismisses reasoning as post hoc rationalization (Link 2). However, it must be stressed that four of the six links in the model are reasoning links, and three of these links (Links 3, 5, and 6) are hypothesized to have real causal effects on moral judgment.

Link 3, the reasoned persuasion link, says that people's (ex post facto) moral reasoning can have a causal effect – on *other people's* intuitions. In the social intuitionist view, moral judgment is not just a single act that occurs in a single person's mind but is an ongoing process, often spread out over time and over multiple people. Reasons and arguments can circulate and affect people, even if individuals rarely engage in private moral reasoning for themselves.

Link 6, the reflective judgment link, allows that people may sometimes engage in private moral reasoning for themselves, particularly when their initial intuitions conflict. Abortion may feel wrong to many people when they think about the fetus but right when their attention shifts to the woman. When competing intuitions are evenly matched, the judgment system becomes dead-locked and the "master" (in Hume's metaphor) falls silent. Under such circumstances one may go through repeated cycles of Links 6, 1, and 2, using reasoning and intuition together to break the deadlock. That is, if one consciously examines a dilemma, focusing in turn on each party involved, various intuitions will be triggered (Link 6), lead-ing to various contradictory judgments (Link 1). Reasoning can then be used to construct a case to support each judgment (Link 2). If reasoning more successfully builds a case for one of the judgments than for the others, the judgment will begin to feel right and there will be less temptation (and ability) to consider additional points of view. This is an account of how a "makes sense" epistemology (Perkins et al., 1983) may become a "feels right" ethic. We use conscious reflection to mull over a problem until one side feels right. Then we stop.

Link 5, the reasoned judgment link, recognizes that a person could, in principle, simply reason her way to a judgment that contradicts her initial intuition. The literature on everyday reasoning (Kuhn, 1991) suggests that such an ability may be common only among philosophers, who have been extensively trained and socialized to follow reasoning even to very disturbing conclusions (as in the case of Socrates or the more recent work of Peter Singer [1994]), but the fact that there are at least a few people among us who can reach such conclusions on their own and then argue for them eloquently (Link 3) means that pure moral reasoning can play a causal role in the moral life of a society.

If the social intuitionist model is correct as a description of human moral judgment, it may be possible to use the model to get reasoning and intuition working more effectively together in real moral judgments. One approach would be to directly teach moral thinking and reasoning skills, thereby encouraging people to use Links 5 and 6 more often. However, attempts to directly teach thinking and reasoning in a classroom setting generally show little transfer to activities outside of the classroom (Nickerson, 1994), and because moral judgment involves "hotter" topics than are usually dealt with in courses that attempt to teach thinking and reasoning, the degree of transfer is likely to be even smaller.

A more intuitionist approach is to treat moral judgment style as an aspect of culture and to try to create a culture that fosters a more balanced, reflective, and fair-minded style of judgment. The "just community" schools that Kohlberg created in the 1970s (Power, Higgins, & Kohlberg, 1989) appear to do just that. By making high school students create their own rules, enforce their own discipline, and vote on numerous policies, Kohlberg created an environment where students enacted democracy. By putting students and teachers on an equal footing (all had just one vote; all used first names only; all sat in a circle on the floor at community meetings), Kohlberg created an environment where students and teachers enacted equality. Years of such implicit learning, coupled with explicit discussion, should gradually tune up intuitions (Fiske, 1999; Lieberman, 2000) about justice, rights, and fairness, leading perhaps to an automatic tendency to look at problems from multiple perspectives. By creating a com-munity in which moral talk was ubiquitous (Link 3, reasoned persuasion) and in which adults modeled good moral thinking, Kohlberg may well have strengthened his students' tendency to use Link 6 (private reflection) on their own. (See Baron, 2000, for more on how cultural beliefs and practices about thinking can help or hinder good thinking.)

The social intuitionist model also offers more general advice for improving moral judgment. If the principal difficulty in objective moral rea-soning is the biased search for evidence (Kunda, 1990; Perkins et al., 1991), then people should take advantage of the social persuasion link (Link 4) and get other people to help them improve their reasoning. By seeking out discourse partners who are respected for their wisdom and open-mindedness, and by talking about the evidence, justifications, and mitigating factors involved in a potential moral violation, people can help trigger a variety of conflicting intuitions in each other. If more conflicting intuitions are triggered, the final judgment is likely to be more nuanced and ultimately more reasonable.

The social intuitionist model, therefore, is not an antirationalist model. It is a model about the complex and dynamic ways that intuition, reasoning, and social influences interact to produce moral judgment.

[. . .]

Conclusion

Rationalist models made sense in the 1960s and 1970s. The cognitive revolution had opened up new ways of thinking about morality and moral development, and it was surely an advance to think about moral judgment as a form of information processing. But times have changed. Now we know (again) that most of cognition occurs automatically and outside of consciousness (Bargh & Chartrand, 1999) and that people cannot tell us how they really reached a judgment (Nisbett & Wilson, 1977). Now we know that the brain is a connectionist system that tunes up slowly but is then able to evaluate complex situations quickly (Bechtel & Abrahamsen, 1991). Now we know that emotions are not as irrational (Frank, 1988), that reasoning is not as reliable (Kahneman & Tversky, 1984), and that animals are not as amoral (de Waal, 1996) as we thought in the 1970s. The time may be right, therefore, to take another look at Hume's perverse thesis: that moral emotions and intuitions drive moral reasoning, just as surely as a dog wags its tail.

Notes

[1]   This is one of Hume's most radical statements, taken from his first book, *A Treatise of Human Nature*. His more mature work, *An Enquiry Concerning the Principles of Morals*, raises reason from a slave to a respected assistant of the moral sense, yet it maintains the basic position that "the ultimate ends

of human actions can never . . . be accounted for by reason, but recommend themselves entirely to the sentiments and affections of mankind" (1777/1960, p. 131).

[2]   Kant responded to Hume's skepticism about the powers of reason. He argued that any rational agent could and should figure out the morally correct thing to do by applying the categorical imperative: "I should never act in such a way that I could not also will that my maxim should be a universal law" (1785/1959, p. 18).

References

Albright, L., Kenny, D. A., & Malloy, T. E. (1988). Consensus in personality judgments at zero acquaintance. *Journal of Personality and Social Psychology*, 55, 387–95.

Ambady, N., & Rosenthal, R. (1992). Thin slices of expressive behavior as predictors of interpersonal consequences: A meta-analysis. *Psychological Bulletin*, 111, 256–74.

Asch, S. (1956). Studies of independence and conformity: A minority of one against a unanimous majority, *Psychological Monographs*, 70(9, Whole no. 416).

Bargh, J. (1994). The four horsemen of automaticity: Awareness, efficiency, intention, and control in social cognition. In J. R. S. Wyer & T. K. Srull (eds.), *Handbook of social cognition*, 2nd edn. (pp. 1–40). Hillsdale, NJ: Erlbaum.

Bargh, J. A., & Chartrand, T. L. (1999). The unbearable automaticity of being. *American Psychologist*, 54, 462–79.

Baron, J. (1995). Myside bias in thinking about abortion. *Thinking and Reasoning*, 1, 221–35.

Baron, J. (1998). *Judgment misguided: Intuition and error in public decision making*. New York: Oxford University Press.

Baron, J. (2000). *Thinking and deciding* (3rd ed.). Cambridge, England: Cambridge University Press.

Bastick, T. (1982). *Intuition: How we think and act*. Chichester, England: Wiley.

Bechtel, W., & Abrahamsen, A. (1991). *Connectionism and the mind: An introduction to parallel processing in networks*. Cambridge, MA: Blackwell.

Berger, P. L., & Luckman, T. (1967). *The social construction of reality*. New York: Doubleday.

Boehm, C. (1999). *Hierarchy in the forest: The evolution of egalitarian behavior*. Cambridge, MA: Harvard University Press.

Bruner, J. S. (1960). *The process of education*. Cambridge, MA: Harvard University Press.

Bruner, J. S. (1986). *Actual minds, possible worlds*. Cambridge, MA: Harvard University Press.

Cacioppo, J. T., & Petty, R. E. (1982). The need for cognition. *Journal of Personality and Social Psychology*, 42, 116–31.

Chaiken, S. (1980). Heuristic versus systematic information processing and the use of source versus message cues in persuasion. *Journal of Personality and Social Psychology*, 39, 752–66.

Chaiken, S., Giner-Sorolla, R., & Chen, S. (1996). Beyond accuracy: Defense and impression motives in heuristic and systematic information processing. In P. M. Gollwitzer & J. A. Bargh (eds.), *The psychology of action: Linking cognition and motivation to behavior* (pp. 553–78). New York: Guilford Press.

Chaiken, S., & Trope, Y. (eds.). (1999). *Dual process theories in social psychology*. New York: Guilford Press.

Chen, S., & Chaiken, S. (1999). The heuristic–systematic model in its broader context. In S. Chaiken & Y. Trope (eds.), *Dual process theories in social psychology* (pp. 73–96). New York: Guilford Press.

Chen, S., Shechter, D., & Chaiken, S. (1996). Getting at the truth or getting along: Accuracy- versus impression-motivated heuristic and systematic processing. *Journal of Personality and Social Psychology*, 71, 262–75.

Cleckley, H. (1955). *The mask of sanity*. St. Louis, MO: C. V. Mosby.

Darley, J. M., & Berscheid, E. (1967). Increased liking as a result of anticipation of personal contact. *Human Relations*, 20, 29–40.

Davis, J. L., & Rusbult, C. E. (2001). Attitude alignment in close relationships. *Journal of Personality and Social Psychology*, 81, 65–84.

de Waal, F. (1996). *Good natured: The origins of right and wrong in humans and other animals*. Cambridge, MA: Harvard University Press.

Devine, P. G. (1989). Stereotypes and prejudice: Their automatic and controlled components. *Journal of Personality and Social Psychology*, 56, 5–18.

Dion, K., Berscheid, E., & Walster, E. (1972). What is beautiful is good. *Journal of Personality and Social Psychology*, 24, 207–13.

Edwards, K., & von Hippel, W. (1995). Hearts and minds: The priority of affective versus cognitive factors in person perception. *Personality and Social Psychology Bulletin*, 21, 996–1011.

Eisenberg, N., Shea, C. L., Carlo, G., & Knight, G. P. (1991). Empathy-related responding and cognition: A "chicken and the egg" dilemma. In W. M. Kurtines & J. L. Gewirtz (eds.), *Handbook of moral behavior and development: Vol. 1. Theory* (pp. 63–88). Hillsdale, NJ: Erlbaum.

Epstein, S. (1994). Integration of the cognitive and the psychodynamic unconscious. *American Psychologist*, 49, 709–24.

Festinger, L. (1957). *A theory of cognitive dissonance*. Stanford, CA: Stanford University Press.

Fiske, A. P. (1999). *Learning culture the way informants do: Observing, imitating, and participating*. Unpublished manuscript, University of California, Los Angeles.

Forgas, J. P. (1995). Mood and judgment: The affect infusion model (AIM). *Psychological Bulletin*, 117, 39–66.

Frank, R. (1988). *Passions within reason: The strategic role of the emotions*. New York: Norton.

Freud, S. (1976). *The interpretation of dreams* (J. Strachey, Trans.). New York: Norton. (Original work published 1900)

Frijda, N. (1986). *The emotions*. Cambridge, England: Cambridge University Press.

Galotti, K. M. (1989). Approaches to studying formal and everyday reasoning. *Psychological Bulletin*, 105, 331–51.

Gazzaniga, M. S. (1985). *The social brain*. New York: Basic Books.

Gazzaniga, M. S., Bogen, J. E., & Sperry, R. W. (1962). Some functional effects of sectioning the cerebral commissures in man. *Proceedings of the National Academy of Sciences, USA*, 48, 1765–9.

Gibbs, J. C. (1991). Toward an integration of Kohlberg's and Hoffman's theories of morality. In W. M. Kurtines & J. L. Gewirtz (eds.), *Handbook of moral behavior and development: Vol. 1. Advances in theory, research, and application* (pp. 183–222). Hillsdale, NJ: Erlbaum.

Gigerenzer, G., & Goldstein, D. G. (1996). Reasoning the fast and frugal way: Models of bounded rationality. *Psychological Review*, 103, 650–69.

Greenwald, A. G., & Banaji, M. R. (1995). Implicit social cognition. *Psychological Review*, 102, 4–27.

Griffin, D. W., & Ross, L. (1991). Subjective construal, social inference, and human misunderstanding. *Advances in Experimental Social Psychology*, 24, 319–59.

Haidt, J. (2003). The moral emotions. In R. J. Davidson, K. Scherer, & H. H. Goldsmith (eds.), *Handbook of affective sciences* (pp. 852–70). Oxford, England: Oxford University Press.

Haidt, J., Bjorklund, F., & Murphy, S. (2000). *Moral dumbfounding: When intuition finds no reason*. Unpublished manuscript, University of Virginia.

Haidt, J., & Hersh, M. (2001). Sexual morality: The cultures and reasons of liberals and conservatives. *Journal of Applied Social Psychology*, 31, 191–221.

Haidt, J., Koller, S., & Dias, M. (1993). Affect, culture, and morality, or is it wrong to eat your dog? *Journal of Personality and Social Psychology*, 65, 613–28.

Hare, R. M. (1981). *Moral thinking: Its levels, method, and point*. London: Oxford University Press.

Harrison, J. (1967). Ethical objectivism. In P. Edwards (ed.), *The encyclopedia of philosophy* (Vols. 3–4. pp. 71–5). New York: Macmillan.

Hume, D. (1960). *An enquiry concerning the principles of morals.* La Salle, IL: Open Court. (Original work published 1777)

Hume, D. (1969). *A treatise of human nature.* London: Penguin. (Original work published 1739–40)

Kagan, J. (1984). *The nature of the child.* New York: Basic Books.

Kahneman, D., & Tversky, A. (1984). Choices, values, and frames. *American Psychologist, 39.* 341–50.

Kant, I. (1959). *Foundation of the metaphysics of morals* (L. W. Beck, Trans.). Indianapolis, IN: Bobbs-Merrill. (Original work published 1785)

Kohlberg, L. (1969). Stage and sequence: The cognitive-developmental approach to socialization. In D. A. Goslin (ed.). *Handbook of socialization theory and research* (pp. 347–480). Chicago: Rand McNally.

Kohlberg, L. (1971). From is to ought: How to commit the naturalistic fallacy and get away with it in the study of moral development. In T. Mischel (ed.), *Cognitive development and epistemology* (pp. 151–235). New York: Academic Press.

Kuhn, D. (1989). Children and adults as intuitive scientists. *Psychological Review, 96,* 674–89.

Kuhn, D. (1991). *The skills of argument.* Cambridge, England: Cambridge University Press.

Kunda, Z. (1990). The case for motivated reasoning. *Psychological Bulletin, 108,* 480–98.

Kunst-Wilson, W. R., & Zajonc, R. B. (1980). Affective discrimination of stimuli that cannot be recognized. *Science, 207,* 557–558.

Lakoff, G. (1996). *Moral politics: What conservatives know that liberals don't.* Chicago: University of Chicago Press.

Lazarus, R. S. (1991). *Emotion and adaptation.* New York: Oxford University Press.

Lieberman, M. D. (2000). Intuition: A social cognitive neuroscience approach. *Psychological Bulletin, 126,* 109–37.

Lord, C. G., Ross, L., & Lepper, M. R. (1979). Biased assimilation and attitude polarization: The effects of prior theories on subsequently considered evidence. *Journal of Personality and Social Psychology, 37,* 2098–109.

Margolis, H. (1987). *Patterns, thinking, and cognition.* Chicago: University of Chicago Press.

Metcalfe, J., & Mischel, W. (1999). A hot/cool-system analysis of delay of gratification: Dynamics of willpower. *Psychological Review, 106,* 3–19.

Moskowitz, G. B., Skurnik, I., & Galinsky, A. D. (1999). The history of dual process notions, and the future of pre-conscious control. In S. Chaiken & Y. Trope (eds.), *Dual process theories in social psychology* (pp. 12–36). New York: Guilford Press.

Newcomb, T. M. (1943). *Personality and social change: Attitude formation in a student community.* New York: Dryden.

Nickerson, R. S. (1994). The teaching of thinking and problem solving. In R. J. Sternberg (ed.), *Thinking and problem solving* (pp. 409–449). San Diego, CA: Academic Press.

Nisbett, R., & Ross, L. (1980). *Human inference: Strategies and shortcomings of social judgment.* Englewood Cliffs, NJ: Prentice Hall.

Nisbett, R. E., & Schacter, S. (1966). Cognitive manipulation of pain. *Journal of Experimental Social Psychology, 2,* 227–36.

Nisbett, R. E., & Wilson, T. D. (1977). Telling more than we can know: Verbal reports on mental processes. *Psychological Review, 84,* 231–59.

Perkins, D. N., Allen, R., & Hafner, J. (1983). Difficulties in everyday reasoning. In W. Maxwell (ed.), *Thinking: The frontier expands* (pp. 177–189). Hillsdale, NJ: Erlbaum.

Perkins, D. N., Farady, M., & Bushey, B. (1991). Everyday reasoning and the roots of intelligence. In J. F. Voss, D. N. Perkins, & J. W. Segal (eds.), *Informal reasoning and education* (pp. 83–105). Hillsdale, NJ: Erlbaum.

Petty, R. E., & Cacioppo, J. T. (1986). The elaboration likelihood model of persuasion. In L. Berkowitz (ed.), *Advances in experimental social psychology* (pp. 123–205). New York: Academic Press.

Piaget, J. (1965). *The moral judgement of the child* (M. Gabain, Trans.). New York: Free Press. (Original work published 1932)

Plato. (1949). *Timaeus* (B. Jowett, Trans.). Indianapolis, IN: Bobbs-Merrill. (Original work published 4th century BC)

Posner, M. I., & Snyder, C. R. R. (1975). Attention and cognitive control. In R. L. Solso (ed.), *Information processing and cognition: The Loyola Symposium* (pp. 55–85). Hillsdale, NJ: Erlbaum.

Power, F. C, Higgins, A., & Kohlberg, L. (1989). *Lawrence Kohlberg's approach to moral education.* New York: Columbia University Press.

Pyszczynski, T., & Greenberg, J. (1987). Toward an integration of cognitive and motivational perspectives on social inference: A biased hypothesis-testing model. *Advances in Experimental Social Psychology, 20,* 297–340.

Rawls, J. (1971). *A theory of justice.* Cambridge, MA: Harvard University Press.

Reber, A. S. (1993). *Implicit learning and tacit knowledge: An essay on the cognitive unconscious.* New York: Oxford University Press.

Robinson, R. J., Keltner, D., Ward, A., & Ross, L. (1995). Actual versus assumed differences in construal: "Naive realism" in intergroup perception and conflict.

Journal of Personality and Social Psychology, 68, 404–17.

Ross, W. D. (1930). *The right and the good.* London: Oxford University Press.

Selman, R. (1971). The relation of role taking to the development of moral judgment in children. *Child Development, 42,* 79–91.

Shavitt, S. (1990). The role of attitude objects in attitude formation. *Journal of Experimental Social Psychology, 26,* 124–48.

Sherif, M. (1935). A study of some social factors in perception. *Archives of Psychology, 27*(187).

Shweder, R. A., & Haidt, J. (1993). The future of moral psychology: Truth, intuition, and the pluralist way. *Psychological Science, 4,* 360–5.

Simon, H. A. (1992). What is an "explanation" of behavior? *Psychological Science, 3,* 150–61.

Singer, P. (1994). *Rethinking life and death.* New York: St. Martin's Press.

Solomon, R. C. (1993). The philosophy of emotions. In M. Lewis & J. Haviland (eds.), *Handbook of emotions* (pp. 3–15). New York: Guilford Press.

Stein, R., & Nemeroff, C. J. (1995). Moral overtones of food: Judgments of others based on what they eat. *Personality and Social Psychology Bulletin, 21,* 480–90.

Tappan, M. (1997). Language, culture, and moral development: A Vygotskian perspective. *Developmental Review, 17,* 78–100.

Thorndike, E. L. (1920). A constant error in psychological ratings. *Journal of Applied Psychology, 4,* 25–29.

Turiel, E. (1983). *The development of social knowledge: Morality and convention.* Cambridge, England: Cambridge University Press.

Turiel, E., Hildebrandt, C., & Wainryb, C. (1991). Judging social issues: Difficulties, inconsistencies, and consistencies. *Monographs of the Society for Research in Child Development, 56,* 1–103.

Wegner, D. (1994). Ironic processes of mental control. *Psychological Review, 101,* 34–52.

Wegner, D., & Bargh, J. (1998). Control and automaticity in social life. In D. T. Gilbert, S. T. Fiske, & G. Lindzey (eds.), *Handbook of social psychology* (4th edn., pp. 446–96). New York: McGraw-Hill.

Wicklund, R. A., & Brehm, J. W. (1976). *Perspectives on cognitive dissonance.* Hillsdale, NJ: Erlbaum.

Williams, B. (1967). Rationalism. In P. Edwards (Ed.), *The encyclopedia of philosophy* (vols. 7–8, pp. 69–75). New York: Macmillan.

Wilson, J. Q. (1993). *The moral sense.* New York: Free Press.

Wilson, T. D. (2004). *Strangers to ourselves: Discovering the adaptive unconscious.* Cambridge, MA: Harvard University Press.

Wilson, T. D., Lindsey, S., & Schooler, T. (2000). A model of dual attitudes. *Psychological Review, 107,* 101–26.

Zajonc, R. B. (1980). Feeling and thinking: Preferences need no inferences. *American Psychologist, 35,* 151–75.

Zimbardo, P. G., LaBerge, S., & Butler, L. D. (1993). Psychophysiological consequences of unexplained arousal: A posthypnotic suggestion paradigm. *Journal of Abnormal Psychology, 102,* 466–73.

38

The Secret Joke of Kant's Soul

Joshua D. Greene

*Two things fill the mind with ever new and
increasing wonder and awe, the oftener
and more steadily we reflect on them: the
starry heavens above me and the moral
law within me.*
— Immanuel Kant

*Kant's Joke – Kant wanted to prove, in a
way that would dumbfound the common
man, that the common man was right:
that was the secret joke of this soul. He
wrote against the scholars in support of
popular prejudice, but for scholars and
not for the people.*
— Friedrich Nietzsche

There is a substantial and growing body of
evidence suggesting that much of what we do, we
do unconsciously, and for reasons that are inaccessible to us (Wilson, 2002). In one experiment,
for example, people were asked to choose one of
several pairs of pantyhose displayed in a row. When
asked to explain their preferences, people gave
sensible enough answers, referring to the relevant
features of the items chosen – superior knit,
sheerness, elasticity, etc. However, their choices
had nothing to do with such features because
the items on display were in fact identical. People
simply had a preference for items on the right-

hand side of the display (Nisbett & Wilson, 1977).
What this experiment illustrates – and there are
many, many such illustrations – is that people
make choices for reasons unknown to them,
and they make up reasonable-sounding justifications for their choices, all the while remaining
unaware of their actual motives and subsequent
rationalizations.

Jonathan Haidt applies these psychological
lessons to the study of moral judgment in his
influential paper, "The Emotional Dog and Its
Rational Tail: A Social Intuitionist Approach to
Moral Judgment" (Haidt, 2001). He argues that
for the most part moral reasoning is a post hoc
affair: We decide what's right or wrong on the
basis of emotionally driven intuitions, and then,
if necessary, we make up reasons to explain and
justify our judgments. Haidt concedes that some
people, some of the time, may actually reason
their way to moral conclusions, but he insists that
this is not the norm. More important for the
purposes of this essay, Haidt does not distinguish
among the various approaches to ethics familiar
to moral philosophers: consequentialism, deontology, virtue ethics, etc. Rather, his radical thesis
is intended, if only implicitly, to apply equally to
the adherents of all moral philosophies, though
not necessarily well to moral philosophers as a
group (Kuhn, 1991).

From The Secret Joke of Kant's Soul, from Walter Sinnott-Armstrong ed., *Moral Psychology, Volume 3: The Neuroscience of
Morality: Emotion, Brain Disorders, and Development*, extract from pages 35–48, 59–66, plus notes © 2007 Massachusetts Institute
of Technology, by permission of The MIT Press.

Moral Psychology: Historical and Contemporary Readings, edited by Thomas Nadelhoffer, Eddy Nahmias, and Shaun Nichols.
© 2010 Blackwell Publishing Ltd except for editorial material and organization © 2010 Thomas Nadelhoffer, Eddy Nahmias, and
Shaun Nichols.

Jonathan Baron (1994), in contrast, draws a psychological distinction between consequentialist and nonconsequentialist judgments, arguing that the latter are especially likely to be made on the basis of heuristics, simple rules of thumb for decision making. Baron, however, does not regard emotion as essential to these heuristic judgments.

In this chapter, I draw on Haidt's and Baron's respective insights in the service of a bit of philosophical psychoanalysis. I will argue that deontological judgments tend to be driven by emotional responses and that deontological philosophy, rather than being grounded in moral *reasoning*, is to a large extent an exercise in moral *rationalization*. This is in contrast to consequentialism, which, I will argue, arises from rather different psychological processes, ones that are more "cognitive," and more likely to involve genuine moral reasoning. These claims are strictly empirical, and I will defend them on the basis of the available evidence. Needless to say, my argument will be speculative and will not be conclusive. Beyond this, I will argue that if these empirical claims are true, they may have normative implications, casting doubt on deontology as a school of normative moral thought.

Preliminaries

Defining deontology and consequentialism

Deontology is defined by its emphasis on moral rules, most often articulated in terms of *rights* and *duties*. Consequentialism, in contrast, is the view that the moral value of an action is in one way or another a function of its consequences alone. Consequentialists maintain that moral decision makers should always aim to produce the best overall consequences for all concerned, if not directly then indirectly. Both consequentialists and deontologists think that consequences are important, but consequentialists believe that consequences are the *only* things that ultimately matter, while deontologists believe that morality both requires and allows us to do things that do not produce the best possible consequences. For example, a deontologist might say that killing one person in order to save several others is wrong, even if doing so would maximize good consequences (S. Kagan, 1997).

This is a standard explanation of what deontology and consequentialism are and how they differ. In light of this explanation, it might seem that my thesis is false *by definition*. Deontology is rule-based morality, usually focused on rights and duties. A deontological judgment, then, is a judgment made out of respect for certain types of moral rules. From this it follows that a moral judgment that is made on the basis of an emotional response simply cannot be a deontological judgment, although it may appear to be one from the outside. Kant himself was adamant about this, at least with respect to his own brand of deontology. He notoriously claimed that an action performed merely out of sympathy and not out of an appreciation of one's duty lacks moral worth (Kant, 1785/1959, chap. 1; Korsgaard, 1996a, chap. 2).

The assumption behind this objection – and as far as I know it has never been questioned previously – is that consequentialism and deontology are, first and foremost, moral philosophies. It is assumed that philosophers know exactly what deontology and consequentialism are because these terms and concepts were defined by philosophers. Despite this, I believe it is possible that philosophers do not necessarily know what consequentialism and deontology really are.

How could this be? The answer, I propose, is that the terms "deontology" and "consequentialism" refer to *psychological natural kinds*. I believe that consequentialist and deontological views of philosophy are not so much philosophical inventions as they are philosophical manifestations of two dissociable psychological patterns, two different ways of moral thinking, that have been part of the human repertoire for thousands of years. According to this view, the moral philosophies of Kant, Mill, and others are just the explicit tips of large, mostly implicit, psychological icebergs. If that is correct, then philosophers may not really know what they're dealing with when they trade in consequentialist and deontological moral theories, and we may have to do some science to find out.

[. . .]

Because I am interested in exploring the possibility that deontology and consequentialism are psychological natural kinds, I will put aside their conventional philosophical definitions and focus instead on their relevant functional roles. As noted earlier, consequentialists and deontologists have some characteristic practical disagreements. For example, consequentialists typically say that killing one person in order to save several others may be the right thing to do, depending on the situation. Deontologists, in contrast, typically say that it's wrong to kill one person for the benefit of others, that the "ends don't justify the means." Because consequentialists and deontologists have these sorts of practical disagreements, we can use these disagreements to define consequentialist and deontological judgments functionally. For the purposes of this discussion, we'll say that con-sequentialist judgments are judgments in favor of characteristically consequentialist conclusions (e.g., "Better to save more lives") and that deontological judgments are judgments in favor of characteristically deontological conclusions (e.g., "It's wrong despite the benefits"). My use of "characteristically" is obviously loose here, but I trust that those familiar with contemporary ethical debates will know what I mean. Note that the kind of judgment made is largely independent of who is making it. A card-carrying deontologist can make a "characteristically consequentialist" judgment, as when Judith Jarvis Thomson says that it's okay to turn a runaway trolley that threatens to kill five people onto a side track so that it will kill only one person instead (Thomson, 1986). This is a "characteristically consequential-ist" judgment because it is easily justified in terms of the most basic consequentialist principles, while deontologists need to do a lot of fancy philosophizing in order to defend this position. Likewise, consider the judgment that it's wrong to save five people who need organ transplants by removing the organs from an unwilling donor (Thomson, 1986). This judgment is "charac-teristically deontological," not because many card-carrying consequentialists don't agree, but because they have to do a lot of extra explaining to justify their agreement.

By defining "consequentialism" and "deonto-logy" in terms of their characteristic judgments, we give our empirical hypothesis a chance. If it turns out that characteristically deontological judgments are driven by emotion (an empirical possibility), then that raises the possibility that deontological *philosophy* is also driven by emotion (a further empirical possibility). In other words, what we find when we explore the psychological causes of characteristically deontological judg-ments might suggest that what deontological

moral philosophy really is, what it is *essentially*, is an attempt to produce rational justifications for emotionally driven moral judgments, and not an attempt to reach moral conclusions on the basis of moral reasoning.

The point for now, however, is simply to flag the terminological issue. When I refer to something as a "deontological judgment," I am saying that it is a characteristically deontological judgment and am not insisting that the judgment in question necessarily meets the criteria that philosophers would impose for counting that judgment as deontological. In the end, however, I will argue that such judgments are best under-stood as genuinely deontological because they are produced by an underlying psychology that is the hidden essence of deontological philosophy.

Defining "cognition" and "emotion"

In what follows I will argue that deontological judgment tends to be driven by emotion, while consequentialist judgment tends to be driven by "cognitive" processes. What do we mean by "emotion" and "cognition," and how do these things differ?

Sometimes "cognition" refers to information processing in general, as in "cognitive science," but often "cognition" is used in a narrower sense that contrasts with "emotion," despite the fact that emotions involve information processing. I know of no good off-the-shelf definition of "cognition" in this more restrictive sense, despite its widespread use. Elsewhere, my collaborators and I offered a tentative definition of our own (Greene, Nystrom, Engell, Darley, & Cohen, 2004), one that is based on the differences between the information-processing requirements of stereotyped versus flexible behavior.

The rough idea is that "cognitive" representa-tions are inherently neutral representations, ones that do not automatically trigger particular behavioral responses or dispositions, while "emo-tional" representations do have such automatic effects, and are therefore behaviorally valenced. (To make things clear, I will use quotation marks to indicate the more restrictive sense of "cognitive" defined here, and I will drop the quotation marks when using this term to refer to information processing in general.) Highly flexible behavior requires "cognitive" representations that can be easily mixed around and recombined as situational demands vary, and without pulling the agent in sixteen different behavioral directions at once. For example, sometimes you need to avoid cars, and other times you need to approach them. It is useful, then, if you can represent CAR in a behaviorally neutral or "cognitive" way, one that doesn't automatically presuppose a particular behavioral response. Stereotyped behavior, in contrast, doesn't require this sort of flexibility and therefore doesn't require "cognitive" representations, at least not to the same extent.

While the whole brain is devoted to cognition, "cognitive" processes are especially important for reasoning, planning, manipulating information in working memory, controlling impulses, and "higher executive functions" more generally. Moreover, these functions tend to be associated with certain parts of the brain, primarily the dorsolateral surfaces of the prefrontal cortex and parietal lobes (Koechlin, Ody, & Kouneiher, 2003; Miller & Cohen, 2001; Ramnani & Owen, 2004). Emotion, in contrast, tends to be associated with other parts of the brain, such as the amygdala and the medial surfaces of the frontal and parietal lobes (Adolphs, 2002; Maddock, 1999; Phan, Wager, Taylor, & Liberzon, 2002). And while the term "emotion" can refer to stable states such as moods, here we will primarily be concerned with emotions subserved by processes that in addition to being valenced, are quick and automatic, though not necessarily conscious.

Here we are concerned with two different kinds of moral judgment (deontological and consequentialist) and two different kinds of psychological process ("cognitive" and emotional). Crossing these, we get four basic empirical possibilities. First, it could be that both kinds of moral judgment are generally "cognitive," as Kohlberg's theories suggest (Kohlberg, 1971).[1] At the other extreme, it could be that both kinds of moral judgment are primarily emotional, as Haidt's view suggests (Haidt, 2001). Then there is the historical stereotype, according to which consequentialism is more emotional (emerging from the "sentimentalist" tradition of David Hume [1740/1978] and Adam Smith [1759/1976]) while deontology is more "cognitive" (encompassing the Kantian "rationalist" tradition [Kant, 1959]). Finally, there is the view for which I will argue, that deontology is more emotionally driven while consequentialism is more "cognitive." I hasten to

add, however, that I don't believe that either approach is strictly emotional or "cognitive" (or even that there is a sharp distinction between "cognition" and emotion). More specifically, I am sympathetic to Hume's claim that all moral judgment (including consequentialist judgment) must have some emotional component (Hume, 1978). But I suspect that the kind of emotion that is essential to consequentialism is fundamentally different from the kind that is essential to deontology, the former functioning more like a currency and the latter functioning more like an alarm. We will return to this issue later.

Scientific Evidence

Evidence from neuroimaging

In recent decades, philosophers have devised a range of hypothetical moral dilemmas that capture the tension between the consequentialist and deontological viewpoints. A well-known handful of these dilemmas gives rise to what is known as the "trolley problem" (Foot, 1967; Thomson, 1986), which begins with the *trolley* dilemma.

A runaway trolley is headed for five people who will be killed if it proceeds on its present course. The only way to save these people is to hit a switch that will turn the trolley onto a side track, where it will run over and kill one person instead of five. Is it okay to turn the trolley in order to save five people at the expense of one? The consensus among philosophers (Fischer & Ravizza, 1992), as well as people who have been tested experimentally (Petrinovich & O'Neill, 1996; Petrinovich, O'Neill, & Jorgensen, 1993), is that it is morally acceptable to save five lives at the expense of one in this case.

Next consider the *footbridge* dilemma (Thomson, 1986): As before, a runaway trolley threatens to kill five people, but this time you are standing next to a large stranger on a footbridge spanning the tracks, in between the oncoming trolley and the five people. The only way to save the five people is to push this stranger off the bridge and onto the tracks below. He will die as a result, but his body will stop the trolley from reaching the others. Is it okay to save the five people by pushing this stranger to his death? Here the consensus is that it is not okay to save five lives at the expense of one (Fischer & Ravizza, 1992; Greene et al., 2004; Greene, Sommerville, Nystrom, Darley, & Cohen, 2001; Petrinovich & O'Neill, 1996; Petrinovich et al., 1993).

People exhibit a characteristically consequentialist response to the *trolley* case and a characteristically deontological response to the *footbridge* case. Why? Philosophers have generally offered a variety of *normative* explanations. That is, they have assumed that our responses to these cases are correct, or at least reasonable, and have sought principles that *justify* treating these two cases differently (Fischer & Ravizza, 1992). For example, one might suppose, following Kant (1785/1959) and Aquinas (1265–72/1988), that it is wrong to harm someone as a means to helping someone else. In the *footbridge* case, the proposed action involves literally using the person on the footbridge as a trolley stopper, whereas in the *trolley* case the victim is to be harmed merely as a side effect. (Were the single person on the alternative track to magically disappear, we would be very pleased.) In response to this proposal, Thomson devised the *loop* case (Thomson, 1986). Here the situation is similar to that of the *trolley* dilemma, but this time the single person is on a piece of track that branches off of the main track and then rejoins it at a point before the five people. In this case, if the person were not on the side track, the trolley would return to the main track and run over the five people. The consensus here is that it is morally acceptable to turn the trolley in this case, despite the fact that here, as in the *footbridge* case, a person will be used as a means.

There have been many such normative attempts to solve the trolley problem, but none of them has been terribly successful (Fischer & Ravizza, 1992). My collaborators and I have proposed a partial and purely descriptive solution to this problem and have collected some scientific evidence in favor of it. We hypothesized that the thought of pushing someone to his death in an "up close and personal" manner (as in the *footbridge* dilemma) is more emotionally salient than the thought of bringing about similar consequences in a more impersonal way (e.g., by hitting a switch, as in the *trolley* dilemma). We proposed that this difference in emotional response explains why people respond so differently to these two cases. That is, people tend toward consequentialism in the case in which the emotional response

is low and tend toward deontology in the case in which the emotional response is high.

The rationale for distinguishing between *personal* and *impersonal* forms of harm is largely evolutionary. "Up close and personal" violence has been around for a very long time, reaching far back into our primate lineage (Wrangham & Peterson, 1996). Given that personal violence is evolutionarily ancient, predating our recently evolved human capacities for complex abstract reasoning, it should come as no surprise if we have innate responses to personal violence that are powerful but rather primitive. That is, we might expect humans to have negative emotional responses to certain basic forms of interpersonal violence, where these responses evolved as a means of regulating the behavior of creatures who are capable of intentionally harming one another, but whose survival depends on cooperation and individual restraint (Sober & Wilson, 1998; Trivers, 1971). In contrast, when a harm is *impersonal*, it should fail to trigger this alarmlike emotional response, allowing people to respond in a more "cognitive" way, perhaps employing a cost-benefit analysis. As Josef Stalin once said, "A single death is a tragedy; a million deaths is a statistic." His remarks suggest that when harmful actions are sufficiently impersonal, they fail to push our emotional buttons, despite their seriousness, and as a result we think about them in a more detached, actuarial fashion.

This hypothesis makes some strong predictions regarding what we should see going on in people's brains while they are responding to dilemmas involving personal versus impersonal harm (henceforth called "personal" and "impersonal" moral dilemmas). The contemplation of personal moral dilemmas like the *footbridge* case should produce increased neural activity in brain regions associated with emotional response and social cognition, while the contemplation of impersonal moral dilemmas like the *trolley* case should produce relatively greater activity in brain regions associated with "higher cognition."[2] This is exactly what was observed (Greene et al., 2004; Greene et al., 2001). Contemplation of personal moral dilemmas produced relatively greater activity in three emotion-related areas: the posterior cingulate cortex, the medial prefrontal cortex, and the amygdala. This effect was also observed in the superior temporal sulcus, a region associated with various kinds of social cognition in humans and other primates (Allison, Puce, & McCarthy, 2000; Saxe, Carey, & Kanwisher, 2004). At the same time, contemplation of impersonal moral dilemmas produced relatively greater neural activity in two classically "cognitive" brain areas, the dorsolateral prefrontal cortex and inferior parietal lobe.

This hypothesis also makes a prediction regarding people's reaction times. According to the view I have sketched, people tend to have emotional responses to personal moral violations, responses that incline them to judge against performing those actions. That means that someone who judges a personal moral violation to be *appropriate* (e.g., someone who says it's okay to push the man off the bridge in the *footbridge* case) will most likely have to override an emotional response in order to do it. This over-riding process will take time, and thus we would expect that "yes" answers will take longer than "no" answers in response to personal moral dilemmas like the *footbridge* case. At the same time, we have no reason to predict a difference in reaction time between "yes" and "no" answers in response to impersonal moral dilemmas like the *trolley* case because there is, according to this model, no emotional response (or much less of one) to override in such cases. Here, too, the prediction has held. Trials in which the subject judged in favor of personal moral violations took significantly longer than trials in which the subject judged against them, but there was no comparable reaction time effect observed in response to impersonal moral violations (Greene et al., 2004; Greene et al., 2001).

Further results support this model as well. Next we subdivided the personal moral dilemmas into two categories on the basis of difficulty (i.e., based on reaction time). Consider the following moral dilemma (the *crying baby* dilemma): It is wartime, and you and some of your fellow villagers are hiding from enemy soldiers in a basement. Your baby starts to cry, and you cover your baby's mouth to block the sound. If you remove your hand, your baby will cry loudly, the soldiers will hear, and they will find you and the others and kill everyone they find, including you and your baby. If you do not remove your hand, your baby will smother to death. Is it okay to smother your baby to death in order to save yourself and the other villagers?

This is a very difficult question. Different people give different answers, and nearly everyone takes a relatively long time. This is in contrast to other personal moral dilemmas, such as the *infanticide* dilemma, in which a teenage girl must decide whether to kill her unwanted newborn. In response to this case, people (at least the ones we tested) quickly and unanimously say that this action is wrong.

What's going on in these two cases? My colleagues and I hypothesized as follows. In both cases there is a prepotent, negative emotional response to the personal violation in question, killing one's own baby. In the *crying baby* case, however, a cost-benefit analysis strongly favors smothering the baby. After all, the baby is going to die no matter what, and so you have nothing to lose (in consequentialist terms) and much to gain by smothering it, awful as it is. In some people the emotional response dominates, and those people say "no." In other people, this "cognitive," cost-benefit analysis wins out, and these people say "yes."

What does this model predict that we will see going on in people's brains when we compare cases like *crying baby* and *infanticide*? First, this model supposes that cases like *crying baby* involve an increased level of "response conflict," that is, conflict between competing representations for behavioral response. Thus, we should expect that difficult moral dilemmas like *crying baby* will produce increased activity in a brain region that is associated with response conflict, the anterior cingulate cortex (Botvinick, Braver, Barch, Carter, & Cohen, 2001). Second, according to our model, the crucial difference between cases like *crying baby* and those like *infanticide* is that the former evoke strong "cognitive" responses that can effectively compete with a prepotent, emotional response. Thus, we should expect to see increased activity in classically "cognitive" brain areas when we compare cases like *crying baby* with cases like *infanticide*, despite the fact that difficult dilemmas like *crying baby* are personal moral dilemmas, which were previously associated with emotional response (Greene et al., 2001).

These two predictions have held (Greene et al., 2004). Comparing high-reaction-time personal moral dilemmas like *crying baby* with low-reaction-time personal moral dilemmas like *infanticide* revealed increased activity in the anterior cingulate cortex (conflict) as well as the anterior dorsolateral prefrontal cortex and the inferior parietal lobes, both classically "cognitive" brain regions.

Cases like *crying baby* are especially interesting because they allow us to directly compare the neural activity associated with characteristically consequentialist and deontological responses. According to our model, when people say "yes" to such cases (the consequentialist answer), it is because the "cognitive" cost-benefit analysis has successfully dominated the prepotent emotional response that drives people to say "no" (the deontological answer). If that is correct, then we should expect to see increased activity in the previously identified "cognitive" brain regions (the dorsolateral prefrontal cortex and inferior parietal cortex) for the trials in which people say "yes" in response to cases like *crying baby*. This is exactly what we found. In other words, people exhibit more "cognitive" activity when they give the consequentialist answer.[3]

To summarize, people's moral judgments appear to be products of at least two different kinds of psychological processes. First, both brain imaging and reaction-time data suggest that there are prepotent negative emotional responses that drive people to disapprove of the personally harmful actions proposed in cases like the *footbridge* and *crying baby* dilemmas. These responses are characteristic of deontology, but not of consequentialism. Second, further brain imaging results suggest that "cognitive" psychological processes can compete with the aforementioned emotional processes, driving people to approve of personally harmful moral violations, primarily when there is a strong consequentialist rationale for doing so, as in the *crying baby* case. The parts of the brain that exhibit increased activity when people make characteristically consequentialist judgments are those that are most closely associated with higher cognitive functions such as executive control (Koechlin et al., 2003; Miller and Cohen, 2001), complex planning (Koechlin, Basso, Pietrini, Panzer, & Grafman, 1999), deductive and inductive reasoning (Goel & Dolan, 2004), taking the long view in economic decision making (McClure, Laibson, Loewenstein, & Cohen, 2004), and so on. Moreover, these brain regions are among those most dramatically expanded in humans compared with other primates (Allman, Hakeem, & Watson, 2002).

Emotion and the sense of moral obligation

In his classic article, "Famine, Affluence, and Morality," Peter Singer (1972) argues that we in the affluent world have an obligation to do much more than we do to improve the lives of needy people. He argues that if we can prevent something very bad from happening without incurring a comparable moral cost, then we ought to do it. For example, if one notices a small child drowning in a shallow pond, one is morally obliged to wade in and save that child, even if it means muddying one's clothes. As Singer points out, this seemingly innocuous principle has radical implications, implying that all of us who spend money on unnecessary luxuries should give up those luxuries in order to spend the money on saving and/or improving the lives of impoverished peoples. Why, Singer asks, do we have a strict obligation to save a nearby drowning child but no comparable obligation to save faraway sick and starving children through charitable donations to organizations like Oxfam?

Many normative explanations come to mind, but none is terribly compelling. Are we allowed to ignore the plight of faraway children because they are citizens of foreign nations? If so, then would it be acceptable to let the child drown, provided that the child was encountered while traveling abroad? Or in international waters? And what about the domestic poor? This argument does not relieve us of our obligations to them. Is it because of diffused responsibility – because many are in a position to help a starving child abroad, but only you are in a position to help this hypothetical drowning child? What if there were many people standing around the pond doing nothing? Would that make it okay for you to do nothing as well? Is it because international aid is ultimately ineffective, only serving to enrich corrupt politicians or create more poor people? In that case, our obligation would simply shift to more sophisticated relief efforts incorporating political reform, economic development, family planning education, and so on. Are all relief efforts doomed to ineffectiveness? That is a bold empirical claim that no one can honestly make with great confidence.

Here we find ourselves in a position similar to the one we faced with the trolley problem. We have a strong intuition that two moral dilemmas are importantly different, and yet we have a hard time explaining what that important difference is (S. Kagan, 1989; Unger, 1996). It turns out that the same psychological theory that makes sense of the trolley problem can make sense of Singer's problem. Note that the interaction in the case of the drowning child is "up close and personal," the sort of situation that might have been encountered by our human and primate ancestors. Likewise, note that the donation case is not "up close and personal," and is not the sort of situation that our ancestors could have encountered. At no point were our ancestors able to save the lives of anonymous strangers through modest material sacrifices. In light of this, the psychological theory presented here suggests that we are likely to find the obligation to save the drowning child more pressing simply because that "up close and personal" case pushes our emotional buttons in a way that the more impersonal donation case does not (Greene, 2003). As it happens, these two cases were among those tested in the brain imaging study described earlier, with a variation on the drowning child case included in the *personal* condition and the donation case included in the *impersonal* condition (Greene et al., 2004; Greene et al., 2001).

Few people accept Singer's consequentialist conclusion. Rather, people tend to believe, in a characteristically deontological way, that they are within their moral rights in spending their money on luxuries for themselves, despite the fact that their money could be used to dramatically improve the lives of other people. This is exactly what one would expect if (1) the deontological sense of obligation is driven primarily by emotion, and (2) when it comes to obligations to aid, emotions are only sufficiently engaged when those to whom we might owe something are encountered (or conceived of) in a personal way.

[. . .]

Two patterns of moral judgment

The experiments conducted by Greene et al. (2001, 2004), Small and Loewenstein (2003), Baron et al. (1993), Kahneman et al. (1998), Carlsmith et al. (2002), Sanfey et al. (2003), de Quervain et al. (2004), and Haidt et al. (2000, 1993) together provide multiple pieces of independent evidence that deontological patterns

of moral judgment are driven by emotional responses while consequentialist judgments are driven by "cognitive" processes. Any one of the results and interpretations described here may be questioned, but the convergent evidence assembled here makes a decent case for the association between deontology and emotion, especially since there is, to my knowledge, no empirical evidence to the contrary. Of course, deontologists may regard themselves and their minds as exceptions to the statistically significant and multiply convergent psychological patterns identified in these studies, but in my opinion the burden is on them to demonstrate that they are psychologically exceptional in a way that preserves their self-conceptions.

Why should deontology and emotion go together? I believe the answer comes in two parts. First, moral emotion provides a natural solution to certain problems created by social life. Second, deontological philosophy provides a natural "cognitive" interpretation of moral emotion. Let us consider each of these claims in turn.

First, why moral emotions? In recent decades many plausible and complementary explanations have been put forth, and a general consensus seems to be emerging. The emotions most relevant to morality exist because they motivate behaviors that help individuals spread their genes *within a social context*. The theory of kin selection explains why individuals have a tendency to care about the welfare of those individuals to whom they are closely related (Hamilton, 1964). Because close relatives share a high proportion of their genes, one can spread one's own genes by helping close relatives spread theirs. The theory of reciprocal altruism explains the existence of a wider form of altruism: Genetically unrelated individuals can benefit from being nice to each other as long as they are capable of keeping track of who is willing to repay their kindness (Trivers, 1971). More recent evolutionary theories of altruism attempt to explain the evolution of "strong reciprocity," a broader tendency to reward cooperative behavior and punish uncooperative behavior, even in contexts in which the necessary conditions for kin selection (detectable genetic relationships) and reciprocal altruism (detectable cooperative dispositions) are not met (Bowles & Gintis, 2004; Fehr & Rockenbach, 2004; Gintis, 2000). These theories explain the widespread human tendency to engage in cooperative behaviors (e.g., helping others and speaking honestly) and to avoid uncooperative behaviors (e.g., hurting others and lying), even when relatives and close associates are not involved. Moreover, these theories explain "altruistic punishment," people's willingness to punish antisocial behavior even when they cannot expect to benefit from doing so (Boyd, Gintis, Bowles, & Richerson 2003; Fehr & Gachter, 2002; Fehr & Rockenbach, 2004). Other evolutionary theories make sense of other aspects of morality. For example, the incest taboo can be explained as a mechanism for avoiding birth defects, which are more likely to result from matings between close relatives (Lieberman, Tooby, & Cosmides, 2003). Finally, the emerging field of cultural evolution promises to explain how moral norms (and cultural practices more broadly) develop and spread (Richerson & Boyd, 2005).

[. . .] In short, when Nature needs to get a behavioral job done, it does it with intuition and emotion wherever it can. Thus, from an evolutionary point of view, it is no surprise that moral dispositions evolved, and it is no surprise that these dispositions are implemented emotionally.

Now, onto the second part of the explanation. Why should the existence of moral emotions give rise to the existence of deontological philosophy? To answer this question, we must appeal to the well-documented fact that humans are, in general, irrepressible explainers and justifiers of their own behavior. Psychologists have repeatedly found that when people don't know why they're doing what they're doing, they just make up a plausible-sounding story (Haidt, 2001; Wilson, 2002).

[. . .]

The tendency toward post hoc rationalization is often revealed in studies of people with unusual mental conditions. Patients with Korsakoff's amnesia and related memory disorders are prone to "confabulation." That is, they attempt to paper over their memory deficits by constructing elaborate stories about their personal histories, typically delivered with great confidence and with no apparent awareness that they are making stuff up. For example, a confabulating patient seated near an air conditioner was asked if he knew where he was. He replied that he was in an air-conditioning plant. When it was pointed out that he was wearing pajamas, he said. "I keep

them in my car and will soon change into my work clothes" (Stuss, Alexander, Lieberman, & Levine, 1978). Likewise, individuals acting under posthypnotic suggestion will sometimes explain away their behaviors in elaborately rational terms. In one case, a hypnotized subject was instructed to place a lampshade on another person's head upon perceiving an arbitrary cue. He did as instructed, but when he was asked to explain why he did what he did, he made no reference to the posthypnotic suggestion or the cue: "Well, I'll tell you. It sounds queer but it's just a little experiment in psychology. I've been reading on the psychology of humor and I thought I'd see how you folks reacted to a joke that was in very bad taste" (Estabrooks, 1943; Wilson, 2002).

Perhaps the most striking example of this kind of post hoc rationalization comes from studies of split-brain patients, people in whom there is no direct neuronal communication between the cerebral hemispheres. In one study, a patient's right hemisphere was shown a snow scene and instructed to select a matching picture. Using his left hand, the hand controlled by the right hemisphere, he selected a picture of a shovel. At the same time, the patient's left hemisphere, the hemisphere that is dominant for language, was shown a picture of a chicken claw. The patient was asked verbally why he chose the shovel with his left hand. He answered, "I saw a claw and picked a chicken, and you have to clean out the chicken shed with a shovel" (Gazzaniga & Le Doux, 1978; Wilson, 2002). Gazzaniga and LeDoux argue that these sorts of confabulations are not peculiar to spilt-brain patients, that this tendency was not created when these patients' intercerebral communication lines were cut. Rather, they argue, we are all confabulators of a sort. We respond to the conscious deliverances of our unconscious perceptual, mnemonic, and emotional processes by fashioning them into a rationally sensible narrative, and without any awareness that we are doing so. This widespread tendency for rationalization is only revealed in carefully controlled experiments in which the psychological inputs and behavioral outputs can be carefully monitored, or in studies of abnormal individuals who are forced to construct a plausible narrative out of meager raw material.

We are now ready to put two and two together. What should we expect from creatures who exhibit social and moral behavior that is driven largely by intuitive emotional responses and who are prone to rationalization of their behaviors? The answer, I believe, is deontological moral philosophy. What happens when we contemplate pushing the large man off the footbridge? If I'm right, we have an intuitive emotional response that says "no!" This nay-saying voice can be overridden, of course, but as far as the voice itself is concerned, there is no room for negotiation. Whether or not we can ultimately justify pushing the man off the footbridge, it will always *feel* wrong. And what better way to express that feeling of non-negotiable absolute wrongness than via the most central of deontological concepts, the concept of a *right*: You can't push him to his death because that would be a violation of his *rights*. Likewise, you can't let that baby drown because you have a *duty* to save it.

Deontology, then, is a kind of moral confabulation. We have strong feelings that tell us in clear and uncertain terms that some things *simply cannot be done* and that other things *simply must be done*. But it is not obvious how to make sense of these feelings, and so we, with the help of some especially creative philosophers, make up a rationally appealing story: There are these things called "rights" which people have, and when someone has a right you can't do anything that would take it away. It doesn't matter if the guy on the footbridge is toward the end of his natural life, or if there are seven people on the tracks below instead of five. If the man has a right, then *the man has a right*. As John Rawls (1971, pp. 3–4) famously said, "Each person possesses an inviolability founded on justice that even the welfare of society as a whole cannot override" and, "In a just society the rights secured by justice are not subject to political bargaining or to the calculus of social interests." These are applause lines because they make emotional sense. Deontology, I believe, is a natural "cognitive" expression of our deepest moral emotions.

This hypothesis raises a further question. Why just deontology? Why not suppose that all moral philosophy, even all moral reasoning, is a rationalization of moral emotion? (This is the strong form of the view defended by Jonathan Haidt, 2001, whose argument is the model for the argument made here.)[4] The answer, I think, is that consequentialist moral judgment is not driven by

emotion, or at least it is not driven by the sort of "alarm bell" emotion that drives deontological judgment. The evidence presented earlier supports this hypothesis, suggesting that consequentialist judgment is less emotional and more "cognitive," but it doesn't explain why this should be so. I argued earlier that there is a natural mapping between the content of deontological philosophy and the functional properties of alarmlike emotions. Likewise, I believe that there is a natural mapping between the content of consequentialist philosophy and the functional properties of "cognitive" processes. Indeed, I believe that consequentialism is inherently "cognitive," that it couldn't be implemented any other way.

Consequentialism is, by its very nature, systematic and aggregative. It aims to take nearly everything into account, and grants that nearly everything is negotiable. All consequentialist decision making is a matter of balancing competing concerns, taking into account as much information as is practically feasible. Only in hypothetical examples in which "all else is equal" does consequentialism give clear answers. For real-life consequentialism, everything is a complex guessing game, and all judgments are revisable in light of additional details. There is no moral clarity in consequentialist moral thought, with its approximations and simplifying assumptions. It is fundamentally actuarial.

Recall the definition of "cognitive" proposed earlier: "Cognitive" representations are inherently neutral representations, ones that, unlike emotional representations, do not automatically trigger particular behavioral responses or dispositions. Once again, the advantage of having such neutral representations is that they can be mixed and matched in a situation-specific way without pulling the agent in multiple behavioral directions at once, thus enabling highly flexible behavior. These are precisely the sorts of representations that a consequentialist needs in order to make a judgment based on aggregation, one that takes all of the relevant factors into account: "Is it okay to push the guy off the bridge if he's about to cure cancer?" "Is it okay to go out for sushi when the extra money could be used to promote health education in Africa?" And so on. Deontologists can dismiss these sorts of complicated, situation-specific questions, but consequentialists cannot, which is why, I argue, that consequentialism is inescapably "cognitive."

Some clarifications: First, I am not claiming that consequentialist judgment is emotionless. On the contrary, I am inclined to agree with Hume (1740/1978) that all moral judgment must have some affective component, and suspect that the consequentialist weighing of harms and benefits is an emotional process. But, if I am right, two things distinguish this sort of process from those associated with deontology. First, this is, as I have said, a weighing process and not an "alarm" process. The sorts of emotions hypothesized to be involved here say, "Such-and-such matters this much. Factor it in." In contrast, the emotions hypothesized to drive deontological judgment are far less subtle. They are, as I have said, alarm signals that issue simple commands: "Don't do it!" or "Must do it!" While such commands can be overridden, they are designed to dominate the decision rather than merely influence it.

Second, I am not claiming that deontological judgment cannot be "cognitive." Indeed, I believe that sometimes it is. (See below.) Rather, my hypothesis is that deontological judgment is affective at its core, while consequentialist judgment is inescapably "cognitive." One could, in principle, make a characteristically deontological judgment by thinking explicitly about the categorical imperative and whether the action in question is based on a maxim that could serve as a universal law. And if one were to do that, then the psychological process would be "cognitive." What I am proposing, however, is that this is not how characteristically deontological conclusions tend to be reached and that, instead, they tend to be reached on the basis of emotional responses. This contrasts with consequentialist judgments which, according to my hypothesis, cannot be implemented in an intuitive, emotional way. The only way to reach a distinctively consequentialist judgment (i.e., one that doesn't coincide with a deontological judgment) is to actually go through the consequentialist, cost-benefit reasoning using one's "cognitive" faculties, the ones based in the dorsolateral prefrontal cortex (Greene et al., 2004).

This psychological account of consequentialism and deontology makes sense of certain aspects of their associated phenomenologies. I have often observed that consequentialism strikes

students as appealing, even as tautologically true, when presented in the abstract, but that its appeal is easily undermined by specific counterexamples. (See the earlier discussion contrasting people's real-world motives and abstract justifications for punishment.) When a first-year ethics student asks, "But isn't it obvious that one should do whatever will produce the most good?" all you have to do is whip out the *footbridge* case and you have made your point. Whatever initial "cognitive" appeal consequentialist principles may have is quickly neutralized by a jolt of emotion, and the student is a newly converted deontologist: "Why is it wrong to push the man off the footbridge? Because he has a *right*, an inviolability founded on justice that even the welfare of society as a whole cannot override!" Then it's time for a new counterexample: "What if the trolley is headed for a detonator that will set off a nuclear bomb that will kill half a million people?" Suddenly the welfare of society as a whole starts to sound important again. "Cognition" strikes back with a more compelling utilitarian rationale, and the student is appropriately puzzled. As this familiar dialectic illustrates, the hypothesis that deontology is emotionally based explains the "*NEVER!* – except sometimes" character of rights-based, deontological ethics. An alarmlike emotional response presents itself as unyielding and absolute, until an even more compelling emotional or "cognitive" rationale comes along to override it.

This hypothesis also makes sense of certain deontological anomalies, which I suspect will turn out to be the "exceptions that prove the rule." I have argued that deontology is driven by emotion, but I suspect this is not always the case. Consider, for example, Kant's infamous claim that it would be wrong to lie to a would-be murderer in order to protect a friend who has taken refuge in one's home (Kant, 1785/1983). Here, in a dramatic display of true intellectual integrity, Kant sticks to his theory and rejects the intuitive response. (He "bites the bullet," as philosophers say.) But what is interesting about this bit of Kantian ethics is that it's something of an embarrassment to contemporary Kantians, who are very keen to explain how Kant somehow misapplied his own theory in this case (Korsgaard, 1996a). Presumably the same goes for Kant's views of sexual morality (Kant, 1930, pp. 169–71; Kant, 1994). Modern academics are no longer so squeamish about lust, masturbation, and homosexuality, and so Kant's old-fashioned views on these topics have to be explained away, which is not difficult, since his arguments were never terribly compelling to begin with (see the epigraph). If you want to know which bits of Kant contemporary Kantians will reject, follow the emotions.

Notes

Many thanks to Walter. Sinnott-Armstrong, Jonathan Haidt, Shaun Nichols, and Andrea Heberlein for very helpful comments on this chapter.

[1] Kohlberg was certainly partial to deontology and would likely say that it is more "cognitive" than consequentialism.

[2] It turns out that determining what makes a moral dilemma "personal" and "like the footbridge case" versus "impersonal" and "like the trolley case" is no simple matter, and in many ways reintroduces the complexities associated with traditional attempts to solve the trolley problem. For the purposes of this discussion, however, I am happy to leave the personal-impersonal distinction as an intuitive one, in keeping with the evolutionary account given earlier. For the purposes of designing the brain imaging experiment discussed later, however, my collaborators and I developed a more rigid set of criteria for distinguishing personal from impersonal moral violations (Greene et al., 2001). I no longer believe that these criteria are adequate. Improving these is a goal of ongoing research.

[3] It is worth noting that no brain regions, including those implicated in emotion, exhibited the opposite effect. First, it's not clear that one would expect to see such a result since the hypothesis is that everyone experiences the intuitive emotional response, while only some individuals override it. Second, it is difficult to draw conclusions from negative neuroimaging results because current neuroimaging techniques, which track changes in blood flow, are relatively crude instruments for detecting patterns in neural function.

[4] Haidt (2001), however, believes that philosophers may be exceptional in that they actually do reason their way to moral conclusions (Kuhn, 1991).

References

Adolphs, R. (2002). Neural systems for recognizing emotion. *Curr Opin Neurobiol 12*, 169–77.

Allison, T., Puce, A., and McCarthy, G. (2000). Social perception from visual cues: Role of the sts region. *Trends Cogn Sci 4*, 267–78.

Allman, J., Hakeem, A., and Watson, K. (2002). Two phylogenetic specializations in the human brain. *Neuroscientist 8*, 335–46.

Aquinas, T. (1988). Of killing. In *On law, morality, and politics*, W. P. Baumgarth, and R. J. Regan, eds. (Indianapolis/Cambridge, Hackett Publishing Co.), pp. 226–7.

Baron, J. (1994). Nonconsequentialist decisions. *Behavioral and Brain Sciences 17*, 1–42.

Baron, J., Gowda, R., and Kunreuther, H. (1993). Attitudes toward managing hazardous waste: What should be cleaned up and who should pay for it? *Risk Analysis*, 183–92.

Botvinick, M. M., Braver, T. S., Barch, D. M., Carter, C. S., and Cohen, J. D. (2001), Conflict monitoring and cognitive control. *Psychol Rev 108*, 624–52.

Bowles, S., and Gintis, H. (2004). The evolution of strong reciprocity:

Cooperation in heterogeneous populations. *Theor Popul Biol 65*, 17–28.

Boyd, R., Gintis, H., Bowles, S., and Richerson, P. J. (2003). The evolution of altruistic punishment. *Proc Natl Acad Sci U S A 100*, 3531–5.

Carlsmith, K. M., Darley, J. M., and Robinson, P. H. (2002). Why do we punish?

Deterrence and just deserts as motives for punishment. *J Pers Soc Psychol 83*, 284–99.

de Quervain, D. J., Fischbacher, U., Treyer, V., Schellhammer, M., Schnyder, U., Buck, A., and Fehr, E. (2004). The neural basis of altruistic punishment. *Science 305*, 1254–8.

Estabrooks, G. H. (1943). *Hypnotism* (New York, E. P. Dutton).

Fehr, E., and Gachter, S. (2002). Altruistic punishment in humans. *Nature 415*, 137–40.

Fehr, E., and Rockenbach, B. (2004). Human altruism: Economic, neural, and evolutionary perspectives. *Curr Opin Neurobiol 14*, 784–90.

Fischer, J. M., and Ravizza, M., eds. (1992). *Ethics: Problems and principles* (Fort Worth, TX, Harcourt Brace Jovanovich College Publishers).

Foot, P. (1967). The problem of abortion and the doctrine of double effect. *Oxford Review 5*, 5–15.

Gazzaniga, M. S., and Le Doux, J. E. (1978). *The integrated mind* (New York, Plenum).

Gintis, H. (2000). Strong reciprocity and human sociality. *J Theor Biol 206*, 169–79.

Goel, V., and Dolan, R. J. (2004). Differential involvement of left prefrontal cortex in inductive and deductive reasoning. *Cognition 93*, B109–21.

Greene, J. (2003). From neural 'is' to moral 'ought': What are the moral implications of neuroscientific moral psychology? *Nat Rev Neurosci 4*, 846–9.

Greene, J. D., Nystrom, L. E., Engell, A. D., Darley, J. M., and Cohen, J. D. (2004). The neural bases of cognitive conflict and control in moral judgment. *Neuron 44*, 389–400.

Greene, J. D., Sommerville, R. B., Nystrom, L. E., Darley, J. M., and Cohen, J. D. (2001). An fmri investigation of emotional engagement in moral judgment. *Science 293*, 2105–8.

Haidt, J. (2001). The emotional dog and its rational tail: A social intuitionist approach to moral judgment. *Psychological Review 108*, 814–34.

Haidt, J., Bjorklund, F., and Murphy, S. (2000). Moral dumbfounding: When intuition finds no reason (unpublished manuscript, University of Virginia).

Haidt, J., Koller, S. H., and Dias, M. G. (1993). Affect, culture, and morality, or is it wrong to eat your dog? *J Pers Soc Psychol 65*, 613–28.

Hamilton, W. D. (1964). The genetical evolution of social behaviour. *Journal of Theoretical Biology 7*, 1–52.

Hume, D. (1978). A treatise of human nature, L. A. Selby-Bigge, and P. H. Nidditch, eds. (Oxford, Oxford University Press), pp. xix, 743.

Kagan, S. (1989). *The limits of morality* (New York, Oxford University Press).

Kagan, S. (1997). *Normative ethics* (Boulder, CO, Westview Press).

Kahneman, D., Schkade, D., and Sunstein, C. R. (1998). Shared outrage and erratic rewards: The psychology of punitive damages. *Journal of Risk and Uncertainty 16*, 49–86.

Kant, I. (1930). *Lectures on ethics* (Indianapolis/ Cambridge, Hackett).

Kant, I (1959). *Foundation of the metaphysics of morals* (Indianapolis, Bobbs Merrill).

Kant, I. (1983). *On a supposed right to lie because of philanthropic concerns*. (Indianapolis/Cambridge, Hackett), pp. 162–6.

Kant, I. (1994). The metaphysics of morals. In *Ethical philosophy* (Indianapolis, IA, Hackett).

Kant, I. (2002). *The philosophy of law: An exposition of the fundamental principles of jurisprudence as the science of right* (Union, NJ, Lawbook Exchange).

Koechlin, E., Basso, G., Pietrini, P., Panzer, S., and Grafman, J. (1999). The role of the anterior prefrontal cortex in human cognition. *Nature 399*, 148–51.

Koechlin, E., Ody, C., and Kouneiher, F. (2003). The architecture of cognitive control in the human prefrontal cortex. *Science 302*, 1181–5.

Kohlberg, L. (1971). From is to ought: How to commit the naturalistic fallacy and get away with it in the study of moral development. In *Cognitive development and epistemology*, T. Mischel, ed. (New York, Academic Press), pp. 151–235.

Korsgaard, C. M. (1996a). *Creating the kingdom of ends* (New York, Cambridge University Press).

Kuhn, D. (1991). *The skills of argument* (Cambridge, Cambridge University Press).

Lieberman, D., Tooby, J., and Cosmides, L. (2003). Does morality have a biological basis? An empirical test of the factors governing moral sentiments relating to incest. *Proc R Soc Lond B Biol Sci 270*, 819–26.

Maddock, R. J. (1999). The retrosplenial cortex and emotion: New insights from functional neuroimaging of the human brain. *Trends Neurosci 22*, 310–16.

McClure, S. M., Laibson, D. I., Loewenstein, G., and Cohen, J. D. (2004). Separate neural systems value immediate and delayed monetary rewards. *Science 306*, 503–7.

Miller, E. K., and Cohen, J. D. (2001). An integrative theory of prefrontal cortex function. *Annu Rev Neurosci 24*, 167–202.

Nisbett, R. E., and Wilson, T. D. (1977). Telling more than we can know: Verbal reports on mental processes. *Psychological Review 84*, 231–59.

Petrinovich, L., and O'Neill, P. (1996). Influence of wording and framing effects on moral intuitions. *Ethology and Sociobiology 17*, 145–71.

Petrinovich, L., O'Neill, P., and Jorgensen, M. (1993). An empirical study of moral intuitions: Toward an evolutionary ethics. *Journal of Personality and Social Psychology 64*, 467–78.

Phan, K. L., Wager, T., Taylor, S. F., and Liberzon, I. (2002). Functional neuroanatomy of emotion: A meta-analysis of emotion activation studies in pet and fmri. *Neuroimage 16*, 331–48.

Ramnani, N., and Owen, A. M. (2004). Anterior prefrontal cortex: Insights into function from anatomy and neuroimaging. *Nat Rev Neurosci 5*, 184–94.

Rawls, J. (1971). *A theory of justice* (Cambridge, MA, Harvard University Press).

Richerson, P. J., and Boyd, R. (2005). *Not by genes alone: How culture transformed human evolution* (Chicago, University of Chicago Press).

Sanfey, A. G., Rilling, J. K., Aronson, J. A., Nystrom, L. E., and Cohen, J. D. (2003). The neural basis of economic decision-making in the ultimatum game. *Science 300*, 1755–8.

Saxe, R., Carey, S., and Kanwisher, N. (2004). Understanding other minds: Liking developmental psychology and functional neuroimaging. *Annual Review of Psychology 55*, 87–124.

Singer, P. (1972). Famine, affluence and morality. *Philosophy and Public Affairs 1*, 229–43.

Small, D. A., and Loewenstein, G. (2003). Helping a victim or helping the victim. *Journal of Risk and Uncertainty 26*, 5–16.

Smith, A. (1976). *The theory of moral sentiments* (Oxford, England, Oxford University Press).

Sober, E., and Wilson, D. S. (1998). *Unto others: The evolution and psychology of unselfish behavior* (Cambridge, MA, Harvard University Press).

Stuss, D. T., Alexander, M. P., Lieberman, A., and Levine, H. (1978). An extraordinary form of confabulation. *Neurology 28*, 1166–72.

Thomson, J. J. (1986). *Rights, restitution, and risk: Essays, in moral theory* (Cambridge, MA, Harvard University Press).

Trivers, R. L. (1971). The evolution of reciprocal altruism. *Quarterly Review of Biology 46*, 35–57.

Unger, P. K. (1996). *Living high and letting die: Our illusion of innocence* (New York, NY, Oxford University Press).

Wilson, T. D. (2002). *Strangers to ourselves: Discovering the adaptive unconscious* (Cambridge, MA, Harvard University Press).

Wrangham, R., and Peterson, D. (1996). *Demonic males: Apes and the origins of human violence* (Boston, Houghton Mifflin).

39

Moral Intuitionism Meets Empirical Psychology

Walter Sinnott-Armstrong

. . . if this be all, where is his ethics? The position he is maintaining is merely a psychological one.
(Moore 1903: §11, 11)[1]

G. E. Moore's diatribe against the naturalistic fallacy in 1903 set the stage for most of twentieth-century moral philosophy. The main protagonists over the next sixty years were intuitionists and emotivists, both of whom were convinced by Moore that empirical science is irrelevant to moral philosophy and common moral beliefs. Even in the 1970s and 1980s, when a wider array of moral theories entered the scene and applied ethics became popular, few moral philosophers paid much attention to developments in biology and psychology.

This isolation must end. Moral philosophers cannot continue to ignore developments in psychology, brain science, and biology. Of course, philosophers need to be careful when they draw lessons from empirical research. As Moore and his followers argued, we should not jump straight from descriptive premises in psychology or biology to positive moral conclusions or normative conclusions in moral epistemology. That would be a fallacy.[2] Nonetheless, psychology can still affect moral philosophy in indirect ways. That

is what I want to illustrate here. I will trace an indirect path from empirical premises to a normative conclusion in moral epistemology. In particular, I will argue that some recent research in psychology and brain science undermines moral intuitionism.

1. What is Moral Intuitionism?

Some philosophers define moral intuitionism as the structural view that there are many moral values or requirements with no systematic unification or ranking. Other philosophers see moral intuitionism as the metaphysical view that moral properties are non-natural. Neither of these views concerns me here. I mention them only to set them aside.

The kind of moral intuitionism that is my target here is a position in moral epistemology, which is general epistemology applied to moral beliefs. The deepest challenge in moral epistemology, as in general epistemology, is raised by a skeptical regress argument: Someone is justified in believing something only if the believer has a reason that is expressible in an inference with premises that the believer is already justified in believing. This requires a chain of inferences that must continue infinitely, close into a circle, or

From Walter Sinnott-Armstrong (2006). Moral intuitionism meets empirical psychology. In T. Horgan and M. Timmons (eds.), *Metaethics After Moore* (Clarendon Press, Oxford, 2006), pp. 339–58, 362–5. Reprinted with permission of Oxford University Press.

stop arbitrarily. Academic skeptics reject all three options and conclude that there is no way for anyone to be justified in believing anything. The same regress arises for moral beliefs (cf. Sinnott-Armstrong 1996: 9–14; 2002a).

The simplest way to stop this regress is simply to stop. If a believer can work back to a premise that the believer is justified in believing without being able to infer that premise from anything else, then there is no new premise to justify, so the regress goes no further. That is how foundationalists stop the regress in general epistemology. Moral intuitionists apply foundationalism to moral beliefs as a way to stop the skeptical regress regarding moral beliefs.

The motivation behind moral intuitionism is not always to stop the skeptical regress,[3] but that use of moral intuitionism is common and is what concerns us here, so we can use it to decide among possible definitions of moral intuitionism. What we need to define is the weakest version of moral intuitionism that is strong enough to solve the regress problem that would lead to moral skepticism. Here it is:

Moral intuitionism is the claim that some people are adequately epistemically justified in holding some moral beliefs independently of whether those people are able to infer those moral beliefs from any other beliefs.[4]

Several features of this definition are worth highlighting.

So defined, moral intuitionism is not about knowledge. It is about justified belief. This makes it normative. Psychologists sometimes define intuitionism as a descriptive claim about the nature and origins of moral beliefs (see Haidt 2001). Such descriptive claims are not intended to stop the skeptical regress; so they do not concern me here.

More specifically, the defining claim of moral intuitionism is about what is *epistemically* justified because moral skeptics win if the only justification for holding moral beliefs is that those belief states have beneficial practical effects. Similarly, moral skeptics win if some moral beliefs are inadequately justified but none is *adequately* justified, that is, justified strongly enough that the believer ought to believe it as opposed to denying it or suspending belief.[5] Accordingly, I will henceforth use 'justified' as shorthand for 'adequately epistemically justified'.

To say that moral believers are justified independently of an inferential ability is just to say that they would be justified even if they lacked that ability, that is, even if they were not able to infer those beliefs from any other beliefs. This independence claim can hold even when moral believers are able to infer those moral beliefs from other beliefs as long as they do not need that inferential ability to be justified.[6] This notion of need will become prominent later.

I infer a belief when I go through a reasoning process of which the belief is the (or a) conclusion and other beliefs are premises. A believer is able to draw such an inference when the believer has enough information to go through a reasoning process that results in this belief if he had enough incentive and time to do so. This ability does not require self-consciousness or reflection about the beliefs or abilities. All that is needed, other than general intelligence, is for the requisite information to be encoded appropriately in the believer's brain at the time of belief.[7]

Some moral intuitionists claim only that certain moral beliefs are justified independently of any actual inference. However, that weak moral intuitionism is not enough to stop the skeptical regress. Even if whether certain moral beliefs are justified does not depend on any actual inference, it still might depend on the believer's ability to infer them from other beliefs. The ability to draw an inference cannot make a belief justified if beliefs in the inference's premises are not themselves justified. This requirement is enough to restart a skeptical regress. Thus, to meet the skeptical challenge, moral intuitionists must make the strong claim that some moral believers are adequately epistemically justified in holding some moral beliefs independently of any ability to infer the moral belief from any other belief.[8] So that's what they claim.

Although this claim is strong, it has many defenders. Rational intuitionists see basic moral beliefs as analogous to beliefs in mathematical axioms, which are taken to be justified independently of inference. Moral sense theorists assimilate particular moral beliefs to perceptual beliefs, which are supposed to be justified independently of inference. More recently, reliabilists hold that any belief is justified if it results from a reliable process, regardless of whether that process has anything to do with any inference. I group these views together under my broad definition of moral intuitionism because my arguments will apply to them all.

Under my definition, there are at least two ways to deny moral intuitionism. Moral intuitionists claim that some moral believers would be justified even if they did not have any ability to infer their moral beliefs from any other beliefs. Some opponents object that moral beliefs always depend on some inference or inferential ability. However, the evidence (cf. Haidt 2001) strongly suggests that people often have moral beliefs that do not result from any actual inference. It is harder to tell whether any moral beliefs are independent of any ability to infer. Nonetheless, I will grant for the sake of argument that some moral beliefs are spontaneous in the sense that they are independent of any inference or inferential ability.

Other opponents of moral intuitionism deny that moral believers are ever justified in holding such spontaneous moral beliefs if they lack certain inferential abilities. This conclusion follows if inferential abilities are always needed for a moral believer to be justified. That is what I will try to show.

2. When is Confirmation Needed?

We cannot answer this question directly. If a moral intuitionist baldly asserts that we do not need inferential abilities to back up our spontaneous moral beliefs, then this assertion begs the question. Similarly, if a critic of moral intuitionism baldly asserts that we do need inferential abilities to back up our spontaneous moral beliefs, then this assertion also begs the question. Neither side can win so easily. We need a less direct method.

One alternative uses analogies to non-moral beliefs. This path is fraught with peril, but it might be the only way to go. What this approach does is appeal to non-moral cases to develop principles of epistemic need and then later apply those principles back to moral beliefs. Let's try it.

I will formulate my principles in terms of when confirmation is needed, but they do not claim that the believer needs to go through any process of confirming the belief. The point, instead, is only that some confirmation needs to be available at least implicitly as information stored somehow in the believer that gives the believer an ability to infer the belief from some other beliefs.[9] The question is when some such confirmation is needed in non-moral cases.

Suppose that I listen to my daughter in a piano competition. I judge that she played great and her rival was mediocre. Am I justified in trusting my judgment? Not if all I can say is, 'Her performance sounded better to me.' I am too biased for such immediate reactions alone to count as evidence. I still might be justified, if I am able to specify laudable features of her performance, or if I know that others agree, but some confirmation seems needed. Generalizing,

Principle 1: confirmation is needed for a believer to be justified when the believer is partial.

This principle also applies to direct perceptual judgments, such as when I believe that my daughter played middle C at just the right time in the midst of her piece. This partly explains why we prefer umpires, referees, and judges not to be parents of competitors. Even reliabilists can admit this principle because partiality often creates unreliability.

Second, imagine that each of us adds a column of figures, and I get one sum, but you get a different sum. Maybe I would be justified in believing that I am right if you were my child and I was helping you with your homework. However, if you are just as good at arithmetic as I am, then, when we get different answers, we need to check again to find out who made a mistake before either of us can be justified in believing that his or her answer is the correct one. We owe each other that much epistemic respect. The best explanation of this natural reaction seems to be

Principle 2: confirmation is needed for a believer to be justified when people disagree with no independent reason to prefer one belief or believer to the other.

This principle also applies when the person on the sidewalk looks like Tom Cruise to me but not to you. If I have no reason to believe that I am better than you at this identification, then I am not justified in believing that your belief is incorrect or that mine is correct.

A third principle concerns emotions. When people get very angry, for example, they tend to overlook relevant facts. They often do not notice excuses or apologies by the person who made them angry. We should not generalize to all emotions, but we can still endorse something like this:

Principle 3: confirmation is needed for a believer to be justified when the believer is emotional in a way that clouds judgment.

This explains why jurors are dismissed from a case that would make them too emotional. This principle applies even if their emotions do not bias them towards either side, so it is distinct from Principle 1, regarding partiality.

Next consider illusions. At least three kinds are relevant here. First, some illusions are due to context. Objects look larger when they are next to smaller objects, and they look smaller when they are next to larger objects. Since our estimates of their sizes are affected by their surroundings, we are not justified in trusting our estimates until we check their sizes in other circumstances or by other methods.

A second group of illusions arises from generalizations. For example, an oval that is shaded on top looks concave, but an oval that is shaded on the bottom looks convex. The explanation seems to be that our cognitive apparatus evolved in circumstances where the light usually came from above, which would produce a shadow on the top of a concave oval (such as a cave opening) and on the bottom of a convex oval (such as an egg). Since we often overextend generalizations like this, we are not justified in trusting beliefs that depend on such generalizations until we check to determine whether our circumstances are exceptional.

The third kind of illusion involves heuristics, which are quick and simple decision procedures. In a passage with a thousand words, how many seven-letter words have the form '_ _ _ _ in _'? How many seven-letter words have the form '_ _ _ _ ing'? Most people estimate more words have the latter form, although that is impossible, since every word of the form '_ _ _ _ ing' also has the form '_ _ _ _ in _'. Why do people make this simple mistake? They seem to test how likely something is by trying to imagine examples and guessing high if they easily think of lots of examples. This is called the availability heuristic (Kahneman *et al.* 1982). Most people easily produce words that end in 'ing', but they have more trouble coming up with words that end in 'in _' because they do not think of putting 'g' in the last place. In cases like this, the availability heuristic is misleading. Accordingly, they do not seem

adequately epistemically justified in trusting beliefs based on such heuristics until they check on whether they are in circumstances where the heuristics work.

This quick survey of three common kinds of illusion suggests

Principle 4: confirmation is needed for a believer to be justified when the circumstances are conducive to illusion.

This principle would apply as well to many other kinds of illusions.

A fifth and final principle considers the source of a belief. If you believe that George Washington never told a lie, and if this belief comes from a legend spread by Washington's allies to gain power, then you are not justified in believing the legend, though it still might be true. Even if you believe only that Washington was unusually honest, this belief might be a lingering effect of this childhood story, and then its origin makes this belief need confirmation. The point can be generalized into something like

Principle 5: confirmation is needed for a believer to be justified when the belief arises from an unreliable or disreputable source.

This principle also explains why we do not view people as justified in beliefs based only on prejudice and stereotypes.

These five principles, although distinct, complement each other. When a belief is partial, controversial, emotional, subject to illusion, and explicable by dubious sources, then all of these principles apply. In such cases, they work together to make it even clearer that confirmation is needed for justified belief. Even if not all of these principles apply, the more that do apply, the clearer it will be that there is more need for more confirmation. We might think of this as a sixth principle.

I do not claim that these principles are precise or that my list is complete.[10] What I do claim is that these principles or some close relatives seem plausible to most people and are assumed in our shared epistemic practices. I also claim that they make sense because they pick out features that are correlated with reliability and other epistemic values.

Most importantly, I claim that these principles apply in all areas of belief. My illustrations include beliefs about arithmetic, language, history, identity, value, sound, size, and shape, but the same principles apply in scientific research, religion, and so on. The main question here is whether they apply to moral beliefs. Admittedly, morality might be a special case where these principles do not apply. However, unless someone can point to a relevant difference between these other areas and moral beliefs, it seems only fair to apply these same standards to moral beliefs when asking whether moral beliefs are justified. So that's what I will do.

3. When are Moral Beliefs Justified?

Some of these principles can be applied only with the help of empirical research. Others are easier to apply. Let's start with the easy ones.

Partiality

Principle 1 says that partiality adds a need for confirmation. But what is partiality? A judge is often called partial when the judge's self-interest is affected by the outcome of the case. However, if the judge's self interest does not influence the judge's decision, so the judge would have made the same decision if the judge's self-interest had not been involved, then it is natural to say that the judge's decision is not partial, even if the judge is partial. Analogously, believers can be called partial whenever their beliefs affect their self-interest either directly or indirectly (by affecting the interests of people whom they care about). Beliefs are then partial only when the believer's self-interest influences whether the believer holds that belief. Thus, a partial believer can hold an impartial belief (or can hold it impartially) if the believer has an interest in holding the belief, but that interest does not influence whether the believer holds that belief.

Partiality of a belief can't be all that triggers Principle 1. To see why, recall the examples that motivated Principle 1. Because I am biased in favor of my daughter, even after watching her play in the piano competition, I need confirmation to be justified in believing that my daughter played better than her rival. Maybe my interest in her

victory did not influence my assessment, but the danger of such influence is enough to create a need for confirmation. Admittedly, if I can rule out such influence, then I can be justified in believing that my daughter played better, but the only way to rule out such influence involves independent confirmation. Thus, confirmation seems needed when the believer is partial, even if the believer is not actually influenced by that partiality, so the belief is not partial. Since confirmation is also needed when the belief is partial, Principle 1 requires confirmation when either the believer or the belief is partial.

To apply this principle to moral beliefs, we need to determine whether moral beliefs affect our self-interest either directly or indirectly. The answer seems clear: Moral beliefs affect us all. It can be very expensive to believe that we are morally required to help the needy, but it can be even more expensive if others do not believe that they are morally required to help us when we are in need. It can also cost a lot to believe that we have to tell the truth or to keep a promise. And all of us know or should know that, if killing, stealing, lying, cheating, and promise-breaking were generally seen as morally permitted, then we would be more likely to get hurt by others doing such acts. Life would be more 'solitary, poor, nasty, brutish, and short', as Hobbes put it. Moreover, if an individual did not see such acts as immoral, then he or she would be more likely to do them and then to be punished in various ways – 'if not by law, by the opinion of his fellow creatures', as Mill said. Special interests also arise in special cases: Women and men know or should know that, if abortion is not seen as morally permissible, then they, their friends, or their daughters will be more likely to suffer more. Moral beliefs about affirmative action affect the interests of the preferred groups and also the non-preferred groups. And so on. Indeed, on many views, what makes an issue moral in nature is that interests are significantly affected by the judged actions. Since moral beliefs about actions affect those actions, our moral beliefs themselves affect our interests at least indirectly. Finally, social groups often form around and then solidify moral beliefs (cf. Chen and Tetlock et al. as discussed in Haidt 2001). People who believe that homosexuality is immoral find it harder to get along with homosexuals and easier to get along with homophobes. Conversely, people who believe that homosexuality is not immoral find it harder to get along with homophobes and easier to get along with homosexuals. Some might try to fake moral beliefs in order to get along, but few of us are good enough actors, and those who believe that homosexuality is immoral usually also believe that they ought not to pretend otherwise in order to get along with homosexuals. Thus, our moral beliefs affect our social options as well as our actions.

Many moral beliefs might seem to have no effect on us. If I believe that it was immoral for Brutus to stab Caesar, this moral belief by itself will not change my social options or rule out any acts that I could do today. Still, given universalizability, my judgment of Brutus seems to depend on a principle that does apply in other cases where my self-interest is involved more directly. Arguments from analogy also might force me to take a moral stand that affects my interests. Thus, any moral belief can affect my self-interest indirectly.

Because our moral beliefs affect our self-interest so often in so many ways at least indirectly, we cannot be justified in assuming that any of us is ever fully impartial as a moral believer. Even if our self-interest is not involved in some exceptional case, we still need a reason to believe that our self-interest is not affected in that case, since we know or should know that such effects are very common and often hidden. The facts that partiality is so common in this area and so difficult to detect in ourselves are what create a need for confirmation of all moral beliefs, according to Principle 1.

Disagreement

Principle 2 says that disagreement creates a need for confirmation. Many people seem to think that this principle is easy to apply to moral beliefs because moral disagreement is pervasive. In their view, people from different cultures, time periods, social classes, and genders disagree about a wide variety of particular moral judgments and general moral principles.

Actually, the extent of moral disagreement is not obvious. One reason is that people who seem to disagree are often judging different actions or using different concepts. Also, many apparently moral disagreements are really factual, since those who seem to disagree morally would agree in their moral judgments if they agreed about the facts.

Still, straightening out concepts and non-moral facts seems unlikely to resolve all apparently moral disagreements. One reason is that people often express different moral beliefs about hypothetical cases where all of the facts are stipulated, so these moral believers seem to accept the same non-moral facts. Admittedly, descriptions of these situations usually leave out important facts, and moral believers might interpret the hypothetical cases in light of different background beliefs. But there still seem to be lots of cases where all relevant non-moral facts are agreed upon without leading to agreement in moral belief.

This claim is supported by a study in which Jana Schaich Borg and I surveyed fifty-two undergraduates at Dartmouth College, using thirty-six scenarios, including the well-known side-track and fat-man trolley cases. In both cases, five people tied to a track will be killed by a runaway trolley if you do nothing, and the only way to save the five is to kill one other person.[11] In the side-track version, you can save the five only by pulling a lever to divert the trolley onto a side-track where it will run over one victim. In the fat-man variation, you can save the five only by pushing a fat man in front of the trolley so that his body will stop the trolley before it hits the five. In two rounds, 35 per cent then 43 per cent of our subjects said that it would be wrong to divert the trolley onto the side-track. When the same scenario was described with more vivid language, 61 per cent then 45 per cent judged diversion wrong in the two rounds. In contrast, 76 per cent in the first round then 88 per cent in the second round judged it wrong to push the fat man. (Interestingly, there were still 35 per cent in the first round and 18 per cent in the second round who said that they would push the fat man.) These percentages did not change much with more vivid language. Thus, we found significant disagreement about the very cases that philosophers often cite to support their theories.[12]

There is, admittedly, more agreement about other cases: Would it be wrong to push the fat man in front of the trolley just because you are angry at him for beating you at golf when killing him will not save or help anyone else? I hope and expect that 100 per cent would answer, 'Yes.' But what would that show? The universality of moral beliefs about cases like this one could hardly be used to justify any moral theory or any controversial moral belief.[13] Such cases cannot get moral intuitionists all that they seem to want.[14]

Moral intuitionists might respond that all they claim is that *some* moral beliefs are non-inferentially justified. One case seems enough to establish that claim. However, the fact that there is so much disagreement in other cases affects the epistemology of cases where there is no disagreement. Compare a box with one hundred thermometers. We know that many of them don't work, but we are not sure how many. If we pick one thermometer arbitrarily from the box, and it reads 77 degrees, then we are not justified in believing that the temperature really is 77 degrees, even if we were in fact lucky enough to pick a thermometer that works. Of course, if we confirm that this thermometer works, such as by testing it against other thermometers, then we can use it to form justified beliefs, but we cannot be justified in trusting it before we confirm that it works.[15] Similarly, if we know that many moral intuitions are unreliable because others hold conflicting intuitions, then we are not justified in trusting a particular moral intuition without some reason to believe that it is one of the reliable ones. If we know that everyone agrees with that particular moral intuition, then we might have reason to trust it. But that is just because the known agreement provides confirmation, so it does not undermine the point that some confirmation is needed, as Principle 2 claims.

Emotion

Next consider Principle 3, which says that emotions that cloud judgment create a need for confirmation. It is hard to tell whether this principle applies to moral beliefs. Philosophers and others have argued for millennia about whether moral beliefs are based on emotion or on reason. They also argue about which emotions, if any, cloud judgment. How can we resolve these debates? Luckily, some recent empirical studies suggest an answer.

Haidt and his group have been accumulating an impressive body of behavioral evidence for what they call the social intuitionist model:

This model suggests that moral judgment is much like aesthetic judgment: we see an action or hear a story and we have an instant feeling of approval or disapproval. These feelings are best thought of as affect-laden intuitions, as they appear suddenly and effortlessly in consciousness, with an affective valence (good or bad), but without any feeling of having gone through any steps of searching, weighing evidence or inferring a conclusion. (Greene and Haidt 2002: 517)[16]

Haidt's behavioral evidence dovetails nicely with independent brain studies. Moll's group found that brain tissue associated with emotions becomes more activated when subjects think about simple sentences with moral content (e.g. 'They hung an innocent') than when they think about similar sentences without moral content (e.g. 'Stones are made of water') (Moll *et al.* 2001) or disgusting non-moral sentences (e.g. 'He licked the dirty toilet') (Moll *et al.* 2002a).[17] Similar results were found with pictures in place of sentences (Moll *et al.* 2002b).

Studies by Joshua Greene and his colleagues are even more fascinating because they distinguish kinds of moral beliefs (2001).[18] Greene's group scanned brains of subjects while they considered what was appropriate in three kinds of dilemmas: non-moral dilemmas, personal moral dilemmas, and impersonal moral dilemmas. A moral dilemma is personal if and only if one of its options is likely to cause serious harm to a particular person other than by deflecting an existing threat onto a different party (Greene and Haidt 2002: 519). A standard personal moral dilemma is the fat-man trolley case. A paradigm impersonal moral dilemma is the side-track trolley case. These different moral cases stimulated different parts of the brain. While considering appropriate action in impersonal dilemmas, subjects showed significant activation in brain areas associated with working memory but no significant activation in areas associated with emotion. In contrast, while considering appropriate action in personal dilemmas, subjects showed significant activation in brain areas associated with emotion and under-activation (below the resting baseline) in areas associated with working memory. It is not obvious what to make of these results. Brain scientists do not know how to interpret under-activation in general. Nonetheless, one natural speculation is this: When asked about pushing the fat man, subjects react, 'That's so horrible that I can't even think about it.' Emotions stop subjects from considering the many factors in these examples. If this interpretation is correct, then many pervasive and fundamental moral beliefs result from emotions that cloud judgment.[19]

Some moral intuitionists might argue that there is no need to consider anything else when the proposed action is the intentional killing of an innocent fat man. It might even be counterproductive to consider additional factors, since they might lead one away from the correct belief. Such responses, however, assume that it is morally wrong to push the fat man, so they beg the question here. When asking whether a moral belief is justified, we should not assume that the only relevant factors are those that would be relevant if the belief were true. Ridiculous moral beliefs could be defended if that method worked.

Still, moral intuitionism is hardly refuted by these experiments because Greene's results must be replicated and interpreted much more carefully. (Some initial replication can be found in Greene 2004.) All I can say now is that such brain studies seem to provide some evidence that many moral judgments result from emotions that cloud judgment.

Additional evidence comes from Wheatley and Haidt (2005). They gave participants the post-hypnotic suggestion that they would feel a pang of disgust whenever they saw either the word 'take' or the word 'often'. Participants were later asked to make moral judgments about six stories designed to elicit mild to moderate disgust. When a story contained the word that elicited disgust in a participant, that participant was more likely to express stronger moral condemnation of acts in the story. Moral judgments were then affected by elements of the story that could not determine the accuracy or acceptability of those moral judgments. In that sense, emotions clouded their judgment. Because independently caused emotions can distort moral beliefs in such ways, moral believers need confirmation in order to be justified in holding their moral beliefs.

Illusions

To apply Principle 4 to moral beliefs, we again need empirical research, but this time in cognitive science rather than brain science. I mentioned three kinds of illusions that should be considered separately.

The first kind of illusion occurs when appearances and beliefs depend on context. An interesting recent example comes from Peter Unger, who found that the order in which options are presented affects beliefs about whether a given option is morally wrong. He also claims that people's moral beliefs about a certain option depend on whether that option is presented as part of a pair or, instead, as part of a series that includes additional options intermediate between the original pair (Unger 1996: 88–94).[20] Since order and intermediate options are not morally relevant factors that could affect the moral wrongness of the judged option, the fact that moral beliefs are affected by these factors shows that moral beliefs are unreliable in such cases. That is why confirmation is needed. One still might confirm one's moral belief by reconsidering the issue in several contexts over time to see whether one's moral belief remains stable, but that is just a way of seeking confirmation, so it does not undermine my point that confirmation is needed.

The second kind of illusion arises from overgeneralization. Such illusions also affect moral beliefs. Jonathan Baron even argues that all 'nonconsequentialist principles arise from overgeneralizing rules that are consistent with consequentialism in a limited set of cases' (1994: 1). But one need not accept consequentialism in order to admit that many people condemn defensible lying, harming, and love-making because they apply generalizations to exceptional cases. We probably disagree about which moral beliefs are overgeneralizations, but we should agree that many people overgeneralize in ways that create illusions of moral wrongness. In any such case, the moral believer could argue that this case is not an exception to the generalization, but, as before, that is just a way of seeking confirmation, so it does not undermine my point that this kind of illusion creates a need for confirmation.

Heuristics, which are quick and simple decision procedures, also create illusions in morality. One reason is that many moral beliefs depend on consequences and probabilities, for which we often lack adequate evidence, and then we have to guess these probabilities. Such guesses are notoriously distorted by the availability heuristic, the representative heuristic, and so on.[21] Even when moral beliefs do not depend on probability assessments, moral beliefs are affected by the so-called 'I agree with people I like' heuristic (cf. Chaiken and Lord, Ross, and Lepper as discussed by Haidt 2001). When people whom we like express moral beliefs, we tend to go along and form the same belief. When people whom we dislike oppose our moral beliefs, we tend to hold on to them in spite of contrary arguments. This heuristic often works fine, but it fails in enough cases to create a need for confirmation.

In addition to these three kinds of illusions, moral beliefs also seem subject to framing effects, which were explored by Kahneman and Tversky (1979). In one famous experiment, they asked some subjects this question:

> Imagine that the US is preparing for an outbreak of an unusual Asian disease which is expected to kill 600 people. Two alternative programs to fight the disease, A and B, have been proposed. Assume that the exact scientific estimates of the consequences of the programs are as follows: If program A is adopted, 200 people will be saved. If program B is adopted, there is a 1/3 probability that 600 people will be saved, and a 2/3 probability that no people will be saved. Which program would you choose?

The same story was told to a second group of subjects, but these subjects had to choose between these programs:

> If program C is adopted, 400 people will die. If program D is adopted, there is a 1/3 probability that nobody will die and a 2/3 probability that 600 will die.

It should be obvious that programs A and C are equivalent, as are programs B and D. However, most subjects who chose between A and B favored A, but most subjects who chose between C and D favored D. More generally, subjects were risk averse when results were described in positive terms (such as 'lives saved') but risk seeking when results were described in negative terms (such as 'lives lost' or 'people who die').

The question in this experiment was about choices rather than moral wrongness. Still, the subjects were not told how the policies affect them personally, so their choices seem to result from beliefs about which program is morally right or wrong. If so, the subjects had different moral beliefs about programs A and C and about programs B and D. The only difference within each pair is how the programs are framed or described. Thus, descriptions seem to affect moral beliefs. Descriptions cannot affect what is really morally right or wrong. Hence, these results suggest that such moral beliefs are unreliable.

Moral intuitionists could claim that moral intuitions are still reliable when subjects have consistent beliefs after considering all relevant descriptions. But then moral believers would need to know that their beliefs are consistent and that they are aware of all relevant descriptions before they could be justified in holding moral beliefs. Framing effects distort moral beliefs in so many cases that moral believers need confirmation for any particular moral belief.

To see how deeply this point cuts, consider Warren Quinn's argument for the traditional doctrine of doing and allowing, which claims that stronger moral justification is needed for killing than for letting die. In support of this general doctrine, Quinn appeals to moral intuitions of specific cases:

> In Rescue I, we can save either five people in danger of drowning at one place or a single person in danger of drowning somewhere else. We cannot save all six. In Rescue II, we can save the five only by driving over and thereby killing someone who (for an unspecified reason) is trapped on the road. If we do not undertake the rescue, the trapped person can later be freed. (1993: 152)

Most people judge that saving the five is morally wrong in Rescue II but not in Rescue I. Why do they react this way? Quinn assumes that these different intuitions result from the difference between killing and letting die or, more generally, doing and allowing harm. However, Tamara Horowitz uses a different distinction (between gains and losses) and a different theory (prospect theory) to develop an alternative explanation of Quinn's moral intuitions:

> In deciding whether to kill the person or leave the person alone, one thinks of the person's being alive as the status quo and chooses this as the

neutral outcome. Killing the person is regarded as a negative deviation. . . . But in deciding to save a person who would otherwise die, the person being dead is the status quo and is selected as the neutral outcome. So saving the person is a positive deviation. . . . (1998: 153)

The point is that we tend to reject options that cause definite negative deviations from the status quo. That explains why subjects rejected program C but did not reject program A in the Asian disease case (despite the equivalence between those programs). It also explains why we think that it is morally wrong to 'kill' in Rescue II but is not morally wrong to 'not save' in Rescue I, since killing causes a definite negative deviation from the status quo. This explanation clearly hinges on what is taken to be the status quo, which in turn depends on how the options are described. Quinn's story about Rescue I describes the people as already 'in danger of drowning', whereas the trapped person in Rescue II can 'later be freed' if not for our 'killing' him. These descriptions affect our choice of the neutral starting point. As in the Asian disease cases, our choice of the neutral starting point then affects our moral intuitions. Horowitz adds, 'I do not see why anyone would think the distinction [that explains our reactions to Quinn's rescue cases] is morally significant, but perhaps there is some argument I have not thought of. If the distinction is not morally significant, then Quinn's thought experiments do not support one moral theory over against another' (1998: 155).

Admittedly, Horowitz's explanation does not imply that Quinn's moral intuitions are false or incoherent, as in the Asian disease case. It does not even establish that his moral intuitions are arbitrary. As Mark van Roojen says, 'Nothing in the example shows anything wrong with treating losses from a neutral baseline differently from gains. Such reasoning might well be appropriate where framing proceeds in a reasonable manner' (1999).[22] Nonetheless, the framing also 'might well' *not* be reasonable, so the epistemological dilemma remains: If there is no reason to choose one baseline over the other, then our moral intuitions seem arbitrary and unjustified. If there is a reason to choose one baseline over the other, then either we have access to that reason or we do not. If we have access to the reason, then we are able

to draw an inference from that reason to justify our moral belief. If we do not have access to that reason, then we do not seem justified in our moral belief. Because framing effects so often lead to incoherence and error, we cannot be justified in trusting a moral intuition that relies on framing effects unless we at least can be aware that this intuition is one where the baseline is reasonable. So Horowitz's explanation creates serious trouble for moral intuitionism whenever framing effects could explain our moral intuitions.

The doctrine of doing and allowing is not an isolated case. It affects many prominent issues and is strongly believed by many philosophers and common people, who do not seem to be able to infer it from any other beliefs. If moral intuitions are unjustified in this case, doubts should arise about a wide range of other moral intuitions as well.

Origins

Some previous principles look at origins of individual moral beliefs, but Principle 5 considers the social origins of shared moral beliefs. The two issues are related insofar as many of our moral beliefs result from training and social interaction.

Specifically, Principle 5 claims that problematic social origins create a need for confirmation. To apply this principle, we need to ask whether moral beliefs have problematic social origins. The social origins of moral beliefs might be problematic in two ways. First, moral beliefs might be caused by factors that are unrelated with the truth of those beliefs. Second, the origins of moral beliefs might be immoral according to those moral beliefs. I will focus on the latter case.

Are the origins of our moral intuitions immoral by their own lights? Friedrich Nietzsche suggests as much when he argues that Christian morality results from slaves cleverly overcoming their superiors by re-evaluating values. Insofar as Christian morality condemns such subterfuge and self-promotion, Christian morality condemns its own origins, if Nietzsche is correct (Nietzsche 1966).[23] Similarly, Michel Foucault argues at length that moral beliefs express or result from social power relations. Yet these moral beliefs themselves seem to condemn the very kind of power that leads to these beliefs. But I don't want to rely on Nietzsche or Foucault, at least not in this context, so I will consider Gilbert Harman's explanation of the common moral belief that harming someone is much worse than failing to helping someone in need:

> whereas everyone would benefit equally from a conventional practice of trying not to harm each other, some people would benefit considerably more than others from a convention to help those who needed help. The rich and powerful do not need much help and are often in the best position to give it; so, if a strong principle of mutual aid were adopted, they would gain little and lose a great deal, because they would end up doing most of the helping and would receive little in return. On the other hand, the poor and the weak might refuse to agree to a principle of non-interference or non-injury unless they also reached some agreement on mutual aid. We would therefore expect a compromise [that] would involve a strong principle of non-injury and a weaker principle of mutual aid – which is just what we now have. (1977: 110; cf. Scheffler 1982: 113)

Remember also that rich and powerful people have always controlled the church, the media, and culture, which in turn affect most people's moral beliefs. In this context, Harman's claim is that the self-interest of the rich and powerful in making everyone believe that harming is worse than failing to help can explain why so many people believe that harming is worse than failing to help. But our moral beliefs also seem to condemn such self-serving indoctrination by the rich and powerful, since morality is supposed to consider everyone's interests equally. Thus, if Harman is correct, morality condemns its own origins, as Nietzsche and Foucault claimed.

The point is not that such moral views are internally inconsistent, self-condemning, or even self-defeating. The point is only that there are grounds for doubt when beliefs come from disreputable sources. Defenders of such moral beliefs must admit that the sources of their beliefs are disreputable if Harman's explanation is accurate. Then they need additional support for their beliefs beyond the mere fact that those beliefs seem correct to them.

These speculations about the origins of moral beliefs are mere armchair psychology. Perhaps more support could be obtained from the literature on sociobiology or evolutionary psychology.

Still, these explanations are likely to remain very controversial. Luckily, I don't need to prove them here. I claim only that these undermining accounts are live possibilities. They seem plausible to many people and have not been refuted.

That would not be enough if I were arguing for the falsehood of a certain moral belief, such as Christian morality (from Nietzsche) or the prevalence of non-injury over mutual aid (from Harman). However, I am not drawing any substantive moral conclusion. To do so would commit a genetic fallacy, but my argument is different. My point lies in moral epistemology, and I reach it indirectly. If these disreputable origins are live possibilities, then moral believers need some independent confirmation that their beliefs are not distorted by such disreputable origins. This need for independent confirmation then undermines moral intuitionism.

Togetherness

Don't forget that Principles 1–5 complement each other. If I am right, moral beliefs are partial, controversial, emotional, subject to illusion, and explicable by dubious sources, so all of the principles apply. However, even if not all but only several of them apply, these principles still work together to make it clear that confirmation is needed for justified moral belief. That undermines moral intuitionism. It also shows how empirical research can be indirectly relevant to normative moral epistemology.

[. . .]

Some

Many opponents object that, even if Principles 1–5 apply to some moral beliefs, they do not apply to all moral beliefs. As I admitted, some moral beliefs are not controversial. For example, almost everyone (except moral nihilists) agrees that it is morally wrong to push the fat man in front of the trolley just because you are angry with him for beating you in a game. Such cases also do not seem due to context, heuristics, overgeneralization, or framing effects. Still, such moral believers are partial and emotional (as Greene's experiments suggested). So Principles 1 and 3 do seem to create a need for confirmation even in such clear cases.

Furthermore, if very many moral beliefs need confirmation, the others cannot be immune from this need. To see why, compare a country with lots of barn façades that look just like real barns when viewed from the road (Goldman 1976). If someone looks only from the road, then he is not justified in believing that what he sees is a real barn, at least if he should know about the barn façades. The barn façades are analogous to situations that produce distorted moral beliefs. Since such distortions are so common, morality is a land of fake barns. In such areas, confirmation is needed for each justified belief, even for those beliefs formed in front of real barns. Analogously, confirmation is needed for each spontaneous moral belief, even when the common distorting factors are absent. We need to get off the road and look closer. At least when we should know that moral beliefs in general are so often subject to distortion, we cannot be justified in trusting any moral belief until we confirm that it is an exception to the rule that most moral beliefs are problematic. So moral intuitionists cannot claim that any moral believers are justified without confirmation.

This point can be presented as a dilemma: If a moral believer is an educated modern adult, then she should know that many moral beliefs are problematic in the ways indicated by Principles 1–5. She either knows or does not know that her moral belief is an exception to the trend. If she does not know this, she should accept a significant probability that her belief is problematic. Then she cannot be justified without confirmation. Alternatively, if she does know that her moral belief is exceptionally reliable, then she has enough information to draw an inference like this: My moral belief is exceptionally reliable. Exceptionally reliable beliefs are probably true. Therefore, my belief is (probably) true. If this moral believer does not have the information in these premises, then it is hard to see why we should call her justified. So, either way, moral intuitionism fails.

Skepticism

A common objection is that my argument leads to general skepticism, since every inference has premises, so the demand for an inference cannot always be met. However, my argument does not generalize so easily. If my belief that a pen is in front of me is not subject to disagreement or illusions and has no disreputable sources, and if I am neither partial nor emotional about pens, then I might be justified in holding that non-moral belief without being able to support it with any inference. Thus, my argument against moral intuitionism does not lead to general skepticism.

My argument still might seem to lead to moral skepticism. If so, and if moral skepticism is unacceptable, then something must be wrong with my argument. However, my argument does not by itself lead to moral skepticism. My thesis is not that spontaneous moral beliefs are not justified, but only that they are not justified non-inferentially because they need confirmation. Such confirmation still might be possible somehow. Even if moral intuitionism is rejected, there are other non-skeptical methods in moral epistemology, including coherentism, contractarianism, contractualism, contextualism, and naturalism (Sinnott-Armstrong 1996: 31–41). Moral skepticism arises only after all of these other approaches fall. So my argument does not by itself support moral skepticism.

Besides, even if these other approaches also fail, so my argument plays a role in a larger argument for moral skepticism, that does not show that anything is wrong with my argument, unless one assumes that moral skepticism is unacceptable. Why assume that? I accept a limited Pyrrhonian version of moral skepticism. So I, at least, will not be dismayed if my argument takes one step in that direction.[24]

Anyway, my goal here has not been to argue for moral skepticism. My goal has been to argue against moral intuitionism. More generally, I tried to show one way in which empirical research in psychology and brain science might be relevant to normative moral epistemology. If I succeeded in that enterprise, I will happily leave moral skepticism for another occasion.

Notes

[1]   Here Moore was discussing the claim that the object of desire is not pleasure, but his charge against naturalism extended much further.

2   Although some such arguments are formally valid. See my 2000: 159–74. I add the qualification 'positive' because 'Bertie and Madeleine are dead' might entail 'It is not the case that Bertie ought to marry Madeleine.'

3   As George Pappas reminded me, part of foundationalism can be separated from the denial of skepticism. Foundationalists can be skeptics if foundationalism claims only that a believer is justified in a belief only if the belief is either non-inferentially justified or inferable from non-inferentially justified beliefs. Non-skeptical foundationalists merely add that some beliefs are justified. Analogously, moral intuitionism could be seen as a claim about the structure of justification separate from any denial of skepticism. Nonetheless. I will define moral intuitionism to include the denial of moral skepticism because almost all actual moral intuitionists do deny skepticism and because I am concerned with whether moral intuitionism can succeed as a response to skepticism.

4   Although I define moral intuitionism in terms of 'some' believers and 'some' moral beliefs, all actual moral intuitionists claim that a significant group of believers and beliefs can be justified non-inferentially. It also might seem odd that a theory counts as moral intuitionism on my definition if it holds that some beliefs based on testimony are justified independently of any inference or inferential ability. However, my arguments will apply to such views, so I see no pressing need to complicate my definition so as to avoid these problems.

5   I will discuss pro tanto justifiedness in responses to objections below. For more detail on kinds of justifiedness, see my 2002b: 17–25.

6   Compare Ross 1930: 29: 'without any need of proof'. (Since not all inferences are proofs, and Ross does not mention abilities, he might not deny the need for an inferential ability.) Contrast Moore (1903: 77), who sees moral intuitions as unprovable. Moore's stronger claim is not needed to stop the skeptical regress. Notice also that opponents of moral intuitionism, who claim that an inferential ability is *necessary*, do not have to claim that any inferential ability is *sufficient* to make any moral belief justified. At least the moral belief must also be *based on* the inferential ability. Other necessary conditions might also have to be met. Opponents of moral intuitionism can hold that an inferential ability is needed without specifying what, if anything, else is needed and, so, without specifying what is sufficient for justified moral belief.

7   The relevant notion of ability, then, is not the same as when I am able to become justified in believing that there are ten coins in my pocket because I could take them out of my pocket and count them. To have an ability of the relevant kind, I must be able to infer the belief from other beliefs that I already have without gaining any new information. I hope that it is also clear that, when I write about needing 'an inferential ability', I am not referring to a general ability to draw just any old inference, or any inference of a certain form. What is at issue is the ability to infer the specific moral belief from other beliefs.

8   The stronger claim is also needed for moral intuitionism to contrast with its traditional opponent, moral coherentism, since coherentists do not claim that believers must actually draw inferences in order to be justified.

9   Confirmation need not always be evidence, since I want confirmation to include defeater defeaters, that is, reasons to discount what would otherwise keep a belief from being justified.

10   One additional principle might claim that confirmation is needed when errors are costly. This principle applies to moral beliefs insofar as moral errors are costly.

11   These cases originate from Foot 1967. If such cases seem unrealistic, see the real case at www.cnn.com/2003/US/West/06/21/train.derail.ap/index.html.

12   For more evidence of disagreement, see Haidt *et al.* 1993.

13   Compare Descartes's 'I think,' which is nowhere near enough to ground science. Notice also that I am talking about actual moral beliefs, not possible moral beliefs. There might be an infinite number of possible moral beliefs that would garner agreement from everyone who understands them. However, there still might be a high rate of disagreement among the actual moral beliefs that people bother to form. That is what matters when we ask whether our actual moral beliefs are justified.

14   Some intuitionists might claim agreement on qualified general principles, such as that it is morally wrong to kill anyone in a protected class without an adequate reason. Of course, those who accept this formula still disagree about which class is protected and which reasons are adequate. Similarly, although many people (today!) agree that all moral agents deserve respect, different people count different acts as violating that rule by showing disrespect. It is not clear whether to count agreement on such indeterminate formulas as real moral agreement. See Snare 1980.

15   According to Bayesians, if the temperature feels to us as if it is about 70 degrees, so we start with that assumption, then the fact that this thermometer reads 77 degrees should make us move our estimate towards 77 degrees. How much our estimate should increase depends on our prior assumption about

how many thermometers work. This might make it seem as if the thermometer reading can lead to justified belief. However, if our initial estimates (about temperature and the percentage of working thermometers) are unjustified, then I doubt that one reading can ground justified belief. Besides, many of us do not form any of the initial estimates that are needed to start Bayesian reasoning.

[16] See also Haidt 2001. Of course, many other judgments cause emotional reactions 'suddenly and effortlessly'. But Haidt argues that emotions drive or constitute moral judgments rather than being effects of those judgments.

[17] It would be interesting to test reactions to negations, such as 'They did not hang an innocent' and 'He did not lick the dirty toilet.'

[18] This article also reports timing studies that confirm the different roles of emotion in different moral beliefs.

[19] Philosophers should notice that what Greene calls 'personal dilemmas' include most proposed counterexamples to consequentialism. If those intuitions are unjustified, then Greene's study might help consequentialists defend their moral theory, even if other intuitions are not affected.

[20] Unfortunately, Unger does not describe the method or precise results of his informal survey, so there is room for more careful empirical work to test his claims. Some philosophical support comes from moral paradoxes, which often arise through the mechanisms that Unger describes. One example is the mere addition paradox of Parfit 1984, in which B seems worse than A when the two are compared directly, but it seems not worse than A when Parfit interjects A+ and Divided B as options intermediate between A and B.

[21] Kahneman et al. 1982. Lackey 1986: 634, suggests how such heuristics might explain conflicting moral intuitions about nuclear deterrence.

[22] Van Roojen might admit that Horowitz's argument undermines moral intuitionism, since he defends a method of reflective equilibrium that is coherentist rather than foundationalist.

[23] I am not, of course, endorsing Nietzsche's speculations.

[24] See Sinnott-Armstrong 2006. My version of Pyrrhonism denies that any particular contrast class is the relevant one in the sense that believers need to rule out all alternatives in that class in order to be justified without qualification. That view might seem to conflict with my claim here that moral beliefs need inferential confirmation. However, there might be no need to rule out any particular contrast class, even if there is a need to give evidence of a certain kind.

References

Baron, J. (1994). 'Nonconsequentialist Decisions'. *Behavioral and Brain Sciences*, 17: 1–42.

Foot, Philippa (1967). 'The Problem of Abortion and the Doctrine of Double Effect'. *Oxford Review*, 5: 5–15.

Goldman, A. (1976). 'Discrimination and Perceptual Knowledge'. *Journal of Philosophy*, 73: 771–91.

Greene, J. et al. (2001). 'An fMRI Investigation of Emotional Engagement in Moral Judgment'. *Science*, 293: 2105–8.

Greene, J. and Haidt, J. (2002). 'How (and Where) does Moral Judgment Work?' *Trends in Cognitive Science*, 6: 517–23.

Greene, J. et al. (2004). 'The Neural Bases of Cognitive Conflict and Control in Moral Judgment.' *Neuron*, 44: 389–400.

Haidt, J. (2001). 'The Emotional Dog and its Rational Tail: A Social Intuitionist Approach to Moral Judgment'. *Psychological Review*, 108: 814–34.

Haidt, J. et al. (1993). 'Affect, Culture, and Morality, or is it Wrong to Eat Your Dog?' *Journal of Personality and Social Psychology*, 65: 613–28.

Harman, G. (1977). *The Nature of Morality*. New York: Oxford University Press.

Horowitz, T. (1998). 'Philosophical Intuitions and Psychological Theory'. In M. DePaul and W. Ramsey (eds.), *Rethinking Intuition: The Psychology of Intuition and its Role in Philosophical Inquiry*. Lanham, MD: Rowman & Littlefield.

Kahneman, D., Slovic, P., and Tversky, A. (eds.) (1982). *Judgment under Uncertainty: Heuristics and Biases*. Cambridge: Cambridge University Press.

Kahneman, D. and Tversky, A. (1979). 'Prospect Theory: An Analysis of Decision under Risk'. *Econometrica*, 47/2: 263–92.

Lackey, D. (1986). 'Taking Risk Seriously'. *Journal of Philosophy*. 83: 633–40.

Moll, J. et al. (2001). 'Frontopolar and Anterior Temporal Cortex Activation in a Moral Judgment Task: Preliminary Functional MRI results in Normal Subjects'. *Arq. Neuropsiquiatr*, 59: 657–64.

Moll, J. et al. (2002a). 'Functional Networks in Emotional Moral and Nonmoral Social Judgments'. *Neuroimage*, 16: 696–703.

Moll, J. et al. (2002b). 'The Neural Correlates of Moral Sensitivity: A Functional Magnetic Resonance Imaging Investigation of Basic and Moral Emotions'. *Journal of Neuroscience*, 22: 2730–6.

Moore, G. E. (1903). *Principia Ethica*. Cambridge: Cambridge University Press.

Nietzsche, F. (1966). *Genealogy of Morals*. In *Basic Writings of Nietzsche*, ed. and trans. W. Kaufmann. New York: Random House.

Parfit, D. (1984). *Reasons and Persons*. Oxford: Clarendon Press.

Quinn, W. (1993). 'Actions, Intentions, and Consequences: The Doctrine of Doing and Allowing', repr. in *Morality and Action*. New York: Cambridge University Press.

Ross, W. D. (1930). *The Right and the Good*. Oxford: Oxford University Press.

Scheffler, S. (1982). *The Rejection of Consequentialism*. Oxford: Clarendon Press.

Sinnott-Armstrong, W. (1996). 'Moral Skepticism and Justification'. In W. Sinnott-Armstrong and M. Timmons (eds.), *Moral Knowledge?* New York: Oxford University Press.

Sinnott-Armstrong, W. (2000). 'From "Is" to "Ought" in Moral Epistemology'. *Argumentation*, 14: 159–74.

Sinnott-Armstrong, W. (2002a). 'Moral Skepticism', in Edward N. Zalta (ed.), *The Stanford Encyclopedia of Philosophy* (Summer 2002 edn.), http://plato.stanford.edu/archives/sum2002/entries/skepticism-moral/.

Sinnott-Armstrong, W. (2002b). 'Moral Relativity and Intuitionism'. *Philosophical Issues*, Realism and Relativism, 12: 305–28.

Sinnott-Armstrong, W. (2006). Moral Skepticism. New York: Oxford University Press.

Snare, F. (1980). 'The Diversity of Morals'. *Mind*, 89: 353–69.

Unger, P. (1996). *Living High and Letting Die*. New York: Oxford University Press.

van Roojen, M. (1999). 'Reflective Moral Equilibrium and Psychological Theory'. *Ethics*, 109: 846–57.

Wheatley, T., and Haidt, J. (2005). 'The Wisdom of Repugnance: Hypnotically-Induced Disgust Makes Moral Judgments More Severe' (unpublished manuscript. University of Virginia).

Sources

The editor and publisher gratefully acknowledge the permission granted to reproduce the copyright material in this book.

1 *A Discourse of Natural Religion* from *A Discourse concerning the Unchangeable Obligations of Natural Religion, and the Truth and Certainty of the Christian Revelation*. First printed, 1709. This text taken from corrected 7th edition (1728).

2 *An Inquiry into the Original of Our Ideas of Beauty and Virtue*, from *An Inquiry into the Original of our Ideas of Beauty and Virtue*. First printed 1725. This text taken from revised 4th edition (1738).

3 *An Essay on the Nature and Conduct of the Passions and Affections, with Illustrations on the Moral Sense*, Treatise II: Illustrations Upon the Moral Sense, from Treatise II: Illustrations Upon the Moral Sense, 3rd edition, London 1742.

4 *Enquiries Concerning the Principles of Morals*, from An Enquiry concernnging the Principles of Morals by David Hume, Esq; London Printed for A. Millar, over_against Catberine_Street in the Strand. 1751 pages 197–212.

5 From Immanual Kant, *Groundwork for the Metaphysics of Morals* (translated by Allen Wood). (Yale University Press 2002), pp. 18–21. Reprinted with permission of Yale University Press.

6 Abridged from Lawrence Kohlberg, *The claim to moral adequacy of a highest stage of moral judgment. The Journal of Philosophy*, 70 (1973), pp. 630–5, 641–6. Reprinted with permission.

7 From Robert James Blair. A cognitive developmental approach to morality: Investigating the psychopath. *Cognition*, 57 (1995), 2–3, 5–18, 20–5. Reprinted with permission of Elsevier

8 From Michael Smith (1994). *The Moral Problem* (Blackwell) (pp. 60–71 & pp. 185–9).

9 From Shaun Nichols (2002). How psychopaths threaten moral rationalism. *Monist*, 85, pp. 285–303. Reprinted with permission of The Monist.

10 From *Republic*, Book II, from *The Republic* by Plato Written 360 BCE Translated by Benjamin Jowett.

11 From Thomas Hobbes, *Leviathan*. Text edited by A.R. Waller. Cambridge University Press, 1904. Excerpts from Chapters 11, 13, 14, and 15. pp. 81–6, 97–103. Thomas Hobbes and Ferdinand Tonnies (ed.). *The Elements of Law Natural and Politic*. Simpkin, Marshall, and Co., 1889.

12 Excerpts from Sermon 5 "Upon Compassion"; and Sermon 11 "Upon the Love of Our Neighbor" from Joseph Butler, *Fifteen sermons preached at the Rolls Chapel*, excerpts from Sermon 5 "Upon Compassion"; and

Sermon 11 "Upon the Love of Our Neighbor." London: printed by W. Botham, for James and John Knapton, 1729. pp. 78–9, 147–64.

13 Excerpts from Treatise II: An Inquiry concerning Moral Good and Evil, from Francis Hutcheson, *An Inquiry into the Origin of our Ideas of Beauty and Virtue*, excerpts from Treatise II: An Inquiry concerning Moral Good and Evil. First printed, 1725. Text here is from revised 4th edition, London, 1738.

14 From Dan Batson (March, 1990). How social an animal: The human capacity for caring. *American Psychologist*, 45, 3. American Psychological Association, Inc. (pp. 336, 339–46)

15 From Robert Trivers (March, 1971). The evolution of reciprocal altruism. *Quarterly Review of Biology*, 46, 1. The University of Chicago Press. pp. 35–9, 45, 47–57.

16 From Eliot Sober and David Wilson (2000). Summary of *Unto Others: The Evolution and Psychology of Unselfish Behavior*. First published in *Journal of Consciousness Studies*, Vol. 7, No. 1–2 (2000), pp. 185–9, 194–206. © Imprint Academic, Exeter, UK.

17 From Barry Schwartz (Sep. 1993). Why Altruism is Impossible . . . and Ubiquitous. *The Social Service Review*, 67, 3. The University of Chicago Press, pp. 314–26, 337–43.

18 From Plato, Benjamin Jowett (trans.) and Maurice Francis Egan (introduction), *Dialogues of Plato: Containing the Apology of Socrates, Crito, Phaedo, and Protagoras*, Revised Edition. (The Colonial Press 1900), pp. 154–79, 194–7, 207–8.

19 From Aristotle, *Nicomachean Ethics*, Martin Ostwald (trans.) (Macmillan Publishing, 1962), pp. 29–44, 170–3. Editor's brackets and most footnotes removed.

20 Abridged version of 'Behavioural study of obedience' by Stanley Milgram (2001) in *Conflict, Order and Actions: Readings in Sociology*, Edward Ksenych and David Liu, Canadian Scholars Press inc. Reprinted with kind permission of Alexandra Milgram.

21 From Lee Ross and Richard E. Nisbett. *The Person and the Situation: Perspectives of Social Psychology*. (Temple University Press, 1991) pp. 1–8, 18–20, 30–5, 41–4, 48–50.

Reprinted with the kind permission of the authors.

22 From John Doris (1998). Author's excerpts from Persons, situations, and virtue ethics. *Noûs*, 32, 4. Blackwell Publishers Inc., 1998, excerpts from pp. 504–30 Reprinted with permission of Wiley-Blackwell.

23 From Rachana Kamtekar (2004). Author's excerpts from Situationism and virtue ethics on the content of our character. *Ethics* 114. The University of Chicago, April 2004. Reprinted with permission of The University of Chicago Press.

24 From Maria Merritt (2000). Virtue ethics and situationist personality psychology. *Ethical Theory and Moral Practice* 3. Kluwer Academic Publishers, Netherlands, 2000. (excerpt from pp. 365–7, 369–83).

25 From Aristotle, *Nicomachean Ethics*, Martin Ostwald (trans.) (Macmillan Publishing, 1962) pp. 52–68.

26 From Thomas Reid, *Essays on the Active Powers of Man*. Book IV, Chapters 1 and 2. Originally published in 1788. Spelling and capitalization have been normalized.

27 Extracts from *Poetry* Translated by L A Magnus, New York Macmillan 1909 XV 268pp & *The Complete Works of Friedrich Nietzche, vol. 16, The Twilight of the Idols*, translated by Anthony M Ludovici, New York Macmillan 1911 (Unwin 1899).

28 From B.F. Skinner, *Beyond Freedom and Dignity* New York: Alfred A. Knopf, 1971/1989, pp. 5–9, 10–22, 198–201, 205–6, 211–15. Reprinted with permission of Hackett Publishing Company Inc.

29 From Daniel Wegner and Thalia Wheatley (1999). Apparent mental causation: Sources of the experience of will. *American Psychologist*, 54, 7. American Psychological Association, pp. 480–92. Reprinted with permission of the American Psychological Association.

30 From Eddy Nahmias (2005). Agency, authorship, and illusion. *Consciousness and Cognition*, 14, 771–85. Reprinted with permission of Elsevier Limited.

31 From Roy Baumeister (2008) Free will in scientific psychology. *Perspectives on Psychological Science*, Volume 3, No. 1. Association for Psychological Science, 2008.

pp. 14–19. Reprinted with permission of Wiley-Blackwell.

32 Original paper for this volume by Alfred Mele.

33 From Henry Sidgwick (1838–1900), *The Methods of Ethics*, Book I, Chapter VIII Sections 2, 3, and 4, Book III, Chapter 1, Sections 1, 4, and 5.

34 From W.D. Ross (1930). *The Right and the Good*, Chapter 2. Oxford: Clarendon Press, 1930. Reprinted with permission of Oxford University Press.

35 From Judith Jarvis Thompson (1985). The Trolley Problem. *The Yale Law Journal*, 94: 1395. The Yale Law Journal Company, 1985. pp. 1395–1401, 1403–6, 1409–10. Reprinted by permission of The Yale Law Journal Company, Inc.

36 From Peter Unger, *Living High and Letting Die: Our Illusion of Innocence* (Oxford University Press, 1996), pp. 3–13, 14–23. Reprinted with permission of Oxford University Press.

37 Excepts from Jonathan Haidt (2001). The emotional dog and its rational tail: A social intuitionist approach to moral judgment. *Psychological Review*, 108, 4. The American Psychological Association, Inc., 2001. (pp. 814–23, 828–34).

38 From Walter Sinnott-Armstrong ed., *Moral Psychology, Volume 3: The Neuroscience of Morality: Emotion, Brain Disorders, and Development*. extract from pages 35–48, 59–66, plus notes © 2007 Massachusetts Institute of Technology, by permission of The MIT Press.

39 From Walter Sinnott-Armstrong (2006). Moral intuitionism meets empirical psychology. In T. Horgan and M. Timmons (eds.), *Metaethics After Moore* (Clarendon Press, Oxford, 2006), pp. 339–58, 362–5. Reprinted with permission of Oxford University Press.